STRUCTURED INEQUALITY
in Canada

STRUCTURED INEQUALITY in Canada

edited by

John Harp
Carleton University

and

John R. Hofley
University of Winnipeg

Prentice-Hall of Canada, Ltd. Scarborough, Ontario

Canadian Cataloguing in Publication Data

Main entry under title:

Structured inequality in Canada

Bibliography: p.

ISBN 0-13-854596-0

1. Poor - Canada - Addresses, essays, lectures.
2. Income distribution - Canada - Addresses, essays,
lectures. 3. Social classes - Canada - Addresses,
essays, lectures. I. Harp, John, 1928- II. Hofley,
John R., 1939-

HC120.P6S87   339.4'6'0971   C80-094260-4

Prentice-Hall, Inc., Englewood Cliffs, New Jersey
Prentice-Hall International, Inc., London
Prentice-Hall of Australia, Pty. Ltd., Sydney
Prentice-Hall of India Private Limited, New Delhi
Prentice-Hall of Japan, Inc., Tokyo
Prentice-Hall of Southeast Asia (Pte.) Ltd., Singap̃

Production Editor: Veronica Orocio
Designer: Gail Ferreira
Compositor: Dimensions in DesignType Ltd.

ISBN 0-13-854596-0

80 81 82 83 84 85 HR 5 4 3 2 1

Printed in Canada by Hunter Rose Company, Ltd.

Contents

IV STRATEGIES AND PROGRAMS 401

Acknowledgements

A book such as this requires the cooperation of a large number of people. Many of the articles were prepared especially for this volume by colleagues from across Canada, who responded patiently to our deadlines and editorial comments. The strengths of the volume are a reflection of their excellent work. We would also like to express our thanks to those colleagues and journals who gave permission to reprint previously published articles.

Three anonymous reviewers commented on an earlier version of the manuscript. Their reviews were detailed and highly constructive, and we have tried to respond to their suggestions.

Over the past two years, three persons have assisted us in the preparation of the bibliography — Ros Usiskin, Norma Hanson, and Bob White. Carleton University and the University of Winnipeg provided grants to cover some of the costs of typing. Elinor Loos at the University of Winnipeg and Debbie Devries and Norma Cordukes at Carleton University were immensely helpful in the typing of materials for this book.

Our thanks to Jane Springer who did an excellent job of editing the manuscript. Her comments and suggestions were lucid and perceptive.

We also wish to thank the people at Prentice-Hall. Marta Tomins was simultaneously prodding and helpful, and Veronica Orocio capably saw the volume through its many production stages with the help of Gail Ferreira, Heather McClune, Joe Chin, and Rand Paterson.

Finally, we are grateful to our wives and families for putting up with the presence of "the book" as graciously as we could expect.

Preface

A basic theme underlying this collection of articles on poverty in Canada is that explanations of both the nature and sources of inequalities in our society are a function of the perspective(s) investigators use in analyzing the problem. Not only are there differences in the sources and basic explanations for the condition but there are differences in the ways in which certain key concepts are defined. For example, liberal perspectives on the problem tend to seek the causes of poverty in individual characteristics capable of adaptation by the individual himself or herself, whereas a Marxist perspective views poverty as emerging from the contradictions of capitalism. So whereas a liberal perspective would make recommendations for changing the individual, a radical viewpoint would argue for a transformation of the whole social structure and the elimination of classes.

Our earlier volume on the subject of poverty in Canada, written a decade ago, failed to treat the basic causes of poverty. Indeed, our surprise at the apparent paradox of poverty amid such affluence was widely shared by many writers of the period. What we lacked at that time was the insight provided by viewing poverty and inequality as a contradiction of capitalism. In the present volume we seek the causes of poverty in what have been referred to as "the basic system-defining institutions of capitalism," namely class and the state.

While not all articles in this volume view "class" from a Marxist perspective, the majority hold to the broad Marxist argument that class is not an individual characteristic but a relation between those who own the means of production and those who are wage laborers. Obviously, this relationship is complex.

One illustration of this complexity is the relationship between class and the state in Canada. From a Marxist political economy perspective, the state in a capitalist society serves certain purposes, one of which is to protect private property, thereby supporting the "class" that owns and controls the means of production. This is by no means a clear-cut purpose, visible to all Canadians. Classes are not fixed "things," nor is the state. Both must be examined historically and specifically within the Canadian context. (See Panitch's article in this volume for an elaboration. See also Reg Whitaker's article, "Images of the State in Canada" in Panitch, 1977:28-68.)

A number of articles in this volume examine aspects of the political economy of poverty in Canada. In its most simplistic sense the term "political economy" is used to refer to the sources and distribution of wealth and the ways in which they relate to other aspects of society's structure. Throughout the volume, an effort is made to link macro and micro patterns (e.g., the macro level problems of social class inequality and unequal distribution of resources with the micro level processes of individual socialization and control).

The collection is organized into four sections. It begins with the Basis of Concern, which attempts to set the stage for the problem empirically and to treat some key methodological issues.

In Section II we present a number of perspectives on the study of poverty. Hofley's article raises the critical issues and the articles which follow are exemplars of a Marxist, a culture of poverty, and a functionalist viewpoint respectively. The final article in this part is the classic statement by Georg Simmel, a symbolic interactionist perspective emphasizing a person's conception of himself or herself and society's definition of him or her.

Section III includes articles on the sources of variation of inequalities, grouped under three headings: "The State and Social Class Analyses," "Regions and Regionalism" and "The Political Economy of Specific Groups." All of these articles share a rather broad political economy perspective and focus on particular problems.

Finally, Section IV consists of several articles on strategies and programs that document the abysmal record of the capitalist state in its attempts to ameliorate conditions of inequality. The articles offer confirmation that despite the efforts of the federal and provincial governments during the past two decades to redistribute income and wealth, the results have been negligible. The Canadian state basically operates within the confines of a capitlist economy, and its general thrust is to protect the interests of the dominant class. As long as this is true, structured inequalities will persist.

We would be remiss in our role as social scientists if we failed to acknowledge the need for further analysis. Studies should be undertaken to show more clearly the linkages between the major system-defining institutions of capitalism (i.e., class relations, the state and the economy), and the structural bases of inequality. Analysis should not become an end in itself. Nevertheless, with all due regard to Marx's eleventh thesis on Feuerbach — "The philosophers have only interpreted the world, in various ways; the point is to change it" — challenges to existing economic arrangements and prevailing ideology must be based on careful critical studies of societal systems rather than on polemical rhetoric.

I

The Basis of Concern

Introduction

Inequality is not one-dimensional. It appears in a variety of guises in our society — racial, ethnic, sexual, religious, regional, political, and economic. This book will present the reader with data documenting most of these inequalities, but the present section focuses on the unequal distribution of income in Canada and the problems of measuring this distribution. In addition, Jordan's article will offer us a much-needed discussion of the philosophical and logical issues involved in the concept of equality.

A common assumption made by governments and many citizens during the 1960s and 1970s was that the extent of inequality was diminishing, largely because of massive government spending in areas such as welfare and unemployment insurance and because of more equitable tax deductions. The first two articles provide little empirical support for this premise.

The first article, from the *Canadian Fact Book on Poverty*, documents the extent of poverty in Canada and its differential impact on groups such as the young, the old, and women. The data also demonstrate that among the poor, a majority depend on transfer payments for survival. While there has been some improvement in the plight of the poor, it has been minimal.

The second article by Gillespie examines in greater detail the redistributive effects of transfer payments on the distribution of income. Unlike the data in the first article which concentrates on the poor, Gillespie's data give a more complete picture of income distribution for the whole population. His analysis shows that while the poor received some increase in their share of resources in the 1960s and the early 1970s, this has been eroded. "On the other hand, the considerable gain of the rich during the 1960s has persisted during the early 1970s, thus giving the rich an improvement in their 'share' over time." It is apparent that during the past two decades, income inequality has remained relatively untouched.

The third article, taken from a Health and Welfare research report entitled *The Distribution of Income in Canada: Concepts, Measures, and Issues*, highlights the importance of understanding how inequality is measured and considers the strengths and weaknesses of a number of measures. The report also raises the issue that is the focus of Jordan's article: the normative definition of equality. Jordan admonishes us to be careful in distinguishing between descriptive ("18.4% of families in Canada live below the poverty line") and normative ("This is terribly unjust") statements concerning equality.

Jordan also cautions us to consider carefully the arguments of both Marxists and structural functionalists, who are constantly in debate over the issue of inequality. The Marxists stress that the ideas of the ruling class are in every age the ruling ideas, while structural functionalists argue that normative consensus is a cultural universal. Are our ideas about equality and inequality those of the ruling class? If so, is this why we accept as "natural" the immense inequalities in income documented in this section? Or is there general consensus that inequality is a "good" in the normative sense? Jordan's article is a first-rate introduction to these issues, which surface continually throughout the volume.

The Extent of Poverty in Canada*

Introduction

What do Canadians mean when they say someone is living in poverty? If we refer to our fellow Canadians we probably mean that an individual or family has a very low level of income by Canadian standards and consequently cannot afford as much or as good a quality of life. While there are many Canadians who are just surviving, the poor in Canada generally are able to obtain the bare necessities of life, including shelter, food, clothing and health care. This maintenance of life is possible largely through the various services and income support plans operated by public and private agencies.

In comparison with other parts of the world, especially some areas of the Third World, those who are living in poverty here in Canada could be considered well off. There, poverty can mean *real* poverty: starvation, malnutrition, pestilence, tatters for clothing and makeshift shelters built from scrounged materials. Yet in comparison with other parts of the world, some of the Scandinavian countries, for instance, Canada has not done enough to reduce the number of people living in poverty.

While poverty has been with us for thousands of years, the world has not been very successful in producing an objective and operational definition of poverty. There are significant difficulties in determining what should be measured and how:

> Individual or family resources clearly should be measured comprehensively. Current money income, for example, does not tell the whole story although it probably constitutes the single most important resource. An accurate assessment of an individual's or family's situation must include knowledge as to what net assets they own and what non-marketed income they produce, in addition to their money income. None of these sources are easy to measure or are adequately recorded in official statistics. Furthermore, the assessment of individual and family resources is complicated by the fact that income is a flow over time. Income varies with the life cycle; periods of low income can be followed by periods of high income, or the reverse. The view of how many resources an individual/family has will obviously be affected if a longer or shorter time period is selected: lengthening the period over which income is measured will lessen evident poverty and shortening the accounting period will increase it.
>
> Money income is an incomplete measure of individual/family resources, but it is the one measure about which most is known and on which most attention has been focused.[1]

*From *Canadian Fact Book on Poverty, 1979*, Donald M. Caskie, Canadian Council on Social Development, Ottawa.

Poverty Lines

The poverty line is one of the principal methods of defining and measuring poverty. As such, this approach suffers from exclusive emphasis on money income, but is the main methodology developed for assessing income insufficiency in an aggregate fashion.

There are two principal approaches to the creation of poverty lines: the absolute and the relative, with a wide range of possibilities between these two extremes.

The absolute approach creates a poverty line that is considered the minimum requirement for an individual's or family's basic necessities of food, clothing and shelter. A poverty line created in this fashion yields an amount of money that is absolutely necessary for physical survival.

These poverty lines are absolute to the extent that it is possible to establish basic economic needs or subsistence levels without reference to prevailing community standards. In theory at least, absolute poverty lines have no relation to the standard of living enjoyed by other Canadians.

By contrast, the relative approach takes into account the overall distribution of poverty in terms of income inequality, or as a shortfall from community standards. The relative approach thus attempts to estimate the resources required for personal dignity and social survival and is hence a measure of social as well as economic well-being.

Both approaches have limitations. The absolute approach yields a minimal or subsistence level that has very little relation to the creation and maintenance of social well-being. Since the income needs suggested by the absolute approach are quite low, it is possible for some to agree that the incidence of "real" poverty is diminishing as the various income support programs improve their coverage and benefits.

On the other hand, the relative approach can be criticized because it will always define some people as poor. It can also be argued that, taken to this extreme, the relative approach implies that income equality would be achieved if all Canadians enjoyed the same standard of living.

Despite these difficulties, poverty lines are a reasonable method of measuring poverty, so long as the assumptions on which they are based are clearly stated, and so long as they are carefully interpreted. While they are far from perfect as operational and analytical tools, they are a useful starting point from which to address the issue of poverty.

In Canada, there are five major poverty lines accepted on a national basis, as well as several regional or local lines. The five principal lines are:

1. The updated Statistics Canada poverty line;
2. The revised Statistics Canada poverty line;
3. The Canadian Council on Social Development poverty line;
4. The updated poverty line first created by the Special Senate Committee on Poverty in the early 1970s; and
5. The revised Statistics Canada poverty line according to size of area of residence.

While none of these lines is either completely absolute or completely relative, generally the Senate line is regarded as the most relative, followed by the CCSD line, the revised Statistics Canada line and the updated Statistics Canada line.

Updated Statistics Canada

The first Statistics Canada poverty line was established in 1961 and was based on the knowledge that the proportion of income spent on basic necessities increases as income decreases. Consumer expenditure surveys indicated that in 1961, Canadians spent an average of 50% of their income on food, clothing, and shelter. More or less arbitrarily, Statistics Canada established that those individuals or families required to spend more than 70% of their income on basic necessities should be considered as living in poverty.

Revised Statistics Canada

Beginning in 1973, Statistics Canada began to compile the "revised" poverty line. The revised line is based on a 62% criterion, since Canadians on average now spend a smaller percentage of their income on the basic necessities. The original line has been updated to take account of inflation. The 1976 data, as published by Statistics Canada in *Income Distributions by Size in Canada*, have been adjusted using the all-item consumer price index. Since Statistics Canada does not publish a national revised line comparable to the other three lines, it was necessary to produce one using as a basis the five lines differentiated by size of area. This was created by applying the population distributions by size of area for low-income families and unattached individuals respectively to the low-income poverty lines by size of area as follows:

$$\text{for unattached individuals} \quad \frac{\begin{array}{c}\text{income for one person per size of area}\end{array} \times \begin{array}{c}\text{total number of low-income unattached individuals per each size of area}\end{array}}{\text{total number of low-income unattached individuals}} = \begin{array}{c}\text{income for all unattached individuals}\end{array}$$

$$\text{for families} \quad \frac{\begin{array}{c}\text{money income for each family size per each size of area}\end{array} \times \begin{array}{c}\text{total number of low-income families per each size of area}^*\end{array}}{\text{total number of low-income families}} = \begin{array}{c}\text{income for families by size of area}\end{array}$$

*Not differentiated by size of family
Note: A separate calculation is made for each family size, i.e., 2, 3, 4, 5, 6 and 7+ persons per family.

Canadian Council on Social Development

While the two Statistics Canada lines are based primarily on the absolute or subsistence approach, the Canadian Council on Social Development line presents a measurement of relative poverty. The basis for the CCSD line is the Statistics Canada estimate of average family income. The definition of income includes pre-tax wages, interest, business profits, unemployment insurance benefits, etc., but does not include capital gains, inheritance or income in kind. In calculating the CCSD lines, average Canadian family income is considered representative of a family of four (the average size of Canadian families), and the poverty line for a family of four is calculated as 50% of the average income figure. Adjustments are then made for family size, with a family of one receiving a weight of three units; a family of two receiving five units; a family of three, six units; a family of four, seven units; and each subsequent addition to family size being assigned an added unit.

Average family income for 1978 was calculated by updating the Statistics Canada estimate of family income (*Income Distributions by Size in Canada*), using the annual percentage increase in per capita personal income. (Personal income data is presented in Statistics Canada's *National Income and Expenditure Accounts*. Population data is presented in Statistics Canada's *Quarterly Estimates of Population for Canada and Provinces*.)

Special Senate Committee on Poverty

The Senate Committee poverty line was originally calculated following the procedure outlined in the committee's report, "Poverty in Canada." The Senate line is somewhat complicated to calculate because it requires annual data on family composition as well as total personal income taxes paid by Canadians. Since this information is not available until at least two years after the fact, it is necessary to use an estimating procedure. Since the Senate committee poverty line has consistently been 56% of average family

Table 1

Comparison of Selected National Poverty Lines, Canada, 1978

| | $ | | | |
| | *Statistics Canada* | | | |
Size of Family Unit	*Updated*	*Revised*	*CCSD*	*Senate*
1 Person	3,527	4,459	4,549	5,096
2 Persons	5,878	6,281	7,572	8,481
3 Persons	7,051	8,015	9,089	10,179
4 Persons	8,226	9,531	10,605	11,876
5 Persons	}	10,656	12,121	13,575
6 Persons		11,696	13,638	15,209
7 Persons	} 9,403	}	15,154	16,972
8 Persons			16,660	18,660
9 Persons		} 12,824	18,176	20,357
10 Persons			19,692	22,055

Source: Based on Statistics Canada, *Income Distributions by Size in Canada*.

income (as prepared by Statistics Canada), this figure has been used in estimating the more recent poverty line statistics. This line was updated for 1978 using the same approach as for the CCSD line, including the calculation of average family income.

Table 1 indicates the difference among the poverty lines for the year 1978. The updated Statistics Canada line has the lowest level of income required for an upper limit and therefore includes the fewest number of people of any of the four definitions of poverty. Conversely, the Senate line has the highest upper limit. The revised Statistics Canada and the CCSD lines fall in between these extremes.

The difference between the extremes of the updated Statistics Canada and the Senate lines is quite substantial, amounting to $1,596 for one person and $3,650 for a family of four. The former amount is 45% of the updated Statistics Canada line for one person while the latter represents 44% of the same line for a family of four. As noted earlier, however, the underlying philosophies of these various poverty measures must be kept in mind in evaluating the adequacy of the income levels they propose.

Quintile Distributions and Number of Poor in Canada

Quintile distributions are a relatively simple tool for measuring the way income is distributed throughout the entire population of the country. The population is divided into five equally sized groups according to the ascending order of total income. Thus, each fifth of the population can be assigned its particular share of the total income. As with poverty lines, quintile distributions are useful as starting points for further enquiry into the question of income distribution.

Considerable caution must be exercised in using the quintile distribution of income as a measure of the general equity of income distribution throughout society. While the trends and proportions are certainly illustrative, they may also mask reality. A small family with an income in the second quintile may well be better off than a large family with an income in the middle quintile. The maintenance of a chronically ill parent or the education of a child with learning disabilities may reduce a family with income in the middle or fourth quintile to poverty levels.

There have been very few changes since 1967 in the percentage distribution of income of Canadian families and unattached individuals. As Table 2 indicates, percentage distribution has remained extremely stable. Between 1967 and 1977, the poorest 20% of families and individuals continued to receive about 4% of total income, while the richest 20% received just over 42%. For families, the lowest quintile has about 6% of income while for individuals this quintile received approximately 3.5% of the income of individuals.

The upper limits of income quintiles have increased considerably since 1967. Table 3 shows that the upper limit of the lowest quintile for families and unattached individuals in 1976 had risen from $2,592 to $5,798, an amount of 124% more than that of the comparable quintile in 1967. The comparable increases for the remaining quintiles for the same period are: 130% (second quintile), 145% (middle quintile), and 151% (fourth quintile). As can be seen, the growth in the upper limits between these two points in time has been greater for the upper quintiles. The growth in the upper limits of the lowest quintile has been greater for individuals (146%) than for families (130%).

It is clear that all of the poor are not confined just to the lowest-income quintile. According to Table 4, those unattached individuals living at or below the CCSD and Statistics Canada poverty lines in 1976 were in the category receiving up to 13.2% of total income in Canada, but this figure jumped to 28.3% for those living at or below the Senate line. Families of four living at or below both the updated and revised Statistics Canada poverty lines were in the group receiving 5.9% of total income, while those families who were at or below the CCSD and Senate lines were included in the group getting 18.4% of income. These percentages have all increased from the comparable percentages for 1971, except for the case of individuals at or below the CCSD line.

Table 2

Percentage Distribution of Total Income of Families and Unattached Individuals by Population Quintile for Selected Years 1967 - 1976*

Population	1967	1969	1971	1972	1973	1974	1975	1976	Average 1967-76
All Families and Unattached Individuals									
Lowest quintile	4.2	4.3	3.6	3.8	3.9	4.0	4.0	4.1	4.0
Second quintile	11.4	11.0	10.6	10.6	10.7	10.9	10.6	10.4	10.8
Middle quintile	17.8	17.6	17.6	17.8	17.6	17.7	17.6	17.3	17.6
Fourth quintile	24.6	24.5	24.9	25.0	25.1	24.9	25.1	24.8	24.9
Highest quintile	42.0	42.6	43.3	42.9	42.7	42.5	42.6	43.4	42.7
Families									
Lowest quintile	6.4	6.2	5.6	5.9	6.1	6.3	6.2	5.9	6.1
Second quintile	13.1	12.6	12.6	12.9	12.9	13.1	13.0	12.5	12.8
Middle quntile	18.0	17.9	18.0	18.3	18.1	18.2	18.2	17.9	15.1
Fourth quintile	23.6	23.5	23.7	23.7	23.9	23.6	23.9	23.8	23.7
Highest quintile	38.9	39.7	40.0	39.1	38.9	38.8	38.8	39.9	39.3
Unattached Individuals									
Lowest quintile	3.6	3.9	2.9	3.5	3.2	3.5	3.9	4.3	3.6
Second quintile	8.5	8.2	8.0	8.5	8.6	8.7	8.9	8.9	8.5
Middle quintile	15.9	15.3	14.8	14.7	15.2	15.7	15.5	15.1	15.3
Fourth quintile	26.2	25.7	25.8	25.1	24.9	25.6	25.6	25.1	25.5
Highest quintile	45.8	46.9	48.6	48.1	48.1	46.5	46.1	46.7	47.1

*A family is defined by Statistics Canada as a "group of individuals sharing a common dwelling unit and related by blood, marriage or adoption," and an unattached individual as a person living alone or rooming in a household where he or she is unrelated to other household members.

Source: Based on Statistics Canada, *Income Distributions by Size in Canada.*

Table 3

Upper Limits of Income Quintiles for Families and Unattached Individuals
for Selected Years 1967-1976

Population	1967	1969	1971	1972	1973	1974	1975	1976
				$				
All Families and Unattached Individuals								
Lowest quintile	2,592	2,952	3,110	3,420	3,980	4,627	5,038	5,798
Second quintile	4,824	5,520	6,275	6,735	7,620	8,927	9,793	11,112
Middle quintile	6,807	8,000	9,295	10,137	11,286	13,060	14,565	16,664
Fourth quintile	9,468	11,111	12,941	14,009	15,943	18,238	20,598	23,782
Families								
Lowest quintile	3,900	4,318	4,927	5,515	6,321	7,480	8,214	8,952
Second quintile	5,949	6,900	8,044	8,941	9,948	11,765	12,997	14,577
Middle quintile	7,794	9,126	10,669	11,698	13,149	14,288	17,224	19,533
Fourth quintile	10,379	12,185	14,196	15,432	17,633	20,174	22,823	26,226
Unattached Individuals								
Lowest quintile	1,140	1,320	1,384	1,620	1,764	2,106	2,400	2,810
Second quintile	1,792	2,132	2,199	2,413	2,760	3,384	3,624	4,269
Middle quintile	3,418	4,000	4,296	4,500	5,000	6,240	6,705	7,526
Fourth quintile	5,200	6,280	6,959	7,298	8,008	9,684	10,422	11,866

Source: Based on Statistics Canada, *Income Distributions by Size in Canada.*

Table 4

Percentage of Total Income Received by Families and Unattached
Individuals Living at or below Selected Poverty Lines, 1971 and 1976,
Using Upper Limits of Income Quintiles as Cut-Off Points

Poverty Line	Families (4 persons as norm)		Unattached Individuals	
	1971	1976	1971	1976
Updated Statistics Canada	5.6	5.9	10.9	13.2
Revised Statistics Canada	N/Av*	5.9	N/Av*	13.2
CCSD	18.2	18.4	25.7	13.2
Senate	18.2	18.4	25.7	28.3

*Not available.
Source: Statistics Canada, *Income Distribution by Size in Canada.*

Composition and Characteristics of the Poor

The general trend during the 1970s has been for the incidence of poverty in
Canada to decline according to the approach used in Statistics Canada's
revised low-income cut-offs. The changes in this trend, however, have not
altered significantly the composition or rate of incidence of those living in
poverty, at least for the years under consideration here, namely 1973 and

1976. Data is provided for 1967, but note that the cut-offs are different for this year, being lower in amount owing to the methodology employed.

For almost all of the characteristics that are considered here, the incidence of poverty is much higher for individuals than for families. In 1976 the incidence for individuals (34.3%) was three times that for families (11.2%), as indicated in Table 5a.

One factor stands out very prominently in the characterization of poverty in Canada — the importance of employment income. The absence of employment and the resulting shortfall in income is the major element separating the poor from the non-poor. Several factors, including old age or youth, sex of head, low educational qualifications, and shortage of job opportunities, figure prominently in any discussion of this lack of employment income.

The following discussion compares the variations in incidence for both families and unattached individuals, but does not consider the differences in the magnitude of incidence involved. In Table 5a, the rates of incidence of poverty are discussed under five key areas: geographical location, personal and family factors, educational levels, labor force and income characteristics. The data presented in Tables 5a through 5n are for the years 1967, 1973, and 1976, and distinguish between the incidence of poverty for families and unattached individuals. Tables 5a to 5n use the revised definition of low income developed by Statistics Canada (except for 1967 which is on an updated basis). If the same analysis were applied to the CCSD and Senate committee poverty lines, most incidences would be higher.

Geographical Characteristics

By Region   The incidence of low income in 1976 is greatest for families in the Atlantic region and individuals in Quebec, and least for families in Ontario and unattached individuals in British Columbia. This is the same pattern as in 1967. But in 1973, B.C. had the lowest incidence for both groups and the Prairies the highest among individuals. Between 1973 and 1976, the only region to show an increase in incidence was British Columbia, and this only for families.

Table 5a

Proportion of Families and Unattached Individuals in Each
Region Who Have a Low Income by Region

Region	1967 Families	1967 U.I.	1973 Families	1973 U.I.	1976 Families	1976 U.I.
Atlantic	33.8	50.0	19.0	44.9	14.1	38.7
Quebec	19.9	41.8	15.4	40.8	12.1	40.4
Ontario	12.2	33.0	10.7	37.7	9.7	32.5
Prairie	23.0	39.1	16.5	45.5	11.4	34.5
British Columbia	15.9	30.7	8.9	37.1	11.0	26.4
Canada	18.4	38.9	13.4	40.2	11.2	34.3

By Size of Area of Residence Families in rural areas have the highest like-lihood of low income, while those in cities with a population of 100,000 - 499,999 have the lowest. For individuals, the greatest incidence is reported in small urban areas and the least in cities with a population of 30,000 - 99,999. This is a change from 1973 when the lowest incidence for both groups was found in cities of 500,000 and over. This latter pattern was also recorded in 1967.

The only increase in incidence between 1973 and 1976 was for families living in cities with a population of 500,000 and over.

Table 5b

Proportion of Families and Unattached Individuals with a Low Income by Size of Area of Residence

Size of Area of Residence	1967 Families	U.I.	1973 Families	U.I.	1976 Families	U.I.
500,000 and over	10.3		11.4	37.1	12.5	32.8
100,000 - 499,999	10.6	32.0	11.9	38.2	8.1	33.1
30,000 - 99,999	12.1		12.2	41.8	11.1	30.3
15,000 - 29,999	15.6	50.8	11.8	37.3	10.7	31.3
Small urban areas	21.8	51.2	16.0	49.8	11.5	43.4
Rural areas	40.5	58.3	17.3	47.4	13.3	37.8
All areas	18.4	38.9	13.4	40.2	11.2	34.3

Table 5c

Proportion of Families and Unattached Individuals with a Low Income by Farm and Non-Farm Residence

Farm and non-farm Residence	1967 Families	U.I.	1973 Families	U.I.	1976 Families	U.I.
Resident on farm	N/Av	N/Av	21.8	53.9	18.8	N/Av
Non-resident on farm	N/Av	N/Av	12.8	39.7	10.7	34.3
All residents	18.4	38.9	13.4	40.2	11.2	34.3

Farm or Non-Farm Residence Farm residents have a much higher chance of being poor than non-farm residents. This pattern was also evident in 1973.

Personal Characteristics

Sex of Head The incidence of poverty among families and individuals has consistently been much higher for female heads of family units. A slight in-crease in incidence was registered for female heads of families between 1973 and 1976.

Table 5d

Proportion of Families and Unattached Individuals with a Low Income by Sex of Head

Sex of Head	1967 Families	U.I.	1973 Families	U.I.	1976 Families	U.I.
Male	16.2	30.2	10.8	31.9	8.2	25.9
Female	36.3	47.1	41.6	47.2	42.8	41.2
Both sexes	18.4	38.9	13.4	40.2	11.2	34.3

Age of Head   For both families and individuals, the highest likelihood of being poor occurs among those who are 24 and under or 65 and over. For individuals the chance is also high in the age group 55 - 64.

The incidence increased between 1973 and 1976, only for families whose head was 24 or under and for individuals age 35 - 44.

Table 5e

Proportion of Families and Unattached Individuals with a Low Income by Age of Head

Age of Head	1967 Families	U.I.	1973 Families	U.I.	1976 Families	U.I.
24 and under	14.6	38.3	16.0	40.6	18.3	43.2
25 - 34	14.9	12.0	11.7	16.5	9.1	13.2
35 - 44	15.7	15.9	12.6	18.7	10.1	20.5
45 - 54	14.6	25.1	9.6	31.4	8.4	21.9
55 - 64	17.7	39.9	12.3	42.4	9.8	33.8
65 - 69	31.1	55.9	21.4	51.7	14.0	46.4
70 and over	42.0	68.3	26.2	66.6	23.3	58.1
All ages	18.4	38.9	13.4	40.2	11.2	34.3

Table 5f

Proportion of Families and Unattached Individuals with a Low Income by Size of Family Unit

Size of Family Unit	1967 Families	U.I.	1973 Families	U.I.	1976 Families	U.I.
1 person	N/Av	38.9	0.0	40.2	0.0	34.3
2 persons	N/Av	0.0	16.0	0.0	13.9	0.0
3 persons	N/Av	0.0	11.4	0.0	11.0	0.0
4 persons	N/Av	0.0	10.3	0.0	8.4	0.0
5 persons or more	N/Av	0.0	14.4	0.0	10.1	0.0
All sizes	18.4	38.9	13.4	40.2	11.2	34.3

Size of Family Unit The incidence of poverty among families in 1973 and 1976 was highest where there were just two persons and lowest with four persons.

The incidence of poverty among unattached individuals shows a drop between 1973 and 1976; with the high rate of unemployment between 1976 and 1979, it is likely that the incidence of poverty in this group is now higher.

Number of Children under 16 In general, for both 1973 and 1976, the likelihood of poverty increased directly in proportion to the number of children under 16 years.

Table 5g

Proportion of Families and Unattached Individuals
with a Low Income by Number of Children under 16

Number of Children under 16 Years	1967		1973		1976	
	Families	U.I.	Families	U.I.	Families	U.I.
None	19.3	38.9	12.0	40.2	10.0	34.3
1 child	13.9	0.0	11.5	0.0	10.5	0.0
2 children	14.1	0.0	12.8	0.0	11.5	0.0
3 children	19.3	0.0	16.5	0.0	14.4	0.0
4 or more children	25.7	0.0	25.2	0.0	18.1	0.0
All families	18.4	38.9	13.4	40.2	11.2	34.3

Table 5h

Proportion of Families and Unattached Individuals
with a Low Income by Birthplace

Birthplace	1967		1973		1976	
	Families	U.I.	Families	U.I.	Families	U.I.
Canadian-born	N/Av	N/Av	13.5	38.8	11.4	32.5
Non-Canadian-born	N/Av	N/Av	13.0	44.7	10.4	40.3
All birthplaces	18.4	38.9	13.4	40.2	11.2	34.3

Birthplace In 1973 and 1976, Canadian-born families had a higher chance of being poor than those born outside of Canada, but the difference was very small. The situation was reversed for individuals, as the foreign-born displayed a considerably higher likelihood of living in poverty than Canadian-born.

Educational Background of Head

There is a general tendency for the incidence of poverty to increase in inverse proportion to the level of education attained by the head. However, between 1973 and 1976, there are some indications that the incidence among families and unattached individuals has increased for those heads with post-secondary education, and particularly for individuals with a university degree.

Table 5i

Proportion of Families and Unattached Individuals with a Low Income by Education of Head

Education of Head	1967 Families	U.I.	1973 Families	U.I.	1976 Families	U.I.
0 - 8 years			21.7	63.0	17.8	54.6
Some high school, no post-secondary	19.5	41.4	11.1	33.6	10.2	26.1
Some post-secondary					7.5	33.8
Post-secondary diploma			6.4	30.9	5.2	23.1
University degree	3.5	9.1	3.3	12.5	3.8	21.3
All levels of education	18.4	38.9	13.4	40.2	11.2	34.3

Labor Force Characteristics

Labor Force Status of Head As can readily be guessed, the incidence of being poor is many times greater for those not in the labor force.

Table 5j

Proportion of Families and Unattached Individuals with a Low Income by Labor Force Status of Head

Labor Force Status of Head	1967 Families	U.I.	1973 Families	U.I.	1976 Families	U.I.
In labor force	13.1	22.8	8.7	21.7	6.4	16.7
Not in labor force	45.9	71.0	36.3	69.2	30.9	59.0
All	18.4	38.9	13.4	40.2	11.2	34.3

Occupation of Head The chance of living in poverty is higher for those families and individuals whose head is engaged in farming. It is lowest for those heads who are managers or professionals, although amongst individuals this advantage is not always that large.

Weeks Worked by Head As might be expected, the incidence of poverty declines as the number of weeks worked increases. Yet the incidence is consistently higher for those who work one to nine weeks than for those who do not work at all. In fact, it is not until the head has worked 20 weeks or more that there is a significant difference in incidence between those working and those not working.

Table 5k

Proportion of Families and Unattached Individuals with a Low Income by Occupation of Head

Occupation of Head	1967 Families	U.I.	1973 Families	U.I.	1976 Families	U.I.
Managerial	6.7	9.4	1.6	11.1	1.1	7.9
Professional	3.3		4.3	18.5	3.9	13.8
Clerical	5.6	13.3	8.3	17.1	7.3	15.4
Sales	7.2	13.8	7.9	27.0	5.0	13.4
Service	16.7	20.0	15.8	40.2	14.6	33.0
Farming	29.6	53.8	23.7	39.7	17.1	N/Av
Processing & machining	10.8	18.8	5.3	17.7	3.9	N/Av
Product fabrication			6.9	20.5	5.5	11.5
Construction			8.5	10.8	5.8	N/Av
Transport	14.9	10.3	8.5	17.6	4.5	7.1
All occupations	18.4	38.9	13.4	40.2	11.2	34.3

Table 5l

Proportion of Families and Unattached Individuals with a Low Income by Weeks Worked by Head

Weeks Worked by Head	1967 Families	U.I.	1973 Families	U.I.	1976 Families	U.I.
None	49.2	75.2	40.1	72.1	34.6	66.8
1 - 9 weeks	56.8	86.7	48.3	76.7	36.8	N/Av
10 - 19 weeks	46.2	62.7	37.7	70.7	33.0	60.5
20 - 24 weeks	41.3	44.0	25.7	44.5	17.8	33.4
30 - 39 weeks	30.1	28.2	16.5	29.0	13.1	13.5
40 - 49 weeks	18.4	22.2	12.3	10.8	12.1	17.2
50 - 52 weeks	10.1	13.9	6.0	13.2	4.1	7.5
All	18.4	38.9	13.4	40.2	11.2	34.3

Table 5m

Proportion of Families and Unattached Individuals with a Low Income by Number of Earners

Number of Earners	1967 Families	U.I.	1973 Families	U.I.	1976 Families	U.I.
None	N/Av	N/Av	53.9	74.8	45.9	64.2
One	N/Av	N/Av	16.0	20.4	14.1	16.7
Two	N/Av	N/Av	4.9	0.0	3.2	0.0
Three or more	N/Av	N/Av	2.6	0.0	1.7	0.0
All	18.4	38.9	13.4	40.2	11.2	34.3

Numbers of Earners   There is a dramatic drop in the likelihood of poverty as the number of earners increases.

Major Source of Income

Those families and individuals who have wage and salary income have the lowest incidence of poverty, whereas those who depend on transfer payments have the highest likelihood. Those who depend on income from self-employment have a greater chance of being poor than those receiving wages and salaries.

Table 5n

Proportion of Families and Unattached Individuals with a Low Income by Major Source of Income

Major Source of Income	1967		1973		1976	
	Families	U.I.	Families	U.I.	Families	U.I.
No income	100.0	100.0	100.0	100.0	100.0	100.0
Wages and salaries	9.0	18.1	6.0	18.2	4.0	
Net income from						14.5
self-employment	40.4	40.4	20.4	37.0	15.8	
Transfer payments	75.8	88.5	60.4	83.9	50.1	74.3
Other money income	28.1	30.2	16.9	23.4	13.5	17.4
All sources of income	18.4	38.9	13.4	40.2	11.2	34.3

Note: Sources for Tables 5a-5n are Statistics Canada, *Income Distributions by Size in Canada, 1973,* and *1976,* and *Statistics on Low Income in Canada, 1967.* Data for 1967 are in reference to the updated poverty line while 1973 and 1976 data are based on the revised line.

The Young and the Old: Particular Victims of Poverty

In identifying the characteristics that are common to the poor in Canada, special attention must be paid to the significance of the age and sex of the family head. The influence of these two factors is dramatically shown in Table 6, which presents the percentage distribution of families and un-attached individuals according to income groups, age and the sex of family heads.

Table 6 indicates that in 1976, the average income for those under 25 and over 65 years of age was about half that for all age groups combined. Families headed by individuals under 25 and over 65 had average incomes of $9,654 and $8,786 respectively. Well over half the families in these two groups had an annual income of less than $10,000.

The sex of the family head is a major factor in determining family income. Male heads of families received an average income of $18,273, more than twice that of female heads, who averaged $7,502. Most striking is that 67.7% of elderly woman in Canada lived on an annual income of less than $5,000 in 1976. The average income of all families headed by women over 65 was only $5,675.

Table 6

Percentage Distribution of Families and Unattached Individuals by Income Grops, Age and Sex of Head, 1976

Income Group	All Age Groups	Age of Head Under 25	Age of Head 65 and Over
All Families and Unattached Individuals			
Under $5,000	16.4	30.4	41.5
$ 5,000 - $10,999	23.0	34.2	35.5
$11,000 - $14,999	14.4	16.0	8.0
$15,000 - $19,999	16.7	11.9	7.1
$20,000 and over	29.7	7.6	8.0
AVERAGE INCOME $	16,095	9,654	8,786
Male Head			
Under $5,000	9.2	19.9	26.2
$ 5,000 - $10,999	20.2	30.5	43.7
$11,000 - $14,999	15.2	21.6	10.3
$15,000 - $19,999	19.4	17.3	9.5
$20,000 and over	36.0	11.2	10.4
AVERAGE INCOME $	18,273	11,737	10,620
Female Head			
Under $5,000	45.3	51.1	67.7
$ 5,000 - $10,999	33.7	41.5	21.6
$11,000 - $14,999	10.5	5.5	4.1
$15,000 - $19,999	5.9	1.2	2.9
$20,000 and over	4.7	0.7	2.9
AVERAGE INCOME $	7,502	5,541	5,675

Source: Statistics Canada, *Income Distribution by Size in Canada.*

Expenditure Patterns and Inflation

Expenditure Patterns

Those living in a state of poverty have considerably different expenditure patterns from those with higher incomes. Table 7 indicates that, in 1976, families in the lowest-income quintile, which includes those families living in poverty, spent a greater proportion of their income on food and shelter than those in the other four quintiles. In fact, the lowest-income group still spends over half of their income (53.2%) on the basic essentials, namely food, shelter and clothing. But the poor spent less proportionally on travel and transportation, security and contributions, and much less on personal taxes; the percentage of their expenditures for clothing is similar to the other quintiles.

Obviously these percentage differences should not be taken to mean that poor families actually spend more money on food, for instance, than

Table 7

Patterns of Family Expenditure by Family Income Quintile, 1976

	%	%	%	%	%
Personal taxes	6.1	14.3	17.0	19.7	25.1
Security and contributions	4.4	6.0	6.6	7.5	8.9
Other	26.5	23.8	23.1	22.5	21.2
Travel & transportation	9.8	13.6	12.8	12.6	12.5
Clothing	7.3	7.0	7.2	7.2	7.2
Shelter	22.1	16.8	16.1	14.8	12.1
Food	23.8	18.5	17.3	15.7	12.9
	Lowest	Second	Middle	Fourth	Highest
			Quintile		

Source: Based on unpublished data from Statistics Canada, consumer income and expenditure division.

do those in the other quintiles. An accurate comparison of the expenditure patterns of different income groups requires analysis of the proportions that each group spends on the various items. Hence, those in the lowest-income quintile in 1976 spent almost a quarter of their income on food, or in dollar terms, approximately \$2,057. Those in the second quintile spent a fifth on food, or \$2,725 approximately, while those in the upper-income quintile paid out about 13% of their income on food, or about \$4,458. Thus, the proportion of the income of the poor going for basic needs such as food and housing is much higher than that of those in the other income quintiles, but the actual dollar amounts spent are in fact much lower.

Table 8 indicates that between 1969 and 1976 the expenditure pattern of the average family did not change significantly. The major change was the decrease in the share of income going to current consumption, which declined from 77.4% to 73.5%. This shift was due mainly to the increased share of income being allocated to personal taxes, an increase from 15.6% of income to 19.1%. The share of expenditures for food declined by just over one percentage point. Clothing and medical/health care decreased by approximately one percentage point each, while shelter was reduced by half a percentage point. Some of these changes are accounted for by the shifts in responsibility for social programs from the private/personal sector to the public sector.

In addition to presenting a general picture of expenditure patterns for Canadian families, Table 8 also indicates some interesting changes in the characteristics of the Canadian family. Between 1969 and 1976, average family size decreased slightly from 3.63 to 3.32 persons. The average age of the family head stayed almost the same. The percentage of families with the wife working full-time increased moderately from 16.3% to 22.1%. Small increases were also seen in the proportion of families who owned homes and either cars or trucks.

Table 8

Patterns of Expenditures for Families of Two or More Persons, Based on Surveys of 8 Canadian Cities, 1969 and 1976

Item	1969		1976	
Family characteristics				
Average family size (no.)	3.63		3.22	
Average age of head (yr.)	44.0		43.8	
Average net income before taxes ($)	10,560.1		20,768.9	
Percentage				
Who own home	55.0		57.1	
Who own car or truck	77.9		79.8	
With wife employed full-time	16.3		22.1	
Percentage of total expenditure spent on:				
Food	17.3		16.2	
Shelter	15.6		15.1	
Rented living quarters		(5.7)		(4.7)
Owned living quarters		(6.5)		(7.1)
Other housing		(.9)		(.8)
Water and fuel		(2.6)		(2.5)
Clothing	8.1		7.2	
Travel and transportation	12.2		12.5	
Other	24.1		22.5	
Household operation		(4.1)		(3.8)
Furnishings and equipment		(4.6)		(4.9)
Personal care		(2.1)		(1.4)
Medical and health care		(3.2)		(2.0)
Smoking and alcoholic beverages		(3.6)		(3.2)
Recreation		(3.5)		(3.8)
Reading		(.6)		(.5)
Education		(1.0)		(.7)
Miscellaneous		(1.4)		(2.2)
Total current consumption	77.4		73.5	
Securities	4.7		5.2	
Gifts and contributions	2.3		2.1	
Personal taxes	15.6		19.1	
Total	100.0		100.0	

Source: Based on Statistics Canada, *Urban Family Expenditure 1972,* Table 7, for 1969 data; and Statistics Canada, *Urban Family Expenditure 1976, Selected Tables* (mimeograph), Table 4, for 1976 data.

Table 9

Consumer Price Indexes for All Items and Specific Components,
Canada 1965-1978 (1971 = 100)

Year	Food	Housing	Clothing	Trans-port-ation	Health and Personal Care	Recrea-tion, Educa-tion, and Reading	Tobacco and Alcohol	All-Items Index
Group weight as a percentage of total*	*24*	*32*	*11*	*16*	*4*	*7*	*6*	*100*
1965	83.4	77.3	83.8	80.7	79.4	77.9	81.7	80.5
1966	88.7	79.5	87.0	82.6	81.8	80.1	83.7	83.5
1967	89.9	82.9	91.4	86.1	86.0	84.1	85.8	86.5
1968	92.8	86.7	94.1	88.3	89.5	88.3	93.6	90.0
1969	96.7	91.2	96.7	92.4	93.8	93.5	97.2	94.1
1970	98.9	95.7	98.5	96.1	98.0	96.8	98.4	97.2
1971	100.0	100.0	100.0	100.0	100.0	100.0	100.0	100.0
1972	107.6	104.7	102.6	102.6	104.8	102.8	102.7	104.8
1973	123.3	111.4	107.7	105.3	109.8	107.1	106.0	112.7
1974	143.4	121.1	118.0	115.8	119.4	116.4	111.8	125.0
1975	161.9	133.2	125.1	129.4	133.0	128.5	125.3	138.5
1976	166.2	148.0	132.0	143.3	144.3	136.2	134.3	148.9
1977	180.1	161.9	141.0	153.3	155.0	142.7	143.8	160.8
1978	211.2	172.9	144.5	160.7	165.0	146.9	157.4	175.1

*These weights, indicating the components' relative importance, are based on 1967 expenditures and have been incorporated since May 1973; prior to May 1973, the weights reflected 1957 expenditures.

Source: Statistics Canada, *Canada Year Book 1976-77* (Ottawa, 1977), Table 21.15, p. 1022; *Canadian Statistical Review* (July 1978), p. 66.

Inflation

The much higher rates of inflation in the 1970s have made the problem of poverty more difficult for many people. It is true that, if averages are struck for all of the poor taken together, their incomes have increased a little more than the overall increase in the consumer price index (CPI). Thus at this average level, the real income of the poor has increased slightly, but by the late 1970s the average poor person was neither much worse off nor much better off than in 1970, allowing for inflation. However, the averages conceal enormous differences of experience among the poor. For many such people, their money incomes have gone up by less than the CPI; their real incomes were reduced absolutely by inflation. For others, whose money incomes have increased significantly faster than the CPI, somewhat above-average improvements in real incomes have occurred. But the overall CPI understates the impact of inflation on the poor during the 1970s, since they spend a higher proportion of their income on the essentials of life. Two of these essentials, food and shelter, have been subject to the highest rates of inflation.

Table 9 shows that food, which absorbs a quarter of the income of those in the lowest-income quintile, has experienced the greatest increase in the rate of inflation of any component in the consumer price index. In June 1978, the food index was 211.2 while the all-items index was 175.1. Housing at 172.9 was very close to the all-items figure and health/personal care at 165.0 was not far behind. These three essentials of life have experienced greater inflation than the non-essentials such as tobacco and alcohol. Fortunately for the poor, the clothing index rose considerably slower than the housing and food indexes, although the cost of clothing rose almost 50% between 1970 and 1978.

NOTES

1.   Ontario Economic Council, *Issues and Alternatives 1976: Social Security*, p. 3.

On the Redistribution of Income in Canada*

W. IRWIN GILLESPIE

In order to focus programs on those who need them, we must define, with as much clarity as possible, the essential components of a minimum standard for satisfactory living — not a subsistence standard but one which allows for dignity and decency.

Prime Minister Pierre Elliott Trudeau,
House of Commons Debates (1968)

The "sense of a Canadian community" is at once the source of income redistribution between people and regions in Canada and the result of such measures.

We believe the Government of Canada must have the power to redistribute income, between persons and between provinces, if it is to equalize opportunity across the country.

Prime Minister Pierre Elliott Trudeau,
Income Security and the Social Services
(1970, 68 and 60)

...the Parliament of Canada must continue to play a role in the income security system: ... it has a responsibility to combat poverty by way of a fair distribution of income among people across Canada; and it has a responsibility to promote national unity through preventing extremes in income disparities across the country.

The Hon. Marc Lalonde, Minister of National
Health and Welfare, *Working Paper on Social
Security in Canada* (1973, 38)

*From "Tax Essay," *Canadian Tax Journal,* Vol. XXIV, No.4, July-August 1976.

This paper is a condensed version of W. Irwin Gillespie, "The Redistribution of Income in Canada," Carleton Library Series (Toronto: Macmillan of Canada, 1980). I wish to express my appreciation to Carleton University and the Canada Council (Grant No. S71-1999) for research assistance and financial support. I am grateful to Jenny Podoluk, Gail Oja, Boriss Mazikins, Isabel McWhinney and Harry Champion of Statistics Canada for assistance with the data on income and expenditures; and I am especially indebted to Nicholas LePan for research assistance. I am thankful for the helpful comments on an earlier draft of the study by David Dodge, Jim Johnson, Richard Kerr, Nicholas LePan, Allan Maslove, Gail Oja, Tom Rymes and Eugene Smolensky. For any remaining errors, I am fully responsible.

Introduction

A myth is in the process of becoming entrenched in the Canadian body politic. Like all myths, this one is based on partial bits of reality and fantasy and serves to arm men and women against the supposed wrath of the gods, while at the same time providing solace to the troubled psyche which seeks to explain its historical predicament. Fortunately this myth can be expunged with benefit to all.

We refer to the myth that Canadian society has become increasingly more redistributive away from the rich to the poor during the postwar period. The claim that Canadian governments have been succesful in increasing the degree of redistribution such that the share of command over resources of the poor has increased considerably at the expense of the rich has moved off the popular podium into the popular literature.[1] The claim may also lie behind recent provincial and federal moves to "tighten up on welfare clients", restrain spending on unemployment insurance payments and expand tax loopholes for the rich.[2] It is a claim that does not hold up under closer examination. It is a well-documented fact that the distribution of money income in Canada did not change significantly between 1951 and 1974.[3] The poorest one-fifth of Canadians had 4.4% of money income in 1951 and 4.0% in 1974; the richest one-fifth had 42.8% of money income in 1951 and 42.4% in 1974 (see Table 1). Such constancy over 23 years obscures some variation during the interim. The distribution of income became slightly less unequal during the 1950s and early 1960s, more unequal during the late 1960s through 1971, and slightly less unequal since 1971.[4]

The constancy in the distribution of money income has puzzled most observers, because it occurred during a period when Canadian governments were introducing new transfer programs and expanding old transfer programs. This expansion of transfer programs has not led to a reduction in the inequality of income: rather, it has held that inequality virtually steady.

The distribution of money income is a partial measure of the extent to which governments redistribute resources, since it includes transfer payments only, and does not encompass government redistribution effected by taxes paid and the value of government services and goods received. Consequently, many observers believe that if all government redistributive actions generated by taxes, transfers and the value of government services were accurately measured and accounted for in a "true" measure of income distribution, then the record of the postwar period would reveal a substantial reduction in "true" income inequality in Canada.

Unfortunately the data to test such a hypothesis for the entire postwar period do not exist. The evidence now available permits us to examine in detail the 1961 through 1969 period and make a reasoned judgment about the 1969 through 1974 period. Both sources of evidence support a set of conclusions which undermine the myth of a public sector increasingly redistributive in favour of the poor at the expense of the rich. This essay examines the evidence on the redistribution of income.

Table 1

Percentage Distribution of Total Incomes by Quintiles of Families and Unattached Individuals, Selected Years, 1951-74, Canada

	1951	1957	1961	1965	1969	1971	1972	1973	1974
All Units									
Lowest quintile	% 4.4	4.2	4.2	4.4	4.3	3.6	3.8	3.9	4.0
Second quintile	11.2	11.9	11.9	11.8	11.0	10.6	10.6	10.8	10.8
Third quintile.	18.3	18.0	18.3	18.0	17.6	17.6	17.8	17.7	17.8
Fourth quintile.	23.3	24.5	24.5	24.5	24.5	24.9	25.0	25.2	25.0
Highest quintile	42.8	41.4	41.1	41.4	42.6	43.3	42.9	42.4	42.4
Total	100.0	100.0	100.0	100.0	100.0	100.0	100.0	100.0	100.0
Upper Limits of Income Quintiles: All Units									
Lowest quintile	$ 1,260	$ 1,650	$ 1,930	$ 2,403	$ 2,952	$ 3,110	$ 3,420	$ 3,983	$ 4,500
Second quintile	2,310	3,040	3,586	4,340	5,520	6,275	6,735	7,608	8,720
Third quintile.	3,180	4,200	4,950	6,032	8,000	9,295	10,137	11,213	12,847
Fourth quintile.	4,320	5,870	6,630	8,344	11,111	12,941	14,009	15,800	17,962
Highest quintile	—	—	—	—	—	—	—	—	—

SOURCE: Statistics Canada, *op. cit.,* 1972, 1973b, 1974 and 1975. The data for 1951 through 1961 are for non-farm units only. The data for 1965 and later years are for farm and non-farm units.

In Part II, the methodology of fiscal incidence studies which measure the redistributive impact of the public sector are discussed. In Part III, the tax, expenditure and fiscal incidence findings for 1969 are analysed. In Part IV, the fiscal incidence findings for 1961 are compared with the findings for 1969, in order to analyse the change in fiscal incidence over time. In Part V, the results of Part IV are tentatively extended into the early 1970s. The conclusions are summarized in Part VI.

Part II — Methodological Framework

The extent to which governments redistribute income among family units has been examined with the aid of fiscal incidence studies.[5] This paper summarizes the empirical results of Gillespie (1975):

Fiscal incidence is a measure of the change in relative income positions of family units in response to the taxation and public expenditure policies of the entire public sector. Theoretically it is a general equilibrium problem, *par excellence* — the impact of the total public sector on the redistribution of income. Any instrument of budgetary policy, be it a tax instrument or an expenditure instrument, has the potential to affect both the flow of income from its sources to a family unit relative to other family units, and the uses to which such income can be put by a family unit relative to other family units. Analysis of the former in terms of income sources effects, and the latter in terms of income uses effects, provides the foundation upon which the total redistributive effects of the public sector can be developed.[6]

The income base from which the changes in relative income positions of family units generated by the total public sector are measured is crucially important — and unfortunately, is not unambiguously obvious. One can conceive of introducing a public sector into a purely private economy and measuring the distributive effect of taxes and public expenditures as a percentage of income prior to the introduction; that is, income in the absence of a public sector. The comparison income base is broad income, Y, and the experiment is represented by the ratio $\frac{B + R - T}{Y}$, where B, R and T are government expenditures on goods and services, transfer payments, and tax payments, respectively.

Broad income is built up in the following manner. To money income (wages and salaries, net farm income, income from unincorporated enterprises, dividend income, rental income, interest income, and government transfer payments) are added the imputed income items of the national accounts: food and fuel grown and consumed on the farm, imputed rental income of owner-occupied homes and imputed services of financial intermediaries. Several additions to income are made, either because the receipt increases a family unit's command over resources — inheritances, bequests and net capital gains — or because certain adjustments are called for to render the income base consistent with the conceptual analysis: retained corporate earnings, share of corporation profits tax falling on capital, backward-shifted share of the social security taxes, etc. The deduction of transfer payments results in broad income, Y.

Alternatively, one can conceive of removing a public sector from an economy that includes it and measuring the distributive effect of taxes and public expenditures as a percentage of income prior to the removal; that is, income in an economy that includes the public sector. The comparison income base here is adjusted broad income, $Y + B + R - T$, where the benefits from government expenditures on goods and services, and the value of transfer payments are included in income, and tax payments are excluded from income. The experiment is represented by the ratio $\frac{B + R - T}{Y + B + R - T}$. The derivation of broad and adjusted broad income is provided in Table 2.[7]

The fiscal incidence results are built up in three stages: tax incidence, expenditure incidence and fiscal incidence. The empirical estimation of tax incidence is fairly straightforward. Hypotheses are made about the incidence of various taxes by broad economic categories of consumer outlays or factor incomes. Such hypotheses are drawn from the body of theoretical literature and empirical evidence on the theory of taxation. These hypotheses are then translated into distributional changes by size classes of income. The resulting distribution of tax payments is a quantification of theoretical deductions, and to the extent that the hypotheses are valid, one should get a close approximation of the effects of tax policy on the distribution of income. Finally, the distribution of tax payments by income class is expressed as a percentage of the distribution of income resulting in effective tax rates by income class, $\frac{-T}{Y}$ and $\frac{-T}{Y + B + R - T}$ for the broad and adjusted broad income base respectively.

The empirical estimation of expenditure incidence is less precise than tax incidence, primarily because any hypotheses about the distribution of the benefits from government expenditures are less well developed. Transfer payments, such as family allowance payments, old age pensions, etc., can be treated like negative taxes and analysed analogously. Their benefits may remain with the original recipients or they may be shifted to other groups, and hypotheses about transfer incidence can be extracted from the literature in much the same way as hypotheses about tax incidence.

Public expenditures on goods and services pose a different problem, because while ideally one wants to estimate the distribution by income class of the "benefits estimated to be received by" members of the community, practically the only manageable measure is the estimation of the "costs incurred on behalf of" members of the community.[8] These costs are treated as a component of the incomes of certain families in the community. Hypotheses are developed concerning the beneficiary groups on whose behalf public expenditures are made, and the cost is allocated to beneficiaries by the distribution of the beneficiary group by size classes of income. These expenditures, such as education and roadbuilding, have become designated as "specific", because it is considered that they can be allocated to clearly delineated beneficiary groups. When the distribution of total public expenditures by income class is expressed as a percentage of the distribution of income, the result is a set of effective expenditure rates by income class, $\frac{B + R}{Y}$ and $\frac{B + R}{Y + B + R - T}$, for the broad and adjusted broad income base respectively.

Table 2

Total Expenditure Incidence for Alternative General Expenditure Hypotheses, Using the Broad Income Base, Canada, 1969 (Percentages)

Line	Expenditure Incidence	under $2,000	$2,000- 2,999	$3,000- 3,999	$4,000- 4,999	$5,000- 5,999	$6,000- 6,999	$7,000- 9,999	$10,000- 14,999	$15,000 & over	Total
						Family Money Income Class					
	All levels of government, for general expenditures — assumption:										
1.	A (family units)	444.9	189.6	112.7	80.7	63.3	52.2	42.5	29.9	19.3	44.4
2.	B* (broad income).	297.0	148.8	94.0	70.5	57.5	52.1	43.1	34.2	27.7	44.4
3.	C (capital income)	324.3	161.6	102.4	75.0	57.2	51.2	38.3	25.2	32.4	43.7
4.	D (disposable income)	291.4	146.5	102.8	71.6	57.9	51.4	42.8	33.4	28.0	44.4
5.	E (Aaron-McGuire methodology) . .	301.5	147.1	91.5	67.2	53.9	48.3	45.1	34.7	27.9	44.3

*The standard case.

Source: Gillespie, *op. cit.*, 1980: Table 4.13 and Table D-11.

Given the patterns of tax incidence and expenditure incidence, the estimation of fiscal incidence follows directly. One subtracts the distribution of effective tax rates by income class from the distribution of effective expenditure rates by income class to effect a distribution of the net fiscal incidence rates by income class. These results indicate whether the average family unit of any income class is a net gainer from, or a net contributor to, the redistributive mechanism of the total public sector.

Part III — Tax, Expenditure, and Fiscal Incidence, 1969

Tax Incidence

The estimates of tax incidence are derived by allocating tax payments of all three levels of government according to the standard hypotheses concerning the incidence of such taxes by factor shares or consumer outlays, and then by the distribution of such items by size classes of income.[9] The distribution of tax payments is expressed as a percentage of the distribution of broad income in order to effect the pattern of effective tax rates of Table 4.

The total tax incidence (line 24) is regressive over the first four income brackets (up to an income level of $5,000), virtually proportional over the next four income brackets (from $5,000 to $15,000), and mildly regressive throughout the remainder of the measured income scale.

The federal tax incidence (line 8), is regressive over the first three income brackets and virtually proportional for the remainder of the measured income scale. This federal pattern is made up of a number of forces working in opposite directions. The individual income tax is progressive throughout, though not nearly so progressive over the upper income brackets as one might expect. The corporate income tax is regressive up to an income level of $6,000, and with some variation, progressive beyond. The regressivity over the lower income brackets is caused partly by the portion of the tax that is assumed to be shifted forward to consumers, and partly by the fact that family units in the lowest income brackets (probably the retired elderly), own a larger proportion of corporate shares than those in the middle-income brackets do. The general sales tax, selective excise taxes and import duties — all of which are allocated on the basis of some variant of consumption expenditure — show regressivity virtually throughout, with some proportionality over the $5,000 to $9,999 income range.

The provincial tax incidence (line 17), shows a similar general pattern: regressive over the first four brackets, virtually proportional for the next four, and mildly regressive over the top two measured income brackets of the income scale. The inclusion of medical-hospital premiums and other taxes adds an additional degree of regressivity over the lowest income brackets. The local tax incidence (line 23), is regressive throughout the measured income scale. The property tax is the major contributor to this regressive pattern throughout.

In general, then, tax incidence is regressive up to an income level of about $5,000, and beyond an income level of $15,000, with proportionality in between. This regressivity of the total tax structure is crucial when considerations of tax equity are involved. In total, 36% of all family units are affected by the regressiveness of the total tax system up to an income level of $5,000.

The tax incidence results for the adjusted broad income base differ somewhat. The total tax incidence pattern demonstrates less regressivity over the lower income classes and progressivity over the $4,000 through $14,999 income when compared with the broad income results.

The results of Table 4 are based on the standard shifting assumptions of Table 5. Experimentation with alternative shifting hypotheses for taxes

Table 3

Total Tax Payments, Canada 1969

Revenue Source	Tax Payments		Tax Payments Exclusive of Exported Portions[a]	
	Millions of $ (1)	% (2)	Millions of $ (3)	% (4)
1. Individual income tax	7,730	30.	7,730	31.
2. Corporate income tax	3,701	14.	2,682	11.
3. General sales taxes	3,981	15.	3,976	16.
4. Selective excise taxes[b]	2,649	10.	2,649	11.
5. Property Tax	2,825	11.	2,825	11.
6. Social security taxes.	1,863	7.	1,863	8.
7. Medical-hospital, poll taxes	660	3.	660	3.
8. Import duties	818	3.	818	3.
9. Succession and estate taxes	242	1.	242	1.
10. Other taxes[c]	1,438	5.	1,408	5.
11. Total tax payments	25,907	100.	24,853	100.

[a]Most tax exportation occurs as a result of the extensive foreign ownership of Canadian Industry. See Gillespie, *op. cit.*, 1980, Part II.

[b]Selective excise taxes include excises on alcohol, tobacco, fuel oil and several minor commodities.

[c]Other taxes include: motor vehicle license revenues, natural resource revenues, taxes on premium income of life insurance companies, business taxes, and several minor taxes on amusements, etc.

Note: Details may not add to totals, owing to rounding.

Source: Gillespie, *op. cit.*, 1980, Tables A-3 and A-3a, derived from Statistics Canada, *Financial Statistics of Federal, Provincial and Local Governments, 1969*, Cat. Nos. 68-211, 68-203, 68-204 and 68-202 (Ottawa: Information Canada, 1972). The taxes shown here exclude all non- tax revenues, such as sales of goods and services, fines and penalties, net revenues from own enterprises (except alcohol monopolies), postal revenues, foreign exchange, etc. Taxes on income going abroad and credits and payments to non-residents of $248 million are excluded, since it is assumed that the burden of such taxes falls on non-resident Canadian family units, and thus should be excluded from a study of fiscal incidence. Social security taxes from the *National Accounts* and other sources are included in the totals.

Table 4

Tax Incidence: Effective Tax Rates Using the Broad Income Concept, Canada, 1969

Line	Tax	under $2,000	$2,000-2,999	$3,000-3,999	$4,000-4,999	$5,000-5,999	$6,000-6,999	$7,000-9,999	$10,000-14,999	$15,000 & over	Total
						Family Money Income Class					
	FEDERAL TAXES										
1	Personal income tax	2.0	2.8	4.0	5.2	6.6	7.5	8.9	11.0	11.2	9.3
2	Corporation income tax	9.3	4.9	3.8	3.5	2.4	3.2	2.5	2.5	4.9	3.3
3	General sales taxes	13.3	7.4	5.5	4.8	4.5	4.4	4.1	3.8	2.6	3.8
4	Selective excise taxes	5.3	2.9	2.3	2.0	2.1	1.9	1.7	1.5	.8	1.5
5	Social security taxes	2.9	2.7	3.4	4.1	4.7	4.1	3.7	2.7	1.2	2.8
6	Customs import duties	4.8	2.6	1.9	1.7	1.6	1.6	1.5	1.4	.9	1.4
7	Succession and estate taxes	.5	.3	.3	.2	.1	.1	.1	.1	.3	.2
8	*Total federal taxes*	38.2	23.6	21.2	21.5	21.9	22.9	22.3	23.0	22.1	22.3
	PROVINCIAL TAXES										
9	Personal income tax	.8	1.1	1.6	2.0	2.5	2.9	3.4	4.3	4.3	3.6
10	Corporation income tax	3.4	1.8	1.4	1.2	.9	1.1	.9	.9	1.6	1.2
11	General sales tax	8.9	5.8	4.8	3.5	3.4	3.2	3.0	2.8	1.8	2.8
12	Selective excise tax	7.2	4.6	3.7	3.8	3.7	3.7	3.4	3.1	1.7	2.9
13	Social security taxes	.3	.2	.3	.3	.4	.5	.5	.3	.2	.3
14	Medical-hospital premiums	8.9	3.2	2.1	1.6	1.6	1.3	1.1	1.0	.6	1.1
15	Succession and estate taxes	.7	.4	.4	.3	.2	.2	.1	.1	.4	.2
16	Other taxes	5.3	3.1	2.2	2.1	1.8	2.0	1.8	1.8	1.8	1.9
17	*Total provincial taxes*	33.2	20.2	16.3	14.9	14.4	15.0	14.1	14.2	12.4	13.8
	LOCAL TAXES										
18	General sales tax	—	—	—	—	—	—	—	—	—	—
19	Property Tax	22.8	12.7	7.5	6.1	5.3	5.1	4.7	4.3	3.5	4.7
20	Business Tax	1.8	.9	.6	.4	.5	.5	.5	.4	.3	.4
21	Poll taxes	.1	—	—	—	—	—	—	—	—	—

22	Other taxes	.2	.1	.1	.1	—	—	—	—	—	—
23	TOTAL LOCAL TAXES	24.8	13.7	8.2	6.6	5.8	5.6	5.3	4.8	3.8	5.2
24	TOTAL ALL TAXES	96.3	57.5	45.8	43.0	42.2	43.4	41.7	42.0	38.3	41.3

Note: Details may not add to totals, owing to rounding.

Source: Gillespie, op. cit., 1975, Table D-3.

Table 5

Shifting Assumptions for Fiscal Incidence Study, Gillespie, 1975

Line	Item	Shifting Hypothesis	Distributive Series
Tax Hypotheses			
Federal Taxes			
1.	Individual income tax	not shifted	individual income tax payments
2.	Corporation income tax	capital owners (.5) / consumers (.5)	dividend income / total consumption
3.	General sales tax	consumers of taxed items	consumption of commodities subject to federal sales tax
4.	Selective excise taxes		
	i) alcohol	alcohol consumers	alcohol consumption
	ii) tobacco	tobacco consumers	tobacco consumption
	iii) other excises	other consumers	total consumption
5.	Social security taxes		
	i) unemployment insurance	labour taxed	unemployment insurance payments
	ii) Canada/Quebec pension plans	labour taxed	CPP/QPP covered wages and salaries
	iii) public service pensions contributions	labour taxed	other pension payments
6.	Customs import duties	consumers of imported items	consumption of imported commodities
7.	Succession and estate taxes	recipients	succession and estate income

Table 5 continued

Provincial Taxes

8. Individual income tax	not shifted	(.5)	individual income tax payments
9. Corporation income tax	capital owners	(.5)	dividend income
10. Provincial sales tax	consumers		total consumption
	consumers of taxed items		consumption of commodities subject to provincial sales tax
11. Selective excise taxes			
i) alcohol	alcohol consumers		alcohol consumption
ii) tobacco	tobacco consumers		tobacco consumption
iii) fuel oil	vehicle users		number of miles driven
iv) other excises	other consumers		total consumption
12. Social security taxes			
i) workmen's compensation	labour covered		workmen's compensation payments, covered wages
ii) public service pension contributions	labour taxed		other pension payments
13. Medical-hospital premiums	unshifted		prepaid public health plan payments
14. Succession and estate taxes	recipient		succession and estate tax income
15. Other taxes			
i) motor vehicle licences	commercial users	(.5)	total consumption
	passenger vehicle users	(.5)	automobile purchases
ii) taxes on premium income of life insurance companies	policy owner		personal insurance expenditures
iii) natural resource revenues			
a) royalties	consumers		total consumption
b) rental payments	resource owners		dividend income
iv) amusement taxes	consumers		admission to events
v) capital stock taxes	capital owners		dividend income

Municipal Taxes

16. General sales tax	consumers		admission to events
17. Property tax			
a) *on land*			
i) business	capital owners		dividend income

ii) farm	farm capital owners		farm income
iii residential	residential capital owners		rental income
b) *on improvements*			
iv) business	consumers		total consumption
v) farm	consumers of food		consumption of food
vi) residential:			
owner-occupied	owner	(.67)	value of owned home
renter-occupied	renter	(.33)	rent expenditures
18. Business taxes	consumers		total consumption
19. Poll taxes	unshifted		family units
20. Other taxes	consumers		total consumption

Expenditure Hypotheses

Federal Expenditures

21. Education	post secondary students		post secondary students
Highways			
i) non-user share	property owners	(.67)	value of owned homes
	property renters	(.33)	rent expenditures
ii) passenger vehicles	passenger vehicle users		number of miles driven
iii) transport vehicles	consumers of transported products		consumption of transported products
22. Other transportation	passenger consumers	(.5)	other transportation services, beyond the city
	consumers of transported products	(.5)	consumption of transported products
23. Public health and housing			
i) general public health	family units		family units
ii) hospital care	users of hospital services		hospital users
iii) general housing expenditures	family units		family units
24. Social security and veterans			
i) unemployment insurance	unemployment insurance recipients		unemployment insurance benefit income
ii) old age benefits	old age benefit recipients		old age pension income
iii) family allowances	family units with children		family allowance income
iv) veteran's benefits	veteran family units		veteran family units
v) public service pensions	pension recipient		other retirement pensions

Table 5 continued

25. Regional economic expansion			
i) national unity share	family units	(.25)	family units
ii) real output gains	consumers	(.09)	total consumption
	urban family units	(.02)	urban family units
	labour in lagging regions	(.14)	wages and salaries in lagging regions
	capital owners	(.50)	dividend income
iii) inefficiency share			
26. Manpower			
i) growth and stability gains	trainees	(.37)	manpower trainees
	all family units	(.38)	broad income
ii) equity gains	trainees	(.15)	manpower trainees
iii) regional balance	all family units	(.10)	broad income
27. Agriculture	farm owners		farm income
28. Interest on public debt	recipients		interest income on public debt
29. General expenditures (pure public)	all family units		broad income
Provincial Expenditures			
30. Education			
i) elementary and secondary	students		children, 5-17 years
ii) post-secondary	students		post-secondary students
31. Highways			
i) non-user share	property owners	(.67)	value of owned homes
	property renters	(.33)	rent expenditures
ii) passenger vehicles	users		number of miles driven
iii) transport vehicles	consumers of transported items		consumption of transported products
32. Other transportation	passenger consumers	(.5)	other transportation services, beyond the city
	consumers of transported items	(.5)	consumption of transported items
33. Public health and housing			
i) general public health	family units		family units
ii) hospital care	users of hospital services		hospital users

iii) general housing expenditures	family units	family units
34. Social security and veterans		
i) Canada Assistance Plan and other social security	recipients of CAP benefits	other transfer income
ii) public service pensions	pension recipient	other retirement pensions
35. Manpower	trainees	manpower trainees (.52)
	all family units	broad income (.48)
36. Agriculture	farm owners	farm income
37. Interest on public debt	recipients	interest income on public debt
38. General expenditures: Assumption B	all family units	broad income
Municipal Expenditures		
39. Education	elementary and secondary students	children, 5-17 years
40. Public health and housing		
i) general public health	family units	family units
ii) hospital care	hospital users	hospital users
iii) sanitation		
a) commercial use(.33)	consumers of commercial services	total consumption
b) residential use (.67)	property users	weighted average of value of owned home and rent expenditures
iv) general housing expenditures	family units	family units
41. Social security and veterans other social security benefits	recipients	other transfer income
42. Interest on public debt	recipients	interest income on public debt
43. General expenditures: Assumption B	all family units	broad income

Source: Gillespie, *op. cit.*, 1980, *passim* and Appendix A. For each item the assumptions of the standard case have been chosen. The reader is referred to Tables 3.5 and 4.11, respectively, for alternative assumptions on both the tax and expenditure sides of the analysis.

(about which there is still some debate in the literature) resulted in no change in the general pattern of total tax incidence, although there was some change in the magnitudes of effective tax rates.[10] If it is assumed that the corporate profits tax is borne entirely by shareowners, total tax incidence is less regressive over the lower income brackets and slightly less regressive over the upper income brackets. If it is assumed that sales and excise taxes are borne by factor owners, total tax incidence is considerably less regressive over the lower income brackets and virtually proportional over the upper income brackets. If it is assumed that the share of property tax falling on renter-occupied housing units is borne by the landlord rather than by the tenant, total tax incidence is slightly less regressive over the upper income brackets.

Expenditure Incidence

The estimates of expenditure incidence are derived by allocating the transfer payments and expenditures of all three levels of government according to the standard hypotheses concerning the distributional effects of such expenditures by factor shares, consumer outlays or other beneficiary group classification. Such items are then allocated according to income.[11] The distribution of expenditure benefits is expressed as a percentage of the distribution of broad income in order to effect the pattern of effective expenditure rates of Table 7.

These rates make possible a comparison between the amount of public expenditures incurred on behalf of different family units. The magnitudes can be misleading if they are interpreted as levels of economic welfare, especially at the very low end of the income scale where, as broad income approaches zero (e.g., a unit dependent on the old age pension), the expenditure rate approaches infinity. The family unit in such a case does not experience an infinite level of economic welfare; public expenditures do, however, have a greater effect relative to the income of a family unit in the lowest income bracket than they do for a family unit in the next highest income bracket. For this reason primarily, we believe that attention should be focused on the general expenditure incidence pattern rather than on the exact numerical value of the effective expenditure rates.

The total expenditure incidence (line 31) is regressive throughout, and sharply regressive up to an income level of $5,000 and beyond an income level of $7,000.[12] In short, the general pattern of expenditure incidence is favourable to those in the lower income brackets throughout the measured income scale.

The federal expenditure incidence (line 12) is initially sharply regressive, more gradually regressive up to an income level of $10,000 and virtually proportional beyond. The difference between the highest two income brackets is not large enough to suggest regressivity, given the margin for error in a study of this nature. The major forces contributing to the regressivity over most of the income scale are expenditures on social security and veterans, public health, and housing and manpower. The relative weight of social security recipients, family units and hospital users, and

Table 6

Total Public Expenditures, Canada, 1969*

Line	Expenditure	Public Expenditures Millions of $	%
1	Education expenditures	5,239.0	20.0
2	Highway expenditures	1,316.0	5.0
3	Other transportation expenditures	571.0	2.0
4	Public health and housing expenditures	4,189.0	16.0
5	Social security and veterans payments	4,632.0	17.0
6	Regional economic expansion expenditures	212.0	1.0
7	Manpower expenditures	544.0	2.0
8	Agriculture expenditures	690.0	3.0
9	Interest on the public debt	1,890.0	7.0
10	Total specific expenditures	19,285.0	73.0
11	General expenditures	7,253.0	27.0
12	Total, all expenditures	26,538.0	100.0

* Excludes that part deemed exported to foreigners.

Source: Gillespie, 1980: derived from Statistics Canada, *Financial Statistics of Federal, Provincial and Local Governments, 1969,* Cat. Nos. 68-211, 68-203, 68-204 and 68-202 (Ottawa: Information Canada, 1972), Table A-11.

manpower trainees in the lower income brackets accounts for the considerable contribution of the above three public expenditure categories to the overall regressive pattern.[13] Interest payments on the public debt reflect a regressive pattern up to an income level of $5,999 and are mildly progressive beyond. This U-shaped schedule of rates is accounted for by the two major owners of the debt. The regressive pattern over the lower income brackets is weighted by family-unit holders of Canada Savings Bonds and other readily marketable securities, and the progressive feature over the upper income brackets is weighted by debt held by chartered banks and corporations.

Total provincial expenditures (line 23) are regressive throughout the entire income range, especially at the extremes. The education expenditures pattern, while regressive over the very lowest and highest income brackets, is virtually proportional from an income level of $2,000 through $10,000. The existence of relatively high rates in the first bracket reflects primarily the distribution of post-secondary-education students in family units in this income bracket. The incidence of public health and housing expenditures is sharply regressive over the first few income brackets and virtually proportional up to an income level of $10,000, after which it becomes mildly regressive. The high rates over the first few income brackets are accounted for by the weight of hospital users and housing units.

The total local expenditure incidence pattern (line 30) is regressive up to an income level of $4,000, virtually proportional from $4,000 through $10,000 and mildly regressive beyond an income of $10,000. At the local

Table 7

Tax Incidence: Effective Tax Rates Using the Broad Income Base, Canada, 1969

Line	Tax	under $2,000	$2,000-2,999	$3,000-3,999	$4,000-4,999	$5,000-5,999	$6,000-6,999	$7,000-9,999	$10,000-14,999	$15,000 & over	Total
	FEDERAL EXPENDITURES										
1	Education...............	5.2	2.2	1.8	1.9	1.7	1.4	.9	.5	.4	.9
2	Highways...............	0.6	.3	.2	.2	.2	.2	.2	.2	.1	.2
3	Other transportation.....	3.2	2.1	1.3	1.1	.9	.8	.8	.8	.6	.8
4	Public health and housing ..	28.0	9.9	4.8	3.4	2.7	2.2	1.6	1.1	.5	1.8
5	Social security and veterans..	106.2	49.9	24.0	13.6	9.4	7.2	4.3	2.7	1.5	6.3
6	Regional economic expansion	1.0	.4	.4	.3	.3	.3	.3	.3	.5	.4
7	Manpower..............	12.9	6.9	4.5	2.8	1.5	.9	.3	—	—	.7
8	Agriculture.............	2.5	3.0	2.3	1.7	1.0	.5	.5	.5	1.2	.8
9	Interest on debt........	7.2	3.8	3.7	2.6	1.4	1.8	1.8	1.3	2.6	2.0
10	Total specific expenditures...	166.8	78.8	43.0	27.6	19.2	15.3	10.8	7.5	7.4	13.9
11	General expenditures* (B) ...	6.8	6.8	6.8	6.8	6.8	6.8	6.8	7.0	6.8	6.8
12	Total federal expenditures ...	173.6	85.4	49.8	34.4	26.0	22.1	17.5	14.5	14.2	20.7
	PROVINCIAL EXPENDITURES										
13	Education................	11.5	8.5	8.2	8.0	7.8	7.7	6.4	4.0	2.1	4.9
14	Highways................	7.4	4.2	3.0	2.8	2.5	2.5	2.5	2.1	1.1	2.0
15	Other transportation......	.4	.2	.2	.2	.1	.1	.1	.1	.1	.1

Family Money Income Class

16 Public health and housing	61.4	21.9	11.0	7.7	6.2	5.0	3.8	2.6	1.2	4.2
17 Social security and veterans	15.0	8.0	5.7	3.6	2.4	1.9	1.0	.5	.2	1.3
18 Manpower	2.8	1.5	1.0	.6	.4	.3	.1	.2	—	.2
19 Agriculture	1.0	1.1	.9	.6	.4	.2	.2	.2	.4	.3
20 Interest on debt	3.3	1.9	1.1	1.0	.7	.6	.5	.5	.7	.6
21 Total specific expenditures	102.7	47.2	31.0	24.4	20.2	18.2	14.5	10.2	5.9	13.7
22 General expenditures* (B)	2.3	2.3	2.3	2.3	2.3	2.3	2.3	2.3	2.3	2.3
23 Total provincial expenditures	105.1	49.6	33.3	26.7	22.5	20.5	16.8	12.5	8.2	16.0
LOCAL EXPENDITURES										
24 Education	2.8	4.1	4.4	4.1	4.0	4.5	4.1	2.7	1.2	2.9
25 Public health and housing	7.0	3.0	1.8	1.4	1.2	1.1	1.1	.9	.5	1.0
26 Social security and veterans	2.7	1.1	.6	.4	.2	.2	.1	.1	—	.2
27 Interest on debt	2.9	1.6	.9	.5	.5	.6	.5	.4	.5	.5
28 Total specific expenditures	15.4	9.8	7.8	6.4	6.0	6.4	5.7	4.1	2.3	4.6
29 General expenditures* (B)	2.9	3.0	3.1	3.0	3.0	3.0	3.0	3.0	3.0	3.0
30 TOTAL LOCAL EXPENDITURES	18.4	12.9	10.9	9.4	9.0	9.5	8.7	7.1	5.3	7.6
31 Total expenditures: all levels of government	297.0	148.8	94.0	70.5	57.5	52.1	43.1	34.2	27.7	44.4

Note: Details may not add to totals, owing to rounding.

Source: Gillespie, *op. cit.*, 1975, Table D-6; general expenditure assumption B allocates item proportional to broad income.

level, education expenditures are progressive over the first two brackets (reflecting the distribution of children of school age in families in these income brackets), virtually proportional to $10,000 and mildly regressive beyond. Not surprisingly, social security payments are more heavily weighted towards the lower income brackets and virtually proportional beyond an income of $3,000.

The use of the adjusted broad income base in deriving estimates of expenditure incidence results in a pattern of total expenditure incidence that is much less extreme but still highly favourable to the lower income brackets and regressive throughout the entire measured income scale. And while there are some differences at finer levels of disaggregation, one can conclude that the overall pattern of the total results is remarkably similar for both income bases: general regressiveness throughout the entire income range.

The results of Table 7 are based on the standard distributional hypotheses of Table 5. Given the greater state of uncertainty concerning these expenditure hypotheses (compared with the tax hypotheses), we experimented with several alternative assumptions for almost every expenditure category. The alternative experiments had some effect on the magnitudes of the effective rates but no significant impact on the general pattern of total expenditure incidence.[14] When an alternative distributive series is used to allocate the costs incurred on behalf of hospital-care users, total expenditure incidence is less regressive over the lower income brackets. If it is assumed that transfer payments connected with social insurance legislation (unemployment insurance, the Canada and Quebec Pension Plans, etc.) are incurred on behalf of family units that wish to minimize the cost of providing certain forms of humanitarian social welfare to family units that are less well-off, total expenditure incidence becomes much less regressive over the lower income brackets and slightly less regressive over the upper income brackets. The general pattern of total expenditure incidence is still regressive throughout the measured income scale, but it is less regressive for the assumption of prudent humanitarians benefiting compared with the standard assumption of transfer payment recipients benefiting.[15] The difference in results is great enough to underline the importance of future theoretical and empirical work in the distributive aspects of transfer payments.[16]

We have designated pure public goods — those available in equal amounts for all family units — as "general" expenditures.[17] Fiscal incidence studies usually provide an array of alternative assumptions concerning the distribution of benefits from pure public goods,[18] and our assumptions are summarized in Table 2. In our standard case (underlying the results of Table 7), it is assumed that family units benefit from "general" expenditures in proportion to their broad income. Alternatively, it is assumed that family units benefit equally (assumption A), benefit in proportion to their flow of capital income (assumption C), and benefit in proportion to their disposable income (total income-using activities) (assumption D).

The total expenditure incidence pattern for assumptions A, B and D is roughly similar. The magnitudes of the rates vary considerably but the relative effect is very much the same: the incidence pattern is favourable to those in the lower income brackets throughout the measured income range (see Table 2). When "general" expenditures are allocated by capital income (assumption C), the incidence of total expenditures is regressive up to an income level of $14,999 and progressive beyond this range. Given an expected greater concentration of investment income over the upper income ranges, this pattern is not surprising. This is the only major qualification to the standard pattern of total expenditure incidence.

Aaron and McGuire have recently developed a more rigorous methodology for allocating the benefits of pure public goods among family units. Given an efficient level of provision, the income value of a pure public good to a household is "a fraction of the total value of the public good, (that is) proportional to the reciprocal of (the household's) marginal utility of private good expenditure".[19] When "general" expenditures are allocated according to the Aaron-McGuire methodology, the pattern of total expenditure incidence is not changed and the effective rates are not significantly different from the results of the standard case.[20]

Fiscal Incidence

The estimates of fiscal incidence are derived by subtracting the distribution of effective tax rates, (Table 4), from the distribution of effective expenditure rates (Table 7). The results are presented in Table 8. A positive value for the effective fiscal incidence rate for any income bracket indicates that the family units in the bracket are net gainers from the redistributive mechanism of the public sector. A negative value indicates that they are net contributors to the redistributive mechanism. A positive value for the effective fiscal incidence rate for the total row reflects an overall deficit for the period in the government budget; a negative value reflects an overall surplus.[21]

The fiscal incidence estimates for all three levels of government are found in Table 8 and Figure 1. Fiscal incidence for the total public sector is positive and regressive up to an income level of about $10,000 (although it is relatively small over the $7,000 - $9,000 income range) and negative and regressive from an income level of $10,000 on. Family units in the lower income brackets are net gainers from the redistributive mechanism, while family units beyond an income of $10,000 are net contributors to the redistributive mechanism.[22] The general fiscal incidence pattern is the result of a regressive tax incidence pattern and an expenditure incidence pattern that is even more sharply regressive (favourable to the lower income classes). The outcome is redistribution from higher income family units to lower income family units. The same conclusion holds for the adjusted broad income base.

The overall pattern of federal fiscal incidence is positive and regressive up to an income level of $6,000, negligible over the $6,000 to $6,999 income range, and negative and regressive from $7,000 to $15,000, after which it becomes proportional.[23] Family units in the highest income brackets ($15,000 and over) are net contributors to the federal redistributive mechanism, but relative to family units in the next lowest income class, they do not contribute more heavily. In short, the federal sector is not as heavily redistributive as one might expect over the higher income brackets.

Table 8

Fiscal Incidence, Using the Broad Income Concept, Canada, 1969 (Percentages)

Family Money Income Class	Federal	Provincial	Local	Total, All Levels
Under $ 2,000	135.3	71.8	−6.5	200.7
$ 2,000 - 2,999	62.9	29.4	−0.2	93.9
3,000 - 3,999	28.5	17.0	2.7	48.2
4,000 - 4,999	12.9	11.7	2.8	27.5
5,000 - 5,999	4.1	8.1	3.2	15.6
6,000 - 6,999	−0.8	5.6	3.8	8.6
7,000 - 9,999	−4.8	2.6	3.5	1.3
10,000 -14,999	−8.4	−1.7	2.3	−7.8
15,000 and over	−8.0	−4.2	1.5	−10.8
Total	−1.6	2.0	2.4	2.8

Note: Details may not add to totals, owing to rounding.
Source: Gillespie, *op. cit.*, 1975, Table D-9, for the standard case.

Figure 1

Fiscal Incidence

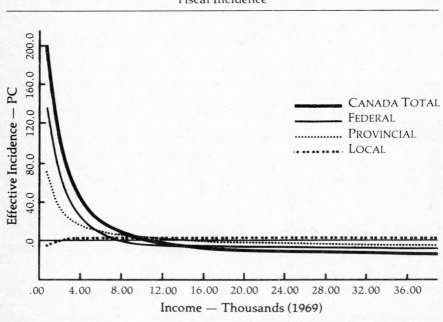

The overall pattern of provincial fiscal incidence is positive and regressive up to an income level of about $10,000 and negative and regressive beyond an income level of $10,000. The provincial redistributive mechanism results in a break-even income at a higher income level (about $9,000 - $9,999) than the federal redistributive mechanism (about $6,000 - $6,999), and it is continuously redistributive throughout the measured income scale. In fact, it is the increasing relative redistribution over the two highest income brackets at the provincial level that outweighs the federal effect to generate the total public sector continuous redistribution.

The pattern of fiscal incidence at the local level differs markedly from those of the other two levels of government. In the first place, the local public sector has an overall deficit of 2.4%, which appears as an augmentation of the positive values in the fiscal incidence estimates. Transfers from the other government levels and borrowing by local governments make such apparent gains possible. Except for the two extremes of the income scale, there is virtually no redistribution at the local level; most family units are gainers and roughly to the same degree. Given these findings, we conclude that the mechanism at the local level redistributes away from family units with incomes less than $2,000 to those with incomes above $3,000.

We noted earlier that none of the alternative tax shifting hypotheses and only two of the alternative expenditure distributive effects hypotheses had a significant impact on the resultant pattern of incidence rates. We examined the fiscal incidence estimates for the public health adjustment, the social security adjustment (the prudent humanitarians) and the general expenditure alternatives. The overall pattern of fiscal incidence for the standard case is not altered by the use of alternative hypotheses concerning expenditures, except when it is assumed that the benefits of general expenditures accrue to family units in relation to capital income. In such cases, net contributors in the upper-middle income range ($10,000 - $14,999) contribute relatively more to the redistribution to the poor than those in the highest income bracket do.

The above findings support the conclusion that the total public sector in Canada was broadly redistributive from higher income classes to lower income classes in 1969. In addition, the public sector was redistributive in such a way that the gainers with higher income gained relatively less from, and the net contributors with higher incomes contributed relatively more to, the redistributive mechanism of the public sector.

Part IV — Income Redistribution in Canada, 1961-1969

This section compares the empirical estimates of fiscal incidence for 1961 and 1969 in order to illuminate the nature of the change during this period.[24] Given the inflation money income between 1961 and 1969, the money income brackets used to classify family units did redistribute income from the upper-middle and richest income classes to the poorest and in the two years will not be directly comparable, and the effective rates measure of fiscal incidence will be less useful for describing changes through time than for describing the state of redistribution at one point of time. Accordingly, we have recast our results in a Lorenz measure of fiscal incidence; for a given percentage distribution of family units in each year, the percentage of income redistributed is compared.[25]

The results are provided in Table 9. The Lorenz grouping of family units (column (2)) is neither of quintiles nor quartiles since it emerges from the data constraints inherent in the fiscal incidence studies for 1961 and 1969. The 1969 distribution of family units has been adjusted to be consistent with the 1961 distribution.[26] The Lorenz groups are also designated by characterized income classes, the median family unit falling within the middle-income class.

The Lorenz measure of redistributed income during 1961 is contained in column (3) for the Panel A results. Lorenz groups one and two gained from the redistributive process of the public sector; groups four and five were contributors to the redistributive process; and the median group was a very slight gainer. In other words, the public sector in 1961 did redistribute income from the upper-middle and richest income classes to the poorest and lower-middle-income classes; the poorest income class was a net gainer of 2.7% of total income, while the richest income class was a net contributor by 3.3% of total income. For the Panel A results the share of total income gained by or contributed by each Lorenz group is shared by all family units within that group. The Lorenz measure of redistributed income for 1969 (column (4)) demonstrates that the public sector in 1969 did redistribute income from the upper-middle and richest income classes to the poorest and lower-middle-income classes (consistent with the findings of Table 8).

Column (5) is especially important, since it captures the *change* over time in the redistributive activity of the public sector. There was a change during the 1960s which favoured groups one, two and five at the expense of groups three and four. The total public sector has become more redistributive over time, but it is redistribution away from the middle and upper-middle-income classes to the extremes of the income scale — both the poorest income classes and the richest income class.

Given the uneven proportion of family units within each Lorenz grouping, it is not a straightforward matter to consider the effects of the changes in income shares of Panel A in terms of individual family units. Consequently we have converted the results of Panel A into the shares of income received by a representative percentile of family units within each Lorenz group and presented them in Panel B.[27] The most interesting results are in column (5). We noted above that the change in the redistributive activity of the public sector during the 1960s favoured groups one, two and five at the expense of groups three and four. This change in redistribution provided net gains to a representative percentile of family units in the poorest income class which are twice as large as the net gains to a representative percentile of units in the lower-middle-income class. However, the net gains to a representative percentile of family units in the richest income class are the largest of all; three times larger than the gains to the poorest representative

Table 9

Fiscal Incidence in Canada, 1961-69, Using the Lorenz Measure of Fiscal Incidence

Line	Lorenz Grouping (Income class) (1)	Family Units in Lorenz Group (2)	Fiscal Incidence (% of Total Income Redistributed) 1961 (3)	1969 (4)	Change in Fiscal Incidence 1961-1969 (5)
Panel A:	Share of total income redistributed within each Lorenz Grouping				
1.	Group one (poorest)	21.7	2.7	3.6	+0.9
2.	Group two (lower-middle)	25.5	2.5	3.0	+0.5
3.	Group three (middle)	25.5	0.1	-0.1	-0.2
4.	Group four (upper-middle)	22.2	-2.0	-3.7	-1.7
5.	Group five (richest)	5.0	-3.3	-2.7	+0.6
6.	Total	100.0	0.0	0.0	0.0
Panel B:	Share of total income redistributed for a percentile of family units within each Lorenz Grouping				
7.	Group one	1.0	0.124	0.166	+0.042
8.	Group two	1.0	0.098	0.118	+0.020
9.	Group three	1.0	0.004	-0.004	-0.008
10.	Group four	1.0	-0.090	-0.167	-0.077
11.	Group five	1.0	-0.660	-0.540	+0.120
12.	Total	1.0	1.0	1.0	1.0

Source: Gillespie, op. cit., 1975, Table C-12.

family unit. In short, *the increasing contributions of middle- and upper-middle-income Canadians to the redistributive mechanism of the public sector during the 1960s generated the major gains to rich Canadians; each rich Canadian family gained three times more than each poor Canadian family and six times more than each Canadian family in the lower-middle-income class.*[28]

We wish to be quite clear about the conclusions that can be drawn from the empirical results of this section. During 1969 the total public sector did redistribute income away from upper-middle and rich representative Canadian family units towards poor and lower-middle representative Canadian family units (column (4), Panel B). Between 1961 and 1969, however, the net contribution of the representative rich Canadian family unit *fell* and the net contribution of the representative upper-middle-income Canadian family unit *rose*. A representative poor family unit also gained, but not nearly as much as a representative rich family unit. In short, the Canadian public sector during the 1960s did not become substantially more redistributive away from the rich towards the poor; it became somewhat more beneficial towards the poor, and considerably more beneficial towards the rich.

By 1969 the distribution of total command over resources which emerged after the redistributive activity of all three levels of government was as set forth in Table 10. Whether the focus is on the distribution of total command over resources across all income classes, or on the share of such command held by a representative percentile of Canadians in each income class, the results are similar. There was — and is — a substantial inequality of the distribution of command over resources. A representative rich family unit had almost twelve times the total income (after all public sector redistribution had taken place) of a representative poor family unit. Some would judge, as we do, that there is still too great an inequality in the distribution of command over resources in an economy as rich as Canada's.[29]

Table 10

The Distribution of Total Command over Resources,* Canada, 1969

Income Class (% of family units)** (1)		% of Total Command over resources	
		Within each income class (2)	For a percentile of family units within each income class (3)
1. Poorest	(21.7)	6.9	0.318
2. Lower-middle	(25.5)	17.9	0.702
3. Middle	(25.5)	25.7	1.008
4. Upper-middle	(22.2)	32.0	1.441
5. Richest	(5.0)	17.6	3.520
Total	(100.0)	100.0	1.000

*   The adjusted broad Income concept.
** The Lorenz groupings of Table 8.
Source: Gillespie, *op. cit.*, 1980, Table C-12.

Part V — Income Redistribution beyond 1969

Since there are no adequate data for a more up-to-date fiscal incidence study,[30] a rigorous test of redistribution since 1969 is not possible. Sources do exist, however, which will permit a reasoned judgment on redistribution during the 1970s.

The inequality of family money income rose significantly in 1971 and declined moderately through 1974 (see Table 1). By 1974 the share of total family money income of the poorest fifth of Canadian family units was 7% below its 1969 level.[31].

Family money income, as defined by Statistics Canada, includes all transfer payments received by families and individuals. Therefore it includes the transfers resulting from the improved unemployment insurance scheme, the expanded family allowance payments, improved old age security pensions, manpower training allowances, indexing of federal social security payments, and the improved provincial social welfare transfers. In other words, family money income includes one of the three components of fiscal incidence as measured by this paper. However, unless the contribution of the two remaining components of the fiscal incidence amount (the public expenditure component and the negative tax component) received by the poorest income quintile *increased* by a much larger amount than it did during the 1960s, the impact upon adjusted broad income (the total command over resources) in 1974 would result in a *decline* in the share of the poorest income quintile.

It is very unlikely that tax changes during the 1970s would operate to improve the relative position of the poorest family units at the expense of the richest family units. Tax reform was preceded by the elimination of federal estate taxes, and through time most provinces have followed suit (or indicated an intention to do so) by eliminating succession duties. Such changes will benefit the upper-middle and rich income classes relative to the poorest income classes. The 1971 tax reform legislation included half of all net capital gains in the income tax base and lowered the top marginal tax rates; the former would increase and the latter decrease the relative tax payments of the upper-middle-income classes and the rich. The corporate profits tax was gradually lowered and the corporate tax rate on profits of manufacturing and processing was cut significantly; both actions would benefit the rich and to a lesser extent some poor with capital income, relative to the middle-income family units.

Finally, during the early 1970s there have been a proliferation of tax incentives to savings (all of which benefit the rich relative to the poor)[32] and personal income tax cuts, which provide no benefits for the very poor (whose incomes are too low to be taxable). On balance, it is more likely that the share of taxes of the poorest quintile of family units has increased relative to the share of taxes of the rich. Therefore the relative position of the poor has probably deteriorated, but it may have remained stable owing to the tax component of fiscal incidence during the 1970s.

It is more difficult to judge whether the change in government expenditures (as opposed to transfer payments) during the 1970s has effected an

the relative position of the poorest family units at the ex-
st family units. The fact that the composition of govern-
goods and services has remained stable suggests that little
taken place. The emergence of medicare as a full-fledged program would probably improve the relative position of the poor compared
with the rich (given the benefit patterns of Table 6). The expansion of
federal regional economic expansion expenditures has improved the position of rich family units relative to poor family units.[33] On balance, then,
the net effect of such changes could well be to leave the relative fiscal incidence measure unchanged.

We believe that neither the tax component nor the expenditure component of fiscal incidence improved the relative position of the poor between
1969 and the present. In fact, the weight of our argument suggests that the
tax component could have facilitated a deterioration. We are prepared to
adopt the more conservative position that there was no substantial change
in the relative economic position of the poor and rich owing to the tax and
expenditure component of fiscal incidence. As a result, the change in family
money income can be taken as a good proxy of the overall change in total
command over resources during the 1970s. *The poor, in terms of their
relative command over resources, were slightly worse off in 1974 than they
were in 1969.*

Part VI — Summary and Conclusions

We have examined the factual basis for the myth that governments during
the recent postwar period have substantively redistributed larger "shares"
of income away from the rich towards the poor. The empirical evidence
does not support the mythology.

During 1969 the total public sector was broadly redistributive from
higher income classes to lower income classes. This redistribution was made
up of a pattern of tax incidence that was regressive over the poorest 36% of
all family units and mildly regressive over the upper income classes as
measured in this paper. In addition, the pattern of expenditure incidence
was sufficiently favourable to the poor to outweigh the tax incidence and effect a positive income redistribution to the poor.

Between 1961 and 1969 the net contribution of a representative rich
Canadian family unit fell and the net contribution of a representative upper-
middle-income Canadian family unit rose. Therefore a representative rich
Canadian family unit gained and a representative upper-middle-income
family unit lost during the 1960s. A representative poor family unit also
gained during the 1960s, but much less than the rich. In short, during the
1960s the public sector became somewhat more beneficial to the poor and
considerably more beneficial to the rich, primarily at the expense of upper-
middle-income family units.

Between 1969 and 1974 the quintile distribution of family money income became less favourable for the poorest fifth of Canadians. Given the
changes in taxes and government expenditures during the 1970s, it is unlikely that there was any improvement in fiscal incidence for the poor relative

to the rich from these sources. Consequently, the change in the distribution of family money income can be taken as a good proxy of the change in relative income shares inclusive of government redistributive activity. It follows that the poorest fifth of Canadian family units, in terms of relative command over resources, was slightly worse off in 1974 than in 1969.

The evidence does not support the belief that over time governments have been successful in increasing the degree of redistribution from the rich to the poor such that the "share" of command over resources of the poor has increased significantly. Quite the contrary; the small relative gain of the poor during the 1960s has been eroded during the early 1970s, leaving the poor with no improvement in their "share" over the longer period. On the other hand, the considerable gain of the rich during the 1960s has persisted during the early 1970s, thus giving the rich an improvement in their "share" over time. For the most part, the relative improvement of the rich has been at the expense of the median and upper-middle-income families. The distribution of command over resources in Canada is still a long way from providing the poor with a standard of living which "allows for dignity and decency".

NOTES

1. Douglas H. Fullerton, "A Society Transformed: Robin Hood Runs out of Funds" (May 1976), 91 *Saturday Night*, pp. 1-23. D.G. Hartle, "On Prophets and Power: A Comment on the Prime Minister's Revelations" (Spring 1976), II *Canadian Public Policy - Analyse de Politiques*, pp. 249-55. Tom Velk, "Good News: Changes in Income Distribution" (May 1976) *Canadian Forum*, pp. 21-23.

2. The Hon. John N. Turner, *Budget Speech, November 18, 1974* (Ottawa 1974), and *Budget Speech, June 23, 1975* (Ottawa 1975), Department of Finance, Government of Canada. The Hon. Donald S. Macdonald, *Budget Speech, May 25, 1976* (Ottawa 1976), Department of Finance, Government of Canada.

3. These dates encompass the first and last years for which comprehensive data on the distribution of income are available. The point was cogently made by the Hon. Mr. Marc Lalonde: "So the 'shares' of family income enjoyed by these several income classes have remained remarkably stable over 20 years, *despite* the enormous increases in social security payments. If anything the relative position of the lowest income group has deteriorated." The Hon. Marc Lalonde, "Income Distribution: A question of Community Ethics," Speech to the Empire Club of Canada (Toronto, October 31, 1974), p. 7 (emphasis original). Keith Horner and Neil MacLeod, *Changes in the Distribution of Income in Canada*, Staff Working Papers, No. Z-7507, Health and Welfare Canada, Policy Research and Long Range Planning (Welfare) (Ottawa: May 1975). Roger Love and Michael C. Wolfson, *Income Inequality: Statistical Methodology and Canadian Illustrations*, Statistics Canada, Cat. 13-559 (Ottawa: Information Canada, March 1976). Statistics Canada, *Income Distributions by Size in Canada, 1969*, Cat. 13-544 (April 1972); unpublished data (1972); *Income Distributions by Size in Canada, 1971*, Cat. 13-207 (August 1974); and *Income Distributions by Size in Canada, 1974: Preliminary Estimates*, Cat. 13-206 (October 1975).

4. This observation is based on the gini coefficient measure of Income Inequality (Horner and MacLeod, *op. cit.*, p.21; Love and Wolfson, *op cit.*, p.75). See Ap-

pendix Table A-1 for the quintile distribution of income for selected years during the 1951-74 period.

5. David A. Dodge, "Impact of Tax, Transfer and Expenditure Policies of Government on the Distribution of Personal Incomes in Canada" (March 1975), 21 *Review of Income and Wealth*, pp. 1-52. W. Irwin Gillespie, "Effect of Public Expenditures on the Distribution of Income" in R.A. Musgrave (ed.), *Essays in Fiscal Federalism* (Washington, D.C.: Brookings Inst., 1965), pp. 122-86; *The Incidence of Taxes and Public Expenditures in the Canadian Economy*, Studies of the Royal Commission on Taxation, No. 2 (Ottawa: Queen's Printer, 1967). James A. Johnson, *The Incidence of Government Revenues and Expenditures*. A Study Prepared for the Ontario Committee on Taxation (Toronto: Queen's Printer for Ontario, 1968). R.A. Musgrave, K.E. Case and H. Leonard, "The Distribution of Fiscal Burdens and Benefits" (July 1974), 2 *Public Finance Quarterly*, pp. 259-312. Tax Foundation Inc., *Tax Burdens and Benefits of Government Expenditures by Income Class, 1961 and 1965*, Research Publication No. 9 (New York: 1967).

6. The income sources; income uses dichotomy is drawn from Musgrave's seminal discussion of general equilibrium effects of budget policy. R.A. Musgrave, *The Theory of Public Finance* (New York: McGraw-Hill, 1958). For a more complete discussion of the theory of fiscal incidence as derived from such general equilibrium analysis, see Gillespie, *op. cit.*, 1967, and *op. cit.*, 1975, and Johnson, *op. cit.* We use the term "family unit" to encompass families and unattached individuals as defined by Statistics Canada.

7. For alternative views of the appropriate income bases for measuring total fiscal incidence, see the following sources. G.A. Bishop, "The Tax Burden by Income Class, 1958" (1961), XIV: 1 *National Tax J.* pp. 41-59. A.R. Prest, "The Budget and Interpersonal Distribution," Proceedings of the Prague Congress of the International Institute of Public Finance, 1967, in (1968), pp. 1-2, *Public Finance*, pp. 80-98. Alan J. Peacock and J.R. Shannon, "The Welfare State and the Redistribution of Income" (August 1968), *Westminster Bank Review*, pp. 1-16. Eugene Smolensky and Morgan Reynolds, "The Post Fiscal Distribution: 1961 and 1970 Compared" (December 1974), 27 *National Tax J.*, pp. 515-30. Jacob P. Meerman, "The Definition of Income in Studies of Budget Incidence and Income Distribution," Studies in Domestic Finance, No. 6, Public and Private Finance Division, Development Economics Department, International Bank of Reconstruction and Development mimeo (July 1974).

    We adopt the orthodox assumption that budget incidence is neutral with respect to the distribution of factor payments (see Gillespie, *op. cit.*, 1980 Part II). The radical critique takes issue with the "neutrality" assumption by arguing that the theory of the state underpinning orthodox fiscal incidence studies is incorrect. It argues that the state, when it emerges, biases the original distribution of factor income against the poor and in favour of the propertied or dominant classes — any later redistribution through transfer payments may return the poor to their original relative position, but does not provide net benefits to the poor. David M. Gordon, "Taxation of the Poor and the Normative Theory of Tax Incidence" (May 1972), LXII *American Economic Review, Papers and Proceedings*, pp. 319-28. W. Norton Grubb, "The Distribution of Costs and Benefits in an Urban Public School System" (March 1971), XXIV *National Tax J.*, pp. 1-12, Stephan Michelson, "The Economics of Real Income Distribution" (Spring 1970), *Review of Radical Political Economics* 75-86. Larry Sawers and Howard Wachtel, "Activities of the Government and the Distribution of Income in the United States", paper delivered at the 13th General Conference of the International Association for Research in Income and Wealth Balantonfured, Hungary, September 1973). This is not the place to deal with the radical alternative in detail; it is enough to point out that a reader who accepts the radical critique will judge this paper as overestimating the redistributive benefits to the poor.

8. The limitations of this approach have recently come under more critical scrutiny. Grubb, *op. cit.* Michelson, *op. cit.* R. Kerr, "An Analysis of the Methodology of Fiscal Incidence Studies", mimeo (Ottawa: Carleton University, 1974).

9. The taxes allocated are found in Table 3 for 1969, the latest year for which comprehensive consumer expenditure data exist (a necessary prerequisite for fiscal incidence estimation). The shifting hypotheses used are summarized in Table 5 for the standard case. These hypotheses are based on fairly widespread acceptance in the literature, and are not dissimilar to other studies. Dodge, *op. cit.* Allan M. Maslove, The Pattern of Taxation in Canada, Economic Council of Canada (Ottawa: Information Canada, 1972).

10. Gillespie, *op. cit.*, 1980, Table 3.6

11. The government expenditures allocated are found in Table 6 for 1969. The distributional hypotheses are found in Table 5.

12. Throughout this paper we are using the terms regressive, proportional and progressive in their strictly technical sense: that is, an effective rate that declines as income increases — whether it be a tax rate, an expenditure rate or a fiscal incidence rate — is defined as a regressive rate. As a result, a regressive expenditure rate is one which is favourable to family units in the lower income brackets and becomes less favourable as income increases.

13. One of the distorting aspects of a study of this sort on the expenditure side of the public sector is that the cumulative effects of a number of disparate programs, benefiting very different groups in the Canadian economy, suggest that the average family unit experiences a favourable average effective expenditure rate over the lower income brackets. The true picture would probably suggest that certain socio-economic groups within these income brackets experience a favourable effective expenditure rate for one program and not for the other programs. The problem of the average rate not representing any family unit within the income class is most pressing for these expenditures.

14. Gillespie, *op. cit.*, 1980, Table 4, 12.

15. The theoretical foundation of social insurance schemes benefiting prudent humanitarians can be drawn from the orthodox literature or the radical literature. The following sources represent the orthodox viewpoint. R.A. Musgrave, "The Role of Social Insurance in an Overall Programme for Social Welfare" in W.G. Bowen *et al.* (eds.), *The Princeton Symposium on the American System of Social Insurance, Its Philosophy, Impact and Future Development* (New York: McGraw-Hill, 1968), pp. 23-46. Harold M. Hochman and James D. Rogers, "Pareto Optimal Redistribution" (September 1969). LIX *American Economic Review*, pp. 542-57, and "Pareto Optimal Redistribution: A Reply" December 1970), LX *American Economic Review*, pp. 997-1002. Mark V. Pauly, "Efficiency in the Provision of Consumption Subsidies" 1970), 1 *Kyklos*, pp. 33-57. The following sources represent the radical viewpoint: Michelson, *op. cit.*, and Sawers and Wachtel, *op. cit.*

16. Experimentation with distributive assumptions for education expenditures, regional economical expansion expenditures and manpower expenditures resulted in very little change in the magnitudes of effective expenditure incidence and no change in the general pattern of incidence. Gillespie, *op. cit.*, 1980.

17. Musgrave, *op. cit.*, 1958, Paul A. Samuelson, "The Pure Theory of Public Expenditure" (November 1954), XXXVI *Review of Economics and Statistics*, pp. 387-89.

18. Gillespie, *op. cit.*, 1965, and *op. cit.*, 1967. Johnson, *op. cit.* Musgrave, Case and Leonard, *op. cit.* Tax Foundation Inc., *op. cit.*

19. Henry Aaron and Martin McGuire, "Public Goods and Income Distribution" (November 1970), 38 *Econometrica*, p. 911.

20. Table 2, line 5. We applied the Aaron and McGuire methodology along with the (σ) factor of 1.55 as derived by Maital: See Shlomo Maital, "Public Goods and Income Distribution: Some Further Results" (May 1973), 41 *Econometrica*, pp. 561-68; "Is Redistributive Taxation a Myth?" paper delivered at the Canadian Economics Association Meetings, mimeo. (June 1973).

21. Designating a budgetary deficit as positive and a budgetary surplus as negative may be confusing. However, given the conceptual framework within which we are working, wherein government expenditures are analysed as an addition to the incomes of family units and tax payments are analysed as a subtraction from the incomes of family units, the result follows directly. We also note that the deficit associated with our conceptual framework is a more complex notion than the usual definition of a deficit; it includes the budgetary effects of active stabilization policy (which should or should not be adjusted for, depending on the model of income determination presumed to hold) and the effects of a differential in the exported fraction of taxes and government expenditures (which should not be adjusted for). For a detailed discussion of the issues involved, see Gillespie, *op. cit.*, 1967, pp. 164-73, and *op. cit.*, 1975, Part V, pp. 1-5.

22. Family units that are, on balance, neither gainers from nor contributors to the redistributive mechanism are referred to as break-even family units; the income bracket which they occupy is designated as the break-even income bracket. Given the possible errors associated with a study of this nature, any fiscal incidence rate less than $+1\%$ and greater than -1% is treated as a break-even rate.

23. The possible errors associated with a study of this nature are such that the difference between the two effective fiscal incidence rates over the highest two brackets are probably not significant. As a result, we conclude that fiscal incidence at the federal level becomes proportional over the higher income brackets.

24. The empirical estimates for 1961 are drawn from Gillespie, *op. cit.*, 1967. The income base of this work had to be adjusted to render it comparable with the income base of the 1975 study. See Gillespie, *op. cit.*, 1980, Part VI, and Tables C-1, C-11 and C-12.

25. See Musgrave, *op. cit.*, 1958, pp. 223-27, for a description of a Lorenz curve as a measure of inequality. See Gillespie, op. cit., 1980, Part VI, for a more detailed discussion of the derivation of the Lorenz measure of income redistribution.

26. See Gillespie, *op. cit.*, 1980, Appendix Table C-10, for a complete description of the methodology underlying the adjustment of the Lorenz groupings to a common 1961 basis. The poorest income class includes family units with incomes up to $1,999 in 1961 and up to $3,199 in 1969. The lower-middle-income class includes family units with incomes from $2,000 - 3,999 in 1961 and from $3,200 - 6,399 in 1969. The middle-income class includes family units with incomes from $4,000 - 5,999 in 1961 and from $6,400 - 9,799 in 1969. The upper-middle-

income class includes family units with incomes from $6,000 - 9,999 in 1961 and from $9,800 - 17,500 in 1969. The bracket limits for 1969 are approximate, given the nature of the adjustment procedure.

27. In carrying out the conversion, it was necessary to assume a rectangular distribution of the relevant income base across the Lorenz distribution.

28. Recall that in 1969 a poor family unit had income less than about $3,200 and a rich family unit had income in excess of $17,500 (given the definitions of poor and rich used in this study).

29. The poorest income class of Table 5 had an upper income bound of approximately $3,200 in 1969. Even if every family unit in this income class had an income of $3,199, it was, in our view, much too inadequate to sustain a decent and dignified standard of living in Canada in 1969. It follows that we do not judge it to be a "fair" distribution of income.

30. Distribution of income data is now available on an annual basis; however, the next completely comprehensive survey of consumer expenditures (both farm and non-farm family units) was conducted by Statistics Canada in 1978, and is being analysed.

31. In this section the poor are defined as those family units falling within the lowest quintile of all family units; during 1974 they had 4.0% of total money income and no family unit had an income exceeding $4,500 (see Table 1).

32. The major tax incentives to savings have been the registered home ownership savings plan, the $1,000 interest and dividend deduction and the expansion of registered retirement savings plans (already in place in 1969), the latest improvement of which was included in MacDonald, *op. cit.*

33. W.I. Gillespie and R. Kerr, "The Impact of Federal Regional Economic Expansion Policies on the Distribution of Income in Canada", monograph prepared for the economic Council of Canada, mimeo. (Ottawa: April 1976).

On the Interpretation of Changes in Inequality*

KEITH HORNER

While income distribution studies are usually motivated by questions of social justice, the connection between social justice and income inequality is not simple and no "just" level of inequality has been proposed.[1] Perfect equality is not suggested as a target because many income differences are clearly just and desirable. These include differentials corresponding to the different income needs of large and small families, differentials resulting from variation in individual preferences for work versus leisure, saving versus consumption, or city life versus country life, and differentials which compensate for differences in the riskiness, difficulty or attractiveness of different jobs. On the other hand, income differentials resulting from discrimination, monopoly, and involuntary unemployment would be condemned as unjust by most people. Less clear-cut examples include income differentials due to inherited wealth and differences in income levels between age cohorts due to productivity growth over time.

When these different sources of income inequality are considered, it is tempting to conclude that an ideal income distribution would exhibit a level of inequality neither close to zero nor close to the existing level. However, any normative conception of income inequality must take into account other considerations as well. One is the degree of mobility of families within the income distribution; another is the apparent demand for certain types of income uncertainty or income inequality as reflected in the popularity of lotteries. A third consideration is the relationship between current incomes and past effort or self-denial; an individual may have a relatively high income today because he saved more and consumed less than others in the past. And finally, the question of how people value changes in their absolute income levels as opposed to changes in their relative income positions is important if it is concluded that redistribution (beyond some point) is inimical to economic growth. These additional considerations complicate the relationship between income inequality and social justice.

The lack of an acceptable inequality norm may lead one to question the purpose of monitoring inequality levels or studying the distribution of income. Why not concentrate instead on monitoring and correcting situations of social injustice such as involuntary unemployment, monopolies, discrimination, and legislation preferential to particular groups? One

*From Social Security Research Reports, *Research Report No. 4*, Health and Welfare Canada, 1977.

answer to this suggestion is that the ultimate consequences of most actions by governments, firms, and individuals are difficult to perceive or to relate to these actions. Monitoring changes in inequality and attempting to understand their causes may provide the best means of identifying practices and regulations which have undesirable effects on the position of particular groups in society.

The lack of a clear target level of inequality complicates the assessment of the significance of changes in inequality. The problem is aggravated by the existence of a variety of family income definitions and summary inequality measures.

Inequality in Family Size-Adjusted Income

One criticism of estimates of inequality among family units is that they involve comparing the incomes of families of different sizes and therefore different income needs. A simple way to overcome this problem is to divide all family incomes by family size and to estimate the level of inequality in per capita income. A drawback of this approach is that it neglects the differing income needs of adults and children and the economies of scale available to larger families. The adjustment made here is to divide family incomes by the factors 1, 1.67, 2, 2.33, 2.67, and 3, corresponding to family sizes of one to six and over.[2] Note that adjustment factors like these could be elaborated to take into account regional variation in living costs or other variables of interest. With this family size correction made, the distribution of "adjusted" income can be defined in either of two ways: over the population of family units or over the population of individuals. The difference is that the adjusted income of a family of size seven would appear once in the former case but seven times in the latter. The latter method gives equal weight to the (adjusted) incomes of all individuals no matter what size of family they are in. The results of both methods of family-size adjustment are shown in Table 1.

Table 1

Income Inequality in Canada, 1973, before and
after Adjustment for Family Size

| | Quintile Shares (%) | | | | | |
	1	2	3	4	5	Gini
1. Incomes of census family units (CFU)	3.5	9.8	17.5	25.4	43.9	0.410
2. Family size-adjusted incomes of CFUs						
a. Family unit basis	5.1	11.0	17.4	24.5	41.9	0.373
b. Individual basis	6.0	12.4	17.8	23.9	39.9	0.339

Source: Statistics Canada, *1974 Survey of Consumer Finances microdata tape*, "Census Families, 1973 Income." Calculations by National Health and Welfare.

Line 1 gives the quintile shares and Gini Coefficient for census family units (i.e., families and persons not in families) before any adjustment for family size. Line 2.a shows how the income distribution appears when the income of each family unit is divided by the family-size adjustment factor appropriate for that family unit. The effect of this adjustment is to reduce the Gini by about 9% and raise the income shares of the bottom two quintiles. This change in measured inequality reflects the concentration of "persons not in families" in the lower quintiles of the unadjusted distribution and the concentration of large-size families in the top quintiles. In line 2.b of the Table, the distribution of family size-adjusted income is converted from a family unit basis to an individual basis. This is done by applying to the adjusted income of each family unit a frequency equal to the number of individuals in the family unit. The result of this conversion is to provide yet a lower estimate of income inequality. The Gini is reduced by a further 9% and the income share of each of the bottom three quintiles is increased. Placing an increased emphasis on the incomes of individuals in large families lowers inequality because inequality is less among large families than among smaller families and persons not in families.

Poverty and Inequality

In most Western countries, the focus of social concern with income inequality has been on the situation of the least advantaged groups. The ideal that all groups should be able to participate fully in society has its strongest expression in the equal and universal distribution of voting rights and in the principle of equality under the law. In the economic sphere, it has found major application in the provision of financial aid to those whose incomes fall below agreed minimum levels. Historically, these basic minima were set at subsistence levels since large segments of each country's population lived at subsistence. With the rapid growth in real income levels since World War II, poverty has increasingly been defined in social or relative terms, as a form of alienation or exclusion from the normal activities of the society. Given the social, economic, and physical structure of our communities, a certain income level is seen as being the minimum necessary to permit full membership in society, and this minimum must relate to the income levels of other families in the community.

Poverty that is defined by absolute (e.g., subsistence) poverty lines will decline over time so long as low-income families have any share in the community's economic growth. "Absolute" poverty, therefore, can be eliminated over time without requiring any reduction in income inequality. Poverty defined in relation to the average or median income of the community, on the other hand, cannot be reduced without a corresponding change in the income distribution. This raises the question of how great a decline in inequality would be produced by the elimination of poverty (where poverty is defined in the narrow sense of income shortfalls from a poverty line). For example, if an increase in the income of poor families implies an increase in the community's average income and thus an increase in the (relative) poverty line, it might be concluded that relative poverty cannot be eliminated without at the same time eliminating income inequality.

To examine this question, estimates are made of the change in inequality that would result from moving all low-income families up to a poverty line.[3] The poverty line proposed in the *Real Poverty Report* (Adams et al., 1971) is selected for this exercise since it is a relative poverty line which rises in proportion to increases in average family income and since, in 1973, it lay in the middle of the range of proposed low-income lines.[4] Two cases are considered: one in which the transfer is financed by a surtax on higher income families so that average family income does not change, and another in which the transfer is financed out of income increases due to economic growth. The first case requires an absolute reduction in the post-tax incomes of families above the poverty line while the second case does not. Since the total income of the community rises in the second case though, the poverty line and poverty gap (i.e., the required total transfer) rise accordingly.

The results are presented in Table 2. Line 1 shows the initial distribution of income over census family units (CFUs). Lines 2.a and 2.b show the effects on inequality of the tax-transfer package. Line 2.a shows the effect of transferring $3.6 billion or about 4.8% of family income to poor families so as to bring them all exactly to the poverty line. Line 2.b shows the additional effect on inequality of increasing the taxes of higher income families by $3.6 billion. Line 3 shows the effects on inequality of eliminating poverty by transferring an increase in total community income to families below the poverty line. Here the transfer required is $4.1 billion or 5.5% of total family income, and the final poverty line for a family of four is $6,601.

In the tax finance case, the elimination of poverty is found to reduce the Gini by 17%, from 0.410 to 0.342, about two-thirds of the reduction being associated with the transfer and one-third with the tax increase. In the case where the transfer is financed from economic growth, the Gini is reduced by only 13% despite the somewhat increased poverty line. In both cases the

Table 2

Effect on Inequality of Eliminating Poverty
(*Real Poverty Report* Poverty Line, 1973)

| | Quintile Shares (%) | | | | | |
	1	2	3	4	5	Gini
1. Incomes of CFU	3.5	9.8	17.5	25.4	43.9	0.410
2. Tax-financed transfer						
a. Post-transfer	5.9	10.9	17.0	24.3	42.0	0.363
b. Post-tax and transfer	6.8	11.0	17.3	24.1	40.7	0.342
3. Growth-financed transfer	6.1	11.1	17.0	24.1	41.7	0.358

Source: Statistics Canada, *1974 Survey of Consumer Finances microdata tape,* "Census Families, 1973 Income." Calculations by National Health and Welfare.

Table 3

Inequality among Husband-Wife Families Where the Husband
Is in the Age Group 35-54 and Is Fully Employed

| | | Quintile Shares (%) | | | | |
	1	2	3	4	5	Gini
a. All family units	3.5	9.8	17.5	25.4	43.9	0.410
b. Husband-wife families, 35-54, fully employed	9.6	15.0	18.6	23.3	33.4	0.241

Source: Statistics Canada, *1974 Survey of Consumer Finances microdata tape,* "Census Families, 1973 Income." Calculations by National Health and Welfare.

relative income gains are shared by family units in the bottom two quintiles and the relative income declines concentrated in the top two quintiles.

The most important observation from these results is that the change in the Gini (whether 13% or 17%) and the changes in quintile shares appear quite modest considering that the event simulated is the complete elimination of the poverty gap using poverty lines that are considerably higher than present minimum wage or social assistance benefit levels. Much the greatest part (83% to 87%) of inequality (as measured by the Gini or quintile shares) is unrelated to poverty. The elimination of poverty, even with poverty lines defined relative to average income, would definitely *not* require the elimination of inequality.

Inequality in a Chosen Subpopulation

A final approach to the interpretation of inequality estimates is suggested in Thurow (1973). Thurow's idea was to see how much inequality would remain if some undesirable components of inequality connected with personal handicaps, involuntary unemployment and wage and job discrimination against blacks, women and others were removed from consideration. Examining not family incomes but earning levels among white fully-employed males, he found that the Gini for this group was 40% lower than that for the incomes of all income recipients.

An example of this kind of benchmark is provided in Table 3. For reasons of data availability and comparability with the inequality estimates in Tables 3.a and 3.b, family unit incomes rather than individual earning levels are considered. By limiting the population to husband-wife families where the husband is between 35 and 54 years of age, the major effects of differing family size and position in terms of lifecycle earnings (i.e., apprentice level wages) are removed. Following Thurow, the population is further limited to families where the husband is fully employed in order to remove the effects of involuntary unemployment, desirability, forced retirement, etc. This provides only a crude estimate of "money income inequality resulting from choice," however, because some effects of discriminatory wage differentials may remain while some families where the husband is voluntarily unemployed or out of the labor force may be eliminated. While no adjustment has been made for family size differences within this group, the effect of such an adjustment would be minor.

In this subpopulation, the level of inequality is markedly lower than for the total population; the Gini is lower by 41% (0.241 compared with 0.410), while the income share of each of the bottom three quintiles is higher and the shares of the top two lower. The differences between this group of families and the total population (which include differences in family size, wage rates, and work experience) explain a larger part of measured inequality than either the family size or poverty corrections. They also explain, more than do the other corrections, income inequality among the higher income families (i.e., the share of the top quintile is considerably reduced relative to the shares of quintiles three and four).

NOTES

1. See the following article by Z.A. Jordan, "The Concept of Inequality in the Social Sciences."

2. These adjustment factors are equivalent to the Family Size Equalizer Points defined in the report of the Special Senate Committee on Poverty (Senate, 1971). They were based in turn on the relationships between Statistics Canada's low-income cutoffs for families of different sizes which were derived from the examination of family expenditure patterns. (See Podoluk, 1968:185.) These adjustment factors were determined for economic families so their application to census families here is merely illustrative.

3. The transfer simulated would not be acceptable in practice because of its 100% tax rate on other income and consequent work disincentive. A negative income tax program, sufficient to completely eliminate poverty, would involve transfers to families above the poverty line. It would be more costly and have a greater effect on inequality than the one simulated.

4. For a family of four in 1973, the *Real Poverty Report* poverty line was $6,601; the Statistics Canada revised low-income cutoff, for community size 30,000-99,999 was $6,230 (Catalogue 13-207:16); the Senate Committee poverty line (updated) was $7,231; the Canadian Council on Social Development poverty line was $6,358, calculated according to the method outlined in Ross (1975).

The Concept of Social Inequality in the Social Sciences

ZBIGNIEW A. JORDAN

Justice, fairness, and equity (in its non-legal sense) are commonly used interchangeably. In the discourses of social philosophers, justice and fairness are often distinguished, the former being applicable to social institutions — "justice is the first virtue of social institutions, as truth is of systems of thought" — and the latter, to the relations among individuals, to their equal basic rights as moral persons and thus, to the principles that secure those rights (Rawls, 1972). Equity is synonymous neither with justice nor with fairness. Equity, even in everyday language, means taking into account special needs. For instance, we make allowances for the handicapped or the industrially disabled; equitable claims, then, are just because they remove the inequalities due to extraneous circumstances. Equity involves the allocation of unequal shares in the presence of morally relevant differences and applies the rule that unlike cases should be treated differently. Adam Smith and John Millar, neither of whom was an egalitarian, supported the demands of equity in the above sense (Smith, 1961:88; Lehman, 1969:345). "Equity," writes a British moral philosopher, "requires inequality of initial distribution (a) to meet special need, in order to achieve real equality and (b) to meet special desert" (Raphael, 1946:132). Thus defined, equity is a redundant term, since it occurs in normative statements derivable from the principle of formal justice and is hardly distinguishable from distributive justice. It is true that the term "equity" has frequently been used in recent American studies concerning people's perception of, and evaluative response to, the application of socially accepted rules of distribution.[1] In this case, however, the substitution of equity for social equality involves an implicit claim that the justice of any particular distribution of scarce resources, in relation to human expectations (evaluative responses), is not only amenable to empirical research, but also can be decided by empirical criteria alone. This claim is an example of the naturalistic fallacy, which will be dealt with later. For conceptual consistency and out of respect for an age-old tradition that has given the idea of social justice its rich, descriptive, and emotive meaning, I will use the terms social equality and social inequality, rather than equity and inequity.

The Concept of Social Equality

The concept of social equality is at least as old as Plato and Aristotle. Aristotle distinguished between justice in its wider sense and justice in its more narrow sense, pointing out that the predicate "unjust" applies both to the conduct of a man who breaks the law (positive law or moral law) and the man who takes more than his share.

> In the popular mind the description 'unjust' is held to apply both to the man who takes more than his due and to the man who breaks the law. It follows that the man who does not break the law and the man who does not take more than he is entitled to will be 'just'. 'Just' therefore means (a) lawful and (b) what is 'equal', that is, fair (1955:140).

Lawfulness or legality, the universal justice in Aristotle's terminology, is a more comprehensive concept than particular justice, that is, equality or fairness, for everything unfair is unlawful, but it is not the case that everything unlawful is unfair. Aristotle divided particular justice into distributive justice and corrective justice. Corrective justice is exercised by the judge in settling disputes in private transactions or business deals, where it serves the purpose of correcting any unfairness that may arise. Distributive justice is concerned with the distribution of honor or money or such other possessions of the community as can be divided among its members (Aristotle, 1955:144-45). The principle of distributive justice involves at least two persons and two shares, and allocates shares to persons in proportion to their relative equality or inequality. If the persons are not equal, their shares will not be equal either. Injustice or inequality may arise as much from treating unequals equally as from treating equals unequally (Aristotle, 1955:145-47). The concept of distributive justice reflects Aristotle's belief that there is no equality among men, either in nature or society. Two socially equal individuals are equal in some respects and unequal in others and thus, the question as to which differences are relevant and which are not is of crucial importance. Aristotle considered all forms of government which were established on the principle that people are equal as entirely unsound (1947:Chs. 12, 13).

The idea that all men are equal, insofar as they all are citizens of the universe, was introduced by the Stoics and reinforced by the Christian religion, which taught that all men were equal before God. But as long as most men lived at a subsistence level and in ignorance of the cause of their conditions, the belief that they were equal before God had no implications for the extreme inequality in social life and, as Marx argued, merely provided them with comforting expectations and reconciled them to their fate. Thus, the Aristotelian distinction of justice as lawfulness and justice as equality or fairness was rediscovered only towards the end of the 18th century; since then the idea of social equality has become one of the most complex concepts of social and political philosophy, and one of the most treasured of human values. It was Rousseau's statement in *Social Contract,* "Man is born free; and everywhere he is in chains" (1947:3) that led the authors of the American Declaration of Independence to the proclamation of the self-evident truth that "All men are created equal." This proclamation was incorporated into the French Declaration of Rights of Man and Citizens of 1789, where we read, "Men are born and live free and equal in their rights." *The Manifeste des Egaux* told the people of France that for 1,500 years they lived in slavery and misery and that it was their destiny to realize equality. "Equality," it stated in the resounding rhetoric that resembles another manifesto published 50 years later, "is the first principle of Nature, the most elementary need of man, the prime body of any decent association among human beings" (Babeuf, 1972:91). It was equality before the law (extended to political equality and universal franchise by the radicals in the 19th century), however, that was the objective of all those who, in earlier centuries, in the American War of Independence and the French Revolution, struggled and fought for equality. The concept of social equality was introduced to make clear that the impartiality of justice, lawfulness, and equality before the law did not abolish inequalities in social life in France or anywhere else.

Since the French Revolution, there has been a gradual erosion of the belief in the inevitability and desirability of social inequality, for which social, political, and moral philosophers have been responsible, and which have been translated into deeds by the successful and abortive revolutions of the last 200 years. The erosion has been further abetted by the ancient doctrine of natural rights. This doctrine was used for different and incompatible purposes in ancient Greece and Rome, in the Middle Ages, and in the modern era of the 17th and 18th centuries. The Reformation made a claim for the autonomy of the individual conscience against the dogma of the Church. The reassertion of the individual belief in religious matters led to the demand for political liberties which, through representative institutions, would protect the individual and his property from the arbitrary power of the King. Among the various versions of natural rights, Locke's doctrine was politically perhaps the most influential. Unlike Hobbes, Locke denied that all rights were acquired by entering civil society. On the contrary, according to Locke, the primary function of the state was to protect the individual's rights to life and liberty and, above all, his rights of property. These were the individual's natural rights, inalienable and indefeasible, attributable to men as their inherent characteristics *qua* men, and hence no government could withhold them. The utilitarians took advantage of Locke's notion of natural rights and J.S. Mill incorporated it into the utilitarian doctrine. "When we call anything a person's right," wrote Mill, "we mean that he has a valid claim on society to protect him in the possession of it" (Mill, 1968:49). Natural right was defined as a claim recognized by the state, and thus lost the sort of validity it had originally as a claim which transcended any positive law.

During the revolutionary periods of the 18th and 19th centuries, the concept of natural right acquired a different connotation. Man has natural rights which are prior to the state in the sense that man *qua* man has those rights regardless of their recognition by the state. For Babeuf, equality meant equality of rights in the new sense of the term. Private property violates fundamental human rights because, as Babeuf puts it, "the earth belongs to none and its fruits to all" (Babeuf, 1972:54). The extension of human rights beyond the scope of claims recognized by the state was endorsed, to a certain extent, by even such a conservative philosopher as Hegel (1962:65-70) and by such a radical thinker as Marx, who made it the cornerstone of a revolutionary transformation of society. The socialists argued that this reconstruction was necessary because the society's protection of the rights of some made it impossible to satisfy the rights of all. "Rights," wrote Harold Laski, "are those conditions of social life without which no man can seek, in general, to be himself at his best. For since the State exists to make possible that achievement, it is only by maintaining rights that its end may be secured. Rights, therefore, are prior to the State in the sense that, recognized or not, they are that from which its validity derives" (1948:91).

The connection between the doctrines of natural rights and the demand for political and social justice should now be clear. In Sir Isaiah Berlin's words, "it is doubtless true that most ardent champions of equality were, in fact, believers in human rights in some sense" (1955-56:302). The connection between the beliefs in social equality and human rights raises questions about the procedure used in testing the validity of claims to human rights. While the claims of legal or moral rights can be justified by reference to laws and rules accepted in a given society, it is much more difficult to follow the same course with regard to human rights. It is possible to argue that human rights are legitimate moral rights, which are derivable from certain moral principles, but these principles are bound to be so general that they allow sharply different or even incompatible interpretations and they turn out to be insufficient to resolve conflicts of opinion and interests.

A more satisfactory explication of the concept of natural rights, in the contemporary sense of the term, can be found in T.H. Marshall's rightly famous lecture, "Citizenship and Social Class." Marshall's main thesis is derived from Alfred Marshall's postulate that there is "a kind of basic human equality associated with the concept of full membership of a community — of citizenship, in the reformulation of T.H. Marshall — and that this basic equality is not inconsistent with the inequalities which distinguish the various economic levels of society" (1963:72). Or to put it differently, the inequalities of the social class system may be acceptable provided the equality of citizenship in three main areas — civil, political, and social — is recognized. Citizenship is a status enjoyed by all full members of a community who are equal with respect to the rights and duties citizenship endows. "There is no universal principle that determines what those rights and duties shall be, but societies in which citizenship is a developing institution create an image of an ideal citizenship against which achievement can be measured and towards which aspirations can be directed" (1963:87). Unlike the imperative rules of morals, which prescribe certain conduct for everyone but give others no claims or rights of any kind, citizenship relies on imperative-attributive rules, where the obligation of one side is the right of other, and vice versa (Petrazycki, 1955:47). Citizenship alters the pattern of social inequality and class relationships. It is responsible for the compression of income distribution at both ends of the scale. It extends the area of common culture and common experience and stabilizes certain status differences, mainly through the systems of education and occupation. Hence, class distinctions which are present in status differences continue to exist side by side with an extending area of citizen rights and duties. Inequalities are tolerated provided they do not spring from hereditary privileges.

Therefore, inequalities exist within a society that is viewed as egalitarian in the sense that it provides a universally real and enforceable status of citizenship. Men are not equal, but they can share an extending range of equal rights. A society where social arrangements are determined by the equality of citizenship seems to provide an alternative to what is called a non-egalitarian classless society, as in the United States and the U.S.S.R. (Ossowski, 1963:Ch. VII). In the former, social equality results from the rights of citizenship; in the latter, social equality is based on the claim of classlessness, "classlessness" being defined differently in the two respective countries.

Is the Proposition "All Men Are Equal" Descriptive or Normative?

The word "equality" is applied to indicate the result of a comparison or measurement of objects with respect to the degree they both possess a certain characteristic, regardless of whether this result is expressed in terms of an ordinal or interval scale. The proposition "All men are equal" is elliptical as long as it does not specify some characteristic or characteristics common to all men. Only if they are specified is the proposition in question complete and, if they are descriptive, either true or false.

It is convenient and advisable to accept Rousseau's distinction between the two kinds of inequality among men. He called the first kind of inequality natural or physical because it is established by nature, and consists in a difference of age, health, bodily strength, and the qualities of the mind or of the soul. Rousseau used the term "moral or political inequality" to refer to differences determined by convention or consent. This kind of inequality consists of the different privileges which some men enjoy to the prejudice of others; such as that of being more rich, more honored, more powerful, or even in a position to exact obedience (1947:160). I will call these two kinds of inequality "natural inequality" and "social inequality", respectively. Rousseau's distinction has exercised a conceptual as well as a socially powerful influence. It initiated what de Tocqueville called "a great revolution" which everybody saw but by no means judged in the same way — the universal, gradual, but as de Tocqueville put it, fated progress of the equality of conditions. "Does anyone imagine," he wrote, "that democracy, which has destroyed the feudal system and vanquished kings, will fall back before the middle classes and the rich?" (1968:5, 8).[2]

It should be clear that if the statement "All men are equal" is taken to be descriptive, it states a false proposition; men are never equal with respect to any natural or social characteristics. In the sense discussed, all societies were and are inegalitarian. We could rescue the truth of the proposition "All men are equal" at the price of turning it into a triviality, by saying that all men are equal with respect to the characteristics which each man must possess as a member of the human species. The supporters of egalitarianism, in its radical or extreme form, believe the truth of the proposition in question in the evaluative terms of humanity common to all persons, but I will not discuss egalitarianism in this context.

Unlike the economists, who are fully aware of the distinction between the descriptive and prescriptive or the objective and normative notions of inequality in the distribution of income or wealth, the sociologists have considerable difficulty making the same distinction in their own studies of social inequality. It is self-evident that some rank ordering of people according to a characteristic capable of gradation need not involve differences in rank, that is, differences on a scale of social inferiority and superiority (physical inequalities are an instance in point). But this is not the case with the rank ordering of social inequalities. For many sociologists, inequality of reward means an objective difference in the size and nature of the reward and refers to a network of social relationships which in no way involves an evaluation. For instance, Kingsley Davis and Wilberforce E. Moore write that "if the rights and perquisites of different positions in a society must be unequal, then the society must be stratified, because that is precisely what stratification means" (1970:370; cf. Fallers, 1973:29). If taken literally, this statement is a harmless tautology, because it says "If the rights and perquisites of different positions in a society must be unequal, then they are unequal." But Davis and Moore wish to state a universal characteristic of every society, namely, that it always possesses a certain amount of institutionalized inequality or that inequality is ubiquitous in human societies (1970:370; Moore, 1970:395), where inequality is an evaluative and not a descriptive term. They start with an evaluative statement, to a certain degree informative in content, and then derive from it the conclusion that social stratification is equated with unequal rewards, the latter purporting to be a descriptive difference of rank order unaffected by any value presuppositions.

The protagonists and supporters of the functional theory of stratification do not realize that any distribution of rewards can be legitimately challenged as to its fairness, since it involves a selection of one particular measure of the inequality of reward and this selection inevitably introduces some normative considerations. These normative considerations can never be ignored, even in the relatively simple case of comparing the widely accepted statistical measure of income variation in two different populations, P_1 and P_2, by the Gini coefficient of the Lorenz curve. If, for the sake of simplicity, we do not ask whether the Gini coefficient corresponds to our sense of social equality, the statement "P_1 enjoys a lesser degree of inequality than P_2" does not commit us to recognize the income distribution in P_1 as being more just than that in P_2. More generally, if the Gini coefficient decreases, this does not necessarily mean that there has been a decline in the inequality of income. "The degree of inequality cannot, in general, be measured without introducing social judgements" (Atkinson, 1975:47). In some way or another, the measures of social inequality combine factual and normative criteria and the best thing to do is recognize this explicitly. Gunnar Myrdal's advice, given in connection with the methodology of social policy formulation, applies to the case in point as well. "Value premises should be introduced openly. They should be explicitly stated and not kept hidden as tacit assumptions. They should be used . . . to determine the direction of our positive research. They should thus be kept conscious and in the focus of attention throughout the work" (1958:36-37). Myrdal's advice helps us keep values at the center of any investigation, including the studies of stratification. To define stratification in terms of any and all institutionalized differences of privileges among the adult members of society is not only more useful (Runciman, 1974:56; cf. Parkin, 1971:17,26) but conforms with what the sociologist actually does when he investigates various differences in social rank and the institutionalized arrangements underlying the distribution of privileges.

There are, of course, some sociologists who make a distinction between the normative and descriptive components in the study of stratification and who try to relate the normative aspects of social inequality to the diversity of value assumptions, that is, to the class-bound and class-differentiated views of normative order within a given society (Parkin, 1971:Ch.3). Frank Parkin argues that values are neither imposed on individuals, nor do the individuals construct their social worlds in terms of a wholly personal vision, and without drawing heavily upon the organizing concepts which are part of a public meaning system (1971:82). The "meaning system" seems to signify a class-differentiated normative order of society. Similarly, André Béteille claims that social inequality can be studied both as fact and as value; he emphasizes that the normative criteria of income, occupational or descent status (kinship, race, and ethnicity), need not be consistent with each other and, further, that they may even be sharply at variance with the unstated values (1969:365-68).

The difficulty we tend to experience in the studies of stratification is partly terminological and partly logical. As a rule, inequality is used as a descriptive term to refer to the differentials in the distribution of such resources as income, wealth, social status, and so forth, as well as to the evaluations of those differentials which may or may not conform to the standards of social equality. Studies of stratification fail to logically resolve or even see the problem of relating statements about differentials to the evaluating statements (about those differentials) which involve, implicitly or explicitly, some criteria of social equality. Sometimes these studies suggest that the factual statements about differentials entail evaluative statements, that is, they confuse facts with values by ignoring the intervening step from what is the case to what ought to be. This classic fallacy, of deriving value judgments from statements of fact, is all the more likely to be made in sociology, where value statements are rarely, if ever, purely prescriptive. Apart from their prescriptive mode, value statements involve a descriptive or informative content of meaning. Comparative statements about the Gini coefficient, or the distribution of wealth in corresponding deciles and quartiles for two different countries, provide examples of evaluative statements that include a descriptive content.[3]

In his book *Relative Deprivation and Social Justice*, W.G. Runciman emphasizes that the relation between social inequalities and feelings of relative deprivation is a legitimate problem in social investigations and that an adequate evaluation of this relation presupposes a theory of justice (1972:Ch.12). In other words, the determination of the degree of relative deprivation in various groups or strata of a society (at a specific period of time) is a matter of empirical research, but an evaluation of these empirical findings is a normative task to be accomplished on the basis of a theory of justice, a task which is irreducible to statements of fact. Runciman prefers the theory developed by John Rawls to any other, but he does not claim that Rawls' theory provides a complete and unique resolution of all the problems of social justice. In a later publication Runciman argues, however, that the validity of the indicators of institutionalized inequalities of wealth, prestige, or power is a problem of empirical fact. "To say that any suggested parameter is relevant to stratification is to say that it can, in principle, be related to the distribution of privilege; and it is then a matter for empirical investigation to specify this relation both as accurately and as generally as can be done" (1974:67). In this context, Runciman seems to argue that the criteria of evaluation can be determined by empirical investigations or that what ought to be is derived from what is the case. Runciman's fallacy can also be found in other writers concerned with stratification and social equality (see, for example, Matras, 1975:312).

At least since Hume we have been aware of the dualism of facts and values, or, as Karl Popper prefers to say, of the asymmetry of propositions and decisions through which standards of evaluation are established and/or adopted. Whenever we are faced with a fact, we can evaluate it and ask whether it conforms to certain accepted standards. However, we cannot reverse this mode of procedure, because standards and values are set by our own decisions, while facts exist independently of the standards and values we decide to adopt. Max Weber used to state in his methodological writings, over and over again, that an evaluation cannot be derived from empirical investigations and it is indeed outside their province; there is no legitimate passage but, as he put it, only a leap from the "is" category to the "ought" category. Knowledge of the irreducibility of facts and values has become rare among social scientists today and, hence, we are frequently exposed to ambiguous language and fallacious arguments in studies concerned with differences in rank ordering or with rank differentials and social equality.

The dualism of facts and values does not exclude the use of factual information and rules of logic in arriving at evaluations; it only precludes the former from providing conclusive evidence for the latter. We may and do challenge the validity of a standard as being right or wrong, high or low, relevant or irrelevant. Every standard can be evaluated by another standard, and, in the light of such criticism, can be rejected or upheld. Since evaluative statements are matters of judgment in which factual information and logic play a part — standards are always applied to facts and their application is subject to the rules of logic to a certain extent — evaluative statements set up problems to be resolved by a careful weighing of the information available, an explicit adoption of evaluative criteria, and a precise distinction of the moral issues involved. It is naive and misleading to believe that the evaluation of various social differentials in terms of social equality is a more or less complex finding derived from the investigation of facts.

Karl Popper has pointed out that the rational and imaginative analysis of the consequences of a moral theory has a certain analogy in scientific method; they are both accepted or rejected by an investigation of their concrete and practical consequences. However, in the case of a moral theory there are no results through observation or experimental tests by which it can be tested, apart from the verdict of our conscience (1966:Vol.II,233). Max Weber made a similar point by distinguishing the ethics of responsibility from the ethics of ultimate values, which, being distinct, may supplement each other in certain cases. Because the consequences of our moral beliefs may influence our evaluation and their applicability to the facts of social differentiation, the clarity of thought and language in the statement of these beliefs (in our case, the beliefs concerning the idea of social equality) is of utmost importance. For this reason, the remaining part of this article is devoted to the conceptual analysis of social equality as a prerequisite to arriving at rational and valid evaluative judgments of the facts discovered by stratification studies. It is one of the beliefs of a rational man that in the world of values, as in the world of facts, we can learn through criticism.

The Principle of Formal Justice and Its Inadequacy

As a rule, the proposition "All men are equal" is understood, knowingly or unknowingly, to be a prescription or norm, and hence neither true nor false, but right or wrong, socially, morally or politically. As a prescription, "All men are equal" means "All men ought to be equal, that is, treated alike." Perelman calls that norm the principle of formal or abstract justice, according to which beings of one and the same essential category must be treated in the same way. People belong to an essential category if they possess one characteristic, the same and the only one, to which regard must be had in the administration of justice (Perelman, 1963:16). This principle is as formal as Aristotle's universal justice, because it does not allow decisions regarding which categories are essential and which are not, nor does it specify the kind of treatment to be adopted in a particular case of concrete justice (such as "to each according to his merit," "to each according to his needs," "to each according to his work," and so forth). Therefore, it lays down only a necessary condition of social equality.

It is easy to see that the principle of formal justice is not a sufficient condition of social equality. Let us assume that our essential categories are the Whites and the Blacks or the rich and the poor. If each member of a particular category were treated the same way as every other member of that category, but the forms of the treatment were discriminatory against Blacks or against the poor, the principle of formal justice, lawfulness or legality would have been preserved according to its demands, but the resulting state of affairs would be incompatible with the idea of social equality. The principle of formal justice may result in treating a Black man differently from a White man, or a poor man differently from a rich man, only because he is Black or poor. Hans Kelsen has emphasized that Aristotle's concept of justice as lawfulness or, for that matter, any other equivalent principle (e.g., the principle of formal justice), has no content. Hence, any legal order, privilege or social inequality may be justified by the concept of justice as conformity to positive law (Kelsen, 1971:127).

Perelman's principle of formal justice is not sufficient unless the essential categories are relevant and the differential treatment for each essential category is appropriate to the circumstances and thus justifiable. Without these additional stipulations, the principle of formal justice may be used to inflict all kinds of gross social inequalities upon people. It is also clear that the formulation of the additional necessary conditions of social justice is a very difficult and complex task. Whether a certain essential category is relevant or a certain differential treatment appropriate is a moral question. In answering it we commit ourselves to moral principles, which cannot be conclusively accepted or rejected; they are ultimately adopted as a matter of faith.

The Method of Eliminating Arbitrariness

One way of eliminating those cases where the principle of formal justice justifies real inequality is to eliminate the element of arbitrariness in the rules of concrete justice (social equality), that is, in the content of the rules themselves.

> The formulas of concrete justice lay down or imply essential categories whose members ought to be treated in a certain way, the same for all. To regard such a formula as unjust amounts to questioning either the classification it lays down or the treatment it provides for the members of the different categories (Perelman, 1963:48).

A rule is arbitrary if neither the classification nor the treatment can be justified. We can eliminate or reduce the arbitrariness of the rules of social justice if we respect the prescription "All men ought to be treated alike," unless the rational grounds for treating a certain group differently and unequally have been established. These rational grounds are provided by relating a claim for better treatment to the relevant differences of conditions. Whenever there is a relevant difference of circumstances, there is a rational or reasonable ground for treating a given category differently. Bernard Williams states this demand very briefly: For every difference in the way men are treated a reason should be given, and this reason should be both relevant and socially operative (1964:123). The principle of equal consideration of interests starts with the interests of those persons affected by certain distinctive conditions or the consequences of a social policy, but it justifies the differences in treatment in a similar way. According to this principle, everyone has the claim to have one's interests considered alongside those of every member of the prospective essential category in Perelman's terminology (S.I. Benn, 1971:157).

Ideally, the justification of the rules dividing, let us say, one essential category into two different ones, and establishing a different treatment for their respective members, would consist in deriving the two rules from a more general principle. This way of justifying inequalities of treatment is rare; in most cases, we rely on a combination of empirical evidence and moral persuasion. This kind of justification cannot be conclusive, leaves much room for factual and evaluative disagreement, and delays or makes impossible the implementation of a social policy. It also reminds us that different value commitments underlie different conceptions of social equality, and that equality is one value among many values with which it may come into conflict. There is no simple rule for resolving problems of this nature and there is no *a priori* reason why equality should have precedence over every other value.

Recognized Inequalities

So far, I have assumed that all men are equal in some sense of this term, although they are not treated as being equal, and I have tried to explicate the concept of equality in such a way that the proposition "All men are equal" is not a platitude, a falsehood, or a principle that may be used to entrench inequalities in the name of justice. It should be recognized that the concept of equality can be applied in such a way that it produces consequences exactly opposite to those intended, and it must have the support of other values or ideals so that the demand for equality, as an end in itself, does not suppress other universal human claims. The *philosophes* of the Enlightenment had no doubts, whatsoever, that human ends and ideals were invariably compatible. Modern man has at least a modicum of Weberian pessimism and accepts the possibility of a conflict between ultimate values. Isaiah Berlin, a man at home in the history of ideas and open-minded in his outlook, has expressed very well the mood and way of thinking of modern man. The pursuit of equality, he wrote, may come into conflict with other human aims, be they what they may — such as the desire for happiness or pleasure, or for justice or virtue, or colour and variety in a society for their own sake, or for liberty of choice as an end in itself, or for the fuller development of all human faculties (Berlin, 1955-56:319). Isaiah Berlin has expanded on de Tocqueville's insight that liberty and equality are in fact distinct and, under some circumstances, antagonistic. The danger of despotism might increase with equality (1968:Vol.II, Part II,Chs.1-5).

Let us now analyze the concept of equality in a different way. It appears to be an undeniable fact that all societies have been inegalitarian. Hence, the problems of distributive justice are perhaps more important, from a practical point of view, than any form of egalitarianism. In this case, we do not make the presumption that men are equal or should be treated as equal, but we recognize some inequalities as inherent in the nature of men, that is, in the variety of their endowments. We are concerned, therefore, with the distribution of available resources, material and immaterial, in proportion to some recognized natural and/or social differences, and with making the distribution as just as possible. These assumptions need not endorse the classical liberal doctrine that, given equality before the law and political equality, society should be viewed as governed by rules similar to those in a game of chance which apply to all indiscriminately. It is an established fact of history that if the rules of a game of chance are allowed to operate in a society defined in terms of the liberal doctrine, these rules are not fair, since, from the beginning, the dice are loaded to the advantage of some and the disadvantage of many. The principle of distributive justice is perfectly compatible with the demand for the abolition of some inequalities on the grounds of their being unjustifiable. In general, the principle of distributive justice is compatible with the principle of equal consideration of interests; it may recognize everyone's right to question the fairness of the distributive pattern in force, especially with respect to the resources and rewards which most people desire and work for, such as property (income), prestige (status), recognition, power, or the pursuit of specific interests.

The Various Rules of Distributive Justice and the Canon of Need

There are many rules or canons of distributive justice: to each according to his needs, to his merit (that is, skill, social utility or natural capacity), to his achievement, to his work (productive effort), to his contribution to the common good or public interest, to his socially useful services, and so forth. All the rules of distributive justice must allow for the restrictive conditions that the total amount of resources and rewards to be distributed is in short supply or at least limited. Each pattern of distribution has some intended and some unintended consequences. Our ability to appraise the outcome and relative justice of alternative distributions has to rely on intuition rather than on the application of some precise, operationally defined, criteria of comparison. Vested interests, the desire for power, or the presumption of privilege are not the only obstacles to a fair distribution. Our factual ignorance and poor judgment may also be responsible for errors and injustice in the accepted pattern of distribution.

While in their broad formulations the rules of distributive justice are relatively clear, their meaning and implications become elusive whenever they must be translated into directives for action. In order to make this point, let us consider the rule "To each according to his need." It has precedence over "To each according to his work," as well as over the other canons, for the latter rule is not equitable; it does not and cannot make provisions for the special needs of the aged, the disabled, or those unable to work. Finally, the rule "To each according to his need" has a moral appeal which the other rules lack. The obligation to provide for those of our fellow men who cannot provide for themselves has its moral roots in the world religions (the ideal of the brotherhood of man). The belief that society has the moral obligation to provide for all its members, however small their contribution to the common welfare, was forcefully expressed by the 19th-century socialist thinkers, the Saint-Simonians, Louis Blanc, Proudhon, and Karl Marx. Numerous contemporary writers have also argued convincingly that evaluations of social inequality from the viewpoint of need should take priority over evaluations based on the criteria of ability, talent, merit or service, since the former seems to have, as one of them put it, "greater use for the complex idea that we call humanity" (Sen, 1973:103). It is safe to say that a system of social equality established by the criteria of need enjoys universal acceptance, if not in fact, then at least in the commitment to the belief.

Need is a determinate thing in comparison with merit, achievement, service or the contribution to the public good. It is sufficient to state a need in order to indicate what has to be done to satisfy it (although the question of how the satisfaction of a need should be implemented may still remain unresolved). Furthermore, need can frequently be ascertained beyond any possible doubt, while most of the other criteria of distributive justice are not amenable to empirical testing. The patterns of distribution based on criteria other than the criterion of need are determined by norms that are rarely explicitly stated and rarely enjoy wide recognition and support.

If we consider the whole wide range of human needs, the determinate character of need turns out to be more apparent than real. At a common sense level, the term "need" indicates the lack or absence of something — food, water, clothing, shelter — which are essential in order to survive. "The assertion that a man needs food is very much like saying that a man must eat. . . . It prescribes one of a set of standard goods. It usually functions as a diagnostic term with remedial implications. It implies that something is wrong with a person if certain conditions are absent" (Peters, 1960:17-18). But this analysis of the concept of need should not blind us to the fact that a prescription or norm underlies the recognition of a need. This norm prescribes that the state of health or survival cannot be maintained unless men eat, have clothing and shelter. The norm is so obvious and well established that we fail to notice that the recognition of a need involves the compliance to a norm.

The indispensability of norms can no longer be ignored when we pass from biological needs, related directly to survival, to what are commonly called "basic needs." Basic needs, in one sense of the term, are relative to the standard of living of a given community and are determined in relation to the median or average income of that community. But basic needs is often used in another sense, as the standard of living a man deserves and is entitled to. It then includes not only the bare necessities but also the need for affection, respect, recognition, relaxation, and other often unmeasurable rewards, which vary from one individual to another. While some needs in the set of basic needs are amenable to empirical testing, others are indeterminate and extremely vague. Furthermore, basic needs, regardless of the sense of the term, are selected and determined by socially accepted norms, which can be applied effectively only if there is at least broad agreement on what they imply.

There are still other needs, which people claim as indispensable to the exercise of their occupation or profession — the need for education, self-fulfilment, and so forth. All such claims can be challenged on factual and/or normative grounds, and the satisfaction of such needs by a distributive criterion requires a socially binding norm, which is difficult to formulate and which does not easily gain the necessary social approval.

If an equitable pattern of distributive justice is hard to achieve even in the relatively easy case governed by the criterion of need, this difficulty is bound to increase considerably when other rules of distributive justice are applied. This may be one reason why the principle of fairness or distributive justice is being increasingly replaced by the demand for equality of opportunity.

Equality of Opportunity

"Equality of opportunity" has been defined as "a claim of every man to an equal chance of developing his capacities and pursuing his interests" (Raphael, 1955:87). Such a claim is purely normative and was originally related to the negative idea of social liberty, that is, to the absence of social restraints. The liberal social philosophy of the 19th century, as represented for instance by J.S. Mill, assumed that the absence of social restraints was a sufficient condition for all men to enjoy equality of opportunity. That liberal view has been rejected on the grounds that something more is necessary, since the absence of social restraints may be simply a matter of appropriate legal provisions. Equality of opportunity today refers to the requirement that the distribution of advantages and disadvantages at the starting point of a career be fair, and it often involves remedial action, aid, and support in training. In this interpretation, equality of opportunity presupposes a highly advanced degree of distributive justice, and, as far as I can see, is its outcome rather than its condition. The present-day emphasis on equality of opportunity may spring from the vague realization that equal shares or equal treatment for all men is not always in the interest of social justice and that distributive justice is only imperfectly realizable. Yet if equality of opportunity means giving everyone an equal chance with everybody else, equality of opportunity would not differ from games of pure chance. In the games of pure chance the distribution of gains and losses cannot be said to be just or unjust, fair or unfair; people are simply lucky or unlucky. Furthermore, equality of opportunity in the sense of equal chance could not prevail unless all ties between parents and children were eliminated, thus preventing lucky and unlucky parents from passing on to their children their own advantages and disadvantages, respectively. As in Plato's perfect state, the family would have to be destroyed, since the family would disrupt the workings of the social game of pure chance.

For most North Americans, equality of opportunity actually means the principle of fair competition, where the criteria of fairness are left to the participants' discretion. This kind of equal opportunity does not differ from the game of chance played with loaded dice, in which people were bound to become more and more, instead of less and less, unequal. If in such circumstances "the lucky and the competent . . . do better for themsleves than the unlucky and incompetent," comments an American sociologist, "why should we feel guilty about this?" (Jencks, 1972:3,7,9).

Equality of opportunity is sometimes used in a similar manner, as the line of perfect equality (the diagonal) in income distribution is used to evaluate the extent of the difference of income by the Gini coefficient. Equality of opportunity is first defined as perfect mobility, that is, the equal chance for everyone to attain any social position. More precisely, perfect mobility describes a situation where occupational opportunity of every member of a given population is independent of his inherited occupational status and thus, the occupational distribution of the sons is statistically unrelated to the occupation of the fathers. The deviation of the prevailing mobility pattern from the perfect one (expressed as the ratio of the actual percentage of sons in the same occupational category as their fathers to the expected percentage under conditions of perfect mobility) is called the "index of occupational inheritance." This index measures the extent to which actual mobility differs from egalitarian mobility (Matras, 1975:394ff). It is clear that the concept of perfect mobility and that of the measure of occupational inheritance are not purely descriptive; they involve implicitly the evaluative assumption that perfect mobility is, and should be, accepted as a characteristic of an egalitarian society. The criticism of the Gini coefficient as a measure of the social inequality of income also applies to the use of the index of occupational inheritance as a measure of equality of opportunity.

The strong support for the expansion of education in Western societies has many sources, one of them being the belief that it will increasingly extend equality of opportunity. The demand for the equality of educational opportunity is not necessarily based on the principle that the same kind of education should be made available to all young people. Talents are diverse; to speak of their equality does not make sense. Men are not equal in their natural capacities, and to treat them equally in this respect would serve no useful purpose. The expansion of education would conform to the principles of justice if each child were provided with the kind of education to which his or her ability best fit, that is, if the *means* for the fulfilment of everyone's natural capacity were equally, though not identically, distributed. Whether this kind of equal opportunity is feasible or could actually lead to the desired ends remains to be seen. Equality of opportunity as an equal chance of education, regardless of ability, might lead to what Michael Young calls "the rise of meritocracy" — the allocation of social positions according to a uniform standard of testable ability to carry out the duties of those positions. The rise of meritocracy is a fantasy, but even for most egalitarians, a frightening one. Young wished to make the point, which escapes the attention of many of his readers, that certain kinds of equal opportunity are likely to produce highly repulsive forms of social inequality.

It appears that some kinds of egalitarianism are unacceptable or objectionable on both social and moral grounds. Also, the principle of distributive justice has some self-destructive potentialities for what we call "good society." (I refer to the fact that whenever goods are distributed, the gain of one man is the loss of another.) Under these circumstances, we may come to the conclusion that a specific idea of egalitarianism, one that enjoins respect for the human person — the Kantian categoric imperative — is the only safe cornerstone for a social philosophy and social policy guided by an enlightened idea of equality. The equality of citizenship of an over extending range of real and enforceable rights, is perhaps one of the most promising realizations of the Kantian idea.

Conclusions

One of the main conclusions of this paper can be expressed in the proposition that social inequality is associated with differences in social positions, but cannot and should not be equated with them. The knowledge of the differences in the distribution of income, wealth, privilege, rights, power or influence is indispensable in evaluating the social inequality prevalent in a given society. But the most detailed and accurate knowledge of the purely quantitatively unequal distribution of various resources is vastly different from the value judgment made concerning the justice and injustice of this distribution. Dennis Wrong has argued that stratification and inequality should be conceptually distinguished, because they are independent of each other (1964:13). The difference is not so much conceptual as indicative of the order of categories we use in the examination of stratification and social inequality, respectively. In Kantian language, the categories of stratification theories are constitutive, in that they are required in order to gain any knowledge of stratification. However, the categories applied in the investigation of social inequality are regulative and not constitutive. They do not serve the purpose of acquiring knowledge about real objects, their properties or relations, but restrict or regulate our evaluative statements made on the basis of what we come to know by means of constitutive categories. We use constitutive ideas as cognizing subjects, and we use regulative ideas as moral agents. It follows from this distinction that there is no logical relation between statements concerning stratificational distinctions on the one hand, and value judgments concerning social equality and inequality as characteristics of a system of stratificational distinctions, on the other.

We must distinguish between a descriptive and a normative language, the distinction being defined in terms of the rules governing the use of each type of language. The rules of a normative language concern the use of words which occur either in value judgments and prescriptions or in statements providing reasons for the acceptance or rejection of value judgments and prescriptions. There are numerous normative languages and they differ in respect to our adopted point of view, The selection of a certain normative language as a means of judging or prescribing things according to a standard, is determined by the consideration of whether we wish to judge or prescribe things from a legal, economic, aesthetic, or moral viewpoint. Within each point of view there may exist different standpoints and different normative languages. A moral standard for judging or prescribing has no distinctive or inherent characteristic which differentiates it from a legal or an economic standard. A standard is distinctively moral — and a standard of social equality or inequality is moral — if in its justification we appeal to some relevant rules (where "relevant" means "pertaining to" and in this case, "pertaining to a moral point of view"). One standpoint, within a moral point of view, differs from another by the kind of rules believed to be relevant in the justification of moral evaluations and prescriptions. As stated earlier, we have no intersubjectively valid criteria for the acceptance or rejection of a moral theory or standpoint; we accept or reject them by comparing them with what our conscience tells us, and the verdict of conscience may vary from one individual or one group of individuals to another.

Judgments expressing the degree of social equality or inequality according to a moral standard are invariably a solution to the problem. The problem involves two irreducible elements: a set of findings concerning the differences in the distribution of certain scarce resources, and a set of moral principles or standards whereby the differential distribution of scarce resources are morally evaluated. Since there are no standards of absolute rightness, absolute justice or absolute social equality, the solution of the problem is bound to be tentative and problematic. While we should continue to search for the best solution to our problem, we should never mislead ourselves into believing that we have actually found it. For in view of the nature of a moral theory and the multiplicity of moral theories in any given society, such a belief would be erroneous as well as socially and morally disastrous.

We could make better progress in solving the problem of social equality and inequality if the enormous amount of work and ingenuity expended on stratification studies were accompanied by an investigation of the various moral beliefs actually held in the same society. Knowingly or unknowingly, in one form or another, most social scientists subscribe to the Marxian claim that the ideas of the ruling class are, in every age, the ruling ideas, or to the orthodoxy of structural functionalism, that normative consensus is a cultural universal. Moral scientists could also make a contribution, in the application of moral standards or norms, by studying the peculiar logic of the concept of social equality. As the preceding discussion of this logic should have demonstrated, perhaps nowhere else is the road to hell so paved with good intentions as in the unenlightened efforts toward the creation of a society of free and equal men.

NOTES

1. See, for example, Cook (1975:372-88) and the literature referred to in this article.
2. Some 60 years later, Durkheim, another conservative thinker, was equally aware that the discrepancy between the distribution of social functions and of natural talents (between social inequalities and natural inequalities) produced by the progress of industrialization and generating numerous social conflicts, could not last. Durkheim wrote that unlike in the earlier societies, men now find inequalities intolerable (1960:374-81).
3. The threefold division of predicates into descriptive, evaluative, and prescriptive can be found in Hare (1963:Sec.2.8). Hare's division can be extended to statements.

REFERENCES

Aristotle. *Ethics*. Harmondsworth: Penguin, 1955.
_____. *Politics*. London: Everyman's Library, 1947.
Atkinson, A.B. *The Economics of Inequality*. Oxford: Clarendon Press, 1975.
Babeuf, G. *The Defense of Gracchus Babeuf*. New York: Schocken Books, 1972.
Benn, S.I. "Egalitarianism and the Equal Consideration of Interest," in H.A. Bedau, ed., *Justice and Equality*. Englewood Cliffs, N.J.: Prentice-Hall, 1971, pp. 152-67.

Berlin, I. "Equality," in *Aristotelian Society Proceedings,* Vol. 56 (1955-56), pp. 301-26.

Béteille, A. "The Decline of Social Inequality?" in A. Béteille, ed., *Social Inequality.* Harmondsworth: Penguin, 1969.

Cook, K.S. "Expectations, Evaluations and Equity," *American Sociological Review,* Vol. 40 (1975), pp. 372-88.

Davis, K. and W.E. Moore. "Some Principles of Stratification," in M.M. Tumin, ed., *Readings on Social Stratification.* Englewood Cliffs, N.J.: Prentice-Hall, 1970.

Durkheim, E. *The Division of Labor in Society.* Glencoe: The Free Press, 1960.

Fallers, L.A. *Inequality: Social Stratification Reconsidered.* Chicago: University of Chicago Press, 1973.

Hare, R.M. *Freedom and Reason.* Oxford: Clarendon Press, 1963.

Hegel, G.W.F. *Philosophy of Right.* Oxford: Clarendon Press, 1962.

Jencks, C. *Inequality: A Reassessment of the Effect of Family and Schooling in America.* Harper: Colophon Books, 1972.

Kelsen, H. *What Is Justice?* Berkeley and L.A.: University of California Press, 1960.

Laski, H.J. *A Grammar of Politics,* 5th ed. London: Allen and Unwin, 1948.

Lehman, W.C. *John Millar of Glasgow.* Cambridge: The University Press, 1960.

Marshall, T.H. *Sociology at the Crossroads and Other Essays.* London: Heinemann Educational Books, 1963.

Matras, J. *Social Inequality, Stratification, and Mobility.* Englewood Cliffs, N.J.: Prentice-Hall, 1975.

Mill, J.S. *Utilitarianism, Liberty, Representative Government.* London: Everyman's Library, 1968.

Moore, W.E. "But Some Are More Equal Than Others," in M.M. Tumin, ed., *Readings on Social Stratification.* Englewood Cliffs, N.J.: Prentice-Hall, 1970.

Myrdal, G. *Value in Social Theory.* London: Routledge and Kegan Paul, 1958.

Ossowski, S. *Class Structure in the Social Consciousness.* New York: The Free Press of Glencoe, 1963.

Parkin, F. *Class Inequality and Political Order.* London: MacGibbon, 1971.

Perelman, C. *The Idea of Justice and the Problem of Argument.* London: Routledge and Kegan Paul, 1963.

Peters, R.S. *The Concept of Motivation.* London: Routledge and Kegan Paul, 1960.

Petrazycki, L. *Law and Morality.* Cambridge: Harvard University Press, 1955.

Popper, K.R. *The Open Society and Its Enemies,* 5th ed., Vol. 1-2. New York: Harper Torchbooks, 1967.

Raphael, D.D. "Equality and Equity," *Philosophy,* Vol. 21 (1946), pp. 118-32.

_____. *Moral Judgment.* London: Allen and Unwin, 1955.

Rawls J. *A theory of Justice.* Oxford: Oxford University Press, 1972.

Rousseau, J.J. *The Social Contract and Discourses.* London: Everyman's Library, 1947.

Runciman, W.G. *Relative Deprivation and Social Justice.* Harmondsworth: Penguin, 1972.

_____. "Towards a Theory of Social Stratification," in F. Parkin, ed., *The Social Analysis of Class Structure*. London: Tavistock, 1974.

Sen, A. *On Economic Inequality*. Oxford: Clarendon Press, 1973.

Smith, A. *The Wealth of Nations*, Vol. 1-2. London: Methuen University Paperbacks, 1961.

de Tocqueville, A. *Democracy in America*, Vol. 1-2. London: Fontana Library, 1968.

Williams, B. "The Idea of Equality," in Laslett and Runciman, eds., *Philosophy, Politics and Society*, 2nd series. Oxford: Basil Blackwell, 1969.

Wrong, D.H. "Social Inequality without Social Stratification," *Canadian Review of Sociology and Anthropology*, Vol. 1 (1964), pp. 5-16.

II

Perspectives on Inequality

Introduction

There is a striking diversity of approaches to the analysis of inequality. Waxman, in *The Stigma of Poverty*, distinguishes between two perspectives: the cultural and the situational. He explains that

> the culturalists see the poor as manifesting unique patterns of behavior and values; to escape from their poverty, they must be taught to change their behavior and values. Since their values and patterns of behavior have been internalized over generations through socialization, the change will, of necessity, be a slow and difficult process. . . . To effect a change insofar as poverty is concerned, the situationalists argue, requires not changing the poor themselves, but rather changing their situation by *correcting the restrictive social structure* (Waxman, 1977:26-27, emphasis ours).

The writer associated most often with the cultural perspective is Oscar Lewis. His article *The Culture of Poverty* (reprinted here) stimulated a far-reaching debate that continues to this day. (See, for example, Valentine, 1969, and Waxman, 1977.) Unfortunately, much of the debate has been the result of a very superficial reading of his paper. Waxman's summary of Lewis' work applies only to half of his argument, for Lewis states that "the culture of poverty is not just a matter of deprivation or disorganization." He continues:

> It is a culture in the traditional anthropological sense that it provides human beings with a design for living, with a ready-made set of solutions for human problems and so serves a significant adaptive function.

This culture of poverty is a creation of a capitalist society, and for Lewis, the individual and cultural characteristics of fatalism, helplessness, dependence and inferiority are *adaptive traits* that a significant proportion (about 20%) of the poor possess in order to cope with being victims of a particular social structure. If and when major changes occur in the social structure, the culture of poverty — though not necessarily poverty — will disappear. Lewis concludes his article thus:

> By creating basic structural changes in society, by redistributing wealth, by organizing the poor and giving them a sense of belonging, of power and of leadership, revolutions frequently succeed in abolishing some of the basic characteristics of the culture of poverty even when they do not succeed in curing poverty itself.

Clearly, Lewis subscribes to both the cultural and the situational perspectives outlined by Waxman.

Lewis makes a distinction between the condition of poverty and *being poor*. Most Canadians would argue that peasants living in medieval England or those in contemporary agrarian societies (for example, in India, China, Latin America) were or are living in poverty. But were they or are they *designated* as poor?

This distinction is at the root of Simmel's article *The Poor*. For Simmel, the poor are a social category that emerges through societal definition (Coser, 1965:140; see also Marx, 1912:805-8). He points out that the provision of assistance through private charities or through the state (for example, welfare), reinforces the distinction between the social condition of poverty and the individual who is poor.

> If we take into consideration this meaning of assistance to the poor, it becomes clear that the fact of taking away from the rich to give to the poor *does not aim at equalizing their individual positions and is not, even in its orientation, directed at suppressing the social difference between the rich and the poor.*

The very granting of assistance not only creates the poor person, Simmel suggests, but it makes the poor person into an object of the activity of the group and places him at a distance from the whole, which at times makes him live as a *corpus vile* by the mercy of the whole and at times, because of this, makes him into its bitter enemy. However, Simmel notes that while those who receive assistance are poor and are often seen in very negative terms, there are also many people who are poor who do not receive assistance. Many of these are the so-called "working poor."

Gans, in his article *The Positive Functions of Poverty and Inequality*, recognizes the existence of different groups of poor people and the "relativity of poverty" that this implies. He also stresses that the positive functions aid in the persistence of *nonpoor groups*. These functions (Gans names 15) maintain the distance between the nonpoor and the poor and partially explain why most nonpoor have little desire to alter a system by which they benefit. Gans suggests that only when the persistence of poverty becomes dysfunctional for the nonpoor — or when the poor can obtain enough power to change the system of social stratification — will poverty begin to disappear.

What is a system of stratification? While there are various answers to this question, most scholars agree that it is the existence of inequalities in a given society. However, as Johnson points out in his article *The Development of Class in Canada in the Twentieth Century*, much analysis of inequality in Canada has tended to stress culture or subjective attitudes of individuals, rather than the analysis of class in a Marxist sense, as causes of inequality.

For Johnson, class carries a precise definition which relates not to the attitudes of individuals, but to their external material relationships centered on those created by the productive process. He proceeds to offer a historical and socioeconomic analysis of classes in Canada, namely, the petite bourgeoisie, the capitalist class, and the working class.

Since Johnson's analysis of class in Canada was first published in 1972, two major works by Wallace Clement (*The Canadian Corporate Elite* and *Continental Corporate Power*) have provided us with more detailed evidence that support Johnson's assertions concerning the dominance in Canada of finance capital (banks, trust and insurance companies) and American imperialism. Johnson's article documents the inequalities that result from a capitalist, exploitative system, and asserts that any full understanding of the phenomena of inequality requires a class analysis rooted in a knowledge of Canadian history.

While poverty is an example of inequality, our society contains other inequalities that may or may not be best understood from a class perspective. The difficulty lies in understanding what factors have produced and continue to reproduce the present social structure. As Westergaard and Resler have remarked:

> Poverty has been rediscovered. . . . But to single out "the poor" for special attention in practice runs the risk of emphasizing the specific to the neglect of the general (1976:19).

What causes inequality? Can all inequalities be explained by a Marxist analysis of classes? Will exploitation cease when the capitalist mode of production dies or is overturned in a revolution? What is the relationship between class and power? Will power always be present in some form in every society? If so, will those with power use it to distribute goods and services in an egalitarian manner? If not, by what criteria will decisions be made in a classless society? If classes, as Johnson defined them, are abolished, what will our society be like? Are classlessness and equality synonymous terms?

Hofley's article attempts to demonstrate that they are not, and that too often we confuse the terms. He points out that all of the above questions need to be asked, but some are asked only by those working within a classlessness problematic, and others only by those writing within an equality problematic. There is no doubt that almost all present inequalities in Canada are class-related, but will the abolition of classes in a Marxist sense destroy the inequalities or simply alter the form they take?

It is essential that whatever theoretical approach we utilize to increase our understanding and explanation of structured inequality in Canada, we must make that approach's assumptions and concepts as clear as possible before we test it. Otherwise, we are doomed to an ideological analysis of events, and a continuing capacity to talk past one another. Such a situation will not further our knowledge of Canadian society, nor will it begin a process whereby Canadians will move to significantly alter existing inequalities. Our own preference for a perspective which emphasizes the political economy of inequalities in Canada will become readily apparent from our choice of articles for subsequent sections.

Classlessness versus Equality:
An Agonizing Choice*

JOHN R. HOFLEY

All societies distribute goods and services. Some hunting and gathering societies, for example, distribute them in a quite egalitarian manner. Others, for example, contemporary industrial societies such as Canada, distribute goods and services in a very unequal manner. We do not have to be trained social scientists to see this inequality.

However, it is not enough to know that inequality exists. As social scientists, we want to offer *explanations* for its existence. In addition, many people (both lay and professional) wish to initiate changes in our society that would reduce or abolish inequality.

As Canadians we know that Canada is a rich country relative to the majority of countries in the world. We often refer to our nation as a land of opportunity, freedom, and equality. Perhaps, for many Canadians, this last statement seems true. Yet, as the data in Section I of this book have shown, the *actual* distribution of goods and services is very unequal, and this inequality has not altered much since the turn of the century.[1]

We knew that there were some people in Canada having a "rough time," but in general most of us were "doing quite well, thank you!" However, our complacency about inequality was rudely shocked in the 1960s when study after study in Canada and other industrial countries demonstrated that not only do we have *some* "poor" people in rich nations, but in fact we have a *lot* of poor people. At the same time, other studies showed that Canada has a number of very rich persons and families, albeit a small number when compared to the number who were and are poor.

All political parties in Canada were shocked by the extent of poverty and consequently, the Canadian government began a "semi-official" war on poverty.[2] Politicians and most social scientists were optimistic that a solution could be found.

However, as we know from personal attempts to solve problems, a solution is very much a function of how we see and define a problem. In other words, how we go about reducing inequality and poverty depends to a large extent on our explanation of its creation and existence.[3] To answer the questions, "Why is there inequality?" and "How do we abolish it?" we must make explicit assumptions concerning a variety of factors such as human nature, society, social class, power, elites, etc. For example, we may

*I would like to express my thanks to colleagues in Australia and Canada who commented on an earlier draft of this paper in seminars during 1977 and 1978.

ask if people are poor because they are genetically inferior, because they are paid too little, and if so, if this is because their bosses are "greedy", and whether greed is part of human nature or a learned characteristic, and so on.

Unfortunately, very few social scientists reflect on questions of this sort. Much of the work documenting inequality in Canada has focused primarily on presenting "facts." For example, the Senate report, *Poverty in Canada, The Real Report on Poverty,* Statistics Canada reports, and the report of the Canadian Council on Social Development (reprinted in Section I of this book) present income distributions that are highly similar. Yet this does not mean that everyone sees these "facts" in the same way, that is, that the explanations offered are identical. Often such reports do not even attempt an explanation. When they do, the *words* used to explain inequality are often identical, but the *meaning* of the word(s) may be either unclear or substantially different. For example, what does the word "inequality" mean to you? To some, it refers to the unequal distribution of goods and services such as income or education; others refer to unequal privileges, or hierarchical ranking of occupations, ethnic groups, etc. Still others refer to inequality in terms of property relations between those who own property and those who do not.

Thus, two different authors can argue, for example, that Canada's "class system" creates poverty. However, unless the authors have made *explicit* their definitions of "class," the reader can become quite confused. The identical word "class" may be used within frameworks that are, in reality, quite distinct.

One of the purposes of this paper is to demonstrate that analyses of poverty and wealth in Canada emanate from at least two distinct "problematics."[4] I will call these the *classlessness* and *equality* problematics. Each operates with different sets of assumptions, especially in two key areas:[5]

1. The analysis of "class" (production versus distribution).
2. The analysis of "power" and "exploitation".

Clearly, the first area is the more important one, but the second is intimately linked to it.

Thus, we find social scientists using identical words in their analyses of Canada's political economy, yet the conceptual meanings of these words are often unclear or "hidden." For example, if we read the Economic Council of Canada reports of 1968 and 1969, *The Real Poverty Report* and the Senate report, *Poverty in Canada,* and such books on Canadian stratification as John Porter's *The Vertical Mosaic,* Wallace Clement's *The Canadian Corporate Elite* and *Continental Corporate Power,* we will see that the questions asked are often couched in either an empiricist problematic[6] or a problematic that does not clearly separate the concepts of "class" and "inequality." This usually results in theories and solutions that appear on the surface to be either similar or susceptible to synthesis when they may in fact be distinct and lead us in very different directions.

For example, the Senate report begins by saying that the welfare system has clearly outlived its usefulness (xiii) and that the economic system creates poverty (xv). One might expect the report would proceed to raise questions about the nature of the system, but it does not; it is firmly entrenched in a problematic that is not only empiricist, but one in which there is no concept of class, that is, one which defines "classes primarily in terms of common structural positions within the social organization of production" (Wright, 1978:2).

The senators move quickly away from a critical analysis of the overall structure of the economy to talk about *attitudes* — "a central cause of poverty is a social attitude which is reflected in economic policies" (38) — and management — "the poor are casualties of the way we manage our economy and society" (xxvii). The Senate report is working within what I have called an "equality" problematic. Classes are seen as "aggregates of persons distinguished principally by wealth and income" (Forcese, 1975:14). It follows then that to reduce inequality, Canada should institute a guaranteed annual income (GAI).

Clearly, the GAI approach has nothing to do with establishing a classless society. It is still rooted in utilitarian philosophy in that it suggests that we can define the "good" as having "x" dollars, the attainment of which is only a technical problem (cf. Passmore, 1970:203 and Jordan's article in this volume). A more recent example of this position can be found in the Economic Council of Canada's move towards adopting *social indicators* such as crime rates, incidences of diseases, and housing conditions as mechanisms to measure the success or failure of social policies (see especially their reports between 1969 and 1974).

The *Real Report on Poverty* does a much better job of articulating a "structural" argument for the existence of poverty, that is, inequality in terms of *access* to resources in the society. Yet it also recommends a GAI. Thus this report shares the same problematic as the Senate report. It offers us an analysis of inequality, not of classlessness. In Chapter II, "The Production of Poverty," we find an analysis of capitalism but no mention of class. It ignores one of Marx's dictums:

> Economics is not concerned with things but with relations between persons, and in the final analysis between classes; these relations however are always *bound to things and appear as things* (Marx, 1970a:226).

Marxists who tend to operate within a "classlessness" problematic often assume that the abolition of the capitalist mode of production will bring about equality.[7] Non-Marxists tend either to ignore class, or define class in a fundamentally different way, robbing the concept of its relational base to the ownership of the means of production, thereby emphasizing class as a position rather than as a relation.

Thus, Dennis Forcese in *The Canadian Class Structure* defines classes as "aggregates of persons distinguished principally by wealth and income" (14). Others talk about ethnic classes, racial classes, women as a class, etc. These types of analyses I would group under the equality problematic. Their underlying premise is that our society is moving towards the reduction of certain inequalities, and that this can be effected within a capitalist class structure.

Production and Distribution

Every society's economic system is made up of four parts: production, distribution, exchange, and consumption. There is, however, considerable disagreement as to the relative importance of each component and, in turn, its relationship to inequality in a society.

As stated earlier, the two problematics differ in two important areas: (1) production and distribution, and (2) power and exploitation. A problematic that focuses on classlessness argues that the mode of production in any society is the dominant factor, and that distribution, exchange, and consumption are *dependent* on the mode of production. Marx expresses this fundamental point in a number of places.[8]

> The distribution of the means of consumption at any time is only a consequence of the distribution of the conditions of production themselves. The latter distribution, however, is a feature of the mode of production itself (Marx, 1947:27).

> A distinct mode of production thus determines the specific mode of consumption, distribution, exchange, and the specific relations of these different phases to one another (Marx, 1970b:137).

In *The German Ideology,* he poses the question explicitly: "Does distribution form an independent sector alongside and outside production?" He answers:

> The structure of distribution is entirely determined by the structure of production. Distribution itself is a product of production, not only with regard to the content, for only the results of production can be distributed, but also with regard to the form, since the particular mode of men's participation in production determines the specific form of distribution, the form in which they share in distribution (Marx, 1970b:135).

In recent years many contemporary Marxist thinkers have stressed this point. Edward Nell, in an essay on the differences between orthodox and Marxian economic theory, writes that "The central distinction between the two visions, then, lies in the treatment of production and distribution" (Blackburn, 1972:83). Westergaard and Resler, in their analysis of Great Britain, also stress the dominance of the capitalistic mode of production over distribution:

> The central role of private ownership in shaping the pattern of distribution arises in two ways: directly because it is the concentration of private property which has the major part in explaining the continuing accumulation of a very large share of national output in few hands; indirectly, because the workings of both the labour market and of state economic activity reflect the prevailing influences of business views and interests in the assumptions by which everyday economic affairs are conducted in a capitalist society (Westergaard and Resler, 1975:52).

The bourgeoisie is the class that owns the means of production and that ultimately determines distribution. Class, then, for Marx, is not an individual characteristic but a relation to those who own the means of production. Thus, for Marx, inequality cannot be divorced from a class analysis of contemporary capitalist societies.

On the other hand, the problematic that begins with the concept of equality argues, following Weber, that the mode of distribution can be not only analytically separated from production, but that *within any given mode of production* there can be a wide range of distribution, both individual and social. This range results in inequality, or with certain changes, could lead to increased equality. This unequal distribution he called "class."

> A class in the distributive sense is not an entity (as in Marx) but a construct by means of which we can speak of each and every member of the class (Jordan, 1971:23).

Weber was aware of the Marxian argument that contradictions in the capitalistic structure of the mode of production, that is, class conflict, could lead to revolution. However, Weber reasoned that this is only one of several possible outcomes:

> . . . such conflicts as that between land owners and outcast elements. . . may lead to revolutionary conflict. . . . It may, on the contrary, be concerned in the first instance only with a redistribution of wealth (Weber, 1964:426).

Weber and others (e.g., Porter, 1964; Forcese, 1975; and with some reservation, Clement, 1975 and 1977) who fall within what I have called the equality problematic do not deny the importance of the mode of production. What they suggest is that *every society*, regardless of the mode of production (i.e., including a socialist society that has abolished classes), must still face the problem of equality of distribution.

Weber and others[9] suggest that current inequalities in distribution are not just a function of a capitalist mode of production. Resources are fought over by a wide range of groups and collectivities that cut across class lines.

Perhaps the clearest representative of the approach that stresses distribution is American sociologist Gerhard Lenski. In both *Power and Privilege* and *Human Societies* he acknowledges the importance of the mode of production but shows that there are tremendous inequalities in all types of societies and that the range of these inequalities varies *within* a given mode of production. Thus, he defines stratification, not from the point of view of Marxian analysis of class, but as the analysis of distributive systems. Lenski suggests that the basic question is "Who gets what and why?" For him, the answer rests on an analysis of power, not of social class. "Power will determine the distribution of nearly all of the surplus possessed by a society" (Lenski, 1966:44). Much of North American sociology utilizes this Weberian notion of class. We even call the analysis of classes the study of stratification. This has led many to *equate* a class analysis à la Marx with stratification.[10] Unfortunately, this confuses rather than clarifies matters. To replace the use of the word "class" in the Weberian, distributive sense, I shall use the term "equality". When I use the word "class," it is in the Marxist sense of the term.

We must be aware, as Althusser has noted, that scholars look at and use such words as class and equality in a theoretical way, that is, within a given problematic. He writes:

> [Science] can only pose problems on the terrain and within the horizon of a definite theoretical structure, its problematic, which constitutes its absolute and definite condition of possibility, and hence the absolute determination *of the forms in which all problems must be posed,* at any given moment in the science (Althusser, 1970:25).

Power and Exploitation

The second basic area of difference lies in the two problematics' handling of power. At the risk of some exaggeration, I would argue that the classlessness problematic does *not* concern itself with power as a concept. It is true that power is *implicit* in all of Marx's works, but it is never developed as a *concept.*[11] As Jordan has noted: "In contrast to his overriding interest in power there is relatively little systematic reflection on power in Marx's writings" (Jordan, 1971:55). Marx was primarily concerned with the concept, not of power, but of *exploitation.*[12] For Marx, the aim of all capitalist production is the production of "surplus-value." The concept of surplus-value is woven intricately into his concept of class.[13] Exploitation presupposes a relationship between a capitalist who owns and controls the means of production and a worker who is free to sell his/her labor-power to capital. Marx notes in *Capital:*

> The sporadic application of cooperation on a large scale in ancient times, in the middle ages and in modern colonies, reposes on relations of dominion and servitude, principally on slavery. The capitalistic form, on the contrary, presupposes from first to last, the free wage-labourer, who sells his labour-power to capital (Marx, 1912:367).

It is clear from the above quote, as well as from the rest of his works (especially *Capital* and the *Grundrisse*), that Marx did not see power as a phenomenon unique to capitalism. We can also assume that Marx did not expect that the abolishment of the capitalistic mode of production would bring an end to the use of power, albeit a power not based on private property. Yet, unlike Weber, Marx spent very little time wrestling with this problem. Why?

I think the French structuralist school, led by such writers as Louis Althusser and Nicos Poulantzas, are partially correct when they suggest that Marx wanted to put forward a concept, surplus-value, that would be devoid of any subject or subjectivity. Marx wanted to develop a science that would be objective in the sense that its central concepts would be part and parcel of a structure, and therefore independent of the observer. Class and exploitation, for Marx and those in the classlessness problematic, are *not* phenomena defined by subjective attitudes or feelings.

In my estimation, the best illustration of this Marxian class emphasis can be found in John Westergaard's and Henrietta Resler's stimulating work *Class in a Capitalist Society*, an empirical study of contemporary Great Britain. The authors use the words "equality" and "power," but always within a class problematic. "Property, profit and market...remain the prime determinants of inequality" (Westergaard and Resler, 1975:17). In their lengthy discussion of power, Westergaard and Resler argue, following Marx, that power in Great Britain is closely linked to the bourgeois class, although much of the exercise of power rests on "anonymous social mechanisms and assumptions" (143). They write:

> First, there is power inherent in anonymous social mechanisms as well as in identifiable groups or individuals. Second, power derives more from the routine application of effectively unchallenged assumptions than from the manifest dominance of one faction, group, interest or policy over others in open conflict. Third, the institutionalization of conflict involves just that kind of unspoken adoption of key assumptions, behind which there is pragmatically dictated agreement but no legitimation through positive consensus (147).

They then go on to demonstrate that these key assumptions are capitalistic and support the interests of the bourgeoisie. Thus, inequalities persist and will continue to be present as long as Britain's class structure remains capitalistic. I agree with this analysis.

However, what is left out of Marx's as well as Westergaard's and Resler's class problematic is important: there is a failure to recognize and explain inequalities in societies, both pre-capitalistic and post-capitalistic (i.e., socialist) that arise from the use of power to effect the distribution of goods and services. It is this "gap" that Weber and others recognized and attempted to fill.[14]

Since Weber, a whole host of writers have sought to demonstrate that power is found in all social forms of organization and that one cannot simply wipe it away by saying that its existence is totally dependent on the mode of production. Weber saw power as having a variety of resources, some of which are clearly class-based, but many of which are based on factors such as ethnicity, status, nationality, etc. Thus, for Weber:

> "Power" (Macht) is the probability that one actor within a social relationship will be in a position to carry out his own will despite resistance, regardless of the basis on which this probability rests.
>
> All conceivable qualities of a person and all conceivable combinations of circumstances may put him in a position to impose his will in a given situation (Weber,1964:153).

Many who write within a class problematic often criticize Weber's use of power as being hopelessly tied to individuals, rooted in a subjectivity that rules out any sociological analysis. However, as Clegg remarks:

> Although Weber is . . . frequently castigated for being "methodologically individualist" in his concept of "power," this is only correctly observed if one chooses not to consider the context in which Weber developed his concern with "power."
>
> For Weber individual social actions are *not* motivated either by an insatiable desire for power or for certainty, but by collectively recognized and publicly available social rules which orient individual social actions in rationally structured ways (Clegg, 1975:31).

The thrust of Weber's historical analyses and much of the literature on elites suggest that the Marxian concept of class does not subsume the concept of power and vice versa.

Thus, for persons analyzing poverty and inequality within an "equality" problematic, power cannot be seen simply as a result of the capitalist mode of production. Also, abolishing the capitalist mode of production will *not* abolish power, and thus inequalities of condition would still persist.[15] This is not to say that we should not analyze classes, but as Jordon notes:

> Historically and sociologically it is always enlightening to relate the action of a government to the prevailing class structure, class interests and class conflicts. But not all action and functions of the State can be explained by the assumption that state power is an organization of the propertied class, an instrument by which one group dominates others or which is used by the rulers to the disadvantage of the ruled (Jordon, 1971:59-60).

Or as Camus and Balandier have written:

> There is no equality in the world of power and the masters calculate, at a usurious rate, the price of their own blood (Camus, 1953:81).

> Power is strengthened by the accentuation of inequalities, which are its precondition, just as it is the precondition of their maintenance (Balandier, 1970:37).

I am not suggesting that one or the other problematic is correct, or holds the truth. What I am suggesting is that unless we explicitly recognize the two approaches, their different assumptions, and their use of concepts, we will continue to talk past one another.

Where do we go from here? Can we synthesize the two approaches? Can we somehow build an explanation of wealth and poverty that takes into account both the concepts of class and power? What does each problematic tell us about structured inequality in Canada and the nature of Canadian society? The remainder of this paper is a tentative sketching of some possibilities.

I think a synthesis of the two problematics is not possible at the moment. At this point, we must make the problematics more explicit and test them empirically. We need studies done on Canada that focus on class in the Marxian sense, exploring the existence of class antagonisms and how they can be abolished.

> And Canadian sociologists certainly have not given the subject of *class* the attention it demands, in spite of the importance class relations have had in shaping the Canadian past and are having in shaping the present (Watson, 1978:347).

This approach would use the word "power" because it would have to analyze the social formation of Canada, that is, its concrete political, religious, and legal orders (see Poulantzas, 1975:22-24).

However, such a problematic would confine itself quite clearly to a class analysis of Canadian society. Income, whether in the form of wage-labor or as a Guaranteed Annual Income, is not a solution, nor can money be seen as "neutral." For Marx, "Money is not a thing, it is a social relation" (1973:81). A GAI is already built into the capitalist mode of production.

> Whenever the dominant relationship of production consists of capital and wage-labour, there is continuity of wage-labour, insofar as there is a fixed wage for the worker. Wherever wage-labour exists, it exists (McClellan, 1971:57).

Thus, to economists who argue that the worker should have a stable income, Marx ironically states:

> Contrary to the capitalist, the worker benefits from a certain stability of income, which is more or less independent of the great adventures of capital. In just the same way, Don Quixote consoled Sancho Panza: Certainly he had to take all the blows, but he had no need to be courageous (McClellan, 1971:56).

Thus, from the perspective of a class problematic, even though a GAI may be introduced, increased or supplemented, such a move does not alter class relations. A GAI treats money as a thing, consumption as individual and independent of the mode of production,[16] and ignores the fact that wage differentials are the effect of class barriers (Poulantzas, 1975:20).

> Social inequalities (between groups or individuals) are only the effect, on the agents, of the social classes, i.e., of the objective places they occupy, which can only disappear with the abolition of the division of society into classes (Poulantzas, 1971:17).

A class problematic then forces us to look for *historical relationships between classes*. We recognize, as E.P. Thompson notes in his monumental *The Making of the English Working Class*, that:

> Class is a social and cultural formation . . . which cannot be defined abstractly, or in isolation, but only in terms of a relationship with other classes, and, ultimately, the definition can only be made in the medium of time — that is, action and reaction, change and conflict. . . . But class itself is not a thing, it is a happening (Thompson, 1963:939).

Another insight a class problematic offers is to demonstrate that much of a society's emphasis on differences in income, sex, education, religion, ethnicity, etc., together with its insistence that all are equal before the law, that is, as citizens, is the result of ideology. Behind all these facts are hidden class relationships.

> The major point is that the peculiar way in which the modern state emancipates many by declaring that the real differences between men shall not affect their standing as citizens, and hence leaves these differences intact, not only leaves relations of domination and conflict in civil society untouched, but inevitably these real social relations infect the political sphere as well. The modern state, in contrast with feudalism, declares wealth, education, occupation, religion, race, in short all the real distinctions *non-political* distinctions. Only in this way can it claim to stand for the *common* interests of the citizens. Yet how can wealth be unpolitical when it provides access to the means of political persuasion? (Marx, 1970b:10).

Or as Giddens notes: "Ideology must be studied in relation to the social relationships in which it is embedded" (Giddens, 1971:41). We need studies done within this problematic[17] on ideologies in Canada. We must analyze in what sense the language debates in Canada,[18] the struggle for nationalism, regional disagreements, ethnicity, and sexism cloud the issues of classlessness and/or equality — that is, are ideological.

This class problematic also might enable us to analyze more clearly the phenomenon of social mobility. Too often, sociologists see in mobility evidence of a classless society, or a dynamic society. For example, Clement writes:

> In a dynamic society there is a high degree of vertical mobility and a maximum use of talent. Such a society has yet to exist, but theoretically it is known as a "meritocracy". In such a society it is assumed that there could be both a highly structured society controlled by elites and open recruitment to these elites. In a liberal-democracy based on corporate capitalism this is highly problematic because of the way privilege is transmitted.
>
> Those who concentrate on making contemporary capitalist societies meritocratic examine only one dimension of stratification, that associated with opportunity. Unless they also understand that condition delimits whether a society will be dynamic or not, they will be frustrated in their attempts to gain open recruitment (Clement, 1975:2-3).

Studies of social mobility usually fail to distinguish between places and agents (Poulantzas, 1975:33). All social mobility does is circulate agents; the class structure remains untouched. As Poulantzas has noted, if all the bourgeoisie became proletariat and vice versa, there would be no change in class relations. This is not to deny the *ideological* force of such mobility; although the actual amount of mobility may be relatively small, it does serve to obfuscate class relations and emphasize personal relations.

Thus, while the class problematic can, in my view, offer us excellent leads such as the above, it does have some "ignorances" that stem from "inside." The equality problematic, if it becomes conceptually tighter, can assist us in analyzing these ignorances.

Earlier we noted that power resides in all social organizations. It is *not* a phenomenon that can be removed by a revolution. This approach does not concur at all with the Marxist attempt to see power as solely dependent on class relations. One cannot simply define power away, or argue, by definition, that when classes are abolished, power and domination are abolished. Listen to Marx trying to do this:

> When, in the course of development, class distinctions have disappeared, and all production has been concentrated in the hands of a vast association of the whole nation, the public power will lose its political character. Political power, properly so called, is merely the organized power of one class for oppressing another. If the proletariat during its contest with the bourgeoisie is compelled, by the force of circumstances to organize itself as a class, if, by means of a revolution, it makes itself the ruling class, and, as such, sweeps away by force the old conditions of production, then it will, along with these conditions, have swept away the conditions for the existence of class antagonisms and of classes generally and will thereby have abolished its own supremacy as a class (Marx, 1948:55).

In this quotation, Marx ignores the individual nature of "power." Because we *call* it "public power" does not mean that the power cannot be used by those in key positions within the organization of a socialist mode of production to distribute resources unevenly. As Giddens notes about Weber:

Power is not, for Weber, a "third dimension" . . . . [Weber] is quite explicit about saying that classes, status groups and parties are all "phonomena of the distribution of power" (Giddens, 1973:44).

Because those who work within a class problematic focus on the mode of production and exploitation, they often ignore or casually brush aside questions about power and, for example, its relationship to human nature:

Marxism has to come to grips with the conservative argument: that there is something in human nature that invites inequality no matter what we do (Becker, 1975:51).

Robert Heilbroner poses two related questions concerning power that need to be asked and explored: (1) "Why [does] power exert such a temptation for mankind?" and (2) "Why [has] power adduced such acquiesence, such rationalization, even such welcome, from those over whom it has been exercised?" (Heilbroner, 1978:36). It is likely, in the near future, that only scholars working within an "equality" problematic will treat such questions seriously. [19]

On the whole, Marx, unlike the other authors who concentrate on equality and power, sees inequality pretty well disappearing with the abolition of social classes though there will still be some inequalities.

The removal of all social and political inequality is also a very questionable phrase in place of the "abolition of all class differences". Between one country and another, one province and another and even one place and another there will always exist a certain inequality in the conditions of life, which it will be possible to reduce to a minimum but never entirely remove (Marx, 1947:55).

That these inequalities of condition will not be translated into other inequalities is something we must take on "faith." This is why I have partially called the paper "an agonizing choice." In a sense, the word "choice" is misleading, since for many Marxists the movement towards a classless society is inexorable, though there is room for human intervention.

However, the word "agony" is appropriate, because as Cole has remarked:

[Marx's] concern was with the struggle to arrive at the new society, not with the use to which men would put their emancipation when they had achieved it (Cole, 1962:viii).

And Passmore has noted:

Marx was, however, extremely reluctant to describe in detail what Oscar Wilde called 'the soul of man under socialism'. He was contemptuous of Utopias, of any attempt to draw up a blue-print for the future (Passmore, 1970:237).

If Marx and Engels, then, reject the classical ideal of a final perfection, they are still committed to the Phoenix myth, the myth of a fresh start, a "breaking

through" which will carry men if not to perfection then at least to a condition
which permits of unlimited improvement (Passmore, 1970:238)

Alvin Gouldner, in his *The Coming Crisis of Western Sociology,* writes
that "to explore the character of a sociology, to know what a sociology is,
therefore, requires us to identify its deepest assumptions about man and
society" (Gouldner, 1970:28). He goes on to say:

> But when [Sociology] is acting self-consciously, it can at least put these
> assumptions to the test; it can appraise which are warranted and which are
> unfounded (Gouldner, 1970:28).

This paper has attempted to delineate two problematics whose assumptions
concerning the nature of class and power differ. Sociology can enlarge its
understanding and explanation of *both* class and inequality only when we
face these differences. If we continue to ignore these assumptions, see the
two problematics as equivalent, or prematurely synthesize them, our explanations of poverty and wealth will be vacuous.

Only when we recognize these differences can we move towards a basic
alteration of Canadian society, one in which the pernicious consequences of
inequality are removed. In my view, the abolition of classes, in the Marxist
sense, is a necessary condition for the removal of inequalities in Canada,
but it is not a sufficient condition. The classless society leaves us without
classes, but does it leave us without inequalities? The "equalitarian" society
may leave us equal in condition, but will such a society inevitably be so
bureaucratic, so leveled that it will dehumanize the species rather than freeing it? Perhaps in the process of making empirical analyses within at least
these two theoretical frameworks, the agonizing choice, if there is one, will
become clearer.

NOTES

1. See the excellent work by Leo Johnson, *Poverty in Wealth,* rev. ed. Toronto:
   New Hogtown Press, 1977.

2. Canada officially launched its war on poverty in 1968 when it commissioned a
   Senate committee, headed by Senator David Croll, to investigate poverty in
   Canada and its solutions, and report to Parliament. This report, *Poverty in
   Canada,* was tabled in 1971. Another report, *The Real Poverty Report,* was
   published just prior to the above, by a group led by Ian Adams, who broke
   away from the commission. These two reports followed a documentation of the
   extent of poverty in 1968 by the Economic Council of Canada in its 5th Annual
   Report, and again it its 6th Annual Report.

   Recently, the Economic Council of Canada has moved into the area of
   social indicators, and its annual reports since 1969 ignore poverty *per se.* The
   two poverty reports recommended the adoption of a guaranteed annual income
   (GAI) utilizing a negative income tax mechanism so as to keep alive the work incentive. The federal government and the Province of Manitoba recently completed a $17 million experiment on the GAI (see Gilbert's article in this book).
   We now have more data on the poor than anyone could possibly use.

3. Cf. David Lane (1971:11).

4. I am aware of the epistemological issues surrounding Althusser's (1969, 1970)
   concept of the problematic. However, in this paper I am using the term as a

pedagogical device to highlight what I think are some fundamental differences in the way we look at and explain the political economy of Canada. Unless these differences are made explicit and faced "head-on," I cannot see us advancing better explanations of our political economy, nor can I see us fostering significant social changes that would assist the oppressed.

5. Cf. Blackburn's comment: "The very notion that social research can be conducted other than on the basis of the prior development of concepts and theories is held to be ideological. The choice of a particular field of investigation, the choice of a given range of concepts with which to investigate the field, all express assumptions about the nature of society and about what is theoretically significant and what is not" (1972:9-10).

6. For Althusser (1970:32ff.), the empiricist sees knowledge present in the object and in its operation. Empiricism tends to confuse a technical instrument, e.g., a "model," with the concept of knowledge. The empiricist knows his knowledge of wealth and poverty is not identical with wealth or poverty, but he believes that the two (the knowledge and the object) are not two objects, but really only one with two parts. Thus, an empiricist can argue, for example, that poverty and the absence of money are identical. An excellent illustration of this confusion within an empiricist problematic can be seen in the Senate report. The senators argued that poverty was the result of our economic system. Yet one of their recommendations was to establish a Council of Applied Research that would *not* be "concerned with theoretical . . . research problems." The problematic, and hence the recommendations, eliminates questions about the structure right off!

7. I am not suggesting that all Marxists are insensitive to the distinction between classlessness and inequality. For example, as American Marxist sociologist Erik Olin Wright explains: "The underlying premise of a Marxist class analysis is that while the diverse dimensions of social inequality cannot be reduced to class inequality, nevertheless class relations play a decisive role in shaping other forms of inequality" (1978:1.).

8. See also *The German Ideology* (1970b:129-36) and the *Grundrisse* (McClellan, 1971:25-35).

9. See Parkin (1974) and Clegg(1975).

10. Compare Giddens' critique of the work of Dahrendorf on this point (Giddens, 1973:78).

11. The one place, to my knowledge, where Marx explicitly defines power is in a footnote in the first volume of *Capital*, where he distinguishes between power based on land, personal relations of dominion and servitude, and power based on money (Marx,1912:163). His historical works on France also show that he was sensitive to important power variations within as well as between social classes. See especially *The Eighteenth Brumaire* (1963).

12. See Martin Nicolaus' article in Blackburn (1972), especially pp.321-22.

13. Marx wrote: "The rate of surplus-value is therefore an exact expression for the degree of exploitation of labour-power by capital, or of the labourer by the capitalist" (1912:241). It is interesting to note that one of the fundamental disagreements between the work on class by the American Erik Olin Wright, and the work of Poulantzas in France is over the distinction between surplus-value and surplus-labor. See Wright (1976).

14. For an earlier article that compares Marx's concept of class with Pareto's concept of power, see Aron (1950). As I noted in footnote 8, Wright is aware of the problem. However, to date, he has concentrated his efforts on the concept of class, not of power.

15. Two extremely provocative and recent attempts to explain inequalities are

Ernest Becker's *Escape From Evil* and Marvin Harris' *Cannibals and Kings.*

16. For an excellent analysis of this approach, see Althusser (1970:165-81).

17. The recent resurgence of Marxist political economy in Canada should provide us with these sorts of studies over the next decade or two. (For example, see Clement, Drache, Panitch, and Teeple.) However, when we read these studies we should be sensitive to the possible confusion of the two problematics within a given work. For example, Clement's two major works are devoid of a "class" analysis, and Drache (1978) in his essay on the history of political economy in Canada first of all suggests that a political economy perspective can be *either* materialist or non-materialist, yet when he attempts to explain the demise of the political economy approach in the 1950s and 1960s, he notes that "The break with political economy was a break with materialism" (9). Also, note Archibald's facile fusion of Marx and Weber in his very interesting work *Social Psychology as Political Economy* (1978:123).

18. See special issue of *Canadian Review of Sociology and Anthropology*, Vol. 15, 2 (1978), especially the article by John Jackson, p.140.

19. Two other areas where the two problematics vary are in discussions about the *state* and *technology*. The equality problematic agrees with Marx that the state is not a neutral instrument, but it also argues that the state's existence is not simply a result of class conflict nor will it disappear with the abolition of classes. As Clement remarks: "But to say the corporate elite has a disproportionate impact on the state system is not to say they are not distinct institutional domains and bases of power. On the other hand, as a model of liberal-democracies, these distinct domains of power do not mean that power should be viewed piecemeal. Rather, it should be analyzed as a whole by placing these distinct bases in relationship to each other — both in terms of class recruitment and their structural relationships — by examining their relative powers."

As Clement and others have noted, it is critical, in the Canadian context, that we not confine our analyses of power to our national boundaries. I might add that the same is true for any class analysis. Since the capitalist mode of production knows no national boundaries, the proletariat of Canada's class system may not be living as Canadian citizens, but in other parts of the world. We have only begun to systematically explore this possibility.

With technology, we come to another area where the two problematics differ. Marx sees machinery as "neutral," its use dependent upon the mode of production. (See *Capital*, 1912:445-68). Lenski argues that while the two are interrelated, technology creates problems in any distributive system. Following Weber, Lenski demonstrates that the existence of a complex technology forces a society to organize decision-making in a hierarchical manner. For any person who wishes to explore this area, I recommend highly the work of Braverman, Ellul, and Nell's article in Blackburn, 1972.

REFERENCES

Adams, Ian et al. *The Real Poverty Report.* Edmonton: Mel Hurtig Publishers, 1971.

Althusser, Louis. *For Marx.* London: Allen Lane, 1969.

Althusser, Louis and E. Balibar. *Reading Capital.* London: New Left Books, 1970.

Archibald, W. Peter. *Social Psychology as Political Economy.* Toronto: McGraw-Hill Ryerson, 1978.

Aron, Raymond. "Social Structure and the Ruling Class," *British Journal of Sociology*, Vol. 1 (Nov. 1950), pp. 1-16; Vol. 1 (June 1950), pp. 126-43.

Balandier, Georges. *Political Anthropology*. London: Allen Lane, 1970.

Becker, Ernest. *Escape from Evil*. New York: The Free Press, 1975.

Blackburn, Robin, ed. *Ideology in Social Science*. Glasgow: Fontana/Collins, 1972.

Braverman, Harry. *Labor and Monopoly Capitalism*. New York: Monthly Review Press, 1974.

Camus, Albert. *The Rebel*. London: Penguin, 1953.

Clegg, Stewart. *Power, Rule, and Domination*. London: Routledge and Paul, 1975.

Clement, Wallace. *The Canadian Corporate Elite*. Toronto: McClelland and Stewart, 1975.

_____.*Continental Corporate Power*. Toronto: McClelland and Stewart, 1977.

Clement, Wallace and Daniel Drache. *A Practical Guide to Canadian Political Economy*. Toronto: James Lorimer, 1978. .

Cole, G.D.H. "Introduction" to *Capital*. London: Everyman Library Edition, 1962, pp. v-xxv.

Connell, R.W. *Ruling Class, Ruling Culture*. London: Cambridge University Press, 1977.

Drache, Daniel. "Rediscovering Canadian Political Economy," in Wallace Clement and Daniel Drache, *A Practical Guide to Canadian Political Economy*. Toronto: James Lorimer, 1978, pp. 1-53.

Economic Council of Canada. *Annual Reports, 1968-1974*.

Ellul, Jacques. *The Technological Society*. New York: Vintage Books, 1964.

Forcese, Dennis. *The Canadian Class Structure*. Toronto: McGraw-Hill Ryerson, 1975.

Giddens, Anthony. *Capitalism and Modern Social Theory*. London: Cambridge University Press, 1971.

_____. *The Class Structure of Advanced Societies*. London: Hutchison University Library, 1973.

_____. "Classical Social Theory and the Origins of Modern Sociology," *American Journal of Sociology*, 81 (1975), pp. 703-29.

Gouldner, Alvin. *The Coming Crisis of Western Sociology*. New York: Avon Books, 1970.

Harris, Marvin. *Cannibals and Kings*. New York: Vintage Books, 1978.

Heilbroner, Robert. "Inescapable Marx," *New York Review of Books* (June 1978), pp. 33-37.

Heron, Craig, ed. *Imperialism, Nationalism, and Canada*. Toronto: New Hogtown Press, 1977.

Johnson, Leo. *Poverty in Wealth*. Toronto: New Hogtown Press, 1977.

Jordon, Z. "Karl Marx as a Philosopher and Sociologist," in *Karl Marx*. London: Michael Joseph, 1971, pp. 9-67.

Lane, David. *The End of Inequality?* Middlesex: Penguin, 1971.

Lenski, Gerhard. *Power and Privilege*. New York: McGraw-Hill, 1966.

Lenski, Gerhard and Jean Lenski. *Human Societies*. New York: McGraw-Hill, 1971.

Marx, Karl. *Capital*, Vol. 1. Chicago: Charles H. Kerr, 1912.

_____. *Critique of the Gotha Program*. Moscow: Foreign Languages Publications, 1947.

_____. *Manifesto of the Communist Party*. Moscow: Foreign Languages Publications, 1948.

_____. *The 18th Brumaire of Louis Bonaparte*. New York: International Publishers, 1963.

_____. *A Contribution to the Critique of Political Economy*. Moscow: Progress Publishers, 1970a.

_____. *The German Ideology*, C.V. Arthur, ed. New York: International Publishers, 1970b.

_____. *The Poverty of Philosophy*. New York: International Publishers, 1973.

McClellan, David. *Marx's Grundrisse*. London: Macmillan, 1971.

Milner, Sheilagh and Henry Milner. *The Decolonization of Quebec*. Toronto: McClelland and Stewart, 1973.

Nell, Edward. "Economics: The Revival of Political Economy," in Robin Blackburn, ed., *Ideology in Social Science*. Glasgow: Fontana/Collins, 1972, pp. 76-95.

Panitch, Leo, ed. *The Canadian State*. Toronto: University of Toronto Press, 1977.

Parkin, Frank, ed. *The Social Analysis of Class Structure*. New York: Harper and Row, 1974.

Passmore, John. *The Perfectability of Man*. London: Duckworth, 1970.

Penner, Norman. *The Canadian Left*. Scarborough, Ont.: Prentice-Hall of Canada, 1977.

Porter, John. *The Vertical Mosaic*. Toronto: University of Toronto Press, 1964.

Poulantzas, Nicos. *Classes in Contemporary Capitalism*. London: New Left Books, 1975.

Poverty in Canada. Senate Report to the House of Commons, Chairman, Senator David Croll, 1971.

Teeple, Gary, ed. *Capitalism and the National Question in Canada*. Toronto: University of Toronto Press, 1972.

Tepperman, Lorne. *Social Mobility in Canada*. Toronto: McGraw-Hill Ryerson, 1975.

Thompson, E.P. *The Making of the English Working Class*. London: Penguin, 1963.

Watson, G. Llewellyn. "The Poverty of Sociology in a Changing Canadian Society," *Canadian Journal of Sociology* (1976), pp. 345-62.

Waxman, Chaim I. *The Stigma of Poverty*. New York: Pergamon Press, 1977.

Weber, Max. *The Theory of Social and Economic Organization*. Glencoe: The Free Press, 1964.

Westergaard, John and Henrietta Resler. *Class in a Capitalist Society*. New York: Basic Books, 1975.

Wilensky, Harold L. *The Welfare State and Equality*. Berkeley: University of California Press, 1975.

Wright, Erik Olin. "Class Boundaries in Advanced Capitalist Societies," *New Left Review*, 98 (1976), pp. 3-41.

_____. "Race, Class and Income Inequality," Madison, Wisconsin: Institute for Research on Poverty.

The Development of Class in Canada in the Twentieth Century*

LEO A. JOHNSON

There is, in all likelihood, no greater point of division between non-Marxist and Marxist intellectuals in North America than that which arises over the definition, importance, and purpose of the study of class. Primary to this division is the degree to which the non-Marxist (or "liberal") intellectual depends upon the measurement of the subjective attitudes of individuals as his basis of analysis. In contrast, the Marxist measures or defines his categories by the objective relations of those studied. Thus, the liberal, when dealing with class, uses the subjective perceptions of individuals as his primary conceptual framework, and tends to downgrade or dismiss external objective criteria; while the Marxist, beginning with his objective criteria for class, assumes a direct relationship between the objective condition of individuals and their conscious understanding and activity — an expectation which, in the short run at least, is frequently disappointed. While it can be argued that neither basis for analysis automatically creates a distorted or useless perspective, it is important to recognize that serious misconceptions about the development of class in Canada have occurred in the conclusions of both groups and that these are the result of weaknesses in their methodological approach.

Class, to the North American liberal intellectual, relates primarily to the subjective rank-recognition of an individual's status held by his peers.[1] Thus the categories that have been developed within this framework (essentially, upper, middle, and lower class) offer little basis for the analysis of problems which reach beyond the world of ideas, attitudes, and ideology. The liberal scholar is likely to be little concerned with long-range understanding of why certain social or economic phenomena (such as revolutions) occur, but rather contents himself with the investigation of short-term activities of groups (for example, voting), to which investigations of the consciousness or attitudes of individuals in them has generally provided satisfactory answers. Where more profound or searching questions are raised, the liberal intellectual's response traditionally has been to examine the correlations between material conditions and personal attributes of individuals (especially attitudes towards work) and to assume that the latter have caused the former. Only occasionally has this view been seriously challenged by radical scholars such as C. Wright Mills and Gabriel Kolko.[2]

*From G. Teeple, *Capitalism and the National Question in Canada.* Toronto: University of Toronto Press, 1972.

Moreover, concentration on the consciousness of individuals has tended to create a strong emphasis on "culture" as a causative factor in social behavior. Since in North America there exists a great degree of superficial cultural homogeneity at least at the level of the consumption of, and a general conditioned desire for, mass-produced material goods, social analyses which incorporate as a primary input such generally shared subjective characteristics naturally fail to find significant class differentiations among social groups or individuals; and class as an analytical tool, therefore, has had little intellectual, social, or political value.

To a Marxist scholar, however, class carries a precise definition which relates, not to the attitudes of individuals, but to their external material relationships centred on those created by the productive process. Thus class definitions and relations differ between societies where the means and modes of production are different.[3] In a capitalist society, it is argued, three fundamental relationships to the means of production exist: the capitalist class or bourgeoisie, who own the means of production and purchase the labor power of others to operate it; the petite bourgeoisie or independent commodity producers, such as farmers and craftsmen, who both own and operate their means of production; and the proletariat who do not own their means of production and therefore are required to sell their capacity to work — that is, their labor power — in the market place. Marx recognized that in any society such divisions are never so clear cut or all-inclusive. Thus special-interest and functional social groupings which cut across class lines or existed in an adjunct or parasitic relationship to the main classes (such as white collar "clients" of the bourgeoisie, or the demoralized "lumpen-proletariat") were deemed worthy of analysis as well.[4] Moreover, Marxists have always recognized that while an individual may objectively belong to one class, subjectively he may suffer from "false consciousness" and behave as though he belonged to another and therefore act in ways which in fact injure himself and his class peers.

This concentration on the individual's relationship to the means of production stems from the Marxist idea that the farther a worker is from control of his means of production, the greater is his alienation, and consequently the greater will be his potential for revolution and the attainment of the socialist state. Moreover, Marx's studies concluded that in a capitalist society there were certain inherent class antagonisms and relationships which made the ultimate collapse of the capitalist system a certainty. What must be emphasized, however, and what has frequently been forgotten by leftists, is that Marx concerned himself with the general analysis of the process of change and revolution within capitalist society, and not with the description or prediction of particular historical developments or the individual strategies that revolutionary groups would be required to undertake to meet the unique social and political formations of their own society.

The development of Marxist theory occurred within the context of what was perhaps the most vigorous intellectual debate of the 19th century. No scholar investigating the development of Marxist thought can fail to be impressed by the diversity of approach, concern for sources, factual accuracy, and scientific approach, and the spirited and self-critical debate which hammered out the central themes of Marxist thought over the four decades prior to the publication of *Capital*.[5] Unfortunately, when one looks back over Canada's political and intellectual history there is little evidence on the Canadian left of the deep concern for factual accuracy, indigenous theoretical elaboration, and insight into the unique circumstances of national class development which has characterized European Marxist thought. In most cases the little intellectual work that has been undertaken is devoted almost entirely to polemics rather than analysis.[6]

The failure of Canadian Marxists to recognize fundamental differences in the origins and development of class and class relations in Canada from those in Europe (and more recently Asia) has resulted in serious errors in both analysis and political leadership. In particular, lack of indigenous analysis has led to a failure of the left's "time sense"; that is, even when Canadian developments have paralleled classical models, the left has failed to recognize the precise degree or stage in the development of the paradigm. As a result of these failures, political leadership of Canadian Marxists has been almost uniformly disastrous — indeed, for the most part is has consisted of little more than seizing upon any spontaneous unrest that may arise, proclaiming it "the Revolution," and leading it into direct conflict or confrontation with the dominant social forces where it either has been crushed or has collapsed when the short-term conditions have been alleviated. As a result, left leadership is generally and rightfully distrusted in Canada by the very classes whose interests it desires to serve. In this circumstance, most Marxists in Canada have betrayed the first principle of the Marxist intellectual tradition — to be "scientific": to know the facts, and to understand events within the particular historical context of their occurrence.

A second serious consequence of the left's neglect of analysis is the lack of a firm basis from which to criticize the various faddish and superficial theories that appear in the academic community. Thus we are confronted with "youth as class," "worker as an objectively reactionary force," "the sexually repressed middle class as proto-fascists," and simple-minded responses, pro and con, on the question of Canadian nationalism. Since the main questions regarding class in Canada have seldom been asked, let alone answered, the left in Canada has become the victim, just as liberal intellectuals have, of a situation where all ideas about class are equally plausible, and where statements about class are reduced either to the level of opinions and ideology, or to facile applications of analytical models drawn from foreign and historically different circumstances.

This article is both a response to the situation and a challenge to other socialists and Marxists to begin the process of indigenous analysis and criticism which has proved so fruitful in the development of correct analysis and successful political strategy elsewhere. Since the investigation is in its initial stages, few comments about political strategy will be offered, although the facts themselves suggest major criticisms of both "new" and "old" left positions.

The reader should be aware of two considerations relating to the statistics cited in the pages that follow. First, the Dominion Bureau of Statistics and the Taxation Department (the two main sources) do not use the same definitions of occupation, and consequently disparities in numbers exist in reference sources. Since the purpose of this work is to establish historical tendencies rather than absolute conditions, the discrepancy between sources provides no serious problem — particularly since both sources yield results showing identical tendencies. Secondly, it must be remembered that a study covering forty years embraces two generations. To the casual reader processes of impoverishment or proletarianization occurring over that long a period may seem to occur with great rapidity and drama, whereas in real life the process may be so slow (1 or 2% per year) that the individual being impoverished may experience no more than a growing malaise, a sense of uneasiness, or a feeling of helplessness.

Finally, it must be remembered that the political activist who draws his knowledge of impoverishment and exploitation and his perception of the need for major social change from statistics rather than from the direct experience of those processes runs the risk of describing them in a language of such force, drama, and sweeping importance that the very people of whom he is talking fail to recognize their own lives and life experiences in his words. The finest analysis is pointless if it is not faithfully presented to and fully understood by those whom it was designed to benefit.

The Petite Bourgeoisie

In Canada, historically, the petite bourgeoisie has been comprised of two groups, the independent commodity producers such as farmers, fishermen, and craftsworkers, and the small bourgeois businessmen, such as retailers, independent salesmen, and rentiers.

Social and Political History

During the early part of the 19th century, Canada's history was dominated by the struggles of the farmers and small businessmen — the classical petite bourgeoisie — against the domination of aristocratic elements such as the Family Compact and Château Clique. By 1848 with the granting of responsible government and the introduction of elective local government, most of the ideals of these groups had been achieved. Of course, the landless agricultural workers were still disenfranchised, as were the poorer proletarian urban elements, but the more prosperous crafts workers and skilled tradesmen — in the words of the period, those who had "a stake in society" — had been accommodated.

While certain "radical" elements such as the Clear Grit and Rouge parties continued to argue for universal or household franchise, such an ideal was clearly opposed to the interests of the petite bourgeoisie and labor aristocracy, and was strongly rejected for many years by all enfranchised groups.

By the 1870s, however, a cloud had begun to cover their peaceful horizon. The development of a capitalist mode of production and distribution with the resultant destruction of the small local manufacturing and distribution centers, and the growing tendency towards monopoly control of prices, tariffs, freight and interest rates, began to force the independent commodity producers to find means of defending their interests against the growing power of the large capitalists.

At the same time, the crafts workers also were coming under attack by the new capitalist mode of production. By 1872, consciousness of their own interests produced the first major concerted effort to win better working terms by the creation of organizations such as the Toronto Trades Assembly and the Nine Hours League, as well as Canada's first labor-oriented newspaper.[7] By the 1880s, the capitalist mode of production, which utilized large amounts of unskilled labor, had begun to make significant inroads in the ranks of skilled crafts workers, and ancient and respected crafts such as shoemakers (the Sons of St. Crispin as they styled themselves) were in serious decay.[8]

As might be expected, the two groups most affected by the new capitalism discovered that they shared a common interest in combining against monopoly, centralization of production and distribution, and the competition of cheap labor. As a result of their common problems and their similar position in the economic structure, which at least provided them with common enemies, the monopolists and bankers, from 1870 to the present there is a recurring pattern of alliances between farmers and better paid workers, either as third party movements or as advanced wings of one of the "old" parties. In the 19th century these groups tended to support the Macdonald Conservative party and, in the 20th, the King Liberals.

Since both old parties generally placed the interests of capitalists and big businessmen ahead of those of the farmers and workers, the latter found themselves forced at times of extreme stress to undertake a long series of third party and extra-parliamentary strategies. Surprisingly, the literature concerning these groups almost entirely fails to recognize both the continuity of leadership between them, and the fact that the central issues which spurred their creation stemmed from a single problem — the deterioration of their status in the developing capitalist economy. Thus, the Nine Hours movement, the Grange, Patrons of Industry, the progressive farm-labor alliances of the 1920s, and the Social Credit and CCF parties in 1930s and 1940s represented the interests of farmers and workers as they attempted to defend themselves against the erosion of their position.

Over the years, as the two old parties competed with each other and the third party groups for support, considerable concessions were made to working class elements, who gradually were granted the franchise and a degree of protection from the grosser sorts of exploitation and poverty in exchange for their votes.

Since the purpose of these concessions was to win working class support for existing economic, political, and ideological positions, they were usually made before demands for improved social justice by working class elements had led to the growth of class consciousness. Only in the First World War and the depression did exploitation and hardship develop to the point where consciousness of the working class emerged — only to be undermined by Mackenzie King's recognition of the dangers it presented, by his introduction of social legislation designed to reduce tension, and the vigorous repression of radical leadership.

As a result of these historical social and political developments working class elements traditionally have entered the political arena on terms and conditions set by the on-going struggle between the petite bourgeois and capitalist classes. It would appear that so long as this struggle holds center stage, and no great political or economic errors are made by the capitalist protagonists, the growth of working class consciousness will be slow — particularly when a minority of strongly unionized and highly paid workers enjoy a standard of living conducive to property ownership, a high standard of commodity consumption, and the attainment of other externals of petit bourgeois status. It is in the light of these understandings that one should consider the significance of the current stage of decline of the petite bourgeoisie.

Over the past 40 years, the petite bourgeoisie has come under more extreme pressure. As a result they have declined both in income and numbers relative to the general population. Statistics provided by the Department of National Revenue single out five groups of petite bourgeois which provide an insight into the rapidity of their decline as a significant class. As Table 1 points out, these groups in 1968 (farmers, fishermen, independent businessmen, investors, and self-employed salesmen) not only realized little income from their capital investment, but their earned income was below average as well. As a result of their decline in prosperity relative to that of the general society their numbers have shown a marked decline in relative numbers from 14.7% of income earners in 1948 to 10.9% of earners in 1968 — a loss of over 25% in just 20 years.

The Independent Commodity Producers

Among the independent commodity producers, the farmers have been particularly hard hit. The decline in numbers of independent farmers is not, of course, a new story. While the number of occupied farm units in Canada increased in Canada as a whole between 1901 and 1941, this increase came almost entirely from the expansion of agriculture into unsettled areas of the Prairies and British Columbia. In the long-settled areas, a decline in number of farm units was already under way as early as 1901-11 in the Atlantic region.[10] Over the years the decline has accelerated as competition and the rapid expansion of capital investment in agriculture have forced the weak or undercapitalized farm out of business.

One cause of the reduction in the number of occupied farms is the rapid growth in size of farm units. This increase in size of units has occurred in all areas, but has been especially pronounced in the prairies. But farmers in the Atlantic region experienced great changes in the 1951-61 period, when the number of occupied farms dropped by 47.6% while average size increased from 112 to 168 acres.[11]

Along with decline in numbers and increase in farm size, significant changes in patterns of ownership have occurred also. In the areas under greatest economic stress, the Atlantic and Prairie regions, absentee ownership, generally corporate, has made significant inroads. By 1961, fully 42% of all Prairie farms were absentee-owned. In contrast in Quebec, Ontario, and British Columbia owner-occupied farms remained a high proportion of all units.[12]

Table 1

The Independent Petite Bourgeoisie, 1948-68[9]

	1948	1958	1968
Total income earners	3,662,030	5,530,496	8,495,184
Total petite bourgeoisie	559,480	731,481	928,713
Petite bourgeoisie as a percentage of all earners	14.7%	13.3%	10.9%
Average income: all earners	$2,091.30	$3,299.75	$4,918.00
Average income: petite bourgeoisie	2,518.80	3,659.20	4,601.90
Petite bourgeoisie income (1949 dollars)	2,596.70	2,925.00	2,965.10
Petite bourgeoisie income as a percentage of average	120%	111%	94%

Table 2

Farm Income, 1948-68[13]

	1948	1958	1968
Number of farmers	190,090	205,331	291,553
Farmers as a percentage of all earners	5.19%	3.71%	3.43%
Average income of farmers	$1,619.81	$2,234.13	$3,244.36
Farmer income (1949 dollars)	1,669.91	1,785.88	2,090.44
Farm income as a percentage of average	78%	68%	66%

Related directly to the rapid decrease in numbers of farm units and increase in unit size is a rapid increase in capitalization and decrease in farm employment. Thus while there has been only a slight increase in acreage cultivated between 1931 and 1961, farm capitalization has increased by almost 450%. At the same time the farm labor force has declined by almost 50%. With the over-all growth in the labor force, the agricultural sector has declined drastically from 28.79% in 1931 to 10.23% in 1961.[14]

Over the years, economists and government officials have justified the decimation of agricultural workers and farm owners on the grounds that higher capitalization and larger farms would lead to increased productivity and a higher standard of living for farmers. As Table 2 demonstrates, farmers have responded by increasing capitalization from $4 billion in 1931 to more than $19 billion in 1961. Moreover, farm productivity, measured in persons supplied with food and fiber per farm worker has tripled in the same period, from 11 per farm worker in 1935 to 31 in 1962.[15] Despite this enormously increased investment and productivity, farm incomes are falling farther below average. Although the per capita purchasing power of farmers increased by about 20% between 1948 and 1968, this increase was less than one-half the average gain of other income earners. As Table 2 points out, farm incomes declined from 78% to 66% of average. Thus, while productivity increased by 60% between 1948 and 1958, income increased by only 5%.

Moreover, farmers as well as consumers are exploited by the monopoly situation which exists in the food processing and distribution industry. As a result, an increasing share of the consumer's dollar is going to the agribusiness middlemen. Because the farmer is economically vulnerable in comparison to the corporate giants who buy his products, he continues to fall farther and farther behind other sectors in income, despite increased investment and productivity.[16]

A major result of the abandonment and consolidation of farm units and the rise of absentee agribusiness has been the creation of an underclass of dispossessed rural dwellers. The rural dispossessed (those who have been forced off their farms) now make up one-third of the population of the Maritimes.[18] Moreover, not only are the non-farm rural Maritime residents maintained through additions from the farm sector, but their average age is declining rapidly, indicating that they are likely to be a permanent feature of Maritime society and economy.[19] While economists have attempted to justify the forced reduction in size of farm numbers by their economic claims of increased income for those farmers remaining, they have ignored entirely the hardships experienced by those forced from the land who are either incapable of making the transition to urban living, or who, because of their lack of skills, are incapable of being absorbed in the urban economy. Thus, just as 19th century government policy created a laboring class in Canada, so 20th century policies have helped bring into existence an under-class of dispossessed farmers.[20]

Not only have the remaining farmers undergone a process of relative impoverishment — and for those who are forced off the farms, proletarianization — but even those who have remained on the farm have experienced a severe erosion of status. As their income from farming falls farther and farther below average, farmers are forced to turn more and more to wage labor in an attempt to maintain their standard of living. Of course, as Table 3 demonstrates, the lower income farmers are subjected to this process to a greater degree than are those with higher incomes; however, both income groups are clearly undergoing the same process. Thus, even those farmers who retain ownership of their farms have lost much of their cherished independence.

Perhaps the most dramatic example of an independent commodity producing group who have declined to the level of the proletariat is provided by the recent strike of fishermen at Canso, Mulgrove and Petit de Grat, Nova Scotia. In spite of a long and historic tradition of rugged individualism, the rise to dominance of a few powerful fish processors and competition from floating foreign fish factories had so eroded the fishermen's independence, that by the 1960s, their legal and historical description of co-adventurers had become a mockery of their poverty. Working 16 hours a day, 12 days in each two-week cycle, their incomes were as little as $2500 a year. Meanwhile, Nova Scotia's archaic labor laws

Table 3
Source of Income of Farmers, 1948-68[17] (Percentages)

	Farmers with Taxable Incomes		Farmers with Non-Taxable Incomes	
	Farming	Wages & Salaries	Farming	Wages & Salaries
1948	91.1	4.3	90.6	5.1
1958	82.3	8.5	83.1	8.9
1968	76.2	11.0	64.6	20.0

continued to class them not as employees but as small entrepreneurs in partnership with the dominant companies and hence not eligible for the legal protection of union certification. Thus it became necessary for the fishermen and their families to fight a bitter seven-month strike in order to win the legal rights of other proletarianized groups.[21]

The Independent Petite Bourgeoisie
Other independent sectors of the petite bourgeoisie are undergoing processes of impoverishment and proletarianization similar to those experienced by the farmers. As Tables 4 and 5 demonstrate, the process of relative impoverishment is not as far advanced among other sectors of the petite bourgeoisie as among farmers. As Table 6 demonstrates, independent businessmen and salesmen are experiencing the same process of proletarianization that occurred among farmers still owning their independent means of production. With their numbers reduced from their numerical and political dominance of the 1850s to a mere 10.9% of income earners in 1968, it is clear that the whole petite bourgeoisie is reaching the last stages of destruction. Little remains of their former power except their myths and ideals, which are perpetuated by the major capitalists and independent professionals as the first line of defence against those who would question the legitimacy of private ownership of the means of production.

It would be difficult to over-estimate the economic and historical significance of the destruction of the independent petite bourgeoisie and in particular of the independent commodity producers. For the past century, Canada's history has been shaped by their losing struggle against the maturing capitalist economy. During this period the consciousness of the emerging proletariat has been dominated by the "progressive" and "populist" idealism of the petite bourgeoisie, and has, again and again, been diverted from its own best interests into a struggle for goals appropriate only to a "respectable" class of property owners. On the only two occasions when working class people acquired sufficient autonomy of vision to make their own demands and to undertake strategies which seemed to contain the possibility of the attainment of a classless society (in 1919 in the One Big Union and the general strike, and in the 1930s with the rise of the Communist party of Canada), the workers found their erstwhile allies, the petite bourgeoisie, lined up solidly with the capitalists against them in a strategy of state repression. Given the numerical predominance of the petite bourgeoisie at those points in time, as well as the high level of their conscious class self-interest, the likelihood of a working class triumph was very small. There a socialist strategy which drew its analysis from the European experience and concentrated on politics and confrontation tactics rather than social development would appear to have been badly timed, unless significant sectors of the petite bourgeoisie could have been persuaded to join the workers in a socialist revolution.

Table 4
Business Operators' Incomes, 1948-68[22]

	1948	*1958*	*1968*
Total income earners	3,662,030	5,530,496	8,495,184
Total business operators	241,770	301,070	351,621
Percentage of all income earners	6.6%	5.4%	4.1%
Average income of business operators	$2,951.80	$4,031.00	$5,166.90
Average income (1949 dollars)	$3,043.10	$3,301.50	$3,329.20
Average business operators' income as a percentage of average income	141%	129%	105%

Table 5
Independent Salesmen's Incomes, 1948-68[23]

	1948	*1958*	*1968*
Total income earners	3,662,030	5,530,496	8,495,184
Total independent salesmen	29,010	63,323	25,274
Percentage of all income earners	0.8%	1.1%	0.3%
Average income of independent salesmen	$3,291.90	$4,674.10	$5,957.80
Real average income (1949 dollars)	$3,393.70	$3,736.30	$3,383.80
Average independent salesmen's income as a percentage of average income	157%	142%	121%

Table 6
Source of Income: Farmers and Retail Traders, 1948-68[24] (Percentages)

	Farmers		*Retail Traders*	
	Farming	*Wages & Salaries*	*Business Income*	*Wages & Salaries*
1948	90.9	4.6	—	—
1958	82.7	8.7	83.6	8.3
1968	73.4	12.8	78.5	12.0

With the decline of the petite bourgeoisie, a completely new situation has arisen in Canada. First of all the triumph of the capitalist in this century-long stuggle with the petite bourgeoisie means that the essential class composition of Canadian society has been greatly simplified. In a situation where some 83% of Canadians depend upon wages and salaries for their income, the loyalty of the majority of the population to the principle of private ownership of the means of production must be greatly weakened. Thus, traditional appeals to the working class and classical strategies which were inappropriate in the Canadian class situation in 1920 or 1940 may now take on a new validity as the essential class conflict shifts to one between the working class and the capitalist owner.

Second, while the ideological remnants of the petite bourgeoisie-capitalist struggle are likely to linger on for some time to come (indeed, it is now to the advantage of the capitalist to confuse the situation by the perpetuation of populist and progressive ideals), the significant fact is that the petite bourgeoisie itself can no longer serve effectively as the first line of defence against a genuinely class-conscious working class. Finally, a disillusioned petite bourgeoisie itself can make significant contributions to a socialist revolution, particularly in the early stages. It can be argued, therefore, that the failure of the left in Canada in previous periods should not be explained simply as a failure of analysis and timing. Tactics and theoretical analysis which may be valid for a struggle between capital and labor should not be discarded out of hand simply because they failed at a time when the major conflict was occurring between the petite bourgeoisie and the capitalist class. Rather, they must be re-examined within the context of Canadian society and history and be accepted, modified, or rejected as they appear useful in the changing Canadian context.

The Capitalist Class

The Structure of Capitalism in Canada

More than a decade ago, a brilliant husband-and-wife team, L.C. and F.W. Park, wrote a remarkable book, *The Anatomy of Big Business,* which has been entirely ignored by Canadian academics. Their work is a detailed, well-documented study of capitalism in Canada which points out the class relations and corporate ties that bind together the small group of big businessmen that control the Canadian economy.

Commenting on the importance of the concentration of ownership and control of the major means of production in Canada, the Parks argued that: "The power of the [big businessmen] is a class power, that this group, the most important sector of the ruling class, own the means of production in Canada and their power is based on this ownership.

"Now the means of production are in fact owned by . . . the handful of giant corporations, [but] corporations also have owners, and in the last analysis, after stripping away the holding companies that complicate the picture, the financial groups in control of the corporations control them on the basis of owning a controlling interest . . .

"Those who own the controlling interest generally do not manage the corporations they control. Managers can be hired — and fired . . . The fact that the controlling group may play a smaller role in active management does not mean that their power over the corporation and their managers is less. The power remains and is exercised whenever big decisions have to be made."[25]

Over the years, a number of lists have been prepared naming the major capitalists in the country.[26] While authors have given lists of various lengths (from a high of 922 down to the proverbial 50), all authors agree that a very small group of men control the main components (industrial and financial) of the economy, and that they are linked together in complex patterns of intercorporate ownerships, cross directorships, and social relations.

In Canada, the central institutions of capitalist control are the network of banks, trust companies, and insurance companies which accumulate the savings of the ordinary citizen into vast pools of money which are made available to the industrial and investment interests of the bank directors and corporate owners. The largest of these networks, the Bank of Montreal—Royal Trust—Sun Life—CPR—Steel Company of Canada group,[27] controls assets of more than $20 billion — an amount equal to more than one-fifth of Canada's annual gross national product.[28] As Ashley pointed out in 1957, the 30 directors of the Bank of Montreal held among them more than 220 corporate directorships. Similarly, the 20 directors of the Royal Bank held 240 corporate directorships including 12 in Montreal Trust; 22 directors of the Canadian Bank of Commerce held 225 directorships including 7 in National Trust; and 20 directors of the Bank of Nova Scotia held 220 directorships including 5 in Eastern Trust.[29]

A second method of approaching the activities and relations of the capitalist class is that used by John Porter. Porter's method consisted of an examination of the boards of directors of the 183 "dominant" corporations — those manufacturing establishments employing more than 500 workers in 1952. According to this method of examination: "The [Canadian] economic elite, then, consists of the 922 individuals who hold the 1,317 directorships. Of these, 203 individuals, about 22%, hold more than one directorship in the dominant corporations. Most of them of course hold directorships in other corporations which are not classified as dominant. The 203 who hold more than one directorship hold altogether 598 (or 45.3%) of all directorships. The largest number of directorships [in dominant corporations] is ten (E.P. Taylor)."[30]

Porter demonstrates the significance of banks and major insurance companies as central elements in the concentration of economic power. Especially striking are the large number of interconnections held by directors of the Bank of Montreal, Royal Bank, and the Bank of Commerce. They hold 200 of the 297 directorships on the dominant corporations and 34 of the 55 directorships on the largest Canadian insurance companies.[31]

Similarly, the Sun Life, Mutual Life, and Confederation Life insurance companies held central positions, their directors holding 107 of the 188 directorships in leading corporations held by directors of Canadian-owned insurance companies. Such a concentration of power in six financial corporations is made even more impressive when one remembers these corporate directors meet together on the boards of directors of their innumerable smaller industrial interests as well.[32]

These groupings are not accidental or impermanent. For example, an examination of the directorships held by the directors of the Bank of Montreal in 1968 shows that the degree of interconnection between the major components of the Bank of Montreal network has, if anything, increased. In addition, the network has been widened to include several other important corporations. A similar situation exists among the other banks.

Not only have the corporate networks spread, but their assets have greatly increased over the years. The values of assets of the major banks have grown enormously between 1951 and 1971.[33] This vast increase, in both greater concentration and asset value, has meant that greater and greater power over the economy has been acquired by the corporate directors.

A crucial element in the rapid growth of assets of the major capitalists has been the absence of a capital gains tax in Canada.[34] In Canada, the wealthy can escape the effects of high personal income tax by not paying corporate profits out of the treasury to the dividend holders. Thus a "growth-oriented" bank like the Bank of Nova Scotia paid out only 50% of its net profits after corporation taxes in 1971, while other banks tended to pay out about two-thirds of their profits.[35] By exploiting tax laws in this way, the Bank of Nova Scotia increased its assets by 71% between 1951 and 1971, from $874,000,000 to $7,085,000,000.

Over the past 60 years the vast growth of wealth and concentration of power in the capitalist class has been reflected in the enormous increase in economic power wielded by certain individuals. Whereas in 1913, the most significant capitalist was Senator Robert McKay who held directorships in corporations whose assets totalled $1,600,000,000, by 1957 standards he would not have ranked in the top 100. In that year the corporate director who ranked one hundredth on the list was Norman Dawes with directorships controlling assets of $2,200,000,000, while first place was held by Charles Dunning fo the Bank of Montreal network with directorships of $10,800,000,000[37] — a total now surpassed by every director of Canada's three major banks.

Not only does corporate control rest in the hands of a very few powerful men, but the most ownership of shares, and the resultant benefits of dividends and capital gains go to a limited number of individuals as well. In 1968 for example, 1,311 wealthy individuals owned among them $1,156,540,000 in shares, or about 9% of all shares held in Canada — an amount equivalent to that owned by the 4,000,000 lowest income earners in the country.[38]

As Table 7 shows, over the past 20 years there has been a broadening of shareholding among upper income groups (in the 6th to 9th deciles) and a decline in the proportion of shares held by both the top 10% and bottom half of income earners. It would appear that, during a period when independent ownership has become less and less viable, those who would formerly have aspired to an independent petit bourgeois status have made an attempt to maintain an element of participation in the capitalist sector of the economy by acquisition of stock in the giant corporations. During a period of a shortage of technical and managerial skills when wages and salaries were high, this acquisition of shares undoubtedly gave them a sense of ownership and status otherwise denied to them. It should be noted that industrial giants such as Bell Telephone have taken great care to cater to

Table 7

Percentage of All Shares Held by Income Level, 1948-68[36]

	1948	*Percentage of All Shares* *1958*	*1968*
Top 1% of all income earners	57	51	42
96th to 99th percentile of income earners	21	21	20
91st to 95th percentile of income earners	5	7	10
Total, top decile of income earners	83	79	72
9th decile of income earners	4.6	5.4	6.8
6th, 7th and 8th decile of income earners	1.9	4.9	11.4
Total, 6th-9th deciles	6.5	10.3	18.2
Bottom 50% of income earners	10.5	10.7	9.8

these attitudes among its employees, hoping to improve employee performance by encouraging them to purchase a few shares each through salary deductions and incentives. Finally, it should be noted that only a very small proportion of Canadians own shares. In 1968, only 870,852 out of 8,495,184 income earners (10.3%) possessed so much as one share.[39] Thus the vast majority of the benefits of capital gains go to the few wealthy shareholders.

In terms of power over the economy, the extreme concentration of share ownership in the top 1% of income earners allows almost total control — not merely because of the huge proportion directly owned, but because a high degree of concentration in a few hands permits easy organization of those shares for decision-making purposes.

Canadian Capitalism and Imperialist Development

No change in the state of the Canadian bourgeoisie has as much significance, or is likely to have such important long-range effects, as the take-over of the Canadian economy by the American-based multinational corporation. For the parent corporation the take-over of the Canadian means of production satisfied three main needs: the defence and expansion of the capitalist system; the creation of a stable corporate monopoly free from the uncertainties of the market place; and a field for profitable investment of capital.[40] By 1969 about 8,700 Canadian concerns were controlled by non-residents, and foreign capital was invested directly or indirectly in some 12,000 Canadian concerns. In all, 74% of petroleum and natural gas, 65% of mining and smelting, and 57% of manufacturing were foreign-controlled. In 1969, foreign residents owned assets in Canada valued at $46.9 billion.[41] In the same year, total share capital held by Canadian private individuals was about $14.0 billion.[42]

While it is perfectly understandable that foreign corporations would want to take over control of Canadian industry and natural resources, it is perhaps not so clear why Canadian businessmen would so eagerly co-operate in this process. It is not until one examines the corporate ideology of the Canadian businessman, the assumptions he accepts, and his economic interests that some understanding appears.

As the Parks said of the Canadian businessman: "It is not in terms of their birth or citizenship that [they] are un-Canadian but in terms of their outlook . . . The problem and source of danger to the future of Canada lie in the fact that those who control the key sectors of the economy have taken as their premise that US capital is and will be dominant, that Canadian development is necessarily subordinate to and dependent on ('integrated with') the drive of US groups for their own benefit."[43] Even a casual glance through *Industrial Canada,* the monthly journal of the Canadian Manufacturers Association, is enough to convince oneself of the accuracy of the Parks' statement.

Gerard Filion, president of Marine Industries Ltd. (controlled by the Simard family of Quebec), vice-president of the General Investment Corporation of Quebec (the provincially funded development corporation), and 1971 president of the Canadian Manufacturers Association, demonstrated his complete acceptance of the dominance of the multinational corporation in his inaugural speech, "Multi-national corporations are a phenomenon of the contemporary economy; they are here to stay and it is necessary to adjust to this fact . . . It isn't all that important that multinational corporations control large industrial, commercial and financial holdings in Canada."[44]

Norris R. Crump, chairman of CPR, director of the Bank of Montreal, International Nickel, Mutual Life, and 17 other corporations, demonstrated how little interest most major Canadian capitalists have in Canadian economic unity when he addressed the same meeting. Crump demanded substantial changes in Canadian tariff and economic policies whose results would have the effect, in his words, of: "(1) Increasing the attractiveness of imported manufactured goods in Western Canada and the Maritimes; (2) Allowing Quebec and Ontario to integrate their economies more fully into the heartland of North America, so reducing their dependence on Western and Maritime markets; (3) Permitting Canada, particularly Western Canada, to integrate more fully with the Pacific Rim countries [i.e., Japan], which are more and more becoming their natural trading partners."[45]

These businessmen's attitudes to the exploitation of the natural resources of Canada and the underdeveloped nations was couched in the full-blown rhetoric of the multinational ideology. As Gerard Filion expressed it: "We are witnessing a new phenomenon in the world economy, that is the internationalization of raw materials. Heretofore, countries were rich because they possessed coal, iron ore, wood, cereals, or water power. This is no longer the case today. Japan has demonstrated that a country's chief natural resource is the brains of its managing class and the ability of its workers. The internationalization of raw materials is an advantageous phenomenon for the world economy as a whole. Every measure aimed at restricting the export of raw materials from countries that have them in abundance to those who do not counter to the general prosperity of humanity and peace between nations and men."[46] That the "internationalization" of raw materials is a one-way street from the poor to the rich countries appears to have escaped Mr. Filion's attention.

R. Rea Jackson, Chairman of Socony Mobile Oil Company, speaking to the US National Military-Industrial Conference in 1958 was much more explicit. In discussing the growing strategy crisis created from American capitalism by the rapidly depleting reserves of crucial metals, oil, and energy, Jackson pointed out that: "In the old days, a country faced with such a shortage of materials would simply have moved out and grabbed colonies, under some pretext or other . . . Our tradition, or at least a healthy part of our tradition, is the policy of asking for an 'open door' for trade."[47] The chief difficulty facing the US in the acquisition of raw materials by the "open door" method was the nationalism of the countries owning them.[48] As the conclusions of the Military-Industrial Conference pointed out, to the US, "Strategy means 'the mobilization, integration, and prudent management of the political, economic, educational, technological, industrial, scientific, cultural, ideological, and spiritual resources of the entire nation.' "[49] Corporate internationalism offers a crucial ideological weapon in breaking down national resistance to American acquisition of the needed raw materials. Its acceptance by the major Canadian capitalists creates a most serious threat to Canada's autonomy and, ultimately, the welfare of its citizens.

The fact that Canadian businessmen accept the ideology of corporate internationalism is not merely the result of a triumph of American propaganda. Rather, it is a reflection of their personal and corporate interests and goals as well. While a good deal is known and written about the huge degree of American ownership of Canadian industry and raw materials — the Parks, Kari Levitt, Mel Watkins, and others have made excellent contributions to that field of study[50] — much less is known of the relationships of Canadian capitalists to American capital.

Among Marxists and socialists it is often argued that Canadian capitalists are simply servants and front-men for American economic imperialism. But, in reality, the relationship is much more complex. Study suggests that a few Canadian capitalists are, at least temporarily, still members of a national bourgeoisie with few or no ties to foreign capital or business activities. Others, the majority, are deeply involved in multinational corporate business either as dependent businessmen engaged as suppliers or distributors of American goods and technology or managers of American corporate activities in Canada. A final group, again a minority, have reached the status of multinational capitalists themselves where they operate independently or as partners of other multinational interests. For the latter two groups American multinational corporate ideology serves not merely as a strategic weapon for American capitalism, but provides Canadian businessmen with an explanation and justification of their current activities and provides a goal and model for their future.[51]

Perhaps the best example of the Canadian capitalists who have achieved partnership with foreign capital at the international level is that provided in 1970 by the creation of the "Orion" group of financial corporations owned jointly by American, British, German, and Canadian banking interests — Chase Manhattan Corporation, National Westminster Bank, Westdeutsche Landsbank, and Royal Bank respectively. The function of the Orion group is to finance and manage multinational expansion in the Third

World. With such enormous assets behind it (the parent banks possessed $58.7 billion in assets in 1970[52]), undoubtedly it will quickly make its presence felt.

The significance of Orion's creation for Canadian capitalists lies in the fact that, at the top, multinational ideology serves their interests as much as it does those of American, Japanese, French or German capitalists. Thus at the level of Lord Thompson of Fleet with his world-wide newspaper and television empire, E.P. Taylor, and Garfield Weston with the British and Canadian commodity cartels (which are now expanding rapidly in the United States), and Noah Timmins with his vast resource holdings, Canada has become merely a geographic location, among many, where they do business. Lesser capitalists such as the Simards, Stephen Roman, or R.A. Brown, Jr,[53] with aspirations of moving up to the multinational level, see amalgamation of their holdings with existing multinational corporations as the quickest method of reaching that level. Major Canadian capitalists do not, however, relate to national or multinational capital at a single level. They may at one time direct or manage a wholly owned American subsidiary in Canada, direct the activities of a Canadian-owned multinational corporation, and own or control one or more Canadian businesses which have no multinational interests.

Perhaps the best example of the precise relationship between the major Canadian multinational capitalists and US capital is provided by their opposition to the attempt by Rockefeller interests to expand into Canadian banking through the take-over of the Mercantile Bank. While Canadian bankers had been quite content to oversee and, indeed, to co-operate in the take-over of Canadian industries, and to manage them once they were in American hands, it was quite a different story when the Rockefeller-controlled Citibank threatened to replace them. As the Parks notes: "The Canadian groups as well as the Canadian government involved are acting within limits defined by their idea of what the traffic will bear. They want the junior partnership and the profits following from it to continue. Any struggles with their US rivals and allies is over the division of profit."[54]

For the indigenous Canadian capitalist who has not yet entered into multinational operations, economic nationalism and strategies in opposition to the growth of multinationalism may well make good sense, both from the point of personal commitment and a maximization of personal profits. After all, when one's financial and industrial interests are entirely in Canada, a "buy Canadian" policy is no more than good sense. One must, however, view the nationalistic protestations of these businessmen with a certain amount of reserve since most multinational and foreign-owned corporations were once owned by Canadian capitalists who, like Stephen Roman and R.A. Brown Jr, saw their opportunity to maximize profits by selling out to foreign capitalists.

The close relationship of government and business in Canada has been too well documented to require more than a comment upon current developments. While the two old parties have always been financed by big businessmen, and important figures in the business world such as C.D. Howe, Louis St Laurent, Mitchell Sharp, Robert Winters, and James Richardson have moved easily from boardroom to cabinet and back, currently even closer ties with business are being created at all levels of government.

Jean Luc Pepin, federal minister of Industry, Trade and Commerce, in his address to the Canadian Manufacturers Association in 1970, made it clear that he attempted to keep himself informed about business and its needs by meeting with as many businessmen and organizations as time permitted, and visiting as many plants as possible in order to get first-hand knowledge of their operations. As he put it, "politicians and officials are generally quite keen to work with businessmen."[55]

Pepin, however, stated that under his direction the present government had gone much farther than previous governments had in introducing capitalists into the active creation and implementation of policies within his department. To do this he had created an "Advisory Council composed of some 40 leading businessmen, representing various sections of industry and geographic regions, with whom my officials and myself meet four times a year. This council is a very useful forum to us and I dare say to members also. Other ministers are setting up similar bodies.

"Representation progressively leads to active participation in the formulation and implementation of policies. In certain cases, we have already reached that objective, either because the evolving situation must be kept under constant review (automobile industry) or because a new strategy of development must be defined (shipbuilding, chemicals, textiles . . .)

"Practically all of the operation line branches in my department have their own more or less formal committees or advisory groups."[56]

It is little wonder, therefore, that the federal government's policies on foreign ownership and multinational dominance reflect the same approving attitudes as those expressed by the multinational Canadian capitalists.

Equally interesting is the newly created civil service training system called Career Assignment Program. Under CAP middle level civil servants are selected for a 12-week management course then assigned to service in university or business administration for a two-year period on an exchange basis. As Pepin expressed the direction of planned development for CAP, "Plans are to increase the number of industrial participants to 18 a year by 1971 and to have an equal number of government employees on assignment in the private sector."[57] Thus, the thrust of current government planning is to facilitate the participation of capitalists in government planning and administration by training civil servants in industrial management techniques, and presumably, providing them with a better understanding and greater acceptance of the aims, goals, strategies, and ideology of capitalism.

In summary, the Canadian capitalist class consists of a small group of enormously powerful men whose structural relations are undergoing rapid change. Caught up in the ideology of growth and multinationalism, the small capitalist accepts being swallowed up by a large Canadian or foreign (especially American) corporation as an inevitable process in which his disappearance as an autonomous capitalist is compensated for by his participation as a very junior partner of the very powerful.

The process of consolidation of capitalism is very far advanced, but on a multinational, not a national, basis. The huge American, British, German, French, and Japanese capitalist structures all reach into Canada, while a few equally powerful capitalist structures originating in Canada reach into other countries. The ideology of multinationalism therefore has Canadian as well as foreign beneficiaries and advocates. The power of these giants, both foreign and domestically based, is greatly enhanced by their close association with government, to say nothing of their ownership and control of the media, university boards of governors, and other aspects of the national ideological apparatus. In their search for international economic power, they are quite willing to accept (and indeed to advocate) the economic dismemberment of Canada and the rape of raw materials and natural resources.

Any political strategy which is based upon the expectation of an alliance with a Canadian national bourgeoisie is, I should think, doomed to be disappointed. The major Canadian capitalists are as committed to economic imperialism as their American counterparts, while the small capitalist dreams of joining their ranks when the time is ripe. Moreover, the low-level branch plant manager is, at best, a weak reed to lean on. As one observer recently pointed out, the lower-level manager of the branch plant has no room to maneuver. "He's just like any other piece of equipment in that plant. If he gives too much trouble, then he's replaced. If he starts stomping around and saying, 'Well dammit, we're running this show . . .' then he's in trouble."[58]

Finally, it is important to distinguish between the capitalist class, which is composed of individuals who have names, identities, and individual as well as class interests, from the productive apparatus (the corporations) which they control. The enemies of the working class are not the factories, mines, and transportation systems upon which they labor, but the system of ownership and exploitation and those individuals who defend it and benefit from its continuance. Confusion on this point has created a dangerous situation where many young people assume that it is work, itself, which is alienating, not the structure of exploitive and dehumanizing social relations surrounding production in the capitalist system.

The Working Classes

As capitalism has grown and developed in Canada, the composition of the labor force has changed in two distinct ways. First, a larger and larger proportion were drawn from pre-capitalist and pre-industrial occupations, such as agriculture and menial labor, into the capitalist labor market and machine-related production, and second, within the capitalist sector itself, changes in composition have occurred. Related to these changes has been the gradual decline of the status and independence of client groups such as the professional occupations.

The most striking aspect of these changes, as pointed out earlier, has been the decline and absorption of the petite bourgeoisie, especially that of the farmers. As Table 8 points out, between 1901 and 1961 farm workers declined from 40.3% of the work force to 10.2%. Equally important was the decline of menial laborers from 7.2 (12.0 in 1911) % in 1901 to 5.4% in 1961. In all, therefore, those sectors which were least involved in capitalist production declined from 47.5% of the work force in 1901 to 15.6% in 1961. This drop in proportion has been reflected in the growth of the white collar sector from 15.2% in 1901 to 38.6% in 1961, and of the manual workers, outside the menial labor sub-sector, from 25.0% in 1901 to 29.5% in 1961. Other sectors remained relatively stable during this period.

Apologists for capitalism and technology have fastened upon the phenomenon of the rapid rise of the white collar worker as a major justification for the capitalist system, often arguing that the creation of an enormous class of middle management where status is high and alienation low effectively refutes Marxist assumptions that capitalist modes of production create a huge number of alienating tasks. Some "futurologists" will go so far as to argue that eventually all menial (blue collar) work will be eliminated and that "leisure" is the great problem remaining to be solved.[59] Closer analysis of changes within the major sectors as set out by census analysts, however, strongly challenge these assumptions. Moreover, analysis of income distribution suggest that within the past two decades fundamental changes have occurred within the Canadian economy which go far beyond mere occupational redistribution.

Fundamental to an analysis of these changes is the recognition that two sub-categories of labor — farmers and menial laborers — have largely disappeared. Since both of these categories are essentially products and remnants of the pre-capitalist mode of production, analysis of the industrial capitalist sector requires an examination of proportional changes with these sectors removed (see Table 9). It is clear from the figures that the great change in composition of the labor force in the capitalist sector occurred in the 1901-21 period when the white collar sector increased from 29.3% to 43.6% of the work force, while the manual sector declined from 47.6% to 37.5%. Between 1921 and 1941 there was a general decline in the white collar sector and an increase in manual sector, which was reversed in the next 20 years. Thus, by 1961, proportions were only slightly changed from what they had been in 1921. Finally, there has been a steady decline in the primary sector even when agriculture is removed.

The White Collar Sector

Over the past 60 years, the white collar sector has been the most volatile group in the working class, showing both the most rapid over-all growth and the widest fluctuations. Internal analysis of its composition demonstrates the same characteristics, with the most rapid growth occurring in the professional and clerical sectors.[63] As Table 10 shows, however, much of this proportional growth is due to the decline of the pre-capitalist sectors. Once this factor is removed, a relatively stable internal distribution appears. When the white collar sector is examined within the industrial capitalist portion of the economy alone, it becomes clear that only the clerical sub-sector has experienced any large degree of growth. While other sectors have grown, they have done so at average or below average rates.

An examination of the changes in internal distribution within the white collar sector emphasizes the growth of the clerical sector. Made up largely of low-paid female labor (the female proportion of the clerical sub-sector has increased from 22% in 1901 to 61.5% in 1961), the rapid growth of this sub-sector must raise serious questions about the effects of automation on the white collar worker.

In the 19th century, the effect of the introduction of new technology was to reduce labor costs by breaking down complex skills into simple repetitive machine-defined tasks. This process required highly skilled technicians and supervisors but eliminated the need for crafts workers with an intermediate level of skills. While workers in the clerical and professional sectors have increased, the proprietary, managerial, commercial, and financial service sectors — the intermediate skill levels — have declined. It would

Table 8

Total Labor Force, Distributed by Major Occupational Groups, 1901-61[60] (Percentages)

	1901	1911	1921	1931	1941	1951	1961
White collar	15.2	16.8	25.1	24.5	25.2	32.4	38.6
Manual	32.2	36.1	31.3	33.8	33.4	37.7	34.9
Service	8.2	7.7	7.1	9.2	10.5	8.6	10.8
Primary	44.4	39.4	36.3	32.5	30.6	20.1	13.1
Not stated			.2		.3	1.2	2.6

Table 9

Work Force, Distribution outside Agricultural and Menial Labor Sectors, 1901-61[61] (Percentages)

	1901	1911	1921	1931	1941	1951	1961
White collar	29.0	31.3	43.6	40.9	37.1	41.9	45.7
Manual or blue collar	47.6	44.9	37.5	37.6	39.9	40.0	35.0
Service	15.6	14.5	12.3	15.4	15.5	11.1	12.8
Primary	7.8	9.6	6.3	6.2	7.1	5.3	3.4
Not stated	—	—	.3	—	.4	1.7	3.1

Table 10

White Collar Sector, Proportion When Agricultural and Menial Labor Sectors Are Removed from the Labor Force, 1901-61[62] (Percentages)

	1901	1911	1921	1931	1941	1951	1961
Proprietary & managerial	8.2	8.6	12.5	9.4	8.0	9.7	9.4
Professional	8.8	6.9	9.6	10.0	9.8	9.6	11.7
Clerical	6.1	7.1	11.8	11.3	10.6	13.9	15.3
Commercial & financial	5.9	8.7	9.7	10.2	8.7	8.7	9.3
All white collar	29.0	31.3	43.6	40.9	37.1	41.9	45.7

seem, therefore, that the process of proletarianization-through-automation that destroyed the crafts workers in the 19th century may be repeated among the white collar workers in the 20th.

While no useful Canadian study has yet been done which examines the consequences of these changes for Canadian white collar workers, a striking study has been done in the United States by Judson Gooding which suggests the direction which developments in Canada are likely to take. As Gooding points out, the most important consequence of the automation of office work has been a deep-seated and growing alienation among white collar workers: "These workers — clerks, accountants, bookkeepers, secretaries — were once the elite at every plant, the educated people who worked alongside the bosses and were happily convinced that they made all the wheels go around. Now there are platoons of them instead of a privileged few, and instead of talking to the boss they generally communicate with a machine.

"The jobs are sometimes broken down into fragmented components, either for the convenience of those machines or so that the poorly educated graduates of big-city high schools can perform them. Despite their air-conditioned, carpeted offices — certainly the most lavish working quarters ever provided employees in mass — the sense of distance and dissociation from management has increased sharply, and the younger white collars are swept by some of the same restlessness and cynicism that afflict their classmates who opted for manual labor. All too often, the keypunch operator spends the workday feeling more like an automaton than a human being."[64]

Moreover, whereas white collar workers used to enjoy job security, they are now as subject to the vagaries of the capitalist labor economy as are the blue collar workers. One business school professor has remarked "White collars are where administrators look to save money, for places to fire. It's the law of supply and demand. Once you're in big supply, you're a bum."[65]

The deterioration in white collar morale is not just a passing phenomenon born of the recent economic down-turn. For example, in the United States, Opinion Research Corporation of Princeton, New Jersey, recently surveyed 25,000 white collar workers in 88 major American companies. Their conclusions were that job satisfaction for white collar workers had markedly declined in many crucial aspects. As Judson Gooding concluded: "There is a terrible, striking, contrast between the fun-filled, mobile existence of the young opulents of America as shown on television, and the narrow, constricting, un-fun existence that is the lot of most white collar workers at the lower job levels. You can't buy much of what television is selling on the salaries these young workers earn; about all you do is stay at home watching those good things go by on the screen. The result is frustration, sometimes bitterness, even anger. Workers in this stratum cannot but notice that the federally defined poverty standard is climbing toward their level from below, while above them the salary needed to enjoy the glittery aspects of American life soars even higher, further and further out of reach. For many, the office is the real world, not only a livelihood but a focus of existence. They expect it, somehow, to be more than it has become."[66]

In Canada, as in the United States, a major result of this growing alienation has been the appearance of white collar unions which have become the most rapidly expanding sector of the labor movement. Although still far from complete, the process of the proletarianization of the white collar worker must eventually have profound effect upon future class struggles.

The Professionals

During the past 30 years the professionally trained person has been the greatest beneficiary among either the petit bourgeois or working class sectors. In particular, the self-employed individuals in the elite professions such as doctors, dentists, and lawyers have enjoyed enormous increases in incomes over the past 20 years. As Table 11 shows, these increases have run far ahead of the average, with doctors heading the parade. Indeed, so rapid and so exorbitantly have doctors' incomes increased that in 1968 the 17,846 doctors and surgeons in independent practice received as much net income as did the more than half-million inhabitants of Newfoundland. While increases in income in the professional sector undoubtedly are primarily the result of higher demand created by the increased size and complexity of industrial units, the higher level of skills required in commercial and legal transactions, and the wide-spread demand created for health and medical services by the higher standard of living and collective medical insurance plans enjoyed by many Canadians, the creation and control of professional monopolies has contributed a good deal to their wealth.[67]

Professionally trained workers have made up a steadily increasing part of the labor force, expanding from 4.6% in 1901 to 10.0% in 1961; but, as pointed out before, much of this increase is simply a reflection of the overall development of the white collar sector of the capitalist economy. Curiously enough, despite the rapid increase in numbers of professionally trained persons (in 1931 there were 238,077 professionals in the work force; in 1961 this number had increased to 634,271) and the high incomes earned

Table 11

Independent Professionals: Comparison of Incomes, 1948-68[69]

	1948	1958	1968
Total number of independent professionals	24,670	44,712	53,609
Percent of all income earners	.67	.81	.63
Average income of independent professionals	$5,551.70	$10,333.40	$19,908.20
Weighted average income (1949 dollars)	$5,723.40	$ 8,260.10	$12,827.40
Professionals' income: percent of average	265	313	405
Doctors' income: percent of average	362	440	592
Lawyers' income: percent of average	368	385	468
Dentists' income: percent of average	246	317	397
Engineers' & architects' income: percent of average	325	409	431

by some categories of independent professionals, there has been an over-all decline in the proportion of professionals in independent practice. For example, in 1951 there were 35,138 registered nurses in the work force, of whom 3,920 were self-employed; in 1961, while the numbers of registered nurses had risen to 61,553, so few were privately employed that the taxation department no longer reported the category separately.[68]

Engineers and architects — professions which have enjoyed great demand with the rapid expansion of technology — present a similar picture. In 1951 there were 24,992 professionally trained engineers and 1,740 architects in the work force; of this number a total of 2,210 (8.3%) were self-employed. In 1961, while their numbers had grown to 35,721 engineers and 2,940 architects, only 2,785 (7.2%) were self-employed. With the rapid proliferation of engineering schools in the 1960s, it is likely that this process will be greatly accelerated.

Even among the more independent sectors of professionals some deterioration of independence is observable. For example, the proportion of self-employed dentists declined from 93.5% in 1951 (4,310 of 4,608) to 92.0% in 1961 (5,025 of 5,473). Similarly the proportion of independent lawyers showed a modest decline from 62.0% in 1951 (5,600 of 9,038) to 61.7% in 1961 (7,433 of 12,068). Only doctors and surgeons, the highest paid profession, have stood against this tendency, increasing their proportion of self-employment from 67.5% in 1951 (9,670 of 14,325) to 70.9% in 1961 (15,088 of 21,266). Over all, the proportion of all professionally trained persons in independent practice has declined from 9.2% in 1951 (35,270 of 385,676) to 8.1% in 1961 (51,530 of 634,271).

The gradual erosion of their privileged positions is keenly felt by the professionals who have adopted a number of strategies to slow the loss of autonomy. For example, the medical profession staged a strike in Saskatchewan in 1962 when provincial medicare was introduced,[70] and almost repeated the performance in Quebec in October 1970. Nor are doctors alone in their uneasiness. A report presented at a recent meeting of professional engineers pointed out that an analysis by their public relations committee showed that the engineer had "not as high an estimate of his place in society as he once did. And the public does not regard his position as highly as formerly, either."[71]

In his examination of the petite bourgeoisie, Sandy Lockhart has argued that the proletarianization process has been masked by two factors: the transformation of the dispossessed petit bourgeois into the white collar worker within the capitalist production apparatus, and the storing up of surplus labor in the rapid expansion of faculty, staff, and students in institutions of higher education.[72] Now, of course, with the declining status of the white collar worker, and the recent surpluses in university graduates, it would appear that those transformations, in future, will be much less satisfactory, and that safety valve for middle class anxiety will be closed.

The Blue Collar Sector

Like the white collar sector of the labor force, the blue collar sector — the classical proletariat — has undergone some important changes during the

Table 12

Proportional Distribution within the Blue Collar Sector, 1901-61[76]

	1901	1911	1921	1931	1941	1951	1961
Mfg. & mechanical workers	49.4	38.0	36.4	34.0	47.9	46.2	47.0
Construction	14.6	13.0	15.0	13.9	14.1	14.9	15.2
Trans. & communications	13.7	15.8	17.6	18.9	19.2	20.9	22.3
Laborers	22.4	33.0	31.0	33.4	18.9	18.0	15.6
Total	100.1	98.8	100.0	100.0	100.1	100.0	100.1

past 70 years. As Table 12 demonstrates, when the proportional changes within the blue collar sector are examined, three distinct periods stand out. First, the period 1901-11 shows a huge decline in the proportion of manufacturing and mechanical workers from 49.4 to 38.0% of blue collar sector. At the same time the proportion of menial laborers rose from 22.4 to 33.0%. During the second period, from 1911 to 1931, the proportion of menial workers remained constant at 33% of the blue collar sector, while manufacturing and mechanical workers declined from 38 to 34%. The third period, 1941 to 1961, saw a remarkable reversal of the 1901-31 trends: the proportion of laborers declined sharply to 18.9% in 1941 and continued to decline to 15.6% in 1961, while the manufacturing and mechanical sector jumped sharply to 47.9% in 1941 where it remained until 1961. These drastic shifts in proportions within the blue collar sector demonstrate the need to examine two significant aspects of Canadian economic life — immigration policy and its effects on strategies of capital investment, and the particular characteristics of capitalist development within Canada.

High immigration[73] and large-scale capital formation drastically transformed the Canadian economy from small-scale craft production to large-scale machine production based upon readily available cheap labor during the era of Macdonald's National Policy. This expansion of capital and transformation to a capitalist mode of production accelerated rapidly during the 1890-1910 period. Despite the rapid expansion of production, the enormous immigration of the 1896-1911 period (the labor force increased by 52.8% between 1901 and 1911) created a huge surplus of low-skilled laborers which effectively halted the transformation towards capital intensity. Real wages dropped sharply from 1900 to 1915, and laborers' wages did not return to 1900 levels until 1925. Despite the high level of capital accumulation built up in 1910, it would appear that capital was directed into expansion of facilities rather than towards intensification of production.[74] As a result, while there had been a rapid increase in capitalization, labor productivity actually underwent a slight decrease. High levels of immigration encouraged a shift towards the use of menial labor, particularly in the mines and forests of the West. Of course, employers seized the opportunity presented by the abundance of cheap labor to reduce wages, with the result that numerous bitter strikes were fought, bringing frequent repression by the army and the creation of the federal Department of Labour as a means of social control.[75]

During the 1910-20 period, and primarily as a result of the First World War, the economy was greatly diversified, particularly into the refining of non-ferrous metals. During this period, steel production almost doubled. Shortage of capital, however, as well as the continued abundance of low-cost labor reduced capital intensity almost to 1900 levels and resulted in a further decline in the manufacturing and mechanical employment sub-sector and created a further increase in the use of menial labor. By 1920, while large-scale manufacturing and capitalist production had almost entirely eliminated crafts production, still it had not created modern capital-intensive production. Rather a large and increasing proportion of the work force was engaged in essentially pre-industrial (and thereby, essentially pre-capitalist) forms of menial labor. In other words, while capitalist social labor relations had been established, capitalist industrial modes of production in many regions and occupations, had not. On the other hand, the expansion of capitalist production and particularly the creation of large manufacturing units necessitated the creation of a large white collar apparatus to manage it. It should be noted again, however, that the size of the white collar sector is proportional to the manufacturing and mechanical sector.

The years 1920 to 1930 witnessed both the period of greatest capital expansion and the first period in which real incomes of workers began to rise above 1900 levels. While menial labor continued at a high level, within the capitalist labor sector investment, productivity and labor purchasing power all began to rise sharply. Indeed, investment per worker reached it highest point in history in 1930 as speculative fever and over-expansion gripped the economy. While menial laborers were still isolated outside the technologically advanced sectors of the industrial economy, for the first time competition for their low-wage services from the industrial sector began to pull their real wages upward. Moreover, with the huge expansion of physical plant created in the over-speculation of 1920-30, the basic facilities were established which would allow their incorporation within the capital intensive industrial sector when economic conditions warranted it. The depression delayed that process for a decade.

One of the most striking aspects of the 1930s is the huge increase in purchasing power enjoyed by those who managed to remain employed during the depression. While the general index of wages declined from 48.8 in 1930 to 43.2 in 1935 and then rose to 50.8 in 1940 (1949 = 100), the retail price index dropped from 75.2 in 1930 to 59.9 in 1935 then rose only to 65.7 in 1940. The decline in price of food and other agricultural products, of course, provided the largest part of the decline in the cost of living.[77] Despite the favorable position of manufacturing workers, the extremely high level of unemployment (about 20% in 1933)[78] gradually eroded the position of the menial laborers until their real incomes in 1940 fell almost to the 1900 level again. On the other hand, the average purchasing power index of all workers continued to increase, with the result that those employed within the industrial sector became a relatively high-paid labor aristocracy whose economic situation was, for the first time, markedly superior to that of the non-industrial menial labor sector.

It was the Second World War, and C.D. Howe's program of industrialization and rapid expansion of the capitalist sector through guaranteed wartime profits, which finally completed the transformation of the Canadian economy to industrial capitalism and finally incorporated most of Canadian labor into advanced modes of industrial capitalist production.[79] This process, of course, required large shifts of population from the Prairie and Maritime regions to central Canada and British Columbia, as well as a large-scale movement from rural to urban centers. By 1950, the only significant major pools of menial labor remaining were in rural Quebec and the Maritimes, with lesser pools in eastern and northern Ontario and the Prairies. This condition persists to the present.

During the 1940-50 period three additional fundamental changes occurred in the relationship of the composition of capital and labor. First, there was a sharp decline in capital intensity per worker employed. Second, productivity levelled off. And third, real average incomes of workers rose sharply although the large discrepancy between average wage rates and the wages of laborers continued. The decline in capital intensity, as Wood and Scott have pointed out, can be related to the development of tertiary or service industries which have lower capital-output and capital-worker ratios.[80]

By 1961, the capitalist economic system was virtually all-encompassing in Canada, taking in the vast majority of the work force and employing them in both capitalist social relations and in capital-oriented modes of production. The growth and development of capitalism, however, had not followed a regular pattern of growth and transformation. Rather, it had been subjected to large and dramatic convulsions in the relationship of capital and labor, each of which created a period of unrest and heightened labor consciousness.

In response to the agitation by those most deeply injured by these convulsions, a long series of government welfare programs were introduced that were aimed at reducing tensions. Since average purchasing power has risen steadily since 1921 these programs found ready acceptance by those not directly injured. Because the development of capitalism within a non-capitalist society yields enormous profits as pre-capitalist modes of production are over-thrown and replaced by more efficient methods and organizations of production, and because the new capital-intensive technology allowed the exploitation of the virgin environment of Canada to a degree never before attempted, the capitalist system could allow a high and increasing standard of living to the favored sectors of the work force. Thus during development of the capitalist system in Canada, the capitalists have been able to stabilize the proletariat while destroying or incorporating within it the pre-capitalist formations. Moreover, one of the major consequences of the development of capitalism is a growing specialization and differentiation of production which contributes to creating and deepening divisions within labor.

As Wood and Scott have emphasized, a major long-run determinant of capital-output ratios is the size and richness of the stock of natural resources.[81] During the 19th century, political economists reasoned that since the stock of land and resources was limited, it would be necessary, if growth took place, to increase capital investment ratios to keep pace with declining accessibility of natural resources and to augment the lessening fertility of marginal land. In the 20th century, however, this reasoning has generally been ignored because new discoveries of easily accessible and high quality natural resources, new crops and livestock varieties, and the development of new technology which allowed the use of plentiful materials when scarce resources gave out, combined to mask the fundamental correctness of earlier perceptions.

Today, the forest and mining industries are already showing the effects of scarcity and depletion of high-quality reserves. For example, in the 1945-50 period, when there was a general decline in capital-output and capital-labor ratios, the resource industries showed a sharp increase in capital intensity.[82] This tendency continues to the present. Moreover, certain other economic sub-sectors (such as steel, automobiles, and chemicals) have shown capital intensity increases as well. Thus, while the major trend has been toward the development of a low-capital tertiary sector, other significant sectors stand against the decline of capital intensity.

The growing differentiation of capital-labor and capital-output ratios among the various industrial sectors has had significant effects on both the wage structure and the distribution of economic activity in Canada. As capital intensity rises in an industry, and as monopoly increases generally, certain segments of organized labor have found themselves in a very advantageous position vis-à-vis other sectors of labor. In industries such as mining, steel, automobiles, and chemicals, where capital intensity is high, and where it is relatively difficult or impossible to transfer operations without enormous capital loss, labor unions have won high wages. In large part, this is because high capitalization creates high fixed costs, which create losses during strikes when no production is occurring. Moreover, because of the near-monopoly situation in these sectors, the corporations are capable of passing increased labor costs on to the consumer in the form of higher prices. A similar situation exists in the construction industry. As Gilbert Burck reports: "Although many contractors resist union demands, a contractor usually finds it easy and profitable to cooperate with unions. For so long as he cooperates, he simply bases his bids on costs and tacks on a suitable profit. If the costs of building a mile of highway doubles, so do his revenues and his profit."[83]

In contrast to organized labor in the capital-intensive sectors, workers in labor-intensive industries find themselves at a distinct disadvantage. Where manufacturing or service industries require low levels of skills and little fixed capital for permanent facilities (such as electronics assembly and clothing manufacturing), or where competition still exists (such as in the textile and furniture industries), workers are forced to accept low wages, or to see their employer either move to a low-wage area or go out of business. Since areas with high rates of unemployment offer the best opportunities for successful exploitation of low-wage labor, government programs which facilitate the movement of labor-intensive industries into Quebec, eastern and northern Ontario, the Maritimes, or the West have the effect of fixing these areas as permanent low-wage localities.[84]

Moreover, because highly capitalized facilities are extremely costly to operate below optimal levels of production, there is a tendency among industries with capital-intensive operations to concentrate production in the most capital-intensive facilities when the volume of production falls off.[85] Because such an action causes labor costs to rise, there is a counter-tendency to move to greater and greater specialization so that aspects of an industry previously incorporated in the main production center can, by technology, be transformed into labor-intensive operations and transferred to low-wage areas. By this mechanism, hinterland areas become more and more frozen into low-skill, low-income patterns and made ever more dependent upon the metropolitan centers for economic decision-making.[86] Of course, for central Canada, this mechanism provides a two-way process when so much of Canadian industry is foreign owned. Just as high-wage, capital-intensive operations are centralized from the Maritimes and the West to the Montreal and Toronto-Hamilton regions, so do multinational corporations (whether Canadian or American) have a tendency to concentrate high-capital, high-wage operations in the United States.[87]

For the workers, these movements of capital have created a profound cleavage between the well-organized high-wage capital-intensive sector and the low-wage earners who have either weak unions or are unorganized. While the former are, economically at least, the beneficiaries of economism and tend to be conservative or apolitical, the latter find themselves helpless to better their conditions; therefore they either tend toward anti-unionism (because high wages in unionized sections force prices upward) or are open to appeals from paternalistic politicians who promise pie-in-the-sky reforms. Thus the high-wage sector condemns the low-income earner for his "laziness" and his "lack of ambition" (which, it is claimed, causes high taxes to support "welfare bums") while the low-income earner fears the "power" and "greed" of the strong unions. The capitalist-owned media and the well-paid influential media commentators, of course, are delighted to enhance these prejudices and cleavages by condemning both unions and the poor. This situation is likely to continue as long as purchasing power continues to rise for highly paid unionized workers while low-wage workers continue to be unorganized. Only when the fragmented poorly paid sectors are organized is greater solidarity likely to appear.

Despite their basic conservatism, not all elements among the highly paid unionists are closed to radicalization. Despite increases in purchasing power, the stresses of automation and the dehumanization of the workplace under highly organized and specialized production has brought about an increasing alienation even among the best paid workers. In a perceptive article in *Fortune,* Judson Gooding has pointed out that in American automobile factories, "The deep dislike of the job and the desire to escape become terribly clear twice each day when shifts end and the men stampede out the plant gates to the parking lots, where they are sometimes actually endangering lives in their desperate haste to be gone."[88] But alienation goes much deeper than merely a desire to escape the work place. It affects production as well. "For management, the truly dismaying evidence about new worker attitudes is found in job performance. Absenteeism has risen sharply; in fact it has doubled over the past ten years at General Motors and at

Ford . . . Tardiness has increased, making it even more difficult to start up the production lines promptly when a shift begins — after the foreman has scrambled around to replace missing workers. Complaints about quality are up sharply. There are more arguments with foreman, more complaints about discipline and overtime, more grievances. There is more turn-over . . . Some assembly-line workers are so turned off, managers report with astonishment, that they just walk away in mid-shift and don't even come back to get their pay for the time they have worked . . . In some plants worker discontent has reached such a degree that there has been overt sabotage. Screws have been left in brake drums, tool handles welded into fender compartments (to cause mysterious, unfindable, and eternal rattles), paint scratched, and upholstery cut."[89]

In Canada similar tendencies are observable, particularly in Quebec where serious attempts at politicization of the workers and the creation of a "united front" among the three major unions has been undertaken. Despite these initial signs, however, radicalization of the better paid workers is still a long way off.

Women in the Labor Force

Over the past 60 years, the changing nature of the economy has produced important effects on the role and status of women within the work force. As Table 13 points out, while the proportion of female workers in the work force has doubled from 13.3% in 1901 to 27.8% in 1961, there are some surprises involved in its distribution. For example, in spite of the songs of praise for "Rosy the Rivetter" in the Second World War, the degree of change in the proportion of women in the manual labor sector was very small. Indeed, the male-female proportion in that sector has remained almost completely stable over the past 70 years despite huge over-all transformations.

In contrast to the situation in the manual sector, the female proportion of the white collar sector has risen sharply from 20.6% in 1901 to 41.3% in 1961. Moreover, when the distribution of labor within the white collar sector is examined, even more drastic changes can be observed. As Table 14 points out, the proportion of females in white collar occupations has increased in all sub-sectors except among the professionals, the best paid and most prestigious category. The most striking changes have occurred within the clerical and commercial and financial sub-sector which have tripled their proportions of female labor during that period.

It is not, however, until one examines the proportional distribution of occupations within the female white collar work force that the full impact of these changes can be observed. Thus while Table 14 demonstrated that women had maintained their proportion of the professional sub-sector and increased their proportion of the professional and managerial sub-sector from 3.6% in 1901 to 10.3% in 1961, Table 15 shows that these sectors have not kept pace with the over-all growth of the female labor force. In fact, with the rapid increase in the female labor force, a situation has been created where the average status of women has sharply declined. Whereas in 1901, 67.4% of women were employed in the "desirable" proprietorial

Table 13

Female Workers as a Percentage of the Labor Force, and of Major Sectors, 1901-61[90]

	1901	1911	1921	1931	1941	1951	1961
Total labor force	13.3	13.4	15.5	17.0	19.8	22.3	27.8
White collar sector	20.6	23.8	29.5	31.5	35.1	38.1	41.3
Manual sector	12.6	10.4	10.4	8.5	11.0	11.5	10.6
Service sector	68.7	65.3	58.9	63.0	65.1	55.4	57.8
Primary sector	1.1	1.5	1.6	1.9	1.5	3.1	9.2

Table 14

Female Workers as a Proportion of All Workers in White Collar Sub-Sectors, 1901-61[91]

	1901	1911	1921	1931	1941	1951	1961
Proprietorial & managerial	3.6	4.5	4.3	4.8	7.2	8.9	10.3
Professional	42.5	44.6	54.1	49.5	46.1	43.5	43.2
Clerical	22.1	32.6	41.8	45.1	50.1	56.7	61.5
Commercial & financial	10.4	19.2	23.1	23.1	29.4	35.2	36.7

Table 15

Distribution of Occupations within the Female White Collar Work Force, 1901-61[92]

	1901	1911	1921	1931	1941	1951	1961
Proprietorial & managerial	5.1	5.3	4.2	3.5	4.5	5.9	5.0
Professional	62.3	41.8	39.7	39.0	35.0	26.0	27.2
Clerical	22.5	30.4	38.6	39.0	41.0	49.5	49.8
Commercial & financial	10.2	22.4	17.5	18.5	19.5	19.1	18.0

and managerial and professional categories, in 1961 only 32.2% were in these sub-sectors. On the other hand, the clerical, and commercial and financial subsectors had risen from 32.7 to 67.8%. As the director of the women's bureau of the Federal Department of Labour pointed out, the general picture shows: "women as clerical and office workers; sales clerks and waitresses, telephone operators; and stewardesses of airlines; but there is a dearth of planners, executives and managers in the total scene."[93]

In contrast to the changes among female white collar workers, among male white collar workers, proportional distribution between the "desirable" and "undesirable" occupations has remained stable for 60 years.[94] Thus the process of the proletarianization of the white collar workers described earlier consists, in the main, of the proletarianization of

Table 16
Female Labor Force Participation Rate, 1931-61[95]

	1931	1941	1951	1961
Married women	3.5	4.5	11.2	22.0
Single women	43.8	47.2	58.3	54.1
Other women	21.3	17.2	19.3	22.9
Total	19.3	20.3	24.1	29.5
Married women as a percentage of all women in labor force	10.0	12.7	30.0	49.8

the female sector of the white collar workers. Male white collar workers have generally escaped the effects of this process.

Among the most significant aspects of the growth of the female labor force is the rapid increase in the number of married female workers. As Table 16 shows, the proportion of married females who are workers has risen sharply from 3.5% in 1931 to 22% in 1961, and married workers of all female workers from 10.0 to 49.8% in the same period. This pattern has continued to the present. In 1969, 31.2% of all married women were in the labor force, and married women made up 55.8% of all female workers.[96] As two researchers have pointed out: "While the labor force participation of married women in Canada and elsewhere has increased dramatically over the last few decades, the labor force participation of men, especially those in their prime working years (from 25 to 55) has remained steady at a figure just short of 100%."[97]

Thus the social forces which are bringing married women into the labor force have not noticeably altered the proportion of males who are either working or looking for work. In contrast to the continued increase in participation rates in the labor force of married females, single females participation reached a peak of 58.3% in 1951 and has declined steadily since that date. In 1961, the single female participation rate was 54.1%, and in 1969, it was 48.6%.[98]

Recent studies show that a major cause of married women entering the work force is still economic hardship. As Spencer and Featherstone concluded after a lengthy study of motivating and limiting factors: "There is clear and convincing evidence that a married woman is less likely to be in the labor force the higher the level of family income available, exclusive of her earnings." Moreover, "The greater the value of debts incurred by the family the more likely the wife is to be in the labor force."[99] Sylvia Gelber dismissed the argument that for most women a job is a pastime rather than a necessity. Adding up the estimated 331,434 women who are the sole support of their families, 925,000 single working women and an estimated 678,035 working wives whose husbands have a median income of $6,454 a year, she said it is safe to assume that most women work "because of economic need."[100]

The rapid increase in the proportion of married women in the labor force has created deep strains in the basic unit of Canadian social organization, the male-dominated nuclear family. Canadian concepts of "normal" family relations were imported from Europe and developed strong role attachments in which the male parent was the indispensible element of its economic existence. As married women became more deeply involved in the labor force in the past 30 years (in 1969, 31.6% of married women were in the labor force) the more the "duties" society had attached to her role as wife and mother came into conflict with her new status as breadwinner. Indeed, the more she came to accept the values of her new role as a worker, the more unjust appeared the dual demands of homemaker and worker. Moreover, it was an easy extension from the discovery that women are exploited and discriminated against in the work place to the analogy that her traditional secondary and complimentary role in the family was exploitative as well. From this logical progression came fundamental questions concerning all aspects of the female role and role conditioning, social and economic relations of female workers, and male-female relations in general. The progressively deeper involvement in the labor force by married women is likely to heighten the questioning.

Conclusion

Over the past 70 years fundamental changes have occurred in all aspects of class relations in Canada. With the decline of the petite bourgeoisie and the consolidation and maturation of capitalism, a new situation — one more closely resembling Marx's delineation of a capitalist economy — has emerged. Today we are entering a new era of Canadian history where the primary conflict of social forces is moving from one between the capitalist and petit bourgeois modes of production, to a conflict of capital and labor within the capitalist production system.

While the growing concentration of capital, the gradual proletarianization of all divisions of labor (and the rising discontent among workers which is the result of the proletarianization process), and the more recent phenomenon of a rapid impoverishment of the lower levels of income earners, all point toward the development of the classical Marxist model, a warning must be given. Such movements, if history is to be our guide, are matters of decades, not months or years. Therefore, those prophets who predict the immediate collapse of the capitalist system are failing to observe that it is only now reaching its full maturity in Canada. Thus while these conditions are inevitably bound to bring about higher levels of spontaneous unrest and an increased capacity among workers to understand the real nature of their exploitation, it is unlikely that the critical confrontation between capital and labor will be upon us in the immediate future. The timing of that point in history, of course, will depend largely upon the effectiveness of socialists in communicating the true state of affairs to the society around them.

NOTES

1. See various articles in *Canadian Society,* B.R. Blishen *et al.* eds. (Toronto 1968), and Charles C. Hughes *et al.*, *People of Cove and Woodlot* (New York 1968).

2. C. Wright Mills, *The Power Elite* (New York 1959), and Gabriel Kolko, *Wealth and Power in the United States* (New York 1962). See especially an excellent article by John R. Hofley, "Problems and Perspectives in the Study of Poverty," *Poverty in Canada,* John Harp and John R. Hofley, eds. (Scarborough 1971), 101-16.

3. While *Capital* remains the definitive work on basic analysis of class relations within the capitalist system, there are several other works which serve as an introduction to the Marxist system of thought and analysis. Of these the *Communist Manifesto, The Economic and Philosophic Manuscripts of 1844,* and *Theories of Surplus Value* are especially valuable to the student.

4. See for example K. Marx, *Capital,* 1, chap. XXV, "Nomad Population."

5. See especially Ernest Mandel, *The Formation of the Economic Thought of Karl Marx* (New York 1971).

6. Outstanding exceptions to this criticism are the work of L.W. and F.C. Park and Stanley B. Ryerson in English, and Gilles Bourque and his associates in French, all who have made valuable contributions to establishing the principles of Marxist analysis in Canada.

7. It must be emphasized, however, that the *Ontario Workman* represented primarily the point of view and interests of the labor aristocracy or crafts workers rather than that of the low-paid menial workers.

8. *Trades Unions Advocate* (Toronto), 13 July 1882.

9. Department of National Revenue, *Incomes of Canadians,* 1948, 1958, 1968 (Ottawa, 1950, 1960, 1970). Calculations are my own.

10. Agricultural Economics Research Council of Canada, *Rural Canada in Transition,* eds. Marc-Adelard Tremblay and Walter J. Anderson (1968), 30.

11. *Ibid.,* 31.

12. *Ibid.,* 29.

13. *Incomes of Canadians.*

14. *Census of Canada,* appropriate years. Calculations are my own.

15. *Rural Canada in Transition,* 184.

16. Department of Agriculture, Publication 1354 (1068), cited in John W. Warnock, "The Farm Crisis," *Essays on the Left* (Toronto 1971), 125.

17. *Incomes of Canadians.* In 1968, 49% of farmers and taxable returns. Calculations are my own.

18. *Rural Canada in Transition,* 12. Note that the definition of "rural" population changed between 1941 and 1951. The new definition of rural gives somewhat higher totals; thus the new definition overstates (by about 10%) the actual degree of change.

19. *Ibid.,* 17. See also Leroy F. Stone, *Migration in Canada* (Ottawa 1969), 53, 227. As D.A. Curtis points out in the latter work, some 41.4% of all out-migrants from farms who remain in the same province will end up in the non-farm rural category. In addition 33.0% of those who leave the farm and migrate to another farm will fall into the non-farm rural category as well.

20. See Marx, *Capital,* 1, chap. XXV, for a description of the nature and economic functions of an underclass in the capitalist economy.

21. For descriptions of the causes and events of this strike, see *Last Post,* 1, nos. 5 and 8.

22. *Incomes of Canadians.*

23. *Ibid.*

24. *Ibid.*

25. *Anatomy of Big Business* (Toronto 1962), 43. Perhaps the most revealing study of the aims, methods, and function of corporate directors is the autobiography of Alfred P. Sloan, *My Years with General Motors* (New York 1953). As Sloan points out, the board of directors of GM contained both "external" and "internal" directors — the former represented the shareholders, the latter were executive-level employees. He makes it clear that the former were in complete control of long-range policy and the latter were responsible for the implementation of the goals established for the corporation. The key measure of performance and control, he points out, was "rate of return on investment."

26. For example see *Grain Growers Guide,* 25 June 1913; *Macleans Magazine,* 12 Oct. 1957.

27. C.A. Ashley, "Concentration of Economic Power," *Canadian Journal of Economics and Political Science,* XXVII, no. 1 (Feb. 1957), 106. Ashley points out that directors of the Bank of Montreal held 13 directorships on the board of the Royal Trust, 10 on CPR, 6 on the Steel Co. of Canada, and 5 on Sun Life.

28. See *Globe and Mail* (25 Dec. 1969). By 1971, the assets of the Bank of Montreal alone totalled $10,165,397,000, an increase in size of 49% in just three years. See *Globe and Mail,* 3 Dec. 1969.

29. Ashley, "Concentration," 106-7.

30. John Porter, "Concentration of Economic Power and the Economic Elite in Canada," *Canadian Journal of Economics and Political Science,* XXII, no. 2 (May 1956), 210. For his study, Porter does not include the directorships of 13 corporations (10 US-owned) who kept no separate record of Canadian activities; nor does he include the 243 American and 64 British residents who are directors of the remaining 170 dominant corporations which are the basis of the study.

31. *Ibid.,* Appendix B, Table IV, 220.

32. *Ibid.,* Table V.

33. *Globe and Mail,* 25 Dec. 1969 and 4 Dec. 1971.

34. Porter, "Concentration," 220, Table IV, and *Globe and Mail* (25 Dec. 1969). Between 1951 and 1968 assets of the ten largest Canadian-owned insurance companies grew by 206%, from $4,203,000,000 to $12,980,000,000.

35. *Globe and Mail,* 7 Dec. 1971.

36. Figures compiled from *Incomes of Canadians,* 1950, 1960, and 1970, Table 2, "All Returns by Income Classes."

37. Park and Park, *Anatomy,* 49-50.

38. *Incomes of Canadians,* 1970, Table 15. Calculations are my own.

39. *Incomes of Canadians,* 1970, Table 15.

40. The best exposition of the strategic need of the US to acquire control of foreign resources is that by R. Rea Jackson, "America's Need for a New National Economic Strategy," *National Strategy in an Age of Revolution* (the minutes of the National Military-Industrial Conference) ed. George B. Huszar (New York 1959), 134-43. Jackson represented the Rockefeller interests. See also Kari Levitt, *Silent Surrender* (Toronto 1970).

41. *Globe and Mail* (3 Dec. 1971).

42. Calculated at a 20:1 price/yield ratio from Table 15, *Incomes of Canadians,* 1969.

43. Park and Park, *Anatomy,* 51.

44. *Industrial Canada,* June 1971, 13.

45. *Ibid.,* July 1971, 49.

46. *Ibid.,* June 1971, 13.

47. Jackson, "America's Need for a New International Economic Strategy," 140.

48. *Ibid.,* 142.

49. *National Strategy,* etc., Appendix, 271. Although little known, this annual series of conferences, begun in 1955, offers excellent insight into the thinking of the American military-industrial élite, since virtually every branch of the American military, education, industry, and government was represented at the highest level.

50. The following works provide an excellent introduction to the topic of American ownership: *Gordon to Watkins to You,* eds. Dave Godfrey and Mel Watkins (Toronto 1970); *Inter-Corporate Ownership* (Ottawa 1969); James Laxer, *The Energy Poker Game* (Toronto 1970); Kari Levitt, *Silent Surrender* (Toronto 1970); L.C. and F.W. Park, *Anatomy of Big Business* (Toronto 1962); *Report of the Task Force on the Structure of Canadian Industry* (the Watkins Report) (Ottawa 1968); A.E. Safarian, *Foreign Ownership of Canadian Industry* (Toronto 1966).

51. For example, E.S. Jackson, president of Manufacturers Life Insurance Co., in his address to the annual meeting made clear the basis for his opposition to Canadian economic nationalism. His concern was that legislating Canadian ownership would lead to retaliatory action by other countries. With about 75% of its business transacted outside Canada — more than 50% in the US alone — any legislation limiting foreign ownership might bring retaliation which would seriously affect Manufacturers Life's foreign interests. *Globe and Mail,* 23 Dec. 1971.

52. *Fortune,* Aug. 1971, 156.

53. The Simard family are strong backers of the anti-nationalist Liberal government in Quebec. Gerard Filion, the anti-nationalist president of the Canadian Manufacturers Association, is president of the Simard-controlled Marine Industries Ltd., while Robert Bourassa, premier of Quebec, is a son-in-law of one of the Simards. Stephen Roman attempted to sell Denison Mines, the largest remaining Canadian-controlled uranium mine, to US interests, while R.A. Brown Jr, president of Home Oil, attempted to sell out to US interests as well. Both the latter moves were blocked by the federal govenment because of the huge public outcry.

54. Park and Park, *Anatomy,* 51.

55. *Industrial Canada,* June 1970, 25.

56. *Ibid.,* 25-6.

57. *Ibid.,* 26.

58. *Toronto Star,* 18 Dec. 1971.

59. Charles K. Brightbill, *The Challenge of Leisure* (Englewood Cliffs, NJ 1963); Ralph Glasser, *Leisure: Penalty or Prize?* (London 1970); Norman P. Miller, *The Leisure Age: Its Challenge to Recreation* (Belmont, Calif. 1966).

60. Noah M. Meltz, *Manpower in Canada 1931-1961* (Ottawa 1969), Table A.1.

61. Meltz, *Manpower.* Calculations are my own.

62. *Ibid.*

63. *Ibid.*

64. Judson Gooding, "The Fraying White Collar," *Fortune,* Dec. 1970, 78.

65. Quoted in *Ibid.*

66. *Ibid.*

67. The doctors, for example, fought for years to prevent competition by foreign-trained doctors by rigidly excluding all but those trained in the white English-speaking world. The current warfare by the dental profession against denturists is of a similar nature. See for example the prosecution of denturists in Nova Scotia, *Toronto Star*, 22 Dec. 1971.

68. Meltz, Table B.1., 62, and *Incomes of Canadians*, 1953 and 1963. All figures on professional employment in this section are taken from these sources.

69. *Incomes of Canadians*, 1950, 1960, 1970. Calculations are my own.

70. For a good account of the Saskatchewan doctors' strike see R. Badgley and S. Wolfe, *Doctors' Strike* (Toronto 1967).

71. *Kitchener-Waterloo Record* (20 Dec. 1971).

72. R.S. Lockhart, "The Proletarianization of the Petite Bourgeoisie," MA thesis, Simon Fraser University, 1969.

73. In the mid-1820s British colonial policy undertook to create a class of landless laborers requisite to the development of a capitalist state by the manipulation of land-granting policies. See Leo A. Johnson, "Land Settlement, Population Growth and Social Structure in Home District, 1794-1851," *Ontario History*, LXIII, no 1 (March 1971), 41-60.

74. Data for capital stocks and value of production is from O.J. Firestone, *Canada's Economic Development 1867-1953* (London 1958), Table 77, 209. Data income indexes are from M.C. Urquhart and K.A. Buckley, eds. *Historical Statistics of Canada* (Toronto 1965). Series DI-11 and D40-59, pp. 84 and 86. Calculations which follow are my own.

75. Stuart M. Jamieson, *Times of Trouble: Labour Unrest and Industrial Conflict in Canada, 1900-66*, Study no 22, Task Force on Labour Relations, Privy Council Office, Ottawa. See also Frank T. Denton, *The Growth of Manpower in Canada* (Ottawa 1970), 6.

76. Meltz, *Manpower*, 58. Calculations are my own.

77. Urquhart and Buckley, *Historical Statistics*, Series DI-11 and D40-59, pp. 84 and 86.

78. O.J. Firestone, Table 6, p. 58.

79. Leslie Roberts, *C.D.: The Life and Times of Clarence Decatur Howe* (Toronto 1957).

80. Royal Commission on Canada's Economic Prospects, Wm. C. Wood and Anthony Scott, *Output, Labour and Capital in the Canadian Economy* (Ottawa 1958), 269.

81. *Ibid.*, 262.

82. *Ibid.*, 263.

83. This is true in much of the construction industry as well. See Gilbert Burck, "The Building Trades Versus the People," *Fortune* (Oct. 1970); Restrictive Trade Practices Commission, *Road Paving in Ontario* (Ottawa 1970); L.A. Skeoch, *Restrictive Trade Practices in Canada* (Toronto 1966).

84. Recent movement of General Instrument Co. and Clairetone Electronics to Nova Scotia, Hamilton Cottons to Mount Forest, Ontario, and Sperry-Gyro from Ontario to Quebec are all examples of the mobility of low-skilled labor-intensive industries leaving areas with rising wages for low-wage areas.

85. For example, when the Dominion Steel and Coal Co. (Dosco) opened its new large-scale facilities in Hamilton, Ontario, it closed its Nova Scotia operations, even though the Nova Scotia operations were still profitable, in order to operate

the capital-intensive Hamilton plant at closer to optimal production levels. The Nova Scotia plant was sold to the Nova Scotia government and workers. It continues to operate profitably.

86. An examination of the *Economic Atlas of Ontario* (Toronto 1969) provides ample evidence of this process. In particular the maps showing the movement to and concentration of the metal trades in the Toronto region provides an excellent case study.

87. The Massey-Ferguson Company provides the best example of a "Canadian" multinational company concentrating its capital-intensive operations and center of decision-making in the US. Tacit recognition of this process is contained in the Canadian government's creation of the Auto Pact in order to retain a minimum amount of automobile manufacturing in Canada.

It would appear that the only exception to this pattern of centralization and specialization occurs when entirely new capital is invested. While the General Motors plant at Ste Thérèse, Quebec, and Ford's new plant at Talbotville are examples of expansions within the central area, wholly new operations such as Volvo and Michelin tire in Nova Scotia suggest that when new capital investment occurs in heavy industry, it may seek out low-wage areas — particularly when heavily subsidized by government grants. Since such wholly new heavy investments occur but rarely, they will probably have little effect on the over-all picture.

88. Judson Gooding, "Blue-Collar Blues on the Assembly Line," *Fortune,* July 1970, 69.

89. *Ibid.* For similar accounts see *Atlantic,* Oct. 1971.

90. Meltz, *Manpower,* Table A.4, p. 61. It should be noted that in the years 1921 to 1961 an average of 20% of working females gave no occupational information.

91. *Ibid.,* Table A.4.

92. *Ibid.* Calculations are my own.

93. Speech to the Pioneer Women of Canada, 23 Nov. 1971, in *Globe and Mail,* 24 Nov. 1971.

94. Meltz, *Manpower.* Calculations are my own.

95. Byron G. Spencer and Dennis C. Featherstone, *Married Female Labour Force Participation: A Micro Study* (Ottawa 1970), 12. Statistics from the 1931 census are for the age group 10 and over. Statistics from the 1941-51 censuses are for the age group 14 and over. Statistics from the 1961 census are for the age group 15 and over. For a more detailed study of labor force characteristics see Frank T. Denton.

96. *Married Female Labour Force,* 13.

97. *Ibid.*

98. *Ibid.*

99. *Ibid.,* 84.

100. *Globe and Mail,* 24 Nov. 1971.

The Culture of Poverty*

OSCAR LEWIS

Poverty and the so-called war against it provide a principal theme for the domestic program of the Johnson Administration. In the midst of a population that enjoys unexampled material well-being — with the average annual family income exceeding $7,000 — it is officially acknowledged that some 18 million families, numbering more than 50 million individuals, live below the $3,000 "poverty line." Toward the improvement of the lot of these people some $1,600 million of federal funds are directly allocated through the Office of Economic Opportunity, and many hundreds of millions of additional dollars flow indirectly through expanded federal expenditures in the fields of health, education, welfare, and urban affairs.†

Along with the increase in activity on behalf of the poor indicated by these figures there has come a parallel expansion of publication in the social sciences on the subject of poverty. The new writings advance the same two opposed evaluations of the poor that are to be found in literature, in proverbs, and in popular sayings throughout recorded history. Just as the poor have been pronounced blessed, virtuous, upright, serene, independent, honest, kind, and happy, so contemporary students stress their great and neglected capacity for self-help, leadership, and community organization. Conversely, as the poor have been characterized as shiftless, mean, sordid, violent, evil, and criminal, so other students point to the irreversibly destructive effects of poverty on individual character and emphasize the corresponding need to keep guidance and control of poverty projects in the hands of duly constituted authorities. This clash of viewpoints reflects in part the infighting for political control of the program between federal and local officials. The confusion results also from the tendency to focus study and attention on the personality of the individual victim of poverty rather than on the slum community and family and from the consequent failure to distinguish between poverty and what I have called the "culture of poverty."

The phrase is a catchy one and is used and misused with some frequency in the current literature. In my writings it is the label for a specific conceptual model that describes in positive terms a subculture of Western society with its own structure and rationale, a way of life handed on from

---

*Copyright 1966 by Oscar Lewis. An expanded version of this article appears in *La Vida*, by Oscar Lewis. Reprinted as it appeared in *Scientific American*, October, 1966, by permission of Randon House, Inc.

†*Editor's note*: These figures apply to the U.S.A., 1965.

generation to generation along family lines. The culture of poverty is not just a matter of deprivation or disorganization, a term signifying the absence of something. It is a culture in the traditional anthropological sense in that it provides human beings with a design for living, with a ready-made set of solutions for human problems, and so serves a significant adaptive function. This style of life transcends national boundaries and regional and rural-urban differences within nations. Wherever it occurs, its practitioners exhibit remarkable similarity in the structure of their families, in interpersonal relations, in spending habits, in their value systems, and in their orientation in time.

Not nearly enough is known about this important complex of human behavior. My own concept of it has evolved as my work has progressed and remains subject to amendment by my own further work and that of others. The scarcity of literature on the culture of poverty is a measure of the gap in communication that exists between the very poor and the middle-class personnel — social scientists, social workers, teachers, physicians, priests, and others — who bear the major responsibility for carrying out the antipoverty programs. Much of the behavior accepted in the culture of poverty goes counter to cherished ideals of the larger society. In writing about "multiproblem" families, social scientists thus often stress their instability, their lack of order, direction, and organization. Yet, as I have observed them, their behavior seems clearly patterned and reasonably predictable. I am more often struck by the inexorable repetitiousness and the iron entrenchment of their lifeways.

The concept of the culture of poverty may help to correct misapprehensions that have ascribed some behavior patterns of ethnic, national or regional groups as distinctive characteristics. For example, a high incidence of common-law marriage and households headed by women has been thought to be distinctive of Negro family life in this country, and has been attributed to the Negro's historical experience of slavery. In actuality, it turns out that such households express essential traits of the culture of poverty and are found among diverse peoples in many parts of the world and among peoples that have had no history of slavery. Although it is now possible to assert such generalizations, there is still much to be learned about this difficult and affecting subject. The absence of intensive anthropological studies of poor families in a wide variety of national contexts — particularly the lack of such studies in socialist countries — remains a serious handicap to the formulation of dependable cross-cultural constants of the culture of poverty.

My studies of poverty and family life have centered largely in Mexico. On occasion some of my Mexican friends have suggested delicately that I turn to a study of poverty in my own country. As a first step in this direction I am currently engaged in a study of Puerto Rican families. Over the past three years my staff and I have been assembling data on 100 representative families in four slums of Greater San Juan and some 50 families of their relatives in New York City.

Our methods combine the traditional techniques of sociology, anthropology, and psychology. This includes a battery of 19 questionnaires, the administration of which requires 12 hours per informant. They cover the residence and employment history of each adult; family relations; income and expenditure; complete inventory of household and personal possessions; friendship patterns, particularly the *compadrazgo*, or god-parent, relationship that serves as a kind of informal social security for the children of these families and establishes special obligations among the adults; recreational patterns; health and medical history; politics; religion; world view and "cosmopolitanism." Open-end interviews and psychological tests (such as the thematic apperception test, the Rorschach test, and the sentence-completion test) are administered to a sampling of this population.

All this work serves to establish the context for close-range study of a selected few families. Because the family is a small social system, it lends itself to the holistic approach of anthropology. Whole-family studies bridge the gap between the conceptual extremes of the culture at one pole and of the individual at the other, making possible observation of both culture and personality as they are interrelated in real life. In a large metropolis such as San Juan or New York the family is a natural unit of study.

Ideally our objective is the naturalistic observation of the life of "our" families, with a minimum of intervention. Such intensive study, however, necessarily involves the establishment of deep personal ties. My assistants include two Mexicans whose families I have studied; their "Mexican's-eye view" of the Puerto Rican slum has helped to point up the similarities and differences between the Mexican and Puerto Rican subcultures. We have spent many hours attending family parties, wakes, and baptisms, responding to emergency calls, taking people to hospital, getting them out of jail, filling out applications for them, hunting apartments with them, helping them to get jobs or to get on relief. With each member of these families we conduct tape-recorded interviews, taking down their life stories and their answers to questions on a wide variety of topics. For the ordering of our material we undertake to reconstruct, by close interrogation, the history of a week or more of consecutive days in the lives of each family, and we observe and record complete days as they unfold. The first volume to issue from this study is to be published next month under the title of *La Vida, a Puerto Rican Family in the Culture of Poverty — San Juan and New York* (Random House).

There are many poor people in the world. Indeed, the poverty of the two-thirds of the world's population who live in the underdeveloped countries has been rightly called "the problem of problems." But not all of them by any means live in the culture of poverty. For this way of life to come into being and flourish it seems clear that certain preconditions must be met.

The setting is a cash economy, with wage labor and production for profit and with a persistently high rate of unemployment and underemployment at low wages, for unskilled labor. The society fails to provide social, political, and economic organization, on either a voluntary basis or by government imposition, for the low-income population. There is a bilateral kinship system centered on the nuclear progenitive family, as distinguished from the unilateral extended kinship system of lineage and clan. The dominant class asserts a set of values that prizes thrift and the accumulation of wealth and property, stresses the possibility of upward mobility, and explains low economic status as the result of individual personal inadequacy and inferiority.

Where these conditions prevail, the way of life that develops among some of the poor is the culture of poverty. That is why I have described it as a subculture of the Western social order. It is both an adaptation and a reaction of the poor to their marginal position in a class-stratified, highly individuated, capitalistic society. It represents an effort to cope with feelings of hopelessness and despair that arise from the realization by the members of the marginal communities in these societies of the improbability of their achieving success in terms of the prevailing values and goals. Many of the traits of the culture of poverty can be viewed as local, spontaneous attempts to meet needs not served in the case of the poor by the institutions and agencies of the larger society because the poor are not eligible for such service, cannot afford it, or are ignorant and suspicious.

Once the culture of poverty has come into existence it tends to perpetuate itself. By the time slum children are six or seven they have usually absorbed the basic attitudes and values of their subculture. Thereafter they are psychologically unready to take full advantage of changing conditions or improving opportunities that may develop in their lifetime.

My studies have identified some 70 traits that characterize the culture of poverty. The principal ones may be described in four dimensions of the system: the relationship between the subculture and the larger society; the nature of the slum community; the nature of the family; and the attitudes, values, and character structure of the individual.

The disengagement, the nonintegration, of the poor with respect to the major institutions of society is a crucial element in the culture of poverty. It reflects the combined effect of a variety of factors including poverty, to begin with, but also segregation and discrimination, fear, suspicion, and apathy and the development of alternative institutions and procedures in the slum community. The people do not belong to labor unions or political parties and make little use of banks, hospitals, department stores, or museums. Such involvement as there is in the institutions of the larger society — in the jails, the army, and the public welfare system — does little to suppress the traits of the culture of poverty. A relief system that barely keeps people alive perpetuates rather than eliminates poverty and the pervading sense of hopelessness.

People in a culture of poverty produce little wealth and receive little in return. Chronic unemployment and underemployment, low wages, lack of property, lack of savings, absence of food reserves in the home, and chronic shortage of cash imprison the family and the individual in a vicious circle. Thus for lack of cash the slum householder makes frequent purchases of small quantities of food at higher prices. The slum economy turns inward; it shows a high incidence of pawning of personal goods, borrowing at usurious rates of interest, informal credit arrangements among neighbors, use of secondhand clothing and furniture.

There is awareness of middle-class values. People talk about them and claim some of them as their own. On the whole, however, they do not live by them. They will declare that marriage by law, by the church or by both is the ideal form of marriage, but few will marry. For men who have no steady jobs, no property, and no prospect of wealth to pass on to their children, who live in the present without expectations of the future, who want to avoid the expense and legal difficulties involved in marriage and divorce, a free union or consensual marriage makes good sense. The women, for their part, will turn down offers of marriage from men who are likely to be immature, punishing, and generally unreliable. They feel that a consensual union gives them some of the freedom and flexibility men have. By not giving the fathers of their children legal status as husbands, the women have a stronger claim on the children. They also maintain exclusive rights to their own property.

Along with disengagement from the larger society, there is a hostility to the basic institutions of what are regarded as the dominant classes. There is hatred of the police, mistrust of government and of those in high positions, and a cynicism that extends to the church. The culture of poverty thus holds a certain potential for protest and for entrainment in political movements aimed against the existing order.

With its poor housing and overcrowding, the community of the culture of poverty is high in gregariousness, but it has a minimum of organization beyond the nuclear and extended family. Occasionally slum dwellers come together in temporary informal groupings; neighborhood gangs that cut across slum settlements represent a considerable advance beyond the zero point of the continuum I have in mind. It is the low level of organization that gives the culture of poverty its marginal and anomalous quality in our highly organized society. Most primitive peoples have achieved a higher degree of sociocultural organization than contemporary urban slum dwellers. This is not to say that there may not be a sense of community and *esprit de corps* in a slum neighborhood. In fact, where slums are isolated from their surroundings by enclosing walls or other physical barriers, where rents are low and residence is stable, and where the population constitutes a distinct ethnic, racial or language group, the sense of community may approach that of a village. In Mexico City and San Juan such territoriality is engendered by the scarcity of low-cost housing outside of established slum areas. In South Africa it is actively enforced by the *apartheid* that confines rural migrants to prescribed locations.

The family in the culture of poverty does not cherish childhood as a specially prolonged and protected stage in the life cycle. Initiation into sex comes early. With the instability of consensual marriage the family tends to be mother-centered and tied more closely to the mother's extended family. The female head of the house is given to authoritarian rule. In spite of much verbal emphasis on family solidarity, sibling rivalry for the limited supply of goods and maternal affection is intense. There is little privacy.

The individual who grows up in this culture has a strong feeling of fatalism, helplessness, dependence, and inferiority. These traits, so often remarked in the current literature as characteristic of the American Negro, I found equally strong in the slum dwellers of Mexico City and San Juan, who are not segregated or discriminated against as a distinct ethnic or racial group. Other traits include a high incidence of weak ego structure, orality, and confusion of sexual identification, all reflecting maternal deprivation; a strong present-time orientation with relatively little disposition to defer gratification and plan for the future; and a high tolerance for psychological pathology of all kinds. There is widespread belief in male superiority and among the men, a strong preoccupation with *machismo*, their masculinity.

Provincial and local in outlook, with little sense of history, these people know only their own neighborhood and their own way of life. Usually they do not have the knowledge, the vision or the ideology to see the similarities between their troubles and those of their counterparts elsewhere in the world. They are not class-conscious, although they are sensitive indeed to symbols of status.

The distinction between poverty and the culture of poverty is basic to the model described here. There are numerous examples of poor people whose way of life I would not characterize as belonging to this subculture. Many primitive and preliterate peoples that have been studied by anthropologists suffer dire poverty attributable to low technology or thin resources or both. Yet even the simplest of these peoples have a high degree of social organization and a relatively integrated satisfying and self-sufficient culture.

In India the destitute lower-caste peoples — such as the Chamars, the leatherworkers, and the Bhangis, the sweepers — remain integrated in the larger society and have their own panchayat institutions of self-government. Their panchayats and their extended unilateral kinship systems, or clans, cut across village lines, giving them a strong sense of identity and continuity. In my studies of these people, I found no culture of poverty to go with their poverty.

The Jews of eastern Europe were a poor urban people, often confined to ghettos. Yet they did not have many traits of the culture of poverty. They had a tradition of literacy that placed great value on learning; they formed many voluntary associations and adhered with devotion to the central community organization around the rabbi, and they had a religion that taught them they were the chosen people.

I would cite also a fourth, somewhat speculative example of poverty dissociated from the culture of poverty. On the basis of limited direct observation in one country — Cuba — and from indirect evidence, I am inclined to believe the culture of poverty does not exist in socialist countries. In 1947 I undertook a study of a slum in Havana. Recently I had an opportunity to revisit the same slum and some of the same families. The physical aspect of the place had changed little, except for a beautiful new nursery school. The people were as poor as before, but I was impressed to find much less of the feelings of despair and apathy so symptomatic of the culture of poverty in the urban slums of the U.S. The slum was now highly organized, with block communities, educational committees, party committees. The people had found a new sense of power and importance in a doctrine that glorified the lower class as the hope of humanity, and they were armed. I was told by one Cuban official that the Castro government had practically eliminated delinquency by giving arms to the delinquents!

Evidently the Castro regime — revising Marx and Engels — did not write off the so-called *lumpenproletariat* as an inherently reactionary and antirevolutionary force but rather found in them a revolutionary potential and utilized it. Franz Fanon, in his book *The Wretched of the Earth*, makes a similar evaluation of their role in the Algerian revolution: "It is within this mass of humanity, this people of the shantytowns, at the core of the *lumpenproletariat*, that the rebellion will find its urban spearhead. For the *lumpenproletariat*, that horde of starving men, uprooted from their tribe and from their clan, constitutes one of the most spontaneous and most radical revolutionary forces of a colonized people."[1]

It is true that I have found little revolutionary spirit or radical ideology among low-income Puerto Ricans. Most of the families I studied were politically conservative, about half of them favoring the Statehood Republican Party, which provides opposition on the right to the Popular Democratic Party that dominates the politics of the commonwealth. It seems to me, therefore, that disposition for protest among people living in the culture of poverty will vary considerably according to the national context and historical circumstances. In contrast to Algeria, the independent movement in Puerto Rico has found little popular support. In Mexico, where the cause of independence carried long ago, there is no longer any such movement to stir the dwellers in the new and old slums of the capital city.

Yet it would seem that any movement — be it religious, pacifist or revolutionary — that organizes and gives hope to the poor and effectively promotes a sense of solidarity with larger groups must effectively destroy the psychological and social core of the culture of poverty. In this connection, I suspect that the civil rights movement among American Negroes has of itself done more to improve their self-image and self-respect than such economic gains as it has won although, without doubt, the two kinds of progress are mutually reinforcing. In the culture of poverty of the American Negro, the additional disadvantage of racial discrimination has generated a potential for revolutionary protest and organization that is absent in the slums of San Juan and Mexico City and, for that matter, among the poor whites in the South.

If it is true, as I suspect, that the culture of poverty flourishes and is endemic to the free-enterprise, pre-welfare-state stage of capitalism, then it is also endemic in colonial societies. The most likely candidates for the culture of poverty would be the people who come from the lower strata of a rapidly changing society and who are already partially alienated from it. Accordingly the subculture is likely to be found where imperial conquest has smashed the native social and economic structure and held the natives, perhaps for generations, in servile status, or where feudalism is yielding to capitalism in the later evolution of a colonial economy. Landless rural workers who migrate to the cities, as in Latin America, can be expected to fall into this way of life more readily than migrants from stable peasant villages with a well-organized traditional culture, as in India. It remains to be seen, however, whether the culture of poverty has not already begun to develop in the slums of Bombay and Calcutta. Compared with Latin

America also, the strong corporate nature of many African tribal societies may tend to inhibit or delay the formation of a full-blown culture of poverty in the new towns and cities of that continent. In South Africa the institutionalization of repression and discrimination under *apartheid* may also have begun to promote an immunizing sense of identity and group consciousness among the African Negroes.

One must therefore keep the dynamic aspects of human institutions forward in observing and assessing the evidence for the presence, the waxing or the waning of this subculture. Measured on the dimension of relationship to the larger society, some slum dwellers may have a warmer identification with their national tradition even though they suffer deeper poverty than members of a similar community in another country. In Mexico City a high percentage of our respondents, including those with little or no formal schooling, knew of Cuauhtémoc, Hidalgo, Father Morelos, Juarez Diaz, Zapata, Carranza and Cardenas. In San Juan the names of Ramon Power, José de Diego Baldorioty de Castro, Ramon Betances, Nemesio Canales, Lloréns Torres rang no bell; a few could tell about the late Albizu Campos. For the lower-income Puerto Rican, however, history begins with Munoz Rivera and ends with his son Munoz Marin.

The national context can make a big difference in the play of the crucial traits of fatalism and hopelessness. Given the advanced technology, the high level of literacy, the all-pervasive reach of the media of mass communications, and the relatively high aspirations of all sectors of the population, even the poorest and most marginal communities of the U.S. must aspire to a larger future than the slum dwellers of Ecuador and Peru, where the actual possibilities are more limited and where an authoritarian social order persists in city and country.

Among the 50 million U.S. citizens now more or less officially certified as poor, I would guess that about 20% live in a culture of poverty. The largest numbers in this group are made up of Negroes, Puerto Ricans, Mexicans, American Indians, and Southern poor whites. In these figures there is some reassurance for those concerned, because it is much more difficult to undo the culture of poverty than to cure poverty itself.

Middle-class people — this would certainly include most social scientists — tend to concentrate on the negative aspects of the culture of poverty. They attach a minus sign to such traits as present-time orientation and readiness to indulge impulses. I do not intend to idealize or romanticize the culture of poverty — it is easier to praise poverty than to live in it. Yet the positive aspects of these traits must not be overlooked. Living in the present may develop a capacity for spontaneity, for the enjoyment of the sensual, which is often blunted in the middle-class, future-oriented man. Indeed, I am often struck by the analogies that can be drawn between the mores of the very rich — of the "jet set" and "café society" — and the culture of the very poor. Yet it is, on the whole, a comparatively superficial culture. There is in it much pathos, suffering, and emptiness. It does not provide much support or satisfaction; its pervading mistrust magnifies individual helplessness and isolation. Indeed, poverty of culture is one of the crucial traits of the culture of poverty.

The concept of the culture of poverty provides a generalization that may help to unify and explain a number of phenomena hitherto viewed as peculiar to certain racial, national or regional groups. Problems we think of as being distinctively our own or distinctively Negro (or as typifying any other ethnic group) prove to be endemic in countries where there are no segregated ethnic minority groups. If it follows that the elimination of physical poverty may not by itself eliminate the culture of poverty, then an understanding of the subculture may contribute to the design of measures specific to that purpose.

What is the future of the culture of poverty? In considering this question one must distinguish between those countries in which it represents a relatively small segment of the population and those in which it constitutes a large one. In the U.S. the major solution proposed by social workers dealing with the "hard core" poor has been slowly to raise their level of living and incorporate them in the middle class. Wherever possible psychiatric treatment is prescribed.

In underdeveloped countries where great masses of people live in the culture of poverty, such a social-work solution does not seem feasible. The local psychiatrists have all they can do to care for their own growing middle class. In those countries the people with a culture of poverty may seek a more revolutionary solution. By creating basic structural changes in society, by redistributing wealth, by organizing the poor and giving them a sense of belonging, of power and of leadership, revolutions frequently succeed in abolishing some of the basic characteristics of the culture of poverty even when they do not succeed in curing poverty itself.

NOTE

1. Franz Fanon, *The Wretched of the Earth*, translated from the French by Constance Farrington. Copyright 1963 by Presence Africaine (New York: Grove Press, 1963), p. 129.

The Positive Functions of Poverty and Inequality*

HERBERT J. GANS

The preceding chapter examined some problems of equality from the perspective of society as a whole, but still other problems are identified when one looks at the functions — or benefits — that inequality provides for specific sectors of society. This chapter examines such functions of poverty and, in a concluding section, of inequality, taking off from the Mertonian analysis of the functions of the urban political machine.

In analyzing the persistence of the political machine, Robert K. Merton wrote that because "we should ordinarily . . . expect persistent social patterns and social structures to perform positive functions which are at the time not adequately fulfilled by other existing patterns and structures . . . perhaps this publicly maligned organization is, under present conditions, satisfying basic latent functions."[1] He pointed out how the machine provided central authority to get things done when a decentralized local government could not act, humanized the services of the impersonal bureaucracy for fearful citizens, offered concrete help (rather than law or justice) to the poor, and otherwise performed services needed or demanded by many people but considered unconventional or even illegal by formal public agencies.

This chapter is not concerned with the political machine, however, but with poverty, a social phenomenon as maligned as and far more persistent than the machine. Consequently, there may be some merit in applying functional analysis to poverty, to ask whether it too has positive functions that explain its persistence. Since functional analysis has itself taken on a maligned status among some American sociologists, a secondary purpose of this chapter is to ask whether it is still a useful approach.[2]

The Nature of Functions

Merton defines functions as "those observed consequences which make for the adaptation or adjustment of a given system," and dysfunctions as "those observed consequences which lessen the adaptation or adjustment of the system."[3] This definition does not specify the nature or scope of the system, but elsewhere in his classic paper, *Manifest and Latent Functions*, Merton indicates that social system is not a synonym for society, and that systems vary in size, requiring a functional analysis "to consider a *range* of units for

---

*From Herbert Gans, *More Equality*. New York: Vintage Books, 1974, pp. 102-26.

146

which the item [or social phenomenon — H.G.] has designated consequences: individuals in diverse statuses, subgroups, the larger social system
and cultural systems."[4]

In discussing the functions of poverty, I shall identify functions for
groups and *aggregates*, specifically, interest groups, socio-economic classes,
and other population aggregates — for example, those with shared values
or similar statuses. This definitional approach is based on the assumption
that almost every social system — and of course every society — is composed of groups or aggregates with different interests and values, so that, as
Merton puts it, "items may be functional for some individuals and
subgroups and dysfunctional for others."[5] Indeed, frequently one group's
functions are another group's dysfunctions.[6] For example, the political
machine analyzed by Merton was functional for the working-class and
business interests of the city but dysfunctional for many middle-class and
reform interests. Consequently, functions are defined as those observed
consequences which are positive *as judged by the values of the group under
analysis*; dysfunctions, as those which are negative by these values.[7]
Because functions benefit the group in question and dysfunctions hurt it, I
shall also describe functions and dysfunctions in the language of economic
planning and systems analysis, as benefits and costs.[8]

Identifying functions and dysfunctions for groups and aggregates rather
than systems reduces the possibility that what is functional for one group in
a multigroup system will be seen as functional for the whole system, making
it more difficult, for example, to suggest that a given phenomenon is functional for a corporation or political regime when it may in fact be functional
only for its officers or leaders. Also, this approach precludes reaching a
priori conclusions about two other important empirical questions raised by
Merton, whether any phenomenon is ever functional or dysfunctional for
an entire society, and if functional, whether it is therefore indispensable to
that society.[9]

In a modern heterogeneous society, few phenomena are functional or
dysfunctional for the society as a whole and most result in benefits to some
groups and costs to others. Given the level of differentiation in modern
society, I am even skeptical that one can empirically identify a social system
called society. Society exists, of course, but it is closer to being a very large
aggregate, and when sociologists talk about society as a system, they often
really mean the nation.

I would also argue that no social phenomenon is indispensable; it may
be too powerful or too highly valued to be eliminated, but in most instances, one can suggest what Merton calls "functional alternatives" or
equivalents for social phenomena, that is, other social patterns or policies
that achieve the same functions but avoid the dysfunctions.

The Functions of Poverty

The conventional view of American poverty is so dedicated to identifying
the dysfunctions of poverty, for both the poor and the nation, that at first
glance it seems inconceivable that poverty could be functional for anyone.

Of course, the slumlord and the loan shark are widely known to profit from the existence of poverty, but they are popularly viewed as evil men and their activities are, at least in part, dysfunctional for the poor. What is less often recognized, at least in the conventional wisdom, is that poverty also makes possible the existence or expansion of "respectable" professions and occupations, for example, penology, criminology, social work, and public health. More recently, the poor have provided jobs for professional and paraprofessional "poverty warriors," as well as for journalists and social scientists, this author included, who have supplied the information demanded since public curiosity about the poor developed in the 1960s.

Clearly, then, poverty and the poor serve a number of functions for affluent groups — households, professions, institutions, corporations, and classes, among others — thus contributing to the persistence of these groups, which in turn encourages the persistence of poverty in dialectical fashion. These functions are not, however, necessarily the causes of poverty, for functions are, by definition, effects and not causes, and my analysis is more concerned with showing how the functions of poverty aid in the persistence of nonpoor groups than with determining the causes of the persistence of poverty. I shall describe 15 sets of such functions — economic, social, cultural, and political — that seem to me most significant.

First, the existence of poverty makes sure that "dirty" work is done. Every economy has such work: physically dirty or dangerous, temporary, dead-end and underpaid, undignified and menial jobs. In America, poverty functions to provide a low-wage labor pool that is willing — or rather, unable to be unwilling — to perform dirty work at low cost.[10] Indeed, this function is so important that in some Southern states, welfare payments have been cut off during the summer months when the poor are needed to work in the fields. Furthermore, many economic activities involving dirty work depend heavily on the poor; restaurants, hospitals, parts of the garment industry, and industrial agriculture, among others, could not persist in their present form without their dependence on the substandard wages they pay their employees.

Second, the poor subsidize, directly and indirectly, many activities that benefit affluent people and institutions.[11] For one thing, they have long supported both the consumption and the investment activities of the private economy by virtue of the low wages they receive. This was openly advocated at the beginning of the Industrial Revolution, when a French writer quoted by T. H. Marshall pointed out that "to assure and maintain the prosperities of our industries, it is necessary that the workers should never acquire wealth."[12] Examples of this kind of subsidization abound even today; for example, poorly paid domestics subsidize the upper middle and upper classes, making life easier for their employers and freeing affluent women for a variety of professional, cultural, civic, or social activities. Conversely, because the rich do not have to subsidize the poor, they can divert a higher proportion of their income to savings and investment and thus fuel economic growth. This in turn can produce higher incomes for everybody, including the poor, although it does not necessarily improve the position of the poor in the socioeconomic hierarchy, since the benefits of economic growth are also distributed unequally.

At the same time, the poor subsidize the governmental economy, because many of them pay a higher percentage of their income in taxes than the rest of the population. Although about a third to a half of the poor get welfare benefits and other transfer payments exceeding what they pay in taxes, those who do not get them are thus subsidizing the many state and local governmental programs that serve more affluent taxpayers.[13] The poor who do not get welfare payments also subsidize federal governmental activities, at least in the sense that they help to provide the taxes that are not paid by the rich who receive tax preferences, such as the reduced tax rate for capital gains.[14] In addition, the poor support medical innovation as patients in teaching and research hospitals and as guinea pigs in medical experiments, reducing the risk for the more affluent patients who alone can afford these innovations once they are incorporated into medical practice.

Third, poverty creates jobs for a number of occupations and professions that serve the poor, or shield the rest of the population from them. As already noted, penology would be minuscule without the poor, as would the police, since the poor provide the majority of their "clients." Other activities that flourish because of the existence of poverty are the numbers game, the sale of heroin and cheap wines and liquors, Pentecostal ministers, faith healers, prostitutes, pawnshops, and the peacetime army, which recruits its enlisted men mainly from among the poor.

Fourth, the poor buy goods that others do not want and thus prolong their economic usefulness, such as day-old bread, fruit, and vegetables that would otherwise have to be thrown out, secondhand clothes, and deteriorating automobiles and buildings. They also provide incomes for doctors, lawyers, teachers, and others who are too old, poorly trained, or incompetent to attract more affluent clients.

In addition, the poor perform a number of social and cultural functions:

Fifth, the poor can be identified and punished as alleged or real deviants in order to uphold the legitimacy of dominant norms.[15] The defenders of the desirability of hard work, thrift, honesty, and monogamy need people who can be accused of being lazy, spendthrift, dishonest, and promiscuous to justify these norms, and as Erikson and others following Durkheim have pointed out, the norms themselves are best legitimated by discovering violations.[16]

Whether the poor actually violate these norms more than affluent people is still open to question. The working poor work harder and longer than high-status jobholders, and poor housewives must do more housework to keep their slum apartments clean than their middle-class peers in standard housing. The proportion of cheaters among welfare recipients is considerably lower than among income-tax payers.[17] Violent crime is higher among the poor, but the affluent commit a variety of white-collar crimes, and several studies of self-reported delinquency have concluded that middle-class youngsters can be as delinquent as poor ones. However, the poor are more likely to be caught when participating in deviant acts, and once caught, more likely to be punished than middle-class transgressors. Moreover, they lack the political and cultural power to correct the stereotypes that affluent people hold of them and thus continue to be thought of as lazy, spendthrift, and so on, whatever the empirical evidence, by those who need living proof that deviance does not pay.[18] The actually or allegedly deviant poor have traditionally been described as undeserving, and in more recent terminology, as culturally deprived or pathological.

Sixth, another group of poor, described as deserving because they are disabled or suffering from bad luck, provide the rest of the population with different emotional satisfactions; they evoke compassion, pity, and charity, thus allowing those who help them to feel that they are altruistic, moral, and practicing the Judeo-Christian ethic. The deserving poor also enable others to feel fortunate for being spared the deprivations that come with poverty.[19]

Seventh, as a converse of the fifth function described previously, the poor offer affluent people vicarious participation in the uninhibited sexual, alcoholic, and narcotic behavior in which many poor people are alleged to indulge, and which, being freed from the constraints of affluence and respectability, they are often thought to enjoy more than the middle classes. One of the popular beliefs about welfare recipients is that they are on a continuous sex-filled vacation. Although it may be true that the poor are more given to uninhibited behavior, studies by Lee Rainwater and other observers of the lower class indicate that such behavior is as often motivated by despair as by lack of inhibition, and that it results less in pleasure than in a compulsive escape from grim reality.[20] Whether the poor actually have more sex and enjoy it more than affluent people is irrelevant; as long as the latter believe it to be so, they can share in it vicariously and perhaps enviously when instances are reported in fictional and journalistic or sociological and anthropological formats.

Eighth, poverty helps to guarantee the status of those who are not poor. In a stratified society, where social mobility is an especially important goal and class boundaries are fuzzy, people need quite urgently to know where they stand. As a result, the poor function as a reliable and relatively permanent measuring rod for status comparison, particularly for the working class, which must find and maintain status distinctions between itself and the poor, much as the aristocracy must find ways of distinguishing itself from the *nouveaux riches.*

Ninth, the poor also assist in the upward mobility of the nonpoor, for as William J. Goode has pointed out, "the privileged . . . try systematically to prevent the talent of the less privileged from being recognized or developed."[21] By being denied educational opportunities or being stereotyped as stupid or unteachable, the poor thus enable others to obtain the better jobs. Also, an unknown number of people have moved themselves or their children up in the socio-economic hierarchy through the incomes earned from the provision of goods and services to the poor, as by becoming policemen and teachers, owning "Mom and Pop" stores, or working in the various rackets that flourish in the slums.

In fact, members of almost every immigrant group have financed their upward mobility by providing retail goods and services, housing, entertainment, gambling, and narcotics to later arrivals in America (or in the city), most recently to blacks, Mexicans, and Puerto Ricans. Other Americans, of both European and native origin, have financed their entry into the upper middle and upper classes by owning or managing the illegal institutions that serve the poor, as well as the legal but not respectable ones, such as slum housing.

Tenth, just as the poor contribute to the economic viability of a number of businesses and professions (see function 3 above), they also add to the social viability of noneconomic groups. For one thing, they help to keep the aristocracy busy, thereby justifying its continued existence. "Society" uses the poor as clients of settlement houses and charity benefits, so as to practice its public-mindedness and thus demonstrate its superiority over the *nouveaux riches* who devote themselves to conspicuous consumption. The poor play a similar function for philanthropic enterprises at other levels of the socio-economic hierarchy, including the mass of middle-class civic organizations and women's clubs engaged in volunteer work and fund-raising in almost every American community. Doing good among the poor has traditionally helped the church to find a method of expressing religious sentiments in action; in recent years, militant church activity among and for the poor has enabled the church to hold on to its more liberal and radical members who might otherwise have dropped out of organized religion altogether.

Eleventh, the poor perform several cultural functions. They have played an unsung role in the creation of "civilization," having supplied the construction labor for many of the monuments often identified as the noblest expressions and examples of civilization, for example, the Egyptian pyramids, Greek temples, and medieval churches.[22] Moreover, they have helped to create a goodly share of the surplus capital that funds the artists and intellectuals who make culture, and particularly "high" culture, possible in the first place.

Twelfth, the "low" culture created for or by the poor is often adopted by the more affluent. The rich collect artifacts from extinct folk cultures (though not only from poor ones), and almost all Americans listen to the jazz, blues, spirituals, and country music which originated among the Southern poor — as well as rock, which was derived from similar sources. The protest of the poor sometimes becomes literature; in 1970, for example, poetry written by ghetto children became popular in sophisticated literary circles. The poor also serve as culture heroes and literary subjects, particularly of course for the Left, though the hobo, cowboy, hipster, and mythical prostitute with a heart of gold have performed this function for a variety of groups.

Finally, the poor carry out a number of important political functions:

Thirteenth, the poor serve as symbolic constituencies and opponents for several political groups. For example, parts of the revolutionary left could not exist without the poor, particularly now that the working class can no longer be perceived as the vanguard of the revolution. Conversely, political groups of conservative bent use the "welfare chiselers" and others who "live off the taxpayer's hard-earned money" to justify their demands for reductions in welfare payments and tax relief. Moreover, the role of the poor in upholding dominant norms (see function 5 above) also has a significant political function. An economy based on the ideology of laissez-faire requires a deprived population that is supposedly unwilling to work; not only does the alleged moral inferiority of the poor reduce the moral pressure on the present political economy to eliminate poverty, but redistributive alternatives can be made to look quite unattractive if those who will benefit from them most can be described as lazy, spendthrift, dishonest, and promiscuous. Thus, conservatives and classic liberals would find it difficult to justify some of their political beliefs without the poor — but then, so would modern liberals and socialists who seek to eliminate poverty.

Fourteenth, the poor, being powerless, can be made to absorb the economic and political costs of change and growth in American society. During the 19th century, they did the backbreaking work that built the cities; today, they are pushed out of their neighborhoods to make room for "progress." Urban renewal projects to hold middle-class taxpayers and stores in the city and expressways to enable suburbanites to commute downtown have typically been located in poor neighborhoods, since no other group will allow itself to be displaced. For much the same reason, urban universities, hospitals, and civic centers also expand into land occupied by the poor. The major costs of the industrialization of agriculture in America have been borne by the poor, who are pushed off the land without recompense, just as in earlier centuries in Europe they bore the brunt of the transformation of agrarian societies into industrial ones. The poor have also paid a large share of the human cost of the growth of American power overseas, for they have provided many of the foot soldiers for Vietnam and other wars.

Fifteenth, the poor have played an important role in shaping the American political process; because they vote and participate less than other groups, the political system has often been free to ignore them. This has not only made American politics more centrist than would otherwise be the case, but it has also added to the stability of the political process for the rest of the population. If the 12% of Americans below the federal poverty line participated fully in the political process, they would almost certainly demand better jobs and higher incomes, which would require some income redistribution and would thus generate further political conflict between the haves and the have-nots. Moreover, when the poor do participate, they often provide the Democrats with a captive constituency, for they can rarely support Republicans, lack parties of their own, and thus have no other place to go politically. This in turn has enabled the Democrats to count on their votes, allowing the party to be more responsive to voters who might otherwise switch to the Republicans.

Functional Alternatives for Poverty

I have described fifteen of the more important functions that the poor carry out in American society, enough to support the functionalist thesis that poverty survives in part because it is useful to a number of groups in society. This analysis is not intended to suggest that because it is functional, poverty *should* persist, or that it *must* persist. Whether or not it should persist is a normative question; whether it must, an analytic and empirical one; but the answer to both depends in part on whether the dysfunctions of poverty outweigh the functions. Obviously, poverty has many dysfunctions, mainly for the poor themselves, but also for the more affluent. For example, the social order of the affluent is upset by the pathology, crime, political protest, and disruption emanating from the poor, and their income is affected by the taxes that must be levied to protect their social order. Whether or not the dysfunctions outweigh the functions is a question that clearly deserves more study.

It is, however, possible to suggest alternatives for many of the functions of the poor. Thus, society's dirty work (function 1) could be done without poverty, some by automating it, the rest by paying the workers who do it decent wages, which would help considerably to cleanse that kind of work. Nor is it necessary for the poor to subsidize the activities they support through their low-wage jobs (function 2), for like dirty work, many of these activities are essential enough to persist even if wages were raised. In both instances, however, costs would be driven up, resulting in higher prices to the customers and clients of dirty work and subsidized activity, with obvious dysfunctional consequences for more affluent people.

Alternative roles for the professionals who flourish because of the poor (function 3) are easy to suggest. Social workers could counsel the affluent, as most prefer to do anyway, and the police could devote themselves to traffic and organized crime. Fewer penologists would be employable, however, and Pentecostal religion would probably not survive without the poor. Nor would parts of the secondhand and thirdhand market (function 4), although even affluent people sometimes buy used goods. Other roles would have to be found for badly trained or incompetent professionals now relegated to serving the poor, and someone else would have to pay their salaries.

Alternatives for the deviance-connected social functions (functions 5-7) can be found more easily and cheaply than for the economic functions. Other groups are already available to serve as deviants to uphold traditional morality — entertainers, hippies, and most recently, adolescents in general. These same groups are also available as alleged or real orgiasts to provide vicarious participation in sexual fantasies. The disabled already function as objects of pity and charity, and the poor may therefore not even be needed for functions 5-7.

The status and mobility functions of the poor (functions 8 and 9) are far more difficult to replace. In a hierarchical society, some people must be defined as inferior to everyone else with respect to a variety of attributes, and the poor perform this function more adequately than others. They could, however, perform it without being as poverty-stricken as they are, and one can conceive of a stratification system in which the people below the federal poverty line would receive 60% of the median income rather than 40% or less, as is now the case — even though they would still be last in the pecking order.[23] Needless to say, such a reduction of economic inequality would also require income redistribution. Given the opposition to

income redistribution among more affluent people, however, it seems unlikely that the status functions of poverty can be eliminated, and these —
together with the economic functions of the poor, which are equally expensive to replace—may turn out to be the major obstacles to the elimination of
poverty.

The role of the poor in the upward mobility of other groups could be
maintained without their being so low in income. However, if their incomes
were raised above subsistence levels, they would begin to generate capital
so that their own entrepreneurs could supply them with goods and services,
thus competing with and perhaps rejecting "outside" suppliers. Indeed, this
is already helping in a number of ghettos, where blacks are replacing white
storeowners.

Similarly, if the poor were more affluent, they would make less willing
clients for upper-class and middle-class philanthropic and religious groups
(function 10), though as long as they are economically and otherwise unequal, this function need not disappear altogether. Moreover, some would
still use the settlement houses and other philanthropic institutions to pursue
individual upward mobility, as they do now.

The cultural functions (11 and 12) may not need to be replaced. In
America, the labor unions have rarely allowed the poor to help build
cultural monuments anyway, and there is sufficient surplus capital from
other sources to subsidize the unprofitable components of high culture.
Similarly, other deviant groups are available to innovate in popular culture
and supply new culture heroes.

Some of the political functions of the poor would be as difficult to
replace as their economic and status functions. Although the poor could
probably continue to serve as symbolic constituencies and opponents (function 13) if their incomes were raised while they remained unequal in other
respects, increases in income are generally accompanied by increases in
power as well. Consequently, once they were no longer so poor, people
would be likely to resist paying the costs of growth and change (function
14), and it would be difficult to find alternative groups who could be
displaced for urban renewal and technological "progress." Of course, it is
possible to design city rebuilding and highway projects that properly reimburse the displaced people, but such projects would then become considerably more expensive, thus raising the price for those now benefitting
from urban renewal and expressways. Alternatively, many might never be
built, thus reducing the comfort and convenience of those beneficiaries.
Similarly, if the poor were subjected to less economic pressure, they would
probably be less willing to serve in the army, except at considerably higher
pay, in which case war would become yet more costly and thus less popular
politically. Alternatively, more servicemen would have to be recruited from
the middle and upper classes, but this also would make war less popular.

The political stabilizing and "centering" role of the poor (function 15)
probably cannot be substituted for at all, since no other group is willing to
be disenfranchised or likely enough to remain apathetic so as to reduce the
fragility of the political system. Moreover, if the poor were given higher incomes, they would probably become more active politically, thus adding
their demands to those of other groups already putting pressure on the

political allocators of resources. They might remain loyal to the Democratic party, but like other moderate-income voters, they might also be attracted to the Republicans or to third parties. While improving the economic status of the currently poor would not necessarily drive the political system far to the left, it would enlarge the constituencies now demanding higher wages and more public funds. The currently poor could also be replaced by new poor immigrants from Europe and elsewhere, who could serve as non-participating "ballast" in the polity, at least until they became sufficiently Americanized to demand a participatory role.

In sum, then, several of the most important functions of the poor cannot be replaced with alternatives, while some could be replaced but almost always only at higher costs to other people, particularly more affluent ones. Consequently, *a functional analysis must conclude that poverty persists not only because it satisfies a number of functions but also because many of the functional alternatives to poverty would be quite dysfunctional for the more affluent members of society.*[24]

Radical Functional Analysis

I noted earlier that functional analysis had itself become a maligned phenomenon and that a secondary purpose of this chapter was to demonstrate its continued usefulness. One reason for its present low status is political; insofar as an analysis of functions, particularly latent functions, seems to justify what ought to be condemned, it appears to lend itself to the support of conservative ideological positions, although it can also have radical implications when it subverts the conventional wisdom. Still, as Merton has pointed out, functional analysis per se is ideologically neutral,[25] and "like other forms of sociological analysis, it can be infused with any of a wide range of sociological values."[26] This infusion depends, of course, on the purposes — and even the functions — of the functional analysis, for as Louis Wirth suggested long ago, "every assertion of a 'fact' about the social world touches the interests of some individual or group."[27] and even if functional analyses are conceived and conducted in a neutral manner, they are rarely interpreted in an ideological vacuum.

In one sense, my analysis is neutral: if one makes no judgment as to whether poverty ought to be eliminated — and if one can subsequently avoid being accused of acquiescing in poverty — then the analysis suggests only that poverty persists because it is useful to many groups in society.[28] If one favors the elimination of poverty, however, then the analysis can have a variety of political implications, *depending in part on how completely it is carried out.*

If functional analysis only identifies the functions of social phenomena without mentioning their dysfunctions, then it may, intentionally or otherwise, agree with or support holders of conservative values. Thus, to say only that the poor perform many functions for the rich might be interpreted or used to justify poverty, just as Davis and Moore's argument that social stratification is functional because it provides society with highly trained professionals could be taken to justify inequality.[29]

Actually, the Davis and Moore analysis was conservative because it was incomplete; it did not identify the dysfunctions of inequality and failed to suggest functional alternatives, as Tumin and Schwartz have pointed out.[30] Once a functional analysis is made more nearly complete by the addition of functional alternatives, it can take on a liberal reform cast, because the alternatives often provide ameliorative policies that do not require any drastic change in the existing social order, although radical functional alternatives are also possible.

Even so, to make functional analysis complete requires yet another step, an examination of the functional alternatives themselves. My analysis suggests that the alternatives for poverty are themselves dysfunctional for the affluent population, and it ultimately comes to a conclusion not very different from that of radical sociologists. To wit: *that social phenomena which are functional for affluent groups and dysfunctional for poor ones persist; that if the elimination of such phenomena through functional alternatives generates dysfunctions for the affluent, these phenomena will continue to persist; and that phenomena like poverty can be eliminated only when they either become sufficiently dysfunctional for the affluent (for example, by high crime rates making their lives miserable even in the suburbs), or when the poor can obtain enough power to change the system of social stratification.*[31]

The Functions of Inequality

The observations about the functions of poverty also apply to inequality; it too has positive functions for many individuals and groups, which must be replaced by functional alternatives if inequality is to be reduced. Moreover, such functional alternatives would hurt the groups that now benefit from inequality, and they can only come into being when the dysfunctions of inequality become so great as to motivate its beneficiaries to reduce it, or when the victims of inequality can obtain power — either to reduce it or to shift it to another group in society.

The functions of inequality are, however, much harder to identify than those of poverty, for inequality is more pervasive than poverty, and it exists in many different ways and at different levels of the socio-economic hierarchy. Thus, inequality between the upper and upper middle classes has different functions than that between the upper and lower classes, or that between parents and their children. Consequently, a functional analysis of the myriad kinds of inequality would require a book of its own, and this chapter can only serve as a model for such an analysis.

Like poverty, inequality has economic, social, cultural, and political functions. Its most important economic functions are to maintain the existing division of labor and to sort people into the existing roles, filling roles for which the supply of labor exceeds the demand by justifying lower wages, and filling those where the supply is insufficient to meet the demand by paying higher ones. At the same time, inequality functions to block access to the most rewarded roles by setting up various obstacles to people's competing for them. For example, it would be inconceivable for a poor man to run for president. In addition, inequality provides a method of rationing scarce resources, frequently by giving them to those who already have them.

Inequality also creates work for a number of occupations that enable people either to cope with inequality and some of its more deleterious consequences. For example, various secular and sacred forms of therapy serve patients who have been hurt by inequality, and religion exists in part because it provides a respected moral code — or another world — in which equality or justice and fairness prevail.

Inequality is of course tautologous with the class hierarchy, but insofar as upward mobility satisfies ego needs for striving and self-fulfillment, providing people with easily visible goals toward which to aspire, it is perhaps the most important noneconomic function of inequality. As for cultural functions, inequality not only helps to create cultural diversity, because differences of income and education result in differences of taste, but it also provides raw material for culture itself, for a great deal of both serious and popular fiction — in the printed, electronic, and visual media — is concerned with coming to grips with inequality, describing its workings, and healing its wounds. Finally, inequality has important political functions, for insofar as politics has to do with the allocation of scarce resources, it could not exist without inequality. In a completely egalitarian society, there would be less need for politicians to determine who gets what, since most resources would be allocated on egalitarian principles.

This brief set of observations cannot do justice to the functions of inequality. For one thing, it has focused only on inequalities of income and power. A more comprehensive analysis would have to deal with the functions of age inequality, which maintains the existence of schools and all other child-rearing agencies that enable young people to become adults but also make sure that the primacy of adult authority and knowledge is upheld; and with the functions of racial, sexual, and all other kinds of inequality.

Whether functional alternatives for inequality can be developed is an open question; indeed, answering this question is a major task for egalitarian policy. Like those of poverty, the various psychological and cultural functions of inequality can perhaps be replaced or at least diverted to less harmful forms, for example, by replacing money and power as goals of upward mobility with competition for excellence in leisure. The economic, social, and political functions of inequality are much harder to substitute for, again because their replacement would be dysfunctional for those who benefit from it. Nor is it realistic to imagine that inequality would ever become so dysfunctional that its beneficiaries would act to abolish it, although it is more realistic to imagine that the unequal would try to obtain political power to reduce it. The poor are too small a minority to have much hope of drastically increasing their power, even by revolutionary means, but the less-than-equal are a much larger proportion of the population however inequality is measured, and if the trends I describe in Part I accelerate, it is possible that functional alternatives for some kinds of inequality will have to be found.

NOTES

1. Robert K. Merton, "Manifest and Latent Functions," in his *Social Theory and Social Structure* (Glencoe, Ill.: Free Press, 1949), pp. 21-82, quote at p. 49, and in subsequent editions.

2. This essay also has the latent function, as S.M. Miller has suggested, of contributing to the long debate over the functional analysis of social stratification presented by Kingsley Davis and Wilbert Moore, "Some Principles of Stratification," *American Sociological Review*, Vol. 10 (April 1945), pp. 242-49.

3. Merton, "Manifest and Latent Functions," p. 50.

4. *Ibid.*, p. 51.

5. *Ibid.*

6. Probably one of the few instances in which a phenomenon has the same function for two groups with different interests is when the survival of the system in which both participate is at stake. Thus, a wage increase can be functional for labor and dysfunctional for management (and consumers), but if the wage increase endangers the firm's survival, it is dysfunctional for labor as well. This assumes, however, that the firm's survival is valued by the workers, which may not always be the case, for example when jobs are available elsewhere.

7. In his 1949 article, Merton described functions and dysfunctions in terms of encouraging or hindering adaptation or adjustment to a system, although subsequently he has written that "dysfunction refers to the particular inadequacies of a particular part of the system for a designated requirement" ("Social Problems and Sociological Theory," in Robert K. Merton and Robert Nisbet, eds., *Contemporary Social Problems*, New York: Harcourt, Brace & Co., 1961, p. 732). Since adaptation and adjustment to a system can have conservative ideological implications, Merton's later formulation and my own definitional approach make it easier to use functional analysis as an ideologically neutral or at least ideologically variable method, insofar as the researcher can decide whether he or she supports the values of the group under analysis.

8. It should be noted, however, that there are no absolute benefits and costs, just as there are no absolute functions and dysfunctions; not only are one group's benefits often another group's costs, but every group defines benefits by its own manifest and latent values, and a social scientist or planner who has determined that certain phenomena provide beneficial consequences for a group may find that the group thinks otherwise. For example, during the 1960s, advocates of racial integration discovered that a significant portion of the black community no longer considered it a benefit but saw it rather as a policy to assimilate blacks into white society and to decimate the political power of the black community.

9. Merton, "Manifest and Latent Functions," pp. 32-36.

10. On the economic functions of the poor and of welfare, see Frances F. Piven and Richard A. Cloward, *Regulating the Poor* (New York: Pantheon Books, 1971).

11. Of course, the poor do not actually subsidize the affluent. Rather, by being forced to work for low wages, they enable the affluent to use the money saved in this fashion for other purposes. The concept of subsidy used here thus assumes belief in a "just wage."

12. T. H. Marshall, "Poverty and Inequality," unpublished paper prepared for a project on stratification and poverty of the American Academy of Arts and Sciences, n.d., p. 7.

13. Joseph A. Pechman, "The Rich, the Poor, and the Taxes They Pay," *The Public Interest*, No. 17 (Fall 1969), pp. 21-44, especially p. 33.

14. For an estimate of how these tax preferences affect different income groups, see Joseph A. Pechman, and Benjamin A. Okner, "Individual Tax Erosion by Income Classes," paper prepared for the United States Joint Economic Committee, January 14, 1972.

15. David Macarov, *Incentives to Work* (San Francisco: Jossey-Bass, Publishers, 1970), pp. 31-33. See also Lee Rainwater, "Neutralizing the Disinherited," in Vernon Allen, ed., *Psychological Factors in Poverty* (Chicago: Markham Pub. Co., 1970), pp. 9-28.

16. Kai T. Erikson, "Notes on the Sociology of Deviance," in Howard S. Becker, ed., *The Other Side: Perspectives on Deviance* (New York: Free Press, 1964), pp. 9-22.

17. Most official investigations of welfare cheating have concluded that less than 5% of recipients are on the rolls illegally, while it has been estimated that about a third of the population cheats in filing income tax returns.

18. Although this chapter deals with the functions of poverty for other groups, poverty has often been described as a motivating or character-building device for the poor themselves, and economic conservatives have argued that by generating the incentive to work, poverty encourages the poor to escape poverty.

19. A psychiatrist has even proposed the fantastic hypothesis that the rich and the poor are engaged in a sadomasochistic relationship, the latter being supported financially by the former so that they can gratify their sadistic needs. Joseph Chernus, "Cities: A Study in Sadomasochism," *Medical Opinion and Review*, May 1967, pp. 104-9.

20. Lee Rainwater, *Behind Ghetto Walls* (Chicago: Aldine Publishing Co., 1970).

21. William J. Goode, "The Protection of the Inept," *American Sociological Review*, Vol. 32 (February 1967), pp. 5-19, quotation at p. 5.

22. Although this is not a contemporary function of poverty in America, it should be noted that today these monuments serve to attract and gratify American tourists.

23. Of course, most of the poor earn less than 40% of the median, and about a third of them, less than 20% of the median.

24. Or as Bruno Stein puts it: "If the non-poor make the rules . . . antipoverty efforts will only be made up to the point where the needs of the non-poor are satisfied, rather than the needs of the poor." *On Relief* (New York: Basic Books, 1971), p. 171.

25. Merton, "Manifest and Latent Functions," p. 43, and "Social Problems and Sociological Theory," pp. 736-37.

26. Merton, "Manifest and Latent Functions," p. 40.

27. Louis Wirth, Preface to Karl Mannheim, *Ideology and Utopia* (New York: Harcourt, Brace & Co., 1936), p. xvii.

28. Even in this case the analysis need not be purely neutral, but can be put to important policy uses, for example by indicating more effectively than moral attacks on poverty the exact nature of the obstacles that must be overcome if poverty is to be eliminated. See also Merton, "Social Problems and Sociological Theory," pp. 709-12.

29. Davis and Moore, "Some Principles of Stratification."

30. Melvin M. Tumin, "Some Principles of Stratification: A Critical Analysis," *American Sociological Review*, Vol. 18 (August 1953), pp. 387-93; Richard D. Schwartz, "Functional Alternatives to Inequality," *American Sociological Review*, Vol. 20 (August 1955), pp. 424-30. Functional analysis can of course be conservative in value or have conservative implications for a number of other reasons, principally in its overt or covert comparison of the advantages of functions and disadvantages of dysfunctions, or in its attitudes toward the groups that are benefitting and paying the costs. Thus, a conservatively inclined policy researcher could conclude that the dysfunctions of poverty far outnumber the functions, but still decide that the needs of the poor are simply not as important or worthy as those of other groups, or of the country as a whole.

31. On the possibilities of radical functional analysis, see Merton, "Manifest and Latent Functions," pp. 40-43, and Alvin Gouldner, *The Coming Crisis of Western Sociology* (New York: Basic Books, 1970), p. 443. One difference between my analysis and the prevailing radical view is that most of the functions I have described are latent, whereas many radicals treat them as manifest: recognized and intended by an unjust economic system to oppress the poor. Practically speaking, however, this difference may be unimportant, for if unintended and unrecognized functions were recognized, many affluent people might then decide that they ought to be intended as well, so as to forestall a more expensive antipoverty effort that might be dysfunctional for them.

The Poor*

GEORG SIMMEL   *Translated by Claire Jacobson†*

Insofar as man is a social being, to each of his obligations there corresponds a right on the part of others. Perhaps even the more profound conception would be to think that originally only rights existed; that each individual has demands which are of a general human character and the result of his particular condition, and which afterward become the obligations of others. But since every person with obligations in one way or another also possesses rights, a network of rights and obligations is thus formed, where right is always the primary element that sets the tone, and obligation is nothing more than its correlate in the same act and, indeed, an inevitable correlate.

Society in general may be regarded as a reciprocity of beings endowed with moral, legal, conventional, and many other kinds of rights. If these rights imply obligations for others, this is simply, so to speak, a logical or technical consequence; and if the unimaginable should happen — that is to say, if it were possible to satisfy every right in such a way that it would not imply the fulfillment of an obligation — society would in no way need the category of obligation. With a radicalism that certainly does not correspond to psychological reality but which could be developed in the sense of an ethical-ideal construction, one could interpret all the prestations of love and compassion, of generosity and religious impulse, as *rights* of the beneficiary. Ethical rigorism has already asserted, in the fact of all these motivations, that the highest to which a man can aspire is to do his duty and that the fulfillment of duty requires by definition precisely that which a self-adulatory way of thinking considers a merit above duty. One more step from this ethical rigorism, and behind every duty of the person with an obligation, there is the right of the claimant; indeed, this seems to be the ultimate and most rational foundation on which the mutual prestations of men may be based.

A fundamental opposition between the sociological and ethical categories manifests itself here. Inasmuch as all relations of prestation are derived from a *right* — in the widest sense of this concept which includes, among other elements, legal right — the relationship between man and man has totally imbued the moral values of the individual and determined his

*Reprinted with the permission of Arnold Simmel and The Society for the Study of Social Problems, from *Social Problems*, Vol. XIII, No. 2, pp. 118-140.

†Translated from Georg Simmel, "Der Arme," Chapter 7 in *Soziologie: Untersuchungen über die Formen der Vergesellschaftung*, Leipzig: Duncker and Humblot, 1908, pp. 454-493. I wish to thank Professor Juan J. Linz for his invaluable assistance in the preparation of this translation.

course. However, in contrast to the undoubted idealism of this point of view, there is the no less deeply based rejection of any interindividual genesis of duty. Our duties (from this standpoint) — it is said — are duties only toward ourselves and there are no others. Their content may be the conduct toward other men, but their form and motivation as duty do not derive from others, but are generated with full autonomy by the self and its own purely internal demands, being independent of anything that lies outside of it. It is only in the case of right that the other is the *terminus a quo* of motivation in our moral actions, but for morality itself he is no more than the *terminus ad quem*. In the final analysis, we ourselves are the only ones responsible for the morality of our acts; we are responsible for them only to our better selves, to our self-esteem, or whatever we wish to call this enigmatic focus which the soul finds in itself as the final judge that decides freely up to what point the rights of others are obligations.

This fundamental dualism in the basic sentiments which govern the course of moral action is exemplified or empirically symbolized by various conceptions that exist in relation to assistance to the poor. The obligations we have toward the poor may appear as a simple correlate of the rights of the poor. Especially in countries where begging is a normal occupation, the beggar believes more or less naively that he has a right to alms and frequently considers that their denial means the withholding of a tribute to which he is entitled. Another and completely different characteristic — in the same category — implies the idea that the right to assistance is based on the group affiliation of the needy. One point of view according to which the individual is merely the product of his social milieu confers upon that individual the right to solicit from the group compensation for every situation of need and every loss. But even if such an extreme dissolution of individual responsibility is not accepted, one may stress, from a social viewpoint, that the rights of the needy are the basis of all assistance to the poor. For only if we assume such rights, at least as a socio-legal fiction, does it appear possible to protect public assistance from arbitrariness and dependence upon a chance financial situation or other uncertain factors. Everywhere the predictability of functions is improved whenever in the correlation between the rights and obligations that underlie them right constitutes the methodological point of departure; for man, in general, is more easily disposed to demand a right than to fulfil an obligation.

To this may be added the humanitarian motive of making it easier for the poor person to request and accept assistance, when by doing so he only exercises his due right; for the humiliation, shame, and *déclassement* that charity implies are overcome for him to the extent that it is not conceded out of compassion or sense of duty or utility, but because he can lay claim to it. Since this right naturally has limits, which must be determined in each individual case, the right to assistance will not modify these motivations in the material quantitative aspect with respect to other motivations. By making it a right, its inner meaning is determined and is raised to a fundamental opinion about the relationship between the individual and other individuals and between the individual and the totality. The right to assistance belongs in the same category as the right to work and the right to life. It is true in this case that the ambiguity of the quantitative limits, which characterizes this as well as other "human rights," reaches its maximum, especially if assistance is in cash; for the purely quantitative and relative character of money makes it much more difficult objectively to de-limit requests than assistance in kind — except in complex or highly individualized cases in which the poor person may make a more useful and fruitful application of money than of assistance in kind, with its providential character.

It is also unclear to whom the rights of the poor ought to be addressed, and the solution of this question reveals very deep sociological differences. The poor person who perceives his condition as an injustice of the cosmic order and who asks for redress, so to speak, from the entire creation will easily consider any individual who is in better circumstances than he jointly liable for his claims against society. This leads to a scale which goes from the delinquent proletarian who sees in any welldressed person an enemy, a representative of the "exploiting" class who can be robbed in good conscience, to the humble beggar who asks for charity "for the love of God," as though each individual had the obligation of filling the holes of the order which God desired but has not fully implemented. The poor man addresses his demands in this case to the individual; however, not to a specific individual, but to the individual on the basis of the solidarity of mankind. Beyond this correlation which allows any particular individual to appear as a representative of the totality of existence with respect to the demands directed to that totality, there are multiple particular collectivities to which the claims of the poor are addressed. The State, municipality, parish, professional association, circle of friends, family, may, as total entities, maintain a variety of relationships with their members; but each of these relationships appears to include an element which is manifested as the right to assistance in the event of impoverishment of the individual. This characteristic is the common element of such sociological relationships, although in other respects they are of highly heterogeneous character. The rights of the poor which are generated by such ties are curiously mixed under primitive conditions, where the individual is dominated by the tribal customs and religious obligations that constitute an undifferentiated unity. Among the ancient Semites, the right of the poor to participate in a meal is not associated with personal generosity, but rather with social affiliation and with religious custom. Where assistance to the poor has its *raison d'être* in an organic link between elements, the *rights* of the poor are more highly emphasized, whether their religious premise derives from a meta-physical unity or their kinship or tribal basis from a biological unity. We will see, on the contrary, that when assistance to the poor derives teleologically from a goal one hopes to pursue in this way, rather than from the casual basis of a real and effective unity among all the members of the group, the rights of the poor dwindle to nothingness.

In the cases examined so far, a right and an obligation seemed to be two aspects of an absolute relationship. Completely new forms appear, however, when the point of departure is the obligation of the giver rather than the right of the recipient. In the extreme case, the poor disappear completely as legitimate subjects and central foci of the interests involved. The motive for alms then resides exclusively in the significance of giving for the giver. When Jesus told the wealthy young man, "Give your riches to the poor," what apparently mattered to him were not the poor, but rather the soul of the wealthy man for whose salvation this sacrifice was merely a means or symbol. Later on, Christian alms retained the same character; they represent no more than a form of asceticism, of "good works," which improve the chances of salvation of the giver. The rise of begging in the Middle Ages, the senseless distribution of alms, the demoralization of the proletariat through arbitrary donations contrary to all creative work, all these phenomena constitute the revenge, so to speak, that alms take for the purely subjectivistic motive of their concession — a motive which concerns only the giver but not the recipient.

As soon as the welfare of society requires assistance to the poor, the motivation turns away from this focus on the giver without, thereby, turning to the recipient. This assistance then takes place voluntarily or is imposed by law, so that the poor will not become active and dangerous enemies of society, so as to make their reduced energies more productive, and so as to prevent the degeneration of their progeny. The poor man as a person, and the perception of his position in his own mind, are in this case as indifferent as they are to the giver who gives alms for the salvation of his own soul. In this case, the subjective egoism of the latter is overcome not for the sake of the poor, but for the sake of society. The fact that the poor receive alms is not an end-in-itself but merely a means to an end, the same as in the case of the man who gives alms for the sake of his salvation. The predominance of the social point of view with reference to alms is shown in the fact that the giving can be refused from that same social point of view, and this frequently happens when personal compassion or the unpleasantness of refusing would move us strongly to give.

Assistance to the poor, as a public institution, thus has a unique sociological character. It is absolutely personal; it does nothing but alleviate individual needs. In this respect, it differs from other institutions which pursue public welfare and security. These institutions attempt to fulfill the needs of all citizens: the army and police, the schools and public works, the administration of justice and the Church, popular representation and the pursuit of science are not, in principle, directed toward persons considered as differentiated individuals, but rather toward the totality of these individuals; the unity of many or all is the purpose of these institutions. Assistance to the poor, on the other hand, is focused in its concrete activity on the individual and his situation. And indeed this individual, in the abstract modern type of welfare, is the *final* action but in no way the *final purpose*, which consists solely in the protection and furtherance of the community. The poor cannot even be considered as a *means* to this end — which would improve their position — for social action does not make use of them, but only of certain objective material and administrative means aimed at suppressing the dangers and losses which the poor imply for the common good. This formal situation is not only valid for the total collectivity, but also for smaller circles. Even within the family there are many acts of assistance, not for the sake of the recipient himself, but so that the family need not be ashamed and lose its reputation owing to the poverty of one of its members. The aid which English trade unions grant to their unemployed members does not purport so much to alleviate the personal situation of the recipient as to prevent that the unemployed, prompted by necessity, would work more cheaply and that this should result in lower wages for the entire trade.

If we take into consideration this meaning of assistance to the poor, it becomes clear that the fact of taking away from the rich to give to the poor does not aim at equalizing their individual positions and is not, even in its orientation, directed at suppressing the social difference between the rich and the poor. On the contrary, assistance is based on the structure of society, whatever it may be; it is in open contradiction to all socialist and communist aspirations which would abolish this social structure. The goal of assistance is precisely to mitigate certain extreme manifestations of social differentiation, so that the social structure may continue to be based on this differentiation. If assistance were to be based on the interests of the poor person, there would, in principle, be no limit whatsoever on the transmission of property in favor of the poor, a transmission that would lead to the equality of all. But since the focus is the social whole — the political, family, or other sociologically determined circles — there is no reason to aid the person more than is required by the maintenance of the social *status quo.*

When this purely social and centralist teleology prevails, assistance to the poor offers perhaps the greatest sociological tension between the direct and the indirect goals of an action. The alleviation of personal need is emotionally so categorical an end-in-itself, that to deprive it of this ultimate purpose and to convert it into a mere technique for the transsubjective ends of a social unit constitutes a significant triumph for the latter. This distantiation between the individual and the social unit — despite its lack of visibility — is more fundamental and radical in its abstractness and coldness than sacrifices of the individual for the collectivity in which the means and the ends tend to be bound together by a chain of sentiments.

This basic sociological relationship explains the peculiar complications of rights and duties which we find in modern assistance to the poor by the State. Frequently we find the principle according to which the State has the obligation to assist the poor, but to this obligation there is no corresponding right to assistance on the part of the poor. As has been expressly declared in England for example, the poor person has no recourse to action for unjust refusal of assistance, nor can he solicit compensation for illegally refused assistance. All the relations between obligations and rights are located, so to speak, above and beyond the poor. The right which corresponds to the obligation of the State to provide assistance is not the right of the poor, but rather the right of every citizen that the taxes he pays for the poor be of such a size and applied in such a manner that the public goals of assistance to the poor be truly attained. Consequently, in the case of negligence in assistance to the poor, it would not be the poor who are entitled to take action against the State, but rather the other elements indirectly harmed by such negligence. In case it should be possible, for instance, to prove that a thief might not have carried out a robbery if the legal assistance requested by him had been granted, it would in principle be the robbed one who would be entitled to claim compensation from the welfare administration. Assistance to the poor holds, in legal teleology, the same position as the protection of animals. No one is punished in Germany for torturing an animal, except if he does it "publicly or in a manner that results in scandal." It is not, therefore, consideration for the mistreated animal but rather for the witnesses that determines punishment.

This exclusion of the poor, which consists in denying them the status of a final end in the teleological chain and, as we have seen, does not even permit them to stand there as a means, is also manifested in the fact that within the modern relatively democratic State public assistance is perhaps the *only* branch of the administration in which the interested parties have no participation whatsoever. In the conception to which we are referring, assistance to the poor is, in effect, an application of public means to public ends; and, since the poor find themselves excluded from its teleology — something that is not the case for the interested parties in other branches of administration — it is logical that the principle of self-government, which is recognized to a varying degree in other matters, should not be applied to the poor and to their assistance. When the State is obligated by a law to channel a stream to provide irrigation for certain districts, the stream is approximately in the situation of the poor supported by the State: it is the object of obligation but is not entitled to the corresponding right, which is rather that of the adjacent property holders. And every time that this centralist interest prevails, the relationship between right and obligation may be altered for the sake of utilitarian considerations. The projected Poor Law of 1842 in Prussia asserts that the State must organize assistance to the poor in the interest of public prosperity. With this objective, it creates legal public bodies which are obligated to the State to assist needy individuals; but they are not so obligated to the latter since these have no legal claim.

This principle acquires an extreme character when the law imposes upon well-to-do relatives of the poor an obligation of support. It would appear at first sight that in this case the poor hold over their well-to-do relatives a *claim* which the State merely secures and makes effective. The inner meaning is, however, a different one. The political community cares for the poor for utilitarian reasons, and gets compensation from the relatives because the cost of assistance would be excessive, or so it considers it. The law does not take into account any immediate obligation of person to person, for example between a wealthy brother and a poor brother; this obligation is purely moral. The law is concerned only with serving the interests of the community, and it does this in two ways: by assisting the poor and by collecting from relatives the cost of assistance. This is, in effect, the sociological structure of the laws pertaining to support. They do not simply purport to give a legally binding form to moral obligations. This is shown in facts like the following. Undoubtedly, the moral obligation of assistance between brothers is a strong imperative. Nonetheless, when in the first draft of the German Civil Code an attempt was made to give it legal sanction, the explanatory reasons acknowledged the extraordinary harshness of such an obligation, but stated that otherwise the cost of public assistance would be too high. This became manifest in the fact that on occasions the legal quota of maintenance exceeds anything that might be required from an individual and moral point of view. The German Imperial Court of Justice sentenced an old man to give up all his possessions — a few hundred marks — for the maintenance of a disabled son, although he argued on plausible grounds that he too would be disabled and that this money was his sole resource. It is very doubtful that one can speak in this case of a moral right on the part of the son. But such a right does not concern the collectivity; the only thing it asks is whether it may have recourse to the relatives in order to impose upon them its obligation toward the poor, in accordance with the general norms.

This internal meaning of the obligation to provide support is also symbolized by the manner in which it is carried out in practice. First, the poor man at his request is assisted, and then a search is made for a son or a father who, eventually and in accordance with his economic situation, is sentenced to pay not the entire cost of assistance but perhaps one half or one third. The exclusively social meaning of the legal rule appears also in the fact that the obligation to provide maintenance, according to the German Civil Code, only occurs when it does not "jeopardize" the "status-adequate maintenance" of the person so obligated. It is at least debatable whether in certain cases assistance is not morally obligatory, even when it adds up to the amounts mentioned above. But the collectivity, nonetheless, renounces such demands in all cases, because the downward mobility of an individual from his "status-adequate" position would result in harm to the status structure of society which would appear to transcend in social importance the material advantages derived from forcing him to that contribution. Consequently, the obligation of assistance does not include a right of the poor person *vis-à-vis* his well-to-do relatives. The obligation of assistance is no more than the general obligation of the State, but transferred to the relatives and without any correspondence to any action or claim whatsoever of the poor person.

The image of a channeled stream which we used previously was, however, inaccurate. For the poor are not only poor, they are also citizens. *As such*, they participate in the rights which the law grants to the totality of citizens, in accordance with the obligation of the State to assist the poor. To use the same image, let us say that the poor are at the same time the stream and the adjacent landowner, in the same sense as the wealthiest citizens could be. Undoubtedly, the functions of the State, which formally stand at the same ideal distance from all citizens, have, insofar as content is concerned, very different connotations, in accordance with the different positions of citizens; and though the poor participate in assistance, not as subjects with their own ends but merely as members of the teleological organization of the State which transcends them, their role in that function of the State, however, is distinct from that of well-to-do citizens.

What matters sociologically is to understand that the special position which the assisted poor occupy does not impede their incorporation into the State as members of the total political unit. This is so despite the fact that their overall situation makes their individual condition the external endpoint of a helping act and, on the other hand, an inert object without rights in the total goals of the State. In spite of, or better yet, because of these two characteristics which appear to place the poor outside the State, the poor are ordered organically within the whole, belong as poor to the historical reality of society which lives in them and above them, and constitute a formal sociological element, like the civil servant or the taxpayer, the teacher or the intermediary in any interaction. The poor are approximately in the situation of the stranger to the group who finds himself, so to speak, materially outside the group in which he resides. But precisely in this case a large total structure emerges which comprises the autochthonous parts of the group as well as the stranger; and the peculiar interactions between them create the group in a wider sense and characterize the true historical circle. Thus the poor are located in a way outside the group; but this is no more than a peculiar mode of interaction which binds them into a unity with the whole in its widest sense.

It is only with this conception that we resolve the sociological antinomy of the poor, which reflects the ethical-social difficulties of assistance. The solipsist tendency of the medieval type of almsgiving of which I spoke by-passed internally, so to say, the poor to whom the action was directed externally; in so doing, it neglected the principle according to which man must never be treated exclusively as a means but always as an end. In principle, the one who receives alms also gives something; there is a diffusion of effects from him to the giver and this is precisely what converts the donation into an interaction, into a sociological event. But if — as in the case previously cited — the recipient of alms remains completely excluded from the teleological process of the giver, if the poor fulfill no role other than being an almsbox into which alms for Masses are tossed, the interaction is cut short and the donation ceases to be a social fact in order to become a purely individual fact.

As we were saying, neither does the modern conception of assistance to the poor consider the poor as ends-in-themselves; but nevertheless, according to it, the poor, although they are located in a teleological series which bypasses them, are an element which belongs organically to the whole and are — on the basis given — closely related to the goals of the collectivity. Certainly neither now nor in the medieval form does their reaction to the donation fall to any specific individual; but by rehabilitating their economic activity, by preserving their bodily energy, by preventing their impulses from leading them to the use of violent means to enrich themselves, the social collectivity gets from the poor a reaction to what it has done to them.

A purely individual relationship is sufficient from the ethical point of view and perfect from the sociological point of view only when each individual is an end for the other — although naturally not merely an end. But this cannot be applied to the actions of a transpersonal collective entity. The teleology of the collectivity may quietly pass by the individual and return to itself without resting on him. From the moment the individual belongs to this whole he is placed thereby, from the beginning, at the final point of action and not, as in the other case, outside of it. Although he is denied as individual the character of an end-in-itself, he participates as member of the whole in the character of an end-in-itself which the whole always possesses.

A long time before this centralist conception of the essence of assistance to the poor became clear, its organic role in the life of the collectivity was revealed through visible symbols. In old England, assistance to the poor was exercised by monasteries and ecclesiastical corporations, and the reason for this, as has been duly noted, is that only the property of mortmain possesses the indispensable permanence on which assistance to the poor necessarily depends. The numerous secular donations derived from booties and penances did not suffice to attain this end, because they were not yet sufficiently integrated into the administrative system of the State and they were consumed without lasting results. Assistance to the poor then became based on the only substantial and fixed point in the midst of social chaos and turmoil; and this connection is shown negatively by the indignation aroused by the clergy sent from Rome to England, because it neglected assistance. The foreign priest does not feel intimately related to the life of the community; and the fact that he does not care for the poor appears as the clearest sign of this lack of connection.

This same link of assistance with the firm substratum of social existence appears clear in the later tie established in England between the poor tax and landed property; and this was cause as much as effect of the fact that the poor counted as an organic element of the land, belonging to the land. The same tendency is manifested in 1861, when part of the welfare charges were legally transferred from the parish to the welfare association. The costs of assistance to the poor were no longer to be carried in isolation by parishes, but rather by a fund to which the parishes contributed in relation to the value of their landed property. The proposition that in order to make a distribution the number of inhabitants should also be taken into consideration was repeatedly and expressly rejected; with it, the individualistic element was completely excluded. A suprapersonal entity, with its substratum in the objectivity of landed property, and not a sum of persons, appeared as the carrier of the obligation to assist the poor. Assistance in this case is so basic to the social group that the local administration only gradually added to this main activity, first the administration of schools and roads, and then public health and the system of registration. Elsewhere, also, the welfare administration has become a basis of political unity because of its success. The North German Confederation decided that in all of the territory of the Confederation no needy person should remain without assistance and that none of the poor in the Confederation should receive a different treatment in one region than in another. If in England external and technical reasons contributed to establish a link between assistance to the poor and landed property, this connection does not lose its profound sociological meaning when the addition of other branches of administration to public assistance institutions led to the crossing of county boundaries by the welfare associations despite the technical disadvantages involved. It is precisely this contradiction in the technical conditions which makes the unity of sociological meaning even more conspicuous.

Consequently, the conception that defines assistance to the poor as an "organization of the propertied classes in order to fulfill the sentiment of moral duty which is associated with property" is completely onesided. Assistance is rather a part of the organization of the *whole*, to which the poor belong as well as the propertied classes. It is certain that the technical and material characteristics of their social position make them a mere object or crossing point of a superior collective life. But, in the final analysis, this is the role that each concrete individual member of society performs; about which one can say, in accordance with the viewpoint temporarily accepted here, what Spinoza says of God and the individual: that we may love God, but that it would be contradictory that He, the whole which contains us, should love us, and that the love which we dedicate to Him is a part of the infinite love with which God loves Himself. The singular exclusion to which the poor are subjected on the part of the community which assists them is characteristic of the role which they fulfill *within* society, as members of it in a special situation. If technically they are mere ojbects, in turn in a wider sociological sense they are subjects who, on the one hand, like all the others, constitute social reality and, on the other hand, like all the others, are located beyond the abstract and suprapersonal unity of society.

Owing to this also it is the general structure of the group that decides the question: Where do the poor belong? If they still exercise any economic activity at all, they belong to the segment of the general economy that includes them. If they are members of a church, they belong to it, insofar as it does not coincide with another group. If they are members of a family, they belong to the personally and spatially defined circle of their realtives. But if they are no more than poor, where do they belong? A society maintained or organized on the basis of tribal consciousness includes the poor within the circle of their tribe. Other societies, whose ethical connections are fulfilled essentially through the Church, will turn the poor over to one or another type of pious associations, which are the answer of the society to the fact of poverty. The explanatory reasons of the German law of 1871 on place of residence for assistance answer this question in the following manner: the poor belong to that community — that is, that community is obligated to assist them — which utilized their economic strength before their impoverishment. The principle just mentioned is a manifestation of the social structure which existed prior to the complete triumph of the idea of the modern State, since the municipality is the place which enjoyed the economic fruits of those who are now impoverished. But the modern mobility, the interlocal exchange of all forces, have eliminated this limitation; so that the whole State must be considered the *terminus a quo* and *ad quem* of all prestations. If the laws actually permit everybody to establish his residence in whatever community he wishes, then the community no longer has an integrated relationship with its inhabitants. If there is no right to oppose establishment of residence on the part of undesirable elements, one can no longer demand of the community a solidary give-and-take relationship with the individual. Only for practical reasons, and then only as organs of the State — thus read the explanatory reasons of the legislation — do the municipalities have the obligation to take over the care of the poor.

This is, then, the extreme condition which the formal position of the poor has attained, a condition in which their dependence on the general level of social evolution is revealed. The poor belong to the largest effective circle. No part of the totality but the totality itself, to the extent that it constitutes a unit, is the place or power to which the poor as poor are linked. It is only for this circle, which, being the largest, has no other outside it to which to transfer an obligation, that a problem pointed out by the practitioners of welfare in the small corporative entities ceases to exist; the fact that they frequently avoid giving assistance to the poor, for fear that once they have taken care of them they will always have them on their hands. We see manifested here a very important characteristic for human sociation, a trait which might be called moral induction: when an act of assistance has been performed, of whatever type, although it be spontaneous and individual and not demanded by any obligation, there is a duty to continue it, a duty which is not only a claim on the part of the one who receives the assistance but also a sentiment on the part of the one who gives. It is a very common experience that the beggars to whom alms are given with regularity consider these very rapidly as their right and as the duty of the giver, and if the latter fails in this supposed obligation they interpret it as a denial of their due contribution and feel a bitterness which they would not feel against someone who always denied them alms. There is also the person in better circumstances who has supported for some time a needy person, fixing in advance the period for which he will do so, and who, however, when he stops his gifts, is left with a painful feeling, as if he were guilty. With full consciousness, this fact is recognized by a Talmudic law of the ritual code "Jore Deah": he who has assisted three times a poor person with the same amount, although he had in no way the intention of continuing the assistance, tacitly acquires the obligation of continuing it; his act assumes the character of a vow, from which only weighty reasons can dispense him, such as, for example, his own impoverishment.

The case just mentioned is much more complicated than the related principle, homologous to *odisse quem laeseris*, which says that one loves the one to whom he has done good. It is understandable that one projects the satisfaction of his own good action on the one who has given him the opportunity for it: in the love for the one for whom he has made sacrifices he loves in essence himself, just as in the hate against the one to whom he has done an injustice he hates himself. The sense of obligation that the good action leaves in the doer of good, that particular form of *noblesse oblige*, cannot be explained with so simple a psychology. I believe that, in effect, an *a priori* condition is involved here: that each action of this type — despite its apparent free will, despite its apparent character of *opus supererogationis* — derives from an obligation; that in such behaviour a profound obligation is implicit which, in a certain way, is manifested and made visible through action. What happens here is the same as in scientific induction: if the similarity is accepted between a past process and a future one, it is not simply because the first one has this or that structure, but because a *law* can be derived from the first process that determines in the same way as it determines any other future process. There must be, therefore, a moral instinct which tells us that the first act of charity already corresponded to an obligation which also demands the second no less than the first action. This is clearly related to the motives which we touched on at the beginning of this study. If, in the final analysis, any altruism, any good action, any self-sacrifice, is nothing but a duty and an obligation, this principle may, in the individual case, be manifested in such a form that any act of assistance is, in its profound sense — if one wishes, from the viewpoint of a metaphysics of ethics — the mere fulfillment of a duty which, naturally, is not exhausted with the first action but rather continues to exist as long as the determining occasion obtains. According to this, assistance given to someone would be the *ratio cognoscendi*, the sign which makes us see that one of the ideal lines of obligation between man and man runs here and reveals its timeless aspect in the continuing effects of the bond established.

We have seen so far two forms of the relation between right and obligation: the poor have a *right* to assistance; and there exists an *obligation* to assist them, an obligation which is not oriented toward the poor as having a right, but toward society to whose preservation this obligation contributes and which the society demands from its organs or from certain groups. But along with these two forms there exists a third, which probably dominates the moral consciousness: the collectivity and well-to-do persons have the obligation to assist the poor, and this obligation has its sufficient goal in the alleviation of the situation of the poor; to this there corresponds a right of the poor, as the correlative end of the purely moral relation between the needy and the well-to-do. If I am not mistaken, the emphasis has shifted within this relation since the 18th century. The ideal of humanitarianism and of the rights of man, mostly in England, displaced the centralist spirit of the Elizabethan Poor Law, according to which work had to be provided for the poor for the benefit of the community. The ideal of humanitarianism substituted for this principle another one: every poor person has a right to minimal subsistence, whether he wants and is able to work or not. On the other hand, modern assistance, in the correlation between moral duty (of the giver) and moral right (of the recipient) prefers to emphasize the former. Evidently, this form is realized above all by private assistance, in contrast to public assistance. We are attempting now to determine its sociological significance in this sense.

First, we should point out here the already noted tendency to consider assistance to the poor as a matter pertaining to the widest political circle (the State), while initially it was based everywhere in the local community. This ascription of assistance to the smallest circle was, first of all, a consequence of the corporative ties that bound the community. As long as the supraindividual organism around and above the individual had not changed from the municipality to the State and freedom of mobility had not completed this process factually and psychologically, it was the most natural thing in the world for neighbors to assist needy persons. To this may be added an extremely important circumstance for the sociology of the poor: that of all the social claims of a non-individualistic character based on a general quality, it is that of the poor which most impresses us. Laying aside acute stimuli, such as accidents or sexual provocations, there is nothing such as misery that acts with such impersonality, such indifference, with regard to the other qualities of the object and, at the same time, with such an immediate and effective force. This has given at all times to the obligation of assisting the poor a specific *local* character. Rather, to centralize it in the largest circle and thereby to bring it about not by immediate visibility but only through the general concept of poverty — this is one of the longest roads which sociological forms have had to travel to pass from the immediate sensate form to the abstract.

When this change occurred, whereby assistance to the poor became an abstract obligation of the State — in England in 1834, in Germany since the middle of the 19th century — its character was modified with respect to this centralizing form. Above all, the State maintains in the municipality the obligation to participate in assistance, but considers the municipality as its delegate; local organization has been made into a mere technique in order to attain the best result possible; the municipality is no longer the point of departure, but rather a point of transmission in the process of assistance. For this reason welfare associations are organized everywhere according to principles of utility — for example, in England, they are organized in such a fashion that each of them may support a workhouse — and they have the deliberate tendency to avoid the partiality of local influences. The growing employment of salaried welfare officials works in the same way. These officials stand *vis-à-vis* the poor much more clearly as representatives of the collectivity from which they receive a salary than do the unpaid officials who work, so to speak, more as human beings and attend not so much to the merely objective point of view as to the human, man-to-man point of view. Finally, a sociologically very important division of functions takes place. The fact that assistance to the poor is still essentially delegated to the municipalities is especially useful for two reasons; first, because every case must be handled individually, something that can only be done by someone close at hand and with intimate knowledge of the milieu, and second because if the municipality has to grant assistance it also has to provide the money, since it might otherwise hand out the funds of the State too freely. On the other hand, there are cases of need in which bureaucratic handling is not a threat, since action can be determined on the basis of objective criteria: sickness, blindness, deaf-mutism, insanity, chronic illness. In these cases, assistance has a more technical character and consequently the State, or the larger institution, is much more efficient. Its greater abundance of means and its centralized administration show their advantages in those cases where personal and local circumstances have little importance. And aside from the qualitative determination of the direct prestations of the State, there is the quantitative determination that particularly differentiates public from private assistance: the State and, in general, public organizations attend only to the most urgent and immediate needs. Everywhere and particularly in England, assistance is guided by the firm principle that only the minimum necessary for the life of the poor should leave the purse of the taxpayers.

All this is intimately related to the character of collective actions in general. A collectivity which comprises the energies or interests of many individuals can only take into account their peculiarities, when there is a structure with a division of labor whose members are assigned different functions. But when it is necessary to perform a united action, whether through a direct organ or a representative organ, the content of this action can only include that minimum of the personal sphere that coincides with everybody else's. It follows, in the first place, that when expenses are incurred in the name of the collectivity, no more may be spent than what the most thrifty of its members would spend. A community which is acting closely together may allow itself to be moved by an impetus of overpowering generosity; but when the will of each individual is not directly known, but has to be inferred by means of representatives, it must be assumed that no one wants to spend more than the strictly necessary. This is not, of course, an unshakable logical necessity — for the contrary thesis would not constitute a logical contradiction — but it corresponds to a psychological dogma which, by the enormous number of its empirical confirmations, has acquired the practical value of the logically demonstrable.

Mass action has the character of a minimum, owing to its need to reach the lowest level of the intellectual, economic, cultural, aesthetic, etc. scale. The law which is valid for all has been designated as the ethical minimum; the logic which is valid for all is the intellectual minimum; the "right to work," postulated for all, can only be extended to those whose quality represents a minimum; affiliation to a party in principle demands that one accept the minimum of beliefs without which it would not exist. This type of social minimum is perfectly expressed in the negative character of collective processes and interests.[1]

Consequently, the fact that the prestation of the total community in favor of the poor is limited to a minimum is entirely in accordance with the typical character of collective actions. The motive for this — that such an action has as its basis only that which can be assumed with certitude in each individual — is also the second reason for this behavior: the fact that assistance to the poor, limited to a minimum, has an *objective* character. It is possible to determine objectively with fair accuracy what is necessary to save a man from physical breakdown. All that exceeds this minimum, all assistance aimed at a positive rise in level, requires less clear criteria and depends on subjective judgments of quantity and quality. I said before that cases of subjectively not-very-differentiated need, and, therefore, not requiring subjective evaluation, are the ones best adapted to State assistance — particularly cases of illness and physical infirmity — while those which have a more individual character are better assigned to the narrower local community. This objective determinability of the need, which favors the intervention of the widest group, is present when assistance is limited to the minimum. We see here again the old epistemological correlation between universality and objectivity. In the field of knowledge, real universality, the acknowledgement of a proposition by the totality of minds — not historical-real, but ideal — is an aspect or expression of the objectivity of this proposition; on the other hand, there may be another proposition which is, for one or many individuals, absolutely certain and possesses the full significance of truth, but lacks this special stamp which we call objectivity. Thus, in practice, one can only in principle request a prestation from the totality on an absolutely objective basis. When the basis is to be judged only subjectively and there is no possibility of a purely objective determination, the demand may be no less pressing and its fulfillment no less valuable, but it will be directed only toward individuals; the fact that it refers to purely individual circumstances requires correspondingly that it be fulfilled by mere individuals.

If the objective point of view goes hand in hand with the tendency to turn over all assistance to the State — a tendency which certainly until now has nowhere been fully realized — the normative measure, whose logical application implies objectivity, is derived not only from the poor but also from the interest of the State. We see manifested here an essential sociological form of the relationship between the individual and the totality. Wherever prestations or interventions are transferred from individuals to society, regulation by the latter tends to be concerned either with an excess or with a deficiency in individual action. In compulsory education the State requires that the individual should not learn too little, but leaves it up to him whether to learn more or even "too much." With the legal workday, the State provides that the employer should not require too much from his workers, but leaves it up to him whether to ask for less. Thus this regulation always refers only to one side of the action, while the other side is left to the freedom of the individual. This is the scheme within which our socially controlled actions appear; they are limited only in one of their dimensions; society, on the one side, sets limits to their excess or deficiency, while on the other side their deficiency or excess is left to the indefiniteness of subjective choice. But this scheme sometimes deceives us; there are cases in which social regulation includes in fact *both* sides, although practical interest only focuses attention on one side and overlooks the other. Wherever, for example, the private punishment of a crime has been transferred to society and objective criminal law, one only takes into account, as a rule, that thereby one acquires greater certainty in retribution, that is, a sufficient degree and certitude in its application. But, in reality, the goal pursued is not only to punish enough, but also not to punish too much. Society not only protects the person who has suffered damage, but also the criminal against the excess of subjective reaction; that is to say, society establishes as an objective measure of punishment that which corresponds to its social interest and not to the desires or interests of the victim. And this occurs not only in relations which are legally established. Any social class which is not too low sees to it that its members spend a minimum on their clothing; establishes a standard of "decent" dress; and the one who does not attain this standard will no longer belong to that class. But it also establishes a limit at the other extreme, although not with the same determination nor in such a conscious manner; a certain measure of luxury and elegance and even at times modernity is not proper, indeed, for this or that group, and he who over-reaches this upper limit is treated on occasion as not belonging fully to the group. Thus the group does not allow the freedom of the individual to expand completely in this second direction, but rather it sets an objective limit to his subjective choice, that is to say, a limit required by supraindividual life conditions. This fundamental form is repeated whenever the community takes over assistance to the poor. While apparently it seems to have an interest only in setting a lower limit to assistance, that is, in seeing to it that the poor should receive the part to which they are entitled — in other words, that they should not receive too little — there is also the other consideration: that the poor should not receive too much. This latter consideration is in practice less significant. The disadvantage of private assistance lies not only in the "too little," but also in the "too much," which leads to laziness, uses the available means in an economically unproductive way, and arbitrarily favors some at the expense of others. The subjective impulse to do good sins in both directions and, although the danger of excess is not as great as that of deficiency, an objective norm — which determines a standard that is not derived from the subject but from the interest of the collectivity — is directed against that danger of excess.

The transcendence of the subjective point of view is as valid for the recipient as for the giver. English public assistance, by intervening only when there is an objectively determined absolute lack of means, renounces the investigation as to whether a person deserves assistance. This is so because the workhouse is such an unpleasant experience that no one except in extreme need, would choose it, and consequently the lack of means is objectively determined. For this reason its complement is private assistance, which is directed to a specific worthy individual and which can select individually, since the State already cares for the most urgent needs. The task of private assistance consists in rehabilitating the poor, who are already protected from starvation, and in curing need, for which the State offers only a temporary alleviation. It is not need as such, the *terminus a quo*, that determines the task of private assistance, but rather the ideal of creating independent and economically productive individuals. The State operates in a casual sense, private assistance in a teleological sense. To put it in other words: the State assists poverty; private assistance assists the poor. A sociological difference of the greatest importance becomes manifest here. Abstract concepts, which crystalize certain elements of a complex individual reality, often acquire life and consequences for practice which would appear to fit only the concrete totality of the phenomenon. This may be seen in very intimate relationships. The meaning of certain erotic relationships cannot be understood in any other way than that one of the parties seeks not the beloved, but love, often with notable indifference toward the individuality of the lover. This is so because what is wished by this person is to receive the emotional value — love — in and by itself. In religious relationships it often seems that the only essential thing is that there should exist a certain kind and a certain quantity of generosity, while its carriers are indifferent; the behavior of the priest or the relation of the faithful to the community is determined only by this general consideration, without taking into account the particular motives which produce and color this sentiment in the individual. In this case there is no particular interest in those individuals, since they only matter as carriers of that impersonal fact or rather they do not matter at all. In the social and ethical perspective there is a rationalism which demands that the interaction of people should be based on absolute subjective truthfulness. Everyone may require the truth as an objective quality of any statement made to him, without taking into consideration the particular circumstances or special qualifications of the statement; there can be no right to truth modified in an individual way by those qualifications or circumstances. The truth, and not the speaker or the listener in their individuality, is the assumption, content, and value of group interaction. The same problem is also the basis of divergences among criminologists. Is the punishment directed at the crime or at the criminal? An abstract objectivism demands punishment because a crime has occurred which requires a reinstatement of the violated real or ideal order. It demands punishment based on the logic of ethics, as a consequence of the impersonal fact of the crime. But, from another point of view, only the guilty subject should be punished; the reaction of punishment results not because the crime has occurred as something objective, but because a subject who expressed himself in the criminal act requires expiation, education, and control. For these reasons, in the degree of punishment, the individual circumstances of the case will have to be taken into account to the same extent as the general fact of the crime.

This twofold attitude may also be adopted with respect to poverty. It is necessary to start from poverty as an objectively determined phenomenon and to attempt to eliminate it as such. Whoever the poor may be and whatever the individual causes that produce it and the individual consequences it produces, poverty requires assistance, compensation for this social deficiency. But, on the other hand, interest may be directed to the poor person, who is assisted unquestionably because he is poor, not for the purpose of eliminating poverty in general *pro rata*, but rather to help this particular poor person. His poverty operates here as an individual and specific characteristic; it serves as the immediate occasion for being concerned with him; but the individual as a whole should be put into such a situation that poverty would disappear by itself. For this reason assistance derived from the first attitude is directed more to the fact of poverty; and assistance derived from the second attitude, on the other hand, to its cause. Incidentally, it is of sociological importance to observe that the natural distribution of the two types of assistance between the State and private individuals is modified as soon as one follows up the casual chain one step further. The State — in England more clearly than elsewhere — meets externally visible need; private assistance attends to its individual causes. But the fundamental economic and cultural circumstances which create those personal conditions can only be changed by the collectivity. The task of changing those circumstances in such a way that they should offer the least chance for impoverishment due to individual weaknesses, unfavorable propensities, misfortune, or mistakes belongs to the collectivity. Here, as in many other respects, the collectivity, its circumstances, interests, and actions, surrounds and affects the individual in his specificity. The collectivity represents a kind of immediate reality to which the elements contribute their own existence, the results of their own life. But, on the other hand, it is also the ground in which individual life grows, a ground in which it grows in such a way that the diversity of individual proclivities and situations contributes an endless variety of unique and colorful manifestations to that overall reality.[2]

The principle that governs assistance to the poor in England and which led us to these generalizations is the direct opposite of the French one. In

France, assistance to the poor is incumbent upon private associations and persons, and the State only intervenes when these are insufficient. This inversion naturally does not mean that in France private persons would take care of the most pressing needs (like the State in England), while the State would handle what exceeds this minimum and is individually desirable (like private persons in England). What the French principle actually implies is that the two levels of assistance cannot, insofar as content is concerned, be separated as clearly and fundamentally as in England. For this reason, in practice, the condition of the poor will frequently be the same in both countries. But it is obvious that in terms of sociological principles there is a fundamental difference. We are dealing here with a particular case of the larger process, by virtue of which the direct interaction which obtains among the elements of the group becomes an action of the unitary and supraindividual community; once this has happened, constant compensations, substitutions, and changes in priority result between both types of social arrangements. Should this tension or social disharmony which is manifested as individual poverty be directly resolved among the elements of society or through the unity formed by all the elements? This is a question which has to be decided in a formally similar way for every aspect of society, even though it is only rarely posed with such clarity and purity as here. This is mentioned here only so that we should not forget to what extent "private" assistance is also a social phenomenon, a sociological form, which no less definitely attributes to the poor a position as organic members of group life — something that may escape superficial observation. This fact acquires particular clarity by virtue of the transitional forms between both levels; on the one hand, the poor tax, and, on the other, the legal obligation of assistance to poor relatives. As long as a special poor tax exists, the relationship between the collectivity and the poor does not have the abstract purity which places the poor in a direct relationship with the whole as an indivisible unity; the State is only the intermediary that channels the no longer voluntary individual contributions to their beneficiaries. As soon as the poor tax becomes part of the general tax obligation and the resources of assistance are drawn from the general income of the State or municipality, this relationship between the total community and the poor has reached its full development; assistance to the poor becomes a function of the totality as such, and not of the sum of individuals, as in the case of the poor tax. When the law requires the assistance of needy relatives, the interest of the totality is expressed in even more specialized terms. Private assistance, which in all other cases is also affected by the structure and teleology of the collectivity, here in a conscious over-emphasis is dominated by it.

We said above that the relationship between the collectivity and its poor contributes to the formation of society in a formal sense as much as the relationship between the collectivity and the civil servant or the taxpayer. We are going to develop this assertion from the point of view which we have just reached in our discussion. We compared above the poor person with the stranger, who also finds himself *confronted* by the group. But this "being confronted" implies a specific *relationship* which draws the stranger into group life as an element of it. Thus the poor person stands undoubtedly *outside* the group, inasmuch as he is a mere object of the actions of the collectivity; but being outside, in this case, is only, to put it briefly, a particular form of being inside. All this occurs in society in the same way as, in the Kantian analysis, spatial separateness occurs in consciousness; even though in space everything is separate and the subject, too, as perceiver, is outside of the other things, the space itself is "in me" in the subject, in the wider sense. If we consider things more closely, this twofold position of the poor — as well as that of the stranger — can be found in all elements of the group with mere variations of degree. However much an individual may contribute positively to group life, however much his personal life may be tied with social life and submerged in it, he also stands *vis-à-vis* that totality: giving or receiving, treated well or poorly by it, feeling inwardly or only outwardly committed to it; in short, as part or as object in relation to the social group as subject, to which he nevertheless belongs as a member, as a part-subject, through the very relationships based on his actions and circumstances. This twofold position, which appears logically difficult to explain, is a completely elementary sociological fact.

We have already seen this in such simple structures as marriage. Each of the spouses, in certain situations, sees the marriage as an independent structure distinct from himself, confronting him with duties and expectations, good things and bad, which proceed not from the other spouse as a person, but from the whole that makes each of its parts an object, in spite of the fact that the whole consists only of these parts. This relationship, this fact of finding oneself simultaneously within and without, becomes more and more complicated and more and more visible as the number of members of the group increases. And this is true not only because the whole then acquires an independence that dominates the individual, but because the most marked differentiations among individuals lead to a whole scale of nuances in this twofold relationship. The group has a special and different relationship with respect to the prince and the banker, the society woman and the priest, the artist and the civil servant. On the one hand, it makes the person into an object, it "handles" him differently, it subjects him or recognizes him as a power standing against power. On the other hand, the group incorporates him as an element of its life, as a part of the whole, which in turn stands in contrast to the other elements. This is perhaps a completely unitary attitude of social reality, which manifests itself separately in these two directions or which appears different from these two distinct viewpoints: comparably, a particular representation stands with respect to the soul, so distinct from it that it can be influenced by the total mood — colored, heightened or toned down, formed or dissolved — while at the same time it is still an integral part of that whole, an element of the soul, of that soul which consists only of the co-existence and interlocking of such representations. In that scale of relationships with the collectivity the poor occupy a well-defined position. Assistance, to which the community is committed in its own interest, but which the poor person in the large majority of cases has no right to claim, makes the poor person into an object of the activity of the group and places him at a distance from the whole, which at times makes him live as a *corpus vile* by the mercy of the whole and at times, because of this, makes him into its bitter enemy. The State expresses this by depriving those who receive public alms of certain civic rights. This separation, however, is not absolute exclusion, but a very specific relationship with the whole, which would be different without this element. The collectivity, of which the poor person is a part, enters into a relationship with him, confronting him, treating him as an object.

These norms, however, do not appear to be applicable to the poor in general but only to some of them, those who receive assistance, while there are poor who do not receive assistance. This leads us to consider the relative character of the concept of poverty. He is poor whose means are not sufficient to attain his ends. This concept, which is purely individualistic, is narrowed down in its practical application in the sense that certain ends may be considered as independent of any arbitrary and purely personal decision. First, the ends which nature imposes: food, clothing, shelter. But one cannot determine with certainty the level of these needs, a level that would be valid in all circumstances and everywhere and below which, consequently, poverty exists in an absolute sense. Rather, each milieu, each social class has typical needs; the impossibility of satisfying them means poverty. From this derives the banal fact that in all advanced civilizations there are persons who are poor within their class and would not be poor within a lower class, because the means they have would be sufficient to satisfy the typical ends of that class. Undoubtedly, it may happen that a man who is really poor does not suffer from the discrepancy between his means and the needs of his class, so that poverty in the psychological sense does not exist for him; just as it may also happen that a wealthy man sets himself goals higher than the desires proper to his class and his means, so that he feels psychologically poor. It may be, therefore, that individual poverty — insufficiency of means for the ends of a person — does not exist for someone, while social poverty exists; and it may be, on the other hand, that a man is individually poor while socially wealthy. The relativity of poverty does not refer to the relation between individual means and actual individual ends, but to the status-related ends of the individual, to a social *a priori* which varies from status to status. The relationship between individual means and actual ends, on the other hand, is something absolute, independent in its basic meaning from anything outside of the individual. It has a very significant sociohistorical difference *which* level of needs each group considers as a zero point above which or below which wealth or poverty begins. In a somewhat complex civilization there is always a margin, often a considerable one, to determine this level. In relation to this problem there are many important sociological differences; for example: the relationship of this zero point to the *real average*; whether it is necessary to belong to the favored minority in order not to be considered poor or whether a class, out of an instinctive utilitarian criterion to prevent the growth of feelings of poverty, sets the boundary below which poverty begins very low; or whether an individual case can modify the boundary, as for example the moving into a small town or into a closed social circle of a wealthy person; or whether the group holds on rigidly to the boundary set between rich and poor.

A result of poverty's being found within all social strata, which have created a typical level of needs for each individual, is that often poverty is not susceptible to assistance. However, the principle of assistance is more extensive than what its official manifestations would indicate. When, for example, within a large family the poorer and richer members give one another presents, the latter take advantage of a good opportunity to give the former a value which exceeds the value of what they have received; and not only that, but also the quality of presents reveals this character of assistance: *useful* objects are given to the poorer relatives, that is, objects which help them to maintain themselves within the level of their class. For this reason, presents from a sociological point of view turn out to be completely different in the various social classes. The sociology of the gift coincides in part with that of poverty. In the gift it is possible to discover a very extensive scale of reciprocal relationships between men, differences in the content, motivation, and manner of giving as well as in that of accepting the gift. Gift, theft, and exchange are the external forms of interaction which are directly linked with the question of ownership and from which an endless wealth of psychological phenomena that determine the sociological process are derived. They correspond to the three motives of action: altruism, egoism, and objective norms; the essence of exchange is in the substitution of some values by others which are objectively equal, while subjective motives of goodness or greed are eliminated since in the pure concept of exchange the value of the object is not measured by the desire of the individual but by the value of the other object. Of these three forms, gift is that which offers the greatest wealth of sociological situations, because here the intention and position of the giver and of the recipient are combined in the most varied ways with all their individual nuances.

Of the many categories which make possible, so to speak, a systematic ordering of these phenomena, the most important for the problem of poverty seem to be the following basic alternatives. On the one hand, does the meaning and purpose of the gift consist in the final condition achieved by it, in the fact that the recipient will have a valuable specific object, or, on the other hand, does it consist in the action itself, in the gift as the expression of the giver's intention, of a love desirous of sacrifice, or of a reaching out of the self which is manifested more or less arbitrarily by the gift? In the latter case, the process of giving is, so to say, its own ultimate end and the question of wealth or poverty evidently plays no role whatever, except in terms of the practical problem of what people can afford. But when the one to whom one gives is a *poor man*, the emphasis is not on the process but on its results: the main thing is that the poor person receives something. Between these two extremes of the concept of gift there are innumerable mixed forms. The more the latter type predominates in its purest form, the more impossible it often is to give the poor person what he lacks in the form of a gift, because the other sociological relationships between individuals are incongruent with that of giving. The gift is almost always possible when a great social distance intervenes or when a great personal intimacy prevails; but it becomes difficult to the extent that social distance decreases or personal distance increases. In the upper classes, the tragic situation frequently occurs in which the needy person would willingly accept assistance and he who is in a well-to-do position would also willingly grant it; but neither can the former ask for it nor the latter offer it. In the higher classes the economic *a priori*, below which poverty begins, is set in such a way that this poverty very rarely occurs and is even excluded in principle. The acceptance of assistance thus excludes the assisted person from the premises of his status and provides visible proof that the poor person is formally *déclassé*. Until this happens, class prejudice is strong enough to make poverty, so to say, invisible; and until then poverty is individual suffering, without social consequences. All the assumptions on which the life of the upper classes is based determine that a person may be poor in an individual sense, that is, that his resources may be insufficient for the needs of his class, without his having to recur to assistance. For this reason, no one is socially poor until he has been assisted. And this has a general validity: sociologically speaking, poverty does not come first and then assistance — this is rather fate in its personal form — but a person is called poor who receives assistance or should receive it given his sociological situation, although per-chance he may not receive it.

The social-democratic assertion that the modern proletarian is definitely poor but not a *poor man* fits this interpretation. The poor, as a sociological category, are not those who suffer specific deficiencies and deprivations, but those who receive assistance or should receive it according to social norms. Consequently, in this sense, poverty cannot be defined in itself as a quantitative state, but only in terms of the social reaction resulting from a specific situation; it is analogous to the way crime, the substantive definition of which offers such difficulties, is defined as "an action punished by public sanctions." Thus today some do not determine the essence of morality on the basis of the inner state of the subject but from the result of his action; his subjective intention is considered valuable only insofar as it normally produces a certain socially useful effect. Thus too, frequently, the concept of personality is not defined by an inner characteristic that qualifies the individual for a specific social role, but on the contrary, those elements of society that perform a specific role are called personalities. The individual state, in itself, no longer determines the concept, but social teleology does so; the individual is determined by the way in which the totality that surrounds him acts toward him. Where this occurs, we find a certain continuation of modern idealism, which does not attempt to define things by an essence inherent to them, but by the reactions that occur in the subject with respect to them. The binding function which the poor person performs within an existing society is not generated by the sole fact of being poor; only when society — the totality or particular individuals — reacts toward him with assistance, only then does he play his specific social role.

This social meaning of the "poor man," in contrast to the individual meaning, makes the poor into a kind of estate or unitary stratum within society. The fact that someone is poor does not mean that he belongs to the specific social category of the "poor." He may be a poor shopkeeper, artist or employee but he remains in this category, which is defined by a specific activity or position. In this category he may occupy, as a consequence of his poverty, a gradually modified position; but the individuals who, in different statuses and occupations, are in this state are not grouped in any way into a particular sociological whole different from the social stratum to which they belong. It is only from the moment they are assisted — perhaps already when their total situation would normally require assistance, even though it has not yet been given — that they become part of a group characterized by poverty. This group does not remain united by interaction among its members, but by the collective attitude which society as a whole adopts toward it. However, an explicit tendency toward sociation has not always been lacking. Thus in the 14th century, for example, there was in Norwich a *Poorman's Gild,* and in Germany the so-called "guilds of the miserables." Some time later we find in the Italian cities a party of the wealthy, of the *Optimates* as they called themselves, whose members were united only by the fact of their wealth. Similar unions of the poor soon became impossible because with the growing differentiation of society, the individual differences in education and ideas, in interests and background, among those who might have belonged to the unions were too great to lend to such groups the necessary strength for true sociation.

It is only when poverty implies a positive *content,* common to many poor, that an association of the poor, as such, arises. Thus, the result of the extreme phenomenon of poverty, the lack of shelter, is that those who find themselves in such a situation in the large cities congregate in specific places of refuge. When the first stacks of hay arise in the vicinity of Berlin, those who lack shelter, the *Penner,* go there to take advantage of the opportunity to spend a comfortable night. One finds among them a type of incipient organization, whereby the *Penner* of each district have a kind of headman who assigns to the members of the district their places in the night shelter and arbitrates their quarrels. The *Penner* scrupulously see to it that no criminal infiltrates them, and, when this happens, they denounce him to the police to whom they often render good services. The headmen of the *Penner* are well-known persons whom the authorities always know how to find when they need information about some obscure character. Such a specification of poverty, as the lack of shelter implies, is necessary today to contribute an element of association. Moreover, one may note that the increase of general prosperity, the greater police vigilance and, above all, social conscience which, with a strange mixture of good and bad motives, "cannot tolerate" the sight of poverty, all contribute to impose on poverty increasingly the tendency to hide. And this tendency to hide logically isolates the poor increasingly from one another and prevents them from developing any feeling of belonging to a stratum, as was possible in the Middle Ages.

The class of the poor, especially in modern society, is a unique sociological synthesis. It possesses a great homogeneity insofar as its meaning and location in the social body is concerned; but it lacks it completely insofar as the individual qualification of its elements is concerned. It is the common end of the most diverse destinies, an ocean into which lives derived from the most diverse social strata flow together. No change, development, polarization, or breakdown of social life occurs without leaving its residuum in the stratum of poverty. What is most terrible in poverty is the fact that there are human beings who, in their social position, are just poor and nothing but poor. This is different from the simple fact of being just poor which each one has to face for himself and which is merely a shade of another individually qualified position. The fact of being just poor and nothing but poor is particularly apparent where expanding and indiscriminate almsgiving prevails, such as during the Christian Middle Ages and in Islamic lands. However, so long as one accepted it as an official and unchangeable fact, it did not have the bitter and contradictory character which the progressive and activistic tendency of modern times imposes on a whole class: a class which bases its unity on a purely passive characteristic, specifically the fact that the society acts toward it and deals with it in a particular way. To deprive those who receive alms of their political rights adequately expresses the fact that they are nothing but poor. As a result of this lack of positive qualification, as has already been noted, the stratum of the poor, notwithstanding their common situation, does not give rise to sociologically unifying forces. In this way, poverty is a unique sociological phenomenon: a number of individuals who, out of a purely individual fate, occupy a specific organic position within the whole; but this position is not determined by this fate and condition, but rather by the fact that others — individuals, associations, communities — attempt to correct this condition. Thus, what makes one poor is not the lack of means. The poor person, sociologically speaking, is the individual who receives assistance because of this lack of means.

NOTES

1. There is a digression here on the negative character of collective behavior which makes no specific reference to poverty. It has been translated by Kurt H. Wolff in *The Sociology of Georg Simmel* (New York: The Free Press, 1964 [paperback edition; 1st edition, 1950]. pp. 396-401. [Translator's note.]

2. Simmel uses a footnote to expound his basic conception of the relationship between the individual and the social, without any specific reference to the topic at hand. Since this footnote states in metaphorical and highly abstract terms ideas much better presented at length in his basic theoretical writings, we decided to leave it out. [Translator's note.]

III

Sources of Variation: The Political Economy of Inequalities

Introduction

In its most simplistic sense, the term "political economy" is used to refer to the sources and distribution of wealth and the various ways in which they relate to other aspects of society's structure.* For our purposes, we wish to emphasize the importance of economic, political, and ideological relations within certain historical contexts as essential elements for understanding the sources of inequality and the ever-widening gap between rich and poor in Canada. We endorse the position stated so succinctly by Watchell:

> Examined from a perspective of radical political economics, poverty is the result of the normal functioning of the principal institutions of capitalism — specifically labor markets, social class, and the state" (1974).

In the following sections on sources of variation of inequalities, articles are grouped under three headings: first, "The State and Social Class Analyses;" second, "Regions and Regionalism"; and finally, "The Political Economy of Specific Groups."

A. The State and Social Class Analyses

Throughout these discussions, special attention is invariably given to the role of the state, a critical component in advanced capitalist societies. Leo Panitch's insightful article identifies the need for a Marxist theory of the state and points out the unique features of the Canadian case. For example, the importance of provincial state power in Canada is best understood, Panitch argues, in terms of the differing class structures of the various regions, which include regional fractions of the bourgeoisie who use the provincial state to express their interests. He adds to the usually accepted functions of the state (accumulation and legitimation) a third, namely coercion, and notes that in the field of social services the Canadian state has lagged behind its stellar performances in the field of capital accumulation.

Despite the pervasive influence of various versions of Marx's conception of class, there is really very little Marxist theory and research on social classes as such. That is, there is a dearth of study which attempts an empirical Marxist class analysis. There are, to be sure, some recent and notable

---

*Gilpin discusses what he terms three prevailing conceptions of political economy: liberalism, Marxism and mercantilism. Briefly he identifies them as follows:

> Liberalism regards politics and economics as relatively separable and autonomous spheres of activities; Marxism refers to the radical critique of capitalism identified with Marx and his contemporary disciples; the essence of the mercantilistic perspective is the subservience of the economy to the state and its interests.

He concludes with his own eclectic definition of political economy as

> The study of the reciprocal and dynamic interaction in international relations of the pursuit of wealth and the pursuit of power (Gilpin, 1975).

For a more detailed explication of the term "political economy," see Wallace Clement and Daniel Drache, *A Practical Guide to Canadian Political Economy* (Toronto: McClelland and Stewart, 1978) and Leo Panitch's article in this section.

exceptions in North America (e.g., Eric Wright's analysis of the U.S. class structure, and Legares, *Des Classes Sociales au Québec*), and on the continent Nicos Poulantzas and Antonio Carchedi have done path-breaking work on the study of class.

Bernier's study of the class situation of a disadvantaged group in a small town in Quebec is a welcome attempt at providing an analysis of poverty in terms of class opposition, that is, in terms of groups which have special and antagonistic positions in the relations of production. He seriously questions the cultural approach, which stresses that the causes of people's disadvantaged position is intrinsic to each person. Bernier notes that this ideological reflection on the group serves at once to justify the difference between the group and the rest of the town. This belief means that no attempt is made to relate the group's condition to relations of capitalist production, that is, to the class antagonism in the community.

He goes on to analyze the *sous proletaires* as a "reserve army" that serves a number of interests of the dominant classes, both ideological and material (for example, their existence as cheap available labor keeps wages of other workers down). Bernier concludes that the "culture of poverty is not an absence of culture or simply a functional adaptation but rather, the adaptation modeled by the predominant ideology ... to specific material conditions made necessary by the capitalist search for profit."

The educational system can also be viewed as part of the state apparatus, an agent of reproduction, and this is the view taken by Harp in *Social Inequalities and the Transmission of Knowledge: The Case against the Schools.* He first examines the historical growth of a system of mass education, arguing that its development under the aegis of the state was undertaken primarily as a means of avoiding potential class conflict. An explication of the concept of equality leads to a discussion of its theoretical significance for sociologists studying equality of educational opportunity. Canadian studies of the topic reaffirm the social class inequalities in our school systems. What is lacking in these analyses is attention to exactly how the schools engage in the process of social and cultural reproduction. In order to answer this question, the article moves to a critical analysis of the work of Bowles and Gintis and of Pierre Bourdieu's theories on cultural reproduction.

In his article on crime and class in Canada, Greenaway advances the general thesis that the relationship often noted between law violation and class has to do with the mode of production, class conflict, the nature of the state and law in Canada, the enforcement of laws, and the operation of legal systems. Pointing out initially that the illegal conduct of the poor is probably exaggerated in official data, Greenaway goes on to emphasize that the law in capitalist societies is structured *a priori* on the basis of social class. Greenaway conducts a critical review of several cultural explanations of deviance and concludes that a partial explanation for lower-class deviance may be that the nature of our political-economic system is such that the decision to violate the law in particular fashion is more often seen by people at that level as being reasonable and desirable. He notes that such an explanation need not entail the existence of a criminal or delinquent subculture.

The Role and Nature of the Canadian State*

LEO PANITCH

The concern of this essay is to identify the framework of a Marxist theory of the state, to explore some of the basic requisites of such a theory, and then to make an attempt to apply it to the study of the Canadian reality. Unfortunately, an undertaking of this kind is all too often dismissed out of hand without much appreciation for what it actually entails. For when one goes back to the *Communist Manifesto's* famous formulation — "the executive of the modern State is but a committee for managing the common affairs of the whole bourgeoisie"[1] — this often conjures up a grotesque image in certain minds. It is assumed that what one *really* means, in the modern Canadian context, is that E.P. Taylor, after having eaten two or three babies for breakfast, calls Pierre Trudeau every morning and, amidst satisfied belches, gives the prime minister instructions on what the government should accomplish that day. To be sure, the idea that the modern state acts at the behest of the dominant class in our society has often seemed much more plausible than the pluralist and social-democratic view of the state as a neutral arbiter between competing groups or classes. A cartoon in the *Grain Growers' Guide* of 1910[2] showed a House of Commons in which the benches were occupied by "fat cats" representing the "meat combine," the "cotton combine," and the "cement trust," led by the man from the "railroads combine." They are sending Laurier and Borden, dressed as parliamentary messengers, out of the House to carry the message of the "real rulers" to the people. This cartoon alone, entitled "How the Country is Governed," tells us more about the Canadian state of that period than many of our history texts. But the real point that must be made in this respect is that an interpretation of the Marxist theory of the state as claiming that the state merely acts on the direct instructions of the bourgeoisie is a crude caricature of the concept of the modern state as "a committee for managing the common affairs of the whole bourgeoisie," a caricature which fails to distinguish between the state acting on *behalf* of the bourgeosie and its acting on their *behest*. As Ralph Miliband has put it: ". . . the notion of common affairs assumes the existence of particular ones; and the notion of the whole bourgeoisie implies the existence of separate elements which make up that whole. This being the case, there is an obvious need for an institution

---

*Reprinted from Leo Panitch, ed., *The Canadian State*. Toronto: University of Toronto Press, 1977.

of the kind they (Marx and Engels) refer to, namely the state; and the state *cannot* meet this need without enjoying a certain degree of autonomy. In other words, the notion of autonomy is embedded in the definition itself, is an intrinsic part of it."[3] For the state to act only at the behest of particular segments of the bourgeoisie would be dysfunctional to it managing the common affairs of that class. For it to accomplish this task, it needs a degree of independence from that class, a "relative autonomy." A crude economistic interpretation of the state makes it in fact impossible to understand the real functions the state performs for the capitalist class.

The notion of the state managing the *common* affairs of the *whole* bourgeoisie, even incorporating as it does the idea of autonomy, is only the starting point for a Marxist theory of the state. And in going beyond that starting point, it is true to say that there is in Marx's own writings no systematic examination of the state to match his work on the capitalist mode of production itself. To be sure, a careful reading of Marx — and not only of his explicitly political tracts, such as the *Eighteenth Brumaire*, but of *Capital* itself — gives us very important insights. When Marx observed in the third volume of *Capital* that despotic states perform both the general function of undertaking "common activities arising from the nature of all communities, and the specific functions arising from the antithesis between the government and the mass of the people,"[4] he was clearly noting the co-ordinating role of the state in all societies, which is undertaken apart from specific class interests, although of course framed within the boundaries set by the mode of production and the relations of production of a given society. And when analyzing the intervention of the state in the economy in the 19th century in the form of ten-hour day legislation and the Factory Acts, Marx showed that the state was by no means immune from the pressure of classes other than the bourgeoisie. He identified two factors that led the English state, ruled directly by capitalists and landlords, to forcibly limit the working day by state regulations: first, the demands of "the working class movement that daily grew more threatening"; and, second, the need for the state to save the bourgeoisie from itself, as the individual capitalist in his relentless drive for profit, far from being protected by some invisible hand, threatened to destroy the very basis of bourgeois wealth and accumulation by "the passion of capital for a limitless draining of labor power" — just as "the same blind eagerness for plunder...exhausted the soil" in the era of commercial farming. The state's role in the class struggle over the ten-hour day was to make the issue resolvable without revolution, and at the same time promulgate the bourgeoisie's common interest, constituting thereby its political unity, so as to prevent blind competition from undermining its dominance. And Marx followed this with an incisive analysis of how the state's action here produced a reactive response in the economy. For to maintain the extraction of surplus value at the same rate as previous to the ten-hour day legislation, capital immediately introduced further mechanization to increase labor productivity per hour. Marx was suggesting here a dialectical relationship between base and superstructure: the state acts out of contradictions produced in the economic base, and once it acts it produces modifications in the economic base.

Finally, we should note the extent to which Marx presaged the growth of the state's role in the economy. Indeed, those who would deny the validity of the Marxist analysis on the basis of modern conditions not fitting with laissez-faire would do well to read *Capital*. For Marx showed clearly there the dynamic of state intervention in the context of an analysis of the regulation of child labor. As soon as the state intervenes at one point by introducing an exceptional law relating to one branch of industry (mechanical spinning and weaving), the necessity for the generalization of factory regulation, for "a law affecting social production as a whole," arises. "There are two circumstances that finally turn the scale: first, the constantly recurring experience that capital, so soon as it finds itself subject to legal control at one point, compensates itself all the more recklessly at other points; secondly, the cry of the capitalists for equality in the conditions of competition, i.e., for equal restrain on all exploitation of labor."[5]

Despite these insights, it nevertheless remains true that the Marxist theory of the state is underdeveloped and, although Lenin, Gramsci, and others have added contributions, there remains much work to be done. It appears that a fully developed theory of the state in capitalist society must meet at least three basic requirements. It must clearly delimit the complex of institutions that go to make up the state. It must demonstrate concretely, rather than just define abstractly, the linkages between the state and the system of class inequality in the society, particularly its ties to the dominant social class. And it must specify as far as possible the functions of the state under the capitalist mode of production. It must undertake these tasks, moreover, not in an ahistoric way but in relation to the way the state's organization, its functions, and its linkages with society vary with the changes in the capitalist mode of production itself, and also vary with the specific conditions of a given social formation. Marxism may give us a method of analysis, but, as Marx himself pointed out in the third volume of *Capital*, this method has to be applied not as an overgeneralization but in a manner that will illuminate concrete empirical and historical circumstances: "The specific economic form, in which unpaid surplus-labor is pumped out of direct producers, determines the relationship of rulers and ruled, as it grows directly out of production itself and, in turn, reacts upon it as a determining element. Upon this, however, is founded the entire formation of the economic community which grows up out of the production relations themselves, thereby simultaneously its specific political form. It is always the direct relationship of the owners of the conditions of production to the direct producers — a relation always naturally corresponding to a definite state in the development of the methods of labor and thereby its social productivity — which reveals the innermost secret, the hidden basis of the entire social structure, and with it the political form of the relation of sovereignty and dependence, in short the corresponding specific form of the state. This does not prevent the same economic basis — the same from the standpoint of its main conditions — due to innumerable different empirical circumstances, natural environment, racial relations, external historical influences, etc., from showing the infinite variations and gradations in appearance, which can be ascertained only by analysis of the empirically given circumstances."[6]

Before turning, with this in mind, to an examination of the specific role and nature of the Canadian state in light of the "empirically given circumstances" of our own society, a few comments are necessary with regard to each of three requisites of a theory of the capitalist state which were mentioned above. One of the very important contributions of Ralph Miliband's *The State in Capitalist Society* is to stress the importance of delimiting clearly the institutions of the state.[7] As Miliband points out, the state is not merely the government, far less just the central government. The state is a complex of institutions, including government, but also including the bureaucracy (embodied in the civil service as well as in public corporations, central banks, regulatory commissions, etc.), the military, the judiciary, representative assemblies, and (very importantly for Canada) what Miliband calls the sub-central levels of government, that is, provincial executives, legislatures, and bureaucracies, and municipal governmental institutions. Although the point itself seems simple once stated, its importance is paramount. It is important, first of all, because of what it leaves out. It leaves out political parties, the privately owned media, the church, pressure groups. These other institutions form part of the political system and no doubt part of the system of power in a liberal-democratic capitalist society, but, unlike the fascist case, they remain autonomous from the state. This is of crucial importance not only theoretically, in the sense that it requires us to explain how these other institutions form part of the system of power through their contribution to political socialization, political recruitment, and social control, but also because it means, in practice, that within the rubric of bourgeois democracy, as opposed to fascism, class conflict does obtain political and industrial expression through the voluntary organizations of the working class. At a general level both forms of the state may be seen as capitalist in their nature, but a specific understanding of the political sphere in each must follow different guidelines.

A second reason for delineating clearly the institutions of the state is that it leads us away from assuming, as social democrats consistently do, that election to governmental power is equivalent to the acquisition of state power. This is, of course, not necessarily true and in most cases is simply untrue, as the example of the Allende regime in Chile demonstrates and as Allende himself understood quite well. In what was probably his last public interview, Allende was asked whether he was turning Chile into a traditional Marxist-Leninist state. Allende's response was to the point. His election, he explained, had not of itself transformed Chile into a socialist country, nor did the fact that a Marxist occupied the office of head of state and leader of the government make the Chilean state socialist or Marxist. He was vice-president of the Senate for four years, and the Senate was not Marxist. He was president of the medical school and nobody could say that the medical school was Marixst.[8] The point here is that the extent to which a government effectively controls the power of the state, indeed even the extent to which it can speak authoritatively in the name of the state, will depend on the balance of forces within the various institutions of the state, such as the bureaucracy, the judiciary, and the military, in terms of the classes *they* represent and the values *they* hold. This will determine how far governmental power is circumscribed by state power.

The second requisite of a theory of the state — that of specifying linkages between the state system and the class structure — is also of key importance. Nicos Poulantzas, whose book, *Political Power and Social Classes,* has already had a substantial impact in the field, has tended to play down the utility of tracing the ties between state personnel and the capitalist class, suggesting that the state's activities on behalf of the capitalist class are determined by deep structural relations rather than by the similar class backgrounds and social positions of state personnel and businessmen. In this way he is able to grant the state "relative autonomy" from the capitalist class while at the same time defining an "objective relation" between the state and and the bourgeoisie which automatically determines that state activities are the expression of the power of the dominant class. The most efficient capitalist state, for Poulantzas, is one that has the *least* direct personal ties to the bourgeoisie, both in terms of mystifying the relationship and in terms of acting as a cohesive factor for the whole bourgeoisie.[9] The problem with this approach, however, is that it tends to remove from the theory of the state a concrete empirical and historical orientation. By establishing by definition the relationship between state and bourgeoisie, one leaves out the central question, to be determined empirically in each instance, of the *extent* to which the state is acting on behalf of the dominant class. As Miliband has put it, in a critique of Poulantzas' "structuralist abstractionism": ". . . one of the main reasons for stressing the importance of the notion of the relative autonomy of the state is that there is a basic distinction to be made between class power and state power, and that the analysis of the meaning and implications of that notion of relative autonomy must indeed focus on the forces which cause it to be greater or less, the circumstances in which it is exercised, and so on."[10]

Turning finally to the question of the specific functions of the capitalist state, a useful framework has been suggested by James O'Connor: "Our first premise is that the capitalistic state must try to fulfill two basic and often mutually contradictory functions — *accumulation* and *legitimization* . . . This means that the state must try to maintain or create the conditions in which profitable capital accumulation is possible. However, the state also must try to maintain or create the conditions for social harmony. A capitalist state that openly uses its coercive forces to help one class accumulate capital at the expense of other classes loses its legitimacy and hence undermines the basis of its loyalty and support."[11] A number of points should be noted in this respect. First of all, there are really three distinct functions identified here: in addition to policies that will foster capital accumulation (for example, subsidies to private industry), and in addition to policies that will foster social harmony (for example, the ten-hour day legislation or social welfare legislation), there is a *coercion function,* that is, the use by the state of its monopoly over the legitimate use of force to maintain or impose social order. The capital accumulation function does not *normally* rely on the coercion function, but operates independently of it. Secondly, the legitimization and capital accumulation functions are by no means necessarily mutually contradictory. A taxation policy aimed at income redistribution for the purpose of legitimization may be contrary to short-term accumulation, but necessary for maintaining accumulation in the long run, indeed even for accelerating it. It should be stressed, finally, that the emphasis given here to the concept of functions need not, if properly employed, give rise to the same problems as are found in other structural-functional approaches. As Eric Hobsbawm has observed: "Marxism is far from the only structural-functionalist theory of society, though it has good claims to be the first of them, but it differs from most others in two respects. First, it insists on a hierarchy of social phenomena (e.g., 'basis' and 'superstructure'), and second, on the existence within any society of internal tensions ('contradictions') which counteract the tendency of the system to maintain itself as a going concern... The importance of these peculiarities of Marxism is in the field of history, for it is they which allow it to explain — unlike other structural-functional models of society — why and how societies change and transform themselves... Today, when the existence of social systems is generally accepted, but at the cost of their a-historical, if not anti-historical analysis, Marx's emphasis on history as a necessary dimension is perhaps more essential than ever."[12]

It should be obvious, in this light, that the exercise of the various state functions is by no means uniform in all periods and in all societies, and that the size and prominence of any one of the three state functions must be examined in light of the "empirically given circumstances" of a particular society. Indeed, what is striking as one turns to an analysis of the Canadian state is how at each point the Canadian state reflects *particular* characteristics which mark it off in a comparative sense from other capitalist states. On the question of state organization one sees that the federal form has always been, and remains, of crucial importance in terms of the power of the provincial segments of the state vis-à-vis the central government. One sees as well that the linkages between the state and the dominant class have been, and remain, not general and abstract but particularly close and intimate. And one sees in terms of state functions that, from its very beginnings, the Canadian state has played a tremendously large role in fostering capital accumulation. Each of these will be looked at in turn. What follows, however, must in no sense be seen as anything more than a tentative and necessarily incomplete approach towards employing Marxist theory to understand the Canadian state.

The utility of delimiting the institutions of the Canadian state, along the lines suggested by Miliband, is clear. Although no such spectacular examples of the distribution of state power as afforded by the Allende case exist in Canadian history, an appreciation of the balance of powers among various state institutions can give us the handle to grasp the limitations placed by the bureaucracy on CCF-NDP governments, and even the tensions between the Diefenbaker government and the federal civil service in the 1957 to 1962 period.[13] Moreover, by drawing the differences between the state system and the broader political system, we can begin to trace more clearly the worrying ways in which there is occurring within Canadian liberal democracy an increasing "statisization" of the political sphere. Specifically relevant here are such developments as state subsidies to political parties' election campaigns or the recent attempts to involve trade unions in the government's "consensus" incomes policy. Although the foray by the state into the regulation of party financing is progressive in the sense that it ostensibly seeks to limit the influence of corporate money on the electoral arena, the introduction of state financing as a substitute, carrying as it does a bias in favor of the existing parties and against new parties, may tend to freeze the extremely limited party alternatives presently available. Similarly, the attempt to incorporate trade unions in an incomes policy is clearly designed to ensure that these working-class organizations, however defective at present as representatives of workers' demands, will be obliged to act explicitly as agencies of social control over their members.

But in following Miliband's suggestive outline of the state system thus far, it is necessary immediately to depart from him in one crucial respect with regard to the Canadian state. For while Miliband argues that amongst Western societies there has been a tendency towards the centralization of state power at the expense of sub-central institutions, this does not hold for Canada where provincial state power has historically been important and has become increasingly more so in recent years. Unfortunately, Marxists in Canada have avoided dealing with this in a serious way, with perhaps the crucial exception of C.B. Macpherson, whose *Democracy in Alberta* remains the best political analysis in the Marxist tradition undertaken in Canada. To be sure, the federal factor has often been used by Canadian politicians to pass the buck on the introduction of progressive social legislation, as a rationale for inaction, and as a means of dividing the working class. Nevertheless, without an understanding of Canada's federal nature the Canadian state cannot be properly analyzed.

The reasons for this dispersion of state power in Canada are complex and many of them hark back to the racial, geographic, and historical factors that Marx spoke of as necessitating a concrete examination of specific societies: the binational nature of Canadian society, the fact that the state was formed as an amalgam of British colonies, and the fact that within Canada there emerged a quasi-colonial relationship between regions, a relationship dominated by central Canada and its bourgeoisie although it itself was dominated from the outside. Moreover, the persistence of provincial state power is to be understood in terms of the differing class structures of various Canadian regions and in terms of the regional fractions of the bourgeoisie. The dominant classes, or rather class fractions, in the provinces, often unable to constitute a unity with their counterparts either through political parties or in economic coalitions, have used the provincial state to express their interests. This was shown by Macpherson with regard to the petite bourgeoisie of Alberta of the 1930s and it has been brilliantly demonstrated by Hubert Guindon with regard to the new middle class of Quebec in the 1960s.[14]

The relentless striving and competition on the part of the provincial governments for American investment in the last two decades, which has been a large factor in the balkanization and quasi-colonization of Canada as a whole, is a product of such factors. Moreover, this perspective is required to understand the Alberta-federal government dispute over oil, which reflects a clear difference of interest within the bourgeoisie between oil and gas interests and manufacturing interests (often both comprador in the nature). That the Ontario, Alberta, and federal governments could come together in an agreement on the Syncrude rip-off is an attestation to the important role the state plays in providing a unity for the bourgeoisie, which cannot be obtained through other mechanisms. This political unity is increasingly being achieved, however, not within the traditional federal institutions but by new and *ad hoc* federal-provincial conferences two or three steps removed from any sort of popular control, even in the liberal-democratic sense of that term.[15] The point, however, is that these developments can only be understood in terms of the fragmented representation of regional bourgeois interests in a federal system.

When we turn from the organization of the state to the second requisite of a Marxist theory, that of specifying the concrete linkages between a state formally based on political equality and a society dominated by the capitalist class, we again immediately note a particularly striking characteristic of the Canadian state — its very close personal ties to the bourgeoisie. Whatever the merits of Poulantzas' contention that the most efficient state is that with the least direct ties to the dominant class, it is a rather academic point as applied to Canada. Without indulging in fantasies of E.P. Taylor and P.E. Trudeau on the telephone, let us remember that the relationship between the first post-confederation cabinets and the financial bourgeoisie and the railway entrepreneurs was not only close — they were often the same people.[16] To take but one example among many, a list of the board of directors of the Grand Trunk Railway reads like a list of the Fathers of Confederation, including Galt and Cartier. T.W. Acheson's study of Canada's industrial elite at the turn of the century reveals that no less than one-third of the members of that elite held political office at some time in their careers.[17]

The story is a repetitive one extending through Mackenzie King, adviser of the Rockefellers, to St Laurent, the corporation lawyer, to Wallace McCutcheon, managing director of Argus Corporation, to the Pearson-Trudeau cabinets on which Drury, Sharp, and Richardson sat as members of the corporate elite in their own right. John Porter's demonstration of the degree of co-optation from business to government and of exit from cabinet to business makes the very concept of an autonomous political elite in Canada a highly tenuous one. The political recruitment role played by political parties in this respect is important. This was evident from the origins of the dominant 19th-century party — the Conservatives — out of the bosom of the Montreal business establishment.[18] And it is no less evident from an examination of the activists in the Liberal and Conservative parties today. A study of these parties' leadership conventions in 1967 and 1968 reveals that these great exercises in participatory democracy were attended by delegates "drawn from a strikingly narrow socio-economic base."[19] Two-thirds had annual incomes of $10,000 or more as compared with 7% of the Canadian population in this income bracket; 40% earned $15,000 or more — only 2% of Canadians had such incomes; 25% earned $20,000 or more — as against 1% of all Canadians. As one would expect from this, 60% of the delegates were executives or professionals, while only 8% were drawn from clerical and other white-collar occupations or from the ranks of skilled or unskilled manual workers.

When we turn to the bureaucracy, we find again particularly strong linkages, with a major tendency, despite the development of a civil service based on the merit principle rather than patronage, for the co-optation of businessmen from the outside. The classic example is that of C.D. Howe's "boys." This architect of federal industrial and commercial policies during the war and in the formative post-war years, according to Mitchell Sharp, "knew every important businessman in Canada, and they seemed to have made a practice of talking to 'C.D.' whether they wanted anything from the Government or not."[20] Howe brought to Ottawa a large number of businessmen to "manage" the Canadian economy and to head publicly owned enterprises, and a number of these men maintained private corporate positions at the same time. As Porter observed: "It was not surprising that a close relationship should develop and career lines become confused between the corporate world and the public service in and around departments which, through planning, regulations, and defence contracts, came into close contact with industry. The result was a growth of a penumbral area of power in which the political, bureaucratic, and corporate elites met, and became linked in such a way as to become a minor power elite."[21] With the recommendations of the Glassco Commission in the early 1960s that these ties and interchanges between business and the civil service be encouraged and the consequent actions in this respect on the part of Liberal governments, this "penumbral area of power" does not appear to have been attenuated. Wally Clement has indeed recently shown that there has been "an increasing interpenetration between the corporate elite and both the state and political systems in the last twenty years," and the "a total of 39.4% of the current economic elite members either were themselves or had close kin in the state system."[22]

The point to be drawn from all this is not that the state in Canada would be independent of the capitalist class without these specific linkages, given the balance of class forces within which the state operates. It certainly does suggest, however, "a confraternity of power" of such dimensions as to permit the clear employment of the term "ruling class" in the political as well as the economic sense in the Canadian case. It suggests, above all, an ideological hegemony emanating from both the bourgeoisie and the state which is awesome, which is reflected in the sheer pervasiveness of the view that the national interest and business interests are at one, and which certainly ensures the smooth functioning of the relationship between the state and the capitalist class. This was clearly evidenced in a frank statement by Jack Pickersgill from his position as head of the Canadian Transport Commission to the Canadian Manufacturers' Association in 1970: ". . . the public generally, and business men specifically, must come to realize that it is just as moral, and just as praiseworthy to operate a railway, an airline, or a trucking firm at a profit as it is to make a profit manufacturing motor cars or packing meat or making steel." Not surprisingly, this statement was questioned by the Canadian Railway Labour Association as showing no little bias in favor of

the rate hikes for Canadian Pacific, which Mr. Pickersgill's CTC was supposed to be regulating. Pickersgill, however, was utterly amazed that
anyone could take exception to his apologia for profit: "I must say," he
said, "that I thought that that statement was as safe as saying one was in
favor of motherhood as one could come and not be accused of banality...
What I was seeking to do was to remove all bias of any kind, without raising a very large question, which I have no intention of raising, as to
whether it is moral to make a profit on anything. I am sure that no one
wants to debate this subject."[23] This disposition to see profit as
motherhood, so widely spread throughout the operations of the Canadian
state, lends particular credence to the concept, sometimes used in political
science, of the "non-decision." The problem is not that political and
bureaucratic officials *decide* to favor capitalist interests in case after case;
it is rather that it rarely even *occurs* to them that they might do other than
favor such interests. The problem is indeed a systematic one.

What must be understood, however, as we move to examine the functions of the Canadian state, is that this ideological hegemony that extends
across the state-corporate sphere in no way inhibits a very large role for the
state in the society; indeed, if one can distinguish between the capital accumulation function on the one hand and the legitimization function on the
other, one can easily see how such close ties would promote a major role for
the state in the former respect. In terms of the capital accumulation function, the Canadian state has generally undertaken four main tasks. It has
provided a favorable fiscal and monetary climate for economic growth via
private enterprise. It has underwritten the private risks of production at
public expense through grants, subsidies, fast write-off depreciation
allowances, etc. (Confederation itself was produced by the desire to
facilitate capital accumulation by guaranteeing loans from London to build
the railways.) It has played a crucial role, via control of land policy and immigration policy, in creating a capitalist labor market and, especially in recent decades, in absorbing the social cost of production of capitalist enterprise through sanitation services, medicare, unemployment insurance,
educational facilities. And it has directly provided the technical infrastructure for capitalist development when this was too risky or costly for private
capital to undertake itself. State ownership of railroads and public utilities
and state construction and operation of airports were never undertaken as
ends in themselves with the aim of managing or controlling the economy,
but always with a view to facilitating further capital accumulation in the
private sphere to the end of economic growth.[24]

What is particularly noteworthy about these activities is how large they
bulked for the Canadian state long before the concentration of capital in the
monopolistic stage found this function duplicated to this extent in other,
more developed, capitalist countries. The Canadian state was *never* a
laissez-faire state and, although it was not always the case that a spade was
called a spade, Canadian economists and historians have well recorded this
function. Indeed, Lord Durham in his famous *Report* of 1839 noted that,
whereas in Europe the main role of the state was defence, in North America
it was active engagement in the construction of communication links in the
new societies.[25] But given the particular nature of the Canadian economy,

this function became much more developed in Canada than in the United States. Writing almost 20 years ago, C.B. Macpherson observed:

> ...one of the main achievements of Canadian economics has been to show in more detail the close interdependence of political and economic structure. The constitutional structure of Canada has been to a large extent determined by the need to secure capital at favorable rates of interest and to promote the expansion of the economy: "Constitutional changes are a part of market operations." (Innis). In turn the political authorities, federal and provincial, have as a matter of course assumed large powers of control and protection, encouragement and regulation of economic life.
>
> This embrace of private enterprise and government is not at all unusual in new countries. In Canada it is the direct result of the fact that the natural resources, abundant but scattered, have always afforded the prospect of highly profitable exploitation and could most rapidly be made profitable by concentrating on the production of a few staples for export — fur and fish in the early days, wheat, forest products and minerals today. This required a heavy import of capital and heavy government expenditure in railways, power developments, irrigation, land settlement, and so on. To support such investment, governments have been driven to all sorts of further encouragement of various industries and regions, notably by way of protective tariffs. They have also been driven to monetary and other regulatory policies to offset the extreme swings of an economy so dependent for its revenue on the unstable demand for and prices of a few staples, and so burdened by the fixed costs of interest on its capital indebtedness. And because the different regions of Canada, being unevenly developed, felt these problems at different times and to different extents, there is constant struggle both within federal politics and between federal and provincial governments for more favorable consideration for every region. In addition, the fact that governments still own or control many rich natural resources, leads to a continuing high degree of government manipulation and regulation.
>
> All this flows directly from the demand of private enterprise; the economy as a whole remains fundamentally a private-enterprise system, but the pattern of prices, markets, and profits is perennially complicated by the manifold involvement of governments and by the pressures on governments which their involvement invites. Just as the Canadian economy is in an exposed position due to its dependence on world prices for staples, so the political system has from the beginning been exposed, to an unusual extent, to the pressures of economic interest groups.[26]

The Canadian bourgeousie, moreover, has not shied away from considerable public ownership as an acceptable means whereby the state could perform the accumulation function. Indeed, the state's activities in this respect were developed so early and in such large proportions that social-democratic politicians in Britain in the 1920s, with characteristic inability — no less remarkable then than now — to understand the true significance of events, actually took inspiration from such public ventures as Ontario Hydro and the CNR as expressions of "the great socialist experiments of the Dominions." This was the view of Arthur Greenwood upon the eve of his entering Ramsay MacDonald's Labor government in 1929. He saw these ventures as "two enterprises (which) stand to the credit of a people whose policy has been decided on grounds of public advantage."[27] A rather more realistic assessment has recently been offered by the historian H.V. Nelles in his masterful account of government-industry relations in Ontario: "From the outset the crusade for public power was a businessmen's movement; they initiated it, formed its devoted, hard-core membership and, most importantly, they provided it with brilliant leadership. By the phrase 'the people's power,' the businessmen meant cheap electricity for the manufacturer, and it was assumed that the entire community would benefit as a result. The socially and politically influential manufacturers turned readily to public ownership primarily because the private electric companies at Niagara refused to guarantee them an immediate, inexpensive supply of a commodity on which they believed their future prosperity depended." Not surprisingly, the operation of Ontario Hydro has always looked more like state capitalism than anything else, ". . . run by businessmen, for businessmen, in what was always referred to as a 'businesslike' manner." Unlike so many of our political analysts, Canadian capitalists have been good at distinguishing between a large state with major accumulation functions and a socialist state. As Nelles puts it: ". . . the positive state survived the 19th century primarily because businessmen found it useful. The province received substantial revenue from the development process and enjoyed the appearance of control over it, while industrialists used the government — as had the 19th-century commercial classes before — to provide key services at public expense, promote and protect vested interests, and confer the status of law upon private decisions. If public functions such as the distribution of hydro-electricity were to the advantage of industry, this expansion of political control was eagerly sanctioned; whereas, if businessmen resented interference (mineral royalties and forest protection regulations, for example), then the scope of government intervention narrowed. . . the structures established to regulate business in the public interest. . . contributed to a reduction of the state — despite an expansion of its activities — to a client of the business community."[28]

It has been the very lack of relative autonomy of the state, the sheer depth of its commitment to private capital as the motor force of the society, which, when combined with a weak indigenous bourgeoisie and a strong financial bourgeoisie cast in the mould of an intermediary between staple production in Canada and industrial empires abroad, explains the lengths to which the state has gone in promoting private capital accumulation not only for the domestic bourgeosie but for foreign capitalists as well. However persuasive the arguments by R.T. Naylor and Clement with regard to the Canadian financial bourgeoisie being particularly suited and willing to make a profit by acting as a conduit for American ownership of Canadian industry, it appears unlikely that the role of the Canadian state in fostering direct American investment is to be understood in terms of the dominant financial fraction of the bourgeoisie having "captured" the state to the detriment of indigenous industrialists. T.W. Acheson has shown that in 1910, at the crossroads of the major growth of American direct investment, manufacturers were much more involved in politics at both the provincial and federal levels than were financiers.[29] A more general, yet more convincing, explanation might be suggested: Macpherson in his study of Social Credit observed that the Alberta petite bourgeoisie supported a strong state with a view to protecting itself against big eastern capital, but because of the strength of its commitment to private property in an age of monopoly capitalism it found the state inexorably drawn into the latter's orbit. We might suggest in a similar way that the Canadian bourgeoisie, both industrial and financial, seeks to build with the aid of a large and strong state a viable national economy on the northern half of the continent, but because of the commitment to private accumulation it comes to rely on American direct investment as the readiest source of capital. This produces the very opposite of the stated intention —not a viable independent bourgeois society, but a dependency on the American Empire. The National Policy, which has been pursued with unwavering commitment by Canadian governments from the time of John A. Macdonald and the CPR to the time of Donald Macdonald and Syncrude, has been based on shifting sands. It involves relying on foreign capital for staple extraction on the assumption that this will create the surplus out of which industrialization in central Canada will grow; and it involves the further assumption that foreign branch plants may take the lead in this industrialization behind tariff walls as good corporate Candian citizens.

In the case of the earlier reliance on British portfolio investment, given the non-perpetuating character of control involved since loans can be paid off, and given the waning of British imperial power generally, this alone did not provide tremendous difficulties for the development of Canadian independence. But this independence from Britain, told so often in our school textbooks as the story of "From Colony to Nation," was but a temporary one, occasioned by a situation in which Britain had lost and America had not yet gained the ability to rule Canada. For as American direct investment permeated Canada with the help of the Canadian state and the financial bourgeoisie, the economic basis of independence was lost. The guiding ideology and function of the Canadian state remained that of providing the basis for capital accumulation to facilitate national economic development, with some discrimination in favor of central Canada in terms of the location of investment, but without discrimination with regard to the origin or nature of the investment. As C.D. Howe succinctly put it in a speech in Boston in 1954: "Canada has welcomed the participation of American and other foreign capital in its industrial expansion. In Canada foreign investors are treated the same as domestic investors."[30] The result of this policy was economic growth indeed, but a distorted growth which removed from the Canadian state, given the sheer dominance of foreign capital over the economy, much of the substance of its political sovereignty. It is the economic basis for a new colonial relationship with the American Empire which, through a foreign policy of "quiet diplomacy," "special status," and an "ear in Washington," resembles very closely the neo-colonial relationship offered to Canada at the turn of the century by Britain in the form of an "imperial cabinet." This was rejected by Laurier on the grounds ". . . that a method of consultation obviously defective and carrying with it in reality no suspensory or veto power, involves by indirection the adoption of that very centralizing system which it had been his purpose to block. . . the policy of consultation gave the Dominions a shadowy and unreal power; but imposed upon them a responsibility, serious and inescapable."[31] In

Canada's voyage from colony to nation to neo-colony, we seem to have exchanged the "shadowy and unreal" independence offered within the British Empire for the "shadowy and unreal" independence tolerated by the Americans.

Turning now to the other functions of the Canadian state, it should be noted — although there is not the space to discuss this here — that in respect of the coercion function the state's use of its coercive powers to maintain or impose social order has also been much in evidence in Canadian history. To this, attest such famous examples as the tight central control of western expansion, the suppression of the Riel Rebellion, the employment of troops against strikers in Winnipeg and mounties against the unemployed in Regina, as well as the ready use of the War Measures Act more recently. What has been least developed, however, is the state's legitimization function. In contrast with the accumulation function where the Canadian state has been a forerunner, at least among the Anglo-American countries, in terms of legitimation the state's role has not been comparatively active, imaginative, or large. Legitimation is being used here not in the sense of state propaganda or statements by politicians that seek to rationalize capital accumulation in terms of its benefits for the whole community, but rather in the sense of concrete state activities such as welfare measures, anti-combines legislation, redistributive taxation, union protection, and governmental consultation with labor representatives. We are speaking of policies directed at the integration of the subordinate classes in capitalist society either through the introduction of reforms which promote social harmony or through the co-optation of working-class leaders via tripartite consultations with government and business — giving them the semblance of power without the substance — so as to employ them as agencies of social control over their members.

Noting that the legitimization function is relatively underdeveloped in Canada does not imply its total absence — it is a requisite of every state. With respect to union rights, it was clearly employed in Canada shortly after Confederation when Macdonald defended the right to strike of the Toronto *Globe's* printers as against the newspaper's owner — the Liberal party leader — George Brown. Macdonald's Trade Union Act of 1872 was a Canadian variant of Disraeli's "aristocratic embrace," conceived in the hope of finding conservative angels within the hard marble exteriors of the working class. But what has been particularly notable about Canadian labor legislation, in comparison with the British and even in comparison with the American, is the extent to which the rights of unionization and free collective bargaining have been hedged around by, even embedded in, a massive legal and penal structure. This places such tremendous statutory restriction on labor and gives such a large role for the law and the courts to play, that the legitimation aspect of labour legislation in Canada's case seems at least balanced, if not actually overshadowed, by the coercive aspect.

In terms of state regulatory policies over business, Canada's first anti-combines legislation (1889) appeared in fact a year before the American Sherman Act. This legislation has never made much of an impact on Canada, however. As Michael Bliss has said of the pre-First World War period: "Canadian anti-combines legislation during these years was insignificant and ineffectual; it did not reflect a serious desire by legislators to resist economic consolidation or restore the forces of the free market."[32] Precisely the same conclusion has been reached for the post-Second World War period by Hugh Thorburn and Bert Young.[33] It is hard to believe that such a policy has garnered much legitimacy for the capitalist system. If it is important, it is in that it indicates so clearly the particular strength of the financial bourgeoisie of this country in that their banking institutions have been largely spared even the embarrassment of investigation, let alone actual "trust-busting" by the state.[34]

In the field of social services the Canadian state has again been a laggard in comparison with its pathbreaking performance in the field of capital accumulation. The "welfare state" was late in coming to Canada and once it came did not outrun by any means the provision of benefits or redistribution of incomes of other capitalist societies.[35] This is in one sense surprising in view of the fact that the major political figure in Canada in this century, Mackenzie King, presaged the welfare state and the neo-corporatist development of union integration within liberal democracy in his *Industry and Humanity* in 1918, and was one of the first writers clearly to do so in the Western world. *Industry and Humanity* made the case for wide dissemination of welfare benefits with a view to laying the basis of labor, capital, and state collaboration in the economy and industry. "Let Labor and Capital unite under the ideal of social service," he exhorted; "the work of material production will go on; not only will it vastly increase, but the whole complexion of Industry will become transformed. No longer will Industry be the battle-ground of rival and contending factions; it will become the foundation of a new civilization in which life and happiness abound."[36] This fundamentally social-democratic view, very similar to that of Ramsay MacDonald in Britain — in fact, more fully developed and more concrete — had virtually no effect on Canadian legislation for the following quarter century, however, despite King's being prime minister for much of that period. Why? The reason is that ideas, if they are socially disembodied in the sense of not correlating with the nature and balance of class forces in a society, can themselves have little impact. The fact that in the pre-Second World War period the petite bourgeousie was the largest subordinate class in Canada[37] and that there was less need on the family farm for the kind of benefits associated with the welfare state, was a major factor in explaining Canada's retardation in this respect. Another key factor was that labor did not pose a *centralized* threat with which the state was forced to deal. The major conflicts of the inter-war years were regionally isolated. It was only during the Second World War, with the tremendous growth of popular radicalism and union consciousness, that the Canadian state turned in a deliberate way towards welfarism. On the night in August 1943 that the Communists won the Cartier by-election (over the CCF's David Lewis) and the CCF won two other by-elections, King wrote in his diary that he hoped that the victory might cause ". . . some of our people to realize that labor has to be dealt with in a considerate way. In my heart, I am not sorry to see the mass of the people coming a little more into their own, but I do regret that it is not a Liberal party that is winning that position for them. It should be, and it can still be that our people will learn their lesson in time. What I fear is we will begin to have defection from our ranks in the House to the CCF.[38]

Canada's "welfare state" legislation was much influenced by Britain's famous *Beveridge Report*,[39] and upon hearing Sir William Beveridge speak in Ottawa in 1943 King proudly noted how his *Industry and Humanity* had anticipated Beveridge's program. This was less true of specific policy proposals than of the philosophy behind them. Beveridge's main concern was with ensuring that the provision of social benefits and the guarantee of full employment would lead to wage moderation as well as political moderation on the part of the working class and particularly to the adoption of a "responsible" accommodative stance by union leaders, who would discipline their members in the context of a more "humane" society. This increased social role for the state combined with a role for unions as agencies of social control over their members — what a prescient London *Times* correspondent in 1943 called a "middle course between Socialism and Fascism"[40] — was indeed central to King's thinking. In a visit to Germany in 1937 King had been above all impressed with the corporative element in German fascism, almost to the total neglect of its effects on the autonomy of working-class institutions and the freedom of working people. After his meeting with Hitler, King wrote in his diary: "Like Henderson, the British Ambassador, I feel more and more how far reaching in the interests of the working classes, are the reforms being worked out in Germany, and how completely they are on the right lines. They are truly establishing an industrial commonwealth, and other nations would be wise to evolve rapidly on similar lines of giving to labor its place in the control of industry; its leisure, its opportunities for education, recreation, sharing, in all particulars, the life which hitherto had been preserved for the privileged classes only. Of all that I have seen on this trip abroad, I have been more impressed and more heartened by what seems to be working itself out in Germany in these particulars than on almost anything else."[41]

These sentiments may give us some insight into the motives behind the introduction of the welfare state in Canada, together with the legal framework established for collective bargaining in the post-Second World War period. Yet, despite these developments, what is in fact surprising about post-1945 Canada is the fact that, unlike almost all western European capitalist states, it has not evolved an institutional mechanism for the integration of the unions in state policy. Whereas other states developed systems of indicative economic planning and incomes policies under which unions are expected to act as agencies of social control over the wage demands of their members, Canada did not. Many reasons might be adduced for this, but a crucial one, raised by the Economic Council itself in its third report, was that there did not exist effective "corps intermediares" in Canada for such a system to operate. It was referring to its doubts that bodies like the CLC and CNTU had the requisite authority over its members to enforce a policy of wage restraint.[42] Rather than union integration, the Canadian state relied on a higher level of unemployment than in Europe to ensure wage moderation.

To be sure, we have seen in recent years an explicit attempt by the federal government at union integration, in the context of an economy beset by high inflation even at levels of unemployment double their post-war rate. That the Canadian labor movement was one of the few in the Western world that turned down participation in a voluntary prices and incomes policy when it was first offered to it (in John Turner's "consensus" talks), indicates, however, the high degree of scepticism with which Canadian labor has come to view the alleged neutrality of the Canadian state between the classes. It is indeed an indication of a crisis of legitimacy that has come to attend a state that has given as much weight to the function of accumulation, to the neglect of its legitimation role, as has the Canadian. While federal and provincial governments stumbled over one another in rushing to hand out subsidies and grants to foreign subsidiaries, total Canadian social security spending as a percentage of GNP in the post- war period was consistently lower than that of any western European country with the exception of Switzerland, and by the mid-1960s was almost half that of West Germany, the Netherlands, France, and Sweden. And although Canadian social expenditure since that time has increased, so that Canada moved from what one scholar termed a "welfare state laggard" to a "middle-range spender,"[43] this has nevertheless taken place in the context of a tax system which while nominally progressive on income tax is in fact regressive when all taxes are taken into consideration. You pay less the more you earn up to $8,000 (1969 dollars) when the tax system then becomes, at best, proportional.[44] At the same time there has been a clear trend for revenues on corporate taxation to fall and for taxes on individuals to rise.[45] This means at a time of fiscal squeeze a situation in which the ratio of state benefits received to taxes paid is declining. When one adds to this the effects of inflation on working people, it is perhaps not surprising that we find that days lost in strikes in Canada per 1,000 workers has recently been higher than in any country in the West with the exception of Italy, amounting to an average of some five million working days lost and 400,000 strikers per year in the 1970s.

The developing contradictions in the role of the Canadian state are seen at another level in the fact that the folly of promoting national development through foreign ownership is also beginning to catch up with the state. This is seen not only in the recent statement by the president of Chrysler Canada, on the question of whether plants will be shut down in Canada to compensate for falling auto sales in the United States, that tells us that "blood is thicker than water" and that any decision in this regard will be a "corporate decision; not a Canadian one";[46] it is also seen in opinion polls which indicate that a majority of the Canadian population favors nationalization of oil and gas production. This too suggests a crisis of legitimacy for a state which, as Syncrude shows, in trying to extricate itself from the dilemma of foreign control, enmeshes itself deeper in it, so that its Foreign Investment Review Agencies are revealed for the empty symbolic exercises they really are.

Both the Canadian oil and gas policy and the highly restrictive statutory incomes policy introduced in the aftermatch of the failed "consensus" talks,[47] indicate the continued emphasis being given by the Canadian state to the accumulation and coercion functions. Moreover, the unity that the Canadian state has been able to forge among the provincial fractions of bourgeoisie around Syncrude, and particularly around the incomes policy despite the incursion it makes into provincial jurisdiction, suggests that the Canadian bourgeoisie is supportive of the state in this regard. Nevertheless, the extent and nature of the opposition of the organized working class to the incomes policy also indicates that class conflict in this country, which has largely been expressed at the industrial level heretofore, is beginning to take on an important political dimension, as evidenced in 1976 in the 22 March mass demonstration on Parliament Hill and the first political nation-wide general strike in Canadian history on 14 October. Although conclusions at this stage must necessarily be highly contingent on many factors, it does appear that the large role played by the state in Canadian society, in the context of industrial militancy, is beginning to lay bare the inconsistency between the apparent legal and political equality of liberal democracy and the socioeconomic inequality of a capitalism protected and maintained by the state. But whether this will have immediate radical consequences, rather than stand as the basis for the development of conservatizing corporatist structures, will only be answered in light of the ensuing struggle.

NOTES

1. Karl Marx and Friedrich Engels, *Selected Works* (Moscow 1969), I, pp. 110-11.
2. Reprinted in Robert Chodos, *The CPR: A Century of Corporate Welfare* (Toronto 1973), between 54 and 55.
3. "Poulantzas and the Capitalist State," *New left Review*, 82 (Nov.-Dec. 1973), p. 85.
4. *Capital* (Moscow 1959), III, pp. 376-77.
5. *Capital* (Moscow 1961), I, pp. 239, 410ff., 490.
6. *Ibid.*, III, p. 772.
7. *The State in Capitalist Society* (London 1969), pp. 49-55; cf.Miliband, "The Capitalist State: Reply to Nicos Poulantzas," *New Left Review*, 59 (Jan.-Feb. 1970), pp. 59-60.
8. Interview with John P. Wallach, in *Genesis*, I, 3 (Oct. 1973), p. 117.
9. See *Political Power and Social Classes* (London 1973), especially pp. 275-321.
10. "Poulantzas and the Capitalist State," pp. 87-88. For the full debate between them, see the articles by Poulantzas and Miliband on "The Problem of the Capitalist State" in R. Blackburn, ed., *Ideology in Social Science* (London 1972), pp. 238-62; also E. Laclau, "The Specificity of the Political: The Poulantzas- Miliband Debate," *Economy and Society*, IV, 1 (Feb. 1975), pp. 87-110; and Poulantzas, "The Capitalist State: A Reply to Miliband and Laclau," *New Left Review*, 95 (Jan.-Feb. 1976), pp. 63-83.
11. *The Fiscal Crisis of the State* (New York 1973), p. 6.
12. "Karl Marx's Contribution to Historiography," in Blackburn, *Ideology in Social Science*, pp. 273-74.
13. See, in this regard, S.M. Lipset, *Agrarian Socialism: The Cooperative Commonwealth Federation in Saskatchewan* (rev. ed., New York 1968), Chap. 12; and John Porter, *The Vertical Mosaic: An Analysis of Social Class and Power in Canada* (Toronto 1965), Chap. 14.

14. On Alberta, in addition to C.B. Macpherson's *Democracy in Alberta: Social Credit and the Party System* (2nd ed., Toronto, 1962), see J.R. Mallory, *Social Credit and the Federal Power in Canada* (Toronto, 1954); on Quebec, see H. Guindon, "Social Unrest, Social Class, and Quebec's Bureaucratic Revolution," Queen's Quarterly, LXXI, 2 (Summer 1964).

15. See, in this regard, D.V. Smiley, *Canada in Question: Federalism in the Seventies* (Toronto, 1972), and R. Simeon, *Federal-Provincial Diplomacy: The Making of Recent Policy in Canada* (Toronto, 1972).

16. See Gustavus Myers, *A History of Canadian Wealth* (Toronto, 1972), pp. 265-66; R.T. Naylor, "The Rise and Fall of the Third Commercial Empire of the St Lawrence," in Gary Teeple, ed., *Capitalism and the National Question in Canada* (Toronto, 1972), pp. 17-18; and Chodos, *CPR*, pp. 20-21.

17. "The Changing Social Origins of the Canadian Industrial Elite, 1880-1910," in B. Porter and R. Cuff, eds., *Enterprise and National Development* (Toronto, 1973), p. 72.

18. See G. Houghham, "The Background and Development of National Parties," in H.G. Thorburn, ed., *Party Politics in Canada* (Scarborough, 1972), pp. 2-3; cf.M. Duverger, *Political Parties* (London 1964), p. XXXIV.

19. J. Lele, G.C. Perlin, and H.G. Thorburn, "The National Party Convention," in Thorburn, *ibid.*, pp. 107-8.

20. Quoted in Porter, *Vertical Mosaic*, p. 430.

21. *Ibid.*, p. 431.

22. *The Canadian Corporate Elite: An Analysis of Economic Power* (Toronto 1975), p. 346.

23. Quoted in Chodos, *CPR*, pp. 16-17.

24. See especially R. Deaton, "The Fiscal Crisis and the Revolt of the Public Employee," *Our Generation*, VIII, 4 (Oct. 1972), pp. 11-51.

25. See H.G.J. Aitken, "Defensive Expansionism: The State and Economic Growth in Canada," in W.T. Easterbrook and M.H. Watkins, eds., *Approaches to Canadian Economic History* (Toronto, 1967), pp. 183-84.

26. C.B. Macpherson, "The Social Sciences," in Julian Park, ed., *The Culture of Contemporary Canada* (Toronto, 1957), pp. 200-1.

27. *The Labour Outlook* (London 1929), p. 32.

28. *The Politics of Development: Forests, Mines & Hydro-Electric Power in Ontario, 1849-1941* (Toronto 1974), pp. 248-49, 490, IX.

29. "Changing Social Origins," p. 72.

30. Quoted in David Wolfe, "Political Culture, Economic Policy and the Growth of Foreign Investment in Canada, 1945-57," unpublished MA thesis, Carleton University, Ottawa, 1973, p. 120.

31. J.W. Dafoe, *Laurier: A Study in Canadian Politics* (1922, Toronto 1963), p. 53.

32. "Another Anti-Trust Tradition: Canadian Anti-Combines Policy, 1884-1910," in Porter and Cuff, *Enterprise*, p. 39.

33. See H.G. Thorburn, "Pressure Groups in Canadian Politics: Recent Revisions of the Anti-Combines Legislation,"*Canadian Journal of Economics and Political Science*, XXX, 2 (May 1964), pp. 157-74; G. Rosenbluth and Thorburn, "Canadian Anti-Combines Administration, 1952-1960," *ibid.*, XXVII, 4 (Nov. 1961); and Bert Young, "Corporate Interests and the State," *Our Generation*, X, 1 (Winter-Spring 1974), pp. 70-83.

34. One must, of course, be careful not to minimize this aspect of the Canadian

state's behavior. For instance, the federal government established in 1919, amidst the economic dislocations and labor unrest of the immediate post-war period, a Board of Commerce to regulate price increases and curb unfair trade practices. There is little reason to doubt T.D. Traves' view of the board's success: "Preservation of the basic component of the existing economic order and integration of disruptive social forces in the established political economy were, broadly speaking, its tasks. In these aims it was partially successful. As a contemporary observer said, '. . . in a general sense public opinion was soothed and the people carried more smoothly over the rocky road of war prices and reconstruction problems than would otherwise have been the case.' The expansion of the Canadian state then, in this case, was intended, and in fact operated in a manner which was fundamentally conservative." "The Board of Commerce and the Canadian Sugar Refining Industry: A Speculation on the Role of the State in Canada," *Canadian Historical Review*, LIV, 2 (June 1974), pp. 174-75. No less significant, however, was the fact that the Board of Commerce failed to become a permanent element on the political scene, having been allowed by the government to wither away barely a year after its establishment.

35. For a history of Canada's snail-like progress in the field of social welfare legislation, see Kathleen Herman, "The Emerging Welfare State: Changing Perspectives in Canadian Welfare Policies and Programs, 1867-1960," in D.I. Davies and K. Herman, eds., *Social Space: Canadian Perspectives* (Toronto 1971), pp. 131-41.

36. *Industry and Humanity* (1918, Toronto 1973), p. 336.

37. See, in this regard, Leo A. Johnson, "The Development of Class in Canada in the Twentieth Century," in Teeple, *Capitalism and the National Question*, pp. 142-53.

38. Quoted in J. Pickersgill, *The Mackenzie King Record, 1939-1944* (Toronto 1960), I, pp. 570-71.

39. *Full Employment in a Free Society, A Report* (London, 1945). For an attestation to Beveridge's impact on Canada, see A. Brady, "The State and Economic Life in Canada," in K.J. Rea and J.T. McLeod, eds., *Business and Government in Canada* (Toronto, 1969), p. 66.

40. "Planning Full Employment," *The Times*, 23 Jan. 1943.

41. 29 June 1937, quoted in the *Citizen*, Ottawa, 11. Jan. 1975.

42. Economic Council of Canada, Third Annual Review: *Prices, Productivity and Employment* (Ottawa 1966), pp. 160-61; cf. Gilles Paquet, "The Economic Council as Phoenix," in T. Lloyd and J. McLeod, eds., *Agenda 1970: Proposals for a Creative Politics* (Toronto, 1968), pp. 135-58.

43. See Harold L. Wilensky, "The Welfare State and Equality" (Berkeley 1975), Table 2, pp. 30-31, and Table 4, pp. 122-24; and his "The Welfare Mess," *Society*, XIII, 4 (May-June 1976), pp. 12-16, 64. I am indebted to Professor Wilensky for making his findings on recent changes in Canada's relative expenditure position available to me in advance of publication.

44. See Allan M. Maslove, *The Pattern of Taxation in Canada* (Ottawa, 1972).

45. See Deaton, "Fiscal Crisis," Table 6, p. 33.

46. Ronald Todgham, quoted in the *Financial Post*, 25 Jan. 1975.

47. For a fuller discussion of the Canadian incomes policy and the ambiguous CLC response to it, see Leo Panitch, *Workers, Wages and Controls* (Toronto, 1976), reprinted in *This Magazine*, X, 1 (Feb.- Mar.1976) and "The Labour Manifesto: Is Corporatism a Strategy for Labour?" *ibid.*, X, 5-6 (Nov.-Dec. 1976).

Sous-Prolétaires Québécois: Class Situation of a Disadvantaged Group*

BERNARD BERNIER

In the past few years, anthropology has concerned itself with the study of disadvantaged groups in regions labeled as underdeveloped (Mexico, Puerto Rico, etc.) as well as in the United States and Canada. The initial thrust into this area was by Oscar Lewis (1961, 1966, 1968, 1969) whose research on "the culture of poverty" has had a great impact. Indeed, even the authors who heavily criticized Lewis's works (see, among others, Valentine, 1968) have always taken a similar approach to his, that is, cultural and "empiricist," an approach which bases its analysis on values and behaviors. I have made a critical analysis of these works and their approach elsewhere (cf. Bernier, 1974) and do not wish to dwell on the subject in this article. Rather, I would like to present a different approach, based on historical materialism, which strives to analyze disadvantaged groups and poverty in terms of social class opposition, that is, in terms of groups which have special and antagonistic positions in the relations of production. To illustrate this, I will use data collected during the study of a disadvantaged group in a small town in Quebec.[1] It will be necessary, before analyzing this group's proletarian situation, to briefly describe the town and the group, to present the group's economic characteristics, its ideologies, and the way in which the group has been used for political purposes. Finally, I will attempt to reinterpret the elements usually included in the term "culture of poverty."

A "Marginal" Group

The studied group lives in a town of 4,500 inhabitants, 60% of whom are francophone and 40% anglophone. The community's primary economic activity is the textile industry. Indeed, two textile factories provide employment for almost half the town's working population. One is modern (Industry No. 1), specializing in luxurious worsted wool[2] and employing 600 persons, over 550 of whom work in the manufacture of the goods. The other (Industry No. 2) is less well equipped, manufactures synthetic plush

---

*Translated by Pierrette Gisiger. Professor Bernier kindly looked over this translation.

and employs 200 people. The rest of the working population is distributed into business, the civil service, small factories, banks, and teaching. The town serves as an administrative center for the area, which remains an important agricultural region, especially for the dairy industry.

The studied group consists of 193 persons from 39 households occupying 38 houses.[3] The group has a special name which identifies it, and a specific geographic location. All the homes, the majority of which are hovels, are concentrated on four streets located in an area bound by two intersecting railway tracks. A genetic disorder, ectodermal dysplasia (a skin disease), affects 16% of the population of the district. The members of the group are poor and many of them are on welfare. Infirmities and debility are widespread. Family groupings are unstable. In short, the group exhibits the characteristics generally attributed to the term "culture of poverty" (Lewis, 1969:801-6).

The Economic Situation

It is at the economic level that the most important characteristics of the group appear. Table 1, which illustrates the types of jobs and the unemployment for 1965 and 1971, enables us to characterize the employment situation and its evolution. During these six years, the unemployment rate tripled from 15% to almost 45%, even when excluding from the unemployed the women who previously held a job and who in 1971 no longer worked. The group's employment situation has deteriorated appreciably and for two reasons:

(1) The difficulties of the local textile industries since 1966.[4] In factory No. 2, the one which is less well-equipped and whose work force is less skilled, close to 20 jobs have disappeared.
(2) The replacement of members in the group by more qualified or more submissive workers. The net result of these trends has been the massive deterioration of employment conditions for the group's members.

The statistics fail to indicate another important aspect of the employment situation of the group's members. Jobs for these people generally consist of manual labor, which requires no skill and is dirty (e.g., being in charge of the boiler or the unpacking of wool in the textile industry, working as street cleaners or in charge of the sewers for the municipality). In 1971, 21 of the 26 employed persons were classified as laborers and at least 8 of these 26 held temporary jobs. Consequently, a good proportion of the group's members do not have permanent jobs and are unemployed for at least a few months each year.

A good portion of the jobs — 40% in 1971 and 50% in 1965 — were in the smallest of the textile factories, which depends on worn machinery and cheap labor for its survival. The jobs are not stable, and the workers can easily be laid off temporarily or permanently, in spite of the presence of a

Table 1

Jobs and Unemployment for the Members of the Group, 1965 and 1971

	1965	*1971*
Jobs in Factory No. 1	2 (1 woman)	2 (1 woman)
Jobs in Factory No. 2	30 (6 women)	11 (1 woman)
Other factory jobs	4	2
Municipal jobs	4 (1 woman)	5
Other jobs	11 (1 woman)	3
Self-employed	1	3
Unemployed	9	20
Total	61	46
Rate of unemployment	15%	45%

union. Thus, from 1966 to 1971 the number of group members employed at this factory decreased from 30 to 11. In 1973, this factory closed its wool-weaving section, laying off almost 30 workers. During these layoffs the members of the group studied are particularly affected as they are considered as casual, unskilled labor, unreliable and subject to absenteeism.

Absenteeism of the people in the group is about 20% higher than average due to three important factors: (1) the assignment to menial and low-paying jobs; (2) the obligation of working more than the normal work week; (3) the use of workers as temporary labor.

As a reserve labor force, the people in the group are given jobs at peak periods of demand which they lose in periods of low demand. So in fact, the labor instability of the group is caused by the reserve army status to which it is assigned before it is employed in the factory.

Without steady employment, and constantly subjected to the fluctuations of demand, the members of the group must still somehow survive. And it is from this that the other important characteristics of the group emerge. The expedient, "la combine," has always been a way of surviving in the neighborhood. Previously, the theft of wood or coal from the railway allowed the members of the group to obtain fuel for winter. Today, car theft is predominant. Some people can dismantle in a few minutes the gear boxes of automobiles being shipped on railway cars. A junkyard owned by one of the members of the group provides a cover for the secondary activities of dismantling the stolen cars, and is linked with sectors of organized crime.

The important source of income apart from employment and criminal activities is unemployment insurance and social security benefits. Because of the type of employment and its temporary nature, and also because of the high unemployment rate, the group's family incomes are extremely low. Indeed, in 1971, the various money sources mentioned did not even assure an average income of $3,000 per year for a family of five.

The consequences of this low level of income are numerous. The houses are generally unsanitary and overcrowded; the furniture is limited; hygiene conditions are inadequate although they have greatly improved since the

1950s when several houses were made of metal advertising panels and had beaten earth floors. (The improvement in the living conditions and hygiene are also evident in the lowered infant mortality rate over the past 20 years; from almost 150 per thousand in the 1940s and 1950s, infant mortality has decreased to about 50 per thousand for the period 1966 to 1971. This last figure is still high but it does indicate a net improvement in the health conditions.) In spite of their improved economic and material conditions over the past 20 years, the standard of living for the group remains universally poor.

The Discriminatory Ideology

The marginal economic situation of the people of the neighborhood is associated with a series of "beliefs" which other people of the town share and disseminate about them. Some of these are based on fact but many are false; and the reasons given to explain the facts mask the real causes. The sum of these beliefs forms a fairly coherent ideology, which stresses the differences between the members of the group and the rest of the townspeople and which ascribes these differences to intrinsic characteristics of the group.

The first characteristic, which is mentioned as much by the townspeople as by the members of the group, is poverty. It is obvious and is stated as something that differentiates the group from the rest of the town's inhabitants. This characteristic is juxtaposed in various ways with other real or supposed aspects of the group. The townspeople attribute the poverty, with reason, to the lack of work available to the members of the group. But generally they see this lack of work as a consequence of laziness, of a poor education or of the unrealiable work habits of the group members. Naturally, they insist that not all the members of the group are alike, and that there are exceptions, but they nevertheless attribute one or another of these three causes of unemployment to the majority of the group. Quebec's economic situation, the breakdown of the textile industry or the class situation of the members of the group are never mentioned as possible causes of unemployment. Rather, the townspeople see the cause lying in the intrinsic and specific characteristics of the group itself.

Unemployment is perceived as the reason for the group's reliance on social security. The general opinion is that the Social Welfare Bureau is very generous to the members of the group and provides them with a livelihood. However, Bureau control over recipients' spending is deemed essential for appropriate use of the funds. Indeed, townspeople focus on what they perceive to be the unreasonableness of purchases made by the members of the group: "Even when unemployed, some have bought themselves new cars or colored televisions." Townspeople stress that there is then nothing left for food or children's clothing and that these people buy on credit even when they have no money. To make up for these foolish expenditures, the members of the group must then steal on the railway. Several townspeople mentioned the well-known association of members of the group to the syndicate: "Not the big syndicate but the little one; ils servent d'hommes de mains." An informer mentioned "confidentially" the presence of hired killers in the neighborhood.

Another characteristic which is deemed widespread in the group is alcoholism. These people supposedly spend the majority of their income on drink and there is nothing left for food. What's more, when they are drunk, they beat their children and fight among themselves. Alcoholism is seen by most people as one of the two major problems of the group.

The other problem is depraved sexual morals. Indeed, all the members of the group are attributed special sexual behaviors including incest, especially between fathers and their daughters ("the fathers initiate their daughters"); sexual promiscuity, generalized between people married and not married, young and old ("there is no age for them; the old sleep with little girls"); and prostitution. They also stress the high rate of illegitimate births, of separation or divorce, and of common-law relationships. According to our informers, the family, "the basic unit of our society," is thus endangered. This is why they prescribe as necessary in many cases, the removal of children from their families and the placing of these children in foster homes where they will be integrated into a "normal" family.

Uncleanliness is viewed as so common that doctors, so the townspeople say, refuse to enter certain houses because they cannot wash their hands or find one clean towel. Finally, they stress the lack of intelligence of these strange and sometimes dangerous people.

As can be seen, the image portrayed of the members of the group is a fairly precise one. It is partly based on actual fact (illegitimate children, separations, common-law relationships, crime, unemployment, and alcoholism) but it exaggerates certain things (sexual behaviors, alcoholism), creates others (prostitution, the presence of hired killers), and assigns to these real or supposed facts intrinsic causes. What is important to note here is that the characteristics attributed to the group are those that are habitually assigned to minorities in similar economic situations (e.g., the Blacks in the ghettos of the United States and the Native Indians in Canada and the United States (cf. among others, Ertel et al., 1970). In fact, although only one member of the group was part Native Indian, several informers assigned an Indian origin to the members of the group. The relation established between the group and other minorities serves to accentuate the difference between the group and the rest of the town and thereby justifies this difference.

The name of "Zoulou," which is given to individuals suffering from ectodermal dysplasia, further accentuates this characteristic. At least two informers wondered about the possible relation with the African people of the same name. One quickly denied any possibility but the other was unable to decide. The name as well as the possible relation to a strange and "savage" people once again accentuates the difference between "ordinary" people and the members of the group; and this is so even when the members of the group having the genetic disorder is only 16%.

As we can see, ideological reflection on the group serves both to justify the difference between the group and the rest of the town and to accentuate it. Obviously, at the abstract level of human rights all recognize that the people in the group are human beings like everybody else. The majority of informers, having noted the improvement in the living conditions over the past 20 years, even predicted the disappearance of the district as a distinct entity. But the recognition of the similarity in the abstract is always accompanied by that of the difference in the concrete. The necessity of obliterating the neighborhood is stressed, but no adequate measure is taken to ensure this. On the contrary, emphasis is placed on the futility of trying to change the situation. However, the use of minimal measures (clearing the streets of snow, donations of clothing, etc.) eases the townspeople's consciences while permitting the group's situation to reproduce itself.

This philosophy is not only indicated by words; it is actualized in structures and customs. The school, the town council, the police force, the factory, the unions, the churches, the local newspaper, all communicate this ideology. For example, the physical appearance of the streets in the neighborhood differs from those of the rest of the town. They are badly paved, they are always muddy, there is no sidewalk. Also, the sewers and drainage system are inadequate, resulting in floods when the snow thaws. The town council takes no initiative to overcome these problems and by its inaction encourages the continuation of the difference in the physical aspect of the neighborhood, thus contributing to the perpetuation of the marginalization of the members of the group.

The education system is the ideological tool which perhaps best guarantees the maintenance of the group. The principal of the elementary school attended by the majority of the children of the group insists that they are dirty and backward. Some teachers, as well as some students, make fun of the children of the group, if not because of the physical disorder which only a few of them have, then because of their worn clothing and rough language. The children of the group are often involved in fights, for which they are often blamed. The school (and the fault rests not solely with the principal and the teachers, but also with the families in which the other children are raised) thus perpetuates discrimination towards the group.

As was pointed out by Bourdieu et al. (170), Baudelot et Establet (1971), and Tort (1974) for France, school is a milieu tailored to the education of upper- and middle-class families, focusing on personal ambition and academic learning. It goes without saying that family education does not adequately prepare the children of the group for such a milieu.

Trapped in an institution that rejects them and which is not adapted to their social class, the children of the group encounter enormous difficulties at school. Indeed, 18 children of the group, of a total of 41 of primary school age, attend a school for retarded children located in another town in the region. Only seven other children from the town attend this school.

Thus the ideology creates the illusion that the difference between group members and the rest of the townspeople is the fault of the individual members of the group, that it has no economic base, and that its explanation and end rest in itself. Contrary to racism or sexism, which makes differences natural by giving them physical or biological causes, the marginalization of this group is based on cultural characteristics (using to that end a genetic particularity found only in a minority). However, there is a "naturalization" of the difference in the sense that the ideology presents it as self-evident.

Economic and Political Value of the Group

The preceding comments on employment and living conditions led to the conclusion that the studied group is part of the "sous-prolétariat." On the one hand, the group's members have no means of production and have only their labor power to sell; on the other hand, the number of chronically unemployed, of temporary workers and of criminals exceeds the number of permanent workers (31 as compared to 15). In fact, the "active" population of the group can be divided into three categories:

(1) The permanent workers who are employed at difficult jobs requiring little skill, in factories where the exploitation of the labor force is more important than the use of productive machines. These workers can be laid off at will.

(2) The temporary workers and chronically unemployed who may have experienced work, but of a difficult, unstable and unsatisfactory nature, and who have resigned themselves to live without work.

(3) The "racketeers" who live from more or less illicit activities.

The third category constitutes what Marx called "lumpen-proletariat," those living from the corruption of the system (Marx, 1960). The second really makes up the reserve labor force, the veritable "sous-prolétariat." They are part of the working class in that they have only their labor power to sell, but they are in general unemployed and find work only during strikes or periods of high demand. It is thus a labor force that is left unemployed until its services are required. This category accounts for at least 25 of the 46 who were active in 1971. As for the permanent workers, their work experience, although sustained, is seldom gratifying. In fact, they consider their work only as a means of obtaining income (an unsatisfactory income at that — the average salary for the employed members of the group was less than $4,500 in 1971) to enable them to live and to participate in the district's leisure activities. If these workers lose their jobs, it is extremely difficult for them to find another. They have then no other alternative than to become chronically unemployed.

It is this class situation of a poorly paid reserve labor force that explains the special characteristics of the group: theft, alcoholism, illegitimate children, common-law relationships, uncleanliness. These characteristics thus arise as consequences of a specific class situation.

These consequences are not in all cases as negative as the discriminatory ideology would have us believe. For example, illegitimate births and common-law relationships do not cause any internal problems: illegitimate children are generally integrated into the mother's family, while common-law couples are generally regarded as legitimate couples. In fact, these practices often facilitate interpersonal relations within the group, by enabling people who no longer get along to separate without any problem, for example.

What is the function of such a group in the town where it is situated? From a purely economic point of view, the members of the group constitute a cheap labor reserve which can be used when temporary workers are needed. It is advantageous, strictly from the point of view of job fluctuations (linked to the fluctuations of the capitalist market) to have a reserve labor force close by. But this reserve labor force has another direct use. Because of its temporary and unstable character, it is less well paid than the regular workforce. It acts therefore as a threat to workers when the latter are looking for salary increases. Thus it serves to keep salaries low in the local industry as a whole.

Because of their use as cheap labor, the members of the group are already identified as being a cause of low salaries. Their use as strike-breakers in the 1940s and 1950s characterized them even more strongly as those in opposition to the immediate interests of the other workers. This labeling is all the easier when the group is concentrated in a well-defined and established district and is assigned a special "culture" and customs different from those of the other workers of the town, who do not need supplementary resources to survive. The effect of these clear distinctions is to mask the common interests of the temporary and permanent workers, and it is this division that allows the management to keep salaries low.

But this is not the only split within the working class caused by the presence of the group. In fact, a majority of the group's members work in the less well-equipped textile factory, the one where the workers are less skilled and less well paid and where the work conditions are the hardest. The other factory hires members of the group only sporadically. The presence of the members of the group in the less mechanized factory leads to a lowering of skill of the labor force in this factory vis à vis that of the other factory. This lowering of skills is consciously promoted by the owner manager of the better equipped factory in order to prevent the union of the workers from both factories in the defense of their common interests. Indeed, he tries to convince his employees that they are the elite of the town's workers. Moreover, he lets it be known that negotiations coordinated by the unions of the two factories would limit the salary increases of his employees as well as worsen their work conditions, and that negotiations without outside interference "between people who know each other" give much better results. The workers are thus urged to restrict negotiations to their own factory and ignore the interests which link them with temporary workers and workers in other factories.

Class Position of the "Sous-Prolétariat"

The social groups which have been analyzed through the concept of the "culture of poverty" are all part of the three social strata present in the group studied in this article: the lumpen-proletariat, the chronically unemployed, and the temporary or poorly paid workers. A class analysis assigns these strata to the working class:[6] their members do not possess any means of production; they have only their labor power to sell. This distinguishes them from the bourgeoisie, which owns or controls the means of production, and from small businessmen. The jobs which they obtain or that they can obtain, are productive[7] and/or manual jobs, which separates them from the employees in the public sector, in banks and in commerce.[8] Nevertheless, these groups form one or rather several strata of the working class and they all share one characteristic: their incomes are not adequate to meet their historically defined needs or means of subsistence (cf. Marx, 1970a, Chap. 6).

The existence of these strata in the working class is essential to capitalist accumulation. The reserve labor force always exists, either because once "maximum employment"[9] is achieved, capitalists use ever more productive machines to decrease the number of employed workers and thus create this reserve; or because through the expropriation of farmers or through immigration (cf. Granotier, 1970), new work forces are injected into the realm of capitalism. In both cases a more or less abundant labor force is created to satisfy the needs of the business concerns.

Furthermore, the poorly paid sector of the proletariat is the one that suffers directly the salary pressures resulting from the presence of a reserve labor force. Relatively unskilled and easily replaceable, these workers are more threatened than skilled workers or those who work in the major sectors. We find the poorly paid labor force in the least productive sectors of the economy (textile and clothing, wood, footwear, food and drinks), precisely those sectors which, because of the low machine productivity and the high competition of products from other countries where labor is cheap, need workers with low salaries to keep themselves in operation with an adequate rate of profit.

These two strata have in fact the same effect on the whole of the working class: they serve to keep salaries low and to divide the working class. It is important to note, with reference to this subject, that certain criteria which already identify sectors of the population (sex, color of skin) are also used to keep these sectors in the disadvantaged portion of the working class and to divide the working class (cf. among others, *Report of the Royal Inquiry Commission on the Status of Women in Canada;* Ertel et al., 1970; Bonacich, 1972).

The specific cultural and social characteristics which are generally included under the term "culture of poverty" remain to be explained. Two important aspects must be underlined. First, the disadvantaged portion of the proletariat must bear, as do all social classes, the dominant ideology, that is, a system of beliefs, more or less coherent and contradictory, which centers on assuring the survival of productive relations and consequently the interests of the dominant classes. The goal of this ideology is to present bourgeois interests as being identical to the general interest, and to integrate all social classes to existing social relations. To effectively ensure this integration, the dominant ideology must adapt itself to diverse material class situations. Indeed, the ideology imparted to the management of business, even if it shares fundamental elements of the ideology of other classes, cannot be in every way similar to that imparted to workers or to the chronically unemployed. In the latter case, the ideology aims to minimize the social dangers posed by the existence of people who are unemployed and without adequate income. To this end it tries to accustom the unemployed to their plight while attributing to them the blame for it. It is clear that this approach is based on a fundamental contradiction: those who have been conditioned to unemployment are not always ready to work when demand creates a need for labor.

Second, the material situation of these strata instigates diverse forms of adaptation which make life easier: theft, unmarried people living together, etc. Living in misery, these strata must organize themselves as well as they can to survive. In fact, the forms taken by this organization can, in certain cases, show certain advantages over bureaucratic and standardized forms of organization in effect in society. On the other hand, some of the forms that are essential to survival under difficult circumstances (conditions arising from the need of capitalism to maintain a reserve labor force) clash with predominant forms of social relationships or with some elements of the predominant ideology. For example, common-law marriages and il-legitimate births constitute organizational forms of the group which may raise doubts about the habitual form of the family. In this light then, the "culture of poverty" is not an absence of culture nor simply a functional adaptation but rather the adaptation modeled by the predominant ideology (and even capable of being in conflict with it) to specific material conditions made necessary by the capitalist search for profit.

NOTES

1. To avoid any trouble that this article or any other subsequent publications could bring to the members of the analyzed group, I will not give its name or that of the municipality where it is situated. The field research was financed by the Arts Council for two and a half years (1970-72), thanks to three research subsidies. I would like to thank here the numerous students who participated in this research: Diane Lessard, Colette Chatillon, Serge Dubuc, Bernard Rioux, Pierre-Paul Gareau, Louis McComber, Suzanne Chartrand, Jean Roy, Michel Duval, Monique Dumont, Douglas Degroot, Pierre Robitaille, Andre Laplante, Bernard Emond, and Louise-Andree Hardy.

2. Wool fabric used in the making of suits for men.

3. The data are from 1971. For the purposes of this article, the 1971 situation is always related in the present tense.

4. These difficulties are shared by the Canadian textile industry as a whole.

5. Obviously a fairly large proportion is concerned. But the fact that it is not the majority who are affected by this disorder permits us to affirm that this characteristic is used to marginalize the group, but that it is not the cause of this marginalization.

6. I must exclude here certain individuals who make their living from "the rackets" but who, having succeeded, have become operation managers rather than bottom-rung laborers.

7. For a more detailed work of the concepts of productive and unproductive work, see Marx, 1970b, Chaps. 1 to 5; Marx, 1971: 191-240; and Berthoud, 1974.

8. For a detailed examination of those various social classes, see Belanger et al., 1974.

9. Full employment does not mean that all the potential workers have a job but rather that the declared unemployment rate situates itself around 1 or 2%, depending on the countries concerned.

REFERENCES

Baudelot, Christian et Roger Establet. *L'Ecole Capitaliste en France*. Paris: Maspero, 1971.

Bélanger, Paul et al. *La division en classes sociales*. Québec: Département de Sociologie, Université Laval, 1974.

Bernier, Bernard. "'Culture de la pauvreté' et analyse de classes,"*Anthropologica*, Vol. 16, No. 1 (1974), pp. 41-58.

Berthoud, Arnaud. *Travail productif et productivité du travail chez Marx*. Paris: Maspero, 1974.

Bonacich, Edna. "A Theory of Ethnic Antagonism: The Split Labor Market," *American Sociological Review*, Vol. 37, Act 72 (1972), pp. 547-59.

Bourdieu, Pierre et Passeron, J.C. *La Reproduction*. Paris: Editions de Minuit,1970.

Ertel, Rachel, et al. *En Marge*. Paris: Maspero, 1971.

Granotier, Bernard. *Les travailleurs immigrés en France*. Paris: Maspero, 1970.

Lewis, Oscar. *The Children of Sanchez*. New York: Random House, 1961.

_____. "The Culture of Poverty," in this volume.

_____: *A Study of Slum Culture*. New York: Random House, 1968.

_____. *La Vida*. Paris: Gallimard, 1969.

Marx, Karl. *Le Manifeste du Parti Communiste*. Paris, 10-18, 1960.

_____. *Le Capital*, Livre I. Paris: Gonthier Flammarion, 1970a.

_____. *Le Capital*, Livre II. Paris: Editions Sociales, 1970b.

_____. *Un Chapitre inédit du capital*. Paris: 10-18, 1971.

La Presse. *La situation économique du Québec*. Supplement, Montréal. (janvier 1974).

Rapport de la Commission Royale d'Enquête sur la situation de la Femme au Canada. Ottawa: Imprimeur de la Reine, 1971.

Tort, Michel, *Le quotient intellectuel*. Paris: Maspero, 1974.

Valentine, Charles A. *Culture and Poverty*. Chicago: University of Chicago Press, 1968.

Social Inequalities and the Transmission of Knowledge: The Case against the Schools

JOHN HARP

Mass Education and Social Class: The Canadian Case

In order to understand the role of the schools in the transmission of knowledge, one must view them as something other than simple socializing agencies imparting "neutral" knowledge and skills to a relatively passive clientele. They must be seen in a broad sociopolitical context, as integral parts of the state apparatus whereby they serve the interests of corporate work and life. More importantly, they are involved in the process of social and cultural reproduction as agents of bourgeois society. Only through the systematic development of such a perspective can the origins of social inequalities in the transmission of knowledge be located. This thesis is abstract and complex, requiring both interpretation and specification; supportive evidence must be found and presented in order to move it beyond the realm of speculation. Some of this work has already been done and this article will draw upon a few of the most salient studies in order to identify critical issues in the area of education.

The article examines three major areas believed to be central to an understanding of social inequalities in the transmission of knowledge. They are the early historical development of a system of compulsory mass education, equality of educational opportunity, and finally, the process of knowledge transmission in the schools. Some attention must be given to the history of mass education if one is to understand educational systems of advanced industrialized societies such as Canada. We choose to begin during the mid-19th century in Upper Canada and Ontario since it is here that both the scope and direction of educational change can be most clearly seen. Indeed, it is during this mid-century period that the transition from an informal and voluntary system to a formal and compulsory education under the supervision of the state occurred (Prentice, 1977).

Elementary and Secondary Education

The development of a system of mass education in Upper Canada and Ontario is treated extensively in an insightful historical analysis by Alison Prentice entitled *The School Promoters*. She looks at how the school promoters of the period, including the celebrated Egerton Ryerson, perceived the social structures of their times and the function of the schools in relation to them. Prentice provides support for her proposition that "Victorian educators' ideas about human and child nature was thus carried over into a world view in which fundamental distinctions were made not only between civilized and savage societies but also within any given society between the respectable classes and the lower order" (Prentice, 1977).

As the school promoters came more and more to see the world in this way, they increasingly became concerned about the potential for conflict between the two great classes of society. The answer was to see the schools as promoters of peace, fostering good relations between the classes and reconciling to some extent two mutually hostile classes. Class conflict or the potential thereof would be eliminated by encouraging the lower classes to take on the values of the upper. This entailed, of course, inculcating discipline in the poor, including respect for private property. Nevertheless — and this is a theme we will pick up later and apply to a more contemporary period — there were certain basic contradictions in the schools' perceived functions. Consolidation and universality were promoted in a class society. Reality soon parted company from the ideal and in Prentice's words:

> The professed goals of bringing all classes into the common schools on the one hand, and of encouraging educational opportunity for the labouring classes and the poor on the other, were seriously compromised by the way in which the two goals conflicted with each other, as well as by countless practical and psychological obstacles to the fulfillment of these ideals (1977).

Although provisions for state-controlled grammar schools were made as early as 1816 in Upper Canada (Wilson, 1970a), there was a distinction made between the type of education to be gained by the masses and by the elite. The elite had access to a liberal and classical education; in Lord Simcoe's words, classical education was for "all sons of gentlemen" and the "children of the principal people of this country," who would become the country's leaders (Wilson, 1970a:193). Despite attempts at this time to enable youth to learn the skills of the trades and mechanics, Simcoe dismissed these efforts, expressing the view that "such education as may be necessary for people in the lower degree of life...may at present be provided for them by their connections and relatives" (Wilson, 1970a:193). The education of the elite took place mainly in private schools, which charged tuition and provided basic training in the classical studies. As levels of education increased, the higher levels remained the prerogative of the upper classes.

The early elitist character of Canadian education was apparent to some in 1867. In an article from the Toronto *Globe* arguing against following the American precedent of educating girls, the writer contends:

> it is not to be overlooked, in any comparison between the American educational system and our own, that an exclusive spirit of class and cast exists here, which is nearly unknown in the States.... It would lead to no good result to discuss the wisdom of such exclusiveness. The fact is indisputable, and cannot be overlooked in any scheme for establishing Provincial higher schools for girls... (quoted in Prentice and Houston, 1975:257).

Continuity of the class structure was thus reinforced by the elitist system of education. The early practice in Canada of providing higher education for members of the elite has changed only slightly over the years. While education has been expanded to provide access for a greater number of individuals, higher education today is distinguished by an over-representation of upper- and middle-class students in the universities, as shown in Table 1. We will have more to say on this issue of accessibility later in our discussion.

The expansion of education in Upper Canada took place in the latter half of the 19th century. Under the supervision of Egerton Ryerson, elementary education was made universal, free, and compulsory. Ryerson's plea for compulsory education was based on his understanding that " 'Education is a public good, ignorance is a public evil,' and therefore every child rich or poor should receive an education sufficient to overcome 'the evils of want and poverty,' and 'fit him to be an honest and useful member of the community.' " (Wilson, 1970b). Education was intended to integrate individuals into the society, but education would also eliminate pauperism, crime, vice, and juvenile delinquency. By improving the nation, an educated people would be "the best security for good government and constitutional liberty" (Wilson, 1970b:218). Ryerson's views were supported both by conservatives in the society, as a means to minimize radicalism and discontent in the lower classes, and by the radicals of the period, who saw free education as a form of social mobility.

The curriculum of the elementary schools was to emphasize a practical education: history, geography, linear drawing, bookkeeping, music, arithmetic, nature study, agriculture, physical education, hygiene, and

Table 1

Occupation of Parents of Post-Secondary Students, 1968-69

	Occupation of Father	Occupation of All Males in Labor Force
	%	
Managerial	22	12
Professional and technical	16	11
Clerical and sales	21	13
Craftsmen and production workers	6	32
Laborers	9	6
Service	6	7
Farming	9	12
Other	11	7
Totals	100	100

Source: Perspective Canada, 1974.

political economy (Wilson, 1970b). While not all of these courses were included in the final curriculum, they indicate that there was a significant difference between the content of elementary education, geared primarily to the needs of lower-class youth, and the classical content of the schools attended by upper-class children. The differences are apparent in the division of secondary education, a division made in 1871 yet never fully instituted due to financial difficulties. The high schools were to teach English, commerce, and natural science, while collegiate institutes were college preparatory institutions emphasizing the study of Greek and Latin (Wilson, 1970b). Thus education in Ontario after the Ryerson years reflected the elitist and conservative nature of higher learning and the practical training of lower-class children.

By the 1870s Canada was on the brink of industrialization, and the new mode of production with its concurrent effects of urbanization and immigration brought many changes to Canadian society which, in turn, imposed new demands on schools (Stamp, 1970a). Spring (1972) outlines the changes in education demanded by industrial society. The new form of society, based on a corporate image stressing cooperation, required the development of a social institution to produce "men and women who conformed to the needs and expectations of a corporate and technocratic world" (Spring, 1972). The school served this function as the major institution of socialization and part of the state apparatus.

Consequently, the development of education in the late 19th and early 20th centuries was closely tied to the needs of the corporate state. The expansion of the system during this period was phenomenal. For example, there were two and a half times as many school-age children in 1876 as there had been in 1846, but the number of children attending common schools had quadrupled (Prentice, 1977). This period is characterized by the "transition from the informal and largely voluntary to formal institutional and compulsory education under the aegis of the state" (Prentice, 1977). The power of the schools, by virtue of the emphasis placed on the integrative function, shows the importance of education to political and economic stability; a successful program of integration would lead to a passivity on the part of the people towards the inequalities of the society, for integration means supplying people with an understanding and acceptance of their role in society.

Vocational and Technical Education

The need for education of a vocational nature to train workers for industrialized Canada appears as early as Ryerson's statement of 1847:

> In the present state of manufacturers, where so much is done by machinery and tools, and so little done by brute labour (and that little diminishing), mental superiority, system order, punctuality, and good conduct — qualities all developed and promoted by education — are becoming of the highest consequence (Prentice and Houston, 1975).

The advent of industrialization caused great concern for many Canadians, who felt this country was being left behind. J.G. Hodgins, Ontario's deputy minister of education, wrote in 1876:

While our immediate neighbours have profited by the example of other Nations, as illustrated at the [Philadelphia] World's Fair, we have been, to all intents idle. Even in our best Schools the teaching of drawing is the rare exception, not to speak of higher Industrial Art Training (Stamp, 1970a).

Not only would the development of vocational training provide skilled labor, but education of a practical sense was perceived as necessary to meet the growing problems of industrialization.

As with other forms of education, the alternate purpose of social control was also evident in vocational education programs. There was a need at the turn of the century not only for a disciplined and stratified labor force in line with the new requirements of capitalism but also for one which would "contain the class conflict that emerged in the forms of ethnic and labor unrest, petit-bourgeois radicalism, and general social upheaval" (Schecter, 1977). This new reform also came with certain clearly recognized tasks of socialization, as shown by the following excerpt from the report of the Royal Commission on Industrial Training and Technical Education.

> The full results of Industrial Training and Technical Education are to be sought through, —
>> The discipline which comes from interest in work. . . . The preservation and strengthening of a spirit of willingness to accept and fill one's place in organized society which implies relative positions and relative degrees of authority" (Prentice and Houston, 1975).

Early advocates of vocational education included the Quebec Council of Arts and Manufacturers, the Manufacturers Association of Ontario, the Nova Scotia Coal Mining industry, Trades and Labour Congress of Canada, Dominion Board of Trade, the National Council of Women, and the most vocal advocate, the Canadian Manufacturers' Association (Stamp, 1970a). Students trained in the industrial schools would be better workers because the qualities required by industrialization would be instilled by the schools.

The Royal Commission on Technical Education understood this function of education and particular attention was given to the education of the working mechanic and foreman to ensure they acquired the dispositions and attitudes necessary to hold supervisory positions in the hierarchical division of labor.[1] With the assistance of federal funds educational systems were to change in response to a changing industrial capitalism that was emerging in the country. Nevertheless, education's primary function continued to be social control. Support of technical education by the bourgeoisie and their political representatives becomes "a further attempt to integrate the working class into capitalism without having to resort to outright coercion" (Schecter, 1977). Ontario, with its more advanced form of industrial capitalism, led the country in the emphasis placed on technical education.

The phenomenal growth and development in vocational technical education occurred during the 1960s. Martell makes the following observations:

> . . .With the offer of assistance from the Federal Provincial Technical and Vocational Agreement, provinces fought to keep pace with the building of

new technical and vocational schools. The result was that for this program the original estimate of 190 million dollars for ten years [made by the federal government for its contributions to all provinces] was exceeded by 79 million within 15 months, with Ontario leading the way. The total cost of the federal government will exceed one billion dollars if the program is fully completed by the provinces (Martell, 1974).[2]

At the secondary level there is some question as to whether the schools actually fulfill their goal of providing specific training which prepares a student for a particular job or group of jobs (Reich and Zeigler, 1972). In addition, the related problem of literacy training for students in these schools has been a subject for debate, as shown by the following excerpt from a Special Report prepared for the Toronto Board.

> The main common characteristic of all these students is that they don't read and write very well, and an examination of the ability levels of the students who have tentatively selected a program in the Vocational Schools for next year suggests that their reading ability is unlikely to show any great improvement in the years to come (Special Education Report, June 1970).

If this particular class of schools is failing in its manifest goal of preparing students for jobs, how are they faring with their latent goal of socialization, of preparing students to fit into the various levels of working-class or middle-class employment? This goal is recognized by no less than the prolific historian of education in Ontario, W.G. Fleming.

> While technical courses continued to aim at the development of certain basic skills, the emphasis for the bulk of the students swung towards technology in the broad sense. There was stress on principles and concepts with transfer value. These changes did not come immediately with the introduction of the new plan in 1961, for a time the main change was quantitative. It was not until 1965 or 1966 that the qualitative differences really became evident. The creation of the colleges of applied art and technology did much to further the idea that secondary school courses were intended, not primarily to prepare the student for a job but rather to give him an appreciation of the role of the machine and a reasonable feeling of self confidence in the face of technology (Fleming, 1972).

Finally then, the changes that occurred in the structure of corporate capitalism required a highly stratified work force whose members were socialized to take their place in the occupational structure by a growing and complex bureaucratic educational system.

Post-Secondary Education

As we stated earlier, a "liberal" or "classical" education was something reserved for the sons and daughters of the upper classes in 19th-century Canada. With the firm establishment of public mass education at the secondary level during the latter part of the 19th century, greater numbers of children of diverse backgrounds attended school. By the end of World War II, a high school education was not uncommon among Canadians. This is not to suggest that education lost its class bias, which persisted both in terms of differences in aspirations and levels of attainment for students from diverse backgrounds (Barrados, 1977).

In the United States by the 1930s a college degree was replacing a high school diploma as the "minimal standard of respectability" (Collins, 1974). Canada has always lagged behind the United States in both kind and amount of post-secondary education available to students. The reasons for this disparity undoubtedly reflect certain differences in the educational systems of the two societies. But as we shall see later, selective mechanisms regarding accessibility are still at work in both societies.

Robert Harris, a noted historian of higher education in Canada, argues for the unique features of Canadian universities in comparison with their American and European counterparts. This uniqueness is present to some degree as early as 1860 and consists in part of an emphasis on classical college courses with less specialization than one finds in the United States. However, no Canadian university restricted its program to the provision of liberal education. Harris also believes that the support for professional education provided by provincial governments was a significant factor in persuading them to provide substantial support for all types of higher education. These things suggest a rather pragmatic, utilitarian approach to education and one which has found its fullest expression in the human capital arguments advanced by the state during the 1960s.[3] At times during this expansionist period for Canadian universities, education became almost a synonym for knowledge and, as some have argued, in a post-industrial society knowledge is also power (Bell, 1975). Universities are seen as the prime producers of knowledge (especially theoretical knowledge) through their research and development linkages. But it bears emphasizing that they are also one of the major institutions through which society manages its stock of knowledge. Universities, no less than other units in the educational system, are an essential instrument in the transmission and legitimation of knowledge in the industrial society (Egglestone, 1977).

Until quite recently the post-secondary non-university educational system in Canada was neither as extensive nor as well developed as that found in the United States. In the late 1960s and early 1970s several Canadian provinces undertook to "rationalize" this sector of education. A recent OECD report describes some of these developments, offering several reasons for the creation of junior colleges:

(1) to relieve the pressure of numbers on the senior institutions sufficiently to avoid the need of creating more universities;
(2) they were inexpensive, comparing the unit costs of the two institutions;
(3) they were a selection device which enabled "border-secondary line" academic students to study at the post secondary educational level and still permitted the senior institutions to weed out the weaker students at mid point in the degree programme (New College Systems in Canada, OECD, Paris, 1972).

The CEGEPS of Quebec are closely linked to the universities because students can enter university from CEGEP and no longer from the *colleges classiques* or the publicly supported or private secondary schools. In contrast, the new colleges in Ontario, Colleges of Applied Arts and Technology (CAAT) were designed to meet the needs of the local community, and their responsibilities were threefold: first, to provide courses of types and levels beyond, and not suited to, the secondary setting; to meet the needs of graduates from any secondary school program, *apart from those wishing to attend university*; and to meet the educational needs of adults and out-of-school youth, whether or not they are secondary school graduates. The omission of transfer courses in this early statement would seem to effectively preclude or at least seriously hinder students who wish to go on from a college of applied arts and technology to a university.

We have argued throughout this section that the development of a system of mass compulsory education under the aegis of the state can best be understood in relation to the nature of the class structure existing within a given sociopolitical and historical context. We began with the early educational promoters of the mid-19th century, including the celebrated Egerton Ryerson, who saw mass education as a means of avoiding potential class conflict. We also discussed the responsiveness of the educational system to the needs of the corporate and technocratic world and in a more recent period the increased bureaucratization of the educational system in order to facilitate social control by the state. Finally, we addressed ourselves to the character and functions of types of post-secondary institutions in Canada.

In the next section we will examine the social origins of students who attend these institutions and the extent to which they serve a "cooling out" function for some students of secondary schools.[4] Since World War II, western industrial societies have expressed concern over equality of access to public education and more recently to various types of post-secondary education. Nowhere has this concern been so emphatically stated as in the United States, where sociologists and economists have provided us with the results of a prolific research program on the subject of equality of educational opportunity. Before examining some of the Canadian work in this area we will attempt a brief explication of the concept of equality so central to these studies.

Equality of Opportunity and Class Specific Education

The concept of equality is central to the discussions of many liberal thinkers, past and present. In fact, it is a fundamental tenet of classic liberalism, proclaiming the individual, rather than family, community or state as the singular unit of society. As criteria for advancement, universalism champions over particularism and institutions of society are arranged in such a way as to fairly regulate the competition. Bell states it succinctly:

> As a principle equality of opportunity denies the precedence of birth, of nepotism, of patronage or any other criterion which allocates place other than fair competition open equally to talent and ambition (Bell, 1973).

During the 18th century Enlightenment, the Lockean version of natural rights gave primacy to the individual. Rights were natural in the sense of being attributable to men as inherent characteristics qua men; consequently no state could withhold them. Laski puts it cogently, "Rights therefore are prior to the state, in the sense that recognized or not they are that from which its validity derives" (Laski, 1948). It is not surprising therefore, that most advocates of equality turn out to be believers in human rights in some sense (Jordan, 1975).

But how can one justify the claims of human rights? Legal and moral rights can be justified with reference to laws and rules accepted in a given society. T.H. Marshall found the answer to human rights in the concept of citizenship. "A basic human equality associated with full membership of a community, of citizenship" (Marshall, 1943). Inequalities are tolerated therefore, provided they do not spring from hereditary privileges.

Others, for example, John Rawls, see the basis of equality in a theory of distributive justice, or equality for reasons of justice (Rawls, 1973). "Justice is the first virtue of social institutions" (Rawls, 1972). Justice and fairness rest on two principles:

(1) Each person has equal right to the most extensive basic liberty, compatible with similar liberty for others.
(2) Social and economic inequalities are to be arranged so that they are:
(a) reasonably to be expected to be everyone's advantage;
(b) attached to positions open to all.

The implications for education and the schools is made quite clear in the following statement:

> . . . there should be equal prospects of culture and achievement for everyone similarly motivated and endowed — chances to acquire cultural knowledge and skills should not depend upon one's class position and so the school system should be designed to even out class barriers (Rawls, 1972).

We shall examine the problems associated with implementing these ideas later in our discussion. For the present we note that Rawls is sufficiently realistic to conclude that you cannot equalize opportunity but, "one can only bend it toward equality of result" (Rawls, 1972).

The meritocratic principle, often used by liberals to rationalize the failures of the system, is rejected by Rawls in part because it violates the difference principle (i.e., "If some persons are to be better off, the lesser advantaged also are to be better off"). It seems that much more is involved here than simple equity, for one is taking into account special needs, or "From each according to his ability; to each according to his needs." The implications of the difference principle for social policy is borne out through the principle of redress, namely to redress the bias of contingencies in the direction of equality. The state moves through certain policies to accept the principle of redress and the representation of the disadvantaged in group terms. However, both the meaning of disadvantaged and the measure of fairness, must be answered within a given social context (Jordan, 1975).[5]

If one can use Parkin's notion of a "public meaning system" which individuals draw upon in constructing their social worlds, then this meaning system, as Jordan points out, "seems to signify a class-differentiated normative order of society" (Parkin, 1971; Jordan, 1975).

This would conceivably lead us to consider typologies of societies. One such scheme provides a normative context for examining equality of access (McRoberts and Gilbert, 1975). Two dimensions of equality are considered here: (1) equality of opportunity to include universalism and insuring that

Figure 1

A Typology of Distributive Systems (Gilbert and McRoberts, 1975)

Equality of Opportunity

		High	Low
	Present	Egalitarian	Communal
		1	2
Equality of Condition		3	4
	Absent	Meritocracy	Stratified

all members of society begin the race the same; (2) equality of condition refers to the allocation of rewards in society. These dimensions, when combined, form the typology of societies shown in Figure 1. They should be seen as a series of ideal types against which one may measure societies of particular sociocultural and historical settings.

The two societal types where equality of condition is present are egalitarian and communal. Lenski singles out this feature of hunting and gathering societies. "If any single feature of hunting and gathering societies has impressed itself upon observers, it is the relative equality of the members" (Lenski, 1966). As for equality of opportunity, the primacy of the kinship system results in a strong collective orientative and particularistic criteria of selection. The egalitarian type, for which there is no empirical referent, displays equalities of both condition and opportunity. The former reveals itself through equality in the distribution of material goods. The only inequalities to be tolerated are those which are part of the authority structure and derive from the division of labor. Equality of opportunity exists in order that each individual may develop his or her potential through education and training.

Societies which lack equality of condition but vary with respect to equality of opportunity are termed meritocratic and stratified, appearing in the third and fourth quadrants respectively. In a meritocratic type, the normative structure is such that inequalities exist in various types of social rewards (e.g., wealth, power, prestige). The ideological basis for meritocracy argues that differences in material inequalities are appropriate when these inequalities arise as differential rewards for varying levels of performance. Presumably performance comes to be determined largely by an individual's genetic component. It has been argued by opponents of this view that a genetic lottery is surely an arbitrary basis for social justice.

Subsequently many of the educational programs of the 1960s (in the U.S., in particular) grew out of a distrust of meritocracy.

Finally we come to the stratified societal type, for which Canada and the United States serve as approximations. This type of society is similar to the meritocratic with respect to the differential distribution of material and non-material rewards. Inequalities result, it seems, from particularistic, ascriptive transmission (e.g., through religion, ethnic, linguistic, sexual, and family groupings in society). However, the main particularistic ascriptive status transmission mechanisms are to be found in the family or the influence of the family as, some have suggested, mediated or maintained and perpetuated by the schools (Gilbert, 1977).

Our historical overview of mass education in Canada illustrated the conflicting ideas of equal opportunity. Some argue the case of needs arising from industrialization requiring a basic education for the labor force, whereas others perceive it as a means used by the ruling class to allay potential class conflict within the society. The arguments in the former case are couched in a liberal ideology, whereas the latter is elaborated within a Marxist perspective.

Fleming reports on the increased attention given the concept of equality of opportunity in Canadian reports on education since World War II, but acknowledges that a greater interest occurred in the United States. However, in 1970, the Economic Council of Canada devoted its Annual Review to the topic, and Canadian studies of equality of opportunity which deal with access to post-secondary education appear more numerous during the 1960s and early 1970s (e.g., the seminal work of Raymond Breton at the University of Toronto, and more recently, the studies conducted by John Porter and his colleagues at Carleton University) (Breton, 1971; Porter, 1978). It is beyond the scope of this paper to systematically review all of the work in this area; nevertheless, we wish to examine some of the recent evidence used in assessing the influence of ascribed characteristics on levels of educational attainment.

Equality of Educational Opportunity:
Selective Research on Cohort Generational Shifts in Schooling:
The Case of Canada and the United States

Although the level of educational attainment of the Canadian population has greatly increased since the turn of the century, great inequities persist. One approach to demonstrating both the sources and trends of these inequities uses a cohort analysis (Barrados, 1977). The exercise is a partial replication of work carried out in the United States by Hauser and Featherman, who cautiously point out the limitations of the technique (i.e., "two forms of misrepresentation, first differentials in marriage, fertility, initial differences in cohort size and mortality in relation to other differences between cohorts result in a somewhat distorted picture of historical reality," and second, a demographic presentation "tends to smooth and prolong processes of social change") (Hauser and Featherman, 1976). Despite these limitations the exercise provides some interesting insights on the subject of inequality and educational attainment.

Barrados is able to report, predictably enough, that successive cohorts of Canadian males (females are excluded from the sample) have attained increasingly higher levels of education. In short, the mean years of education attained by men in the Canadian population as shown in Table 2 have increased regularly from 1907 to 1951 and the variability in education has declined across the cohorts. These general trends are identical with those reported by Hauser and Featherman for the United States. We are cautioned against assuming that no differences in educational attainment exist between the two countries. For example, educational attainment is consistently higher in the United States than it is in Canada. Furthermore, the variability in educational attainment is greater in Canada than reported for the United States. However, levels of educational attainment are found to have been growing at a more accelerated rate in Canada than the United States. Finally, the decelerating rate in educational attainment reported for the United States by Hauser and Featherman does not appear to be occurring in Canada, at least as near as one can judge from these data.

Insofar as equality of educational opportunity is concerned, the traditional regression model is used with several background factors, including father's education and occupation, which account for 54% of the variance in educational attainment. The U.S. study alluded to earlier employs eight variables to explain 34% of the variance. Interestingly enough, a comparison of studies of educational aspirations of high school students in the two countries shows socioeconomic background of parents to be a better predictor in Canada than in the United States (Gilbert, 1974). One hesitates to make too much of these observations, given the possible variations in measurement for the cohort studies and sampling variations in the surveys. They do serve, however, to emphasize that certain background factors or ascribed characteristics continue to predict life chances in societies where the meritocratic ideology is pervasive.

Equality of Opportunity: The Case of High School Dropouts

Despite the fact that greater numbers of students are completing high school today than at any previous period in the history of Canada, the selective character of high school dropouts is a persistent phenomenon. Unfortunately, most of the literature on this topic suffers from the limitations of cross-sectional designs. A recent follow-up study of a sample of Ontario grade eight students originally interviewed in 1971 proves the exception (Porter, Blishen, Barrados, 1977). At the time of the follow-up it was expected that most of these students would be completing their secondary school studies. The authors report that "Higher father's education is found to continue to influence the choice of high school programs even when the effects of school performance, individual self evaluations of ability, and motivation are held constant" (Porter, Blishen, Barrados, 1977). A special study of a subsample of students from lower socioeconomic status backgrounds but with mental ability scores in the upper two-thirds of the distribution was also carried out.[6] It is here that school program looms large as a significant factor affecting educational decisions. It would seem that the early decisions taken by counsellors and teachers in assigning students to streams become even more

Table 2

Percentage Distribution of Post-Secondary Students by Program and Sex

Program	Males (N=65,403)	Females (N=40,784)	N
Post-secondary non-university	22.3	40.0	30,902
Undergraduate university	70.4	56.2	68,698
Post-graduate university	7.3	3.8	6,317
Total			106,187

Source: Marsden and Harvey, 1971.

critical in influencing their educational futures, a finding also emphasized by Breton's earlier work in this area (Breton, 1971).[7]

Returning to the study of school dropouts, perhaps the most significant finding reported by Porter et al. is found in the following succinct statement:

> The dynamics of elementary school participation are predictive of high school program choice and high school attainment (Porter et al., 1977).

This would suggest, at least to the present author, that future studies should focus on the dynamics of teacher-student relationships at the elementary level. Working toward a theory of educational transmissions is an integral part of the research of many neo-Marxist social scientists, some of which we will examine shortly.

In summary then, even a cursory assessment of research conducted by both liberal reformers and neo-Marxists concludes that social class inequalities in our school system are too evident to be denied. At the post-secondary level, as shown by the data in Tables 1 through 7, ascribed characteristics such as gender and father's occupation influence high school programs and university attendance. One also finds that the correlation between parents' social status and years of education attained by individuals who completed schooling three to four decades ago is approximately the same as individuals today or in recent years. An individual's family background continues to be an important predictor of both educational aspirations and attainment in our society. Furthermore, the reduction in inequality for years of schooling has not been matched by an equalization of income distribution in either the United States or Canada.

Although a comprehensive assessment of the effects of education on subsequent employment and economic returns is beyond the scope of the present paper, we would be remiss not to point out the decreasing job openings for highly qualified manpower occupations. In addition, large youth unemployment is surely a significant social issue, and as shown in Table 8, the unemployment rate of the 14 to 24 age group since 1970 has been twice as high as for the 25 and over age groups. Furthermore, it is likely that

Table 3

Educational Attainment of Canadian Males by Cohort

Birth Cohort	Mean Ed. Attn.	S.D.	N
1947-1951	11.81	2.64	707
1942-1946	11.80	3.27	603
1937-1941	11.08	3.58	456
1932-1936	10.51	3.64	456
1927-1931	9.99	3.79	469
1922-1926	9.43	3.73	434
1917-1921	9.21	3.77	415
1912-1916	9.04	3.79	370
1907-1911	8.05	3.95	250

Source: M. Barrados, "Inequality of Educational Attainment in Canada and the U.S.A." CARMAC Project, Carleton University, 1977.

Table 4

Student's Secondary School Program by Father's Occupational Status

	Class I	Class II	Class III	Class IV	Class V	Class VI	Total
5-year	86	83	74	69	56	51	65
4-year	14	16	26	30	43	49	35
N (=100%)	(178)	(212)	(289)	(534)	(1,021)	(299)	(2,530)

Source: Gilbert and McRoberts, 1975.

Table 5

Percentages of Grade 12 Students, in Spring 1971, Expecting to Graduate from University, by Socioeconomic Status of Father

Socioeconomic Status of Father (Blishen Scale)	Percentage of Grade 12 Students Expecting to Graduate from University
Class I (mainly professional)	60
Class II (mainly managerial)	53
Class III (lower managerial) (lower professional)	43
Class IV (skilled)	38
Class V (farmers)	25
Class VI (unskilled)	24
Total	37

Source: Porter et al., 1973.

Table 6

Educational Distribution of Fathers of Post-Secondary Students and of Canadian Population Aged 15 and over

Educational Levels	Canadian Population		Fathers of Post-Secondary Students	
	%		%	
Elementary[1]	37.2		24.9	
Secondary[2]	53.0		51.3	
Some university	5.1		6.2	
Bachelors	2.4		9.2	
		9.8		23.8
First professional	1.2		4.0	
Masters or doctoral	1.1		4.4	
Total %	100.0		100.0	
Total N (000)	13,168.0		661.7	

[1]No formal education, some elementary schooling or elementary completed.
[2]Includes some or completed secondary schooling.
Source: Secretary of State, *Some Characteristics of Post-Secondary Students in Canada*, Ottawa, 1976, Table 3.2, p. 36.

many of these unemployed young people come from the disadvantaged groups of Canadian society and have limited marketable skills. When youth unemployment is related to educational attainment we see clearly the screening function of education in the labor market (Table 10).

The failure of progressive educational reforms is generally conceded by liberal research analysts and Marxists alike; they mainly differ concerning the reasons for failure and the suggested solutions. Bowles and Gintis argue persuasively that one should look to the contradictions inherent in the integrative, egalitarian and personal development functions of schools in societies whose economic life is governed by institutions of corporate capitalism. They point out, for example, that the way in which the school performs the integrative function, through the production of a stratified labor force, is inconsistent with egalitarian and development functions also claimed by the system (Bowles and Gintis, 1975).

In order to examine the root causes of the problem these authors begin with a basic tenet of Marxist social theory, namely that consciousness develops through social relations into which people enter in their daily lives. Consciousness is reproduced not only through the individual's contact with work but also through membership in a social class and the institutions of reproduction (i.e., school and family). In other words, "inequalities and repressiveness in the educational institution are best understood as reflections of the social relations of hierarchy and subordination in the capitalist-economy" (Bowles and Gintis, 1975). Hence we see a parallel between the social relations of the school and those of the economy. It bears emphasizing that the reference is to experience in schooling and not the content of

Table 7

Fathers' Education by Type of Post-Secondary Student

Fathers' Education[1]	Community College				University				Professional	All
	Transfer		Terminal		Undergrad		Graduate			
	F	P	F	P	F	P	F	P		
%										
Elementary or less	25	30	30	35	20	35	20	30	15	25
High school	35	35	45	43	35	40	35	35	35	40
Post-sec. Non-univ.	15	10	12.5	11	10	12.5	10	10	10	10
University	25	25	12.5	11	35	12.5	35	25	40	25
Total	100	100	100	100	100	100	100	100	100	100

(Braces combine Post-sec. Non-univ. and University: Transfer F = 40, P = 35; Terminal F = 25, P = 22; Undergrad F = 45, P = 25; Graduate F = 45, P = 35; Professional = 50; All = 35.)

[1]Elementary or less; some or completed high school; Post-sec. Non-univ. includes business, technical or training, or nursing school, teacher college, junior college, classical college or equivalent; includes some university (no degree, and undergrad, and graduate degree completion).

Source: Secretary of State, *Some Characteristics of Post-Secondary Students in Canada,* Ottawa, 1976, Figure 3.5 adapted, p.37.

Table 8

Fathers' Income by Type of Student

Fathers' Income	Community College				University				Professional	All
	Transfer		Terminal		Undergrad		Graduate			
	F	P	F	P	F	P	F	P		
%										
Less than $5,999	12.5	25	15	32.5	15	37.5	27.5	37.5	20	20
6,000–9,999	22.5	25	30	22.5	20	22.5	17.5	20	15	22.5
10,000–14,999	32.5	22.5	30	27.5	30	20	25	22.5	20	27.5
15,000–19,999	12.5	12.5	17.5	5.0	10	7.5	10	5.0	15	12.5
20,000 plus	20	15	12.5	12.5	25	12.5	20	15	30	17.5
Total	100	100	100	100	100	100	100	100	100	100

Source: Secretary of State, *Some Characteristics of Post-Secondary Students in Canada,* Ottawa, 1976, Figure 3.7 adapted, p. 43.

formal learning. In the Canadian context, Schecter also argues forcibly for this position in his discussion of educational reforms.

> Progressive education was . . . an adaptation of schooling to the new type of character formation required by the changes in corporate capital. These changes required a highly stratified work force that had internalized different norms of behavior according to their place in the occupational structure (Schecter, 1977).

The dominant structure of social relations in capitalist societies reflects the hierarchical division of labor and the bureaucratic authority of corporate enterprise. The lowest levels, for example, will emphasize following rules, middle-class dependability, and the capacity to operate under continuous supervision; the highest levels will emphasize internalization of the norms of the enterprise and sensitivity to interpersonal relations within the organization. Similarly, different levels of education limit and channel activities of students. Even within a given school, students are streamed to conform to different behavior norms. In short, differences within and among schools reflect different backgrounds as well as the future economic positions of the student body.

What evidence can we marshall to support these ideas? Because there is no one study which satisfactorily answers the questions posed, one is forced to borrow selectively from available work of varied quality.[9] This is especially apparent in the radical critique of the U.S. educational system. As stated earlier, we do not lack for studies which show that ascribed characteristics continue to play an important role in predicting both equality of educational opportunity and educational success. What is lacking, however, are studies which focus on the overall structure of relations of the educational encounter which reproduce consciousness.

The structure of relations has, as we stated earlier, important class dimensions which must be examined. Much depends on the degree of class struggle in the society at large and the extent to which social forces are in opposition. At the most abstract level we can conceive of education as "classless; class specific; class confirming or class divisive" (Entwistle, 1976). A classless education in a classless society presupposes both equality of opportunity and equality of condition and we know that the former has not led to the latter. Furthermore one finds scant reference to a class confirming conception of working-class education. It is unlikely that we would find it in the public schools since they are agents of legitimation that encourage the population to maintain an uncritical acceptance of the basic belief and value systems that provide the ideological underpinnings of the state. What one looks for and fails to find is working-class education; what one finds instead is education of the working class.

Schecter's excellent analysis of early educational reforms in Canada proves the exception. He reports, for example, that early school reforms did not lead to an instant invasion of the schools by children of the working class. A reason for this hesitancy by working-class parents to endorse the public schools is described by Schecter as "a resistance to an attempt by upper class trustees and school experts to impose upon [the working class] an institution whose main function was to legitimate their own oppression"

(Schecter, 1977). Schecter gives further documentation of the continuity of working-class resistance to educational reforms imposed from above. For example, he refers to technical education in the following observation.

> In the working class opposition to technical education can be seen that tradition which characterized the ambivalent working class response to an earlier middle class reform, the Mechanics Institute, which, like the friendly society was a nursery for the industrious classes of the community. Lessons learned in the halls would not be forgotten in later years. Among these lessons were

Table 9

Unemployment of the 14-to-24 Age Group, 1967 to 1977

Calendar Year	14 to 24 Age Group No.	%	25 Years and Over %	Total %
1967	130,000	6.8	3.2	4.1
1968	163,000	8.2	3.7	4.8
1969	165,000	7.9	3.6	4.7
1970	224,000	10.4	4.4	5.9
1971	256,000	11.4	4.7	6.4
1972	263,000	11.1	4.6	6.3
1973	251,000	10.0	4.0	5.6
1974	258,000	9.6	3.8	5.4
1975	346,000	12.5	5.0	7.1
1976*	355.000	12.8	5.1	7.1
1977 (September)*	418,000	14.5	6.0	8.3

*15-to-24 age group
Source: Statistics Canada, *Monthly Labour Force Survey*, December 1975, December 1976, and September 1977.

Table 10

Unemployment Rate by Age Group and Level of Education, April, 1975 to 1977

Level of Education	15 - 24 Age Group 1975	1976	1977	Three-Year Average	25 Years and Over 1975	1976	1977	Three-Year Average
				(in %)				
Grades 0 - 8	26.5	23.9	25.0	25.1	8.6	8.4	10.0	9.0
High school (no post-secondary)	13.1	14.0	16.0	14.4	5.1	5.7	7.0	5.9
Some post-secondary	7.9	8.3	12.6	9.6	5.0	4.5	5.3	4.9
Post-secondary certificate or diploma	6.2	6.8	7.9	7.0	3.7	5.1	4.2	4.3
University degree	4.8	4.7	7.3	5.6	2.0	2.5	2.4	2.3
All levels	12.3	12.8	15.1	13.4	5.4	5.8	6.7	6.0

Source: Statistics Canada Special Labour Force Division, *Special Tabulations.*

those of self-help, mutual aid and the gains to be gleaned from literacy (Schecter, 1977).

Such early resistance as documented by Schecter was not sustained by the working class, in part because reforms engendered further reforms, which reinforced the social control functions of the schools. But the basic reasons for this phenomenon are surely to be found in the developing system of class relations.[10]

The more basic issue always centers around the class struggle and the nature of class polarization, for it is here that we must look if we are to understand the reaction of the working class to educational reforms and the role of the school as a part of the state apparatus and an active agent of the ruling class. Rosenblum emphasizes that:

> It is not possible to automatically deduce that capitalist ideology will dominate within the schools simply on the basis that the society is capitalist. That, other things being equal, is surely the situation. But other things are usually in a state of flux. Much depends on the degree of class struggle, or in other words the extent to which social forces are in opposition. If conventional wisdom is being challenged in society at large, it will in all likelihood be under serious examination and criticism within the schools (Rosenblum, 1978).

Nowhere is this clearer than when comparing the system of relations between teachers' organizations and the state in the provinces of Ontario and Quebec (Harp and Betcherman, 1978). In Quebec, teachers' organizations, namely the CEQ, have joined the common front and are openly and actively affiliated with the labor movement, whereas in Ontario, the stance taken by the association of secondary teachers resembles that of a professional association. These positions, which evolved during the 1960s and 1970s, have important implications for teaching and curriculum development in the provinces' school systems.

In Ontario, for example, teachers' organizations such as the OSSTF see education functioning as an instrument to facilitate the integration of the younger generation into the present system and bring about conformity to it, whereas in Quebec, the statements of the CEQ in the early 1970s saw education as part of an exploitative system of class relations and defined the teacher's role as helping students to deal critically and creatively with reality in order to transform their world (Harp and Betcherman, 1978).

In this section we have examined the concept of equality of opportunity as it applies to an industrialized capitalist society such as Canada. We have shown that with regard to equality of access to higher education, ascribed characteristics are still significant predictors. Nor is there any evidence to support the thesis that education has produced equality of condition in society. The source of the problem is to be found in the capitalist mode of production, whereby the schools act as agents of social reproduction reflecting the interests of the dominant class. The task remaining for research in this area is to show how consciousness is created in the school systems and, in the process, to expose the hidden curriculum and the role played by classroom teachers in its transmission. It is to this critical area that we now direct our attention.

The Hidden Curriculum:
Perspectives on Knowledge Transmission

To recapitulate the more significant earlier themes, we have argued that schools are socializing agencies, one of the state apparatuses, and as such serve the interests of corporate work and life in capitalist societies. Teachers are public employees, also defined as "various types of social workers" (Martell, 1974). Given the recent fiscal crisis of the state, funds are needed for new corporate markets and less money is available for education. Consequently, political activity occurs on at least two important fronts: (1) Teachers' unions battle against the fiscal squeeze, and their collective activity can take different forms (as shown by recent moves of teachers' organizations in Ontario and Quebec); and (2) Both within and outside the schools a search continues for a relevant working-class curriculum and/or a radical pedagogy.

It is the second area to which we will devote our attention in this concluding section of the paper. A singular fault with early attempts to understand the dynamics of classroom relations concerns their failure to locate the system of relationships and the school within a broader context of society. The school has an unavoidable relationship with wider society. As Egglestone points out, "The normative and power systems of the school are not only part of the micro systems of the school but also of the macro system of the whole society" (Egglestone, 1977); or as Freire states, "It is impossible to think of education without discussing economic and political power.... If you describe to me the structure of power in a society, the relations of production, I can describe to you the system of education" (Freire, 1972).

Specifically how this relationship is to be examined and understood is a matter of some dispute — whether, for example, greater emphasis should be placed on the structure of relations or on the content of curriculum or, indeed, on both, are debatable issues. One thing seems clear enough, and that is the relevance of concrete historical analyses. Apple and Wexler state the position succinctly:

> Studies of the minutiae of classroom interaction sequences cannot lead to a complete understanding of school knowledge. In order to do this both the focus of interaction provided for in schools and what is selected and taught in these institutions can only be fully understood historically. They must be seen as the result of concrete cultural, economic and political struggles and ideological arguments that have surrounded and provided the content for day to day life in the classrooms. In short one must have that peculiarly Marxist sensitivity to the present as history, if one is to comprehend the relationship between ideology and culture" (Apple and Wexler, 1978).

There is a definite need for a fully articulated political economy of education, one which will clearly show contradictory relationships between the integrative and personal development functions of educational systems. A starting point, at least for some analysts, is the so-called "hidden curriculum," but there is little consensus concerning its composition. For Jackson it is a set of rules of proper school comportment (Jackson, 1968); for King it is the affective, feeling level of the educational experience (King, 1973;); for Durkheim it is moral education (Durkheim,

1961); for Waller it is the culture of the school (Waller, 1965); while Silberman writes simply of "the experience of schooling" (Silberman, 1971). Recently students of radical sociology have directed attention to the basic contradictions between what is often called the official curriculum and the hidden curriculum (Giroux and Penna, 1977). More explicitly, the hidden curriculum is used to refer to "those unstated norms, values, and beliefs that are transmitted to students through the underlying structure of classrooms as opposed to formally recognized and sanctioned dimensions of classroom experience. More specifically, the hidden curriculum is based on a set of structural properties that promote social relations of education that are strongly hierarchical and authoritarian in nature" (Giroux and Penna, 1977). In short, the originating question for research is: What are the latent norms and values that are perpetuated by the hidden curriculum? Or, what are the oppressive structural properties in which the hidden curriculum is grounded?

Richer's detailed study of several kindergarten classes demonstrates that the child, from the very first day of formal schooling, finds himself or herself competing with other children. Differentiation of the children in terms of success or failure is evident in the games played, early printing exercises, in proper school comportment and achieving attention from the teacher. Some children do better than others in motor coordination events and are rewarded accordingly. Games such as Simon Says and Cross the River produce a winner — the former, the best in attentiveness and reflex, and the latter the best jumper in the class. By the middle of the second month in the classes observed, stars were allotted for especially neat printing, these usually accompanied by verbal praise. Show and tell, a period where children talk briefly about items brought from home, became a period where they sought to impress the teacher with their favorite doll, toy soldier, or truck — this inevitably at the expense of their peers. At a more covert level, the children are placed in the position of competing throughout the day for both teacher approval and attention. Regarding the former, children adhering to the teacher's conception of proper school behavior are clearly treated differently from those behaving otherwise. While there are children in the class under observation by Richer and associates who reject (for a while) this competition and refuse to participate, by the end of the first two months of school all the children actively seek the teacher's approval. The teacher accomplishes this through various types of rewards and punishments (Richer, 1977).

Concerning competition for teacher attention, Jackson presents a good description of the competition that constantly exists for this commodity. Given the situation of 30 or so children in a teacher-centered communication structure, "delay, denial, and interruption" are no doubt inevitable and frequent occurrences (Jackson, 1968).

Perhaps the least "hidden" aspect of the hidden curriculum is the transmission of what we would call submission of self. The child learns that he or she must put aside his or her own wishes in favor of the wishes of a recognized authority figure in adult society, in this case the teacher. Children are socialized to accept as rational and right that people above them in a status hierarchy can dictate their behavior, an acceptance that is to be generalized to other organizations they will encounter.

What is typically emphasized in this line of inquiry is that students can and do learn from both the structural properties of the school (e.g., authority relations) and the actions of teachers (e.g., punishing and rewarding various behaviors). What is lacking in most of the earlier work is any linking of these results with the system of class relations existing in the society. One is interested to know, as Miliband suggests, precisely how educational systems at all levels serve as legitimating agencies.[11] A related question centers on how the societal division of labor not only influences the individual success of the student, but also affects variations in the forms of interaction which take place in schools (Apple and Wexler, 1978). Earlier in our discussion we cited the work of Bowles and Gintis on this topic (Bowles and Gintis, 1975). It would be misleading, however, to leave readers with the impression that their innovative development of the thesis of social reproduction is without its critics. There appear to be at least two aspects to the controversy: one concerns how much responsibility the school shares for reproducing the class structure with all its well-documented inequities, while the other focuses on the definition and treatment of that complex concept known as culture (Gorelick, 1977).

First, concerning the indictment of the schools, it bears repeating that the schools do not stand alone in their responsibility for social and cultural reproduction. They are after all only one (albeit an important one) of the state apparatuses. The seminal work by Ray Rist, to which most investigators return when dealing with student social class origins and teachers' expectations, puts the issue squarely:

> The public school system is, I believe, justifiably responsible for contributing to the present structure of the society, but the responsibility is not its alone. The picture that emerges from this study is that the school strongly shares in the complicity of maintaining the organizational perpetuation of poverty and unequal opportunity. This, of course, is in contrast to the formal doctrine of education in this country to ameliorate rather than aggravate the conditions of the poor (Rist, 1970:447).

What needs to be added to Rist's otherwise excellent statement is simply that in the final analysis one must return to the mode of production as the primary set of determining conditions to be interpreted within a given historical context.[12]

The issues are much more complex regarding the second problem, the treatment of culture. Bowles and Gintis have been criticized in part for seeing culture as "a given, to which social institutions correspond and to which children are socialized" (Gorelick, 1977). The argument advanced by one critic emphasizes the dynamic of culture as something which is "continually being produced, reinforced and destroyed in the process of class struggle and structural change"[13] (Gorelick, 1977). Even more basic to these differing views of how culture should be treated in education research are what Egglestone refers to as two ideological models of curriculum (Egglestone, 1977). On the one hand is the perspective in which "curriculum knowledge, like other components of the knowledge system in the social order, is accepted as a received body of understanding" (Egglestone, 1977). In other words, it is non-negotiable.

Alternately, curriculum knowledge can be seen to be negotiable. As Egglestone puts it, "Essentially it is dialectic and manifestly subject to political and other influences, a construction of those who participate in its determination" (Egglestone, 1977). The latter model is referred to as the reflexive perspective. For some Marxists an analysis of curriculum knowledge requires that one come to terms with the thesis of cultural reproduction as treated in the writings of Pierre Bourdieu. An insightful summary of Bourdieu's complex theoretical ideas is given by Kennett:

> Bourdieu's main postulates are: firstly, that society is characterized by repression; secondly, that . . . there is diffused within a social space a cultural capital, comparable to economic capital transmitted by inheritance and invested in order to be cultivated; thirdly, that the true as opposed to the apparent nature of the education system functions to discriminate in favor of those who are the inheritors of this cultural capital; fourthly, that the essentialist view of men implicit in common sense representations of school failure as being due to lack of talents, or of social groups as having certain characteristics which make them fit or unfit for success, is a mystification, an ideology of the dominant group; fifthly, that culture has, despite the theory of art for art's sake, a political function (Kennett, 1973).

The problem is, as always, one of trying to link macro-micro patterns. Macro-level patterns of social class inequality and unequal distribution of cultural capital are linked to micro-level processes of pedagogy, evaluation and curriculum.

Society is seen by Bourdieu as a "particular form of violence," which "seeks to impose meanings, and to impose them as alone legitimate, disguising the power relations which are the source of its strength. By this legitimation the system of power relations, which in reality imposes 'reality', remains unrevealed and the 'reality' functions to maintain the system of power relations" (Kennett, 1973).

We are of necessity, therefore, concerned with the academic culture of the schools, which are not engaged in the dispassionate distribution of objective knowledge, but involved in a process of cultural reproduction which has its origins in a system of class relations. While there is a "danger of reducing all school knowledge to ideological knowledge,"[14] we are interested in which specific groups control curriculum selection in the schools (Apple and Wexler, 1978). In other words, whose cultural capital is being marketed in the schools? The implications of this theory for radical teachers must be emphasized. Their task is in a sense to break the "cultural code" and reveal the underlying system of power relations whereby curriculum knowledge is controlled. Giroux and Penna pinpoint the strategy.[15]

> While radical teachers cannot eliminate the hidden curriculum, they can expose its underlying political values and build objectives, methods and structural properties that offset its worst features. Radical teachers can work within the schools to produce a generation of politically conscious students who will reject the social basis of the hidden curriculum and translate that rejection into a praxis that goes to the root of the problem (Giroux and Penna, 1977).

NOTES

1. The recommendations of the Royal Commission on Technical Education of 1911 were not implemented until 1919, and even then provided $10 million instead of the recommended $30 million (Schecter, 1977). Support came from the lobbying activities of the Canadian Manufacturers' Association, the Trades and Labour Congress, and the Dominion Educational Association.

2. Martel also comments on the increased centralization of the educational bureaucracy in Ontario during the 1960s.

> Ontario experienced a very strong centralizing push (from the state) in the sixties under the rhetoric of decentralization. On the one hand, in giving up its concern with the minutiae of school board operations, the Department of Education assumed a much greater competence to oversee and therefore control the board directions of school board organization and policy. In the 1960s there was the undercutting of the financial powers of local boards and their sharp reduction in numbers. In the seventies this centralization continues into the area of teacher negotiations, as it has for negotiations with all public employees, following mounting pressure to impose direct control over labor costs (Martell, 1974).

3. The 1960s proved to be a period of rapid expansion for Canadian educational systems. The Economic Council of Canada, in its Annual Review of 1970, gives some indication of the magnitude of what is appropriately termed the "educational industry."

> By almost any measure, education is now Canada's biggest industry. There are about 6.5 million full-time students and teachers — nearly a third of Canada's population — involved in education (as well as hundreds of thousands more on a part-time basis) both in the formal education system and in a great variety of training programmes. Expenditures on formal education and vocational traning now account for about 8% of GNP. Education is the largest category (over 20% of total government spending in Canada) and now exceeds $6 billion (Economic Council of Canada 7th Annual Review, Ottawa, 1970).

> In addition, at the post-secondary level for the period 1967-68 to 1976-77, non-university full time enrolment increased from 99,410 to 231,060. Whereas post-secondary university enrolment showed an increase from 253,486 to 382,060 for the comparable period (Statistics Canada: Special Report, 1977).

4. An OECD Report on the Canadian system proves informative.

> In Canada, largely because of the universities' stand but also because of costs, the government tried to divert the student flow and create an attractive new system, complete in itself and closely linked to employment in the paraprofessional level. For the applied programs it will probably succeed.

The authors continue with a note of warning:
> . . . if its [CAATS] excellent students from its best programmes are locked effectively into a dead end, the demand for full formal transfer or even degree granting status will grow.

At another point the authors of the report cautiously suggest, "Possibly Canada has oversold education as an investment (New College Systems in Canada, 1973).

5. At least one investigator explicitly recognizes the relevance of a theory of justice for educational research: "Curriculum and more general educational research needs to have its roots in a theory of justice, one which has as its prime focus increasing the advantage of the least advantaged" (Apple, 1977).

6. At one point in the report, the authors pose the question: "Why should young people whose families have lower socioeconomic status spend less time in high school than young people from families in higher socioeconomic status?" Satisfactory answers to the question are more likely to be found through a class analysis whereby one examines the relationship between class origins and the dominant class bias of the schools. Instead, the authors opt for a treatment of class in a distributive rather than a classifactory sense (Porter, Blishen, Barrados, 1977).

7. On the still broader question of education and social stratification, recent applications of status attainment model to the male labor force in Canadian society concludes with grounds for cautious optimism concerning stratification.

> Canada is a stratified society, of that there can be no doubt. However, over the last forty years it has become slightly less stratified. In looking at the process of status attainment there is some evidence that this process is becoming more open. At least the educational attainment of Canadians is less dependent upon their social origins than it used to be. However, the increasingly strong relationship between educational attainment and socioeconomic status appears to have restructured the degree of opportunity for intergenerational mobility and at the same time placed an even heavier emphasis on the need for openness on the educational institutions of the country (McRoberts, 1975).

8. Needless to say, the so-called correspondence principle is not without its critics even among Marxist scholars. Rosenblum, for example, cites the following problems.

> A number of difficulties with the correspondence theory come quickly to mind. On a conceptual level the classification of some behavioral traits as predictions of conformity to the hierarchical division of labour is questionable. Dependability and cooperation with others as opposed to individualistic and aggressive independence do not necessarily carry a conformist connotation and/or signal lack of creativity. In the same way deferment of gratification can be found among non-conformists and radicals. Even if the schools reproduce the social relations of production behind the backs of students might not they simultaneously reproduce historically specific forms of resistence? Furthermore, the deep seated disparity in socialization experiences within and between different levels of the educational system may not be nearly as complete as correspondence theorists suggest (Rosenblum, 1978).

9. Bleasdale comments on the social division of both cognitive and evaluative knowledge as practised in the schools. Of the former he tells us:

> That streaming provides different kinds of knowledge and skills to children from different socio-economic backgrounds, is no longer disputed. A disproportionate number of working class children are tracked into vocational and commercial programmes in preparation for blue collar and low level white collar service jobs, while a disproportionate number of middle and upper class children are placed in academic programmes in preparation for university and professional or management positions.

He goes on to summarize the situation concerning evaluative knowledge as follows:

> Further evidence points to the social division of evaluative knowledge. Authoritarian norms such as consistency, punctuality, conformity, discipline and external motivation were found to be stressed in high schools, while universities permitted individual autonomy and a more open atmosphere. The rapidly growing community college system in the U.S. and Canada, designed to train future service and middle class workers was also found to reproduce a normative structure similar to that of the high school. What is indicated here is that the education system is capable of accommodating different forms of evaluative knowledge for different levels of role allocation (Bleasdale, 1978).

10. Gintis puts the point succinctly: "that is, the idea of liberating education does not arise spontaneously, but is made possible by emerging contradictions in the larger society" (Gintis, 1972).

11. Miliband puts the case as follows: "Schools may or may not consciously engage in 'political socialization' but cannot in any case avoid doing so, mostly in terms which are highly functional to the prevailing social and political order. In other words educational institutions at all levels generally fulfil an important conservative role and act with greater or lesser effectiveness, as legitimating agencies in and for these societies" (Miliband, 1968).

12. Rist describes the more salient results of his research in the following statement: "For the students of high socio-economic background who were perceived by the teachers as possessing desirable behavioral and attitudinal characteristics, the classroom experience was one where the teachers displayed interest in them, spent a large proportion of teaching time with them, directed little control oriented behaviour towards them, held them as models for the remainder of the class and continually reinforced statements that they were 'special' students" (Rist, 1970).

13. A major point in Gorelick's critique of Bowles and Gintis concerns their treatment of the concept of social class. She especially objects to the conceptualization of class in terms of hierarchy, since "scientifically it compounds two errors: (1) 'Hierarchy' confuses the phenomenal form of the organization of occupational roles with the abstract category of class. (2) 'Hierarchy' turns the qualitative concept of class into an inherently quantitative one more akin to stratification" (Gorelick, 1977).

14. Elizabeth Cagan is one who chooses to emphasize ideology in education, arguing very effectively that American notions of individualism are at the heart of failure of radical educational reform. What is of particular interest here in light of Parsons' earlier comments on the collectivist orientation adopted by the school is the paradox Cagan points out between individualism and conformism, "co-existing as manifestations of the same phenomenon in modern capitalist society. This is what makes it difficult to attain clarity about what must be changed. In our encounters with social institutions such as schools and the work place, we feel ourselves dehumanized and robbed of personal identity. Our response is to withdraw as much as possible from these public arenas, investing our energies instead in personal projects and relationships which appear to reveal our uniqueness and individuality" (Cagan, 1978).

15. Cagan is also one of the few radical educational reformers who does not confine her attention to the schools, but advocates a "deliberate intervention into moral and character development", as well as offering a "number of pedagogical practices which address the explicit curriculum and the hidden one and unite both the structure and content of education around collectivist goals" (Cagan, 1978).

REFERENCES

Apple, Michael W. and Philip Wexler. "Cultural Capital and Educational Transmission: An Essay on Basic Bernstein, Class Codes and Control: Vol. III — Towards a Theory of Educational Transmissions," *Educational Theory*, Vol. 28 (Winter 1978).

Barrados, Maria. "Inequality Educational Attainment in Canada and the United States." Unpublished Report CARMAC PROJECT, Carleton University, Ottawa, 1977.

Bell, Daniel. *The Coming of Post-Industrial Society*. New York: Basic Books, 1973.

Bleasdale, Graham. "Towards a Political Economy of Capitalist Educational Values," *Reading, Writing and Riches*, Nelson and Nock, eds., Between the Lines. Toronto, 1978.

Bowles, Samuel and Herbert Gintis. *Schooling in Capitalist America: Educational Reform and the Contradictions of Economic Life*. New York: Basic Books, 1975.

Breton, Raymond. *Social and Academic Factors in the Career Decisions of Canadian Youth*. Ottawa: Manpower and Immigration, 1972.

Cagan, Elizabeth. "Individualism, Collectivism and Radical Educational Reform," *Harvard Educational Review*, Vol. 48, No. 2.

Coleman, James S. "The Concept of Equality of Educational Opportunity," *Harvard Educational Review*, Vol. 38 (1968).

Durkheim, Emile. *Moral Education*. Glencoe, Ill.: The Free Press, 1961.

Egglestone, John. *The Sociology of the School Curriculum*. London: Routledge and Kegan Paul, 1977.

Entwistle, Harold. *Class, Culture and Education*. London: Meathen and Co. Ltd., 1978.

Fleming, W.F. *Ontario's Educative Society*, Vol. 3, *Schools Pupils and Teachers*. Toronto: University of Toronto Press, 1971.

Freire, P. "Interview with Paulo Freire," in *Times Educational Supplement*, Oct. 20, 1972.

Gilbert, Sid and Hugh A. McRoberts. "Differentiation and Stratification: The Issue of Inequality," in Dennis Forcese and Stephen Richer, eds., *Issues in Canadian Society*. Scarborough, Ont.: Prentice-Hall of Canada, 1975.

Gilbert, Sid. "The Selection of Educational Assertations," in Richard Carlton et al., eds., *Education, Change and Society*. Toronto: Gage Educational Publishing Ltd., 1977.

Giroux, Henry and Anthony Penna. "Social Relations in the Classroom: The Dialectic of the Hidden Curriculum," *Edcentric*, Nos. 40-41 (Spring/Summer 1977), pp. 39-46.

Gorlich, Sherry. "Undermining Hierarchy: Problems of Schooling in Capitalist America," *Monthly Review* (Oct. 1977).

Harp, John and Gordon Betcherman. "Contradictory Class Locations and Class Action: The Case of Secondary School Teachers Organizations in Ontario and Quebec." Paper presented at the American Sociological Association Annual Meeting, San Francisco, 1978.

Harris, Robert. *Higher Education in Canada*. Toronto: University of Toronto Press, 1976.

Jencks, Christopher. "Inequality: A Reappraisal of the Effect of Family and Schooling in America." New York: Harper, Colophon Books, 1972.

Kennett, John. "The Sociology of Pierre Bourdieu," in *Educational Review*, Vol. 25 (June 1973).

Laski, H.J. *A Grammar of Politics*, 5th ed. London: Allen and Unwin, 1948.

Lenski, Gerhard E. *Power and Privilege*. New York: McGraw Hill, 1966.

Marshall, T.H. *Sociology at the Crossroads and Other Essays.* London: Heinemann Educational Books, 1963.

Martell, George, ed., *The Politics of the Canadian Public School.* Toronto: James Lorimer and Co., 1974.

McRoberts, Hugh. "Social Stratification in Canada: A Preliminary Analysis." Unpublished Doctoral Dissertation, Carleton University, 1975.

Miliband, Ralph. *The State in Capitalist Society.* London: Quartet Books Ltd., 1973.

Organization of Economic Cooperation and Development. *New College Systems in Canada.* Paris: OECD, 1972.

Porter, Marion R., John Porter and Bernard R. Blishen. *Does Money Matter?* Toronto: York University, 1973.

Prentice, Alison and Susan E. Houston. *Family, School and Society.* Toronto: Oxford University Press, 1975.

Prentice, Alison. *The School Promoters: Education and Social Class in Mid-Nineteenth Century Upper Canada.* Toronto: McClelland and Stewart, 1977.

Rawls, John. *A Theory of Justice.* Oxford: Oxford University Press, 1972.

Reich, Carole and Suzanne Zeigler. "A Follow Up Study of Special Vocational and Special High School Students," City of Toronto Board of Education, Research Department, Report 102, April 1, 1972.

Rist, Ray C. "Student Social Class and Teacher Expectations: The Self-Fulfilling Prophecy of Ghetto Education," *Harvard Educational Review*, Vol. 40, No. 3 (Aug. 1970).

Rosenblum, S. "The Marxist Theory of Education: A Conceptual Note." Paper presented at the Annual Meeting of the Canadian Sociological and Anthropological Association, University of Western Ontario, May 1978.

Sewell, W., R. Hauser and D. Featherman, eds. *Schooling and Achievement in American Society.* New York: Academic Press, 1976.

Stephen, Schecter. "Capitalism, Class and Educational Reform in Canada," in Leo Panitch, ed., *The Canadian State: Political Economy and Political Power.* Toronto: University of Toronto Press, 1977.

Spring, Joel H. *Education and the Rise of the Corporate State.* Boston: Beacon Press, 1972.

Stamp, Robert M. "Education and the Economic and Social Milieu: The English Canadian Scene from 1870 to 1914," in Donald J. Wilson et al., eds., *Canadian Education: A History.* Scarborough, Ont.: Prentice-Hall of Canada, 1970.

Waller, Willard. *The Sociology of Teaching.* New York: Russell and Russell, 1961.

Wilson, Donald J. "Education in Upper Canada: Sixty Years of Change," in Donald J. Wilson et al., eds., *Canadian Education: A History.* Scarborough, Ont.: Prentice-Hall of Canada, 1970.

Crime and Class: Unequal Before the Law

W.K. GREENAWAY

Introduction — Crime, Class, and Culture

Common knowledge and official statistics have led people to conclude that low status groups are more prone to committing criminal and delinquent acts than those of higher status. Why this might be the case and how the illegal conduct of poor people relative to wealthier folk may be exaggerated in official data is the subject of this article.

People examining the way in which official crime data are constructed often doubt the extent to which such reports represent actual illegal conduct. Instead, such data may be regarded as information about enforcement rather than criminality. Tepperman points out that the legal system in Canada is a vast machine which has the certification of crime as its task. He suggests that to begin with, one can take just about anyone for most of the criminal value of our criminals is added by the machine itself (1977: 26.).

In the same vein, Box (1971:21) concluded a chapter on the social construction of official statistics as follows:

> By conceiving official data as objects fit for study, we have been able to sustain the argument that the end product is not a valid indicator of a country's 'real' extent or pattern of criminal activity. Its formulation and variation is determined by organizational, legal and social pressures, rather than by a rigorous attempt to measure criminal activity accurately.

In particular, Tepperman and Box agree that social class differences in crime rates must at least be qualified. After looking at such unofficial measures as self-report studies in comparison with official ones, Box notes that the unofficial data failed to reveal the significant inter-class differences implied in official statistics. Some have located differences but these have tended to be much smaller than those officially recorded (1971:58-91).

Tepperman allows that Canadian official crime data have a variable and uncertain degree of validity.

> Definitive conclusions cannot be drawn regarding the reasons for differences in criminal convictions by social class, so one must tentatively conclude that some element of both class bias and differential motivation and opportunity for crime enter into making these differences (1977:191).

The data may be both an indication of criminality and an indication of enforcement procedures which do not randomly select subjects for processing.

Very often sociologists attempting to offer explanations for criminality and delinquency have disregarded Tepperman's reminder and have centered on differential motivation and opportunity among working-class and, more particularly, poor people. Class bias is too often ignored, as are the social processes which create and sustain the invidious conditions of poverty (Watson, 1976). Instead, the culture of poverty often becomes an explanation for crime in many of the best known theories of sociologically oriented criminologists.

Literature on the sociology of crime and delinquency is replete with explanations which, in effect, blame the poor for problems of deviance, while ignoring the role of men of power. Perhaps the earliest instance of such an approach in North American criminology grew out of the urban ecology school centered at the University of Chicago. This school carried *social disorganization* as a central theoretical component. Delinquency researchers such as Clifford Shaw (1929) and Frederic M. Thrasher (1927) examined urban areas where boys' gangs and juvenile court cases flourished. Using theoretical ideas based partly on the writings of W.I. Thomas and Florian Znaniecki (1917-18), these researchers explained the existence of delinquency areas as stemming from the social processes going on within them. Rapid social change emanating from large-scale immigration to major U.S. cities had resulted, in their view, in a cultural breakdown. Populations in delinquency areas lacked clear, internalized norms of conduct. In the U.S. such notions were often cited to justify programs which sought to Americanize immigrants, that is, to inoculate them with a vaguely defined set of WASP cultural standards. Crime and delinquency, according to the social disorganizationists, resulted from an absence of cultural *consensus* and an ensuing moral vacuum that existed in some areas of cities.

Later sociologists have taken issue with the moral vacuum part of the social disorganization explanation in particular. Edwin H. Sutherland (1939) began a new trend in criminological investigation of supposed cultural determinants with a re-analysis of the earlier urban ecology studies. Sutherland suggested that delinquency areas were the territorial base for a set of norms and values conducive to the violation of law. The idea is very similar to the culture of poverty concept elaborated by Oscar Lewis in an article in this book. Sutherland held that subcultures themselves, and not the *absence* of rules and standards, *compel* adherents toward the violation of law.

Because Sutherland never took the time to present more than a bare outline of theoretical explication, it is difficult to be sure exactly what he meant. An image of conflict emerges in his criminology text (1939) but the conflict is one of *cultures* rather than classes. Sutherland's explanation came to be labeled "differential association theory," centering on the social psychological mechanisms by which he said cultures and subcultures are transmitted from one generation to the next. One can see in it images of good culture sustained by people who wear ties to work, join the Home and School, keep their substantial lawns and hedges trimmed, and whose children become Girl Guides and Boy Scouts. Its antithesis, bad culture, is the world of leisure-time-on-street-corners, tenements, pool halls and lunch buckets. Though the line of demarcation between the two cultures may have been clear in Sutherland's mind, he recognized that all people will be affected by both. It is cultures, therefore, which are in conflict, even within individual psyches.

Later, an urban anthropologist, Walter B. Miller (1958), carried Sutherland's subcultural explanation further when he suggested that the working class sustains a culture with focal concerns such as toughness and smartness, which automatically place its adherents in conflict with the norms on which laws are based. According to Miller, working-class culture exists autonomously and unfortunately contains prescripts which may lead individuals inevitably into conflict with the dominant culture—the law.

Other writers have developed the subcultural explanation in concert with theoretical ideas advanced by Robert King Merton (1938) to which we will turn in a moment. Albert Cohen (1955), for example, suggested that rather than being autonomous, the subculture which generates delinquency grows out of a reaction formation. Lower-class boys reject what they secretly crave: success by middle-class standards. They band together to form and perpetuate a delinquency subculture which takes the norms of conventional society and turns them upside down. Law violation is "right" by the standards of the delinquency subculture precisely because it is "wrong" by conventional standards, Cohen suggests.

Yet another version of subcultural theory is found in the writings of Cloward and Ohlin (1960). They suggest that alienation from middle-class standards and a perceived blocking of opportunities in terms of such standards leads working-class boys in frustration to erect parallel structures — delinquency subcultures — through which one may obtain recognition and status.

The subcultural explanation for delinquency has been rather decisively called into question. Travis Hirschi (1969), David Matza (1964), and Gresham Sykes (Sykes and Matza, 1957) have revealed that the subcultural approach suffers from many empirical and conceptual deficiencies. In the same vein, Frank E. Hartung (1965) examined crime and delinquency in both Canada and the U.S. in a volume which, ironically, attempts to validate Sutherland's subcultural explanation. While Sykes and Matza and Travis Hirschi concentrate on delinquency, Hartung, a symbolic interactionist social psychologist, contends that virtually all conduct, regardless of its legality or illegality, is the product of learning accomplished through the medium of symbols—words and gestures—imbedded in a culture. While the idea that conduct which violates laws is encompassed within roles that people learn to play is one that is consistent with Sutherland's, Hartung's portrait of culture excludes the good-bad dichotomy which differential association seems to carry. On the contrary, Hartung insists that cultural norms in our society are ambiguous and internally contradictory. One can learn vocabularies of motives conducive to violation of law from *conventional* others (82). An example used by Sykes and Matza as well as by Hartung illustrates this irony: the popularity in penology of the medical model in recent years has led to an increasing sense of irresponsibility (Hartung, 1965:65-72). The idea that one can be driven by unconscious forces and irrational compulsions, whether scientifically valid or not, is an interpretation of one's own conduct which can be learned and used to rationalize illicit behaviors. One can learn, says Hartung (167-73) to conceive of oneself as a person so driven. Clearly, the learning of deviant motives is not confined to those who come into contact with deviant subcultures.

Nevertheless, Hartung insists that all conduct is socioculturally learned (82) and must be so explained. This includes conduct which violates the law. Such reasoning, however, brings the subcultural explanation for deviance to a grinding halt. If there is no bad culture, if conventional culture is ambiguous, inconsistent, and inclusive of vocabularies of motives which generate deviance, and if *all* conduct is generated by identical processes of sociocultural learning, albeit with variations in content, then one cannot explain law violation culturally except in a circular fashion: we deduce the quality of learning from the nature of conduct and the nature of conduct is, in turn, explained by the content of learning.

When we insist, as Hartung, Howard Becker (1963), and the labeling theorists do, that everyone learns deviant motives, the problem becomes one of explaining why some people at some times are more likely to *act* on them. Furthermore, why is it that some who act in violation of the law are more likely than others to be officially sanctioned? These problems take us beyond the realm of cultural explanations.

The idea that a lower-class subculture which causes crime and delinquency has developed as a result of structural factors— limits which the social system places on opportunities and privileges — grew in part out of the ideas of R.K. Merton (1938). Consistent with the structural-functional perspective in sociology, Merton contends that each society has a culture common to virtually all of its members. Because of structural limitations placed upon the opportunities of certain individuals, Merton suggests such people are pressured to ignore cultural prescriptions and instead resort to individual adaptations which are deviant. Merton's ideas have been very attractive to liberal thinkers. As subsequent analyzers of his work have claimed, he was a "cautious rebel" (Taylor, Walton and Young, 1973:101-5). According to Taylor and associates, Merton favored a sociopolitical system wherein differences in power and privilege are based solely on innate differences in talent and the willingness to expend effort unimpeded by the vicissitudes of birth, minority group status, race or other ascribed factors. His ideal was a system where competition reigns and inequality is justified by clear differences in merit. The rejection of systems of gross inequality, however ideologically justified, and the impossibility of a true meritocracy, as well as Merton's failure to extend fully his critique of U.S. liberalism, are reasons given by Taylor and his associates (1973:101-5) for dismissing Merton. Laurie Taylor (1971:148, as quoted by Ian Taylor and associates, 1973:101) criticizes Merton's appreciation of the nature of the social system about which he mildly complains: the system is like a huge slot machine which is rigged. Merton never tells in whose favor it is rigged, who maintains it, who set it up in the first place or who collects the profits from its operation.

In sum, sociological explanations, only a few of which have been cited here, have often accepted the common sense notion that crime and delinquency are peculiarly lower-class problems. They have rarely, until recently, examined the social construction of crime data to determine its accuracy in locating deviance in the social structure. Taking the accuracy of official crime data for granted, criminologists have devoted a great deal of attention to the culture of poverty, expecting to find in it a theory of crime and delinquency. When structural inequality has been recognized, this has often meant examining how unfair competition exists in some anomalous fashion to pressure people to ignore commonly held standards of conduct or to develop and sustain their own deviant standards. Cultural explanations are often geared to blaming the poor even though the subcultural followers of Merton, and Merton himself, were cautiously critical of the actual operation of liberal societies because of the failure of such systems to meet the ideals of meritocracy.

Subcultural explanations have failed to fulfill their intentions. The numerous criticisms of this approach all point to one central problem: "Most poor people do not become criminals and many well-to-do and rich people become crooks" (Hartung, 1965:29).

Even if one could demonstrate that law violation is peculiarly or predominately a lower-class phenomenon and that cultural supports for such conduct do exist among lower-class people in a way in which they do not for others, one would still have to ask, why is this the case? Weak structural explanations like Merton's do not suffice. A more thorough structural analysis is needed.

In the remainder of this article attention is turned to an interpretation of crime and delinquency and its generation and certification by official agencies of state control, from a perspective which attempts to delve into the roots of our social, political, and economic order. Clearly, simple explanations for the apparent relationship between law violation and class are not possible. The relationship has to do with the mode of production, class conflict, the nature of the state and the law in Canada, the operation of legal systems and the enforcement of laws. It may also be dependent on social psychological factors at different class levels.

Law and Dominant Interests

The law, as opposed to other instruments of social control, is a system of rules and sanctions generated and administered by the state. Any analysis of law violation should begin with an examination of the law itself. It has often been remarked in jest that the principal cause of crime is law! Too few sociologists have appreciated the serious implications of this statement. Many have taken law as "given" — a representation of generally held social goals or common cultural values (see, for example, Friedmann, 1959).

Others have conceived law to be the result of the interplay of a multitude of political pressure groups, all of whom exercise a share of power. Small (1978), for example, has analyzed the early development of Canadian narcotics legislation as an outgrowth of a number of social and cultural factors: imbedded and exaggerated ideas about the pharmacological effects of certain substances, racism (especially anti-Asiatic sentiments), and the reform efforts of identifiable groups of moral entrepreneurs. The dynamic of class, as conceived by Marx and elaborated elsewhere in this volume, is absent in Small's analysis, as it is in other liberal-pluralist interpretations.

A Marxist perspective sees the capitalist state and therefore its instrument, the law, as based on relationships of production. The state and the law are largely within the domain of the relatively few people who constitute its ruling class. The Marxist approach holds that rather than reflecting commonly held social values or emanating from the machinations of relatively autonomous and diverse pressure groups, the law in capitalist states pursues the interests of its dominant class. This perspective suggests that to ignore the larger social context in examing law violation among the poor, and to suggest that the conduct of the poor is unrelated to the conduct of the wealthy is an overly-restricted sociological view. The law quite clearly is not an outgrowth of relationships existing solely among the poor. Neither, therefore, is its violation.

The law and law enforcement practices and priorities are structured in a way people may see as natural or universal. The law may be based at times on a consensus which may or may not exist relatively independently of the influence of the media or educational institutions — powerful cultural tools in the hands of dominant groups.[1] Yet laws and law enforcement are not natural, but instead are outgrowths of class relationships. A change in those relationships yields variations in law, a point we will now elaborate.

Most of us reared in Canada and other capitalist countries have been exposed to heavy doses of an ideology which asserts that freedom exists in our system while it does not or did not exist in others. The word freedom has become so emotionally laden that it is difficult to use it in rational discourse. Freedom is, of course, always relative. One has always to ask, "freedom to do *what*?" Recognizing problems with the word and concept of freedom, it can at least be said that social systems vary with respect to the *diversity* of behavior and lifestyles which are tolerated within them. A limited, albeit wide range of conduct exists within capitalist systems. The fact that those systems contain such diversity has often obscured the fact that limits are maintained and opportunities are not the same for everyone living within capitalist systems. Laws operate to set limits on diversity and choice. It is useful, therefore, to examine the nature of law in our society and to begin by looking at its historical development.

Capitalism emerged out of feudalism. In feudalism the dominant class was the aristocracy, which owned the land and controlled those who were attached to land and to the aristocracy by bonds of fealty. Feudalism also comprised a small middle class of merchants, artisans and others who sometimes had a base in the free cities. As commerce and then industry developed, this middle class or *bourgeoisie* first entered into a struggle for social and economic power with the aristocracy and eventually came to supersede them. In contemporary capitalist systems, it is the bourgeoisie which is the dominant class and wage labor is the prevailing mode of production.

In the transition from feudalism to capitalism, a new legal philosophy which accompanied a broader liberal ideology gained force. While the new philosophy and the system of laws and law enforcement which grew out of it unquestionably brought benefits to both dominant and many non-dominant groups, the principal gain was, and still is, realized by the bourgeoisie: they gained dominance through the legitimized right to own, accumulate, control, and exploit private property. This dominance was reinforced by a philosophy which argued that feudal divisions and hereditary rights were no longer useful or rational. This liberal philosophy professed that societies should be conceived as a composite of individuals and that individual rights should replace the perquisites of nobility and the obligations of others. In other words, the bourgeoisie, not just the aristocracy, should be able to own, accumulate, control, and exploit property. Ironic as it may seem, the idea that we live in a society composed of individuals, not classes, thus became entrenched in the liberal ideology in the period in which the bourgeoisie *as a class* struggled to gain its hegemony.

The myth that capitalist societies are based on individual rather than class rights is in part maintained by the complexity of the legal system and the relative diversity of conduct permitted and even encouraged. This is underscored by Baldus (1977:254) in an article entitled "Social Control in Capitalist Societies."

> Aristocratic dominant classes had seen periphery [i.e., non-dominant class] diversity as a threat to their interests and had tried to suppress it. The new dominant bourgeoisie realized not only that this was not possible, but that it was not necessary. It was the historic discovery of the individual capitalist that he could solve the apparent contradiction between his own interests and those of an increasingly diverse periphery by letting others work for him while allowing them to pursue their own personal goals.

The use of diversity to accomplish the goals of class domination is what Baldus (1977:250) calls "complementarity" and it is an important characteristic of social control in capitalist regimes. The concept includes such ironies as the promotion and sale of mass-produced, centrally distributed, and aggressively marketed goods by which people are encouraged to express their individuality. People are given a limited range of choices, but the parameters of choice are controlled and manipulated by elites. The ethic of individualism, behavioral diversity, and the existence of opportunities to make choices, however restrictive, obscures the process of social domination in capitalist societies.

With respect to the law, conduct which may be more probable among the lower classes or among powerless minorities is placed under restrictions of criminal law more frequently than deviant conduct, which is more typical of people at the other end of the social spectrum. Although the extraction of surplus value is consistent with some definitions of theft, appropriating for oneself part of the value produced by workers is not only excluded from the formal definition of theft in our society, but is viewed as natural, right, and even a socioeconomic necessity. Profit is perhaps capitalism's central freedom. Acquiring private property by shoplifting, on the other hand, is deemed illegitimate, even in circumstances where the pursuit of profit leads to marketing practices where people are exhorted daily to accumulate products they do not need, where such goods are displayed openly in an attempt to encourage impulse buying, and where, at the same time, the system creates unemployment and impoverishment. Most people, however, do not regard as arbitrary the restricted definition of theft or the placing of only certain violations of law in criminal codes, with its powerful sanctions, and other violations in less stigmatizing civil codes (Sutherland, 1945).

Anthony Platt (1969), a U.S. social researcher who analyzed the "invention of delinquency," has argued that the philosophy of the juvenile court and official definitions of delinquency were developed with specific reference to the conduct of lower-class, urban, immigrant children. Susan Houston (1978), examining some of the same developments in Canada, suggests that special delinquency processing agencies, along with compulsory schooling, were measures adopted to mold from the lower class a literate and disciplined work force. With such a developmental history, is it surprising that official delinquents are by and large recruited from the lower classes?

Although his argument is too complex to recreate here, John Hepburn (1978) has suggested that law in fact pursues dominant class interests in its very conception even when it appears to provide equal protection to all members of a society, when it appears to be irrelevant to elite interests, or when it appears to be inimical to such interests. He concludes his argument by citing Richard Quinney (1972), who contends that as long as class domination exists "law can be nothing other than official repression."

Addressing a Winnipeg audience, Roland Penner, an attorney, a law professor and former chairman of Legal Aid Manitoba, asked people to use their imaginations:

> Let's suppose I became philosopher-king and I could make any changes I wanted. Suppose I decided that minor social control offences and crimes-without-victims were to be eliminated from the Criminal Code. Also suppose that minor property offenders were to be dealt with in the community rather than in jails. At the same time suppose that I made tax evasion, knowingly polluting the environment, false advertising, fraudulent bankruptcy, and price-fixing crimes which carried automatic jail terms. Now, let's introduce the proverbial 'man from Mars' who always gets into stories like this one. He arrives and I take him on a tour of (the Provincial Jail near Winnipeg). What would he say? 'You sure have a problem with your middle class white people, don't you?'

The point is that the law in capitalist societies is structured *a priori* on the basis of social class. It is structured in a way that determines at the outset that lower-class people will predominate among its violators, at least in the case of criminal law. Pretensions of equality before the law, that is, of fairness in legal *processing*, should not obscure this fact. As Anatole France once remarked, "The law in all its majestic equality, forbids the rich as well as the poor to sleep under bridges on rainy nights, to beg in the streets and to steal bread."

The Poor in the Legal Process

The criminal law may proscribe acts which are most likely or most advantageously committed by lower-class people while, as suggested by Sutherland (1945) in his work on white collar crime, many socially harmful acts — those more likely to be committed by the well-to-do — are covered by less brutal civil prohibitions and sanctions. Or, as Herman and Julia Schwendinger (1970:148-49) argue, acts are not proscribed at all which may be regarded as "criminal" if one defines the word in terms other than existing law in capitalist countries. Such acts might be those relating to imperialism, racism and poverty itself (Schwendingers, 1970:148).

> If the terms imperialism, racism, sexism and poverty are abbreviated signs for theories of social relationships or social systems which cause the systematic abrogation of basic rights, then imperialism, racism, sexism and poverty can be called crimes according to the logic of our argument.

Given that the structure of law itself may be an initial reason that official data contain a preponderance of lower-class violators, let us turn to other factors which add to such a result. Again it is useful to take a historical view.

In the transition from feudalism to capitalism the aristocracy met the threat to its hegemony with brutal force uncharacteristic of its more stable days (Rusche and Kirchheimer, 1939).

> It was not uncommon for those convicted of minor offenses such as begging, theft or mendicancy to receive such punishment as removal of a hand or finger, cutting off or tearing out the tongue, putting out an eye, severing an ear, castration, burning, or torture on the wheel, with capital punishment reserved for all other offenses against the law (Scott and Scull, 1978:150).

Legal philosophers in sympathy with the emerging bourgeoisie were dissatisfied with both the brutality of punishment and the absence of due process afforded by the old system. People such as Cesare Beccaria (c1764, 1963) complained that the arbitrariness and brutality of aristocratic justice were counterproductive. Instead, Beccaria proposed a new system based on individual rather than class rights: a system of equal justice. As well as equality before the law for all citizens, the new system was to administer sanctions swiftly, with maximum certainty and only in such measure to insure that people would be deterred. Sanctions would be related to the amount of social harm done or likely to be done by an infraction rather than according to the personal circumstances of lawbreakers. Thus equality before the law and the primacy of the act rather than the actor became part of the legal ideals which, to a point, were carried forward with the development of capitalism.

While recognition of the individual rights of all citizens to own and control property and to obtain equal justice served the bourgeoisie well in the period of transition from feudalism, these principles served less well when the power of the old middle class was established. As the bourgeoisie became the ruling class their major threat no longer was an aristocracy who might limit their ambitions. Instead, it was the unpropertied and unprivileged, some of whom were taking the ideas of universal democracy and equality altogether too seriously.

Adjustment of the ideals of justice was assisted by the development of "scientific" criminology. Liberal principles of justice had included the idea that all people operate by free will and may therefore be held equally responsible for their actions and may also be more or less equal in their response to deterrent sanctions. In the development of positivist theories lawbreakers were seen as subjects of social, personal, and biological forces beyond their control rather than as *objects* capable of self-determination. The concept of the natural, born, or otherwise unique criminal emerged to explain the concentration of criminality among the "dangerous classes." It could still be maintained that people were political equals, that is, equal in terms of their rights as individual citizens.

Scientific criminology thus set the stage for a return to legal-process-by-class as it existed in a different form in feudal days. Inequality in the legal process could now be disguised as individualized justice. Legal measures could now, with ideological impunity, be adjusted to the presumed circumstances or capabilities of *individuals*. Greater attention paid by law enforcement personnel and more onerous sanctions (sometimes further disguised as "treatment") meted out to the dangerous classes could be rationalized on the basis of putative individual differences rather than class differences.

When an individual today appears in court in Canada the person does not do so solely to account for a particular law violation. All aspects of past life as well as future possibilities are taken into account. This situation Edwin Schur (1969:159) contends, ". . . allows the respectable (middle or upper class) citizen caught in criminal acts a degree of immunity not available to the supposedly less respectable (lower class) colleagues in crime." Throughout the justice system people are dealt with on the basis of the quality of their lives prior to the act and the projected quality of their futures, judged to a large degree by factors associated with social class. The so-called individualization of justice and the exercise of increasingly diversified forms of discretion in the legal system are contemporary characteristics of justice in Canada.

Investigating a number of studies done in Canada and elsewhere, Tepperman (1977:159) concludes, ". . . the evidence suggests that wherever discretion is available it is used in ways ultimately damaging to poor people." Such is the case at virtually every level of the criminal or delinquency processing system.

Discretion in the legal system begins with the deployment of enforcement resources. For a variety of reasons, Box (1971:177-90) suggests, police may be deployed to pay closest attention to lower-class areas. Differential deployment follows a choice of statutes to be enforced, since not all can be enforced with equal fervor. As well, there is a choice made of potential offenders. The police thus begin the process by which a number of people are selected for official processing from among those who might be included by virtue of their conduct relative to the law. The bureaucratically selected population of law violators become subjects of criminological study, and their characteristics, however related or unrelated to their criminal or delinquent conduct, may become the basis for scientific explanations. Buttressed by such authoritative theories and their own experience, the police look for law violators where they have found them before and where they "know" them to exist. As Box emphasizes, this "social construction of reality" takes on a reified existence. The situation is an example of the self-fulfilling prophecy and is reminiscent of the old vaudeville routine where a drunk is seen looking for a lost article beneath a burning street-light surrounded by darkness. Someone asks him what he is doing and he responds that he is trying to find his wallet. "Where did you lose it?" inquires the observer. "About 100 yards that way," he replies. "Well, then why are you looking for it here?" he is asked. "Because the light is better here!" is his slurred response. To a degree at least, crime and delinquency are "found" among the poor because that is where they are sought and the poor have little ability to resist intrusion.

The head of an RCMP Commercial Fraud section once confided to the writer that a lead given to his group would not likely be followed up. The RCMP have too few personnel even to begin to investigate more than a very small portion of the cases which come to their attention. Compare this situation to the concentrated police patrols of lower-class neighborhoods.

Beyond initial deployment practices and decisions to concentrate attention on certain kinds of laws and to give scant attention to others, studies have indicated other ways in which discretion in the justice system operates to the disadvantage of the poor.

An example of the operation of police discretion with respect to juveniles is provided by Nease (1966) in a study conducted in Hamilton, Ontario. She examined official contact and referral in "high delinquency" as compared with other areas in the city. As an initial condition resulting in differential contact, she suggests that there is an over-dependence on the police in poor areas (142). This is similar to a later conclusion by Black and Reiss (1970) in the U.S. that people in poor areas more frequently resort to calling the police for relatively trivial matters. Such a finding does not explain subsequent differences in delinquency processing, however. Nease found that ". . . boys from economically disadvantaged neighborhoods are sent to juvenile courts more frequently than their fellow delinquents from the rest of the city" (141). Such decisions were apparently unrelated to the seriousness of offenses. In other words, the characteristics of an area seem to operate independently of age, religion, nationality, offense or past record to influence the police decision to refer a case to juvenile court rather than to release with a warning.

Having examined the Nease study in a class taught by the author, members of the Winnipeg Police Juvenile Division suggested the following explanation in terms of their own experience: police are reluctant to push a case any further along the official processing route than seems necessary. This is so for two reasons. The first stems from compassion and sometimes from knowledge of labeling research, which suggests that the further a juvenile penetrates into the official system, the more he or she is liable to develop a delinquent self-concept. The second reason for avoiding official channels is that it often involves the officer in a great deal of paperwork, court appearances and other bureaucratic burdens, which bring little personal or organizational reward. Why then should police more frequently push kids from poor areas along the official route? The Juvenile Officers suggest that it has to do with police ability to contact parents or other responsible adults, the perceived cooperativeness of the adults, and a general, subjective assessment of the adequacy of an alleged offender's home. In other words, the conditions of poverty, the attitudes that adults who are poor may, as a result of their own experience, develop toward official representatives of the state, and the subjective assessments of the police may add up to the creation of official delinquents for reasons independent of personal conduct.

Nease's (1966) study of Hamilton delinquents found that juvenile court decisions were less influenced by area than the police decision on whether or not to refer a case to juvenile court, possibly because the police act as a filter prior to the exercise of court discretion. Others have found that the filter continues to operate at the level of juvenile court decisions.

Haldane, Elliott and Whitehead (1972) examined cases passing through the Halifax Family Court. Their results indicate that receiving a "major disposition" is positively associated with "low social class, low income, broken home, unmarried parents, families judged to be unstable, a history of legal involvement on the part of the parent, and an overcrowded home" (240). Although differences in the statistical relationships occurred when offense category was held constant, discrimination — they used the more polite term, "particularism" — based on factors related to class remained. In fact, it was found that juveniles from low social class families were more likely to receive major dispositions for minor infractions than those from the higher social class (241).

In the processing of adult offenders, similar sorts of filtering occur to the disadvantage of lower-class people. Again, the process begins at the level of police contact. While delinquency legislation may be aggreeably ambiguous to many, there is a general expectation, suggests Brian Grosman (1975) in his work on the police in Canada, that criminal law is mechanical and objective in its application. On the contrary, Grosman (1974:90) says that much of what follows in the criminal process depends upon ". . . the individual policeman (sic) who engages in selective enforcement without any real guidance. . . . Obviously law enforcement neither means total enforcement nor equal enforcement when the law enforcement policy is made by individual policemen (sic)."

Discretion is also a major factor affecting outcomes at levels in the justice system beyond the police, as Grosman (1969) found in his study, *The Prosecutor: An Inquiry into the Exercise of Discretion*, an examination of Canadian court procedures. John Hogarth (1971), in a monumental study of decision-making in Ontario's courts, examined regularities of sentencing within very wide limits of discretion given to such courts to administer sanctions.

Precisely what influence social class has upon one's chances of arrest and conviction and how class influences functionaries' use of discretion is not clear in all instances. There is some evidence, however, that poor adults are at a disadvantage in the criminal justice system in ways similar to the demonstrated disadvantage of poor youngsters in the delinquency processing system.

Tepperman (1977:161-65) reviewed a number of studies touching upon poverty, access to legal representation, and one's chances in court. He concluded that there is a difference in the chances of conviction between those who are remanded in custody and those who obtain an interim release. The difference remains when both obtain legal counsel. Likewise, custody tends to increase the chances that one will be imprisoned upon conviction. Tepperman (1977:162) concludes, "These risks fall most heavily on poor people because they are least likely to be able to raise bail."

While it may not be absolutely certain that discretion always works to the disadvantage of lower-class defendants, investigation and processing of so-called white collar crimes is often conducted so as to keep high status law violators out of the courts. In her examination of legislation — municipal, provincial and federal — affecting corporate conduct in Canada, Snider (1978) points out that procedures often dictate that past infractions be ignored if such violations are remedied or if future compliance is assured. Attrition rates for such offenses tend therefore to be much higher than rates for normal, that is, predominately lower-class, crimes. If someone burglarizes your house and is apprehended in circumstances which would clearly yield a conviction, it would not be common for the offender to be released by the police on the promise that stolen articles will be returned and that the offender will go straight. If someone steals from you by deliberately withholding your wages (Snider, 1978), then such is not the case.

Emphasizing the way in which high status law violators are kept out of the courts, Tepperman (1977:163) cites a newspaper report of a Supreme Court of Canada case. A representative of the Department of Revenue frankly admitted that "tax evaders were not prosecuted if they could pay when caught." As C.B. Macpherson (1965:7) said, "All are free, but some are freer than others." The statement could refer to the freedom to violate the law in Canada.

While most studies of judicial processing have centered on restricted bureaucratic practices, a study by Kellough (1977) takes a macrosociological view. She examined the effects which general political and economic conditions have upon patterns of incarceration. Her sociohistorical investigation covers a 29-year period in the Eastern Judicial District of Manitoba. Data indicate a fluctuation in rates of incarceration associated with general social conditions and such fluctuations are "...almost entirely made up by incarcerations of the most powerless groups for 'social control' offenses" (2). (Social control offenses include those related to alcohol, morality, offenses against public order, and vagrancy.)

Here is another important finding in Kellough's research: "...while only slight differences are found in the severity of sentence imposed, the lowest social classes are most apt to serve their full sentence" (2). The recent growth of parole authority and other conditional release procedures in Canada makes this finding all the more important. A study by Waller

(1974) failed to discover a rational basis for parole board decision-making; this leaves open the question of whether parole boards merely grant privileges to those most like themselves in terms of education, lifestyle, and professed values.

If we combine studies which indicate that lower-class people are at a disadvantage in the legal process with evidence (Stebbins, 1971) that the farther one penetrates into the crime and delinquency processing system, the more difficult it is to escape from the "criminal role," one is at least suspicious that the system may be unwittingly exacerbating problems it ostensibly wishes to minimize. A more cynical interpretation (Liazos, 1974) suggests that minimizing crime is a goal superseded in capitalist systems by that of terrorizing lower-class people (who step out of their meagre "place"), thereby keeping their confreres in line.

If we take data from any stage in the legal process, lower-class people prevail, but to what extent this is due to the patterns of conduct of lower-class people we cannot truly estimate.

The Social Psychology of Crime

In attempting to explain crime and delinquency at the individual level, criminologists have tended (if they have not resorted to "personal pathology" explanations) to assert that deviant outcome results from sociocultural learning (Hartung, 1965:37). The desperate conditions of lower-class life, it is often suggested, may force some people to abandon conventional morality (Merton, 1938) and possibly to establish a counter-culture (Cohen, 1955) or an alternative subculture (Cloward and Ohlin, 1960). Thus many of the popular interpretations of crime and delinquency center ultimately upon the social psychology of lower-class people. As emphasized throughout this article, such concentration is unwarranted because criminality, defined by law or by autonomous philosophical criteria (Schwendingers, 1970), occurs at all class levels.

Control theorists such as Travis Hirschi (1969) have examined structural conditions operating at an individual level to create the willingness to violate laws. Hirschi concurs with Nye (1958:5) who claimed that ". . . behavior proscribed as criminal or delinquent need not be explained in any positive sense, since it usually results in quicker and easier achievement of goals than normative behavior." Hirschi (1969:11) suggests that deviance occurs at all class levels and thus ". . . for some men (sic), considerations of morality are important; for others they are not." Applying control theory to an empirical examination of delinquency, Hirschi discovered that it is persons, not cultures, who are deviant: those most likely to commit delinquent acts are those with weak attachments to other people and who have a low stake in conventional conformity.

Low stake in conformity and weak attachments may be endemic among the lower classes, and Hirschi's data do not preclude this. Such factors, in combination with others explored in earlier sections of this article, may help to explain the preponderance of lower-class people in official crime data. Stake in conformity and attachment may help to explain the tendency for particular acts — often those we have come to regard as most serious — to be more predominant among lower-class people. This relationship between deviance and class is suggested in a New Brunswick self-report study (Tribble, 1972), which confined the definition of delinquency to serious matters. Such explanations do not account for all types or instances of law violation, however.

The well-known Watergate Case in the U.S. seems to have resulted from the actions of individuals who tenaciously clung to the reigns of political power. They took foolish precautions to insure that their stake in the system and their control over it would be maintained. Similarly, the alleged violations of civil rights and procedural law by the RCMP — being investigated by the McDonald Commission as this article is being completed — do not appear to be the acts of socially isolated people with a low stake in conformity unless one really stretches a point. Neither do the embezzlers interviewed by Cressey (1953) in his classic study of such offenders appear in the main to be people who have little to lose.

Steven Box (1971:139-61) recognizes the contribution of control theorists, while qualifying their conclusions. He suggests that attachment to others and stake in conformity act in combination with situational factors and that the total circumstances are open to subjective interpretation and misinterpretation by potential deviants. The availability of skills or tools needed to commit deviant acts, the amount of support — social and symbolic — an individual perceives, and an assessment of the chances of being detected and punished are among the factors which influence an individual in the consideration of action at any class level.

It may indeed be the case with respect to particular *forms* of law violation that the circumstances of class and class relationships can be said to create conditions enhancing the choice of deviant alternatives. A partial explanation for lower-class deviance may be that the nature of our political-economic system is such that the decision to violate the law in a particular fashion is more often seen by people at that level as being reasonable and desirable. But such an explanation need not entail the existence of a criminal or delinquent subculture.

Conclusion

The relationship between class and criminality is largely spurious. The definition of some behaviors as criminal while other socially harmful acts are not so defined is, in large part, if not totally, a function of class domination. Thus, the preponderance of poor folk among law violators occurs in part *by definition.*

An examination of contemporary studies and of history suggests that equality before the law is an idea developed in pursuit of bourgeois class interests. It is now, and always has been, a slogan for obscuring important class divisions. Based on an ethic of individualism, it is the ideology by which such divisions are preserved. Individualized justice is a more recent development in the mystification of class relationships.

We must agree with Hagan (1977:63-69), however, when he suggests that, in addition to the victimization of poor people by the law and its agents, one must also accept the idea "that poverty carries with it many socially injurious experiences...(which) lead logically to deviant outcomes." In this regard we examined the social psychology of crime and suggested that circumstances may exist among lower-class people to increase the probability that individuals will choose deviant alternatives. Such conditions may exist at all class levels, of course, but the circumstances of a class may mean that certain *kinds* of law violation are more common at one level than another. Stock fraud offenders are even less common among welfare mothers than are shoplifters among chartered accountants.

Surely no culture of poverty explanation is needed to explain the predominance of lower-class people in jails, police statistics, or other official records of crime and delinquency. Crime and delinquency are social products and, given the nature of Canadian political and economic organization, it should surprise no one that the status of criminal or delinquent is one which is, with few exceptions, reserved for those at the bottom of the social order.

Canadian criminologists have too often relied upon theories grounded in U.S. race and ethnic relations, urban settlement patterns, and an obscurantist liberal ideology. Subcultural explanations not only do not suffice as analytical tools, they tend to blame the poor for social problems which are more properly seen as being the result of the activities of the rich.[2]

As pointed out recently by Morton, Snider and West (1978:2), we have yet to produce a distinctive Canadian political economy of crime. Such an analysis would have to recognize the basis of such organization in the mode of economic production and the historical use of the law in Canada to preserve a social order conducive to dominant class interests.

NOTES

1. For a discussion of the implications for conflict theory of consensus in Canada on some laws and conflicting ideas on others, see the concluding chapter of *Law and Social Control in Canada* (Greenaway, 1978:225-40).

2. The intention here is not to dismiss the very real danger presented by crime and delinquency. Rather, it is to suggest a new perspective. Without a doubt, the solutions prompted by liberal criminologists, if they have done anything at all, have tended to exacerbate problems. Radical solutions, in addition to tackling crime and delinquency indirectly — through political and economic change — may involve dismantling the present "technology of corrections" which includes a hierarchy of agencies ironically dependent for their continued existence on the continuation of crime. Means could be sought to gain cooperation from those directly involved in the vital processes of production, rather than warehousing wrongdoers or treating them. It is to the advantage of workers to reclaim social harmony and lost human resources. Community treatment would thus take on new meaning.

REFERENCES

Baldus, Bernd. "Social Control in Capitalist Societies: An Examination of the Problem of Order in Liberal Societies," *Canadian Journal of Sociology*, 2 (1977), pp. 247-62.

Beccaria, Cesare. *On Crimes and Punishment*, trans. by Paolucci. Indianapolis: Bobbs-Merrill, c. 1964, 1963.

Becker, Howard S. *The Outsiders: Studies in the Sociology of Deviance*. New York: Free Press, 1963.

Black, D.J. and A.J. Reiss. "Police Control of Juveniles, *American Sociological Review*, 35 (1970), pp. 63-77.

Box, Steven. *Deviance, Reality and Society*. Toronto: Holt, Rinehart and Winston, 1971.

Cloward, Richard and Lloyd Ohlin. *Delinquency and Opportunity: A Theory of Delinquent Gangs*. Glencoe, Ill.: Free Press, 1960.

Cohen, Albert K. *Delinquent Boys: The Culture of the Gang*. Glencoe, Ill.: Free Press, 1955.

Cressey, Donald J. *Other People's Money*. Glencoe, Ill.: Free Press, 1953.

Friedmann, Wolfgang. *Law in a Changing Society*. Berkeley: University of California Press, 1959.

Greenaway, W.K. "General Conclusion: Problems and Issues in the Conflict Theory of Law and Social Control," in Greenaway and S.L. Brickey, eds., *Law and Social Control in Canada*. Scarborough, Ont.: Prentice-Hall of Canada, 1978, pp. 225-40.

Grossman, Brian A. *The Prosecutor: An Inquiry into the Exercise of Discretion*. Toronto: University of Toronto Press, 1969.

_____."The Discretionary Enforcement Law," in Craig L. Boydell, Paul C. Whitehead and Carl F. Grindstaff, eds., *The Administration of Criminal Justice in Canada*, 1974, pp. 84-92.

_____. *Police Command: Decisions and Discretion*. Toronto: Macmillan, 1975.

Hagan, John. *Disreputable Pleasures*. Toronto: McGraw-Hill Ryerson, 1977.

Haldane, Lesley H., David H. Elliott and Paul C. Whitehead. "Particularism in the Sentencing of Juvenile Delinquents," in C.L. Boydell, C.F. Gridstaff and P.C. Whitehead, eds., *Deviant Behaviour and Societal Reaction*. Toronto: Holt, Rinehart and Winston of Canada, 1972, pp. 231-43.

Hartung, Frank E. *Crime, Law and Society*. Detroit: Wayne State University Press, 1965.

Hepburn, John. "Social Control and the Legal Order: Legitimated Repression in a Capitalist State," in W.K. Greenaway and S.L. Brickey, eds., *Law and Social Control in Canada*. Scarborough, Ont.: Prentice-Hall of Canada, 1978, pp. 70-84.

Hirschi, Travis. *Causes of Delinquency*. Berkeley: University of California Press, 1969.

Hogarth, John. *Sentencing as a Human Process*. Toronto: University of Toronto Press, 1971.

Houston, Susan. "Victorian Origins of Juvenile Delinquency: A Canadian Experience," in W.K. Greenaway and S.L. Brickey, eds., *Law and Social Control in Canada*. Scarborough, Ont.: Prentice-Hall of Canada, 1978, pp. 168-90.

Kellough, D. Gail. "Incarceration as a Response to Political and Economic Conditions." Unpublished Master's thesis, University of Manitoba, 1977.

Liazos, Anthony. "Class Oppression: The Functions of Juvenile Justice," *The Insurgent Sociologist*, 5 (1974), pp. 2-24.

Macpherson, C.B. *The Real World of Democracy*. Toronto: CBC Publications, 1965.

Matza, David.*Delinquency and Drift*. New York: John Wiley and Sons, 1964.

Merton, Robert K. "Social Structure and Anomie," *American Sociological Review*, 3 (1938), pp. 577-602.

Miller, Walter B. "'Lower Class Culture as a Generating Milieu of Gang Delinquency,"*Journal of Social Issues*, 15 (1958), pp. 5-19.

Morton, M.E., L. Snider and W.G. West. "Towards a Critical Political Economy of Canadian Crime." Paper presented at the Annual Meetings of the Canadian Sociology and Anthropology Association, London, Ont. (May 1978).

Nease, Barbara. "Measuring Juvenile Delinquency in Hamilton," *Canadian Journal of Corrections*, 8 (1966). Reprinted in W.E. Mann, ed., *Social Deviance in Canada*. Toronto: Copp-Clark, 1971, pp. 62-73.

Platt, Anthony. *The Child Savers: The Invention of Delinquency*. Chicago: University of Chicago Press, 1969.

Quinney, Richard. "The Ideology of Law: Notes for a Radical Alternative to Legal Oppression," *Issues in Criminology*, 7 (1972), pp. 1-35.

Rusche, Georg and Otto Kirchheimer. *Punishment and Social Structure*. New York: Columbia University Press, 1939.

Schur, Edwin M. *Our Criminal Society*. Englewood Cliffs, N.J.: Prentice-Hall, 1969.

Schwendinger, Herman and Julia Schwendinger. "Defenders of Order or Guardian of Human Rights?" *Issues in Criminology*, 5 (1970), pp. 123-57.

Scott, Robert and Andrew Scull. "Penal Reform and the Surplus Army of Labor," in W.K. Greenaway and S.L. Brickey, eds., *Law and Social Control in Canada*. Scarborough, Ont.: Prentice-Hall of Canada, 1978, pp. 147-58.

Shaw, Clifford R. *Delinquency Areas*. Chicago: University of Chicago Press, 1929.

Small, Shirley. "Canadian Narcotics Legislation, 1908-1923: A Conflict Model Interpretation," in W.K. Greenaway and S.L. Brickey, eds., *Law and Social Control in Canada*. Scarborough, Ont.: Prentice-Hall of Canada, 1978, pp. 28-42.

Snider, D.L. "Corporate Crime in Canada: A Preliminary Report," *Canadian Journal of Criminology*, 20 (1978), pp. 142-68.

Stebbins, Robert.*Commitment to Deviance*. Westport, Connecticut: Greenwood Publishing, 1971.

Sutherland, Edwin H. *Principles of Criminology*. New York: J.B. Lippincott, 1939.

_____. "Is 'White Collar Crime' Crime?" *American Sociological Review*, 10 (1945), pp. 132-39.

Sykes, Gresham and David Matza. "Techniques of Neutralization: A Theory of Delinquency," *American Sociological Review*, 22 (1957), pp. 664-70.

Taylor, Ian, Paul Walton and Jock Young. *The New Criminology: For a Social Theory of Deviance*. London: Routledge and Kegan Paul, 1973.

Taylor, Laurie. *Deviance and Society*. London: Michael Joseph, 1971.

Tepperman, Lorne. *Crime Control: The Urge toward Authority*. Toronto: McGraw-Hill Ryerson, 1977.

Thomas, W.I. and Florian Znaniecki. *The Polish Peasant in Europe and America*. New York: Alfred A. Knopf, 1917-18. Two Volumes.

Thrasher, Frederic M. *The Gang*. Chicago: University of Chicago Press, 1927.

Tribble, Stephen. "Socio-economic Status and Self-Reported Juvenile Delinquency," *Canadian Journal of Criminology and Corrections*, 14 (1972), pp. 409-15.

Waller, Irvin. *Men Released from Prison*. Toronto: University of Toronto Press, 1974.

Watson, G. Llewellyn. "The Poverty of Canadian Sociology," *Canadian Journal of Sociology* (1976), pp. 345-62.

B. Regions and Regionalism

Regional disparities are engrained in the structure of the Canadian economy. Clement views regionalism as an expression of deeply rooted inequalities and social problems in Canada that can best be understood as part of the broader problem of underdevelopment. More important for our overall perspective on inequality, Clement argues persuasively for an approach that treats regionalism in terms of the total context of Canadian society.

He reviews various regional power structure frameworks used in Canada, takes note of the paucity of empirical work, and affirms the importance of class over geographical distinctions. Regional power structure models have the advantage over traditional elite models, he states, because they "allow for more complex sources of opposition."

Clement continues with his own empirical analysis of Canada's economic elite, offering results similar to those from earlier reports, and documents the economic dominance of central Canada in trade, manufacturing, and finance with Toronto-Montreal as the center of indigenous Canadian capitalism. The reader should be cautious, however, to note the rapid and recent growth of particular types of capital in western Canada, a point overlooked by Clement.

According to Clement, regionalism is an uneven development, and attached to this view are two basic premises:

(1) Uneven economic development occurs when more surplus is extracted than put in.

(2) A region can only be underdeveloped if it is tied to an external economy that is responsible for the underdevelopment. Underdevelopment manifests itself in the economies of various regions and is shown by tax bases the economies provide, distribution of taxable income, and selected evidence on regional disparities in lifestyles.

Clement argues for an understanding of regional inequalities that is developed by investigating the inequalities in several contexts, namely, the international context vis à vis the United States, the interprovincial context vis à vis the western and eastern hinterlands, and the interprovincial context.

Clairmont, Macdonald, and Wien offer us a segmentation approach to the study of poverty and low-wage work in the Maritimes. The segmentation model divides the work world into two broad segments: the central and the marginal. Clearly the Maritime case is one of the working poor, and the concept of a marginal work world is central to this article's analysis. An operational definition of low-wage industries includes those which in 1970 had more than 60% of their full-time workers earning less than $120 per week, and over 50% of the Atlantic provinces' labor force could be placed in the low-wage sector. The authors report that these industries are growing in absolute terms and the compensation gap has not narrowed.

The authors define the marginal work world (MWW) in terms of work settings (establishments) and occupations (in the case of self-employed individuals), which provide for the majority of their work force, or membership employment packages characterized by low wages, limited fringe benefits, little job security, and restricted internal advancement opportunities. They go on to define central work world (CWW) establishments as ones which offer high wages, extensive fringe benefits, internal career ladders, and job security provisions. Within the category one finds considerable variation, including well-organized self-employed occupational groups such as the professions and the highly skilled craft guilds. While much is made by the authors of their focus on work settings or establishments (where they believe segmentation is likely to persist), their subsequent analyses fail to link these establishments to the industrial occupational units which serve in the main as the principal data base.

Following a review of orthodox, Marxist and eclectic (to use their own terminology) approaches to the study of labor markets, the paper turns to determinants of the kind of employment package provided by establishments. Attention is given to the linking mechanism between the marginal and central work worlds (e.g., direct ownership, subcontracting, franchises). The authors refer to this as an evaluation of the MWW, holding however to the position that the CWW/MWW dichotomy has remained intact, albeit with some decrease in the distinction between powerful and powerless firms.

A final section includes some discussion of various attempts to transform the marginal sector, including the organization of occupational groups and the role of unions. Organizational strategies are divided into two major categories, associations grouping together independent producers and unionization strategies. With regard to unionization, the MWW is described as a frontier land that is difficult to settle, secure, and transform. It is in the areas of public administration and community services that the greatest growth of unionization has occurred, but the prospects of unionization for this segment of the labor force, as reported to the authors by union officials, are rather dismal.

A Political Economy of Regionalism in Canada*

WALLACE CLEMENT

Regionalism is but one expression of more deeply rooted inequalities and social problems in Canada. Any dominant class creates problems through its very existence and actions; one such problem is regionalism. To suggest that regional inequalities are "natural" ignores the realities of power and the control some men have over the lives of others. Thus a detailed analysis of the current structure of regionalism would show that it is not the product of some natural phenomenon like geography or resources or even historical accident; rather, it is the product of a series of actions and institutions created and alterable by man.

Regionalism is a sub-set of a larger problem known as underdevelopment. Since little theoretical work from a class or power perspective has been done on regionalism *per se*, it is necessary to begin with some recent models of underdevelopment which can then be applied to the question of regionalism in Canada. While, initially, these models of underdevelopment may seem rather remote, their relevance will soon become apparent. Generally, regionalism in Canada has been examined either interprovincially — that is, on a national scale with Ontario and Quebec as the center and the rest of the provinces as their periphery; or intraprovincially — as, for example, within a province like Ontario with Toronto as the center and the rest of the province as the periphery. Rather than focus exclusively on one or the other of these perspectives, a third overriding approach which links them together and involves broader questions of class structures and Canada's international context will be used. This approach may be regarded as "holistic" in the sense that individual expressions of regionalism cannot be understood in isolation but must be analysed in terms of the total context of Canadian society, itself part of a broader world system.

Regionalism and Development Theory

A number of frameworks based on regional power relationships and used primarily to describe Latin America's relationship with advanced capitalist nations have been developed recently. These models integrate both national

*From David Glenday, Hubert Guindon and Allen Turowetz, eds., *Modernization and the Canadian State*. Toronto: Macmillan of Canada, 1978.

and international relations into their studies of development. They analyse each nation as a total society in terms of the indigenous regional and class power structures while simultaneously taking into account relations between these structures and external centers of power. Central to all these models is an unequal exchange between interdependent units which form a set of asymmetrical associations either within nations or between nations.

According to André Gunder Frank and his "development of under-development" model, "contemporary underdevelopment is in large part the historical product of past and continuing economic and other relations between the satellite underdeveloped and the now developed metropolitan countries." The model is not restricted to international relations; rather, Frank attempts to link internal developments to relationships within as well as outside nations — to what he describes as "a whole chain of constellations of metropoles and satellites." His central thesis is that "within this world-embracing metropolis-satellite structure the metropoles tend to develop and satellites to underdevelop."[1] In other words, there is a chain of exploitive relations between various levels from the local to the regional to the national and international which serves to accumulate power and resources at the highest levels and drain them from the lowest ones.

Johan Galtung offers a variation on the themes presented by Frank. He begins, as did Frank, by focusing on "inequality within and between nations" and specifically analyses the interaction among these inequalities.[2] Using the imagery of "center" and "periphery,"[3] Galtung argues that "there is a disharmony of interest between the Center nation [metropolitan nation] as a whole and the Periphery nation [satellite nation] as a whole" but maintains that this misses an important refinement "because it blurs the harmony of interest between the two centers, and leads to the belief that imperialism is merely an international relationship, not a combination of intra- and inter-national relations."[4] The key mediation party in the Galtung model is the "bridgehead" in the center of the periphery nation. Inequality results from the way interaction takes place and can be identified in terms of sets of elites. In what he calls the "multinational, asymmetrical stage," Galtung argues that "elites have emerged in the Periphery nations, strongly identified with and well harmonizing with the Center elites."[5] One final refinement Galtung introduces has particular relevance to Canada: that is the "go-between" status of some nations, mediating between center and periphery nations in much the same way that the center in the periphery nation mediates in the general model.[6]

Unfortunately, the imagery of the regional power-structure models emphasizes geographical distinctions rather than class distinctions; but, while the capitalist class may be located in metropolitan areas, so is much of the working class. While keeping the overall perspective of international relationships and their intranational implications, recent analysts have paid much more attention to the class structures within these nations and have argued that some elements of these class structures have become "internationalized." Norman Girvan has classified such analyses as "historical/institutional/structural" approaches.[7] Osvaldo Sunkel's work exemplifies this type or approach.[8] Using five main interrelated concepts of "development, underdevelopment, dependence, marginality and spatial imbalances," Sunkel argues:

> A realistic analysis of Latin American development should therefore be based on a conception which assumes our socioeconomic system to be formed by two groups of structural elements: internal and external. Among the internal factors are: the pattern of natural resources and population; political institutions, especially the state; sociopolitical groups and classes; the ideologies and attitudes of different groups and classes; the specific policies followed by the government; etc. The complex of internal and external structural elements, and the interrelations among them, define the structure of the system, and constitute, therefore, the framework within which the functioning of the national system and its processes of structural transformation take place.[9]

More specifically, there are three dimensions of the analysis — process, structure, and system — whereby "it is postulated that underdevelopment is part and parcel of the historical process of global development of the international system, and therefore, that underdevelopment and development are simply the two faces of one single universal process."[10] The most recent phase in these relationships maintains the overall structural asymmetry between nations but, now that they have become "ever more closely integrated — it is necessary to take into account that this new model of international economic relations is based operationally on the transnational conglomerate, a new kind of business organization that has experienced an enormous growth during the last decades."[11]

Sunkel's model, therefore, focuses on developments within center and periphery nations but, in addition, introduces an international category because of his "global perspective." From this wider perspective, two basic components can be identified:

> a) a complex of activities, social groups and regions in different countries which conform to the developed part of the global system and which are closely linked transnationally through many concrete interests as well as by similar styles, ways and levels of living and cultural affinities;
> b) a national complement of activities, social groups and regions partially or totally excluded from the national developed part of the global system and without any links with similar activities, groups and regions of other countries.[12]

Thus, Sunkel's imagery is of a "transnational kernel or nucleus" at the "heart" of the international system which tends to be integrated, plus national segments which tend to be segregated from or marginal to the core of the dominant national and international system. Of central importance in this model is the nature of the relationship which these segregated sectors in both center and periphery have with the transnational integrated sectors. This can be defined in terms of the types of demands the transnational sectors may make upon the marginal sectors and the conflicts which may arise as a result of those demands.

If Galtung's idea of "go-between" nations is coordinated with Sunkel's concept of "integrated and marginalized" segments of the class structures of center and periphery nations, a model of international economic relations and their regional and class implications can be developed. Also, of course, the multinational corporations and the elites which control them mediate between the various structural components of the model. To turn these models into a theory of international and regional capitalism will require a great deal more empirical work, especially as they relate to Canada, but as a guide to this empirical inquiry they are quite useful.

Although there has been some discussion of various regional power-structure frameworks in Canada, very little empirical work has actually been done. What has been undertaken is at the level of the Frank "development of underdevelopment" thesis and not of more recent models such as Galtung's or Sunkel's. Mel Watkins, for example, following in the tradition of Harold Innis, suggests using a "center-margin framework" similar to Frank's model for examining the national capitalist class and "its relationships of dependency or independency with respect to the imperial business class or the imperial bourgeoisie."[13] In so doing, he recognizes the importance of the "metropolis-satellite chain" used by Frank, arguing that in the international framework, "Canada would lie above the line as one of the exploiting nations rather than an exploited nation."[14] But, at the same time, the internal relationships must also be taken into account and it is in this context that Arthur K. Davis's paper, "Canadian Society and History as Hinterland *versus* Metropolis,"[15] fits — particularly his argument that "it is impossible to conceptualize a holistic view of Canadian society apart from American society. This means that the minimal frame of reference for Canada is North American society."[16] As yet, however, very little in the way of theory, model building, or empirical research has been developed from these humble beginnings.

Those who question whether studies of the role of multinationals and their implications for development in Latin America are relevant for Canada should read Philip Mathias's *Forced Growth*[17] for five studies of the relationships established between Canada's weakest provinces and foreign-controlled multinationals. Because of the provincial structure of Canada's state, multinationals, or even giant nationally owned corporations, can and frequently do treat provinces much as they do various countries in Latin America, shifting investment and production schedules according to local conditions and thus "trading off" one province against another. This is also done by "resource-based" companies whose exploration policies define when and where resources will be located and utilized.

These frameworks make particularly promising models for Canadian social science because they reflect a centralist tradition important in Canada's development. Both Innis's staple theory and the Lower/Creighton "Laurentian thesis" point out that this centralist tradition was especially strong when Canada's early colonial links were established and during the early growth of central Canada. Both theses analyze structural power links, binding them into a whole founded on geography, regionalism, and resource extraction. As Watkins has pointed out, "what Innis was talking about [in his staples theory] is [*sic*] areas where the growth process is led by primary exports and the dominant elite within the colony is committed to exports. The staples theory is really a pseudonym for a kind of imperial relationship."[18] One difference between typical elite models, like the one used by John Porter in *The Vertical Mosaic*, and the regional power-structure frameworks outlined here is that the latter allow for recognition of more complex sources of opposition. They see the relationship as one of running conflict whereby Canadians are placed in a "double-bind" between United States and Canadian business interests, both of whom have turned toward the regional hinterlands for their surplus extraction.

Regionalism and Canada's Dominant Class

It should be evident that it is not "Ontario" *per se* which dominates the rest of Canada. It is the capitalist class and its operating arm in the economy, the economic elite, which has always performed and continues to perform this task. This capitalist class resides primarily in parts of the Toronto-Montreal-Ottawa "golden triangle" but is national in scope and influence. Here, for example, are located the six national men's clubs and the head-quarters of the dominant financial institutions — the banks and insurance companies. There are also other regional segments of the capitalist class, in the west and the Atlantic provinces which overlap with the national capitalist class, but the core resides within this triangle. Although little empirical work has been done for Canada within this regional power-structure framework, the remainder of this discussion will provide some empirical application of the model to the question at hand.

Canadian history is rich with details illustrating how the current structure of regionalism developed. The most interesting and important event is probably the National Policy of 1879 which combined programs on immigration, tariffs, and railways to assert a vision of central Canadian dominance and western underdevelopment — a vision designed and put into effect by the ruling class in the Montreal-Toronto axis. This vision dominated the west until 1947 when the Leduc oil find by Imperial Oil transformed that region from the hinterland of central Canada into the hinterland of both central Canada and the United States. As early as 1934, U.S. branch plants in Canada were highly concentrated geographically. Two-thirds of all U.S.-controlled plants were located in Toronto (32%), Montreal (13%), Hamilton (5%), the Niagara Frontier (7%), or nearby border cities (9%). Of all manufacturing establishments in Canada in 1931, 42% were in Ontario and 31% in Quebec, but 66% of the U.S.-controlled plants were in Ontario and 16% in Quebec.[19] Thus, the Ontario-centered branches of U.S. manufacturing firms tended even at this time to reinforce and aggravate the problems of regionalism in Canada. Contemporary data, to be presented later in this essay, illustrate that this pattern persists; first a different expression of regionalism will be analyzed.

Data on Canada's economic elite (the most powerful segment of the capitalist class) show the effects of these historical developments in terms of their implications for the elite structure of Canada. Statistical comparison is made between 1921 (the mean year of birth for the current elite) and 1971 (the most recent census year).

The most striking feature of this table is that it shows every region in Canada, with the exception of Ontario, to be underrepresented in the

Table 1

Birthplace and Residence of the Canadian Economic Elite (Percentages)*

Region	Elite	Birth Pop. (1921)	Percentage Points Difference	Elite	Residence Pop. (1971)	Percentage Points Difference
Atlantic	8.6	11.4	(2.8)	4.0	9.4	(5.5)
Quebec	20.2	26.9	(6.7)	25.2	27.9	(2.7)
Ontario	47.6	33.4	(14.2)	52.4	35.7	(16.7)
Manitoba	7.9	6.9	(1.0)	3.5	4.6	(1.1)
Saskatchewan	4.0	8.6	(4.6)	1.0	4.3	(3.3)
Alberta	5.7	6.7	(1.0)	6.3	7.5	(1.2)
British Columbia	5.9	6.0	(0.1)	7.5	10.1	(2.6)
Total	100	100		100	100	
(N)	(682)			(797)		

*Data in Tables 1, 2, and 3 differ slightly from that in my *Canadian Corporate Elite* (Toronto, 1957), since thay are revised and expanded. See my *Continental Corporate Power* (Toronto, 1977).

economic elite by residence. By birth, only Manitoba and Ontario are over-represented, with British Columbia about equal. The most under-represented region by birth is Quebec, followed by Saskatchewan. By residence, the Atlantic provinces are most underrepresented.

The best way to evaluate regional opportunities for entrance into elite positions is to compare how many make it into the elite by staying in the province of their birth. Not surprisingly, Ontario has the highest retention rate, keeping 85% of the elite born there; it is followed by Quebec, which keeps 80% and then by British Columbia, which keeps 78%. There is then a large drop to Alberta, which keeps 54%, while all others lose over half their natives to other provinces. The greatest proportion of exits are from Saskatchewan (only 22% stay), Manitoba (35% stay), and the Atlantic region (49% stay). For each of the regions, Ontario is by far the greatest receiver of émigrés, particularly from Manitoba (43%), and from Saskatchewan (37% have migrated to Ontario), but also from the Atlantic region (31% of natives now live in Ontario). Ironically, more elites born in Manitoba and Saskatchewan now live in Ontario than remain in these provinces. Ontario also receives the lion's share of those born outside Canada. It has received 50% of the elites born in the United States and 58% of those born in the United Kingdom. It is clear that Ontario is the center of the Canadian economic elite. Those born in the province are overrepresented in the elite and many of those entering the elite from other regions move to Ontario to take up their elite positions.

Ontario's high overrepresentation by birth and current residence among the economic elite is related to the fact that so much of Canada's production is located there. This, in turn, is linked to foreign dominance in the sphere of production, a phenomenon to be explored in detail shortly. Besides being the center of manufacturing, both foreign- and Canadian-owned, Ontario is the center of finance and of the upper-class institutions of

Table 2

Upper-Class Origins in the Canadian Economic Elite by Region

Region	Birth Upper Class (%)	Total	Residence Upper Class (%)	Total
Atlantic	61	59	75	32
Quebec	78	138	73	201
Ontario	58	326	57	419
Manitoba	70	54	67	28
Saskatchewan	19	27	38	8
Alberta	49	39	41	50
British Columbia	53	40	51	60
Total	61	683	61	798

Canada. It combines the paradox of containing over half of the foreign-controlled U.S. comprador elites resident in Canada as well as having very high proportions of the indigenous Canadian elite. In other words, 53% of the U.S. comprador elites (whose main affiliation is with a foreign branch plant in Canada) are resident in Ontario, but so are 55% of the indigenous elite (those primarily associated with a Canadian-controlled company). This paradoxical position is reflected in the following table on class origins by region.

Ontario is lower in upper-class recruitment than the Canadian total because it is the location of such a large share of U.S. comprador elites, a phenomenon to be examined shortly. Even taking this into account, elites west of Manitoba are clearly less upper class in origin both by residence and birth. In part, this reflects the fact that proportionately Alberta and British Columbia have the greatest amount of compradorization but this does not account for Saskatchewan's lower percentage from the upper class. The west's lower level of upper-class recruitment is at least partly attributable to its late start as an immigrant society which, consequently, has not solidified its upper-class institutions.

Changes in the proportion of the upper class born and resident in each area can be attributed to a variety of factors. In the Atlantic region, the increase is the result of a greater proportion of those from outside the upper class leaving the region, since, in actual numbers, elites of upper-class origin living in the Atlantic region have declined between birth and residence. In Ontario and Quebec, on the other hand, the proportion of the upper class has fallen between birth and residence but the actual number of upper-class-origin elites has risen, suggesting an in-migration of people born in the upper class but a greater in-migration from outside that class. Manitoba has lost upper-class-origin elites numerically, as have Saskatchewan and Alberta, but Saskatchewan lost a greater proportion from outside the upper class. British Columbia has gained slightly numerically but dropped slightly in proportion of upper class, suggesting that a slightly greater proportion of the in-migrants have been from outside the upper class.

Generally, region of birth has had an effect on the chances of members of the Canadian economic elite for entry into elite positions. Those from outside the upper class are forced more often to emigrate from their place of birth if they are going to enter into the elite while those of upper-class origins are able to stay in their place of birth.

It is of interest to distinguish the particular economic sectors with which elite members from these various regions become aligned. The western-born are overrepresented in terms of both their proportion in the total elite and their 1921 population base in utilities and resources. Pipelines account for the overrepresentation in utilities; foreign-controlled oil and gas for over-representation in the resource area. In other sectors, particularly finance and manufacturing, westerners are very underrepresented. The center (Ontario and Quebec), on the other hand, is overrepresented in terms of the 1921 population base in all sectors except utilities; in its proportion of the elite, it is also underrepresented in resources. It is highly overrepresented in trade, manufacturing, and finance.

As the data on economic sectors would suggest, westerners are much more likely to be U.S. comprador elites (that is, primarily working for U.S.-controlled companies) than those born anywhere else in Canada. Indeed, their numbers compare well with those of foreign-born Canadian residents: in both groups one quarter are U.S. compradors. On the other hand, eastern-born are most likely to be U.K. compradors, and again their numbers are almost identical to the proportion of foreign-born. These findings reflect the historical associations these regions have had outside Canada — the west with the United States and the east with the United Kingdom. The center, however, is almost 80% indigenous and the east is more indigenous than the west. Thus it can be concluded that central Canada's strength is in the economic activities of trade, manufacturing, and finance; that those from central Canada are more likely to become members of the economic elite, although upper-class origin is a great advantage in this respect; and that the center of indigenous Canadian capitalism is in the Toronto-Montreal axis, where the national upper class also resides and maintains most of its upper-class institutions — the private schools and private clubs.

Interprovincial Regionalism: The International Context

Canada is a particularly fragmented nation. It is a federation of ten provinces and two territories, each of which has increased its demands and power vis-à-vis the central government since the dismantling of the Ottawa war machinery created for the Second World War. But do these political boundaries really explain regionalism in Canada? Are the real regional splits not based more on economics than politics? Is it not the case that northern Ontario, or for that matter all Ontario outside the "golden horseshoe," is just as exploited by outsiders as the Atlantic region or the Prairies? While political fragmentation aggravates regionalism, it is not itself the cause of regionalism. That cause must be found in the uneven economic development of the country and the branch-plant structure of corporate capitalism.

What is meant by "regionalism" in terms of the discussion thus far? Essentially, it means uneven economic development — an unequal sharing of the wealth and and benefits a nation has to offer, expressed in geographical terms. But this definition is not fully adequate. There is also a relationship involved — a region is a region of something else and herein lies the key to the *unevenness* of economic development. It is only uneven when more surplus is extracted than is put in — otherwise it is *undeveloped*, and not *under*developed. A region can only be underdeveloped if it is tied to an external economy that is responsible for the underdevelopment. And only when all those on site who participate in the development share equally in the surplus produced can it be truly developed. If more of the surplus is shipped out than is retained, underdevelopment is occurring. This principle applies equally to class relations or to regionalism, the latter frequently passing for the former.

Upon examination, problems of class and regionalism appear to be closely intertwined. At the most basic level, this is because both are rooted in extractive relationships and both, in Canada, are perpetuated through the institution of private property. This is not to say that there are no extractive relationships in societies which are not capitalist or that they too do not have a type of regionalism, but they have these problems for different reasons and under different circumstances.

Canada is not unequivocally an industrial society. *Part* is industrialized — but the rest is more aptly characterized as a resource hinterland. Most of Canada's industrial capacity is located below a line starting at Windsor, encompassing Toronto, and moving on to Montreal. This is industrial Canada; all other areas base their economies on key resources: in British Columbia on wood, pulp and paper, with some hydro; in the Prairies, on gas, petroleum, potash, and wheat; in northern Ontario and Quebec, on mining, and pulp and paper, plus, again, hydro; in the Atlantic region, on pulp and paper, fish, and some coal, plus hydro in Newfoundland. These outliers feed the "golden horseshoe" and U.S. markets with their resources and, in turn, consume the finished products from there. The different economies in the different parts of the country produce different types of class structures in these regions. At the same time, regional economies are tied to national economies and national ones to international ones. Thus, regional class structures and, contingent upon these, varieties of lifestyle and opportunity, are to some extent dependent upon the way they "fit" into the national and international economic order. Those regions which have surplus extracted from them will have less access to goods, services, and opportunities— including such basics as health care and education — while those in the surplus-extracting areas will have a greater advantage. The overdevelopment of one region depends on the underdevelopment of another; the overdevelopment of the dominant class depends on the underdevelopment of subordinate ones.

Concretely, how does underdevelopment manifest itself in the economies of the various regions? One significant key to its effect on different economies is a study of the tax bases these economies provide to the

Table 3

Distribution of Non-Financial Industrial Taxable Income by Region and Control, 1972 (Percentages)

Control of Companies	Atlantic	Quebec	Ontario	Prairies	B.C.	
U.S.	3.2	18.1	53.5	17.6	7.3	100
Canada	5.2	26.0	41.8	13.4	13.0	100
All	4.5	22.5	45.7	15.9	11.0	100
Population	9.5	28.0	35.7	16.4	10.1	100

Source: Calculated from *CALURA Report for 1972,* Statistics Canada, Ottawa, 1975; *Canada Year Book,* Statistics Canada, Ottawa, 1973.

different provincial governments. This is important because taxes are a major source of the revenues necessary to pay for various social services. It can readily be demonstrated that differing levels of industrial development have a bearing on the resources available to provincial governments.

While Ontario has 36% of the population of Canada, in 1972 it received 46% of the provincial corporate taxes from non-financial companies, 51% of the taxes paid by foreign-controlled companies, and 54% of the U.S.-controlled non-financials. This is especially notable in the manufacturing sector where 72% of Ontario's taxes are from foreign-controlled companies.[20]

Table 3 illustrates two aspects of regionalism. First is the overrepresentation of taxes Ontario receives from industrial corporations compared to the other areas of Canada. Second is the compounded affect of U.S. direct investments on this overrepresentation by Ontario. Consistently for all regions, the distribution of taxable income by Canadian-controlled industrials is much more in line with the population distribution than is the distribution from U.S.-controlled companies. In other words, if it were not for U.S. industrials, the problem of regionalism would not be as serious as it now is for the Atlantic provinces, Quebec, and British Columbia. However, in the Prairies the situation is somewhat different because of oil revenues (a non-renewable resource). This is evident in Table 4 which examines only manufacturing.

Here every area besides Ontario is underdeveloped compared to its population base. However, for only Canadian-controlled manufacturing, Quebec and British Columbia are actually above their proportions of the population. In mining, which provided $279.7 million in taxable income to the provinces in 1972 compared to $3,344.5 million from manufacturing, Alberta alone received one-half of this income ($138.6 million) of which 88% was from foreign-controlled companies. All the other provinces were well below their proportion of the population with Ontario's 22% closest to its 36% of the population. Thus, it can be argued that foreign investment in manufacturing, because it has been so Ontario-centered, and in petroleum, because it has been so Alberta-centered, have added to the problems of regionalism in Canada.

A recent government publication, *Domestic and foreign control of*

Table 4

Distribution of Taxable Income by Region and Control from Manufacturing, 1972 (Percentages)

Control of Companies	Atlantic	Quebec	Ontario	Prairies	B.C.	
U.S.	2.7	18.9	62.2	9.6	6.7	100
Canada	3.6	28.8	43.2	9.8	14.4	100
All	3.1	23.3	53.7	10.2	9.6	100
Population	9.5	28.0	35.7	16.4	10.1	100

Source: See Table 3

Table 5

Regionalism and Percentage of Occupied Dwellings without Amenities, 1971 (Percentages)

	Canada	Atlantic	Quebec	Ontario	Prairies	B.C.
Piped running water	2.7	9.6	0.3	1.1	8.0	1.3
Exclusive use of bath or shower	7.4	27.1	5.8	3.6	12.3	3.3
Exclusive use of flush toilets	4.6	17.5	0.6	2.4	12.0	2.2

Source: Statistics Canada, *Perspective Canada*, Ottawa, 1974, p. 215.

manufacturing establishments in Canada, 1969 and 1970, allows further analysis of the effects of foreign investment on regionalism in Canada by providing additional indicators and refinements. All these indicators show that all provinces except Ontario have lower levels of foreign control in manufacturing than the national average. The extent of foreign control in manufacturing in Ontario is 55% of total employees (compared to the national average of 44%), 58% of salaries and wages (compared to 49%), 59% of value added by manufacturing activity (compared to 51%), and 62% of the value of shipments of goods (compared to 52%).[21] It is clear, then, that Ontario is the center of foreign penetration into Canadian manufacturing. This same publication provides, for the first time, a detailed breakdown of foreign control by intraprovincial divisions in the manufacturing sector. In every geographical division cited, all areas outside Ontario have "no relative shortage or concentration" of Canadian-controlled manufacturing, but again, outside Ontario, there is a relative shortage of U.S.-controlled manufacturing. Within Ontario, all of the Census Metropolitan Areas (CMA) have an over-concentration of U.S.-controlled manufacturing, with the single exception of Hamilton, which is still higher than any other CMA outside Ontario. This government study concludes that, "the predominance of foreign-controlled manufacturing in Ontario, and to a lesser degree in Quebec, parallels the concentration of industrial activity in what is often termed the 'manufacturing belt' stretching from

Windsor to Quebec City....both U.S. and other foreign-controlled manufacturing are more geographically concentrated than Canadian- controlled activity."[22]

How are the inequalities of regionalism expressed in terms of the life-style of Canadians? Table 5 provides some selected indicators which illustrate regional differences in basic amenities.

Even at the most basic level of services, there is wide regional variation when 27% of occupied dwellings from the Atlantic provinces and 12% from the Prairies do not have exclusive use of baths or showers, or when 18% and 12%, respectively, do not have exclusive use of flush toilets.

Predictably, regional variations also occur in income distribution. Incomes in the Atlantic provinces are only 76.5% of the national average, while those from Ontario are 110.8% of the average.[23] In terms of the proportion of low-income families in different provinces (allowing for family size), the differences are even more acute. For example, 34% of the families in Newfoundland and P.E.I. are low-income families, as are 28% in Saskatchewan, 24% in New Brunswick, and 23% in Nova Scotia, but only 11% in Ontario. Not only has Canada not done well in sharing its wealth, it has also been bad at sharing its poverty.[24]

How has the federal government attempted to alleviate these regional inequalities? Certainly not through its own spending programs. As James Richardson pointed out in the House of Commons on June 12, 1972:

> If we examine the figures for federal Government purchasing which has actually taken place over the past six years, we find that under 6% of all purchases have been made in the four Atlantic provinces (10% population). We find that over 40% of these purchases have been made in Quebec (28%), some 44% in Ontario (36%) and under 10% in the region of Canada west (27%).[25]

But then there's DREE (the Department of Regional Economic Expansion). DREE offers examples of how, when the state uses existing corporations to carry out its response to regionalism, it invariably ends up providing subsidies to these corporations rather than resolving the problems of regionalism. DREE's own record can speak for itself:

> Aerovox Canada Ltd. got an industrial incentives grant of $253,950 from the federal government to start a new factory in Amherst, N.S., so it closed its Hamilton, Ont. plant. In Hamilton, 68 jobs were lost; in Amherst, 90 new ones will be created. The company paid an average of $3.23 an hour in Hamilton; it will pay $2 in Nova Scotia.
>
> Celanese Canada Ltd. got four federal grants, totalling $278,628, for modernization and expansion in Drummondville, Montmagny and Coaticook, Que., so it shut down its Montmagny plant and laid off 450 workers. Then Ottawa handed $2,477,600 to two other companies to create 412 new jobs in the old Celanese plant.
>
> Bruck Mills Ltd. got a grant of $843,105 to create 140 jobs in Sherbrook and Cowansville, Que., so it laid off 95 workers in Sherbrook — a net gain of 45 jobs.
>
> Rayonier Quebec Inc., a subsidiary of International Telegram and Telephone of New York, got $13.8 million from Ottawa to create 459 jobs in the pulp industry in Quebec, while Canadian International Paper was laying off 550 workers also in the pulp industry in Quebec.[26]

With such a "rational" system of economic planning in Ottawa and with such great "control" over corporations, it is little wonder that regionalism persists and programs like DREE turn out to be corporate handouts rather than a serious solution to regional inequalities.

As a result of the Regional Development Incentives Act, the federal government has spent $505 million between 1969 and 1975. The bulk of this "incentive" money has gone to private corporations in Quebec (43%) accounting for most (46%) of the value of the capital projects involved. The Atlantic provinces have received 25% of the grants but account for only 19% of the capital projects. Very few of the grants have gone to British Columbia (1%), or Saskatchewan (3%). However, Alberta has received 7% of the grants and 8% of the capital value of the projects, and Manitoba 9% of each. What is most surprising is that Ontario, the center of industry, received 12% of the grants and 15% of the value of capital projects under the program.[27] This allocation of public money to private corporations with the hope of alleviating regional disparities can be a "hit-or-miss" strategy at best since the government does not control these corporations. As the above examples illustrate, the state exerts no influence over the more far-reaching effects of these corporations' national (not to mention multinational) operations — which may involve using public money to update equipment in one plant, or closing down others, or relocating at the public expense in search of cheaper sources of labor. Moreover, in the course of the program, 55% of the grants and 61% of the value of capital projects involved have gone to Quebec and Ontario, the two most industrialized provinces. It is obvious which regions are expanding economically under the watchful eye of the federal government.

Intraprovincial Regionalism: The Single Industry Town

Unless this type of analysis is placed in the context of the regional power-structure framework mentioned previously, it cannot reveal how the structure actually operates within a particular region. How this structure creates the regional disparities within central Canada itself, and the implications of this phenomenon for these underdeveloped regions can be shown by using the data provided in Rex Lucas's *Minetown, Milltown, Railtown.*

By combining the earlier analysis of power at the national level with that provided by Lucas for the local level, and linking them in the manner suggested earlier in the regional power-structure framework, it can be shown that many regional disparities are the outcome of absentee or branch-plant operations of national and multinational corporations.

Lucas's study focuses on "communities of single industry with a population of less than 30,000 in which at least 75% of the working population serves the single industry and its supporting institutional services. ... The communities answering this description are mainly built around resource-based industries and transportation — mining towns, smelting towns, textile towns, pulp and paper towns, sawmill towns and railway towns."[28] Altogether, these include some 636 communities and about one million Canadians.

The inhabitants of these communities, writes Lucas, "know that their situation is bounded by bureaucracy and a precise division of labor which in turn depends on a complex national and international division of labor. They know that their future depends upon impersonal forces outside their community such as head office decisions, governmental policies, and international trading agreements."[29]

Lucas provides a detailed discussion of the total control and paternalism exhibited by the companies which dominate these towns. One example from an interview with an executive of one of these companies illustrates this:

> There doesn't seem to be much double working although husband and wife, when they do work, run into difficulties and we have to cut it out. During the early days, we had a husband and wife both working and the children were running wild in the streets and we had the police moving in — so we had to lay down new rules by which married women were not permitted to work.[30]

Examples of the total control exercised by the companies in these towns could be multiplied a thousandfold but the point of this discussion is to show the processes and consequences of regionalism as they affect larger social developments.

One such development is the relationship between class and ethnicity as suggested nationally in John Porter's *The Vertical Mosaic*. In Railtown, Lucas finds that, "the British have retained all of the top administrative jobs and desirable status-bearing occupations of the railroad. The French and Indians have continued to work in the lower levels of the job hierarchy."[31] He describes how nepotism and insider information are used to maintain ethnic selectivity. "After 60 years of hiring by this process, the British represent 100% of the managerial group, 91% of the train crews, but only 15% of the laborers."[32]

But the class structure within Railtown or any of the other company towns cannot be explained by indigenous forces alone since "Railtown, by definition, has not been in existence long enough to produce resident leading families of great wealth and lineage."[33] The external linkages, like those discussed earlier in the regional power-structure model, are presented most clearly in an interview with one of the residents:

> Everyone knows what everyone else's work is like, what they do and where they fit. . . . the top echelons are scientists and engineers and they really don't push locally to try to achieve high prestige and high status. This is because they don't have to be recognized on the local level or in the local community. Their level of recognition is on a national and international level through their work.[34]

In other words, this resident is aware that the upper levels within the community are more integrated with the international and national power structure than with the local community. Aside from its potential for creating alienation, a subject discussed in detail by Lucas, another important implication of this type of structure is reflected in patterns of mobility into decision-making positions.

As Lucas points out, "the major barrier to upward mobility arises because the upper levels of the hierarchy operate according to a different principle and within a different flow of personnel. The upper echelons are part of an international, national, or company-wide system, rather than a local or community-bound system."[35] As a result, the local population is "trapped" within a low mobility system in which the top positions are filled from outside the community by those from the parent corporation. There is little opportunity for locals to tap into this horizontal mobility system, with the result that they are unlikely to experience vertical mobility. One of the respondents summarized the situation when he said: "The work force on the semi-skilled and unskilled level is drawn almost entirely from the local population. In other words, the local population was used for the main, basic, large proportion of workers; but the necessary specialists are imported."[36]

With such patterns of recruitment, it is clear why the effect of regionalism shows up in the national economic elite. The structures are designed in such a way that they "lock" people into the regional hinterlands. Organizational avenues to top decision-making positions are non-existent. In their place is a system of "transient managers."

Absentee ownership may be defined in terms of the distance from a particular center. The boundaries under consideration must be specified; for example, at the national level foreign ownership is absentee and economic boundaries are not coincident with the nation state. On the community or regional level, absentee ownership refers to branches of firms which are not locally owned but part of larger corporations, themselves either Canadian- or foreign-controlled. The consequences of foreign ownership at the national level and the local level are similar, and include lack of freedom from outside control and decision-making, withdrawal of capital and resources, and a higher degree of uncertainty about the continuation of the branch plant (at each level), since by definition it is peripheral to the overall operation.

In some respects, it does make a difference whether the absentee owners are Canadian or foreign. For example, profits retained within Canada *could* be used to expand industrial activity, thus creating greater surplus and more jobs. Many of the secondary and tertiary spin-offs such as technology development *could* be supported and encouraged within Canada. Also, firms based in Canada might be made subject to greater regulation by the Canadian state.

In other respects, it makes little difference whether the branch plant is Canadian or foreign controlled, particularly at the regional or local level. In either case the major access points to occupational mobility, the major accumulation of surplus, and the sources of decision-making occur outside the area. The community or region within which the branch plant is located is equally vulnerable to decisions taken at head office, be it in Toronto or New York.

Again, this is reflected in the attitudes at the community level in Lucas's study when he says: "In spite of the public declarations about the taking over of Canadian industry by interests in the U.S.A., and the fact that many mining, pulp and paper, and manufacturing industries found in communities of single industries are known to be owned and controlled by shareholders in [the] U.S.A., no evidence was found to support U.S.A. 'they' group feelings. There were no spontaneous references to U.S. ownership in any of the 500 interviews." He quotes one of the residents after direct questioning as saying: "It doesn't really matter who they say owns it."[37]

In summary, regional inequalities in Canada must be placed within several contexts: the international context vis-à-vis the United States, the interprovincial context vis-à-vis the western and eastern hinterlands, and the intraprovincial context such as the Ontario hinterlands outside the "golden triangle". Several frameworks based on regional power-structure analysis have been offered which attempt to establish the links between these regions and the elites who control them. On the international horizon, the multinational corporation is the organization which creates internationalized sectors of the economy; on the regional level, this is accomplished either by national corporations with branches in the regions or by the sub-branches of foreign-controlled branch plants. On the regional level, the equivalent to the international sector is composed of that part of the local structure more attached to the center of the company, that is, its headquarters, than to the company town itself. This is reflected in patterns of mobility and the phenomenon of "transient managers" on the regional level. At several stages in the chain of relationships there are "go-betweens" mediating between the local plant, the branch-plant headquarters, and the multinational or national headquarters. In terms of the overall corporate hierarchy, the local plants in the company towns in Ontario and the rest of Canada described by Lucas are below the headquarters, but some parts of these plants — the management — are integrated with the officials of the headquarters; hence, the phenomenon of vertical mobility and lack of horizontal mobility.

The capitalist class within the "golden horseshoe" and its extension in the economic sphere, the corporate elite, are central to the structure of economic power in Canada. But within the center, only the major urban centers house the dominant class; the rest of the province and the rest of the class structure are as peripheral as the rest of Canada. Moreover, it has been demonstrated that it is not sufficient to look only at internal forces to understand the structure of regional inequality in Canada. It is also necessary to look beyond the political boundaries to the larger economic system of which Canada is a part. From this perspective, it is evident that the effect of foreign, particularly U.S., direct investment is to aggravate the problem of regionalism by concentrating most of Canada's manufacturing capacity within Ontario. Thus the problem of regional inequalities becomes bound up with other problems such as foreign ownership and class inequalities. Decisions of men created these problems; we must now seek to understand them and act to reshape the institutions in which these inequalities are rooted.

NOTES

1. André Gunder Frank, *Latin America: Development or Revolution* (New York, 1969), pp. 4, 6, 9.

2. Johan Galtung, "Structural Theory of Imperialism," *Journal of Peace Research*, 2 (1971), p. 83.

3. The terms "periphery" and "center" as images of international economic relations have been used since at least 1949 by Paul Prebish in his *The Economic Development of Latin America and its Principal Problems* (New York, 1950), p. 1 (originally published in Spanish, 1949).

4. Galtung, "Structural Theory of Imperialism," p. 84.

5. *Ibid.*, p. 96.

6. *Ibid.*, p. 104.

7. For an important overview of the types of analysis which have been performed in Third World countries, see Girvan's "The Development of Dependency Economics in the Caribbean and Latin America: Review and Comparison," *Social and Economic Studies*, 22, 1 (1973), pp. 1-33.

8. Osvaldo Sunkel, "Transnational Capitalism and National Disintegration in Latin America," *Social and Economic Studies*, 22, 1 (1973), pp. 132-76.

9. *Ibid.*, p. 135.

10. *Ibid.*, pp. 135-36.

11. *Ibid.*, p. 139.

12. *Ibid.*, p. 146.

13. Mel Watkins, "The Branch Plant Condition," in A. K. Davis (ed.), *Canadian Confrontations: Hinterland versus Metropolis* (Banff, Alberta, December 1969), p. 35.

14. *Ibid.*, pp. 37-40.

15. Arthur K. Davis, "Canadian Society and History as Hinterland *versus* Metropolis," in R.J. Ossenberg (ed.), *Canadian Society: Pluralism, Change and Conflict* (Toronto, 1971).

16. *Ibid.*, p. 12.

17. Philip Mathias, *Forced Growth: Five Studies of Government Involvement in the Development of Canada* (Toronto, 1971).

18. Watkins, "The Branch Plant Condition," p. 40.

19. Herbert Marshall, Frank Southard, Jr., and Kenneth W. Taylor, *Canadian-American Industry* (New York, 1936; Toronto, 1976), pp. 221-22.

20. Calculated from CALURA *Report for 1972* (Ottawa, 1975), pp. 21-22, Statements 4 and 5.

21. *Domestic and Foreign Control of Manufacturing Establishments in Canada, 1969 and 1970* (Ottawa, 1976), p. 27, Table XIV.

22. *Ibid.*, pp. 18-20, Table VIII.

23. Calculated from *Perspective Canada* (Ottawa, 1974), p. 153.

24. *Ibid.*, p. 161.

25. *The Globe and Mail*, June 17, 1972, p. 7.

26. Walter Stewart, *Toronto Star*, August 12, 1972, p. 1.

27. "DREE tells where it put the money," *The Financial Post*, February 28, 1976, p. 33.

28. Rex Lucas, *Minetown, Milltown, Railtown* (Toronto, 1971), p. 17.

29. *Ibid.*, p. 20.

30. *Ibid.*, p. 52.

31. *Ibid.*, p. 135.

32. *Ibid.*, p. 136.

33. *Ibid.*, p. 151.

34. *Ibid.*, p. 152.

35. *Ibid.*, p. 153.

36. *Ibid.*, p. 155.

37. *Ibid.*, p. 145.

A Segmentation Approach to Poverty and Low-Wage Work in the Maritimes*

DONALD H. CLAIRMONT / MARTHA MACDONALD /
FRED C. WIEN

Introduction

As many reports have indicated, Canada, like other Western industrial countries, exhibits considerable inequality in earnings and household income, high unemployment, a narrow conception of what constitutes work, and large numbers of working poor. In the Maritimes, the locale for our research on inequality and low-wage work, these patterns are of even greater significance. Here a very large proportion (some 52% in 1973) of the families falling under the poverty line have the head of the family, not to mention other members, working during the course of a year; here, too, the scarcity of good jobs is reflected in high levels of unemployment and, as in the United States, in the significant movement over time between programs such as UIC, Manpower training or welfare and low-wage work. Thus a sizable portion of the poor are persons either currently working for low remuneration or likely to do so. In this light, a casualty model of poverty which restricts the issue to the infirm, the uneducated, the old or the single parent can be seen to be extremely limited.

The indirect effects of inequality and low-wage work in determining the general level of poverty in Canada are also considerable. Low-wage work imposes constraints on the development of social welfare measures, restricting the levels of social assistance (as in New Brunswick, where support levels are pegged in relation to the minimum wage) and preventing the implementation of reforms because of their presumed threat to low-wage work (e.g., a guaranteed annual income). Social service case workers in Nova Scotia indicate that income supplementation programs are often shrouded in secrecy lest the army of potential claimants ever come forward.

*This paper emerges from the research being conducted through the Marginal Work World Research Program, based at the Institute of Public Affairs, Dalhousie University. The research program, which is of five years duration (1975-1980), is funded in large part by a program grant from the Canada Council and also by contributions from Health and Welfare Canada and Dalhousie University. The original outline of the research is contained in Clairmont and Wien (1974), and a current list of research reports and papers is available upon request.

Table 1

Industries Grouped by Wage Sector and Ranked by %
Low-Wage, Showing Number of Part-Time, Full-Time, and
Total Workers — Atlantic Provinces, 1971*

Industry Low-Wage Sector	% Low-Wage	Part-Time	Full-Time	Total
Knitting mills	93.2	80	1,330	1,410
Leather industries	92.3	55	330	385
Personal services	91.4	6,375	13,315	19,690
Farms	87.8	6,320	15,400	21,720
Accommodation & food services	86.3	8,475	20,845	29,320
Religious organizations	86.2	1,110	3,885	4,995
Clothing industries	86.0	90	705	795
Textile industries	85.3	210	1,755	1,965
Furniture and fixture mfg.	83.4	105	890	995
Fishing	83.1	4,945	14,525	19,470
Wood industries	82.2	1,475	7,790	9,265
Health and welfare services	80.0	8,140	40,405	48,545
Logging	78.7	3,185	10,460	13,645
Retail trade	78.6	24,475	65,005	89,480
Food and beverage mfg.	77.4	9,465	36,365	45,830
Unspecified industries	74.5	15,915	46,350	62,265
Amusement and recreation services	73.9	2,090	3,075	5,165
Storage	70.1	160	485	645
Finance industries	69.7	1,090	10,650	11,740
Misc. services	69.1	2,405	6,545	8,950
Misc. manufacturing	68.0	185	1,555	1,740
Electrical product mfg.	66.7	240	3,010	3,250
Wholesale trade	64.1	3,440	26,375	29,815
Rubber and plastic prod. mfg.	64.0	115	805	920
Tobacco products mfg.	61.5	15	125	140
Non-metal mineral prod.	60.8	265	2,485	2,750
Forestry services	60.7	265	870	1,135
Totals: Low-wage industries		100,690	335,335	436,025
General contractors	59.1	5,390	31,170	36,560
Printing and publishing	59.0	1,045	3,530	4,575
Quarries and sand pits	58.5	75	300	375
Metal fabrication (except machinery)	58.4	335	4,180	4,515
Insurance and real estate	58.0	715	4,245	4,960
Services to agriculture	58.0	165	385	550
Special trade contractors	57.8	5,225	19,500	24,725
Provincial administration	57.0	2,120	15,260	17,380
Local administration	56.4	1,115	7,535	8,650
Services to business management	56.4	1,690	9,315	11,005

Industry High-Wage Sector	% Low-Wage	Part-Time	Full-Time	Total
Education and related services	56.2	10,840	42,855	53,695
Non-metal mines (except coal)	54.5	210	2,285	2,495
Transportation equipment industries	54.2	495	7,590	8,085
Insurance carriers	53.6	285	3,260	3,545
Mineral fuel mines	52.9	130	5,250	5,380
Transportation	52.7	6,975	39,420	46,395
Machinery mfg. (except electricity)	51.2	70	1,245	1,315
Communications	45.4	2,555	14,290	16,845
Primary metal milling	43.4	245	4,805	5,050
Chemical production mfg.	42.1	400	2,670	3,070
Electrical power, gas and water	38.3	555	8,070	8,625
Services to mining	36.2	75	745	820
Federal administration	31.4	4,260	50,475	54,735
Service to fisheries	31.1	80	505	585
Other government offices	30.7	45	1,120	1,165
Metal mines	28.5	195	6,180	6,375
Paper industries	28.2	1,535	13,550	15,085
Petroleum and coal producers	22.8	70	1,200	1,270
Totals: High-Wage Industries		46,895	300,935	347,830
TOTAL ALL INDUSTRIES		145,585	636,270	783,855

Source: Compiled by Ron Smith (1977) from a Statistics Canada special tabulation of the 1971 census. The percentage of full-time workers earning less than $120 per week ($3 per hour) was calculated by industry. Industries were considered low-wage if this percentage was at least 60%, and high-wage if this percentage was less than 60%.

Directly and indirectly, then, inequality and low wages in the work world are integral to the poverty found in advanced capitalist societies, especially Canada. There is little reason to think that these factors are going to diminish in their significance in the near future. Some studies have shown that earnings inequality has in fact increased over the past two decades (Johnson, 1974; Adams, 1970).

Certainly low-wage work continues to be an important characteristic of the Maritimes. For example, if we define low-wage industries as those which, in 1970, had more than 60% of their full-time workers earning less than $120 per week, over 50% of the Atlantic provinces' labor force could be placed in the low-wage sector (Table 1). Over the 20-year period 1957-1976, the wage gap between low- and high-wage industries grew in both absolute and percentage terms (Smith, 1977). It also appears to be characteristic of industries in the low-wage sector to have had lower rates of increase in nonmonetary compensations in recent years (Wood, 1977). Despite large employment losses in low-wage sectors such as farming, logging, and fishing on the one hand and significant public sector expansion on the high-wage side, the overall employment increase in the low-wage sector was two-thirds that of the high-wage sector. In short, low-wage industries take in a large proportion of the labor force, are growing in absolute terms, and the compensation gap at the very least has not narrowed.

In examining poverty and inequality in the Maritimes, we have found it useful to characterize contemporary North American capitalism in terms of a segmentation model which posits the existence of two broad segments, labeled the marginal and central work worlds (MWW and CWW). In the following section, we will elaborate on the segmentation approach we are using in our current research and contrast it with more orthodox explanations of poverty and low-wage work. Following a theoretical discussion of the origins of segmentation within a region such as the Maritimes, we go on to present some preliminary findings emerging from the research program. These sections are organized around three questions: how segmentation is perpetuated or maintained; how fundamental the segmentation dynamic is in relation to possible change strategies; and what the value of such a framework can be in understanding poverty, inequality and low-wage work in the region. In order to keep the paper to a manageable length, we have chosen to focus each section on a particular illustration of the issue, rather than to cover a broad range of possibilities. Thus, the section on the maintenance of segmentation examines the persistence of the segments despite changing ownership patterns. In discussing change strategies, we focus particularly on organizational attempts among workers in the marginal sector, and we raise the question of the value of a segmentation framework by considering differences in low-wage work in central and marginal segments.

Low Income Work from a Segmentation Perspective

To understand what characterizes a segmentation perspective it is useful to begin with a summary of the competing orthodox economic and socio-logical view of the labor market and wage/income determination. The orthodox model is based essentially on neoclassical economic price theory. In its assumptions and central ideas, the model shares many similarities to structure-functionalism in sociology (Whyte, 1971).[1] In oversimplified terms, a central tenet of the orthodox position is that in the short run, under conditions of perfect competition and equilibrium in the supply and demand for labor, workers' wages equal their marginal revenue products and one wage rate prevails for homogeneous units of labor.

Productivity is in turn linked to the worker's individual qualities such as the level of general education, training, previous work experience and natural ability. In the human capital elaboration of the orthodox model, it is argued that individuals invest in improving their stock of human capital (skills), expecting an adequate return on their investment in the form of higher wages. Employers, for their part, facing a labor supply with a higher reservation or asking wage, will employ an individual at the higher wage so long as the wage demanded is not more than the individual's marginal revenue product. Supply and demand considerations affect the investment choice — individuals will avoid situations where an oversupply of labor to a particular occupation, industry or region has reduced the wage below the cost of the human capital investment, and they will gravitate toward occupations with higher returns.

In the orthodox model, then, wage rates are seen to respond to (and signal) the movement of factors of production, and it is argued that there is a long-run tendency toward equalization of returns. It is suggested that workers have considerable influence and choice over the nature of their employment. Thus, worker sovereignty prevails and present employment situations can be seen as freely chosen (Gordon, 1972). There is little emphasis in the model on how the job structures among which individuals allegedly choose were developed in the first place, and how they affect and limit the range of individual choice.

If equalization in wages has not occurred over the long term, as is demonstrably the case even for workers at comparable levels of education and skills (Bluestone, 1974; Wachtel and Betsey, 1972), some orthodox theorists would argue that the conception of human capital needs to be broadened to include elements which, unfortunately, are more difficult to measure (e.g., the quality of education, the effect of preschool differences in ability, etc.). Alternatively, others would argue that exogenous changes in technology and consumer tastes keep the labor market in a continual state of disequilibrium, though the wage signals still operate to alter the supply and demand for labor in an equilibrating direction.

By way of contrast, a segmentation perspective finds the division of the economy into two or more sectors with unequal returns to be a fundamental feature, which is continuously being reinforced and regenerated, although its characteristics may change over time. The intellectual roots of contemporary segmentation approaches are diverse; for American economists, of significance were the institutionalist school of the 1950s in labor economics (e.g., Kerr, 1954; Dunlop, 1957), the dualistic economic development literature applied to the Third World (e.g., Boeke, 1953; Lewis, 1954) and applied research conducted on race relations (e.g., Myrdal, 1944). The dual labor market model advanced in the late 1960s and early 1970s had, as its immediate reference point, research conducted on ghetto labor markets in several major urban areas (e.g., Bluestone, 1970; Baron and Hymer, 1968; Vietorisz and Harrison, 1970). These studies posited the dichotomization of the labor market into primary and secondary segments on the basis of certain job characteristics:

> ...the primary market offers jobs which possess several of the following traits: high wages, good working conditions, employment stability and job security, equity and due process in the administration of work rules, and chances of advancement. The...secondary market has jobs which, relative to those in the primary sector, are decidedly less attractive. They tend to involve low wages, poor working conditions, considerable variability in employment, harsh and often arbitrary discipline, and little opportunity to advance. The poor are confined to the secondary labor market (Doeringer and Piore, 1971).[2]

At the same time, a somewhat different dualistic perspective was emerging in eastern Canada. Brox (1972), drawing on theoretical literature in economic anthropology (Bohanan and Dalton, 1965; Barth, 1967) examined the Newfoundland fishing industry from a segmentation perspective, in terms similar to that used in the Third World economic development literature:

> The most striking feature of Newfoundland's economy is the dualistic nature of its development. On the one hand, there are modern, sophisticated, technologically up-to-date industries. On the other, economic practices and techniques exist that appear to be almost medieval, such as inshore fishing and especially the processing of salt fish, where no innovation whatsoever seems to have taken place, either in tools or work methods. . . . Most noteworthy is the fact that the traditional fishing population is not mobilized for the trawler fleets — the latest innovation in Newfoundland fishing technology. Traditional inshore fishing continues along-side commercial, large-scale trawler fishing in striking contrast to Scandinavia and especially Iceland, where modernization seems to take place simultaneously in all sectors and regions (Brox, 1972).

In our own case, we have drawn on both of these streams in developing a dualistic perspective in which the two segments are labeled the central and marginal work worlds. The latter is defined in terms of work settings (establishments) and occupations (in the case of self-employed individuals) which provide, for a majority of their work force or membership, employment packages characterized by low wages, limited fringe benefits, little job security and restricted internal advancement opportunities, among other characteristics.[3] Under this definition, if an establishment (or self-employed occupational group) meets the above criteria, then all persons belonging to the establishment or occupation, whether low wage or not, are considered to be part of the marginal work world, part of a social reality in which the actors have a shared external environment and, at least on some dimensions, some common attitudinal and behavioral patterns. Generally, small labor-intensive firms and relatively unorganized self-employed groups, serving an unstable or restricted market, fall into the marginal work world category. Common examples in the Maritimes include motels, textile plants, sawmills, fast food outlets, day care centers, taxi drivers, and food processing establishments. Since the definition is based on the actual employment package available at the establishment level, work settings can fall into the marginal sector even though they may be linked, through ownership, to powerful firms in the core of the economy.

Central work world establishments, in contrast, offer (or are required to provide) high wages, extensive fringe benefits, internal career ladders, and job security provisions. They are characterized by the interfacing of powerful actors on both the employer and employee sides, and include the public sector as well as establishments in the large-scale highly capitalized private sector (e.g., coal mining, steel, petroleum refining, auto assembly or pulp and paper production). Well-organized self-employed occupational groups such as the professions and the highly-skilled craft guilds are also included in the central work world category, with the organization of the *occupation* providing the structure that is provided for other workers by their *establishment.*[4]

While the postulate of pervasive work world segmentation appears to be increasingly attractive to social scientists, not all segmentation approaches select the establishment or work setting as the key defining unit. Some researchers have focused upon the *industry-wide* level (Beck, 1978) while others have seen segmentation in terms of core and peripheral *firms* (Averitt, 1968).[5] Dual labor market theorists have defined segmentation in relation to *job* characteristics. The different operationalizations overlap a great deal in terms of the social reality to which they point but the overlap is by no means complete. Much research is necessary to understand the theoretical implications of the diversity. Compared with our emphasis on the establishment or work setting there are some advantages in the alternative operationalizations. The firm rather than the establishment is the decision-making unit (Simon, 1957); technological imperatives are best appreciated at the industry-wide level where, also, secondary data are more available; and low status jobs, wherever they are found, are highlighted in the dual labor market perspective. Nevertheless, we think our focus on establishments is heuristic since work settings are important units of social reality. Our approach suggests that it matters considerably where low status jobs are located (i.e., by type of establishment). Moreover, it enables us to appreciate the persistence of segmentation at the work setting level along with the increasing integration of the work world at the firm level.

There are a number of important themes in a segmentation view of low wage work. Among the most important is the emphasis on the existence of barriers that restrict individuals from making transitions between the segments. It is argued that barriers exist which restrict a significant number of persons to the marginal segment, for reasons unrelated to their preferences or productive capacities. This has at least two important implications. In the first place, it suggests that individuals in the marginal sector will circulate among jobs and work settings within the sector (e.g., from domestic work to waitressing; from inshore fishing to rural carpentry) more readily than across sectors, even within the same industry (e.g., from small sawmills to the pulp and paper industry).

A second implication is that there is a substantial number of persons confined to the marginal sector who are under-employed there, who have the education, skills and other qualities to perform well in the central sector, or who could easily adapt to employment there if given the opportunity to do so.[6] Segmentation theorists generally reject the orthodox contention that the labor market, as a result of a competitive bargaining process over wages, will serve to assure jobs for all who would like to work; they suggest that the labor market can only determine which individuals obtain the limited opportunities available (Eichner, 1977). Thurow (1975) maintains that the employer, who takes the initiative in determining the number and types of jobs available, is generally indifferent in the short run to the availability of labor at lower wages, particularly in the central sector, where measures have been taken to protect workers from job and wage competition pressures. Job vacancies, rather than wages, signal the reallocation of labor. The point at issue then becomes who, among the large number of qualified individuals, obtains access to the relatively scarce central work

Table 2

Stepwise Pairing of Marginal and Central Workers with a Comparison of Average Earnings at Each Pairing Step*

Step No.	Pairing Variable	No. of Pairs	Average Earnings		Difference	Sign** Test	Paired T-Test	DF
			Central	Marginal				
1.	No. of weeks worked	1,039	4,346.	3,473.	873.	.2225	7.986	1,038
2.	No. of hours per week	1,036	4,371.	3,470.	901.	.2366	8.312	1,035
3.	Sex	1,036	4,360.	3,468.	892.	.2320	8.226	1,035
4.	Occupation	939	4,506.	3,587.	919.	.2280	7.634	938
5.	Age	863	4,476.	3,693.	784.	.2401	6.421	862
6.	Education	593	4,739.	3,872.	867.	.2500	5.656	592

*Source: Compiled by Ron Smith (1977) from the Public Use Sample Tape of the 1971 census (1 in 100 sample for the Atlantic Provinces).

Method: The mean wage was calculated for each occupational/sex group (for full-time workers). Each person was identified as having a wage greater or less than the mean for their group. In each industry the number of persons with earnings less than the mean wage were counted, and industries where at least 60% of workers earned below their respective mean wages were classified as marginal. The remaining industries were classified as central. Then individuals were matched from each sector (MWW and CWW) on each pairing variable in a stepwise fashion, so that the distribution of individuals in each sector sample were identical in terms of the pairing variables. Finally, mean annual earnings were compared between groups at each step of the pairing.

The occupation and industry breakdowns are too aggregated to fully capture our "work setting" focus. Therefore, we have collected primary data on a matched pair sample of workers in CWW and MWW establishments in Moncton (Clairmont & Jackson, 1976). Preliminary results indicate confirmation of unequal returns to education and skill.

**Modification of the Gamma and sign test computed as:

$$\text{Coefficient} = \frac{\text{Concordant pairs} - \text{disconcordant pairs}}{\text{Concordant pairs} + \text{disconcordant pairs}}$$

world positions, with their attendant mobility and on-the-job training opportunities. Thus, there is a situation where substantial differences in employment rewards exist and persist over time, even among workers with similar attributes of skill, education or age (Table 2).

The restricted number of central work world jobs is, consequently, a most important barrier, especially in a region such as the Maritimes. Other barriers that serve to restrict access include unwarranted education requirements (credentialism), licensing and certification provisions, and union restrictions. Ascriptive characteristics such as age, sex, race or class may also serve as barriers to the mobility of certain groups through discrimination.

Another important theme is the relationship between segments; they clearly cannot be examined in isolation. Examples of both conflict and accommodation can readily be found in the region. Exclusionary practices, for example, have the effect of creating a crowding situation in the marginal sector which serves to restrain wages and attempts at organization; this is particularly evident in open-access occupations such as taxi-driving. Within particular industries such as forestry, there is conflict between small local sawmills which serve a specialized or restricted geographical market (e.g., for lobster traps, fish crates, or housing frames) on the one hand, and the large capital-intensive pulp and paper corporations, on the other, which place vast demands on the limited raw material resources of the region.

The marginal sector continues to persist, however, which suggests that it serves important functions for the larger social system with which it is integrated. A particularly interesting examination of the interrelationship of the two sectors is given by Berger (1973) who, in writing about Italy, argues that the "declining classes survive" and segmentation is maintained rather than eroded because the marginal sector provides an element of production flexibility for central firms (e.g., via subcontracting),[7] and political stability for the society as a whole by soaking up fluctuations in employment. She argues that in North America, unemployment insurance programs contribute to the same purpose.

Researchers operating from a segmentation perspective have, in fact, been careful to specify the interconnections among low-wage work on the one hand and other related systems such as the "training economy," the "welfare economy" and the "irregular or hustle economy" (Harrison, 1972). These are argued to have similar characteristics, such as low remuneration, short-term involvement, and limited potential for future advancement. The extensive and frequent mobility of individuals among these subsystems has also been documented (Ferman, 1967; Harrison, 1978; Butler and Buckley, 1978).

Finally, another distinctive feature of segmentation models is that employer and worker behavior and attitudes are said to differ across segments, and therefore that a uniform model cannot be applied; the rules of the game are different within each sector.[8] In contrast to the orthodox model where the causes of a good deal of worker and employer behavior and attitudes are relegated to exogenous factors, segmentation models tend to stress the effect of job structures and the work context on individual behavior and attitudes. Thus low motivation and low job stability on the part of workers in marginal establishments may well reflect a sensible adaptation to employment where stable, long-term, more highly trained employees earn little more than new recruits. The *opportunities* for stable employment and for on-the-job training may also be quite limited by the nature of the jobs available in the marginal sector. A similar argument can be made for the reluctance of entrepreneurs in the marginal sector to adopt new technologies.

Thus, rather than taking labor market structures as given and examining individual "choices" within this context, there is considerable interest among segmentation theorists in understanding the historical and theoretical roots for the development of particular labor market structures — the conditions under which segmented labor markets develop, and the role that factors such as class antagonisms, the nature of product markets, or the labor force requirements of particular firms play in the development of technology and job structures. The following section is devoted to these considerations.

The Origins of Work World Segmentation

Researchers who posit the existence of at least two segments of the work world, characterized by limited intersegment mobility, are not united in their theoretical explanations of the origins of this segmentation. We will group explanations into orthodox, Marxist and eclectic categories. We will also discuss the relevance of these arguments to the problem of low-wage work in the Maritimes.

Orthodox Explanations

We have mentioned that neoclassical labor economics, in its purist form, leaves no room for segmentation to develop. However, neoclassical economists have responded to the mounting evidence of segmentation by suggesting explanations from within the orthodox framework. They retain the neoclassical paradigm, with maximizing behavior, choice and traditional price theory as central elements in the analysis.

The modified approach points to market imperfections which prevent the economy from operating in its competitive (and therefore equalizing) way. Barriers to individual mobility create noncompeting segments of the work world, allowing wages and working conditions to diverge and locking some people into a marginal work world. These barriers include those mentioned in the previous section, as well as incomplete information about job and wage opportunities and sociological factors such as a "culture of poverty" and the geographic/life-style preferences of individuals. Imperfections such as these are seen as exogenous to the economic system and imply both voluntary and involuntary membership in the MWW.

In this approach, "worker sovereignty" retains some meaning, and the wage mechanism still serves to adjust supply and demand in each insulated market. For example, unions restrict access to some jobs, bidding wages up in those markets, and down in the remaining jobs into which non-unionized workers are "crowded." Excess labor supply to the marginal work world, for whatever reasons it occurs, is the main mechanism for keeping wages low in neoclassical explanations of segmentation. Presumably these imperfections could be overcome by policies to improve access to job information, encourage geographic mobility, and restrict discrimination. Such policies in the Maritimes try to get people moving *within* the region, and get them moving *out* of the region to the more developed central work world in Ontario and Alberta. However, the migration which has occurred does not seem to alter the MWW/CWW gap, and often leaves the individual's relative position unchanged (Economic Council, 1977; Smith, 1977; Clark, 1978). Worker immobilities are clearly only part of the cause of excess labor supply and segmentation.

There are other neoclassical explanations of the origins of segmentation, which focus on the demand for labor and operate along with the worker mobility barriers discussed above. In this view, oligopolistic firms arose due to product market imperfections and exogenous technological factors and developed different labor needs than the smaller firms operating in competitive markets. The argument is made that central oligopolistic firms have a need for stability in their work forces to recapture investment in on-the-job training or to ensure efficient use of large capital investments. Thus internal labor markets developed as an efficient way to minimize turnover costs in large capital-intensive organizations. Also, due to market power, central firms could afford to pay wage premiums for a prime labor force, even when elaborate job ladders were not dictated by technology. Petroleum refineries, steel plants and pulp and paper firms are commonly cited examples of this CWW development in the Maritimes.

Firms operating in the MWW, on the other hand, develop different "efficient" strategies in this view. They do not need stable work forces, for reasons such as seasonality (fish plants), uncontrolled fluctuations in demand (longshoring), low training costs (food processing), or low capital investment (personal services). Perhaps they also lack the market power to absorb any wage premiums. It is thus not rational for them to create internal labor markets or pay to hold good employees, though they may prefer a stable workforce if it is costless to them. Thus, motel operators complain of high turnover, though they are unwilling to "buy" lower turnover by paying more than the minimum wage.

The neoclassical model may also introduce government interventions as explanations of segmentation. An example is the role of welfare and unemployment insurance in preventing the equalizing movement of factors of production from taking place, thus creating surplus labor in certain segments. This argument is frequently put forward in the Maritimes to explain the continuing peripheral position of the region (lack of outmigration) as well as intraregional work world segmentation (Courchene, 1978).

The neoclassical adaptation to segmentation is a hodgepodge of mechanisms which could divert the economy from its tendency toward equalization of returns. These explanations do more to describe aspects of the operation of a segmented work world than to account in a systematic way for the original development of segmentation. Too much of the explanation lies in unexplained exogenous developments, such as technology, market "imperfections", and institutional factors of unionization and government intervention. We therefore draw on the Marxist literature for a more comprehensive causal explanation.

Marxist Explanations

In the Marxist paradigm, determining factors in the evolution and operation of capitalism include class conflict, the social relations of production, the creation of surplus value by labor and its appropriation by capital, the relentless momentum of capital accumulation, and the complicit role of the state in protecting the interests of capital. These elements are brought to the analysis of segmented work worlds. The Marxist method of investigation is historical; therefore much emphasis is put on the origins of segmentation. A definition of segmentation from Reich, Gordon and Edwards (1973:359) speaks of the "the historical process whereby political economic forces encourage the division of the labor market into separate sub-markets. . . distinguished by different labor market characteristics and behavioral rules."

The Marxist view of the historical development of labor market segmentation in North America can be summarized in simplified terms as follows.[9] In the 19th century, the spread of competitive capitalism gradually eroded production by independent producers and the petite bourgeoisie. More and more people became dependent on selling their labor power for wages, owning no means of production. In the factories, an increasing homogeneity of workers developed as machines replaced craft skills. The motive for this substitution of capital for labor was twofold — the need for reinvestment of accumulated surplus, and the need to consolidate control of production in the hands of capitalists, not labor. The breakdown of craftsmanship was essential to this control. An excess labor supply (the normal condition in capitalism) kept wage rates low and helped discipline labor.

In the early 20th century, the transition to monopoly capitalism occurred as the natural outcome of the drive for capital accumulation. This concentration of capital resulted in a dualism in the industrial structure — a monopoly sector characterized by competition among a few powerful corporations of increasing size and bureaucracy (and by extensive involvement of foreign and state capital in Canada), and a competitive sector which retained the characteristics of 19th-century capitalism. From this dualism in industrial structures grew dualism in labor markets. In the monopoly sector, large congregations of homogeneous labor created the conditions for increasing class consciousness and resulted in renewed labor militancy in both Canada and the United States. Internal labor markets were created as a further attempt at control over labor, and wage premiums were also introduced, thereby recreating a divisive heterogeneity of labor on capitalist terms. Internal labor markets, in this scheme, are not technologically determined, but are an "efficient" response to the power of undifferentiated labor that may be manifested in union activity, in lack of discipline and productivity, or in costly turnover. Efficiency and social control were two sides of the same coin in the scientific management movement of the 1920s. Internal labor markets often preceded the wage and security demands of the industrial unions in the 1930s and 1940s. These union efforts, in monopoly sector firms, built on the already institutionalized systems of wage and status differentials; they negotiated consistent rules for both the differentials and the allocation of workers, as well as overall increases in the wage scale.

In the competitive sector, the employment practices of early capitalism were continued, including control by simple hierarchy and the use of the reserve army of the unemployed as a disciplining force and as a wage depressant. In addition, the continuing process of capitalist expansion fueled the excess labor supply in this sector, as more and more people left independent commodity production and became wage laborers, and as more and more jobs were replaced by machines in the monopoly sector.[10]

The dualism in the labor market described above interacted with existing divisions by race and sex and locked certain groups into the MWW. The most docile workers at any one time peopled the MWW— they did not need to be "rewarded" to be controlled. Over time, these have included various immigrant groups, women and racial minorities. The implication is that capitalists only improved wages and working conditions when forced by either worker demands or government fiat. Capitalism historically made these improvements in a way which divided the working class and this division served to undermine the development of subjective working-class consciousness.

One implication of this analysis is that employers make the choice to play each employment strategy where it best suits the nature of the production process and the relations of production. A CWW strategy is used where this facilitates needed long-run control and commitment, and a MWW strategy is used elsewhere. Thus we have subcontracting by monopoly sector firms and branch plant establishments in areas with docile or surplus (i.e., low-wage) labor, such as the Maritimes.

A Marxist approach also provides a means of understanding the relationship between regional inequalities and labor market inequalities. The concentration of capital occurs spatially as well as sectorally. Therefore, whole regions such as the Maritimes become reserve armies of labor, with a dominant MWW and small enclaves of CWW establishments.

The Maritime region is a dependent capitalist periphery, characterized historically by the export of surplus capital and the retention of surplus labor.[11] The CWW in the Maritimes is essentially imported. It is found in the public sector, due to national unionization and government ability to pay (based on revenue sharing).[12] It is also found in the mining, steel, and pulp and paper industries, which have historically been owned by "outside" monopoly sector interests and organized by international unions which prevent exploitation of the MWW employment potential of the region. As in most peripheral regions and countries, development has been concentrated in these resource-based, export-oriented sectors which serve the primary product needs of central capital. These sectors provide CWW jobs because the mobility of resource-based capital is limited and this imparts a power to labor (Clark, 1977).[13]

The composition of the MWW in this region is also in line with the

Marxist analysis of the link between dualism in the industrial structure and the work world, and the expectation of unbalanced economic development in the periphery. The MWW in the Maritimes contains footloose outside-owned establishments attracted by cheap labor (electronics assembly), peripheral establishments in industries where capital is being run down (textiles), small establishments in competitive industries (consumer non-durables), remnants of the "traditional" economy (small sawmills and fish processors) whose prolonged (and distorted) existence, Marxists would argue, plays a role in the overall function served by the periphery to central monopoly capitalism (Amin, 1975), and establishments serving local markets, primarily in service and trade, which are still in the labor-intensive stage of capitalist development.

In summary, the major elements we draw from a Marxist explanation of segmentation are as follows. Class conflict (maintaining the control of capital over the production process) is a major factor in the evolution of segmented work worlds. Surplus labor is normal in a capitalist economy and guarantees the continuation of a MWW. Uneven development (*within* a region, and *between* regions) is endemic to capitalism rather than an "imperfection"; thus small reforms will not alleviate segmentation and low-wage work. Finally, the job characteristics presently associated with the CWW and the MWW are subject to evolution, depending on how effective those particular constellations of characteristics are at providing the needed control over labor and profit to capital as economic conditions change.

Eclectic Explanations

There are other explanations of the origins of segmentation in the literature which alter some neoclassical assumptions without wholly or explicitly embracing the alternative Marxist paradigm. We call these explanations "eclectic" because they are not a coherent theory but diverse attempts at explaining segmentation by a variety of researchers drawing on more than one body of theory. They focus on historical and institutional factors and reject or severely modify the neoclassical function of wages as a market-clearing device. Like Marxist explanations, they see segmentation as a normal tendency of modern capitalism. Unlike Marxists, they see some possibilities for intervention without destroying the whole capitalist system.[14] We make use of some of these explanations in developing our own understanding of the origins of segmentation. For example, in explaining labor demand, Michael Piore (1973) begins with the premises that (1) productivity is a function of the division of labor, which in turn is a function of the extent and stability of the market, and (2) the demand for any product has a stable and an unstable portion. This implies a tendency for concentration among large firms to develop in the stable portions of markets and competition among a number of small firms to prevail in the unstable portions. Segmentation on a micro level thus develops historically between firms which capture the stable demand and those which have unstable, or inherently small, markets. The development of technology and the resulting division of labor in each of these types of firms reinforce this dualism and transmit it into the nature of jobs. Both technological change and the tendency for a few firms to capture the stable portion of demand are endogenous in Piore's model (and exogenous in the neoclassical model). CWW and MWW firms then diverge on the kind of labor force required and on their ability to pay. The key causal element generating internal labor markets in this approach is the nature of the product market. A CWW develops from the attempts by firms to reduce their share of the instability in modern capitalism, while an MWW must exist to deal with the ever-remaining instability. The composition and employment characteristics of the two, and the severity of the job segmentation which results, are conditioned by institutional developments (government and labor responses) and change over time.

MWW-tending establishments identified by this causal approach include those serving the unstable portion of large markets (e.g., subcontractors and branch plants), those in markets limited in extent by geography or product type (personal services, retail trade) and those whose product or raw material cannot be inventoried to help smooth production (fish plants, restaurants). Managers interviewed in MWW firms in the Maritimes frequently cited limited and unstable markets as major constraints to productivity increases which would facilitate higher wages.

On the supply side of the work world, CWW-*tending* employers may need to be forced to translate their requirements for stable employees into CWW jobs with high wages (Piore, 1976). In this case, workers too are attempting to reduce their share of instability. The influence of unions was crucial in rigidifying an economy-wide gap between the CWW and the MWW, thus precluding company preferences on the demand side of the labor market from resulting in a continuum of employment characteristics rather than segmentation. Thus the CWW represents the accommodation of capitalist needs for market control and stability and worker demands for economic security, whereas in the Marxist framework the CWW is organized exclusively in the interests of capital.

From our point of view, however, segmentation in the industrial structure, in the regional distribution of economic activity, and in the labor market is structural and normal to capitalism. Barriers to mobility are not just the result of minor imperfections in labor markets. Orthodox explanations tell us how these imperfections operate, but the other explanations tell us where they originate. Economic power differences between companies (capital) and workers (labor), and *within* the classes of capital and labor, interact over time to create a segmented work world, where low-income work cannot be understood or dealt with outside of its particular economic and institutional context.

The Maintenance of Segmented Work Worlds

Our previous discussion of the causes of segmentation suggests that the determinants of the kind of employment package provided by establishments can be grouped around three factors: *the desired labor force* of the establishment, *its ability and willingness to pay*, and *the requirement to pay*. Technology characteristics, product market extent and stability, and the need for control over labor all affect the desired labor force and point to

MWW-tending and CWW-tending establishments. Factors such as profits, ownership characteristics, competition in the product market and the potential for geographic mobility of a particular establishment affect the ability/willingness to pay, and indicate whether an establishment is potentially a CWW employer. Finally, the requirement-to-pay dimension may be affected by the pressures which are brought to bear on a firm by either workers or government to follow a CWW employment strategy. The requirement to pay is low where workers are unorganized, where there is a surplus supply of suitable workers, and where there are no employment alternatives. A high requirement to pay is a necessary, though not sufficient, condition for a CWW employment strategy in all explanations of segmentation.

The interaction of these three factors helps us to understand why an MWW strategy may be maintained despite changes in some underlying variables such as technology, ownership, unionization or level of profits. As an illustration, we will examine in this section the effect of changing ownership patterns in the MWW on the three factors and thus on the employment strategy of establishments.

Based on our case studies of MWW establishments and secondary data analysis, it is clear that the small, family-owned single location MWW firm is a dying breed in the Maritimes (Table 3). We have found a relatively viable, predominantly locally owned, MWW in only one portion of the region — the Acadian and English region of southwestern Nova Scotia, comprising Yarmouth and Digby counties. In our MWW case studies in other areas of the Maritimes, the pattern is one of takeovers, mergers, franchising, threats of takeover, and general fear for the future of the "independent" owner. Of 40 MWW establishments studied in Moncton, New Brunswick (Clairmont and Jackson, 1976), only five were single-location firms. The remaining 35 were split evenly between regional and national or multinational based firms. In another group of 30 "connected" MWW establishments selected randomly from five regions of the Maritimes (see Table 3 for total population of "connected" MWW establishments), 14 began as branch locations, three became connected before 1960, six became connected from 1960 to 1970, and seven became connected from 1970 to 1977. Some establishments go out of business and the employees are channeled into new and growing types of marginal work settings — in the service sector, for example, or in labor-intensive branch plants attracted to the region. Other MWW establishments become linked in a variety of ways to the CWW, including national and multinational companies. Still other MWW establishments become joined together in multiple-location, clearly profitable companies which continue to operate exclusively in the MWW. The increasing control over the entire work world on the part of larger corporations, government, and, to a lesser degree, strong unions is not incompatible with segmentation. Marxists argue that the search for new markets, investment outlets and sources of profit continually expand the domain of the monopoly sector. The employment strategy, however, need not be altered in the newly-acquired territory. Writers such as Piore, who point to the need for different employment strategies in the stable and

Table 3

Numbers of "Connected" and "Unconnected" MWW Establishments in 5 Regions of the Maritimes*

	Manufacturing		Trade		Services	
	Unconnected	Connected	Unconnected	Connected	Unconnected	Connected
North Eastern Nova Scotia (5 counties)	16	8	14	18	9	7
Cape Breton Island (4 counties)	9	5	10	20	7	13
P.E.I. (all)	8	5	13	12	7	6
Fredericton, N.B. (3 counties)	3	4	4	15	5	9
North Eastern N.B. (3 counties)	13	5	2	24	3	3
Total	49	27	43	89	31	38

Total "Connected" = 154   Total "Unconnected" = 123

*"Connected" establishments are part of multi-establishment firms. "Unconnected" establishments are single-location firms. Establishments were identified as MWW by Manpower officials on the basis of employing 20 to 499 workers with ≥60% earning < $4/hr. The five regions were selected from 11 regions in the Maritimes as a population for one study (Apostle and MacDonald, 1977).

Source: The ES-1 listing of establishments with more than 20 employees, Statistics Canada, 1976.

unstable sectors of the economy, do not imply that companies operate exclusively in one sector. There is, then, an appreciation that the MWW takes on a more complex character through these changing ownership patterns, without necessarily losing what we define as its essential characteristics.

Linkages via direct ownership, subcontracting, or franchises with the CWW do not, for the most part, reflect an erosion of the CWW, but rather an evolution of the MWW. Thus McDonald's replaces the local restaurant and Modern Cleaners (Dustbane) replaces the small cleaning operation. In some cases, however, it does represent a decision to carry out production in one sphere rather than another, as when a branch plant locates in a cheap labor area.

Connections of previously independent MWW establishments to firms which have CWW components and connections to profitable firms using MWW strategies throughout their operations (such as motel chains, grocery store chains) do not generally alter their job characteristics. In terms of the approach outlined above, the desired labor force often remains the same and the probable increased ability to pay remains untapped. In many cases this ability to pay is impossible to tap, for although the overall company is viable, the jobs in specific establishments are vulnerable. The company may be interested in the establishment only as long as a MWW strategy can be pursued, and may respond to pressures to pay more by abandoning the location. In some cases, the vulnerability of the "connected" MWW jobs is greater than that of the unconnected jobs they replace, due to the greater mobility of connected capital; the shutdown profit point of a family business is often extremely "uneconomic." There are also examples (or charges) of disinvestment by corporate sector companies in the establishments which they buy out. Even where capitalization of establishments does occur, the lack of a requirement to pay, due to conditions of surplus labor and the difficulties of organizing workers in small establishments, often precludes this from leading to improved employment conditions. The frequent result is similar, but fewer, jobs as capital is substituted for labor. Wages in these firms are still influenced most by the local labor market, particularly in nonurban areas. In addition, legal problems of defining the bargaining unit may make organizing more difficult in multi-establishment firms and thus prevent an increase in the requirement to pay. The point is that the CWW/MWW dichotomy has remained intact, though the distinction between powerful/powerless firms may be decreasing through growing webs of ownership. One major implication of this greater centralization and coordination is the importance of distinguishing between the firm (the corporate entity) and the establishment, as we have done in our research.

Attempts to Transform the Marginal Sector

The foregoing discussion clearly points to the need to consider change strategies bearing on the employment package that establishments are *required* to provide. Although a range of considerations are relevant, including the legislative provisions of governments, we will focus here on the prospects for, and implications of, worker organization in the marginal sector.

Our conception of the marginal work world involves considerable internal diversity. Thus, in discussing organizational strategies, it is useful to make a distinction between groups such as dairy farmers, hairstylists or day care workers, whose members work in very small geographically dispersed work settings and who typically organize on the basis of their occupational group vis-à-vis the market or their customers, and those who organize within the bounds of a particular establishment and across occupational lines, vis-à-vis their employer. In both cases, it can be argued, as Freedman (1977) does, that the point of organization is to establish job shelters, that is, the protection of incumbents of jobs from competition in the market and from the risks of unemployment, disability and old age outside the market.

The Organization of Occupational Groups

With respect to the organization of occupational groups whose members are largely self-employed, we have seen considerable change taking place in the region over the last decade and a half. A number of occupations whose members are in the low to middle income range are becoming better organized, either through their own initiative or through the intervention of external actors. While organizational developments are not automatically translated into the achievement of CWW status (reflected in higher incomes, more stable and secure employment, etc.) and while the process of organizing is not an easy one, there have been some significant developments. In rural occupations such as inshore fishing, for example, licensing and quota regulations as well as occupational organizations have been advanced; dairy farming has seen the development of marketing boards and commissions. Among urban service occupations such as hairstyling and day care services, there have also been organizational and certification developments.

A variety of strategies are used in these attempts to achieve greater institutionalization, as Kerr (1951) would call it. In our research program we have undertaken case studies of seven occupations, including those mentioned above, and are inclined at this point to divide the strategies into two major categories: associations grouping together persons who regard themselves as independent producers, and unionization strategies. There are various subtypes within each category; for example, association strategies may take a semi-professional form, or involve non-professional organizations which nevertheless have licensing or certification procedures. Cooperatives and marketing boards also fit into this category. On the unionization side, craft, white collar and other union models are found. Often there is debate within an occupational group about the relative merits of association or union strategies, as in inshore fishing and taxicab driving, or a shift from one strategy to another over time as conditions change. One of the interesting questions being pursued in the research is to establish the determining conditions by which a particular organizational strategy is selected.

While some occupations have become more institutionalized, two of the cases we have examined, taxicab operators and woodlot owners, have faced substantial obstacles. In addition, the advances made by one group (e.g., hairdressers) may well be made at the expense of another (e.g., barbers) as the clientele shifts from one to the other.

It is also the case that as occupational groups organize, the process of transformation means the exclusion of residual members of the occupations (e.g., part-time fisherman), or the achievement of gains by reducing membership in the occupation, thereby feeding surplus labor into other parts of the marginal sector where access barriers have not been erected.[15] Again, segmentation persists in the absence of an overall strategy directed at its elimination. On the basis of our case studies, it is clear that provincial and federal governments are important actors in these efforts at collective occupational transitions, and their support is a crucial variable in whether or not a successful transformation is made — whether day care workers become certified, or whether small woodlot owners are able to establish a pulpwood marketing board in the face of opposition from the pulp and paper companies. The only alternative source of institutional support for these movements would appear to be the resources of the organized labor movement.[16]

Unionism and MWW Establishments

In addition to these case studies of attempts to organize occupational groups, we have also begun some research on the transformation of marginal work settings through the unionization of employees within establishments. From our Table 1, it appears that more than half of the work force in Atlantic Canada can be classified as being in the MWW. Only about 10% of MWW workers are unionized, as compared with at least 35% of the total work force (Nova Scotia Department of Labour, 1976). If these figures are accurate, then a majority of those working in the CWW — and, of course, an even larger proportion if one excludes groups like management and the armed forces — are members of unions, and the union movement is largely constituted by CWW employees. There are some MWW work settings with a long history of unionization, as in textiles, and there are some large MWW-based unions such as the retail, wholesale, and department store workers. Even the larger, more established MWW-based union locals in the Maritimes, however, do not have the resources and bargaining power of their CWW counterparts.

From the standpoint of unionism, the MWW remains primarily a "frontier land," difficult to settle, secure, and transform. Union organizers face stiff opposition from both independent or family-owned establishments where the ability to pay may be in question, and from large corporations which may have set up an establishment locally to secure cheap or non-unionized labor. They have to organize work settings where there may be a tradition of independence (e.g., rural craftsmen) or a more paternalistic style of employer-employee relations (e.g., small or modest size manufacturing concerns, retail trade operations). They have to win over low-income persons who may be justifiably skeptical of what a union could accomplish.

Part-timers and women, who are disproportionately in the MWW and who may define themselves as secondary household earners, are difficult to organize, as are those who have self-selected non-union work settings. And this organizing has to be done with few resources, with competition rather than cooperation from other unions and on an establishment by establishment basis where the size of each unit is rather small and where turnover is often high.[17] Finally, once having organized an MWW concern, the union representative will generally have to put up with settlements that fall below the collective bargaining average and will be threatened occasionally by "raiding" or decertification.[18]

The significant growth of unionization in Atlantic Canada in recent years has primarily occurred in the areas of public administration and community services (Wood and Kumar, 1976). Industries most likely to spawn MWW establishments — trade, light manufacturing, personal and business services — have witnessed little growth in unionization. The fact that there is relatively little unionization in the industries where MWW-based unions are found sets severe constraints on the effectiveness of collective bargaining in the MWW. In effect, the predominance of non-union establishments means that the strike threat there has few social and economic implications beyond the establishment, an especially vital consideration given the often considerable imbalance in power between companies and workers, the limited strike funds available to union locals in the MWW and the usual problems of mobilizing and maintaining appropriate commitment in MWW establishments.

Preliminary interviews with union officials, perusal of collective agreements and more detailed examination of the MWW in specific regions of the Maritimes (e.g., metropolitan Moncton) indicate little difference in wages between unionized and non-unionized MWW establishments in the same industry. The most obvious advantage of organized MWW workers is in the area of fringe benefits, but perhaps the most important union benefits relate to the regulation of employer-employee relationships and of working conditions generally.

Our research thus far indicates profound differences in collective bargaining clout between MWW-based and CWW-based unions. Sharp differences are also evident in the important union activity of contract administration. Business representatives of locals servicing MWW workers not only have fewer financial and organizational resources, but what they do have is further thinned by the spread of the relatively small membership of the local over a number of distinct establishments or bargaining units. Thus one could not expect the same level of service and contract administration provided by the typical CWW local nor perhaps, in the "composite locals" common in the MWW, the same level of identification by members with their local. It should be noted too that the situation does not appear much different in those instances where a CWW-based union (i.e., a union drawing its core membership from CWW establishments) has organized MWW workers. Finally, our research indicates that CWW-based unions are much more active in the field of social policy and in labor federations and district labor councils.

There appears to be considerable skepticism among union people whom we have interviewed regarding the prospects of unionization in the MWW and the significance of the unionization that might occur there.[19] Furthermore, the fragmentation of the labor movement and the prevalent business-unionism orientation do not suggest the transformation of MWW work settings via unionization under present conditions. However, in other advanced capitalist societies where segmentation is less significant (e.g., Sweden, Australia) the work force is more heavily unionized and significant collective bargaining, guided partly by a strong equality principle, takes place on an industry-wide basis and at the national level (Robinson, 1972).

In North America, strong unionism is thoroughly implicated in the creation and maintenance of segmentation. The widespread contention in the segmentation literature is that the combined forces of monopolization and unionization in the oligopolistic or core sector of the economy have produced segmentation or divergent development as an unplanned outcome (Kahn, 1975). The strong or CWW-based unions shelter the employment of their members, contributing to the process of shifting the costs of societal economic organization onto those workers who are either unorganized or weakly so (Piore, 1973). Their success here has depended as much if not more on the capitalization and monopoly character of CWW operations as upon trade union struggle (Aronowitz, 1973). Without a fundamental change in union ideology and organization, accompanied by an equally basic change in certification and collective bargaining, the transformation of MWW work settings will depend upon similar considerations and, perhaps, extensive government regulation of market forces and working conditions.

Clearly mergers among several MWW-based unions competing for similar workers would have an important effect, and in the limiting case where virtually an entire MWW industry (e.g., fishing) is organized by a single union, MWW-based unionization could be very important in attenuating segmentation. But apart from possible quantitative changes in work world segmentation, the historical pattern of strong unions not having gained a larger portion of the pie for labor in society, and having their gains at the expense of those still unorganized or weakly organized, would continue (Johnson and Miekowski, 1970). Our analysis and research indicate that profound changes are necessary, changes directed at the heart of current power imbalances. There is serious question concerning the extent to which the labor movement and workers can or will pursue such changes. Segmentation is quite compatible with the corporatism characteristic of most western societies. As Janowitz (1976:75) observes, class goals have less and less significance and "the politics of an advanced society is a reflection of its own system of inequality which is characterized by intensive occupational and economic interest group competition." In this situation it not surprising to find, as Goldthorpe discovered, "a general appreciation (among workers) of the extent to which their individual prosperity depended upon the economic fortunes of the firms in which they were employed"; nor is it surprising that CWW workers and their unions could adopt "an increasingly particularistic approach to industrial relations, giving rise to a new corporatism and the consolidation of a new labor aristocracy...oriented to sectional rather than class objectives and eschewing any commitment to radical change in the wider economic or social order" (Goldthorpe, 1974b:157).

The Value of the Framework:
Low-Wage Work in the CWW versus the MWW

In our segmentation perspective not all low-wage workers are in the MWW nor are all workers there receiving low wages; the distinction between MWW and CWW work settings refers to *predominant* wage levels, among other considerations. The obvious question then is, what does it matter whether the low-wage worker is in one sphere or the other? If the segmentation approach is meaningful, especially one which places emphasis on the establishment or work setting rather than on the occupation, then one would expect some significant differences in working conditions, wages/total compensation over time, training/mobility opportunities and attitudes/behavior between the low-wage worker in CWW establishments and his or her counterpart in the MWW. Thus we would expect the low-wage worker in the CWW to be more likely to escape from poverty, to experience wage and occupational mobility. If so, then at least some of the often cited movement out of poverty (most of which is probably related to life cycle) can be seen as a CWW phenomenon.

In a preliminary way the data which we have obtained strongly support the suggestions made above. Low-wage workers in CWW establishments in metropolitan Moncton have been found to earn more, have greater fringe benefits, higher overall job satisfaction, and less relative deprivation and alienation than counterparts (matched on occupation, age, sex, ethnicity, and area of residence) drawn from MWW establishments. It also appears from longitudinal data currently being collected that the low-wage CWW workers are more likely to experience wage and occupational mobility.

For example, Table 4 shows that low-wage CWW workers have gained on the provincial average income over their work careers much more than have their MWW counterparts in this Moncton sample. Particularly significant is the finding that the income mobility pattern for females differs profoundly depending on the sector of employment. Also supportive of the hypothesized segmentation effect is the upward mobility found with a change from the MWW to the CWW and the downward mobility found in the reverse movement, though the number of cases is small.

It can also be argued that the situation of the low-wage worker in the CWW should improve over time relative to other CWW workers. Given the social reality constituted by the establishment, low-wage work may well be incongruent with the control and compliance objectives of management, which depend somewhat upon the image of work organization projected to and assimilated by employees (Edwards, 1975). Hence management in CWW establishments might be more inclined to meet demands of their low-wage employees. Also, given the establishment-specific nature of most skills and the ever-present threat of technological change (greater in CWW work

Table 4

Standardized Income Mobility by Work Pattern Type*

Category	Employment Sector Central Work World Mean Standardized Income Mobility	Marginal Work World Mean Standardized Income Mobility
Overall	1.93 (260)	.51 (252)
Female	2.69 (103)	−.66 (103)
Switchers**	4.37 (55)	−3.32 (14)

*For each respondent a calculation was made to standardize income (to the New Brunswick provincial average) for both the first full-time job that they held and for their 1976 job. The initial standardized income was subtracted from the final standardized income and this result was then divided by the number of full-time years spent in the labor force. Or,

$$\text{Standardized Income Mobility} = \frac{\text{Final Standardized Pay} - \text{Initial Standardized Pay}}{\text{Months in labor force} \div 12}$$

**Switchers are those who had their first job in one sector and then swtiched and stayed in the other sector. They are counted in the sector to which they switched.

Source: Donald H. Clairmont and Winston Jackson, "Income Mobility by Type of Employer," Marginal Work World Project, Institute of Public Affairs, Dalhousie University, 1978.

settings) it may well be in the interests of the more advantaged workers to delicately balance status claims with solidarity behavior (Sabel, 1975); thus there would be reinforcement of those considerations which incline collective bargaining to favor, relatively, the least advantaged. If there is anything to this argument, then one might expect not only a different future for the individual low-wage CWW worker compared with her or his MWW counterpart but also some relative gains vis-à-vis the more well-paid strata of CWW workers.

Our most detailed observations on these relative gains within the CWW are with reference to the public sector in the Moncton area. Within the past few years the low-income workers there such as maids, clerks, caretakers, and laundry workers have experienced very significant improvement in wages and working conditions. Both union and management officials with whom we discussed this situation referred to the "pre-election bonus" of 1974 when the provincial government, faced with both a general strike of its non-professional/technical/managerial workers (virtually all of whom are in the same union) and a provincial election, settled generously with the union. Low-wage workers were particularly favored under the new contract; their wages jumped by almost $70 a week over a two-year span and their working conditions and fringe benefits became comparable to other public sector employees (e.g., maids received four weeks' paid vacation after seven years of service). Not unexpectedly, these changes were accompanied by sentiments of "distributive injustice" on the part of lower level supervisory personnel; one payroll supervisor, referring to the similarity of wages between cleaning and supervisory work, exclaimed "Why should I take all this responsibility then?" That the 1974 occurrence was not simply idiosyncratic is attested to by the fact that the more recent pattern of "cash-across-the-board" wage settlements has effected a further flattening of the wage and salary scale. According to union officials the working policy of the union is to narrow the gap between low-wage and other workers, while maintaining an absolute differential between them.

It appears, then, that the situation of the low-wage workers in the public sector in New Brunswick — and probably throughout the Maritimes — has improved in both relative and absolute terms in recent years. At the same time, keeping down compensation costs remains an important objective of CWW firms and job-sheltering remains a major priority of the CWW workers. Thus, along with the above implications may well go the emergence of a new and more important kind of inequality — the differentiation between regular employees and those designated as part-time, casual and temporary. Yet even here it appears to be against the long-term interests of those regularly employed to allow a significant gap in the wage rate component of the compensation package (i.e., this could have the effect of job devaluation); so to the extent that part-time, temporary personnel are involved in CWW establishments, the inequality there would be based more upon employment status, and possibly fringe benefits, than upon wage differentials.

In our research on the public sector in Moncton, we encountered a significant number of part-time and casual workers, especially in the hospitals. According to management officials, part-timers and casuals are generally covered by union contract, draw similar wages and have preference for available full-time positions; officials also were of the opinion that these persons for the most part preferred their current work arrangement to full-time, regular employment.

Finally, if the theoretical argument developed earlier has merit, then despite the peculiarities of the above example (i.e., public sector, pre-election bonus), similar patterns should be found elsewhere in CWW work settings with respect to the compensation of low-wage workers over time and the relative wage gains among different categories of workers. Recently Velk (1976) has suggested that the working poor have found their position improved considerably over the past decade; in support of this contention he presented a table showing that since 1967 the average annual increase in wage rates for new settlements has been significantly greater than the annual rate of change in the consumer price index. Interestingly, the wage increase data are based on averaging overall collective bargaining units of 500 or more, excluding the construction industry; such units would in our terms represent the CWW, and consequently we interpret the Velk article and more generally the well-known "union effect" (Rees, 1973) as supportive of part of our hypothesis. Also we have found in assessing the position of laborers in the construction industry in Nova Scotia, that over the recent past this category of workers experienced considerable improvement in their compensation package both in absolute terms and relative to the skilled tradesmen. One union official representing construction laborers noted that there is a conscious consensual "agreement" to keep wages roughly 75 cents per hour below that of the tradesmen; as wages have steadily improved this has meant of course that the position of the laborers (the lower-wage employees) continually improved relative to the other workers. If these implications of the segmentation model are valid, it would further direct attention to the nature and structure of work settings rather than to the characteristics of workers and occupations. Further it would suggest that micro stratification processes are conditioned by a segmentation effect. Indeed Tolbert, Horan and Beck (1978) have found in the U.S. that the status attainment process is *not* uniform across economic sectors and they contend that "any attempt to analyze the process of attainment of occupational prestige without reference to the industrial structure of the American economy . . . will result in estimates of basic parameters and interpretations of major findings which are open to question."

Conclusion

In this paper, we hope to have provided an integrated and structural approach to poverty and low-wage work in the Maritimes, although much of the empirical support remains to be presented. It is an integrated approach in the sense that we emphasize in the first place the connection between poverty and low-wage work: a majority of low-income family heads and unattached individuals are working in the Maritimes, and many of those that aren't move regularly back and forth, in and out of employment. Secondly, we stress the connection between work world segments: the dimensions of the marginal work world cannot be understood without reference to the rest of the economy and, indeed, to "non-economic" factors such as the role of the state and the educational system. Discussions of barriers, crowding, the generation of surplus labor, ownership and subcontracting connections inevitably are incomplete without an understanding of linkages between marginal and central segments and the functions of marginality. Finally, we cannot account for the issue at hand without reference to the connection between the Maritimes as a peripheral region to core regions, a consideration that directly affects the type and amount of employment available.

It is a structural approach in the sense that we are attempting to understand low-wage work (and its correlates such as employment instability, lack of job security and advancement opportunities) not from the basis of individual characteristics and alleged shortcomings but rather in terms of the influence of the work context on individual characteristics, and the determinants of the kinds of employment packages provided by establishments. Our focus is not so much on the working poor, or even on low-wage occupations, as it is on a whole sector of the regional society that lies outside the relatively structured and powerful central work world.

NOTES

1. Structure-functionalists posit that the functional importance of work roles (measured largely by the human capital investment required) is the prime deter-

minant of stratification differences (measured by rewards and benefits). Further, Parsons (1971), sees a mobile, homogeneous labor force as increasingly characteristic of modern society. In the Whyte formulation, technological change primarily determines changes in functional importance.

2. In the dual labor market analysis, an important feature of establishments operating in the primary sector is their development of internal labor markets. The term is defined as a set of structured employment relations within the establishment, embodying a set of rules (formal and informal) that governs each job and their interrelationship in such matters as job content, wages, opportunities on the promotion ladder and grievance procedures. Access to the establishment for employment is restricted to a few low-level entry points, and beyond entry-level positions, jobs are filled from within the ranks, often on the basis of seniority, along well-defined mobility structures (which also facilitate on-the-job training). It is argued that much of orthodox theory is not applicable within the internal labor market, but may have some relevance for explaining the characteristics of entry-level positions.

3. We do not mean to imply a negative characterization of the marginal work sector, however. There may well be positive compensating factors that offset the characteristics mentioned above (e.g., greater flexibility in the organization of work, or more control over the work process in some occupations such as in fishing or shipbuilding). Nor do we see the central sector in uniformly positive terms. To some extent, our survey data covering employers and workers in both sectors will shed some light on how the participants evaluate different work structures. We expect to find a good deal of variation within each segment.

4. The two types of organization may well overlap for some occupations (e.g., accountants working in central establishments).

5. In referring to *firms*, we mean the total corporate entity of a company, while the term *establishment* refers to one particular location of work.

6. The resolution of this inequity need not necessarily be achieved through individual mobility out of the occupations and work settings characteristic of the marginal sector. It can also be achieved by restructuring existing work settings through unionization, marketing boards, cooperatives, etc., in order to provide more stable and remunerative employment opportunities.

7. To continue with the forestry example, in the Maritimes, subcontractors in trucking and logging serve to absorb the instabilities in the supply of and demand for logs, thereby cushioning the effect on the corporate sector (Marchak, 1977; Wien and Comeau, 1978).

8. Specific predictions on such factors as the wage determination process and the role of education are developed by Doeringer and Piore (1971), Gordon (1972), and Harrison (1972), among others. A critical review is provided by Wachter (1974), Cain (1976) and Smith (1976).

9. The general pattern is similar in all Western countries that evolved from competitive to monopoly capitalism at the turn of the century. The historical details vary according to the position of the country in the world capitalist system, and its particular institutional characteristics. Canada's continual colonial and neocolonial position meant that capitalism was built on the exploitation and export of natural resources, and that British and American capital (and ideas of efficiency and organization) formed the backbone of our monopoly sector. In addition, Canada experienced a more direct state involvement in the economy than the U.S. (railways, for example). See Gordon (1972), Braverman (1974) and Edwards, Reich and Gordon (1975) for discussion of the U.S. situation, and Rinehart (1975) for a summary of Canadian development.

10. This process is continuing today in the Maritimes with the rise of corporate fishing and farming (as well as licensing and quota schemes which eliminate marginal operators in these sectors), the loss of CWW jobs in sectors such as steel and mining, and the loss of skilled craft jobs such as wooden boatbuilding.

11. Frank (1967) and Amin (1975) are key figures in the theoretical literature on dependent development in the capitalist periphery. See Acheson (1972), Archibald (1971) and Matthews (1977), as examples of the relevance of this approach to the Maritimes.

12. In PEI, for example, government spending exceeds the total value of private production (Courchene, 1978).

13. Attempts to improve wages in "footloose" corporate sector establishments which have located here, such as General Instruments, have resulted in runaway shops.

14. In the Marxist paradigm effective government intervention in the present economic system is impossible because the state primarily serves the interests of capital.

15. An especially vulnerable but expanding area of employment is the service sector where jobs are particularly likely to be low-wage, part-time and unprotected. The Atlantic region generally has the largest proportion of persons employed in the service sector of any Canadian region and the smallest in manufacturing, with the exception of the Prairies (Statistics Canada, 1974). Using U.S. data, Freedman (1977) finds that the proportion of persons employed in the least sheltered jobs has increased from 36 to 46% between 1960 and 1970, with much of the growth taking place in the service sector.

16. The current attempt to organize inshore fishermen in Nova Scotia involves a struggle between a fishermen's association funded until recently by the provincial government and a fishermen's union supported in part by the Canadian Labour Congress. The task of the union organizers is made more difficult by the refusal of the provincial government to change legislation which, at present, excludes fishermen from the provisions of the trade union act.

17. Attempts at unionization at the establishment level may be challenged by the firm on the grounds that it represents too limited a base for an appropriate bargaining unit, as in the case of bank branches.

18. In Nova Scotia since 1974, all but three of the 15 cases of revoked certification involved MWW-based union locals.

19. One union official who represents workers at several MWW establishments stated that the high rate of unemployment in the region acts as a brake on aggressive unionism; otherwise, he added, "I believe if you can't trade, get out! I have come to the conclusion that by negotiating and keeping such companies alive, all you are doing is prolonging the agony. You are not doing the workers any good."

REFERENCES

Acheson, T.W. "The National Policy and the Industrialization of the Maritimes," *Acadiensis*, Vol. 1, No. 2 (1972).

Adams, Ian. *The Poverty Wall*. Toronto: McClelland and Stewart, 1970.

Amin, Samir. "Accumulation and Development: A Theoretical Model," *Review of African Political Economy*, 1 (1975).

Apostle, Richard and Martha Macdonald. "Morphology Survey I:

Methodology Report." Working Paper, Institute of Public Affairs, Dalhousie University, 1977.

Archibald, Bruce. "Atlantic Regional Underdevelopment and Socialism," in Laurier LaPierre, et al., eds., *Essays on the Left*. Toronto: McClelland and Stewart, 1971.

Aronowitz, Stanley. "Trade Unionism in America," in B. Silverman and M. Yonowitch, eds., *The Worker in Post-Industrial Capitalism*. New York: The Free Press, 1974, pp. 410-23.

Averitt, Robert. *The Dual Economy*. New York: Norton, 1968.

Baron, Harold and Bennett Hymer. "The Negro in the Chicago Labor Market," in Julius Jacobson, ed., *The Negro and the American Labor Movement*. New York: Doubleday Anchor Books, 1968.

Barth, F. "Economic Spheres in Darfur," in R. Firth, ed., *Themes of Economic Anthropology*. ASA Monographs, No. 6, London: Tavistock, 1967.

Beck, E.M., P.M. Horan and C.M. Tolbert. "Stratification in a Dual Economy: A Sectoral Model of Earnings Determination," American Sociological Review, Vol. 43 (Oct. 1978).

Berger, Suzanne. "The Uses of the Traditional Sector: Why the Declining Classes Survive," Massachusetts Institute of Technology, Dept. of Economics, Cambridge, Mass., 1973.

Bluestone, Barry. "The Tripartite Economy: Labor Markets and the Working Poor," *Poverty and Human Resources Abstracts*, Vol. 5, No. 4 (July-Aug. 1970), pp. 15-35.

Bluestone, Barry Alan. *The Personal Earnings Distribution: Individual and Institutional Determinants*. Boston: Social Welfare Regional Research Institute, 20 (Nov. 1974).

Boeke, J.H. *Economics and Economic Policy in Dual Societies*. Haarlem, Netherlands: H.D. Willink and Zoon, 1953.

Bohannan, P. and C. Dalton. *Markets in Africa*. New York: Northwestern University Press, 1965.

Braverman, Harry. *Labor and Monopoly Capital: The Degradation of Work in the Twentieth Century*. New York: Monthly Review Press, 1974.

Brox, Ottar. *Newfoundland Fisherman in an Age of Industry: A Sociology of Economic Dualism*. St. John's, Newfoundland: Institute for Social and Economic Research, Memorial University, 1972.

Butler, Peter and Pam Buckley. "Work and Welfare: A Closer Look at Linkages between Income Security and the World of Work." Working Paper, Institute of Public Affairs, Dalhousie University, 1978.

Cain, Glen G. "The Challenge of Dual and Radical Theories of the Labor Market to Orthodox Theory." Institute for Research on Poverty, Discussion Papers, Jan. 1975.

Clairmont, D.H. and W. Jackson. "Comparison with the Public Service Project." Project Outline, Institute of Public Affairs, Dalhousie University, 1976.

Clairmont, Donald and Fred Wien. "Segmentation, Disadvantage and Development: An Analysis of the Marginal Work World, Its Relationship to the Central Work World and Its Role in the Evolving Maritime Provinces." Institute of Public Affairs, Dalhousie University, 1975.

Clark, Peter. "Employer-Employee Relations in Four Types of Firms." Project Outline, Institute of Public Affairs, Dalhousie University, 1977.

Clark, S.D. *The New Urban Poor*. Scarborough, Ont.: McGraw-Hill Ryerson, 1978.

Cornwall, John. "Segmentation Theories in Economics." Draft paper prepared for the Marginal Work World Research Program, Institute of Public Affairs, Oct. 1977.

Courchene, Thomas J. "The Transfer System and Regional Disparities: A Critique of the Status Quo." Dept. of Economics, University of Western Ontario, 1978.

Doeringer, P. and M. Piore. *Internal Labor Markets and Manpower Analysis*. Lexington: D.C. Heath, 1971.

Dunlop, John T. "The Task of Contemporary Wage Theory," in George W. Taylor, ed., *New Concepts in Wage Determination*. New York: McGraw-Hill, 1957, pp. 117-39.

Economic Council of Canada. *Living Together*. Ottawa: Ministry of Supply and Services, 1977.

Edwards, Richard C., Michael Reich and David M. Gordon, eds. *Labor Market Segmentation*. Lexington: D.C. Heath, 1975.

Eichner, Alfred S. "The Human Resources Approach to Labor Economics." Conservation of Human Resources Project, Columbia University, Feb. 1977.

Ferman, Louis A. "The Irregular Economy: Informal Work Patterns in the Ghetto." Dept. of Economics, University of Michigan, 1967.

Frank, Andre Gunder. *Capitalism and Underdevelopment in Latin America*. New York: Monthly Review Press, 1967.

Freedman, Marcia. *Labor Markets: Segments and Shelters*. Montclair, N.J.: Allanheld, Osmun and Co., Universe Books, 1976.

Goldthorpe, J.H. "Social Stratification in Industrial Society," in B. Silverman and M. Yanowitch, eds., *The Worker in Post-Industrial Capitalism*. New York: The Free Press, 1974.

_____. "Affluence and the Workers' Work World," in B. Silverman and M. Yanowitch, eds., *The Worker in Post-Industrial Capitalism*. New York: The Free Press, 1974.

Gordon, David M. *Theories of Poverty and Underemployment*. Lexington: D.C. Heath, 1972.

Harrison, Bennett. *Education Training and the Urban Ghetto*. Baltimore: John Hopkins University Press, 1972.

_____. "How Americans Mix Work and Welfare," *Challenge* (May-June 1978).

Janowitz, M. *Social Control of the Welfare State*. New York: Elsevier, 1976.

Johnson, H. and P. Miezkowski. "Effects of Unionization in the Distribution of Income," *Quarterly Journal of Economics*, 84 (1970).

Johnson, L.A. *Poverty in Wealth*, 2nd ed. Toronto: New Hogtown Press, 1974.

Kahn, L. "Unions and Labour Market Segmentation." Ph.D Dissertation, University of California, Berkeley, 1975.

Kerr, Clark. "The Balkanization of Labor Markets," in E. Wright Bakke et al., eds., *Labor Mobility and Economic Opportunity*. Cambridge: Massachusetts Institute of Technology Press, 1954.

Lewis, W.A. "Economic Development with Unlimited Supplies of Labour." The Manchester School of Economic and Social Studies, May 1954.

Marchak, Patricia M. "Corporate and Non-corporate Labour in a Hinterland Economy: The Case of Interior Forestry Workers in British Columbia." Draft paper prepared for the Polish-Canada Exchange Seminar, May 1977.

Matthews, Ralph. "Canadian Regional Development Strategy: Dependency Theory Perspective," *Plan Canada*, 17, 2 (June 1977).

Myrdal, Gunnar. *An American Dilemma*. New York: McGraw-Hill, 1944.

Nova Scotia Department of Labour. *Labour Organizations in Nova Scotia*. Halifax: Province of Nova Scotia, 1976.

Parsons, T. *The System of Modern Societies*. Englewood Cliffs, N.J.: Prentice-Hall, 1971.

Piore, M.J. "Union Rules: The Changing Character of Work," *Social Policy*, 14, 1 (July-Aug. 1973).

———. "On the Technological Foundations of Economic Dualism." MIT Department of Economics, Working Paper No. 110, 1973.

———. "Essays I." Working draft, MIT Department of Economics, 1976.

Rees, Albert. *The Economics of Work and Pay*. New York: Harper and Row, 1973.

Reich, Michael, David Gordon and Richard Edwards. "A Theory of Labor Market Segmentation," *American Economic Review* (May 1973).

Rinehart, J.W. *The Tyranny of Work*. Toronto: Longman Canada, 1975.

Robinson, D. *Solidaristic Wage Policy in Sweden*. Paris: Organization for Economic Cooperation and Development, 1974.

Sabel, Charles F. "Industrial Conflict and the Sociology of the Labor Market." Unpublished paper, Max Planck Institute, West Germany, n.d.

Simon, Herbert A. *Administrative Behaviour*, 2nd ed. New York: MacMillan, 1957.

Smith, David C. "The Dual Labor Market Theory: A Canadian Perspective." Research and Current Issues, Series #32, Industrial Relations Centre, Queen's University, Kingston, 1976.

Smith, Ron. "The Marginal Work World in the Maritimes: Preliminary Statistical Analysis." Halifax: Institute of Public Affairs, Dalhousie University, 1977.

Statistics Canada. *Perspective Canada: A Compendium of Social Statistics*. Ottawa: Information Canada, 1974.

Thurow, L. *Generating Inequality: Mechanisms of Distribution in the U.S. Economy*. New York: Basic Books, 1975.

Tolbert, Charles, Patrick Horen and E. Beck. *The Dual Economy in American Structure*. Athens, Georgia: University of Georgia, 1978.

Velk, Tom. "Good News: Changes in Income Distribution," *Canadian Forum* (May 1976).

Vietorisz, Thomas and Bennett Harrison. *The Economic Development of Harlem*. New York: Praeger, 1970.

Wachter, Michael L. "Primary and Secondary Labor Markets: A Critique of the Dual Approach," *Brookings Papers on Economic Activity*, 3 (1974).

Wachtel, H. and C. Betsey. "Employment at Low Wages," *The Review of Economics and Statistics* (May 1972).

Whyte, Donald. "Sociological Perspectives on Poverty," in John Harp and John Hofley, eds., *Poverty in Canada*. Scarborough, Ont.: Prentice-Hall of Canada, 1971.

Wien, F.C. and Louis Comeau. "The Socio-Economic History and Structure of South-West Nova Scotia." Working Paper, Institute of Public Affairs, Dalhousie University, 1978.

Wood, W.D. and Pradeep Kumar. *The Current Industrial Relations Scene in Canada*. Kingston, Ont.: Industrial Relations Centre, Queen's University, 1977.

C. The Political Economy of Specific Groups

Articles within this section treat groups, whose positions cannot be entirely understood, as "class phenomena." We refer to women, the aged, and so-called Native Peoples. Their respective positions in society have some features of Weber's negatively privileged status groups. The restrictions to which they are subjected invariably come from outside the group, from the higher status group (Waxman, 1977). We do not wish to suggest, and the articles will bear us out on this, that the system of class relations in society has no effect on these groups. Quite the contrary — for example, the position of the aged vis-à-vis other groups can differ significantly as a result of the system of political and ideological relations characteristic of a given society.

John Myles' article on the aged attempts to show the relationship among the aged, the state, and the structure of inequality. He employs a typology of pension systems which includes two dimensions, the relative benefit level, and a flat or graduated benefit plan. This enables him to discuss the Canadian plan in comparative context; he notes that on an OECD transfer ration, Canada ranked 14th out of 17 nations. In short he tells us that the Canadian pension policy has kept the old population equal (intragenerationally) but poor. This leads him to discuss the broader social functions of pension funds, notably the capital accumulation function, a mechanism providing funds to provinces for economic development. Finally he notes that private pension funds are an effective mechanism for simultaneously securing and obscuring surplus value.

In her article on Native Indians, Kellough examines the treatment Indians receive from federal authorities in different historical contexts. The early period, for example, is characterized by a degree of autonomy, whereas a later period of colonization occurs in which the principles of assimilation and protection often operated in contradiction to each other. She argues forcefully that the institutions associated with the Indian Act have functioned as mechanisms in the expansion of the capitalist system. The metropolis-hinterland model provides an understanding of certain patterns of relationships which have occurred.

Chekki and Hofley's article on women and inequality argues that the position of women in Canada must be understood in the context of the development of monopoly capitalism, particularly in its alteration of work. Housework becomes non-productive work, that is, work having no value, since in a capitalist society only work that receives wages is defined as worthy. The article outlines briefly changes in the occupational and sexual division of labor and the resulting inequality, which cannot be explained simply by biology or educational background. Women at all levels of education and in every occupation receive less pay than do men.

These changes in the workplace intrude upon the family and also affect the family in three areas: day care; fertility and childlessness; and divorce and separation. The analysis of these three areas demonstrate that the family and male/female relationships are undergoing profound changes, both inside and outside the household. The brunt of these changes are borne by women.

The Aged, the State, and the Structure of Inequality

JOHN F. MYLES

In 1966, the Senate Committee on Aging (Senate of Canada, 1966:9) commented:

> Without question the most serious problem encountered by the Senate Committee in the course of its investigation was the degree and extent of poverty which exists among older people.

What was true of the 1960s is equally true of the 1970s. In 1974, over 50% of families headed by individuals aged 65 or over were in the lowest quintile of the Canadian income distribution (Statistics Canada, 1977:55). Among elderly females the problem is particularly acute. In 1975, approximately 59% of unattached (widowed, single and divorced) females between 65 and 69 were below the poverty line of $3,988 established by the Senate Committee on Poverty, and among those aged 70 and over the figure was 78% (Collins, 1978:43). In 1977, 55% of all old age pensioners qualified for the federal government's means-tested Guaranteed Income Supplement (Statistics Canada, 1978b:267), another approximate measure of who is poor among Canada's elderly.

The purpose of this paper, however, is not simply to document once again the facts about aging and poverty in Canada. Rather, my object shall be to identify the mechanisms and processes which produce this situation, on the one hand, and the obstacles which stand in the way of ameliorating it, on the other. As will be shown, the economic position of the elderly is not independent of the forces at work in the economy as a whole. The problems which appear at the level of consumption in the form of low incomes are ultimately rooted in the organization of production characteristic of all advanced capitalist societies. However, while the *source* of the problem is common, the *solutions* which have evolved in different advanced capitalist nations vary considerably; these solutions in turn have major consequences with respect to the location of the elderly in the structure of inequality within each society. The strategy of analysis, therefore, is to begin by identifying those features which are common to all of the advanced capitalist societies with respect to the position of the aged by means of selected comparisons with earlier historical forms of the mode of production. Secondly, I shall identify the specific nature of the Canadian response to the problem of aging through a comparison of the Canadian case with the other advanced capitalist countries.[1] In neither case are the comparisons intended to be comprehensive or exhaustive. Rather, a few select comparisons have been chosen to isolate those aspects of aging which are distinctive of the advanced capitalist countries in general and Canadian society in particular. Both levels of analysis are necessary to understand the economics of growing old in Canada.

The Status of the Aged: The Historical Context

Social gerontologists have given considerable attention to cross-societal variations in the status of the aged. Most frequently the status of the aged in contemporary societies has been contrasted with an idealized view of the position of the aged in pre-industrial societies (see Harlan, 1968). Indeed, this view has been presented in the form of a general theory which argues that "... modernization results in, *inter alia*, a relatively lower status of older people in society" (Cowgill, 1974). Among the factors frequently cited as generating this change are the devaluation of the skills and knowledge of the elderly as a result of changing technology and the education of the young; new patterns of social and geographical mobility which lead to the decline of the extended family and a greater degree of social residential segregation of the aged; and greater productivity, which reduces the marginal value of the labor power of the elderly (Rosow, 1962; Cowgill and Holmes, 1972; Cowgill, 1974).

There is a considerable amount of anthropological evidence, however, which suggests that this truism of the gerontological literature considerably overstates and idealizes the status of the aged in preindustrial societies (Nahemow and Adams, 1974; Harlan, 1968). The veneration provided to the elderly in Chinese civilization can be constrasted with the practice of many nomadic societies of abandoning the aged and infirm. The key to understanding this variation has been well stated by Simmons:

> To put the matter somewhat bluntly, a satisfactory old age depends primarily on the amount of persuasion or coercion that may be exerted on the young and strong to serve and pay homage to the needs and interests of the old and physically feeble (1960:65).

The capacity of the aged to exert control over the young has been primarily determined by the mode of production characteristic of a given society (Goody, 1976:118). Of particular importance is the degree to which control over the means of production is concentrated or dispersed. As Simmons writes:

> ... whenever the existing property of a society becomes concentrated into the hands of a very small proportion of the population, and without adequate means of redistribution, its effectiveness as a means of participation for the majority of old people is greatly diminished. If concentration of property ownership is carried too far, large numbers of old people will become very dependent in an otherwise rich society (1960:77).

Simmons' argument can be illustrated by a comparison of the advanced agricultural and nascent industrial societies with the advanced capitalist societies.

The power of the aged appears to have reached its zenith in the most highly developed agricultural economies due to their systems of land-holding and inheritance (Simmons, 1960:74; McConnell, 1960:470; Goody, 1976:118). Here, the entrenched property rights of the elderly and the dependence of the young on eventual inheritance of this property to gain their own livelihood provided, in Goody's (1976:118) words, ". . . both a carrot for the young and a surety for the old." What was of critical importance for maintaining the status of the elderly was the timing of the transfer of productive property between generations. Its transmission at death provided the most secure basis for the authority of the aged whereas transmission prior to this (e.g., providing younger sons with a bride-price or daughters with a dowry) served to weaken the power of the senior generation (Goody, 1976:118).[2]

From the point of view of the elderly individual, control over productive property meant that retirement involved two separate processes — the first related to gradual withdrawal from productive activities, the second to the transmission of productive resources to the younger generation (Goody, 1976:119). The individual could control the timing and pace of withdrawal from productive activities, on the one hand, and continue to use his ownership rights over productive resources as a source of income and control over the younger generation, on the other. In peasant Europe, a widespread pattern of retirement took the form of a contract which legally bound the heir to provide his elderly parents with certain fixed items of consumption until death (Goody, 1976:120).

During the early period in the development of industrial capitalism a similar situation prevailed. Ownership of productive property was widely dispersed and inheritance a major factor in determining an individual's life chances. The subsequent development of all capitalist economies, however, was marked by the process which Marx referred to as the concentration and centralization of capital. Concretely, countries such as Canada and the U.S. changed from societies composed primarily of independent commodity producers (farmers, fishermen, craftsmen) and small businessmen to societies made up of wage and salary workers who, for the most part, own no productive property (see Mills, 1951; Johnson, 1972). For the small landholder, craftsman and businessman, retirement was a more complex process than simply leaving a job on a specified date. As in the advanced agricultural societies, withdrawal from work was under his control and occurred at a pace of his choosing. After such withdrawal had begun, rights of ownership over productive property could provide both a source of income and a source of control over potential heirs. Such a system might be described as an economic gerontocracy, a system dominated by the aged.

In advanced capitalist societies, in contrast, the majority of the young are dependent on the impersonal operation of the labor market, not their family of origin, to gain a livelihood. Familial resources tend to be transmitted primarily through differential access to education and social skills which enhance the individual's ability to compete in the labor market. This occurs relatively early in the family life cycle, however, and does nothing to enhance the relative power position of the elderly.

In addition, the elderly themselves become dependent on the sale of their labor power for survival, placing the older worker in a highly vulnerable position. This vulnerability of the elderly was already apparent in early 20th-century America. Lubove writes:

> . . . the capacity of the aged for self-support was being undermined. Changes in economic organization and family structure had relegated them to a marginal status in the modern industrial society. The key to the plight of the aged, Rubinow explained, was the increasing dependence of "the majority of mankind. . . upon a wage-contract for their means of existence." The wage-system led to economic superannuation in advance of "physiologic old age." It made no difference if the aged worker remained "fit for productive activity"; he experienced an abrupt and total economic disability if he fell "below the minimum level of productivity set by the employer" (1968:114-15).

For the wage and salary worker, retirement is no longer a process of gradual *withdrawal* from productive activities but, rather, an abrupt *exclusion* from the labor market. Such exclusion is not simply a function of the declining productivity of older workers. Indeed, in many occupations older workers tend to be more, not less, productive. Rather, the retirement of older workers has typically been introduced as a mechanism to solve crises of unemployment during periods of economic decline and recession (Kreps, 1976:279). Lowering the age of retirement and the use of "voluntary" early retirement programs clears the market of older, usually highly paid, workers, opens up mobility opportunities for younger workers and lowers the unemployment rate by limiting the number of those eligible to participate in the labor market.

Here then are the structural origins of the "problem of aging" in the Western capitalist nations. Since the majority of individuals in such societies are dependent on the labor market as their primary source of income, the problem arises as to how those excluded from the labor market are to survive.[3] A small minority of the elderly succeed in accumulating sufficient assets during their work lives to become small rentier capitalists, a sort of "lumpenbourgeoisie" (Mills, 1951), who survive on income from savings and investments. The majority become state dependents, relying on government transfer payments for their income. They make up a major portion of the new lumpenproletariat or what O'Connor (1970) refers to as the postindustrial proletariat, composed of those strata which neither participate in the productive process nor compete for jobs with those that do.

In sum, the problems of the elderly which become manifest at the level of consumption in the form of low incomes originate at the level of production. By virtue of their exclusion from the labor market (an exclusion sanctioned by law) and limited ownership of productive property, the elderly have come to pose a special problem for all advanced capitalist nations. A variety of solutions to deal with this problem have been proposed and implemented. Indeed, a history of the evolution of the myriad pension schemes found in the Western capitalist nations is almost synonymous with the history of the modern welfare state (Wilensky, 1975). In subsequent sections I shall attempt to identify some of the fundamental distinguishing characteristics of these different solutions and in so doing delimit the Canadian response. Since, however, the liberal democracies have placed considerable emphasis on individual solutions and the role of personal savings in meeting the exigencies of old age, it is here that we shall begin our discussion.

Saving for Retirement

The view that individuals should be self-dependent and provide for their old age through personal savings has played an important role in the development of welfare policies of the capitalist nations in general and the Anglo-American democracies in particular (see Rimlinger, 1971). Such a view tends to be held by those imbued with the traditional values of liberal philosophy with its emphasis on individual liberty on the one hand, and the notions of self-help and self-reliance, on the other. In the early part of the twentieth century, Frederick L. Hoffman of Prudential Life Insurance expressed these notions clearly when he argued that the provision of income security measures for the aged would strike at the "root of national life and character" by destroying the nation's "capacity for suffering, self-sacrifice, and self-denial." In his view, the prospect of old age dependency was the "most powerful incentive which makes for character and growth in a democracy" (quoted by Lubove, 1968:117). Lest we think that such views are the product of a bygone age, it is instructive to listen to the 1966 Carter Commission on Tax Reform (quoted by Brown, 1975:111):

> It seems to be generally argued that individuals should set aside a portion of their income in the working years to ensure an adequate command over goods and services in their retirement years. Such private provisions for retirement are thought to foster self-reliance and to reduce the need for the state to provide relief.

More recently, Marc Lalonde (1973:4), in his capacity of Minister of Health and Welfare, remarked:

> ...we believe that Canadians hold the value of *independence* or self-dependence. They expect to meet their own needs through their own efforts, and they expect others to do their best to do the same.

As Brown (1975:111) notes, however, this "bland assumption that all of the population have an adequate margin in their income for saving suggests a certain detachment from the realities of daily living." Based on her examination of income and expenditure data for Canada, Brown (1975:114) concludes that only those highly paid individuals in the top quintile of the income distribution are in a position to put funds aside for their old age. For the majority, current income is consumed in meeting the exigencies of daily living. In a similar attempt to evaluate the role of savings in solving the problem of low income in old age, Kreps (1971:116) concludes that "...the role that can be played by private savings would appear to be a very limited one for families whose incomes during work life fall below the median.... Even when the marginal propensity to save is quite high...savings adequate to maintain the targeted level of consumption are not forthcoming."

For those who are able to save significant amounts the problem is not resolved, however. On the one hand, the *real* value of savings is eroded by inflation while, on the other, their *relative* value is eroded by economic growth. Assuming a rather modest inflation rate of 4%, the real value of $100 at age 65 will be worth only $68 by age 75. An 8% inflation rate will make the same $100 worth only $46 by age 75.

Even in the absence of inflationary effects, the relative value of individual savings (i.e., relative to the standard of living in the larger society) will decline unless there is zero growth in the economy. Since economic growth means that each successive cohort has higher average earnings than the one which precedes it, the concentration of the elderly in the lower end of the income distribution is virtually guaranteed if personal savings are relied on as the major source of income. As Kreps notes:

> ...while growth raises the living standards of workers and owners of capital each year, the real income of the aged person is fixed throughout retirement unless he or she is one of the small percentage of retirees who own equities (1976:277).

Kreps estimates that even with a rather modest growth rate of 2% a year, a worker who saves at a rate to provide him or herself with 100% of current consumption would, by age 75, have a consumption level equal to 48% of that of a worker still in the labor force. Hence while inflation eats away at the real value of personal savings, economic growth reduces their relative value in the economy as a whole.

In general, then, individual effort to meet one's own needs in old age is an illusory one, particularly under conditions of economic growth and/or inflation. The wages and salaries available to most individuals during their working lives are, at best, adequate to meet day-to-day requirements and not sufficient to provide for a prolonged period of withdrawal from the labor market. In all Western countries, therefore, the elderly have become a

Table 1

Major Source of Personal Income, Population 65 and Over Not in the Labor Force by Family Status, Canada 1971

		Family Status			Total
	Head	*Spouse*	*Child*	*Not in Families*	
No income	.84	4.98	15.38	1.55	2.09
Wages and salaries	9.13	2.54	3.85	4.74	5.58
Self-employment	2.47	.48	0	.92	1.29
Government transfer payments	59.93	80.89	61.54	72.68	70.59
Retirement pensions	14.88	1.70	11.54	6.65	8.07
Investment	11.67	8.51	7.7	11.82	11.07
Other	1.09	.90	0	1.62	1.31
	100%	100%	100%	100%	100%
	(n = 4415)	(n = 3114)	(n = 26)	(n = 7262)	(n = 14817)

Source: Computed from Public Use Sample Tapes, Individual File, 1971 Census of Canada.

population which is by and large dependent on government transfer payments for survival. This fact is illustrated for the Canadian case in Table 1, which presents data on the major source of personal income for Canada's elderly population who were not in the labor force in 1971. Personal savings, whether in the form of investments or private retirement pensions, were the major source of income for only 26% of elderly heads of families and 19.14% of all elderly individuals not in the labor market. Government transfer payments, on the other hand, were the major source of income for approximately 60% of family heads and 70.59% of all elderly individuals.

In view of the singular importance of the state and state policy in determining the distribution of income among the elderly, this is clearly a topic which warrants our attention. It is in this area, moreover, where we shall find the specific nature of the Canadian response to the problem of income maintenance in old age. Although the elderly occupy a similar class location at the level of production in the advanced capitalist countries, at the level of consumption there is considerable variation in the fate of the elderly as a result of differential patterns of state intervention.

The Aged, the State, and the Structure of Inequality

For the majority of individuals in capitalist societies, position in the income distribution is determined for the most part by the resources and skills which they bring to the labor market to compete for occupational positions to which differential rewards are attached. During the preretirement years, a structure of income inequality emerges as a result of differential location in the occupational structure. To some degree, the inequalities which are created during the preretirement years will persist into the postretirement period as a result of differential accumulation of assets. As we have noted, however, such assets are quickly eroded and government transfer payments constitute the major source of income for the majority of the elderly. It is clear, therefore, that public policy, rather than market forces, is the major factor determining the structure of inequality in old age. Moreover, the policy decisions which become embedded in public pension structures are crucial for understanding not only the income inequalities which exist *within* the elderly population but also those which exist *between* the elderly and younger generations.

The pension structures of the Western countries developed historically in accordance with two different conceptions of the role of old age pensions. The earliest old age pension scheme, initiated by Bismarck in late 19th-century Germany, was organized along occupational lines. The so-called "Bismarck" countries developed pension schemes in which both contributions and benefits were closely tied to preretirement earnings. Such a pension structure is designed to perpetuate into old age the income differentials among individuals which existed during the preretirement years.

The second tradition is associated with the principles set out by Lord Beveridge that served as the basis for postwar reconstruction in Great Britain. The central idea of the Beveridge report was the concept of the national minimum benefit (see Rimlinger, 1971:149). All citizens, irrespective of social position, were to be provided with the same guarantee of an income sufficient for subsistence. Social security provisions were to be egalitarian in the sense that all recipients were to be treated alike — provided the same level of benefits— irrespective of past earnings or contributions. The intent was to construct a social order based on equality of citizenship rather than on the privileges of class. As Rimlinger (1971:150) suggests: "The social insurance system thus becomes an important instrument of social unification by helping to overcome lingering class antagonisms."

Equality, however, can be a two-edged sword. Although the flat-rate benefits paid under the Beveridge principle minimize inequality *within* the elderly population, they may simultaneously increase inequalities *between* the older and younger generations if benefit levels are low. The elderly will be equal but they will be equally poor within an otherwise wealthy society. In sum, pension systems have an effect both on the degree of inequality which prevails within the elderly population (intragenerational inequality) and between the elderly population and the larger society (intergenerational inequality). The nature of these effects are a function of two major variables. The first we shall refer to as the relative benefit level, that is, the average benefit level relative to the average standard of living in the society as a whole. Intergenerational inequality is inversely related to the relative benefit level. If the average relative benefit level is high, intergenerational inequality will be low because the standard of living of the elderly will approximate that which prevails in the larger society. Conversely, if the relative benefit level is low, intergenerational inequality will be high and the elderly will tend to be concentrated at the bottom of the income distribution.

The second variable concerns the structure of the plan, that is, whether it is of the flat benefit type or graduated in accordance with preretirement income differences. The flat benefit type minimizes intragenerational inequality while the graduated type reproduces preretirement inequalities during the post-retirement years.

Cross-classification of these two variables produces four ideal-typical pension systems. These four types and their associated consequences for the structure of both intragenerational and intergenerational inequality are summarized in Table 2. As Table 2 suggests, a flat benefit structure in which the relative benefit level is high would minimize both intragenerational and intergenerational inequalities. In general, however, most countries which have opted for the flat benefit structure have also opted for a benefit level at, or close to, a national minimum subsistence level (the intent of the Beveridge report) that tends to minimize intragenerational inequality but reinforces intergenerational inequality. The elderly tend to be equal but poor.

Irrespective of relative benefit levels, pension systems in which benefits are steeply graduated preserve a high degree of intragenerational inequality. However, if relative benefit levels are high, intergenerational inequality is minimized and the elderly are prevented from becoming a distinctive status group in the larger society. The level of consumption of a retired plumber will be much like that of a plumber still in the labor force particularly if benefits are indexed to increases in wages and salaries (see below).

Table 2

Pension Systems and the Structure of Inequality

Characteristics of the Pension System		Consequences for the Structure of Inequality	
Relative Benefit Level	*Pension Structure*	*Intragenerational Inequality*	*Intergenerational Inequality*
High	Flat	Low	Low
Low	Flat	Low	High
High	Graduated	High	Low
Low	Graduated	High	High

Most pension structures in existence today have in fact combined elements of the two systems. Those systems which originally began with a flat benefit structure have gradually added on a graduated structure to supplement these minimum benefits, and similarly, most countries provide some minimum guarantee to their elderly citizens. Despite this convergence, however, the pension systems of the Western capitalist nations can still be differentiated according to which of the four types outlined above they most closely approximate. Where does Canada fit into this typology? In order to address this question it is necessary to familiarize ourselves with the basic components of the Canadian old age pension system. Our summary will be brief and the reader is referred to more detailed discussions of the topic to be found elsewhere (see especially Brown, 1975: Schulz et al., 1974; Statistics Canada, 1978b).

The first major legislation related to income for the elderly in Canada was the Annuities Act passed in 1908, which provided pensions on a voluntary basis at a lower cost than the going commercial rates but was viewed "...as a species of insurance and a means of promoting thrift rather than as a type of social legislation or state aid" (Wallace, 1952:127). In 1927, the Old Age Pension Act was passed, by which the federal government offered to reimburse 50% of the costs to any province willing to inaugurate a pension scheme of its own. By 1936 the last of the provinces was included in the program. As Herman notes with respect to the Act:

> The scheme itself was in the nature of poor relief in that a stringent means test was involved and the amount of the pension ($20 per month) was intended to cover minimal needs only (1971:135).

It was not until the Old Age Security Act was passed in 1951 that old age assistance became available to the general population. It provided a flat $40 per month benefit for all those over 70 years of age. Under the Old Age Assistance Act the means-tested benefits of the 1927 Act were maintained for those aged 65 to 69. The age at which one could become eligible for benefits under the Old Age Security Act was gradually reduced until 1970 when it became age 65, thus eliminating the means-tested Old Age Assistance Act. As of January 1978 monthly benefits under the act were $153.44 or $1,841.28 per year. Since 1973 the pension level has been adjusted quarterly to reflect rises in the cost of living. Initially a 2% limit was set, but in 1974 this limit was removed so that it is now indexed by the full amount of the consumer price index quarterly. Finally, in June 1975, the legislation was amended to provide an income-tested spouses allowance for persons aged 60 to 65 who are married to Old Age Security pensioners.

In 1967, the Guaranteed Income Supplement (GIS) was also introduced as an interim measure until the 1966 Canada and Quebec Pensions Plans (see below) could come into effect. It subsequently became a permanent plan and provides a monthly income-tested supplement to pensioners who have little or no other income than that provided by Old Age Security. As of January 1978 single and one-pensioner families eligible for the full supplement received $107.62 per month and two-pensioner families $191.12. The GIS is also indexed by the consumer price index. In addition to OAS and GIS most provinces provide additional means-tested supplement to the population 65 and over (see Brown, 1975:130-32). The combination of these programs provides a flat benefit-type basis to the Canadian old age pension structure.

The final component of the federal system is the Canada Pension Plan (in Quebec, the Quebec Pension Plan), which came into effect in 1966. Participation in the plan is mandatory and both contributions and benefits are wage related. In principle then, the C/QPP had the effect of welding a graduated structure onto a basic flat benefit system. The graduated aspect of the plan is mitigated, however, by an earnings ceiling which is placed on contributions (and hence benefits). Above this level ($9,600 in 1978) the plan effectively becomes a flat benefit system. Since the majority of workers have annual salaries above the ceiling, its overall effect tends to be that of a flat benefit system, reproducing in old age only those inequalities which prevailed in the lower end of the income distribution during the pre-retirement years. In contrast to the pension structures found in countries such as West Germany and Austria, where benefits are steeply graduated even into the higher income levels, the Canadian public pension system more closely approximates a flat benefit type system with some gradation in the lower end of the income distribution. In comparative terms, Canadian public pension policy may be said to minimize intragenerational inequality and in this sense is egalitarian.[4] In contrast, the German system of occupational pensions is inegalitarian in the sense that it is deliberately designed to preserve preretirement income inequalities during the retirement years (see Menzies, 1974).

Although the elderly in Canada may be relatively equal in comparison to other Western countries, the data presented at the beginning of this paper suggests that they are also poor, that is, that intergenerational inequality is high. This, as we have seen, is a reflection of the relative benefit levels of such a system. How does Canada compare to the other Western countries in this respect? Establishing exact empirical equivalences across countries with respect to income and benefits is a notoriously difficult exercise. Many benefits provided to the elderly are not in the form of pensions (e.g., housing subsidies) or may be hidden in taxation schedules. Several studies of the topic, however, suggest that until recently the relative benefits levels provided by the Canadian public pension system have been low by international standards (Schulz et al., 1974; Union of Swiss Banks, 1977; OECD,

1976). For comparative purposes the OECD (1976) uses a measure called the transfer ratio which is conceptually equivalent to our concept of relative benefit levels. It is constructed by dividing the average payment per pensioner by Gross Domestic Product (GDP) per head. For example, an average pension of $500 would be considered less generous in a society where GDP per head is $5,000 (transfer ratio = .10) than in a society where GDP per head is only $1,000 (transfer ratio = .50). By this criterion Canada ranked fourteenth out of the 17 advanced capitalist countries included in the study (OECD, 1976:22). The Canadian transfer ratio for 1972 was .291 whereas for West Germany it was .655. When relative benefit levels were computed on the basis of average earnings rather than GDP per head, Canada still ranked fourteenth out of the 17 countries (OECD, 1976:23). When survivors' benefits are considered, that is, benefits provided to a spouse and family members on the death of the major breadwinner, Canada tends to fare even worse in the international spectrum. In a ten-country comparison conducted by the Union of Swiss Banks (1977:14) Canada ranked last in the relative benefit level provided to widows and remaining family members. This factor is of course particularly important for elderly women, who will be discussed separately below. In effect, then, Canadian public pension policy has produced an elderly population which is equal but poor. This is not to say that there will be no income inequalities among the elderly, only that in comparative terms the Canadian public pension system does not reinforce these inequalities to the degree found in many Western pension systems. At the same time, however, it has exacerbated the degree of inequality between the older and younger generations with the result that the elderly have become a distinctive status group in the larger society rather than being evenly distributed throughout the income hierarchy. In Canada, growing old has also implied a process of growing poor.

More recent data indicate that this picture is changing somewhat as a result of the maturation of the C/QPP. In a 12-country comparison, Haanes-Olsen (1978) found that among the countries studied, the Canadian replacement ratio (i.e., the ratio of post-retirement to pre-retirement income of an average industrial worker) had the highest rate of growth between 1965 and 1975. Whereas in 1972 the replacement ratio for a married couple (i.e., when spouses' benefits are included) was .42, by 1975 it had risen to .57. In effect, for those who have recently retired, relative benefit levels are somewhat higher than for those who retired in earlier years. It will take some time, however, before the effects of this change will show up in the income data for the elderly population as a whole. As of March 1977 only 34.9% of all old age security pensioners were receiving payments from the C/QPP (Statistics Canada, 1978b:175). Moreover, in view of the relatively low cutoff point of the C/QPP, the average relative benefit level will continue to fall below that of most Western European systems.

Thus far our analysis of pension policy and inequality has been done from a purely static point of view; that is, we have considered the consequences of alternative pension systems on the structure of inequality as they would appear on the basis of a synchronic comparative analysis. In order to complete our discussion it is necessary to consider pension policy from a dynamic or diachronic perspective. From the point of view of the elderly individual it is equally important to consider the manner in which a given pension system will maintain or alter his or her economic status over the retirement portion of the life cycle. The crucial variable from this perspective is the manner in which social security benefits are indexed, that is, the way in which they are adjusted over time to take into account changes in the economy as a whole.

Let us begin by considering a pension program which is not indexed, which tends to be the case in private rather than public sector pensions. A worker retires at age 65 and receives a pension, say, of $200 a month until death. As noted above in our discussion of individual savings, over time the real value (i.e., the actual purchasing power) of this benefit will be eroded by inflation while its relative value (i.e., relative to the standard of living in the larger society) will be eroded by economic growth. As we have seen, however, Canadian public pensions are indexed against inflation using the Consumer Price Index as a guide. This is intended to keep the absolute values of benefits intact.[5] In order to maintain the *relative* value of benefits, however, it is necessary to index benefits to increases in the standard of living, because historically wages and salaries have risen faster than inflation. A pension system which does not increase benefit levels in accordance with increases in wages and salaries is effectively lowering relative benefit levels each year and hence increasing the level of inequality between the elderly pensioners and those still in the labor force. The differences in the two forms of indexing can be quite substantial. Expressed as a percentage of the Consumer Price Index (in 1974 constant dollars) the basic old age pension (OAS) rose from 73.94 in 1951 to 108.14 in 1974. However, expressed as a percentage of wages and salaries there was a decline from 17.0 in 1951 to 14.0 in 1974 (Statistics Canada, 1976:283). In effect, while the absolute value of OAS increased its relative value declined. Since the introduction of the Guaranteed Income Supplement in 1967, the combined OAS and GIS as a percentage of Consumer Price Index (in 1974 dollars) increased from 149.12 (1967-68) to 180.19 (1974-75). However, as a percentage of average wages and salaries it remained relatively unchanged — 23.2 in 1967-68 and 23.4 in 1974-75 (Statistics Canada, 1976:284). What this implies at the individual level is that while pensions indexed to inflation keep the absolute value of the pensioner's income intact, the absence of wage-indexed pensions reduces its relative value in the society as a whole by the amount that increases in the standard of living exceed inflation. In effect, the elderly are denied a share of the increased wealth resulting from economic growth. Here too, the Canadian elderly fare poorly in comparison with the elderly in those Western European countries (e.g., West Germany, Austria) where pensions are indexed to wages and salaries and where in principle such a decline is avoided.[6]

In summary, then, Canadian public pension policy has not greatly departed from the original Beveridge principal of providing a minimal subsistence level income for Canada's elderly population. Although the C/QPP introduced an element of gradation to the system and raised relative benefit levels somewhat, the overall effect continues to be that of a flat benefit structure. Canada's adherence to such a structure is based less on notions of classlessness, however, than on the continued commitment of Canadian policy makers to leave a substantial portion of the pension field intact for the private sector to exploit.[7] It is this commitment that underlies the relatively low cutoff point of the C/QPP. Workers who earn above this level — and they are the majority — must turn elsewhere to find ways of maintaining their standard of living in old age. In order to understand this aspect of the Canadian system it is necessary to examine the broader role which pensions and pension policy play in the economies of the advanced capitalist countries. As Warham (1970:58) suggests, social policy is usually designed to solve both the problems of the individuals at whom such policies are directed and the problems of the larger society. Thus far we have considered the degree to which Canadian pension policy resolves or fails to resolve the problems of Canada's elderly population. In order to understand the origins and evolution of these policies, however, it is necessary to shift our level of analysis to the larger society which has produced these policies.

Pensions and Power

In general, the role which pensions and pension funds have played and continue to play in the management of the capitalist economies is not widely understood. Frequently, the rapid expansion of social security for the aged is seen as a more or less natural response of modern democratic political systems to a new "need" and constituency created as a result of industrialization, that is, an increasing number of old people without alternative means of support. To think of pensions simply in terms of their welfare function for individuals, however, is to miss the larger social function which they have played in the development of capitalist societies.

State pensions for the elderly were first introduced in Bismarck's Germany at the end of the 19th century as a weapon in Bismarck's struggle to preserve the traditional German system of political inequality (Rimlinger, 1971:112). Faced with a highly militant labor movement and the emerging power of the Marxist-oriented Social Democrats, social protection and, in particular, social security for the aged was to be used as a vehicle for containing the threat of incipient class warfare. As Rimlinger (1971:121) notes: "Bismarck aimed at the dual objective of lessening worker discontent and of increasing their stake in the stability of the existing order." As Bismarck argued before the Reichstag (quoted by Rimlinger, 1971:121):

> I will consider it a great advantage when we have 700,000 small pensioners drawing their annuities from the state, especially if they belong to those classes who otherwise do not have much to lose by an upheaval and erroneously believe they can actually gain much by it.

In the U.S., Roosevelt's Social Security Act came during a period of widespread unemployment, discontent and a nationally organized grassroots movement, the Townsend Movement, whose objective was the introduction of an income security program for the aged (see Piven and

Cloward, 1971). In his analysis of the introduction of social security in Britain and Sweden, Heclo (1974:291) concludes that first and foremost those programs were seen "... as a palliative technique to prevent social unrest and diminish the appeal of socialism." In effect, social security for the aged has been an important instrument utilized by the capitalist state in creating and maintaining social harmony, that is, in fulfilment of its legitimation function (O'Connor, 1973:6).

During the postwar period, however, pensions and pension policy have become an equally, and perhaps more, important instrument in the process of capital formation and accumulation. In Sweden, for example, the National Pension Insurance, created as a result of legislation which went into effect in 1960, accounted for approximately 46% of total advances on the Swedish credit market in fiscal year 1970-71 (Martin, 1973:18). In effect, the fund has become a singularly important tool in the Swedish government's management of the national economy.

Considerations of capital accumulation have been crucial in the development of all income security programs which grew up in Canada during the postwar period. Such reforms as the Family Allowance Act (1944) and Old Age Security (1951) were clearly seen as part of the Keynesian solution for the survival of capitalism through state regulation of the business cycle. The key to this solution was to increase the rate of private capital accumulation by maintaining a sufficiently high level of consumer demand. This could be done by putting money into the hands of those individuals most likely to spend it — parents with families, the aged, etc. The influential Marsh report (the Canadian equivalent of the Beveridge report) noted:

> The final point in gauging the need and validity of a social security programme in post-war Canada is only indirectly a welfare matter at all, but it is a strategic factor in economic policy generally whose importance cannot be over-emphasized. One of the necessities for economic stability is the maintenance of the flow of purchasing-power at the time when munitions and other factories are closing down... (Marsh, 1943:16).

In a similar vein the federal government pointed out in its proposals for the Dominion-Provincial Conference on Reconstruction of 1945 (quoted by Goffman, 1967:205):

> A significant volume of social security payments flowing into the consumer spending stream will stabilize the economy as a whole and work against a fall in national income. Social security payments, therefore, become a powerful weapon with which to ward off general economic depression.

In short, while at the end of the war the problem of legitimation was not one to be taken lightly, particularly in view of the recent successes of the CCF party in Ontario and Saskatchewan, attention was clearly focused on the potential of social security programs to deal with the problem of capital accumulation.

Although there had been a demand for a wage-related contributory scheme in 1951 (Bryden, 1974:137) it was not until 1965, with the introduction of the Canada/Quebec Pension Plan, that such a scheme was instituted. It was not until the accumulation potential of a contributing program was clearly recognized that it was implemented. The plan came about through a long, complex and frequently dramatic series of federal-provincial negotiations which have been discussed in detail by Simeon (1972). While there had been considerable pressure from Canadian labor for such a plan for some time it is clear that once again it was the accumulation potential of the plan, not the benefits it would provide to pensioners, that was instrumental in leading to its implementation.

Federal and provincial officials who were responsible for negotiating the plan were not from the welfare arms of their respective governments but from their finance departments. As Simeon notes:

> ...they looked at the legislation not as pension or welfare experts but as government finance experts. This meant that in the federal-provincial negotiation there was relatively little attention paid to many important aspects of the plan, and more paid to such matters as disposition of the fund, which was largely irrelevant to the goodness or badness of the plan from the point of view of the contributor (1972:152).

What the Canada Pension Plan ultimately provided was not primarily an improved income maintenance program for the aged but "... a vehicle for providing capital funds to provinces to finance economic development..." (Collins, 1975:243). The huge funds that would be created through employer and employee contributions to the Plan were clearly intended to provide a cheap source of new capital for the provincial governments. They would be allowed to borrow from the fund at interest rates which were lower than those prevailing in the regular bond market. As one provincial official involved in the negotiations remarked (quoted by Simeon, 1972:176):

> The main reason for us was the creation of a large fund. It would provide money for development here and give us more liberty in the money markets. The fund was certainly the main reason for me; it was *the* reason.

The C/QPP was the product of a power struggle between Ottawa and the provinces over the issue of fiscal decentralization and the establishment of a new basis of capital formation at the provincial level. It was a struggle which the provinces clearly won (Simeon, 1972:258). During the four years to March 31, 1974 the CPP had furnished 38% of all provincial borrowing and had, in the words of its advisory committee (quoted by Calvert, 1977:85) become "the backbone of provincial debt financing." For the short term at least, receipts from the CPP far exceed payments to the elderly and as a result have become a major instrument in combating what O'Connor (1973) has labeled the fiscal crisis of the state. In Canada, as in Europe, postwar pension policy has become a crucial factor affecting the state's ability to manage the economy and secure revenues for state expenditures. The funds created through the contributions of workers become available not only for welfare purposes but also to provide the necessary infrastructure for further economic expansion.

What distinguishes Canada (and the U.S.) from most Western European countries, however, is the extent to which the pension field (and hence the pension fund) has been left as an area for the private sector to develop and exploit. Whereas in most West European countries private pension schemes play a relatively minor role in the provision of income for the elderly, Canadian pension policy has been deliberately constructed so as to leave a large share of the pension field to the private sector. As noted previously, this is reflected in the overall flat benefit structure of Canadian public pensions which encourages the development of private plans. Such a policy strategy is not based on consideration of the relative merits of private versus public schemes in meeting the needs of the elderly but rather on the more fundamental issue of who is to control the process of capital formation in Canada, the private sector or the state. As Martin (1973:18) has pointed out, the major issue in the determination of pension policy is the basic structure of the capital market and who controls the funds flowing through it.

As the Canadian business class is well aware, any expansion or improvement in public sector pensions involves a transfer of power from the business class to the Canadian state. While it is widely recognized that many of the problems inherent in existing private pension arrangements (see below) would be overcome by the elimination of all private industrial pensions and the creation of a single national government pension scheme, such a system would effectively starve the private sector of its major source of investment capital, the private pension fund. Based on findings of a study conducted by J.A.G. Grant, chief economist of Wood Gundy Ltd., Calvert concludes that for the period to 1985:

> From 70%-80% of all the new capital needed by industry in Canada, and raised through new bond and stock issues is expected to be furnished by the private pension funds (1977:42-43).

As Calvert, a major spokesman for the business community on the issue of pensions, goes on to note:

> The heavy reliance of the Canadian economy on the growth of the private, actuarially funded pension plans as a source of needed new capital is a fact of life which has to be reckoned with in considering any proposals to change or expand the C/QPP in any manner which would result in a curtailment or slowdown in the growth of these private plans (1977:44).

Indeed, in Calvert's view (1977:44), the C/QPP is to be criticized not for the inadequate benefit levels it provides but because it makes "no contribution at all to capital formation."[8]

The problem is a serious one, which provides the context for a major struggle that must surely occur over the next decade. We noted above that the C/QPP has become the backbone of provincial debt financing because of the current excess of receipts from contribution over payments made to the retired. The excess is a short-term phenomenon, however. Over the next decade there will be a convergence between receipts and payments, thereby depriving the provinces of this source of capital, at which point it will be necessary to expand the pension fund or significantly alter the structure of provincial financing. Any expansion of the fund, however, will generate a major conflict with the Canadian business class since, as Calvert points out, such expansion must occur at the expense of the private plans that are the business community's major source of new investment capital. Indeed the conflict has already reached the level of a cold war, as witnessed by the comments directed at government by the business community's representatives in the media. In its lead editorial of October 12, 1977, for example, the *Globe and Mail* stated:

> Government is already too deep into pension plans — and the savings they represent — for the good of Canada's economic future. We need more savings...but the savings should be in a variety of hands and not subject to the political vagaries of government.

Pension policy, then, is not primarily an issue of individual welfare but rather an issue of power, power to control and allocate the capital generated through the savings put aside by workers for their old age. The business community fears the consequences of these funds falling subject to the "political vagaries of government" and the general increase in government control over the economy that would follow. The alternative is continued and increased reliance on private sector plans. While this may solve the problems of the business community, will it solve the economic problems of the elderly? It is to this issue that we shall turn next.

Pensions and Profits

For the majority of workers, the current government strategy of leaving room for the private sector has not been a particularly effective one. In 1971, only 27.5% of all males and 10.5% of all females over 65 reported receiving income from private retirement pensions (Rashid, 1977:44). As of 1976, only 38.8% of all paid workers in the labor force were covered by private pension plans (Statistics Canada, 1978a:23). Coverage by the industrial sector is very uneven. Virtually all government employees are covered, while in trade and commerce less than 14% of paid workers were covered in 1976 (Statistics Canada, 1978a:23). Pension coverage is also directly related to job status (Cliffin and Martin, 1977:53) and income (Munro, 1977:453). Many of those covered, moreover, will not actually collect full benefits as a result of vesting provisions, which require the worker to have reached a specified age and specified years of service with the firm before being legally entitled to the employer's contribution to the fund. The most usual criteria is attainment of age 45 and completion of 10 years of service. This means that workers in occupations characterized by high levels of job mobility or periodic unemployment will never receive full benefits. Moreover, the majority of private pension schemes are indexed neither to wages nor inflation.[9] The issues of vesting and indexing are the obvious weaknesses of private sector plans from the point of view of employees. It is instructive, therefore, to examine their implications from the point of view of employers and Canadian capitalists generally.

Through the private pension fund the owners of Canadian industry are able to borrow back wages which have already been paid out to workers for investment in their enterprises. Curiously, it may appear, the capitalist class has put itself deeply in debt to its working-class creditors. At first glance, the pension fund might appear to represent a means whereby workers are able to share in and benefit from the further development and growth of the Canadian economy. Indeed, for Peter Drucker (1977), writing of the comparable situation in the United States, this fact represents the arrival of "pension fund socialism" and a fundamental transformation of the social relations of capitalist society. Such a transformation has occurred only at the level of appearances, however. Drucker confounds appearances with reality by first of all assuming that legal ownership of the means of production (the owners of private pension plans hold 30% of the American economy, according to Drucker) is equivalent to actual economic control. More importantly, however, his analysis masks the true significance of the private pension fund, namely that is has become a mechanism by which capitalists are able to reappropriate a significant portion of the wages already paid out to workers, thereby reducing the overall wage bill and enhancing profits. In effect the private pension fund has become an efficient mechanism for simultaneously securing and obscuring surplus value, to use Burawoy's (1978) terminology. How does this occur?

The corporate pension fund consists of assets contributed by both employers and employees, from which pension benefits are to be paid to the worker on retirement. It is generally agreed (see Pesando and Rea, 1977:10-11) that such benefits simply constitute a deferred wage which accrues to the worker on retirement, irrespective of the combination of employer/employee contributions that go into the fund. The question, then, is whether workers actually recoup these deferred wages and if not, to whom do these assets accrue? The answer is that at present only a portion of these wages is returned to workers, while the balance flows into the hands of Canadian capitalists. As such, the pension fund is a means of securing surplus value. An obvious mechanism through which this occurs is vesting provisions. The overall wage bill is lowered since in many instances such wages are never paid out. The second mechanism through which this is accomplished, however — inflation — is both more important and at the same time tends to obscure or hide the fact that such a transfer is taking place.[10]

When the real value of an individual's savings or assets is eroded through inflation, the value lost simply seems to disappear because no direct transfer from one individual to another has occurred. The real value of such wealth, however, is simply redistributed. In general, inflation tends to redistribute wealth from lenders to borrowers. As Pesando and Rea (1977) have shown, it is precisely this process which has made the private pension fund a mechanism for transferring wealth from Canadian workers to Canadian capitalists.

Through their investments in pension funds, the vast majority of employees suffer a real loss in the value of their assets in both the preretirement and postretirement years (Pesando and Rea, 1977:48). This occurs during the *preretirement* years since there is currently no available investment vehicle which is neutral with respect to inflation (Pesando and Rea, 1977:39). When the worker retires the real value of his or her savings has been eroded considerably, thus reducing the value of the benefits upon which he or she can draw. Final earnings plans (plans in which benefits are calculated on the basis of the employee's earnings at the time of retirement) prevent erosion during the preretirement years by transferring the costs of inflation to the employer (Pesando and Rea, 1977:30).[11] However, less than one percent of all plan members had such coverage in 1976 (Statistics Canada, 1978a:37). Indeed, until recently, tax regulations discouraged the growth of such plans. *After retirement*, the pensioner continues to suffer a net loss in real wealth since the pension is fixed in nominal dollars. Fully indexed pensions would prevent such a loss.

To whom does the wealth lost through inflation accrue? Pesando and Rea (1977:41) conclude that only under certain conditions will it accrue to the individual employer (e.g., by lowering his or her real costs of purchasing an annuity for the employee).[12] More generally, the beneficiaries of the wealth transfer will be the issuers of fixed income securities — Canadian finance capitalists. Hence, the transfer is not only hidden from workers but from many individual employers as well.

Just how much of workers' wages are reappropriated in this way is not known. In a discussion of the American situation, Epstein (1977) suggests that pension funds invested in the stock market (about two-thirds of all funds in the U.S.) lost nearly two-thirds of their real value between 1964 and 1974, assuming that pension fund investments did about as well as the market as a whole. Epstein concludes:

> ...from the point of view of the poor pensioners, private enterprise seems to have done them in as effectively as it seems to have done in the public employees of the City of New York who have also become through the purchase of city bonds on their behalf the unwilling part owners of an economy whose former proprietors are trying energetically to abandon it (1977:37).

In view of the important role of inflation in converting the private pension fund into a subsidy for Canadian capitalists, it is hardly surprising that a major object of the private sector's attack on government is the indexed pension plan currently provided to government workers. Should such a habit spread to the private sector a major source of income would be lost. It is argued by the business community that it is impossible for business to provide fully indexed plans which will be actuarially sound, that is, in which payments will be less than or equal to revenues over the long term. As Pesando and Rea (1977:53) point out, however, such an argument simply points to the fact that the investment vehicles made available by the private sector (corporate stocks and bonds) are inadequate for the task. Clearly then, it is the economic vagaries of the business community of which the elderly should beware.

In sum, Canadian workers are being called upon to make their savings available, via the pension fund, to provide the major source of fuel for Canada's economic growth. Not only are they being deprived of the benefits of such future growth because pensions are not indexed to changes in the standard of living, but they are being asked not to require that the full value of their investment be returned, since neither pension funds nor pension benefits are indexed to inflation.

A Note on Women and Pensions

Thus far, little attention has been given to differences which exist within the elderly population. Rather, I have dealt with the elderly population as a whole in considering the structures which determine their economic fate. I should be remiss however, in passing over the special situation of elderly women in contemporary Canada. A comprehensive and excellent review of this topic has been presented elsewhere by Collins (1978) and I shall limit this discussion to some of the highlights of his analysis.[13]

As a result of the greater life expectancy of females, the elderly population is disproportionately female. In 1971, the ratio of females to males among those over 65 was 1.23 and this gap is expected to widen (Collins, 1978:23). As noted earlier, in 1975 approximately 59% of unattached (widowed, single, and divorced) females between 65 and 69 were below the poverty line of $3,998 established by the Senate Committee on Poverty and among those aged 70 and over, the figure was 78%.

Only 28% of women in the total labor force were covered by pension plans in 1974 (Collins, 1978:61) and the majority of these were in government jobs. Vesting regulations which require an employee to be 45 years of age and have 10 years of service to become eligible for employer contributions hit female workers, who have high turnover rates, especially hard. These regulations will deprive many of those covered from ever collecting full benefits. For the majority of women, survivor benefits from their husbands' pensions are particularly important. In 1974, however, less than half of the male labor force covered by private programs (who were in turn a minority of all males in the labor force) were in programs which provided a widow's pension. Hence, the inadequacies of private sector pensions become even more acute when considered from the point of view of the aging female. As a result, the majority of unattached elderly females (and the majority of women will eventually become "unattached" through widowhood) must rely almost exclusively on federal pension schemes (OAS, GIS, C/QPP) and provincial income supplements. As noted above, survivor benefits available under public programs in Canada are among the lowest in the Western world. Canada's elderly women, then, suffer from the double burden of ageism and sexism.

The Economic Status of the Canadian Elderly: Past, Present, and Future

The past several decades of Canadian history have seen considerable growth and expansion of social security measures for the Canadian elderly. An important issue, therefore, is the degree to which these changes have altered the economic position of the Canadian elderly in the society as a whole, and what trends, if any, might be extrapolated to indicate what lies ahead. The crucial issue is the degree to which expanded social security measures have been able to compensate for the increased longevity of the elderly, on the one hand, and their declining labor force participation, on the other. The available data, which are summarized below, suggest that since World War II the elderly have been losing ground in the Canadian income distribution despite the growth of the Canadian welfare state. We use the term "suggest" advisedly, however. The observed trend is the result of the convergence of numerous demographic and social changes and is sensitive to the manner in which such fundamental concepts as income and inequality are measured (see Horner and MacLeod, 1975). The disaggregation of the observed trend into its component parts is a task which has scarcely begun.

In her analysis for the period 1951-61, Podoluk (1968:278) noted that families headed by an individual aged 65 or over were forming a rising proportion of the lowest quintile in the Canadian income distribution. Data presented by Horner and Macleod (1975:24) indicate that the percentage of the elderly in the bottom two quintiles increased from 68.5% in 1951 to 75.1% in 1971. The percentage in the highest quintile declined from 11.7% in 1951 to 6.4% in 1971. A continuation of this trend is also noted for most recent years. Between 1967 and 1974 the percentage of elderly families in the lowest income quintile increased from 51.1% to 53.2% (Statistics Canada, 1977:Table 3.27).

These data, however, derived from the annual Survey of Consumer Finances, utilize a family definition (the "economic family") which may mask real improvements in the economic status of the aged (see Podoluk, 1968:216-17).[14] Minimally, identification of trends over time requires some narrower unit of analysis such as the individual or the married couple and their dependent children (Podoluk, 1968:217). This criterion is more closely approximated by the census family definition.[15] Even with this more restricted definition the trend appears, however. Measured in constant (1971) dollars, the median income for families headed by individuals aged 65 or over increased by 35.75% between 1967 and 1974. For the elderly not in families, the median income increased by 37.72%. The increase for all families, however, was 38.56%. A more relevant standard of comparison is the age cohort immediately adjacent to the elderly in the age structure, namely those aged 55 to 64. For families in this age group the median income increased by 43.35% over this period.[16] Hence, despite the fact that the real income of the elderly population improved over this time period their relative position in the income distribution was declining; that is, the level of intergenerational inequality was increasing.

What of the future? In a period of increasing fiscal conservatism it is difficult to be optimistic about substantial improvements in the economic status of the aged. Moreover, in view of the large expected growth of the elderly as a percentage of the Canadian population (Légaré and Desjardins, 1976) a significant growth in social security budgets will be required simply to maintain present benefit levels. In the short term, the oversupply of young, cheap workers makes it unlikely that there will be any change in the pattern of declining labor force participation among older workers. As the baby boom crests, however, and the supply of younger workers declines, the demand for older workers is likely to increase once again. This assumes, however, that the relative demand for labor in the economy as a whole does not significantly decline as a result of management efforts to make the nation's economy more "efficient."

Perhaps the most crucial factor in the future will be the level of organization and cohesion achieved by the Canadian working class. Analysts of the welfare state have noted that the level of welfare provided in the various advanced capitalist nations is directly related to the level and strength of working class organizations — unions, political parties, etc. (Martin, 1973; Wilensky, 1975). Historically, the Canadian working class has been relatively disorganized and politically weak, divided by regional, ethnic and other social cleavages. A critical issue for the future is whether age will be used as a wedge to further divide Canadian workers or whether they will overcome their collective weakness to demand an adequate level of income for their old age. While the outcome of this impending struggle is unclear it is certain that the issue of the economic status of the elderly looms as one of the major political, social and economic conflicts of the coming decades.

NOTES

1. The exclusion of socialist societies does not imply that the situation of the elderly in these countries is either better or worse than in the capitalist nations. They have been excluded because, while in many instances the consequences of aging may be similar in these countries, their origins are different, and the analysis of these differences would take us too far afield from the present task.

2. As Hugh McRoberts has pointed out to me, however, retention of the dowry by the recipient was frequently made subject to the fulfilment of legally specified conditions. In such cases, the dowry served as a continuing basis of control over the young.

3. It is worth noting that for the top members of the capitalist class such a problem does not arise and indeed old age is also the period of greatest wealth (see Lampman, 1962; Louis, 1968; Streib, 1976). The fundamental division between capital and labor which characterize all capitalist societies results in the strange paradox that while the old are disproportionately poor, the wealthy are disproportionately old.

4. This statement, however, probably should be modified in light of the recent explosion in the development of Registered Retirement Savings Plans. Although not a government program, they are a direct result of government policy which makes personal investments in such plans tax exempt. Participation in such plans is largely confined to those in the upper income levels, not only because of their greater surplus for savings but also because they have more to gain as a result of their higher marginal tax rates (Statistics Canada, 1978a:11). The tax provisions for RRSPs are, in effect, a government subsidy to encourage individuals to save for retirement, but since this subsidy increases as individual income levels increase (National Council of Welfare, 1976:25) the effect is to increase intragenerational inequality among the retired.

5. As Collins (1978:43) notes, however, the CPI is an inadequate measure of the effect of inflation on the elderly because they spend a significantly higher proportion of their income on food and shelter, which have inflated at a significantly higher rate than other components of the index in recent years. What is required is an index based on the budgetary patterns of the elderly.

6. For empirical data on the Western European experience, see Wilson (1974:405-15). In general, since 1958, pension levels in countries such as the

U.K., Germany, the Netherlands and Sweden have risen in a manner which more closely approximates wage increases than price increases.

7. Whether it has compensated for other trends in the economy which increase intergenerational inequality is an issue to which we shall return at the end of the paper.

8. From Calvert's (1977) point of view, the problem of pensions is first and foremost a problem of capital formation (see especially, Chap. 2). Despite this obvious bias, his analysis is an important source document for presenting the views of the Canadian business class. Published by the *Financial Post*, the study was commissioned by the Canadian Pension Conference, an employers' organization representing such firms as Alcan, Bank of Montreal, Dupont, Inco, Royal Trust, and others (see Calvert, 1977:2).

9. These problems do not arise with public sector pensions. The C/QPP provides immediate vesting and indexed benefits.

10. Indeed it would appear that the primary function of vesting provisions is not to lower wages but to control and limit labor turnover (Pesando and Rea, 1977:11).

11. When benefits are based on an average of earnings across more than one year in an inflationary climate, there is a real loss to the employees since averaging is based on dollars with different purchasing power (Pesando and Rea, 1977:41).

12. For a more detailed discussion of this process of redistribution, see Pesando (1978).

13. See also Dulude, 1978.

14. The "economic family" consists of all relatives resident in the same household and related by blood, marriage, or adoption. For the elderly, "doubling up" with relatives often reflects inadequate incomes. As their incomes improve, there is less doubling up, which is reflected in a decline in their total "family income."

15. A "census family" consists of a husband and wife and any unmarried children living with them, or, alternatively, a father or mother and unmarried children resident in the same household.

16. Figures computed from Statistics Canada, *Family Incomes. Census Families* (Cat. 13-208 Annual) for 1967 and 1974.

REFERENCES

Brown, Joan. *How Much Choice? Retirement Policies in Canada.* Ottawa: Canadian Council on Social Development, 1975.

Bryden, Kenneth. *Old Age Pensions and Policy-Making in Canada.* Montreal: McGill-Queen's University Press, 1974.

Burawoy, Michael. "Towards a Marxist Theory of the Labor Process: Braverman and Beyond," *Politics and Society,* 8 (1978), pp. 247-312.

Calvert, Geoffrey N. "Pensions and Survival: The Coming Crisis of Money and Retirement," *Financial Post,* Vol. 71 (1977), p. 35.

Cliffin, S. and J. Martin. *Retirement in Canada,* Vol. I. Ottawa: Health and Welfare Canada, 1977.

Collins, Kevin. "The Canada Pension Plan as a Source of Provincial Capital Funds," in J., Brown, ed., *How Much Choice? Retirement Policies in Canada.* Ottawa: Canadian Council on Social Development, 1975, pp. 243-61.

―――. *Women and Pensions.* Ottawa: Canadian Council on Social Development, 1978.

Cowgill, D. "Aging and Modernization: A Revision of the Theory," in J. Gubrium, ed., *Later Life: Communities and Environmental Policy*. Springfield, Ill.: Charles C. Thomas, 1974, pp. 123-46.

Cowgill, D. and L. Holmes. *Aging and Modernization*. New York: Appleton Century Crofts, 1972.

Drucker, Peter. *The Unseen Revolution: How Pension Fund Socialism Came to America*. New York: Harper and Row, 1977.

Dulude, Louise. *Women and Aging*. Ottawa: Advisory Council on the Status of Women, 1978.

Epstein, Jason. "Capitalism and Socialism: Declining Returns," *New York Review of Books*, 17 (Feb. 1977), pp. 35-39.

Goffman, Irving J. "Canadian Social Welfare Policy," in R.H. Leach, ed., *Contemporary Canada*. Durham: Duke University Press, 1967.

Goody, Jack. "Aging in Nonindustrial Societies," in Robert Binstock and Ethel Shanas, eds., *Handbook of Aging and the Social Sciences*. New York: Van Nostrand Reinhold, 1976, pp. 117-29.

Haanes-Olsen, Leif. "Earnings-Replacement Rate of Old-Age Benefits, 1965-75, Selected Countries," *Social Security Bulletin* (Jan. 1978), pp. 3-14.

Harlan, William. "Social Status of the Aged in Three Indian Villages," in Bernice Neugarten, ed., *Middle Age and Aging*. Chicago: University of Chicago Press, 1968, pp. 469-75.

Heclo, Hugh. *Modern Social Politics in Britain and Sweden: From Relief to Income Maintenance*. New Haven: Yale University Press, 1974.

Herman, K. "The Emerging Welfare State: Changing Perspectives in Canadian Welfare Policies and Programs, 1867-1960," in D.I. Davies and K. Herman, eds., *Social Space: Canadian Perspectives*. Toronto: New Press, 1971, pp. 131-41.

Horner, Keith and Neil Macleod. *Changes in the Distribution of Income in Canada*. Ottawa: Health and Welfare Canada, 1975.

Johnson, Leo. "The Development of Class in Canada in the Twentieth Century," in Gary Teeple, ed., *Capitalism and the National Question in Canada*. Toronto: University of Toronto Press, 1972, pp. 141-83.

Kreps, Juanita, *Lifetime Allocation of Work and Income*. Durham, N.C.: Duke University Press, 1971.

_____. "The Economy and the Aged," in Robert Binstock and Ethel Shanas, eds., *Handbook of Aging and the Social Sciences*. New York: Van Nostrand Reinhold, 1976, pp. 272-85.

Lalonde, Marc. *Working Paper on Social Security in Canada*. Ottawa: Government of Canada, 1973.

Lampman, Robert J. *The Share of Top Wealth-Holders in National Wealth, 1922-1956*. Princeton, N.J.: Princeton University Press, 1962.

Légaré, Jacques and Bertrand Desjardins. "La situation des personne âgées au Canada," *Canadian Review of Sociology and Anthropology*, 13 (1976), pp. 321-36.

Louis, Arthur. "American's Centimillionaires," *Fortune*, 77 (1968), pp. 152-57.

Lubove, R. *The Struggle for Social Security, 1900-1935*. Cambridge: Harvard University Press, 1968.

Marsh, Leonard. *Report on Social Security for Canada*. Toronto: University of Toronto Press, 1975.

Martin, Andrew. *The Politics of Economic Policy in the United States: A Tentative View from a Comparative Perspective.* Beverley Hills: Sage Publications, 1973.

McConnell, John. "Aging and the Economy," in Clark Tibbits, ed., *Handbook of Social Gerontology.* Chicago: University of Chicago Press, 1960, pp. 489-520.

Menzies, Ann. "The Federal Republic of Germany," in Thomas Wilson, ed., *Pensions, Inflation and Growth.* London: Heinemann, 1974, pp. 45-109.

Mills, C. Wright. *White Collar.* New York: Oxford University Press, 1951.

Munro, John. "Pensions for Canadian Workers," *The Labour Gazette,* 77 (1977), pp. 453-56.

Nahemow, Nina and Bert N. Adams. "Old Age among the Buganda: Continuity and Change," in Jaber Gubrium, ed., *Late Life: Communities and Environmental Policy.* Springfield, Ill.: Charles C. Thomas, 1974, pp. 147-66.

National Council of Welfare. *The Hidden Welfare System.* Ottawa: National Council of Welfare, 1976.

O'Connor, James. "Some Contradictions of Advanced U.S. Capitalism" *Social Theory and Practice,* 1 (1970), pp. 1-11.

––––––. *The Fiscal Crisis of the State.* New York: St. Martin's Press, 1973.

OECD. *Public Expenditure on Income Maintenance Programmes.* Paris: OECD, 1976.

Pesando, James. *Private Pensions in an Inflationary Climate: Limitations and Policy Alternatives.* Ottawa: Economic Council of Canada, 1978.

Pesando, James and S.A. Rea. *Public and Private Pensions in Canada: An Economic Analysis.* Toronto: University of Toronto Press, 1977.

Piven, F.F. and R.A. Cloward. *Regulating the Poor: The Functions of Public Welfare.* New York: Vintage Books, 1971.

Podoluk, Jenny. *Incomes of Canadians.* Ottawa: Dominion Bureau of Statistics, 1968.

Rashid, A. *Sources and Distribution of Canadian Income.* Ottawa: Statistics Canada (Cat. 99-721), 1977.

Rimlinger, Gaston. *Welfare Policy and Industrialization in Europe, America and Russia.* Toronto: John Wiley and Sons, 1971.

Rosow, Irving. "Old Age: One Moral Dilemma of an Affluent Society," *The Gerontologist,* 2 (1962), pp. 182-91.

Schulz, James et al. *Providing Adequate Retirement Income — Pension Reform in the United States and Abroad.* Hanover, N.H.: Brandeis University Press, 1974.

Senate of Canada. *Final Report of the Special Committee of the Senate on Aging.* Ottawa: Queen's Printer, 1966.

Simeon, R. *Federal-Provincial Diplomacy: The Making of Recent Policy in Canada.* Toronto: University of Toronto Press, 1972.

Simmons, Leo. "Aging in Preindustrial Societies," in Clark Tibbits, ed. *Handbook of Social Gerontology.* Chicago: University of Chicago Press, 1960.

Statistics Canada. *Social Security: National Programs, 1976.* Ottawa: Statistics Canada (Cat. 86-201), 1976.

––––––. *Perspectives Canada II.* Ottawa: Statistics Canada, 1977.

––––––. *Pension Plans in Canada 1976.* Ottawa: Statistics Canada (Cat. 74-401), 1978a.

_____. *Social Security: National Programs, 1978*. Ottawa: Statistics Canada (Cat. 86-201), 1978b.

Streib, Gordon. "Social Stratification and Aging," in Robert Binstock and Ethel Shanas, eds., *Handbook of Aging and the Social Sciences*. New York: Van Nostrand Reinhold, 1976.

Union Bank of of Switzerland. *Social Security in 10 Industrial Nations*. Zurich: Union Bank of Switzerland, 1977.

Wallace, Elizabeth. "Old Age Security in Canada: Changing Attitudes," *Canadian Journal of Economics and Political Science*, 18 (1952), pp. 125-34.

Warham, Joyce. *Social Policy in Context*. London: Batsford, 1970.

Wilensky, Harold. *The Welfare State and Equality*. Berkeley: University of California Press, 1975.

Wilson, Thomas, ed. *Pensions, Inflation and Growth*. London: Heinemann, 1974.

From Colonialism to Economic Imperialism: The Experience of the Canadian Indian

GAIL KELLOUGH

Introduction

Any effort to alter the impoverished condition of native people must involve an understanding of how Canadian social institutions have impinged upon and retarded the development of that segment of society. Since present opportunities for Indians have been determined by past decisions, these processes must be studied historically. Similarities can be noted between the colonization of native people in Canada and such culturally diverse people as those found in Africa, Latin America, Australia, New Zealand and the United States. Such similarities often go unnoticed and Canadian Indians are frequently thought of as just another ethnic minority. Such an orientation is possible because the "emphasis of most histories subordinates or ignores the Indians' experience " (Patterson, 1972:6).

The history of Canadian Indians, since contact with Europeans, can be seen as occurring in two phases. The early historical period was characterized by a high level of autonomy in which Indians held the initiative for the social, political, and economic aspects of their life. The second phase can be characterized as one in which they lost their autonomy and took on the characteristics of a colonized people. The colonizing of a people is a social process; in the case of the Canadian Indians, this process had its roots in the earliest days of contact. While they enjoyed a high level of autonomy during the earlier period, a mutual interdependence also existed between the two groups. Ultimately, what distinguishes colonizers from colonized is a question of power. When the balance of power shifted in favor of the Europeans, the actual colonial period began.

For purposes of analysis, two levels of power need to be outlined.[1] One level is concerned with the external factors of colonization; this level comprises the structural component whereby the colonizers possess the power to determine the institutions of the colonized. Because there are fundamental conflicts of interest between the colonizers and the colonized over control of the structural component of society, there is a need for normative control. Since society is too complex to be regulated at every turn by force, a conquering nation must find ways to hold down revolt. What is crucial for the success of colonizers is the way they are viewed by those whom they hope to influence. The fact that subordinates accept the power of their superiors, and acquiesce in it, converts mere power into authority. This normative control constitutes the second level of power, in which the colonizers possess the power to define the reality of the colonized. This level is concerned with the internal factors of colonization — the cultural and psychological components. While structural power is concerned with decision-making affecting institutions and living conditions, cultural colonialism consists of the effort to explain and legitimate these conditions.[2]

The structural level can be seen to begin with the institution of the reserves in the late 1800s. The cultural level is more difficult to determine, although it will be suggested that its beginnings can be seen with the government's need to legitimate their taking over of structural control through the signing of treaties. While the colonizers have achieved almost complete structural dominance over Indians, it is not so clear to what extent cultural dominance has been achieved.

Structural Colonialism: The Government and the Indian

With the development of capitalism, imperialist countries began to be attracted to the New World in search of new spheres for the investment of their capital. The demand for furs in Europe provided a ready market for new avenues of profit. At the same time, however, the initial period of contact between Europeans and Indians frequently led to greater prosperity for Indians. European trade goods increased their ability to support themselves on the often sparse resources of the country. Since the fur traders were highly dependent on Indian skills, an economic interdependence grew up between the Indians and the fur traders.

The nature of the fur trade discouraged permanent settlement and "made it desirable to disturb as little as possible the Indians' culture and life style" (Patterson, 1972:107). While their culture was undergoing changes, these changes were not generally imposed by the Europeans. European traits which Indians adopted were woven together with traditional ones into a unique pattern. By the middle of the 19th century, two factors were to seriously undermine the mutual independency. When the importance of the fur trade declined, the era of the fur trade began to give way to the era of the settler and the Indians became a hindrance to western development. Settlement required that they be removed peacefully to restricted portions of their former territory. At the same time, the buffalo were rapidly disappearing from the prairies, taking away the cornerstone of the Indian way of life. The buffalo had been the basic unit of their economic system, and even their political and social customs were formed around the buffalo hunt. The second phase of contact, one in which the Indians lost the initiative for the social, political, and economic aspects of their life, was beginning.

Treaty Days

Most whites of the period strongly favored Indian removal from their ancestral homelands onto reservations, some because they were hungry for land and others because they believed such a move would buffer the corrupting influences of a frontier society. The Indians themselves were divided — many did not understand the terms of the treaties, believing that life would continue in much the same way but with the added benefits of sums of money.

Even where the consequences were foreseen,[3] the Indian nations operated from an unequal power position. The government held the trump card. With the disappearance of the buffalo, the Indians were starving. They had to have food; to get it, they had to "take treaty." From the beginning of the treaty negotiations, the Indians were in an inferior bargaining position, and in most cases, the treaties were offered on a take-it or leave-it basis. In many cases, treaties were negotiated only *after* the arrival of white settlers or *after* the land had already been sold.[4] The government was already buying and selling what was technically still Indian property. It was made clear to the Indians that irrespective of whether the treaties were accepted, the territories in question would be subject to white settlement. The inevitability of the process was expressed by Archibald, Lieutenant-Governor of Manitoba, who reported on negotiations of Treaty Two:

> We told them that whether they wished it or not, immigrants would come in and fill up the country; that every year from this one, twice as many in number as their whole people there assembled, would pour into the province, and in a little while would spread all over it, and that now was the time for them to come to an arrangement that would secure homes and annuities for themselves and their children (Indian Chiefs of Alberta, 1970:28).

The Indians had little option for rejecting the treaties. Aboriginal refugees from the United States made them fully cognizant of the horrors they might suffer should they attempt to defend their lands (National Indian Brotherhood, 1973:4). Outnumbered and outarmed, the most they could hope for was to hold out for certain concessions.

As well as negotiating from different power bases, the two groups of negotiators held different perspectives on the significance of the treaties. The government was simply negotiating treaties to legitimate white ownership of the land they were already using. The treaties were seen as deeds of property giving them the "authority" (in a Weberian sense) to do with the land whatever they desired. For Indians, on the other hand, the treaties were seen as "the beginning of a contractual relationship; whereby the representatives of the Queen would have lasting responsibilities for the Indian people in return for the valuable lands that were ceded to them" (Cardinal, 1969:29). Even further, it was the right to use these lands which Indians were negotiating.[5] Private property in land, as we understand the concept, was unknown to the Indians. While private ownership was *not* an alien notion, and while the control of specific territories by tribes was a familiar concept to many Indian societies, the sense of an individual "owning" of property was incomprehensible to them.[6] Land

> was conceived of as of a piece with the air and the water. To say "This is my piece of land" seemed as illogical as saying "This is my piece of air and this is my piece of water" (Lurie, 1974:34).

From the government point of view, the treaties were not really treaties at all, but deeds of sale by which Indians ceded their land to the government; while to the Indians, they were agreeing to give Europeans unhindered use of the land.

Negotiating from different power bases, holding different perspectives on the significance of the treaties, the Indians were further handicapped in their understanding of what the treaties promised them. A non-literate people, they had a verbal tradition in the making of political alliances; verbal promises were held to be binding on all parties. The written promises contained in the treaties often did not coincide with the verbal ones. For example, government spokesmen promised the Indians that "they would be as free to hunt and fish after the treaty as they would be if they never entered into it" (Cardinal, 40). Yet what actually appeared in written form stated that hunting and fishing were to be subject to such regulations as the government saw fit to make; that they could be restricted for purposes of "settlement, mining, lumbering, trading, or other purposes" (Cardinal, 40).[7]

The treaties, signed in the late 1800s, are not a consensus of values arrived at by two independent peoples. They represent two different views of what was taking place by two parties operating from distinctly different power positions.

Administering the Indians

In 1850, the Canadian government had taken over control of Indian Affairs from the Imperial government. For a time, the administration of Indian affairs through the various departments of government continued; however, this dispersed control was to give way to a more centralized arrangement with the creation of the Indian Affairs Branch. This department held the sole responsibility for all matters pertaining to the native population. "Assimilation" and "protection" became the operating principles of this agency in governing their wards. This new centralization of Indian management to solve administrative problems worked against the basic objective of assimilation by reinforcing the view of Indians as a group apart. The same sort of paradoxes revolved around the establishment of reserves. Indians were to be assimilated into the larger society, while at the same time they were to be isolated from the culture they were expected to assimilate into in order to protect them from the worst features of that society.[8] In practice, the principles of "assimilation" and "protection" often operated in contradiction to each other.

The government treated the whole "Indian problem" as a purely administrative one. The first Indian Act, in 1896, set out the framework for this administration. This Act, like almost all the subsequent legislation which was to protect the Indian people, never reflected the spirit nor the intent of the treaties as the Indians had seen them. It did legalize the colonial-like subordination of native people by regulating all of their institutionalized behavior. Covering such a great part of the everyday life of Indians, the Act left little room for Indian participation in the running of their own affairs; instead it gave the Minister of Indian Affairs the sole discretionary power to authorize use of reserve land and to disallow any bylaws enacted by the band. As well, it placed almost all finances of the reserve under control of the department (Fidler, 1970). Although local government was allowed to operate, it was subordinate to the wishes of the federal department. The colonial principle for such rule is that the "colony" and the "mother country" will be able to operate in a mutually beneficial manner. In practice, however, self-rule by colonies is typically "based on the extent to which it will serve the mother country in exploiting the colony" (Lurie, 1974:36).[9] Colonialism in Canada proved to be no exception. During the signing of the treaties, the government set their precedent by assuming the power to depose certain chiefs and to select more "suitable" chiefs to represent them in negotiations. This selection of new chiefs often resulted in new political relations being forced upon Indian tribes.[10]

The Indian Act also established new political relationships. Under Section 80 of the Act, band councils were established and authorized to make bylaws for the reserve, but such bylaws could be disallowed by the Minister or his agent. The Act provided for Indian agents to act as local managers of reserves, and until very recently, it was mandatory for agents to attend all meetings of the band councils. Until 1969, the agent also acted as Justice of the Peace, with all the powers pursuant to that position. In addition, he was responsible for the fiscal policies of the reserve, and band council expenditures had to be first approved by him. In this man resided all the powers of a veritable dictator and direct rule by the agent often became the reality.[11]

It has been suggested that the system under which Indians came to operate was not unlike the feudal system:

> The Indian Affairs Branch is the lord of the manor. The Indian agent is the local manager. The lord has total control over the lives of his serfs, who neither own their land nor rent it. They are "crofters" permitted to live on the land and farm it but not for their individual benefit. The lord or manager tells them what to plant and when to sow or harvest; he provides the equipment; he tells them when to sell the crop and at what price. He can, if he wishes, tell them to plant nothing at all. Thus, the Indians on their own reservations actually work for the Minister. . . . these funds are kept by Indian Affairs to be spent at the Minister's pleasure. The Minister draws up "projects" on which to spend this money. . . . The system is predicated on the Minister's treating the Indians as a responsible patron would treat inferiors (Robertson, 1970:111-12).

These feudal-like features, however, are not due to a lack of incorporation of Indians into the Canadian economy. On the contrary, we will argue, they are due to, and reflect precisely, the incorporation of Indians into the capitalist system. The institutions conceived in the Indian Act have functioned as mechanisms in the expansion of the capitalist system.[12] The important factor to consider, when noting the feudal-like structure imposed upon Indians by their colonizers, is the dependent status forced upon Indians in their interaction with the government.

The clearest example of the Indians' dependent role is in the area of finances. Before 1913, the total cost of Indian administration "was borne primarily by revenues derived from Indian sources, such as the sale or lease of land" (Patterson, 1972:26). The selling of valuable Indian lands was specifically recognized by the department as a means to reduce the cost of maintenance of Indians. The annual report of 1908 declared that where Indians were holding tracts of land which were in demand for settlement, such land should be sold "to relieve pro tanto the country of the burden of their maintenance..." (Hanks, 1950:31). While Indians were literally paying their own way, the Minister of Indian Affairs had total authority over what land should be sold and the amount to be paid. He could dispose of it as he saw fit. Between 1900 and 1930, Indians parted with their land for the purposes of railway, road, and town development. The National Indian Brotherhood has estimated that as much as half of the original reserve allotment across Canada has been lost through land sales made to benefit railways, oil and coal corporations, farmers and recreation developers. In many instances, the band did not know that part of their reserves were being sold. When they did, they operated from an inferior power position. Lucien M. Hanks (1950) reports how the government cut off rations on an Alberta Blackfoot reserve in order to get Indians to sell prime land desired for white settlement. This move divided the reserve between those who wanted to stop the starvation of their children and those who saw the long-term implications of the sale. Eventually, the pro-selling group won and the money was put "in trust" for the Indians. In other cases, where Indian agents acted conscientiously and wisely in running the band's affairs, it didn't pay the Indians to make money through the selling of land, since in most cases "the money only went to pay the wages of the Indian agent and to cover the administration costs" (Robertson, 1970:32).

The political structure of the reserve community encouraged Indians to accept passively Indian Affairs Branch (IAB) directives. The dependence of Indians upon the agent for their very being made it very unlikely they would do or say anything to anger him. The ability of the chief "was threatened by the power and wealth which was at the disposal of the Indian agent" (Patterson, 1972:10). The councillors lacked any real political authority, had no access to informational channels and were operating in non-traditional forms of association (Dosman, 1972). What representation the Indians had in policies affecting their lives was too minimal to be of any benefit and there was little opportunity for them to develop any political skills.[13]

Economic Development or Economic Imperialism?[14]

While the colonial parallel between Canadian Indians and other conquered people is evident in past administrative policies, the parallel does not end there. The problems of underdevelopment of Indian reserves are precisely the same as those faced by Third World countries. The most common approach to, and analysis of, problems of economic development has been to suggest that underdevelopment is a result of the failure of "backward" peoples to adapt to modern society; that such people need to adopt the proper attitudes and values before they can be incorporated into the capitalist system. Contrariwise, this paper supports the thesis that underdeveloped societies are already a part of world capitalism; indeed, their underdevelopment is a direct result of capitalist expansion in the developed countries. Capitalist development is seen, not only as uneven development between classes, but between countries and within countries and between regions, with some prospering while others stagnate. In Canada, the pattern of development and underdevelopment, of metropolis and hinterland, began with the early staples of fur and cod when European metropoles removed the surplus produce from the Canadian hinterland. These metropole-hinterland relations are not limited to the international level, however, but regions which are hinterlands for larger metropolises of the world economy, in turn, become the metropolises for other hinterlands.[15] For example, "the United States metropolis seeks out its hinterland in Canada; Eastern Canada is a metropolis to the west; the south is a metropolis to the north. From there the series goes no further except in class terms internal to the community" (Elias, 1975:52). In most cases, Indian reserves have been at the bottom of the Canadian hinterland ladder. When communities other than reserves form this lower level hinterland, native Indians form the underclass within that community, an underclass of unemployed who are incorporated into the structures and processes of local capitalism.[16]

The pre-colonial Indian society was relatively undeveloped. This undeveloped nature of Indian social structure was used by the colonizers to justify their claim to power. But real development of Indian reserves has actually been stymied by the colonizers. In the transition from hunting and trapping to agricultural production, the nomadic nature of Indian tribes has often been cited as the reason for lack of reserve agricultural development. In many instances, however, despite promising agricultural starts,[17] the allocation of poor farm land to Indian bands and the expropriation of fertile reserve lands worked against such development. With mass agrarian immigration to the western provinces in the early 1900s, Indian land was in great demand. In some instances, Indians were persuaded to move from prime land to less fertile reserves.[18] In others, pressure was exerted upon Indian farmers by the IAB to sell farm land rather than to expand. One such instance is described by R.N. Wilson (1974). In 1916 and 1917, at a time when western Canada was being urged to greater production of grain, a band of Blood Indians were willing and eager to extend their farming operations; however, lease funds, upon which their farming extension was dependent, were appropriated and used for other purposes. Wilson's research led him to conclude that "there was no reason for holding back the farming development at that time other than the determination of officials in charge to 'freeze' the Indians into a land sale." In due course, poverty forced the Blood Indians to part with a substantial portion of agricultural land since they did not have the resources to respond to the greater production appeal.

The availability of loan money has been and is a critical component in the providing of economic development. Because of financial restrictions within the Indian Act, Indians have always had difficulty in arranging for investment capital and technical assistance for any but the smallest projects. Because title to reserves is vested in the government, Indians cannot arrange bank loans in their own name; hence they have been forced to rely on governmental sources of funding. As a result, natural resources have not been exploited by the Indians themselves. A further example of how Indians are disassociated from the means of production is found in the history of wild rice in Manitoba.[19] Indians, who were the original exploiters of this natural resource, have relinquished most of their control over this economic activity. After many requests for financing, a meeting was held in 1970 to discuss a plan for an Indian-controlled commercial paddy; yet no Indian was present at that meeting. Instead of money to proceed, a botanist was hired for wild rice research.[20] After two years of research, a plan was presented for the organization of a commercial paddy development on the reserve. This plan, however, "amounted to a proposition in which the Fort Alexander Band would have no effective representation on the Board of Directors." (Lithman, 1973:49) At the same time that Indians were experiencing difficulties in financing their wild rice venture, a market was being generated for wild rice and major economic interests began to realize that profits could be reaped from a large-scale marketing of this commodity. Since new production methods have not been made accessible to Indian people, it would appear that future marketing will not be beneficial to them and wild rice will eventually become an exclusively commercial crop dominated by major food chains (Lithman, 1973). Even further, such developments in wild rice mean that Indians will no longer receive the substantial revenue that wild rice picking has previously provided them. The development of the wild rice market has led to further underdevelopment of the Indian reserve.

During the late 1960s, the IAB budget exceeded $62 million per year, yet only $1.5 million was spent on economic development (Fidler, 1970:10). The small amounts of the IAB budget spent on economic development tend to go towards measures typically designed to help out larger industries in need of cheap labor or to provide only short-term employment for Indians. What funds are available for economic development on Indian reserves seem to be geared more to the exploitation of natural resources by outside interests than to the development of human resources under local management. Instead of providing the basis for the growth of an indigenous capitalist class and a level of technology adapted to local circumstances, incentive provided to private firms to locate on reserves has ensured the dominance of imported capital and skills and hence continued dependence on the outside world. Private monopolies of reserve-based firms has limited the mobility of Indians and precluded the evolution of an entrepreneurial class of the classic capitalist kind; and the absence of this class has in turn meant that surplus has continued to be monopolized by outside interests.[21] Indian resources taken over by outside interests has limited the accumulation of capital and kept Indians in a technologically backward world, thus limiting their competition in the labor market.[22]

Canada's heavily populated and highly developed regions dictate the development patterns of Indian reservations and relatively unpopulated northern regions. The words of one northern Indian illustrate the highly exploitative relationship between metropolitan centers and the regions they tap: "First, white men come and take all the beaver, then come back and take all the trees. This time they're even back for the rocks" (Hanks, 1950).

The economic interests of the day are going back again; this time *under* the rocks for oil and pipelines, and back again for the water in the form of power dams. The prevalence of mineral, petroleum, and hydro resources in the north is increasingly inviting exploitation by both Canadian and international capital. The operation of mining, smelting, drilling and flooding, are benefiting outside interests while the ecological disruption and economic costs are borne largely by Indian groups. The exploitation of these resources has resulted in a flow of capital to the south which, at the same time, has disrupted traditional hunting and fishing activities and forced the relocation of formerly self-sufficient Indian communities.[23] During the 1920s, oil corporations turned their attention to the possibility of oil and gas discoveries in the Mackenzie Valley, and the first treaty covering the Northwest Territories was enacted (National Indian Brotherhood, 1973). Today, the Arctic transport corridor, including an all-season highway and oil and gas transmission lines, will supposedly bring jobs to unemployed aboriginal people. In the past, however, the jobs which have been created by resource exploitation or highway building have been of a highly temporary nature, with the more permanent, more desirable jobs being filled by skilled labor imported from the metropolitan areas. Direct employment from pipelines is generally small; for natives it has been even less and mainly in low-paying manual jobs.[24]

While projects such as the James Bay Development, the Mackenzie Valley Highway and the damming of South Indian Lake "all involve the seizure of lands from which Indian societies presently make a living" (Manuel, 1974), industrialization which does not involve such land seizure also affects native Canadians. Chemical wastes from industry have affected Indian people across Canada more severely than any other group.[25] Because they lack any real political power, compensation for native people is too little and comes too late. In 1957, the Ontario Hydro built the Cariboo Dam, which raised the waters of the English and Wabigoon Rivers and drowned the rice crops. These rice crops "were worth as much as $500,000 a year to the people of White Dog and Grassy Narrows reserves" (Macleans, 1971). In the 14-year period from 1957 to 1971, the 1,400 Indians affected received just over $23,000 as compensation. With the rice crops gone, the Indians became wholly dependent upon the fish. As the mercury content rose in the fish, governments were prepared to give grants to industry to locate on clean water, but native people are still eating mercury-polluted fish while settlements are being negotiated.

The colonial parallel of "developed underdevelopment" clearly operates in Canada. As Brett has pointed out:

> Colonialism can be accused of the 'development of underdevelopment' if it can be shown that its impact upon local society was such that it created a situation in which the latter could only continue to function by continuing to accept dependence on the dominant external powers (1973:18).

The deterioration of Indian reserves and resources has clearly benefited both lower level metropoles in Canada and international ones in the U.S. Economic imperialism can be charged when "the formal or informal control over local economic resources (operates) in a manner advantageous to the

Metropolitan power, and at the expense of the local economy" (O'Connor, 1972:118).

The Permanently Unemployed

The logical extension of capitalism is a conversion from labor-intensive methods to capital-intensive ones. Costs of production can be significantly lowered only by decreasing the costs of labor through conversion to non-human power. The demand for labor thus decreases while the numbers of unemployed increases. This body of unemployed workers, often referred to as the industrial reserve army, "has the effect of keeping the cost of labor down for those sectors of the economy still relying upon manpower" (Elias, 1975:111). While some Indians provide a source of labor during periods of expansion, returning to their reserves when such labor is not required, large numbers of the Indian population have never worked in a wage position. They form a group that is an even further extension of the growth of monopoly capitalism — the permanently unemployed.[26] This group is not outside capitalism but is an underclass which is fully integrated into the capitalist structure and performing a vital role in the capitalist economy.[27] The fact that Indians are a racially distinctive group provides "a perpetual, readily identifiable 'lowest' group whose position is 'explained' in racist ideology," thus submerging class similarities shared with their white counterparts (Elias, 1975:50). For instance, computations of national employment rates exclude on-reserve Indians, thus masking the real unemployment figures.[28] In this way, metropolitan power elites confuse regional and class differences, since the perpetuation of regional conflict defuses the potential for class alliance.

The permanently unemployed, those who subsist on welfare, perform additional roles besides that of a psychological scapegoat. They are important in their roles as consumers in that they assure the circulation of significant amounts of money within the community. While white businessmen do not appreciate the problems caused for them by "drunken Indians," they do appreciate the welfare dollars spent in their stores and taverns.

In contrast to what is spent on economic development, approximately 25% of the total IAB budget goes to welfare (Cardinal, 1969). Additionally, many programs developed to assist Indians appear to be designed to keep them on welfare. Robertson (1970) cites one such example occurring at Roseau River in the late 1960s. The IAB began plans to build a new townsite on the reserve. This proposed townsite bore no relation to the economic reality of the Indians' situation on this reserve. The reserve had no economic base; there was barely enough farmland to eke out a living for the four Indian men who had entered into an agreement with Indian Affairs to farm reserve land. The proposed townsite was set up to accommodate the 94 families who lived on the reserve. The IAB did not take into consideration that there was nothing to do around Roseau except farm. If the Indians remained on the reserve and occupied their new homes, they would be destined to remain on welfare. The Indians themselves were never consulted about the townsite. "It is the hallmark of a hinterland that it not only cannot generate its own solutions . . . but it cannot even generate its own problems" (Laxer, 1974:110).

Programs "for the Indian" or the "New" Era of Self-Determination

Well meaning officials of the IAB have spent their careers looking for things they can "do for" the Indians. It is this kind of paternalism which has prevented them from seeing that frequently their notion of what is helpful does not correspond with what the Indian believes to be helpful. Over all the multitude of programs designed to turn Indians into integrated and productive citizens has created the "stigma of perpetually being helped and the frustration of never being allowed to do things for themselves and having little to say about what was done" (Rogers, 1971:288). The IAB demands that Indians manage their own affairs, but on the grounds that they do not know how, never lets them try. As in other forms of colonialism, the IAB starts from the basic premise that government is a matter of knowledge (Cohen, 1971:29). In the case of Indians, administrative efficiency has been purchased at the expense of participatory democracy. Government programs have been designed to force the Indians into the mainstream of white culture. Such policies have been defeated because they have taken

> no account of a background of up to 25,000 years of Indian histories and cultures that had nothing in common with the European based cultures of white men . . . . Solutions were those of the whites, not of the Indians. The white man, rarely understanding the people whose problems he was trying to solve, imposed his ideas of proper solutions on the Indians, who either could not or would not accept them and the programs failed (Josephy, 1971:16).

The principle of "protection" was established early in the colonial relationship. It was part of the "mystification" process the early colonizers developed in order to legitimate the structural takeover of Indian institutions.[29]

The power to manage Indian lives has been jealously guarded by the government. Whenever a program or project has begun to develop which challenges the Indian people to action — to think and to question — it has been quickly dropped. During the 1960s, the federal government decided to act on the charges that they were not listening to Indians. A corps of men were hired to aid Indians in articulating their own needs and concerns. For the first time, Indian workers were to be under the Indian people's direct supervision. But these "community development workers" proved to be too much of a good thing. They stimulated the Indians to clamor for better schools, jobs, housing and health resources. Very quickly, the government began to pull back. Their aims were much different. There was no money for such economic development, and "most of the needs of which people began to speak when they were animated through the Community Development program were going to cost money" (Manuel, 1974:156). Community development workers began to get directives requiring them "to become more responsive to direction from the agent." While the Indian was to be consulted, the worker was now to take his orders from the IAB. "Participation, which began as a way of helping the people to take local initiative, was redefined to mean gaining the consent of the band council for Ottawa desired projects" (Manuel, 1974:155). Within three years, the program, as it was originally conceived, was dead.

Present poverty programs do not work. They are aimed at assimilating the Indian and in keeping him dependent. The "good" Indian is defined in terms of white values and culture and in terms of docile and apolitical behavior.[30] Any actions requiring decision-making independent of the IAB are taken to be inherently political and are vigorously opposed by the government. Dosman (1972) cites an example of an Indian self-help organization in Saskatoon. The "Big Bear Gallery" was organized, controlled and directed by local Indians and Métis, completely independently of the government bureaucracies.

> The reaction of the IAB was clear and effective. The vilification of persons on the Board of Directors was a first tactic and one not to be underestimated . . . another was the withholding of information vital to an organization in the opening stages when many people have to be contacted quickly . . . thirdly, the IAB withheld loans and funds at a crucial stage of development, advising that self-help projects must prove themselves before they could be assisted. When asked what "proving themselves" meant, the Indians were told "self-sufficiency." The IAB gave no reply to the rejoinder that a development loan would hardly be necessary when self-sufficiency had been attained . . . on the other hand financial help was offered for the project if the IAB controlled it (Dosman, 1972:111).[31]

While the Big Bear Gallery was quelled because it refused to relinquish political control, many other self-help groups are dissipated through the very governmental funding that the Big Bear Gallery tried so hard to get. The problem of dependency upon governmental financing is clearly outlined by Loney:

> If they cease to talk to the government, if they cease to expand most of their resources in an endless series of committees, we may reasonably predict that government will cease to fund them, the leaders of the movement will be unemployed and the organizations built on the shaky quicksands of outside funding will quickly collapse (1974:111).

Indian organizations are kept from political action by the very fact of their dependence upon government.

Interviews with government officials could easily convince the uninitiated that every possible self-help program is already operational or about to become so. During the 1960s, there was plenty of lip service given to consulting the Indians concerned before policies were implemented. A perfect example of the kind of "consultation" which occurs when all the facilities and the economic power reside in the hands of the government is the construction of the native pavilion at Expo '67:

> Indian artists had been invited from all across Canada to come and present their conception of the pavilion . . . . Of course, each artist had no other tools with which to work than the canvas and oils or sketchbook and pastels with which he was accustomed to work. No specifications had been laid down. No

funds had been provided to build models... when all the artists had finished telling their stories and were waiting to have the decision, you could feel the anticipation in the air .... But first the department officials wanted to show us something. For over an hour, we were shown coloured slides of a model pavilion building that had been designed on commission from the Department of Indian Affairs. When the designers had finished, they asked what we thought of it .... Well, those slides made the artists' paintings look like pretty amateur stuff .... One Indian artist finally said what they all probably felt: "Well, since you have already spent a quarter of a million dollars to get this far, you might as well go ahead. None of our works are worth a fraction of that (Manuel, 1974:173).

The same type of "consultation" exists for programs concerning the reserves. Indians lacking access to technological "experts" are intimidated by the great show of technology and expertise, and "there is a great temptation to admit that the agencies can, in fact, do everything better than a native institution" (Dosman, 1972:160) Much of what passes for grassroots democracy is really a sophisticated job of salesmanship and Indians become passive consumers of programs.

When programs fail, they contribute to already strong feelings of inadequacy among Indians, without providing a learning experience for further attempts at self-help. As one Indian leader notes:

A better program built upon the failure of an old program is the path of progress. But to achieve this experience, competence, worthiness, sense of achievement and the resultant material prosperity, Indians must have the responsibility in the ultimate sense of the word (Warrior, 1971:88).

While proclaiming a new spirit of "consultation and negotiation" during the 1960s, government officials were quietly preparing policy which would determine the future of Indians as a people. The "White Paper" of 1969 projected the phasing out of the Indian Affairs Department over the next five years. It had finally been recognized that the reserve system, and the clientele branch of government which had arisen to administer the system, were working against assimilation. If Indians were to accept white middle-class norms, they must be forced off the reserves (Cardinal, 1969). To do this, the rights of private property over collective ownership had to be upheld; Indian lands would be given over to the individuals who occupied them.

The new governmental policy revealed almost complete ignorance, or indifference, to what Indian people were saying. The White Paper's starting point was a complete dismissal of Indian treaty rights. The government of the day failed to comprehend the extreme importance native people placed upon such rights. They did not deny that written terms of the treaties were misleading nor that verbal promises had not been kept; they did not consider the IAB, nor the Indian Act, as other than oppressive instruments in their own underdevelopment. What they had been saying was that before any meaningful changes could be made, their fundamental rights must first be settled. Only when their land claims had been negotiated would they have the requisite economic and political power to rewrite the Indian Act in light of their own needs. By forcing "private property" concepts upon Indians, the government was attempting to assimilate them into the capitalistic structure. Such a policy ignores the fact that Indians *already are* structurally occupying the lowest ranks of the white capitalist structure. In formulating the new policy, the government not only ignored the words of Indian leaders but also the historical experience of the seven Indian tribes whose collective land rights had been terminated in the U.S. Closer to home, they ignored the plight of the Métis, who have not even had the cultural refuge of a reserve to flee to when coping in the white man's world. In the face of vocal Indian opposition, the "White Paper" was shelved, but the lesson has not been learned — Indian leaders are still excluded from IAB conferences and meetings held to determine policy.[32] The words of former President Nkrumah of Ghana are relevant to the Indian experience in Canada:

> It is this sum total of these modern attempts to perpetuate colonialism, while at the same time talking about "freedom" which has come to be known as *neo-colonialism* (1965:239).

Individual Mobility versus Group Solidarity

Each new policy that is developed seems to be an attempt to reassert the white Canadian's belief in private property and to divide the Indian people. Such policies are not new but have always characterized the government's attitudes towards Indians. An excerpt from a letter written in 1889 states:

> The policy of the Department is to keep the Indians out of the valley as much as possible and to encourage them to build permanent houses on the plain. With this end in view, the Department is surveying lots of 40 acres each on the beach to give them to individual Indians to encourage individual effort on the part of the Indians and gradually break up the tribal system (Baird Papers, July 27, 1889).

Historically, efforts to encourage individual Indian effort have, at best, only fostered a small clientele of successful Indians and have done nothing to help Indians as a group.[33] The few leading families created by such policies have created further indirect rule by providing some measure of legitimacy for government dictates. The creation of power divisions among Indian bands began with the appointment of "chiefs" by the government during the treaty negotiations and continues today through government appointments. The structure created by the early colonizers limited channels of upward mobility to large-scale organizations dependent upon government support. The Indian Act severely limited opportunities for entrepreneurship without assistance from the state.[34] Government emphasis on individual mobility, rather than collective social action has meant that many native leaders wind up in the employ of the government bureaucracies or their sponsored agencies. By singling out "promising" Indians for advancement, the government hampers the recruitment of leaders for self-help projects by independent native oganizations.[35] Government interests are furthered, but the Indian people, as a whole, are further than ever behind. Their leadership has been creamed off.[36] This co-optation of Indian leadership divides the Indian groups while, at the same time, strengthening the belief in individual advancement. Mobility for the individual has meant little conscious consideration for the needs of the Indian community as a whole.

The government has operated from the belief that the solution to surviving in our society is a strong sense of individual competition. As expected, they have been consistent in their reluctance to allow any collective ownership. If Indians want control over their own lands and institutions, the government has continually insisted that it must be on an individual basis. The 1969 "White Paper" is only the most recent example. In 1946, a Special Joint Committee of the Senate and the House of Commons was created to examine and consider the Indian Act. Repeatedly, this committee had the New Zealand treatment of the Maoris set before it as a model for future government policy (Patterson, 1972). Lands were reserved for the native people in New Zealand, as in Canada, but what was important was that title was placed "directly in their own hands, rather than in the name of the Crown, as has been the case in North America, and without breaking the land up into individual lots on an English model" (Manuel, 1974:237). While evidence clearly showed the Maoris had achieved a better material standard of living and a better relationship with their European neighbors, the Committee decided against the Maori form of communal representation.[37] While the Maoris have not completely escaped the effects of colonialism, such effects have been modified to a marked degree by their ability to control their own land and institutions. Their political status has enabled them to achieve a stronger and more positive racial identity than that achieved by Indians. Significantly, political independence and economic power on a collective basis was rejected for Canadian Indians without their ever being consulted.

Individualistic competition has been the source of many of the Indians' difficulties and therefore cannot be their solution. In a time of monopoly capitalism, the vast majority of working people and capitalists alike must fit into labor unions or big industries or they would not survive economically at all. The paradox is that

> We have been taught to strive to get ahead of the next man, but actually today one's success depends much more on how well one learns to work with one's fellow workers (May, 1953:55).

The most important mechanism for influencing governmental decisions is organizational strength. As well, the traditional strengths of Indian cultures were achieved through working on a communal basis. Instead of channeling communal sharing into collective economic planning, government officials have supported private lots and individual opportunity, thus minimizing potential economies of scale and collective bargaining power (Rothney, 1975). While Indians have resisted the "individualistic ethic" for advancement, they have, nevertheless, been divided amongst themselves and prevented from developing political leadership. Those who have attempted to get their fellow Indians and Métis together for political action have been branded as communists or co-opted into the government.[38]

During the reserve period, the Indians have lacked two things — true self-government and economic strength. Because they lacked an economic base, they have never been able to gain political autonomy. Lacking funds, they have not been able to establish their claims as a priority demanding consideration by federal authorities. Indeed, the Parliament of Canada made it an offense for anyone to attempt to raise funds in order to press Indian claims. In 1927, they amended the Indian Act to read:

> 149A Every person who solicits or requests from any Indian any payment or contribution. . . for the purpose of raising a fund for the prosecution of any claim, which the tribe or band of Indians to which such Indian belongs . . . shall be guilty of an offense (Manuel, 1974:195).

Our economic system is oriented towards the belief that "he who pays the piper, calls the tune." The whole orientation of the capitalist world is to attach strings to monetary help.[39] Consumer's rights are always considered to be subordinate to those supplying the capital. Such an orientation fails to realize that political and social autonomy cannot develop under such conditions. Economic help without self-government, or self-government without an economic base, only creates further economic colonialism and underdevelopment. Indians will be short on technology, on education, and on economic self-sufficiency, so long as they are politically weak, and they are politically weak because they lack economic self-sufficiency and unfragmented leadership. Before a group can operate from a bargaining position of strength, it must first close ranks and organize its institutions in order to represent its needs within the larger society. The search for a new form of life means a search for institutions which will, for once, make decisions in the interests of Indian people. This demand for control of their own communities through autonomy in the educational, political and economic spheres "is profoundly revolutionary, for it poses directly the question of who will have the decision-making power among the most oppressed colonized people on this continent — and what those decisions will be" (Fidler, 1970:12). The government has so far been unable to solve the problems of the Indians for the same reason that developed nations cannot solve the problems of the underdeveloped nations — "the problem in the underdeveloped nations is precisely the presence of the developed nations" (Manuel, 1974:169).

Cultural Colonialism — The Church and the Indian

In most colonial situations, missionary activity can be observed which is complementary to structural colonialism. In Canada, as elsewhere, missionaries played a significant role in the colonizing of Indians. Little is to be gained in assuming an insincerity of motive among the missionaries; most of them, whatever their denomination, were dedicated individuals devoted to carrying the Christian message to "pagan" souls — often at great personal cost. What is seldom recognized, however, is that these well-meaning people bear a great deal of the responsibility for the present conditions of native people in Canada. The government needed the church to prepare the districts for the advent of settlers by persuading the Indians to live peacefully on reservations — a goal which was highly compatible with the missionaries' interest in conversion. As well, missionaries and government officials shared a common ideological background. "Long before the surge of imperialism in the late 19th century, Britsh North Americans had looked upon the Empire as the vehicle and embodiment of a progressive civilization which was designated by Providence to spread its culture, religion and political institutions across the face of the earth" (Berger, 1970:127). Such an ideology provided the supreme rationalization for the colonization of Indians.[40] It was left to the missionaries to convince the Indians that the loss of their lands was for their own good. Indian leader George Manuel expressed it this way:

> Conquest only becomes colonialism when the conquerers try to convince the conquered that the rape of his mother was committed for the sake of some higher good (1974:169).[41]

The Mystification of Experience[42]

Colonizers needed a set of pseudo-justifications for themselves as well as a stereotyped image of those they were colonizing. In order to justify exploitation, Indians were seen as inferior to Europeans and the development of their lands as an inevitable part of the destiny of mankind. Missionaries were among the perpetrators of the myths which provided legitimation for colonial activities.[43] A clear example of the role the church was to play is found in an 1828 missionary address to the Seneca Indians:

> However afflictive to the various tribes is the loss of the lands of their forefathers, the eternal happiness of one Indian, saved through the Blood of the Redeemer, is of far, very far, higher estimation than all the plains and forests...and further, what Red brother, who has the love of Jesus in his heart, would part with this hidden treasure for all beneath the Canopy of Heaven (West Papers, April 19, 1928).

Letters from missionaries in the late 1800s demonstrate their perception of Indians either as cruel savages or as weak children:

> The Indians are in many respects like children. At any time they will act just so foolishly (Baird Papers, March 28, 1890).

> Thankless beyond measure, strangers to truth and right, depraved and filthy in the extreme (Baird Papers, March 28, 1890).

> ...are of the worst type...they typify man having reached the lowest level of the human ladder...living a nomadic and lazy life following the innumerable bands of buffalo (Stewart Correspondence).

Missionaries, with their reports of Indian ways, performed a valuable service for a land-hungry society. Seizure of Indian lands and the banishment of the conquered to reserves could be justified by an ideology that saw natives as savage and uncivilized. If they were subhuman, then their lives were not as valuable as European lives and their property need not be valued in the same way (Manuel, 1974).

The missionaries themselves were products of an era that embraced "social Darwinism" — a belief that "biological evolution also worked in human affairs and world affairs" (Berger, 1970:223). Material progress was the mark of the superiority of the white races. Indigenous people were technologically inferior and, therefore, did not deserve the land because they were incapable of developing it and exploiting its resources. These weaker races needed guidance and knowledge in order to develop an advanced civilization. Missionaries were instruments of God's will that the Anglo-Saxon race provided for guidance to the non-white races of the world, and the colonization of Indian people was seen as being for their own good. It is a natural feature of imperialism that exploitation of conquered people must not be seen as such, but seen rather as benevolence. In achieving this, colonizers must not only mystify the natives, they must mystify themselves as well (Laing, 1967).

Acculturating the Indian

The Indians of Canada were a religious people. Their "fervency of spirit and diligence in prayer" as well as their "good sense of forgiving" and principles of sharing, were noted by incoming missionaries. However, this evidence of the Indians' relationship with a God was strongly qualified:

> They had a zeal of God but not according to knowledge. Besides. . . what did these Indians pray for? Exactly the same as the unenlightened Gentiles did in the days of St. Paul, whose thoughts were confined to this present life only, saying "What shall we eat or what shall we drink, or wherewillall shall we be clothed?" (Hines, 1919:108).

The Indians' religion was concerned with practical, everyday matters, while the white religion was concerned with the hereafter. Herein lies the important distinction between the Christian tradition and the Indian tradition:

> Salvation for the native takes place near the beginning of adult life, whereas for the adherent of the Christian tradition, salvation occurs only after death, if at all. The former spends his life in complete confidence that he has achieved it; the latter is engaged in a life-long attempt to prepare himself for its eventual realization (Zentner, 1970).

Because the white missionary never questioned the basic assumption about the depravity of the Indians, it was necessary to destroy their superstitious customs. Abandoning Indian ways was not enough, however, for if colonialism was to be legitimated, it had to be accepted by the colonized as well as the colonizers. Not only were the Indians to be separated from their religion and traditions but they had to be made to regard their former customs as sinful. Without a sense of sin, the message of salvation would be meaningless. If the Indian could be made aware of the sinfulness of his own society, it was felt that he could then be converted. Whenever an Indian had to be charged with "immorality," the missionaries explained that what they were doing was only for "his own good."[44]

While the old ways were associated with the devil and scorned, an over-simplified Christianity, having little to do with the Indians' own experience, was offered by the missionaries. Converts were continually backsliding into their old habits. Particularly obnoxious, from the missionaries' viewpoint, were the Indian dances and the Indian Potlatch ceremony. One missionary reported:

> (The) dances of these heathen Indians appear to be one of the chains that bind them to their old habits and keeps alive the excitement of former days so fondly cherished by the Indian (Baird Papers, April 17, 1890).

As well, the Indian habit of sharing food and land with needy neighbors was seen as a barrier to progress. How were they to progress if they continually gave their property away?[45] Missionaries of all persuasions prevailed upon the government to outlaw these heathen practices. "So success was their condemnation of the Potlatch ceremony that it was considered an illegal action by virtue of the Indian Act up until 1951" (Waubegshig, 1972:74).

If the Indians were to be "uplifted," they must undergo not only a change of values but a change in their entire way of life. They were urged to adopt the white man's more sedentary ways. Missionaries were instructed that:

> the best benefit you can bestow upon them is to encourage them in settling down and cultivating the soil — such efforts as those going hand in hand with the gospel.[46]

The economic framework and social structure of Indian society were conceived in relation to the environment in a way that satisfied their needs. Yet the missionaries felt that the state of the Indians' degradation came from their nomadic way of life and their lack of a work ethic. In the mid-Victorian culture, work was "a virtue in itself, a process in which character was disciplined and man's nature developed. One was to work in the correct spirit, ever conscious that he was serving God in a secular calling" (Berger, 1970:221). Such an ethic was incompatible with the Indians' nomadic way of living. Father Taché, reporting on the Plains Indians, stated:

> They are generally united in large camps from 60 to 80 lodges and often more, live a nomadic and lazy life, following the innumerable bands of buffalos...if the tribes of the prairies have become the seat of all the vices that degrade man, it is because work is unknown to them (Stewart Correspondence).

The Indians of the period were also ignorant of the value of riches; such ignorance was inconceivable to the European missionaries. Their thinking was dominated by the belief that "progress" was not only good, but inevitable. They believed that all the Indians' problems would vanish if only they could be made to adopt white values and beliefs. While the missionary acknowledged the enormity of this task, he never doubted that it could be achieved. Missionary papers intimate that many in the mission field underestimated the socialization experience on a mature person; culture "was regarded as something like a bad habit which could be shed with training."[47] Differences were thought to exist because the Indian had had no chance to become like the European, but once exposed to a civilized way of life, it was unthinkable that he should choose any other.

In a great many cases, Indians reacted to the ministrations of the missionaries and their innovations with minimal adjustment. They did what they had to do and stopped what they were compelled to stop. But they couldn't be compelled to believe. Still, missionaries optimistically saw signs of assimilation in everything the Indians borrowed from the white man and made their own. Many superifical manifestations were cited as evidence of their success. The appearance of the Indian was taken as an important indicator of his degree of Christianization. One reserve reported:

> At Yellow Calf's, most of the people are still pagans. Many of them come to the meetings dressed in Indian costume, their faces painted and their hair long and plaited with the furs of small animals (Baird Papers, May 14, 1891).

Long hair and buffalo robes were symbols of Indian ways; by blotting out the symbols, the missionary could believe he had civilized the Indian. While no culture remains static, non-Indians assumed Indians were being assimilated because their culture was not what it had been at earliest European contact. Few of these changes reached below the surface to the fundamental roots of Indian culture.

The many requests for "suitable" clothing for the schools had the object of inculcating another Christian virtue — cleanliness.[48] Cleanliness ran second only to Godliness as a requisite characteristic of mission workers, as one testimonial given a prospective *teacher* illustrates: "Mrs. Currie is a pleasant earnest Christian woman and a good housekeeper" (Baird Papers, October 23, 1890).

Missionaries were soundly criticized for any relaxation of standards even where flexibility brought in converts:

> The proportionally large attendance at his school has been secured by accommodating the standard of tidiness in far too great a degree to what the Indians like (Baird Papers, March 14, 1890).

The missionaries were to preserve their superiority at all times; their creed being: "we do not adapt to become like the natives but we must make the natives become like us." Respectability was a Christian requirement of teachers and one which was feared might be compromised by too large a contact with the natives. This concern was greatly intensified with regard to Indian teachers and much attention was given to helping them to remain free of the corrupting influence of those who still followed the old ways.[49]

Educating the Indian

Since the job at hand was to civilize the Indians, and because of the presumed connection between civilization and Christianity, missionaries were delegated sole responsibility for Indian education.[50] This factor had important implications for the type of education Indians received. It was more important for the church's goals that their teachers be upright, God-fearing men and women than that they possess any great degree of academic training or teacher experience. An excerpt from a letter requesting testimonials for prospective teachers, illustrates the main concern of the church when hiring mission personnel:

> The principle (sic) qualifications we require are decided Christian character; a liking for children and work among them, some aptitude in teaching and a

reasonably good English education. Some training in the work of teaching or some experience in it is desirable but not indispensable (Baird Papers, July 18, 1890).

Applicants for teaching positions were more often turned down for a lack of missionary zeal than for any other reason. This often slowed down the work of the missions; few of the applicants attracted to the advertised positions combined the necessary qualifications of "sterling character and missionary zeal."

Not only was the quality of the teachers decidedly inferior, but their school facilities were clearly inadequate. Complaints against overcrowding were frequent. There were continual difficulties over money. There was no clear understanding of what the government was expected to pay for and what was the responsibility of the church. As a result, there were numerous clashes between church and state. The government, while realizing thousands of dollars yearly from the sale of land which was once occupied by Indians, shrugged aside responsibility for Indian education and were reluctant to supply more than the most inferior equipment.

The failure of the missions to assimilate Indians did not rest solely on their inadequate staff or facilities. The most important factor, an ignorance of Indian culture and values, affected the methods used and the content of what was taught. The entire structure and routine of the mission school represented a foreign way of life. Everything the children learned had a quality of fiction to it. The Indian child first learned the English alphabet and recited scriptures, but he never got beyond the words to the concepts which they contained. Report after report cited teacher experiences like the following:

> We find it very difficult to get them to understand what they read, to catch the idea and to express it in their own words... (they) are taught to memorize the Golien Texts, some of the questions in the Catechism, the Ten Commandments, the Lord's Prayer... (Baird Papers, May 2, 1890).

> I saw some very good writing by girls in the second book, but Mrs. Cameron says it is quite mechanical. They don't understand what they write (Baird Papers, May 8, 1890).

When the texts were repeated often enough, they remembered the different combinations of sounds on each page. The books became codes the children must learn to decipher (Robertson, 1970:150).

The teachers acknowledged neither Indian language nor culture. Because they made no attempt to see the world as the Indian saw it, they were continually amazed and frustrated in their efforts. The result was often an even stronger effort to mold the Indian children into white patterns:

> These children are pagan, uncivilized, savage... in every trait of character .... They need oversight, vigilant and ceaseless control, to be moulded and pressured almost day and night (Baird Papers, July 27, 1889).

Whatever the issue, the placement of a school, the amount of school holidays, the needs of the children, the opinions of Indian parents were discounted.

Because education was an essential part of cultural colonialism, absenteeism of Indian children could not be tolerated. Early in the reserve period, it was noted that boarding schools were necessary in order that Indian children could be kept separate from their home influence. But boarding schools were not enough in themselves to keep parents from their children. Truancy and extended holidays were a problem for the teachers even where the school was located some distance from the reserve, and it was a common complaint that Indian parents insisted on interfering in their children's education.

The issue of truant children is an excellent example of the juxtaposition of the cultural and structural components of colonialism. The church needed the power of the government to force children to attend the schools. The basic strategy was the withholding of rations. Hunger was not an inconsequential motivator. By 1874, a report to the Lieutenant Governor stated:

> There were no buffalo on the plains all winter and they have suffered frightfully. They told us that many Indians had eaten their horses, dogs, buffalo skins, and in some cases their snow shoe laces and moccasins and then died (Morris Papers, March 23, 1874).

Reports on the Indians in 1890 amply document the dire straits they had to be in before they acquiesced to the missionary's ministrations:

> The man is sick . . . . He is more like a skeleton than like a living man. He said "Look, my friend, look. Can't you take pity on me? Can you give me something to eat? I am poor and all my flesh is gone; but if I could only get flesh to eat, I think I could get well again." He listened attentively as I spoke to him about the bread of life that cometh from above and as soon as I was through speaking said "When can you let me have a little beef?" (Baird Papers, May 4, 1891).

Missionaries were not completely untouched by the Indians' plight. Much sadness was expressed over the "deplorable" conditions under which Indians were forced to live. At the same time, however, when the government moved to cut off the rations of those who refused to surrender their children, it was generally accepted as the proper policy. The church, with its monopoly on education, and the government, with its monopoly on money and power, formed an unbeatable combination that Indians must succumb to or die.

Religious Division

Although Indians had little chance to reject education for their children, they did have room for some manipulation. Different religious denominations provided some opportunities for Indians to play one off against the other. The late 1800s was characterized by fierce conflicts between churches. From the missionary letters and reports of the period, it would be easy to conclude that organized religion was less interested in "saving" the Indian than in preventing their rivals from doing so. These rivalries often led to feverish rushes to open up new districts.

If poverty forced Indians to give up their children to the white religions, at least the jealousies between the churches gave them an avenue to get the best deal. As long as they had some avenue of resistance open to them, cultural domination was not complete. They quickly perceived that there were several ways in which they could obtain necessities of life. Apples, tea, and flour could be obtained by submitting to baptism by the Catholics or by attending church meetings of the Protestants, and clothing was a frequent reward for bringing their children to school. The use of material bribes by the schools opened up a new means whereby Indians could feed and clothe themselves. Whatever their feelings about the conditions of obtaining such material benefits, there is evidence to suggest they became quite shrewd at getting the most they could from what was otherwise a bad deal. Confused by religions that preached brotherly love and tolerance, but whose actions belied their words, Indians adopted Christian concepts when they were useful and continued to practise their native religions.

While the presence of more than one religious denomination gave Indians some limited opportunity to make decisions affecting their lives, it also divided them. A new opposition was created among Indians of different denominations as well as between converted and heathen. Since more than one denomination was often set up on the same reserve, some families were divided against each other.[51] This fragmentation of the colonized into groups is a common feature of colonialism; it confirms the colonizer's opinion that indigenous people are incapable of governing themselves. Since they cannot agree, decisions must be made for them.

Given the missionaries' experience, it was perhaps inevitable that their reaction towards Indians should be ethnocentric. The European experience of conquest and progress developed in them the arrogance that sees their whole culture as superior to all others. By believing in the basic inferiority of Indians, their "divine right" to rule was established. Even more destructive than this principle of beneficent control was the belief that Indians could be "uplifted" by forcing them to reject their own culture and by imposing white values upon them. What is peculiar to the enforced socialization of a colonized people to a foreign culture, is that it ultimately has the effect of socializing, not for equality, but for dependence. In the end, the colonized define themselves in the terms of their oppressors and become convinced of their own sinfulness. It is one thing for the colonizer to believe in the inferiority of the colonized and control them accordingly; it is quite another thing when, in being "uplifted" the colonized come to believe in their own inferiority. Structural control, regardless of its benevolence, can be more easily overthrown than the education for inferiority which cultural control engenders.

Towards Decolonization

The Indians' Experience of Colonialism

Government agencies have retained power over the structure of Indian society resulting in a division of "spoils" in favor of the dominant white society. But retaining power over Indian institutions has required another kind of power — the power to define reality for Indian people. It has been said that the power to define others is the power to control, that "the most important power that any social group or 'nexus' has is the 'power to define reality' " (Levine, 1975:2). Without this kind of power, the colonizers would have had to maintain physical coercion. Indians have not attempted to overthrow an oppressive system, partly because they have been ill-equipped and ill-organized to do so; but equally as important as these structural constraints are their own internal constraints. The system has conditioned Indians to accept the situation. Their readiness to refrain from militancy in the past involves two aspects — the external pressures by the system in which they participate and their own internal motivations.

Although colonization may be analyzed on both cultural and structural levels, in reality, both levels merge. In Canada, both government and church shared a number of things in common in their relationship with Indians. All groups involved have shared a common belief and attitude towards Indians. "All consider the Indians and Métis as deviants to be brought back to some kind of secular or religious fold" (Dosman, 1972:127). All groups have in common this desire to assimilate the Indians and the belief that this is the best policy. All believe they are acting in the best interest of their "wards" and everything done "to" and "for" Indians is for their own "welfare." The rationalizations of the "caretakers" all share a deep commitment to a sense of division — an "us" and "them" orientation. But this belief in separate natures of racial identity "has not led to a belief in the equal distinctiveness of different racial identities but to a belief in the inherent inequality of these identities" (Rowley, 1970:88).

When one takes the attitude that one's own beliefs are superior, it follows naturally that what is being taught will not incorporate the "inferior" reality of the other. In teaching Indians the "right" way to think, believe and behave, the various agencies of colonialism have paid little attention to the experience of Indians. Missionaries did not encourage or equip the Indian people to know and respond to the concrete realities of their world; rather they were kept "submerged" in a situation in which such critical awareness and response were practically impossible. Education of the missionary kind could not liberate him for life in white society.[52] As Paulo Friere has observed:

> No pedagogy which is truly liberating can remain distant from the oppressed by treating them as unfortunates and by presenting for their emulation, models from among the oppressors (1968:39).[53]

Every solution posed as an answer to the social problems experienced by Indians has paid little attention to the experience of the people themselves. Yet, if we take as axiomatic that "behavior is a function of experience; and both experience and behavior are always in relation to someone or something other than self" (Laing, 1967:22), then it makes no sense to look for solutions by attempting to change behavior. Behavior is only the way we act on our perception of the world. Experience is the way we perceive the world (Levine, 1975:2). Thus, we cannot ignore the relationship between experience and behavior; the situation is impossible to grasp by studying the different people in it singly. It is the relation between actors in a system that is central.

When one realizes the total extent to which the Indians' world has been controlled, it appears that no move is possible. Yet if men are not to become simply objects they must act.[54] But, for the Indian,

> He cannot make a move, or no move without being beset by contradictory and paradoxical pressures and demands, pushes and pulls, both internally, from himself, and externally from those around him. He is, as it were, in a position of checkmate (Laing, 1967:95).

From the earliest days of the reserve period, Indians have been forced into manipulative strategies. Where such strategies have been unavailable to them, their reaction has not been one of acceptance but rather one of passive resistance.[55] Evidence of passive resistance to assimilation efforts can be found in missionary reports such as this one by a Presbyterian missionary:

> When we attempted to pray, our voices could scarcely be heard by reason of the noise made by the old people of the house... this only illustrates the feeling with which we meet on the reserve (Baird Papers, May 14, 1891).

George Manuel notes how those on his reserve resisted the church "silently, but so as to be heard — by not attending on the Sundays when the priest would come around, by drinking on Sunday. In a small community, those are pretty loud actions" (1974:101).

The submissive forms of action and withdrawal with which Indians protect themselves leave little room for the expression of anger, other than through self-abuse. Fanon (1963) has suggested that, in a situation where the oppressed feels himself stripped of his individuality and personality, a fury builds up inside him. This fury is not vented against his real enemy because of the omnipotent power which the oppressor has over him. In the preface to Fanon's *The Wretched of the Earth*, Jean Paul Sartre expresses a similar view:

> If this suppressed fury fails to find an outlet, it turns in a vacuum and devastates the oppressed creatures themselves.... In order to free themselves, they even massacre each other...the man who raises his knife against his brother thinks that he has destroyed once and for all the detested image of their common degradation, even though these expiatory customs don't quench their thirst for blood (1963:18).

For the oppressor, violence in Indian communities is seen as further evidence of the barbaric, uncivilized nature of Indians. What is not seen is that "violence is initiated by those who oppress, who exploit, who fail to recognize others as persons" (Friere, 1968:41). Violent behavior by Indians is a reaction to the violence of the oppressors, however misdirected such behavior might be.

The oppression and violence perpetrated on Indians is directly linked to the capitalist system. Capitalism is characterized by a culture of wealth where "the natural condition of man has been defined as affluence" (Levine,

1975:66). For the oppressor, in this system,

> *having* more is an inalienable right, a right they acquired through their own "effort" with their "courage to take risks." If others do not have more, it is because they are incompetent and lazy, and worst of all, is their unjustifiable ingratitude towards the "generous gestures" of the dominant class. Precisely because they are "ungrateful" and "envious," the oppressed are regarded as potential enemies who must be watched (Friere, 1968:45).

For those who adopt capitalist values, "having" becomes a condition of "being." Everything becomes reduced to the status of objects at their disposal. Since everything in their world can be possessed, humanity also becomes a "thing" to be possessed. From this view, the pursuit of full humanity is seen as subversion, and demands for full and equal rights are put down as being the work of extremists. In the "culture of wealth, politics is extrinsic to the individual's concern, because the individual's primary pursuit is not the public welfare, but his own private well-being" (Levine, 1975:68). Political activism is looked down upon as being unnecessary for freedom. Such beliefs conflict with the Indians' reality where "freedom can only be defined politically because it can only exist collectively" (Levine, 1975:69).

Even those who truly desire to transform the unjust order have not seen that they cannot be the executors of this transformation. The question is whether Indians are to be the subjects of their own world or the objects in someone else's. Anything done to and for Indians must be done by the Indians themselves. One perceptive Indian noted: "We picked up your shoes and tied them on by ourselves. Now we must untie them by ourselves. All we ask is that you quit tying the knots."[56] The self-deprecation by Indians is one such knot that handicaps them in two different but related ways. First, it convinces them that they can do nothing about their own situation,[57] and secondly, it co-opts the sympathy of middle-class Indians who "yearn to be equal to the eminent men of the upper class" (Friere, 1968:49). This phenomenon has been noted by Dosman (1972) in his analysis of the "affluent" Indian, but never more eloquently than by Maria Campbell's old Indian grandmother, Cheechum, who tells her granddaughter:

> Because some of them said "I want good clothes and houses, and you no-good Half-breeds are ruining it for me". ... They fought each other...the white man saw that that was a more powerful weapon than anything else with which to beat the Half-breeds...they try to make you hate your people (Campbell, 1973:47).

Consciousness — A First Step towards Decolonization

Of all the aims of colonialism, there is none worse than the attempt to make the colonized believe they had no indigenous culture of their own; or that what they did have was worthless and something to be ashamed of.[58] If Indians are to become subjects in their own world, they must first of all follow the advice of Becker to

> "Know thyself", know what prevents you from being self-reliant. Know how you were deprived of the ability to make your own judgements; know how the world view of your society was built into your perceptions; know how

those who trained you to see and think literally placed themselves into your mind; know how they became the self upon your self, the "superego" upon your "ego", the voice of conscience whispering behind your voice (1967:259).

It is absolutely essential that Indian people know their history. They have become alienated, not from the white society, but from their own world. Assimilationist policies have only perpetuated and enlarged their problem. A sense of common experience and identity is a first step towards the ending of this alienation. Politics, for Indians, must begin with the recognition that they exist as a distinct group with a distinct culture.[59] But while self-definition is the keystone for political action, it is important to remember that "consciousness is not a goal but rather a pre-condition for action" (Fannon, 1963:35) Consciousness is the base from which political action must grow. Without mass Indian support, the colonial system, which has made them objects in their own world, will not allow change in their social, political and economic environment. The power structure confronting them is oppressive and all-powerful and has every intention of remaining so (Munroe, 1974).

The continuance of cultural colonialism is dependent upon structural colonialism. Historically, missionaries required the support of the government to bring about cultural colonialism, and while both levels of colonialism are dependent upon each other, cultural colonialism cannot continue without structural support. While the overthrowing of colonialism must start with the consciousness of a large number of Indian people, the avoidance of further cultural colonialism is only possible with the ending of structural domination. The insidious colonization of experience can be stopped only *after* the structure of their society is transformed. Whether a radical change in the structure of Indian institutions is possible without a radical change in the structure of Canadian institutions generally is questionable. Nevertheless, given the position of Indians within Canadian society, it appears that their institutions are the logical place for a more general transformation to begin. Equality will not be achieved within the present capitalist structure; Indians need to build a new structure for themselves. If they must operate within a capitalist society, they must do so on a collective basis. Contrary to the general myth, groups have a greater chance to prosper under capitalism when they cooperate on a collective basis. Both self-employed farmers and wage laborers rely on collective action in their struggle against monopoly capital.[60]

Without economic power, Indians will remain subject to the control and pity of their fellow Canadians. With the need for economic power, the recognition of aboriginal rights to land and resources becomes paramount. In Canada today, this issue is recognized as being of the utmost importance by all organized Indian groups. Only through collective political action can these land claims be realized, and only when Indians have control over the resources of those lands will they possess any degree of economic power.

The Fourth World[61]

The greatest barrier to recognition of aboriginal rights and to Indian-white coexistence has been in the basic assumptions which have been made "both about Canada and its history and about Indian people and their culture" (Manuel, 1974:224). The failure of such coexistence has been a failure to accept differences as well as similarities. The history of white-Indian relations "bears witness to our intolerance of different fundamental structures of experience. We seem to need to share a communal meaning to human existence, to give with others a common sense to the world, to maintain a consensus" (Laing, 1967:65). But to insist on a consensus when one does not exist is to believe in the myth, in the liberal ideology that has created the situation which human experience is subordinated to mythology. By insisting on the imposition of this mythology, the agencies involved have invalidated and destroyed the Indians' experience. If they are to reclaim their experience, both Indian and non-Indian must come to realize that there is a valid, lasting Indian identity.

In the words of the African diplomat who pointed out that political independence for colonized peoples was only the Third World: "When native peoples come into their own, on the basis of their own cultures and traditions, that will be the Fourth World" (Manuel, 1974:236).

NOTES

1. The model for two levels of colonialism was adapted from Wilkinson (1974).

2. For analytical purposes, the state and its various agencies can be shown to be the principal tools of structural colonialism. In reality, however, the state and the church each perpetuated both levels of colonialism, differing only in the degree of power they held at the two levels of colonialism. The government provided the structural power which enabled the church to perpetuate cultural colonialism while the church provided legitimation for state control at the institutional level.

3. The more sagacious Indian chiefs spoke prophetically, like the Blackfoot Chief, Many Stars, who proclaimed: "Have your good time now! Times are changing. Buffalo will soon leave. They will be shown to you only by the white men; you will not meet them. There will be no hearthstones to mark where you have camped. People will live on the river bottoms. You will make a living from earth, sell grass, sell rocks, sell trees to get things to eat. The only buckskin will be your moccasins" (Hanks, 1950:12).

4. For instance, the Hudson's Bay Company was given parcels of land in exchange for their rights in the NWT before any treaties had been made with Indians.

5. According to Patterson (1972), cross-cultural misunderstandings and conflict because of different land tenure concepts is one of the most frequently occurring and frequently observed aspects of colonial situations.

6. See Rothney (1975:79-81) for discussion of Indian property concepts.

7. The restrictions that have been imposed clearly have not been of benefit to native people. For example, the Migratory Bird Treaty, signed 60 years ago between Canada and the U.S. restricts legal hunting of migratory game birds from mid-March to the end of August, nearly the whole period when birds are available in the north and during the time when northern people say their need for food is the greatest. The intention of preventing spring shooting was to preserve the stock of birds while leaving unhindered fall and winter hunting by American sportsmen (*Winnipeg Free Press*, March 27, 1976, p. 70).

8. See Hodgets (1955:209) for discussion of this paradox.

9. The use of such indirect rule in the administration of aboriginal people is a widespread colonial practice (see Patterson, 1972).

10. For tribes like the Cree and the Blackfoot, the basic unit of organization was not the tribe, but the band, a smaller group whose political leader derived his authority from personal prestige rather than the powers of his office. These chiefs acted only when a general consensus was reached by the band. Now, however, the new chief, representing the whole tribe, was to play a more powerful role in the matter of negotiating away Indian land (Patterson, 1972).

11. "He could put Indians into prison, determine their sentences...take children away from their parents, decide where an Indian should place his residence and prescribe his daily routine" (Peretti, 1973:40).

12. Frank (1969) notes that while a universal characteristic of capitalism is the monopoly power a metropolis holds over its satellites, this monopoly may vary in form (146). In the case of Indians, this monopoly takes a "feudal" form. This feudal-like structure, entrenched in the Indian Act, is a tool of capitalism rather than feudalism *per se*. As we argue later in this paper, it is capitalism, not the perceived feudalism, as expressed by the Indian Act, that needs to be overturned.

13. Until 1961, Indians were unable to vote unless they renounced their status as Indians (Indian Act, Section 10).

14. The definition of economic imperialism used here is that of James O'Connor: "The economic domination of one region or country over another, specifically, the formal or informal control over local economic resources in a manner advantageous to the metropolitan power, and at the expense of the local economy" (1972:119).

15. The metropolis-hinterland analysis has been articulated best by Andre Gunder Frank (1966, 1967, 1969, 1972).

16. See Elias (1975) for discussion of northern Indians as an underclass.

17. See Rothney (1975) for documentation of promising agricultural beginnings on Canadian Indian reserves.

18. Zaslow (1971) cites one such move where the St. Peter's Reserve, consisting of prime agricultural land, was exchanged for another at Fisher River, "which was better suited to the Indians' occupational interests and threw fewer urban temptations their way."

19. Lithman (1973), in a study of the Fort Alexander Indian reserve, traces the development of wild rice from the days of the early fur trade when it was picked and processed by Indians for local consumption in a subsistence economy, through phases of local consumption mixed with a market economy, to today's paddy production, which produces a commercial crop with major food chains involved in the marketing.

20. Several of the Fort Alexander Indians, who were anxious to expand their wild rice operations, wondered, "Why do they give this kind of money to that university guy when we have to fight like hell to get money for economic development?" (Lithman, 1973).

21. See Brett (1973) for a discussion of the same process in East Africa.

22. The Economic Development Fund (EDF), established to develop Indian reserves, makes no provision for upgrading manpower or for services that will encourage the more highly skilled Indians to stay in the area.

23. For examples of such dislocation caused by the construction of dams on the Peace, Columbia, Kootenay, Iskut and Stekine Rivers in British Columbia, from the alteration of lake levels in northcentral Manitoba and northwestern Ontario

and from the James Bay Development project, see NIB (1973). They estimate that evidence before the courts in the James Bay Development project will seriously impair the livelihood of 8,000 aboriginal people. Whole communities are considered expendable, with no value placed on their collective life and traditions.

24. "During the construction of the Pointed Mountain Pipeline, only 30 native people were employed for a maximum of three months, while 320 workers were brought in from the south. In 1970, after the federal government had invested 9 million in the Panarctic, it had employed only 6 natives at $1.75 an hour" (Laxer, 19:122).

25. The NIB (1973) notes that an estimated 6,200 Indian people have lost their economic base on Lake Winnipeg through the dumping of raw waste into major prairie rivers, while in New Brunswick, a paper company is building a waste disposal line across the St. Basile Indian reserve to a disposal south of the reserve. The latter project is being undertaken without even instituting formal legal arrangements prior to its construction. Moreover, it is fraught with grave environmental consequences.

26. See Elias for analysis of the role of the permanently unemployed Indian in the capitalist economy.

27. Davis (1972:12) noted that the term hinterland "may also usefully denote urban under-classes as well as rural peasantries and rural proletariats."

28. Since 94.8% of Northern Manitoba Indians and 89.8% of Northern Saskatchewan Indians were unemployed in 1969, it is to be expected that the 4.7% national rate for that year would have been drastically altered if reserve figures were included (Elias, 1975:113). It should also be noted, as Elias does, that other groups, such as housewives, form part of the permanently unemployed class.

29. The reaction of the government officials to Indian involvement has often been the same as that of the teacher on an Indian reserve who commented: "If we got the community involved, they'd just haggle and bicker and mess things up and we'd never get anywhere" (Robertson, 1970:59).

30. Dosman (1972) has concluded that urban poverty programs are merely "sterile exchanges of money for more or less good behavior."

31. Interestingly, although help was refused to the Big Bear Gallery, an almost identical project was later supported because the treasurer would be an IAB official (Dosman, 1972:160).

32. See "Indians Protest Their Exclusion," *Winnipeg Free Press*, Sept. 25, 1975. Also note recent developments regarding the federal government's indirect transferring of financial responsibility for Indian programs to the provinces — one of the major White Paper recommendations which was rejected by the Indians.

33. In the 1930s, a farm instructor on one of the reserves decided to purchase more draught horses for reserve families. But when the animals arrived, few families knew how to care for them, and the result was that only two families benefited. The redirection of collective band funds into private hands created power division on the reserve by isolating the two "loading families" (Dosman, 1972:57).

34. See Brett (1973) for colonial parallel in East Africa.

35. See Dosman (1972) for illustrations of how this weapon has fragmented Indian leadership.

36. Various writers have pointed out that the strategy of co-opting leadership, thus providing further indirect rule, is a basic feature of colonialism wherever it is found. See Dosman (1972), Brett (1973), Patterson (1972), Manuel (1974).

37. In the same session of of the Special Joint Committee of 1947, anthropologist Diamond Jenness, in speaking to the Maorie, "called attention to the pride of race among them, and to their degree of progress in political and social matters" (Patterson, 1972:13).

38. See Maria Campbell (1973) for the experience of her family in this regard.

39. This has been put very well by Tax and Stanley (1971:186): "They say, in effect, that as long as we pay the bills, we shall manage your communities. If you think you are competent to manage your own affairs, then cut yourselves off from the financial assistance as well. Money to live on, or freedom; you can't have both, so take your choice."

40. It did not go unrecognized that the conversion of Indians to Christianity could benefit the world of business, as this quote from Governor Simpson's Journal indicates: "They would in time imbibe our manners and customs and imitate us in dress; our supplies would thus become necessary to them which would increase the consumption of European produce and manufactures and in like measure increase and benefit our trade as they would find it requisite to become more industrious and to turn their attention more seriously to the chase in order to be enabled to provide themselves with such supplies" (Merk, Fur Trade and Empire: George Simpson's *Journal*, as quoted by Rothney, 1975:106)

41. The deep feelings the Indian people felt towards the land gives significance to this quotation. Kitty Maracle (*Reply on Behalf of Native Peoples and the Criminal Justice System*, Edmonton, Alberta, 1975) put it this way: "The land is our Mother Earth. We never thought that we could own it nor sell it nor possess it for she is our mother."

42. See R.D. Laing (1967) for the concept of "mystification of experience."

43. The main sources for conclusions drawn in this section of the paper were the Baird papers 1889 to 1891 depicting the Presbyterian experience, Rev. J. Hines' autobiographical book, *The Red Indians of the Plains*, depicting the Anglican experience during the same period, and to a lesser degree, the translated works of Msgr. Taché and the D.A. Stewart Correspondence. See Bibliography for a fuller description of this primary source material.

44. It was often necessary to call upon the government to help through the withholding of rations. As one Indian agent reported, this was generally an effective measure: "One family missed one ration and then decided that it was better to abide by the rules. The other two families held out for several rations and then they succumbed and put away wife no. two" (A.J. Markle, Agent of Blackfoot Reserve).

45. Indian societies generally discouraged the accumulation of individual or family wealth. Any status difference usually resulted from what the individual gave away, not from what he acquired and kept. An effective means of sharing and redistributing wealth was the Indian Potlatch ceremony.

46. Instructions of the Committee to the Rev. W.B. Bompass, returning from and to Mr. A. J. Shaw, Mr. J. Reader, and Mr. J. Hines, proceeding to join the North-west America Mission, delivered April 28, 1874, Archives of the Eccl. Province of Ruperts Land, PAM M/S3301.

47. C.D. Rowley (1970) reports the same assumptions being held by missionaries in Australia.

48. Judith Binney (1968) reported that missionaries in New Zealand were concerned with these same things.

49. One such Indian teacher, Mr. Black, was forced to retire to his reserve due to ill

health. The mission administration were concerned that their "good work" would all be lost. They attempted to relocate him, writing to him that if he remained on the reserve he would be unlikely to get on in the world, and it would be better if he were to "remove from the reserve at the Crowsland and try to make (his) living like a white man" (Baird Papers, 1890).

50. The Canadian government did not participate in the education of Indian children until the early 1950s.

51. At the Muscowpetung reserve in Regina, an Indian father and two of his sons were baptized by the Roman Catholics, and later, the mother and two other sons were baptized by the resident Presbyterian minister. When the father died, all four boys were placed in the Presbyterian school, whereupon the Roman Catholic church wrote to Ottawa to get leave to take "their" charges by force (Baird Papers, Feb. 28, 1890).

52. The educational system under federal auspices continued the use of non-native teachers, instruction wholly in English, curriculum oriented to white culture and values and minimal attempts to produce text materials appropriate to the Indian. In major respects, Indian education is only an extended replication of the original mission program.

53. Paulo Friere (1968), working among contemporary peasants in Brazil, has shown that, when what is being taught is relevant to their experience and their concerns, illiterate people can be taught to read and write in six weeks. Hobart and Brant (1966), in a comparison of the Greenland system of education under Danish administration with that of the Eskimo in the Canadian Arctic, demonstrated how the educational policies of the Danes fostered cultural continuity among the Greenlanders. Their methods included local teachers, local relevance of curriculum content, and instruction given in the mother tongue. "The purpose of education was to assist people to make their living where they were. As a result, illiteracy was abolished a century ago, social separation of Danes and Greenlanders is minimal and a high degree of group self-esteem has been maintained."

54. "To alienate men from their own decision making is to change them into objects" (Friere, 1968:13).

55. For examples of manipulative strategies used by Indians, see Neils Braroe's study of Indian-white interaction in a western Canadian town; also see Robertson (1970) for an analysis of excessive drinking as a form of protest.

56. Words to this effect were spoken by an Indian attending the Ethnic Peoples Conference in Winnipeg during November 1975.

57. "Underdevelopment . . . is perpetuated above all by our collective mentality of dependence and impotence with respect to the supposed superiority of the economic, political, and even the cultural institutions, of the dominant metropolis. It follows that the first step towards an escape from underdevelopment and hinterland status is the self-definition and self-assertion of a society in its own terms" (Kari Levitt, *Silent Surrender*, in relation to Quebec, as quoted in *Canadian Dimension*, Vol. 8, No. 6, 1972:28).

58. Julius Nyerere, President of Tanzania, in speaking of the African experience, used a similar denunciation of colonialism.

59. This does not mean regressing to a culture that no longer exists but involves the creation of a new revolutionary culture. Such a task will remain difficult for Indians until they obtain some influence in the educational structure, both in content and in manner of teaching. Their education to date has stressed individual

achievement at the expense of the collectivity. As far as Indians are concerned, the educational system has been a manipulative system "whose 'real hidden curriculum' is the legitimation of an elite and the indoctrination into a consumer society" (Ivan Illich as quoted by Levine, 1975:73).

60. In contrast to Canadian Indians, "Mennonite settlements, which initially appeared in Manitoba during the 1870's, have experienced steady, relative economic success alongside community economic co-operation" (Rothney, 1975:169). Also see Zaslow (1971) for a study of the Indian village of Metlakatla as a cooperative economic unit.

61. "The Fourth World" is the title of the book by George Manuel and Michael Posluns (1974), which has outlined the Indian experience of colonialism.

REFERENCES

Baird Papers 1889-1891. University of Winnipeg. Mic E 9002, C2B3 No. 9.

Becker, Ernest. *Beyond Alienation.* New York: George Brazillier, 1967.

Berger, Carl. *The Sense of Power: Studies in the Ideas of Canadian Imperialism 1867 - 1914.* Toronto: University of Toronto Press, 1970.

Binney, Judith. *The Legacy of Guilt.* New Zealand: Oxford University Press, 1968.

Braroe, Neils Winther. "Reciprocal Exploitation in an Indian-White Community," in Mark Nagler, ed., *Perspectives on the North American Indians.* Toronto: McClelland and Stewart, 1972.

Brett, E. A. *Colonialism and Underdevelopment in East Africa.* London: Heinemann Educational Books, 1973.

Campbell, Maria. *Half-breed.* Toronto: McClelland and Stewart, 1973.

Canadian Dimension. Kit No. 10. Native People's Kit.

Cardinal, Harold. *The Unjust Society: The Tragedy of Canada's Indians.* Edmonton: M G. Hurtig, 1969.

Cohen, Felix S. "Indian Self-Government," in Alvin M. Josephy Jr., ed., *Red Power: The American Indian's Fight for Freedom.* New York: McGraw-Hill, 1971.

Cummings, Peter A. and Neil H. Mickenberg. *Native Rights in Canada.* Toronto: The Indian-Eskimo Association of Canada, 1972.

Davis, Arthur K. "Metropolis/Overclass - Hinterland/Underclass," *Canadian Dimension,* Vol. 8, No. 6 (Mar./Apr. 1972).

————. "Canadian Society and History as Hinterland Versus Metropolis," in R. Ossenberg, ed., *Canadian Society: Pluralism, Change and Conflict.* Scarborough: Prentice-Hall, 1971, pp. 6-32.

Deprez, Paul. "Education and Economic Development: The Case of Indian Reserves in Canada," *Two Papers on Canadian Indians.* Centre for Settlement Studies: The University of Manitoba, 1973.

Dosman, Edgar. *Indians: The Urban Dilemma.* Toronto: McClelland and Stewart, 1972.

Elias, Peter Douglas. *Metropolis and Hinterland in Northern Manitoba.* Winnipeg: The Manitoba Museum of Man and Nature, 1975.

Fanon, Franz. *The Wretched of the Earth.* New York: Grove Press, 1963.

Fidler, Dick. *Red Power in Canada.* Toronto: Vanguard Publications, 1970.

Frank, Andre Gunder. *Capitalism and Underdevelopment of Latin America.* New York: Monthly Review Press, 1962.

_____. *Latin America: Underdevelopment or Revolution.* New York: Monthly Review Press, 1962.

_____. *Lumpenbourgeoisie: Lumpendevelopment.* New York: Monthly Review Press, 1972.

_____. "The Development of Underdevelopment," *Monthly Review* (Sept. 1966).

Friere, Paulo. *Pedagogy of the Oppressed.* New York: The Seabury Press, 1968.

Gonick, Cy. "Themes," *Canadian Dimension,* Vol. 8, No. 6 (Mar./Apr. 1972).

Hanks, Lucien M. Jr. and Jane Richardson Hanks. *Tribe Under Trust: A Study of the Blackfoot Reserve of Alberta.* Toronto: University of Toronto Press, 1950.

Hines, Rev. J. *The Red Indians of the Plains.* London: Society for Promoting Christian Knowledge, 1919.

Hobart, C. W. and C. S. Brant. "Eskimo Education, Danish and Canadian: A Comparison," *Canadian Review of Anthropology and Sociology* (May 1966), pp. 47-66.

Hodgets, J. E. *Pioneer Public Service, An Administrative History of the United Canadas 1843-1867.* Toronto: University of Toronto Press, 1955.

Indian Chiefs of Alberta. *Citizens Plus.* A Presentation by the Indian Chiefs of Alberta to Right Honourable P. E. Trudeau, Prime Minister, and the Government of Canada, June 1970.

Josephy, A. M. Jr. "The New Indian Patriots," in Alvin M. Josephy Jr., ed., *Red Power: The American Indian's Fight for Freedom.* New York: McGraw-Hill, 1971.

Laing, R. D. *The Politics of Experience.* London: Penguin Books, 1967.

Laxer, James. *Canada's Energy Crisis.* Toronto: James, Lewis and Samuel.

Levine, Paul. *Divisions.* Toronto: CBC Publications, 1975.

Lithman, Y. G. "The Capitalization of A Traditional Pursuit: The Case of Indian Reserves in Canada," *Two Papers on Canadian Indians.* Centre for Settlement Studies: The University of Manitoba, 1973.

Lurie, Nancy G. "Forked Tongue in Cheek or Life Among the Noble Civilage," *The Indian Historian* (Spring 1974).

Manuel, George and Michael Posluns. *The Fourth World: An Indian Reality.* New York: The Free Press, 1974.

Maracle, Kitty. "Reply on Behalf of Native People to Introductory Remarks," given at the National Conference on Native Peoples and the Criminal Justice System held at Edmonton, Feb. 3-5, 1975.

May, Rollo. "Man's Search for Himself," in Ronald V. Urick, ed., *Alienation: Individual or Social Problem.* Englewood Cliffs: Prentice-Hall, 1970.

Morris Papers. Provincial Archives of Manitoba.

National Indian Brotherhood. *Aboriginal People of Canada and Their Environment.* Ottawa: National Indian Brotherhood, 1973.

Nkramah, Kwame. *Neo-Colonialism: The Last Stage of Imperialism.* London: Heinemann Educational Books, 1976.

Nyerere, Julius K. *Freedom and Unity.* London: Oxford University Press, 1966.

————. *Ujamaa: Essays on Socialism.* London: Oxford University Press, 1966.

O'Connor, James. "Imperialism and Underdevelopment," in Robert I. Rhodes, ed., *Imperialism and Underdevelopment.* New York: Monthly Review Press, 1970.

Patterson, E. Palmer. *The Canadian Indian.* Don Mills: Collier Macmillan Canada, 1972.

Peretti, Peter O. "Enforced Acculturation and Indian-White Relations," *The Indian Historian* (Winter 1973).

Robbins, William G. "Extinguishing Land Title," *The Indian Historian* (Winter 1974).

Robertson, Heather. *Reservations Are For Indians.* Toronto: James, Lewis and Samuel, 1970.

Rogers, D., ed. *Pilot, Not Commander.* Ottawa: Anthropologica, St. Paul University, 1971.

Rothney, Russell George. *Mercantile Capital and the Livelihood of Residents of the Hudson Bay Basin: A Marxist Interpretation.* M. A. Thesis, University of Winnipeg, 1975.

Rowley, C. D. *The Destruction of Aboriginal Society.* Canberra: Social Science Research Council of Australia, 1970.

Swankey, Ben. *National Identity or Cultural Genocide? Reply to Ottawa's New Indian Policy.* Toronto: Progress Books, 1970.

Stewart Correspondence. Provincial Archives of Manitoba.

Taché, Father. *French Missions Among the Indians of the North West.* Provincial Archives of Manitoba.

Tax, Sol and Sam Stanley. "Indian Identity and Economic Development," in Alvin M. Josephy Jr., ed. *Red Power: The American Indian's Fight for Freedom.* New York: McGraw-Hill, 1971.

Warrior, Clyde. "We Are Not Free," in Alvin M. Josephy Jr., ed., *Red Power: The American Indian's Fight For Freedom.* New York: McGraw-Hill, 1971.

Waubegshig. *The Only Good Indian.* Toronto: New Press, 1972.

Wayne, Jack. "Colonialism and Underdevelopment in Kigoma Region, Tanzania: A Social Structural View," *Canadian Review of Anthropology and Sociology,* Vol. 12 (Aug. 1975), pp. 316-32.

West Papers. Copy of Address by John Davidson Smith to Seneca Indians, Apr. 19, 1828.

Wilkinson, Gerald. "Colonialism Through the Media," *The Indian Historian* (Summer 1974).

Zaslow, Morris. *The Opening of the Canadian North, 1870-1914.* Toronto: McClelland and Stewart, 1971.

Zentner, Henry. "The Impending Identity Crisis Among Native Peoples," in D. P. Gagnon, ed., *Prairie Perspectives: Papers of the Western Canadian Studies Conference.* Toronto: Holt, Rinehart and Winston of Canada, 1970.

Women and Inequality:
Some Indicators of Change

DAN A. CHEKKI / JOHN R. HOFLEY

During the past decade a large number of articles and books on, about, and for women have appeared in Canada. While the authors may argue about how to understand and explain the situation of women, there is no disagreement on one basic fact — women in Canada experience immense inequality in the workplace and at home.

Two fundamental material sets of conditions affect all our lives, but especially the lives of women. These are work and family. The purpose of this article is to examine women and inequality through an analysis of the changing nature of the work of women in Canada and the structure of the family. Both are best seen as consequences of Canada's economic system, particularly as it has developed since the Second World War.

Work in Canada

To understand fully the relationship between inequality and women in Canada it is necessary to study the development of monopoly capitalism. All social relationships, including those between males and females, those within the family, and those in the work world have been profoundly altered during the past century by the changes in our capitalistic economy.

The wealth created by the economy is distributed according to the needs and wants of the dominant class — in a capitalist society such as ours, this means the owners of the capital and some members of certain professional and managerial groups that have strong linkages with the owners, for example, lawyers, accountants, and doctors. So while it is true that women in every social class have experienced discrimination and oppression, working-class women suffer greater inequalities than middle- and upper-class women.[1]

The roots of women's inequality rest in two fundamental shifts that began at the turn of the century: (1) the decline of the family as a relatively autonomous and economic unit, and (2) the transformation of women into wage-laborers. The first change preceded the second. In the 19th and early 20th centuries, the majority of Canadians still lived in a rural setting, and production was centered in the home (Table 1). As Braverman notes: "So long as the bulk of the population lived on farms or in small towns, commodity production confronted a barrier that limited its expansion" (1974:272). The rural household relied heavily on its own skills for both the production and consumption of food, clothing, and shelter. In addition, the family and the community relied on one another for social life. In general, the young, the sick, and the aged were looked after by members of the community. Women, within this social milieu, played an important role.

With urbanization, the conditions that made it possible to be relatively self-sufficient were destroyed. Goods such as clothing and food were now manufactured. The marketplace began to intervene in the household.

> Thus the population no longer relies upon social organization in the form of family, friends, neighbors, community, elders, children, but with few exceptions must go to market and only to market, not only for food, clothing, and shelter, but also for recreation, amusement, security, for the care of the young, the old, the sick, the handicapped. In time not only the material and service needs but even the emotional patterns of life are channeled through the market (Braverman, 1974:276.)

The consequences for women of this transformation are far-reaching.

Table 1

Percentage of Urban* Population, Canada, 1851-1971

Year	% Urban Population
1851	13.1
1861	15.8
1871	18.3
1881	23.8
1891	29.8
1901	34.9
1911	41.8
1921	47.4
1931	52.5
1941	55.7
1951	62.4
1961	69.7
1971	76.1
1976	76.0

*The term "urban" as defined by Canadian censuses, varies. For the period 1871-1941, it refers to "population living in incorporated villages, towns, cities, regardless of size." For the 1951 census, the term "urban" refers to all persons living in cities, towns, villages of 1,000 persons or over, whether incorporated or not, and urban fringe of census metropolitan areas.

This definition was revised for the 1956 census so as to include urban fringe of major urban areas (i.e., cities with a population of 25,000-50,000). The 1961 and 1966 censuses followed this revised definition.

In the 1971 census, the term "urban" refers to (i) "population of incorporated cities, towns and villages with a population of 1,000 or over, (ii) or unincorporated places of 1,000 persons or over having a population density of at least 1,000 per square mile, or (iii) built up fringes of (i) and (ii) having a minimum population of 1,000 and density of at least 1,000 per square mile."

Source: Statistics Canada, *Typology of the Canadian Population: A Proposal for a Change in the Definition of Urban and Rural Population*, Ottawa, 1978.

Table 2

Labor Force Participation Rates by Sex, 1921-1975

Year	Male	Female
1921	89.8	19.9
1931	87.2	21.8
1941	85.6	22.9
1951	83.9	23.5
1961	79.8	28.7
1971	76.1	36.5
1975	77.2	40.9

Source: Statistics Canada, *Perspective Canada*, Ottawa, 1977, Table 6.1.

As modern, urban, nuclear families become more and more "conjugal," that is, increasingly cut off from their kin and friends for support, the role of "housewife and mother" takes on a new quality. Women have always seen the role as very difficult, burdensome and at many times unpleasant, but they seldom questioned it as severely as they do now. As Dorothy Smith writes:

> The division of labor between the sexes does not as such create a relation of oppression of men against women. It is the constitution of public versus private spheres of action, and the relegation of the domestic to that sphere which is outside history — this is the contemporarily relevant transformation and the contemporary form of oppression (Stephenson, 1973:7).

The work of women then, formerly under their own control, becomes, in an urban and industrialized setting, devalued. The marketplace intrudes upon and transforms women's work. Labor in the household becomes uneconomical. The availability of manufactured goods, albeit cheapened, slowly begins either to drive women out of the household and into industry, or to force them to remain in the "home," but now a home "which is external to the managerial structure and external therefore to that place where the decisions which have consequences for the condition of their existence are made" (Stephenson, 1973:13). Thus, in Canada today, the urban housewife becomes either a "consumer" tangentially linked to an economic system, or a wage-laborer.

> The function of the family as a cooperative enterprise pursuing the joint production of a way of life is brought to an end, and with this its other functions are progressively weakened (Braverman, 1974:277).

Monopoly capitalism has transformed the division of labor. Therefore, a comprehension of women's position in Canadian society must begin with an understanding of overall shifts in the occupational structure and the particular place of women within that structure.

As Table 2 indicates, women have markedly increased their participation in the labor force since 1921. When we consider the marital status of the female, the shift becomes clearly one of an enormous increase in the proportion of married women in the labor force. In 1941, 12.7% of female workers were married; in 1971, 56.7% were married.

Table 3

Percentage of the Total Labor Force in Major Occupational Groups, 1901-1971

Occupation	1901	1911	1921	1931	1941	1951	1961	1971
White-collar	15.2	16.8	25.1	24.5	25.2	32.4	38.6	42.5
Proprietary and managerial	4.3	4.6	7.2	5.6	5.4	7.5	7.9	4.3
Professional	4.6	3.7	5.5	6.4	6.7	7.4	10.0	12.7
Clerical	3.2	3.8	6.8	6.7	7.2	10.8	12.9	16.0
Commercial and financial	3.1	4.7	5.6	6.4	5.9	6.7	7.8	9.5
Manual	32.2	36.4	31.3	33.8	33.4	37.7	34.9	29.2
Manufacturing and mechanical	15.9	13.7	11.4	11.5	16.0	17.4	16.4	13.7
Construction	4.7	4.7	4.7	4.7	4.7	5.6	5.3	5.6
Laborers	7.2	12.0	9.7	11.3	6.3	6.8	5.4	3.2
Transportation and communication	4.4	5.7	5.5	6.3	6.4	7.9	7.9	6.7
Service	8.2	7.7	7.4	9.2	10.5	8.6	10.8	11.2
Personal	7.8	7.5	5.8	8.3	9.3	7.4	9.3	8.9
Protective and other	0.4	0.2	1.3	0.9	1.2	1.2	1.5	2.3
Primary	44.4	39.4	36.3	32.5	30.6	20.1	13.1	7.7
Agriculture	40.3	34.3	32.7	28.8	25.8	15.9	10.2	5.9
Fishing, trapping	1.6	1.3	0.9	1.2	1.2	1.0	0.6	0.3
Logging	0.9	1.5	1.2	1.4	1.9	1.9	1.3	0.8
Mining, quarrying	1.6	2.3	1.5	1.4	1.7	1.3	1.0	0.7
Not stated	–	–	0.2	–	0.3	1.2	2.6	8.5
Not elsewhere classified	–	–	–	–	–	–	–	0.9
All occupations								
Percent	100.0	100.0	100.0	100.0	100.0	100.0	100.0	100.0
Number (in thousands)	1,782.8	2,723.6	3,164.3	3,917.6	4,196.0	5,214.9	6,342.3	8,626.9

Source: Patricia Connelly, *Last Hired, First Fired*, Table 7.4.

What sorts of shifts in the occupational structure have created this increase? What type of work are women doing? Why are married women increasingly going outside the home to work?

The three major shifts in the type of work done in Canadian society since 1901 are: (1) A steady increase in the proportion of persons working in white-collar jobs — from 15.2% in 1901 to 42.5% in 1971; (2) a dramatic decline in primary occupations — from 40.3% in 1901 to 5.9% in 1971; and (3) a rather steady proportion of workers classified as "manual" — 32.2% in 1901 and 29.2% in 1971 (see Table 3).

Tables 4, 5, and 6 examine these shifts by sex to see if both men and women are similarly affected, and where the increasing number of women entering the labor force are going. While the proportion of women doing white-collar work has increased immensely since 1901, a closer inspection of these tables shows that women entering the labor force tend to be within the white-collar category, in clerical fields. For example, in 1971, 32% of all women in the labor force were clerks. As Patricia Connelly explains:

> Clerical work as we now know it is largely a product of the period of monopoly capitalism. ... As small enterprises grew into large corporations, office work... expanded until each function was separated into different sections or departments of the corporation (Connelly, 1978:61).

As women moved into the labor force they did *not* compete with men for jobs. What happened was that jobs became *de facto* segregated by sex (see Tables 7, 8, 9, and 10). The data for 1971 have to be given separately because of changes in the census classification. These data show how remarkably consistent the pattern of job segregation has been since 1941. The consequences of this segregation have been noted by Connelly.

> While occupational segregation prevents female workers from competing directly for individual male jobs, the existence of a distinct female labor market has a competitive effect on the male labor force in the long run.

> Men must continually compete to establish or maintain certain occupations as more highly paid men's jobs. As long as more poorly paid female jobs exist, there is always the danger that male occupations will be re-evaluated on the basis of female occupations and wages (1978:40).

Women then have been forced into the workplace, segregated into certain jobs and utilized by the capitalist class as a source of relatively cheap labor.

Tables 11, 12 and 13 document the inequality in wages between males and females. This inequality cannot, as Table 10 shows, be explained away by saying that women have less education or training than men, because in almost every category the female/male earnings ratio is less than .70. The exceptions are between single and young males and females.

Tables 11 and 12 show that even in professional occupations or in occupations that are "female" the incomes of women are very unequal. Connelly sums up this data extremely well.

When women work outside the home they receive, in general, a lower wage than male workers. Wage differentials favoring men have always existed in Canada. The husband's wage has been expected to support the entire family.

> From the capitalist point of view, women at most need to be paid only enough to support themselves until they marry. Once they marry, the cost of their maintenance and the cost of rearing children will be included in their husband's wage. In this way women's labor comes to have a lower value; it is cheap labor (1978:41).

Thus, women, particularly married women, form a vast pool of cheap labor, what Marx calls a "reserve army."[2] As Braverman remarks:

> Women form the ideal reservoir of labor for the new mass occupations. The barrier which confines women to much lower pay scales is reinforced by the vast numbers in which they are available to capital (1974:385).

In this section we have seen that shifts in the industrial and occupational structure of Canada's economy have significantly altered the roles of women. Women are participating in the labor force, but in jobs that are sexually labeled. Even when they perform the same tasks as men, their wages are significantly lower.

These changes must of necessity affect the nature of the family in our society, both the relationships within the family and the family's relationship to the larger society. The following section will examine briefly a few of these changes.

The Family

Work within the home, despite the increasing participation of married women with children in the labor force, remains primarily the responsibility of women. Pat and Hugh Armstrong, in their book *The Double Ghetto*, write:

> And this work of women is segregated from the work men do in the labor force. Not only are women segregated into a predominantly female workplace, the home, but this workplace is becoming increasingly privatized and isolated from those of all other workers (1978:89-90).

Clearly, this situation will affect not only women but their relationships with their husbands and children. As the family, under monopoly capitalism, becomes increasingly isolated, marriages and families will more and more become tied not through the relationships within the household, but through relationships to the workplace outside.

Women, under such strains, surely will and are adapting to these shifts in the economic system. We would like to examine briefly three possible consequences of these changing patterns in the work world upon the family: day care, fertility and childlessness, and divorce and separation.

Table 4

Percentage of the Female Labor Force in Major Occupational Groups, 1901-1971

Occupation	1901	1911	1921	1931	1941	1951	1961	1971
White-collar	23.6	29.9	47.9	45.4	44.6	55.4	57.4	59.8
Proprietary and managerial	1.2	1.6	2.0	1.6	2.0	3.0	2.9	2.0
Professional	14.7	12.5	19.0	17.7	15.6	14.4	15.6	17.8
Clerical	5.3	9.1	18.5	17.7	18.3	27.4	28.6	34.7
Commercial and financial	2.4	6.7	8.4	8.4	8.7	10.6	10.3	8.4
Manual	30.6	28.0	21.1	16.9	18.5	19.4	13.3	10.1
Manufacturing and mechanical	29.6	26.4	18.0	12.7	15.4	14.6	9.9	7.4
Construction	–	–	–	–	–	0.1	–	0.1
Laborers	0.5	0.1	0.1	1.8	1.4	1.8	1.2	0.9
Transportation and communication	0.5	1.5	3.0	2.4	1.4	2.9	2.2	1.7
Service	42.0	37.6	27.0	34.0	34.4	21.3	22.5	15.2
Personal	42.0	37.5	26.0	33.9	34.3	21.1	22.2	14.9
Protective and other	–	0.1	1.0	0.1	0.1	0.2	0.3	0.3
Primary	3.8	4.5	3.7	3.7	2.3	2.8	4.3	3.7
Agriculture	3.8	4.4	3.7	3.6	2.3	2.8	4.3	3.6
Fishing, trapping	–	0.1	–	0.1	–	–	–	–
Logging	–	–	–	–	–	–	–	–
Mining, quarrying	–	–	–	–	–	–	–	–
Not stated	–	–	0.3	–	0.2	1.1	2.5	10.8
Not elsewhere classified	–	–	–	–	–	–	–	0.4
All occupations								
Percent	100.0	100.0	100.0	100.0	100.0	100.0	100.0	100.0
Number (in thousands)	237.9	364.6	489.1	665.3	832.8	1,163.9	1,760.5	2,961.2

Table 5

Percentage of the Male Labor Force in Major Occupational Groups, 1901–1971

Occupation	1901	1911	1921	1931	1941	1951	1961	1971
White-collar	14.1	14.8	21.0	20.2	20.4	25.8	31.4	33.4
Proprietary and managerial	4.8	5.0	8.2	6.4	6.2	8.8	9.8	5.5
Professional	3.1	2.4	2.9	3.7	4.5	5.4	7.9	10.0
Clerical	2.9	3.0	4.7	4.4	4.5	6.0	6.9	7.6
Commercial and financial	3.3	4.4	5.2	5.7	5.2	5.6	6.8	10.0
Manual	32.5	37.3	33.1	37.2	37.1	42.9	43.2	39.2
Manufacturing and mechanical	13.8	11.7	10.2	11.3	16.2	18.2	18.8	17.1
Construction	5.4	5.5	5.5	5.6	5.8	7.2	7.3	8.5
Laborers	8.2	13.8	11.4	13.2	7.6	8.1	7.1	4.4
Transportation and communication	5.1	6.3	6.0	7.4	7.5	9.4	10.0	9.2
Service	2.9	3.4	3.4	4.1	4.6	4.9	6.3	9.2
Personal	2.6	2.8	2.1	3.0	3.2	3.4	4.3	5.8
Protective and other	0.3	0.3	1.3	1.4	1.4	1.5	2.0	3.4
Primary	50.5	44.8	42.3	38.5	37.6	25.1	16.4	9.9
Agriculture	45.9	38.9	38.1	33.9	31.7	19.7	12.5	7.2
Fishing, trapping	1.8	1.5	1.1	1.5	1.5	1.3	0.8	0.5
Logging	1.0	1.8	1.4	1.3	2.3	2.5	1.7	1.2
Mining, quarrying	1.8	2.6	1.7	1.8	2.1	1.6	1.4	1.0
Not stated	—	—	0.2	—	0.3	1.3	2.7	7.4
Not elsewhere classified	—	—	—	—	—	—	—	1.2
All occupations								
Percent	100.0	100.0	100.0	100.0	100.0	100.0	100.0	100.0
Number (in thousands)	1,544.9	2,358.8	2,675.3	3,252.3	3,363.1	4,051.0	4,581.8	5,665.7

Source: Patricia Connelly, *Last Hired, First Fired*, Table 7.2b.

Table 6

Females as a Percentage of the Total Labor Force in Each Major Occupational Group, 1901-1971

Occupation	1901	1911	1921	1931	1941	1951	1961	1971
White-collar	20.6	23.8	29.5	34.5	35.1	38.1	41.3	48.5
Proprietary and managerial	3.6	4.5	4.3	4.8	7.2	8.9	10.3	15.7
Professional	42.5	44.6	54.1	49.5	46.1	43.5	43.2	48.1
Clerical	22.1	32.6	41.8	45.1	50.1	56.7	61.5	68.4
Commercial and financial	10.4	19.2	23.1	23.1	29.4	35.2	36.7	30.4
Manual	12.6	10.4	10.4	8.5	11.0	11.5	10.6	12.0
Manufacturing and mechanical	24.8	25.9	24.3	18.7	19.1	18.8	16.8	18.5
Construction	*	*	0.1	*	0.2	0.3	0.2	0.9
Laborers	0.9	0.1	0.2	2.6	4.4	6.0	6.1	10.1
Transportation and communication	1.4	3.5	8.4	6.5	5.3	8.2	7.9	8.7
Service	68.7	65.3	58.9	63.0	65.1	55.4	57.8	46.2
Personal	71.7	67.2	68.9	69.6	72.9	64.2	66.4	57.4
Protective and other	2.7	6.8	11.9	2.1	1.8	3.1	5.1	3.9
Primary	1.1	1.5	1.6	1.9	1.5	3.1	9.2	16.4
Agriculture	1.2	1.7	1.7	2.1	1.8	3.9	11.7	20.9
Fishing, trapping	0.2	0.8	0.2	1.0	0.6	0.5	1.1	1.9
Logging	–	–	–	–	–	*	0.2	2.1
Mining, quarrying	*	*	*	–	*	*	*	0.6
Not stated	–	–	23.0	18.0	15.1	20.5	25.8	43.3
Not elsewhere classified	–	–	–	–	–	–	–	13.6
All occupations	13.3	13.4	15.5	17.0	19.8	22.3	27.8	34.3

* less than 0.05% – none

Source: Patricia Connelly, *Last Hired, First Fired*, Table 7.3.

Table 7

Leading Female Occupations, 1941-1961[1]

	1941		1951		1961	
	Female % of Occupation	% of All Women Workers	Female % of Occupation	% of All Women Workers	Female % of Occupation	% of All Women Workers
Stenographers and typists	95.9	9.4	96.4	11.6	96.8	12.2
Sales clerks	41.4	6.8	52.9	8.3	53.6	7.8
Babysitters, maids, and related service workers[2]	96.1	22.8	90.8	9.3	88.9	7.7
School teachers	74.6	7.8	72.5	6.5	70.7	6.9
Tailoresses, furriers and related workers[1 2 3]	67.8	6.2	73.7	6.4	76.2	4.5
Waitresses and bartenders[2]	62.5	2.8	66.7	3.5	70.5	3.6
Graduate nurses	99.4	3.2	97.5	3.0	96.2	3.4
Nursing assistants and aides	71.0	1.0	72.4	1.6	78.9	2.9
Telephone operators	92.6	1.5	96.5	2.6	95.2	2.0
Janitors and cleaners	19.7	0.6	27.5	1.2	31.5	1.8
Totals	74.3	62.1	73.7	54.0	73.6	52.8

[1]"Leading" refers to the ten occupations with the most female workers for which comparable data are available from the 1941, 1951, and 1961 Censuses. They are listed in the order of their 1961 size and according to the 1961 occupational classification. They are not necessarily 1961 occupation classes, the most detailed level at which the data are presented. In several cases, 1961 classes have had to be combined to provide comparability. But with one exception (tailoresses, furriers, and related workers), the occupations listed here were occupation classes, even if somewhat differently defined, in the 1941 Census.

[2]The occupational titles used for female workers are employed here. While the male equivalents "tailor" and "waiter" are unremarkable, the replacement of "maid" by "kitchen helper" is perhaps more noteworthy.

[3]Does not include upholsterers.

Source: Pat and Hugh Armstrong, *The Double Ghetto*, Table 6.

Table 8

Similar Leading Female Occupations, 1971

Occupations	Female % of Occupation		% of All Female Workers	
Stenographers and typists	96.9		12.3	
Secretaries and stenographers (4111)[1]		97.4		9.1
Typists and clerk-typists (4113)		95.6		3.2
Salespersons	51.0		6.7	
Salesmen and salespersons [sic]. commodities. n.e.c.[2] (5135)		21.8		0.6
Sales clerks, commodities (5137)		66.0		6.0
Service station attendants (5145)		4.3		
Personal service workers	93.5		3.4	
Chambermaids and housemen (6133)		95.5		0.5
Babysitters (6147)		96.6		0.8
Personal service workers. n.e.c. (6149)		92.2		2.1
Teachers	66.0		6.4	
Elementary and kindergarten (2731)		82.3		4.5
Secondary school (2733)		44.5		1.9
Fabricators, assemblers, and repairers of textiles, fur, and leather products	76.0		3.4	
Foremen (8550)		27.4		0.1
Patternmakers, markers and cutters (8551)		32.6		0.1
Tailors and dressmakers (8553)		73.0		0.6
Furriers (8555)		48.8		—
Milliners, hat and cap makers (8557)		57.4		—
Sewing machine operators, textile and similar materials (8563)		90.1		2.2
Inspectors, testers, graders, samplers (8566)		84.1		0.1
Fabricators, assemblers, repairers, n.e.c. (8569)		72.3		0.3
Graduate nurses	95.4		3.9	
Supervisors, nursing occupations (3130)		92.8		0.5
Nurses, graduate, except supervisors (3131)		95.8		3.4
Waiters and bartenders	76.6		4.1	
Waiters, hostesses, and stewards (food and beverages) (6125)		82.9		4.0
Bartenders (6123)		14.5		0.1
Nursing assistants, aides, and orderlies	79.2		2.9	
Nursing assistants (3134)		91.9		0.9
Nursing aides and orderlies (3135)		74.4		2.0
Telephone operators (4175)	95.9		1.2	
Janitors, charworkers, and cleaners (6191)	32.4		2.1	
Total	72.0		46.4	

[1]Numbers in parentheses refer to unit group numbers.

[2]N.e.c. means not elsewhere classified: — means less than 0.1%.

Source: Pat and Hugh Armstrong, *The Double Ghetto*, Table 7.

Table 9

Leading Male Occupations, 1941-1961[1]

	1941		1951		1961	
	Male % of Occupation	*% of All Male Workers*	*Male % of Occupation*	*% of All Male Workers*	*Male % of Occupation*	*% of All Male Workers*
Farmers and stock-raisers	97.8	18.9	98.5	13.2	97.7	8.4
Laborers	95.6	7.6	94.1	8.1	93.9	7.1
Operators, road transport	99.8	3.2	99.6	4.5	99.3	5.5
Owners and managers, trade	92.5	3.6	90.1	4.1	88.4	4.2
Carpenters[2]	100.00	2.7	100.0	3.2	98.7	3.3
Sales clerks	58.9	2.4	47.1	2.1	46.4	2.5
Loggers and related workers	100.0	2.4	100.0	2.5	99.9	1.7
Janitors	80.3	0.7	72.5	0.9	68.5	1.5
Owners and managers, manufacturing	97.4	0.8	96.9	1.5	95.6	1.5
Owners and managers, community, business, and personal services	86.2	0.6	81.4	1.3	77.8	1.4
Totals	93.4	42.9	90.8	41.3	87.3	37.2

[1]The points made in note 1 of Table 6 apply to this table as well.

[2]Includes some cabinetmakers and other related workers in 1961 only, when for men they made up 19.0% of the broader occupation.

Source: Pat and Hugh Armstrong, *The Double Ghetto*, Table 13.

Table 10

Leading Male Occupations, 1971[1]

Occupations	Male % of Occupation	% of All Male Workers
Farmers (7112)	96.7	4.3
Supervisors, sales, commodities (5130)	83.2	4.0
Truck drivers (9175)	98.8	3.8
Janitors (6191)	67.6	2.2
Motor vehicle mechanics and repairmen (8581)	99.2	2.1
Farm workers (7182)	53.8	2.1
Carpenters and related workers (8781)	99.4	1.9
Accountants, auditors and other financial officers (1171)	84.0	1.7
Sales clerks, commodities (5137)	34.0	1.6
Other ranks,[2] armed forces (6117)	97.9	1.3
Bookkeepers and accounting clerks (4131)	32.4	1.2
Laborers, other construction (8798)	98.9	1.2
Secondary school teachers (2733)	55.5	1.2
Salesmen and salespersons, commodities, n.e.c. (5135)	78.2	1.1
Shipping and receiving clerks (4153)	89.4	1.1
Welders and flame cutters (8335)	95.5	1.1
Foremen, other construction trades (8780)p	99.4	1.1
Mechanics and repairmen, industrial, farm, and construction machinery (8584)	99.2	1.1
Commercial travellers (5133)	97.1	1.0
Totals	75.5	35.0

[1]As with Table 7 above, a separate table for 1971 is necessary because of the changes made to the occupational classification.

[2]Other than commissioned officers.

Source: Pat and Hugh Armstrong, *The Double Ghetto*, Table 14.

Table 11

Annual Earnings for Full-Year, Full-Time Workers, by Sex, Occupation, Industry, Age, Marital Status, Education, Residence, and Region, Canada, 1971

Variable	Male Earnings	Female Earnings	Female/Male Earnings Ratio
	$	$	
Occupation			
Managerial/professional	11,566	6,492	.56
Clerical	7,139	4,801	.67
Sales	8,377	4,059	.49

Service	6,802	3,389	.50
Primary	5,621	2,656	.47
Blue Collar	7,585	4,008	.53
Other	7,256	4,826	.55
Industry			
Primary and construction	7,746	4,288	.55
Manufacturing	8,329	4,542	.55
Transportation, communication, utilities	8,361	5,461	.65
Trade	7,587	4,187	.55
Finance, service, public administration	8,666	5,157	.60
Age			
15-19	3,286	2,919	.89
20-24	5,600	4,300	.77
25-34	7,944	5,321	.66
35-44	9,141	5,132	.56
45-54	9,095	5,051	.56
55-64	8,191	4,906	.60
65 +	6,124	3,590	.59
Marital status			
Single	5,740	4,771	.83
Married and spouse present	8,650	4,847	.56
Separated, widowed, divorced, married and spouse absent	7,562	4,869	.64
Education			
Elementary or less	6,610	3,638	.55
1-3 years high school	7,681	4,459	.58
4-5 years high school	8,818	5,269	.60
B.A. or first degree	12,768	8,184	.64
M.A. or Ph.D.	14,430	10,259	.71
Residence			
Urban	8,504	4,905	.58
Rural	6,949	4,357	.63
Farm	5,277	3,862	.73
Region			
Maritimes	6,905	3,963	.57
Quebec	7,822	4,702	.60
Ontario	8,825	5,190	.59
Prairies	7,709	4,602	.60
British Columbia	8,853	5,223	.59
All wage earners	8,178	4,826	.59

Note: Occupation, industry, and regional figures are for full-year wage earners in the experienced labor force. Other figures are for full-year, full-time wage earners.

Source: Gail Cook, ed., *Opportunity for Choice,* Table 4.10.

Table 12

Average and Median Income (1) for Selected Occupations by Sex, for Persons 15 Years of Age and Over
Who Worked Full-Time in 1970

Occupation	Average		Median	
	Male	*Female*	*Male*	*Female*
			(2)	(2)
Physicians and surgeons	$28,896	$14,965	(2)	9,694
Lawyers and notaries	21,933	10,469	18,226	9,426
Civil engineers	12,786	9,941	12,379	5,801
Accountants, auditors, and other financial officers	10,545	6,171	9,728	
Chemists	10,135	7,801	9,625	7,721
Secondary school teachers	10,100	8,529	9,901	8,480
Systems analysts, computer programmers and				
related occupations	10,062	7,671	9,959	7,698
Real estate salesmen	8,609	6,095	7,772	5,231
Secretaries and stenographers	8,562	7,884	7,314	4,835
Social workers	8,532	7,733	8,174	7,725
Draftsmen	8,239	5,904	8,211	5,866
Pipefitting, plumbing and related occupations	8,110	6,540	8,032	6,852
Sheet metal workers	7,582	4,862	7,531	4,577
Machinists and machine tool setting-up occupations	7,422	4,363	7,458	4,262

Motor vehicle fabrication and assembling occupations not elsewhere classified	7,226	4,580	7,438	4,426
Carpenters and related occupations	6,819	5,282	6,767	4,884
Truck drivers	6,796	4,712	6,555	4,422
Nurses, graduate, except supervisors	6,677	6,351	6,623	6,446
Motor vehicle mechanics and repairmen	6,561	5,031	6,495	4,797
Telephone operators	6,315	4,379	6,141	4,444
Slaughtering and meat cutting, canning, curing and packing operations	6,254	4,642	6,306	4,667
Tellers and cashiers	5,875	3,894	5,901	3,861
Cabinet and wood furniture makers	5,745	3,935	5,677	3,788
Tailors and dressmakers	5,667	3,262	5,551	3,225
Barbers, hairdressers and related occupations	5,062	3,683	4,431	3,375
Service station attendants	4,597	3,026	4,494	3,143
Waiters, hostesses and stewards, food and beverage	4,435	2,866	4,306	2,794
Fish canning, curing and packing operations	3,978	2,662	3,620	2,452
Farmers	3,864	2,361	2,789	1,459

(1) Employment income only. The median is the income that divides the distribution into two equal parts.

(2) The median could not be calculated as it occurred in one of the open-ended classes in the distribution.

Note: In contradistinction to the other tables in this chapter, these data originate from the 1971 Census. For details, see "Sources."

Source: Statistics Canada, 1977, Table 8.15.

Table 13

1970 Average Incomes for Men and Women from the Largest Female Occupations of 1971

Occupation	Average Income for Men	Average Income for Women	Women's Income as a % of Men's
	$	$	
All occupations	6,574	3,199	48.7
Secretaries and stenographers (4111)	7,312	3,952	54.0
Sales clerks, commodities (5137)	4,262	1,803	42.3
Bookkeepers and accounting clerks (4131)	5,828	3,660	62.8
Elementary and kindergarten teachers (2731)	7,041	5,378	76.4
Waiters (6125)	2,992	1,442	48.2
Tellers and cashiers (4133)	3,813	2,325	61.0
Farm workers (7182)	1,784	1,322	74.1
Nurses, except supervisors (3131)	5,795	4,566	78.8
Typists and clerk-typists (4113)	5,110	3,066	60.0
General office clerks (4197)	5,364	3,326	62.2
Sewing machine operators (8563)	4,663	2,660	57.0
Personal service workers, n.e.c. (6149)	2,583	1,554	60.2
Janitor (6191)	4,220	1,892	44.3
Nursing aides and orderlies (3135)	4,839	3,069	63.3
Secondary school teachers (2733)	9,152	6,762	73.9
Other clerical workers, n.e.c. (4199)	5,552	3,032	54.9
Receptionists and information clerks (4171)	4,144	2,805	67.7
Chefs and cooks (6121)	4,000	2,299	57.5
Supervisors, sales, commodities (5130)	8,255	3,716	45.0
Packaging workers, n.e.c. (9317)	3,524	2,520	71.5
Barbers and hairdressers (6143)	4,655	2,627	56.4
Telephone operators (4175)	4,480	3,108	69.4
Library and file clerks (4161)	3,850	2,847	73.9

[1]Included are all the occupations which in 1971 contained at least 1% of the female labor force. The occupations are listed in the order of the number of women in them. Only those workers with some employment income are included in the calculations of average income.

Source: Pat and Hugh Armstrong, *The Double Ghetto,* Table 9.

Day Care

Table 14 shows that 35.6% of all married women with children participated in the labor force in 1971. This means that the family requires some form of day care, either full-time if the child is under six, or part-time if the child is in school and not yet old enough to take care of himself or herself at lunch and/or after school

Despite the increasing numbers of married women with children in the labor force, and the pressures they have brought to bear on governments and companies for day care facilities, Table 15 shows that most families

Table 14

Female Labor Force Participation by Marital Status
and Level of Schooling, 1971

| *Marital Status* | *All Levels of Schooling* | Participation Rate | | | | |
		Less than Grade 9	*Grades 9-11*	*Grades 12-13*	*Some University*	*University Degree*
Single	53.4	38.2	42.9	68.8	76.0	82.5
Married	35.4	23.6	37.8	46.7	51.7	55.3
No children	35.1	19.3	40.6	53.5	59.4	69.5
Some children	35.6	27.7	36.4	42.7	46.9	44.8
Some under 6	27.6	20.7	26.7	33.6	37.5	37.3
None under 6	41.8	31.7	44.6	51.6	56.1	53.5

Source: Pat and Hugh Armstrong, *The Double Ghetto*, Table 19.

where the mother works rely on some form of unpaid day care, often an older sibling or a relative or neighbor. Even in families where the children do not attend school, only 57% have paid day care. Given the low wages of the majority of jobs women do in Canada, paid day care is very costly and is obviously avoided whenever possible. In addition, when governments in Canada are faced with economic crises such as at present, they cut back social services such as day care. This forces more women to remain at home.

The long-range effects of these child-care arrangments on the children, their relationships with their parent or parents, and the relationship between husband and wife are virtually unknown. Clearly, we must begin longitudinal studies of these phenomena.

Fertility and Childlessness

Changes in the fertility rate may be considered as one of the important indicators of projections couples make of the future. Whether a woman continues in a full-time job or maintains a household full-time, she will be involved with the care and rearing of children for a number of years. Fertility rates, then, are indicators of a considerable commitment by women to bearing, nurturing and rearing children.

However, as we argued earlier in this paper, the family is becoming more and more isolated and market pressures are continually intruding upon the family. Such changes undoubtedly will contribute to a decrease in the desire of some women to have children, or will at least cause some to significantly reduce the number of children in their families.

Table 16 presents three different ways of measuring fertility.[3] Each measure supports the assertion that Canadian families are becoming smaller and that fertility rates have declined steadily since 1961.

These data also show that since 1961 there is a dramatic shift towards completing fertility before the age of 30. Also, between 1941 and 1971, the

average size of the family has declined from 4.5 to 3.7. There is every indication that these trends will continue as more and more women remain in
the labor force and/or return to work as soon as possible after child-
bearing.

As Table 17 indicates, more and more Canadian families are not only
reducing their family size, but, for a variety of reasons, are remaining
childless. The most significant shift between 1961 and 1971 was in the age
group 20 to 24, of whom 26.3% were childless in 1961, but 42% of whom
were childless in 1971. Not all will remain childless, nor can we say with
certainty that the reason for this increase in childlessness is the direct result
of women pursuing careers. But clearly, the presence of children in a marriage where both spouses work will affect the lives of both, and especially
the life of the woman. Unless husbands become more equal partners in
child-rearing, shopping, cooking and cleaning, the primary burden of
children will continue to be placed on the wife's shoulders. Certainly one
way to avoid this type of inequality is to remain childless.

Table 15

Child-Care Arrangements for Children of Mothers Participating in the
Labor Force, by School Status of Children, Canada, 1973 (Thousands)

Child-Care Arrangements	Children Attending School Full-Time		Children Attending School Part-Time		Children Not Attending School	
	No.	%	No.	%	No.	%
Unpaid care, total	270	38	84	44	103	30
Persons over 15 years of age, living in home	116	16	30	16	35	10
Cared for by brother/sister under 16 years old	41	6	18	9	–	–
Cared for by neighbor, relative, etc.	113	16	37	19	61	18
Children looking after themselves	267	37	–	–	–	–
Children have lunch at school	134	19	–	–	–	–
Children do not have lunch at school	133	19	–	–	–	–
Paid-care arrangements	119	17	63	33	198	57
Paid care in mother's home	–	–	26	14	72	21
Day-care center or nursery	–	–	–	–	24	7
Other arrangements	63	9	33	17	35*	13*
Total arrangements reported	719	100	190	100	347	100

*Includes work-oriented arrangements, including mother working only when child is in school
and mother takes child to work.

Sources: Statistics Canada, "Working Mothers and Their Child Care Arrangements in
Canada," *The Labour Force,* September 1975, Tables S-1.5 and S-1.6; Gail Cook, ed. *Opportunity for Choice,* Table 5.2.

Table 16

Fertility Rates, Canada, Selected Years, 1926-73

	Age-Specific Rate							Total Fertility Rate[a]	Gross Reproduction Rate[b]
	15-19	20-24	25-29	30-34	35-39	40-44	45-49		
1926-30	30.0	140.7	174.4	149.4	110.1	48.3	5.8	3,293	1.601
1931-35	27.7	121.7	159.3	136.0	96.8	40.6	5.2	2,937	1.431
1936-40	27.0	119.4	145.8	123.3	84.9	34.0	4.1	2,692	1.310
1941	30.7	138.4	159.8	122.3	80.0	31.6	3.7	2,832	1.377
1946	36.5	169.6	191.4	146.0	93.1	34.5	3.8	3,374	1.640
1951	48.1	188.7	198.8	144.5	86.5	30.9	3.1	3,503	1.701
1956	55.9	222.2	220.1	150.3	89.6	30.8	2.9	3,858	1.874
1961	58.2	233.6	219.2	144.9	81.1	28.5	2.4	3,840	1.868
1966	48.2	169.1	163.5	103.3	57.5	19.1	1.7	2,812	1.369
1971	40.1	134.4	142.0	77.3	33.6	9.4	0.6	2,187	1.060
1972	38.5	119.8	137.1	72.1	28.9	7.8	0.6	2,024	.982
1973	37.2	117.7	131.6	67.1	25.7	6.4	0.4	1,931	.937

a. The number of children born to a hypothetical group of 1,000 women who went through the reproductive years bearing children at the given age-specific ratio.

b. The average number of live daughters that would be born to a hypothetical group of women who are moving through the reproductive years subject to current age-specific fertility rates and having an assumed mortality rate of zero before age 50.

Source: Gail Cook, ed., *Opportunity for Choice,* Statistics Canada, Table 2-8.

Table 17

Percentage of Ever Married Women Who Are Childless, for Selected Age Groups, Canada, 1961 and 1971

Age Group	Percentage Childless	
	1961	*1971*
15 and over	13.7	15.8
15-19	42.3	49.7
20-24	26.3	42.0
25-29	13.6	20.7
30-34	9.7	9.4
35-39	9.2	7.4
40-44	10.3	8.2
45-49	13.1	9.6
50-54	15.2	11.8
55-59	15.5	14.5
60-64	14.6	16.6
65 and over	13.0	15.0

Source: Gail Cook, ed., *Opportunity for Choice*, Statistics Canada, Table 2.11.

Divorce

If we are correct that marriage is seen primarily as a "private" matter, as important to the two persons but to no one else, then we would expect that more and more marriages will end in divorce. Table 18 indicates that this is what has happened. Despite the distortion in divorce rates (due to the changes in legislation in 1968), the evidence suggests increasing conflict in marriages and/or increasing unwillingness to remain in a marriage.

Table 19 shows that despite the fact that women identify most strongly with a family, divorces with children present are also increasing. As Boyd, Eichler and Hofley have noted:

> In spite of their economic vulnerability, women request the divorce in nearly 70% of the cases in which children are involved. This proportion increases with the number of children, reaching 75% in families of seven children or more (Cook, 1977:23).

Given the responsibilities of child care, the inadequacy and expense of day care facilities, the inequalities in wages between men and women, women with children who seek and attain a divorce are clearly more vulnerable to economic trends in our society than are males. The fact that more and more women are taking the step of initiating a divorce clearly illustrates the considerable conflict within many contemporary households.

Conclusion

The family exists within a given set of historically derived material conditions. These conditions produce and reproduce not only economic relationships, but marriages and families. As these conditions change over time, so

Table 18

Divorce Rates, Canada, Selected Years, 1941-73

Year	Number	Crude Divorce Rate[a]	General Divorce Rate[b]	Divorce Rate Index[c]
1941[d]	2,462	21.4	56.2	112.4
1946	7,757	63.1	131.9	263.8
1951	5,270	37.6	88.9	177.8
1956	6,002	37.3	89.5	179.0
1961	6,563	36.0	85.9	171.8
1966[e]	10,239	51.2	117.4	234.8
1967[f]	11,165	54.8	125.1	250.2
1968	11,343	54.8	124.3	248.6
1969	26,093	124.2	279.5	559.0
1970	29,775	139.8	311.5	623.0
1971	29,685	137.6	303.6	607.2
1972	32,389	148.4	325.0	650.0
1973[g]	36,704	166.1	h	h

[a]Number of divorces per 100,000 population.
[b]Number of divorces per 100,000 married persons aged 15 and over.
[c]Number of divorces per 100,000 married couples aged 15 and over.
[d]Newfoundland not included prior to 1951.
[e]Yukon and Northwest Territories are included from 1966 on.
[f]Rates and indexes for 1967-70 and 1972 are based on population estimates.
[g]Preliminary estimate.
[h]Population estimates necessary to calculate rates are not available.
Source: Gail Cook, ed., *Opportunity for Choice*, Statistics Canada, Table 2.3.

Table 19

Divorces* by Number of Dependent Children, Canada, 1969-73

No. of Children	1969 No.	%	1970 No.	%	1971 No.	%	1972 No.	%	1973 No.	%
0	12,061	54.9	13,714	46.9	13,241	44.6	14,305	44.2	15,890	43.4
1	4,101	18.7	6,013	20.6	6,189	20.9	7,078	21.9	8,209	22.4
2	3,124	14.2	5,025	17.2	5,430	18.3	5,956	18.4	6,842	18.6
3	1,586	7.2	2,624	9.0	2,825	9.5	2,963	9.2	3,384	9.2
4	659	3.0	1,180	4.0	1,250	4.2	1,294	3.9	1,520	4.1
5+	453	2.0	682	2.3	737	2.5	768	2.4	859	2.3
Total	21,964	100.0	29,238	100.0	29,762	100.0	32,364	100.0	36,704	100.0
Mean no. of children	n.a.*		1.11		1.17		1.15		1.16	

*The number of divorces mentioned here pertain only to those filed under the new divorce legislation of July 2, 1968.
**Not available.
Source: Gail Cook, ed., *Opportunity for Choice*, Statistics Canada, Table 2.4.

does the nature of the family, particularly relationships between men and women, both inside the household and outside in the labor force. Much research is needed on the precise nature of these changes, their causes and consequences. Clearly, however, available data demonstrate that women, relative to men, suffer the brunt of such changes. The solution to this inequality is not an anti-male feminism but a movement that rises up against the economic conditions that create and reproduce such inequalities.

NOTES

1. Most Marxist feminists make a distinction between "exploitation" and "oppression." All workers, both men and women, are exploited under capitalism, but all women, regardless of class, are oppressed in the capitalist family.
2. For an excellent analysis of this concept as it applies to Canadian women, see Patricia Connelly, *Last Hired, First Fired* (Toronto: The Women's Press, 1978).
3. For a fuller description of these measures, see Gail Cook, ed., *Opportunity for Choice* (Ottawa: Information Canada, 1976), p. 31.

REFERENCES

Archibald, Kathleen. *Sex and the Public Service.* Ottawa: Queen's Printer, 1970.

Armstrong, Pat and Hugh. *The Double Ghetto: Canadian Women and Their Segregated Work.* Toronto: McClelland and Stewart, 1978.

Braverman, Harry. *Labor and Monopoly Capital.* New York: Monthly Review Press, 1974.

Canada. *Royal Commission on the Status of Women.* Ottawa: Information Canada, 1970.

Canadian Review of Sociology and Anthropology, Vol. 12, No. 4 (Nov. 1975).

Connelly, Patricia. *Last Hired, First Fired.* Toronto: The Women's Press, 1978.

Cook, Gail, ed., *Opportunity for Choice.* Ottawa: Information Canada, 1976.

Eisenstein, Zillah R., ed. *Capitalist Patriarchy and the Case for Socialist Feminism.* New York: Monthly Review Press, 1979.

Mitchel, Juliet. *Woman's Estate.* New York: Pantheon Books, 1971.

Ostry, Sylvia. *The Female Worker in Canada.* Ottawa: Queen's Printer, 1968.

Rowbotham, Sheila. *Woman's Consciousness, Man's World.* Harmondsworth, England: Penguin Books, 1973.

Stephenson, Marylee, ed. *Women in Canada.* Toronto: New Press, 1973.

_____. *Women in Canada,* rev. ed. Toronto: General Publishing, 1977.

Westergaard, John and Henrietta Resler. *Class in a Capitalist Society.* New York: Basic Books, 1975.

IV

Strategies and Programs

Introduction

During the past 20 to 25 years, all governments in the Western world have spent a great deal of money on social programs ostensibly geared to reducing inequalities in wealth and power. The term "welfare state" connotes the image of a state giving away millions of dollars to the aged, the sick, and the poor.

However, in the essays contained in this book, we see little evidence to support the commonly held belief that governments in Canada have redistributed wealth in any significant way. As St. Laurent notes in her article, "whichever way you choose to measure income, the multi-million dollar social security system has not significantly reduced income inequality." This is not to deny that in the short run, programs such as unemployment insurance, workmen's compensation, and welfare offer people much-needed assistance. Yet, Westergaard's and Resler's remark about Great Britain is pertinent to our situation in Canada.

> The welfare state does redistribute income. But, as the pattern of the data here confirms, this is redistribution between households at different stages of life far more than it is redistribution between households at markedly different levels of income. It is redistribution within classes far more than it is redistribution between classes (1975:68).

Given the obvious inequalities in Canada, what is being done to reduce them and why are present programs inadequate? The consequences of inequalities can be seen in a wide range of areas — jobs, health, housing, education, child care, etc. We decided that it was important for readers to be aware of the range of social security programs available, to have a brief history of the conflict behind the Orange Paper on Social Security published in 1973, and to examine critically at least three specific policy areas, namely, social welfare, the guaranteed annual income, and housing.

The primary thrust of this section is not to present alternative strategies that would "solve" inequalities in Canada, but to demonstrate that any analysis of existing social security measures must *begin* with a clear elaboration of the premises on which a given policy is based. Inequalities, and therefore the policies geared to their reduction, are not merely the consequences of individual variations. Rather, as Joan St. Laurent notes in her paper:

> Socioeconomic trends, class relationships, and the political strategy of the state all enter into the issue with varying degrees of importance in relation to different programs and during different historical periods.

Johnson's excellent account of the review process by federal and provincial governments of the social security system in Canada highlights one of the main themes of this book, which is the importance of assumptions about the nature of society. Johnson delineates five government strategies and discusses the problems within each. Not one of them examines Canada's basic institutional system. The capitalist mode of production, the work ethic, the separation of work and leisure, among others, are unstated first premises. As Westergaard and Resler point out, there is power inherent in anonymous social mechanisms and assumptions (1975:143). These assumptions are often so taken for granted that they are ignored. Yet they can influence how we see a policy and how we operationalize it or put it into practice. Gilbert's article on the Mincome experiment in Manitoba underscores this point. He notes that with stunning regularity social policies accepted in principle by politicians and by the public are rejected when the operational details become known or the actual consequences are realized.

Johnson points out that the participants in the review process on the guaranteed annual income were concerned about its effects on the work ethic. He notes that they wished to avoid creating a system which apparently gave people a free choice between work and leisure. Gilbert notes the same point more succinctly: the government wanted to make the poor fit in better with the achievement/attainment ethic. This ignores the fact, as St. Laurent points out, that 60% of low-income family units work and do not receive any transfer payments from the state, and that all GAI maximum levels of support are *below* existing poverty lines!

Gilbert asks an important question: Does the government reflect the interests of the people in general or merely the interests of the dominant class? Gilbert's own answer to this question is cynical in that he believes no one can test the differences between "false" and "true" values. The neo-Marxist critique of the GAI and the welfare program in general that is offered in St. Laurent's article is missing in Gilbert's contribution. St. Laurent, following a careful analysis of a variety of data on income distribution, concludes that the lack of redistribution is evidence that government programs act in the interests of the dominant class.

Gordon's article, *Housing as Labor,* is a fascinating attempt at broadening the Marxist discussion of the labor process to include not only class and alienation, but also housing. Thus, housing is not merely a shelter, or a response to a basic need, but a representation of social class, a form of social control. For Gordon, both the labor process and the shelter process have become commodities with the development of capitalism; both are the basis for speculative profit by the capitalist, yet essential for the worker's survival, and both are produced by the legitimating myths of individualism and market access.

The thrust of these reviews, especially St. Laurent and Gordon's, is that any future examination of state policies must begin with a consideration of the relationship of the state to the class that owns and controls the means of production.

Canada's Social Security Review 1973-75: The Central Issues*

A.W. JOHNSON†

This symposium on income security[1] is something of a milestone, it seems to me, in the further development of the Learned Societies of this country. It, like the publication of this new journal *Canadian Public Policy — Analyse de Politiques*, reflects the determination of the societies involved that their respective disciplines should increasingly become as concerned with the public policy issues of the day as they are with the development of their several bodies of knowledge and theory. In a country which is notable for the gulf between the theory and practice of the social sciences, and in particular between academicians and practitioners, this is a development much to be welcomed.

Mine is the straightforward task of attempting to launch the symposium by providing some background on Canada's Social Security Review. This I shall attempt to do in three ways: first, by recounting very briefly how the Review came to be undertaken; secondly, by describing what it is trying to accomplish; and then, finally, by examining the policy issues which seem to me to lie at the heart of this developing reform of the nation's social security system.

The Social Security Review: Its Beginnings

The review by Canada's federal and provincial governments of the nation's social security system was born of discord. Jurisdiction over social security, as we know, is divided by the constitution between the Parliament of Canada and the Legislatures of the Provinces in a complicated, even bewildering, way. The exercise of this jurisdiction by the two orders of government has varied in vigor over time, with each tending to take initiatives independently of the other, and with neither being able independently to accomplish its goals. The long history of constitutional dif-

---

*Since this is a tale of evolving public policy, this paper is necessarily topical. For that reason it must be remembered in the reading of it that it was written in 1975, just two years after the Federal-Provincial Social Security Review began, and at the end of the two-year period set by the Conference of Ministers of Welfare for the Development of "a new overall approach to social security." Reprinted from *Canadian Public Policy — Analyse de Politiques*, 1:4 (Autumn 1975).

†Mr. Johnson, who was formerly Deputy Minister (National Welfare), Health and Welfare Canada, is now President of the CBC.

ferences and sometimes amendments, and of federal-provincial conferences and shared-cost agreements, seemed to reach some kind of culmination in the 1960s, due almost certainly to the aggressive program innovations during those years by the Government of Canada, and the equally aggressive resistance on the part of the Government of Quebec, followed by certain of the other provinces, to the interventions into provincial jurisdiction which were alleged to be inherent in the federal initiatives.

Attempts to resolve these differences took a variety of forms over the past decade. For a period of time the route of *statut particulier* was followed, as the Province of Quebec established its own Pension Plan when the Canada Pension Plan was born, and as that province "opted out," at least symbolically, of shared-cost agreements in the social security field. Not long after, when the forbidding implications of special status became more evident, this course was abandoned by the Government of Canada in favor of an attempt to reduce substantially its influence over provincial social security priorities in all provinces, equally. Then came the series of Constitutional Conferences during which the federal and provincial governments sought to arrive at some kind of consensus as to the division of responsibility which ought to apply in the social security field in any revised constitution.

None of these courses successfully resolved the differences. Indeed the Constitutional Conference of 1971, which held the promise of at least an amending formula being agreed upon, foundered in no small measure upon differences over the constitutional provisions which ought to apply in the social security field. This was followed, in 1972, by a Conference of Welfare Ministers at which several provinces, not only Quebec, demanded the transfer to the provinces of responsibility for the long-established federal family allowances program, along with the fiscal resources to pay for them. And at the same conference all of the provinces joined in insisting that a federal-provincial conference be called to develop better mechanisms for achieving a rationalized social security system in Canada.

In the Throne Speech of January 4, 1973, the Government of Canada responded to this challenge, and the imperatives of social security reform which it itself felt, by proposing for the future a quite different course than had been followed in the past. It was this: that the federal and the provincial governments should together review the whole of the nation's social security system — its policies and programs — and should together develop reforms which would at one and the same time provide individual Canadians with more effective programs, and find new modes for harmonizing and integrating the federal and provincial elements of the system. All of this was to be done within the existing constitutional framework.

The Throne Speech was followed by the publication in April of a federal *Working Paper on Social Security in Canada* — a paper which came to be known, in the inscrutable ways so well-known to Canadians, as the Orange Book, in English, and Le Livre Jaune, in French.[2] In this paper, the Minister of National Health and Welfare advanced on behalf of the Government of Canada not a program blueprint, to be accepted, amended, or rejected by the provinces, but rather a set of strategies and propositions, based upon an explicit statement of premises and principles, as to the broad directions of reform which might be explored by the federal and provincial governments together.

The provinces responded favorably, if somewhat cautiously, to this new approach to federal-provincial relations. They "supported the general objectives which lie behind the strategies and propositions contained in the federal working paper"; "agreed that the proposition put forward in (that) paper would be an appropriate basis for (a federal-provincial) review of the social security system" — along with "the propositions put forward earlier by other governments"; but "recognized that program changes should be made gradually, as and when they have been soundly planned and developed, and as and when resources permit."[3]

The Ministers went on to emphasize that this review of the social security system should be done by governments — under political direction, that is to say — and established a set of federal-provincial working parties under the direction of their deputy ministers to do the required work. Officials, it was made clear, were to develop program options for Ministers to consider, within the strategies and propositions accepted by the Conference, and within the specific direction and priorities prescribed by Ministers from time to time. The deadlines for the review were also agreed upon: two years for the development of a "new overall approach to social security," and one to three years more for the implementation of that approach.

The Approach to a Reformed Social Security System

Thus the Social Security Review was launched. In its substance the *Working Paper on Social Security in Canada* advanced five general strategies for achieving a reformed social security system, along with a series of propositions as to how these strategies might be realized. The first strategy, it was suggested, should be an *employment strategy*, designed to assure adequate and secure incomes to Canadians through employment — not through social assistance or a guaranteed income. The second strategy, the paper went on, should be a *social insurance strategy*. Under it retirement needs and temporary income losses — due to unemployment, sickness or accident — would be met through savings; savings arranged through social insurance plans and through private and employer-employee plans. (The social insurance plans referred to, of course, were the Canada and Quebec Pension Plans, Unemployment Insurance, and the provincial Workmen's Compensation Plans.)

The third strategy — the *income supplementation strategy* — was designed to meet, by way of a guaranteed income, inadequacies of income, whether that income came from employment, or from social insurance plus private savings. The ideal guaranteed income system, it was suggested, should be made up of two elements: first, a "full" guaranteed income to people who are unable to work or to find employment; and, secondly, income supplements for people who are working but whose incomes are, by reason of family size or insufficiency of work, inadequate.

The fourth strategy of the Working Paper suggested that the realization of the first three strategies could for a great many people be realized only if there were available to them a broad range of employment and social services. Under this *social services strategy* the handicapped would receive required rehabilitation and employment-assistance services; single parents with pre-school children would be eligible for day-care services; others might receive at one time or another required counselling, training and job placement services.

The final strategy had to do with the realization of these four policy strategies through a new approach to the development and harmonization of federal and provincial social security programs. This *federal-provincial strategy*, as it was called, advanced the proposition that the prime responsibility for setting guaranteed income or income support and supplementation levels, including the levels of universal allowances, should reside with the provinces, including — and here was the radical innovation — provision for the variation by the provinces, within certain national norms, of the levels of the allowances paid by the federal government. The federal-provincial strategy went on to suggest that the Parliament of Canada should, within this context, establish national norms and minima by which the provinces would be bound — at least where federal programs or finances were involved.

It is tempting to recount the process through which ministers and officials, federal and provincial, have gone in attempting to convert the strategies and propositions into policies and programs. But that must be left to others — when the story is complete and can be told with greater objectivity. My task is simply to summarize, as briefly as I can, the program outlines — in some cases the program blueprints — upon which Ministers have agreed. These are the outlines or blueprints which will serve as the basis for the implementation or operational stage of the Social Security Review, which has now begun.[4] As I proceed, I would ask of you only one thing, as a rather involved and therefore biased observer: that you bear in mind not only the very general character of the agreement which existed among Ministers when the Review began two years ago, but also the dimensions of the task involved in 11 governments attempting to travel down the same road, at more or less the same pace, toward the greater articulation of specific programs, out of very broadly-stated objectives and strategies.

First, let me review the decisions which have been made concerning an *employment strategy*. Ministers are agreed that an employment strategy must be an integral part of any comprehensive social security system. This is not to imply that Ministers of Welfare have come to see themselves as having acquired any general responsibility for employment policy; rather they are suggesting that social and economic policy must be seen together, with security of income through employment being an essential nexus between the two. It is really when general employment policies fail, Ministers are agreed, whether because the policies are not adapted to the needs of particular individuals or because of persistent regional or local problems, that Ministers of Welfare must become involved.

For this reason the Conference of Welfare Ministers, in company with the Minister of Manpower and Immigration, agreed to adopt a Community Employment Strategy "to provide employment opportunities for those Canadians who have particular and continuing difficulty in getting and keeping employment."[5] The Community Employment Strategy should be made up of several elements: making people ready for employment through rehabilitation and special employment training; the adaptation of employment practices so as to make it possible for persons with particular problems to enter into employment; the provision of services such as day or home care facilities to make it possible for people such as single parents to take jobs outside the home; special job-finding services; and, where employment in the general labor market does not exist, the creation of jobs by and within local communities.

All of this was seen by Ministers to be a tall order, given our starting point in Canada. So they agreed to establish some 20 developmental projects across the country, and from these projects to acquire the experience and expertise required to generalize their new community employment program.

Secondly, there is the progress which has been made on the *social insurance strategy*. The Conference of Welfare Ministers recognized early in their deliberations that they would have to address themselves to two aspects of Canada's social insurance plans: first, their adequacy as income replacement schemes; and, secondly, their harmonization, or integration, with the guaranteed income system which was being developed as the "backstop" to inadequate employment income, or insufficient replacement income from social insurance and other savings.

Ministers decided to attach first priority to the adequacy of retirement pensions. Within six months it was agreed that the Canada and Quebec Pension Plans should be amended to increase substantially maximum monthly retirement pensions. This was done by increasing, between 1974 and 1980, the band of earnings upon which the contributions to, and the benefits of, the two Plans would be based. The objective was that these pensions, when combined with the universal Old Age Security pension, would come to constitute a more reasonable proportion of the needs of retired people, and, for people with average earnings, would ultimately be larger than the federal guaranteed income available to people 65 years of age and older. Equally important was the decision that the purchasing power of old age pensions should be fully protected by indexing them to the Consumer Price Index. And there were other important, if rather more detailed, changes to the Canada Pension Plan.

The harmonization of Canada's social insurance plans with the guaranteed income system being developed had, of course, to be deferred until the work on the guaranteed income system had been completed. And because this — the guaranteed income — was by far the most difficult and contentious part of the Social Security Review, the Conference was almost inevitably led to the conclusion that the harmonization issue would have to be deferred until the operational or implementation stage of the Review.

When it came to the *income supplementation strategy*, Ministers focussed their attention at the beginning of the Review on the income needs of two particular groups of the population — those 65 years of age and over, and larger families in Canada whose income from employment was insufficient to meet the costs of raising the family.

The Government of Canada acted, even before the Social Security Review was formally launched, to increase the guaranteed income it was paying to people aged 65 and over. It did this by increasing the universal Old Age Security pensions — paid to everyone over 65 years of age — with the existing income-related Guaranteed Income Supplement being "stacked" on top of the higher universal pensions. Starting at about the same time the provinces — by now four of them — began supplementing the guaranteed income paid by Ottawa.

The same approach was followed in ameliorating the income needs of larger families with low incomes. The universal family allowances were nearly tripled — to $20 per child — and their purchasing power was guaranteed as that of the Old Age Security pensions had been guaranteed in 1972. In recognition of the fact that the higher family allowances would benefit the rich as well as the poor, the Government of Canada subjected the allowances to taxation, thus introducing some redistributive effect. The most radical innovation, however, was to permit the provinces to vary the size of the family allowances paid on the basis of age of child or family size, providing the average per child in the province amounted to $20, and providing a minimum of $12 per child were paid.

When these changes in income support and supplementation had been made — significantly, by way of the "demogrant," or universal payment approach — Ministers turned their minds to the development of a general guaranteed income system for people under 65 years of age. After many months of discussion at both ministerial and official levels, the Conference agreed that a guaranteed or minimum income system, in combination with the higher family allowances, should substantially replace present social assistance plans. It was also agreed that the guaranteed income system should be made up of two tiers or parts: "(full) income support for people who are unable to work or for whom employment cannot be found, and income supplements for people who are working but whose incomes are inadequate." The main characteristics of the system have also been outlined: "that the support levels (should) be set by the provinces; that people on support should receive the rehabilitation and employment services required to make it possible for them to take employment which could be found or created for them; and that income supplementation should contain strong work incentives in terms both of the rate at which supplements would be decreased as family income rose, and of the relative income levels assured to people who were working as opposed to those who were on support."[6]

In addition the provincial ministers reached a consensus at an Interprovincial Conference that any jointly-financed guaranteed income system should contain certain specific national standards, including "minimum and maximum benefit levels . . . , a single national definition of the benefit or support unit . . . , a single definition of income . . . and a regular periodic escalation of benefits."[7] Complementing these criteria are certain other specific proposals the Minister of National Health and Welfare has advanced, including provision for "the retention by the family receiving (full) support of a reasonable amount of miscellaneous earnings (one dollar out of every four)," and "provision that, as family earnings increased as a result of more regular employment, and began to approach the support or guaranteed levels, increased work incentives (should) be provided (by allowing the family to retain two dollars out of every three dollars earned)."[8]

Thus Ministers are now able to say, at the end of the policy stage of their Review, that "a consensus has been reached on the broad features of a new guaranteed income system." And officials have been "instructed to work out the details of an operational design for an income support and supplementation (guaranteed income) system of the kind Ministers (have) agreed upon." Harmonization of the new system with social insurance programs is also "to be completed during the operational design stage," and it has been agreed that "attention should as well be paid to the relationship between the income security system and the tax system."[9]

There remain, it must be said — outside of the technical difficulties of completing the operational design of the guaranteed income system — two outstanding, and outstandingly difficult, problems. They are jurisdiction — which government is to do what in the guaranteed income field — and finance — which government is to pay for what. It was agreed from the beginning of the Review, as Ministers put it, that "we must decide first what must be done, and then on who should do it."[10] But the Review has come to the stage where decisions as to which order of government will pay or "deliver" the income supplements, and as to how much of the costs of income support and supplementation will be borne by the Government of Canada, are essential to any final decision as to the design of the guaranteed income system.

To assist Ministers in the decision as to who should deliver income supplements, the Conference "agreed that it would be helpful for future discussions to have an independent evaluation of alternative delivery systems ...to be considered at a future meeting...."[11] To assist Ministers in evaluating the financing question, the Minister of National Health and Welfare has tabled a proposal that the Government of Canada would be willing to bear about 70% of the *additional* costs of the guaranteed income system (over and above present programs), and an average of 60% of the *total* costs of the system. The financing formula is designed to "bear ²/₃ of the cost of supplementing the incomes of people who are working, but at inadequate incomes," and to "increase (Canada's) share in the lower income provinces of the cost of the guaranteed income paid to people who are unable to work or find employment."

In sum, there is agreement that a guaranteed income system should be implemented in Canada, and agreement as to the general form it should take. The decisions as to the financing of the guaranteed income, the delivery of the income supplements, the operational design of the system, its harmonization with social insurance plans, and the timing of its introduction, remains to be taken during the operational or implementation stage of the Social Security Review.

Agreement on the *social services strategy* came more readily than on any of the other three program, or policy, strategies. The conference of Ministers has agreed on essentially three propositions: first, that social services should no longer be looked upon as attaching solely to "people in need or likely to become in need"[12]; secondly, that it should be recognized that the degree of universality of social services — their availability and the charge made for them — will change over time; and, thirdly, that the priority accorded to social services, both to assist people in entering into employment or "useful endeavor," and to enable them to manage at home instead of being placed in an institution, should be greatly increased.

To accomplish these three goals the Minister of National Health and Welfare has undertaken on behalf of the Government of Canada to introduce a new Social Services Act which would extend federal financial assistance not only in respect of social services being provided to people on guaranteed incomes ("people in need"), but also in respect of the higher priority social services which are being, or might be made available to the public generally, either on the basis of an income-test or on a "universal" basis. Immediate priority would be given to income-tested day-care services, and homemaker and other support services designed to enable the old and the handicapped to continue to function in their homes, and, on a universal basis, to child welfare services (as at present), and a greatly expanded range of rehabilitation services. Finally, the new Act would provide for the federal government to share in the costs of new, or additional, services from time to time, or to increase the degree of universality with which services might be made available and still qualify for federal assistance. Any such changes would be made only after adequate notice to and consultation with the provinces.

These then are the policy and program decisions which Ministers have reached in the Social Security Review — on the employment strategy, the social insurance strategy, the income support and supplementation strategy, and the social services strategy. This outline, while topical and perhaps even cataloguish, is a necessary backdrop to an examination of the more interesting part of the Social Security Review: the central policy issues which arose, and how they were resolved.

The Central Policy Issues

Every participant in the Review will have his/her own version as to the policy issues which emerged in this intensely interesting federal-provincial exercise. But I would identify five: the question as to the place of the work ethic in the social security system; the search for a simplistic solution, through some grand omnibus program; the nature of the guaranteed income system which ought to be adopted; the income redistribution issue; and the place of social services in social security.

The Work Ethic Issue

Probably the most fundamental issue Ministers confronted was the place of the work ethic in the social security system. It underlay the "welfare backlash" — the argument that if only people were prepared to get out and work the welfare problem would be solved; and it underlay the opposing argument that the work ethic was dead and was being replaced by a new-found freedom to choose between work and leisure.

Ministers recognized that the social security system could not be based upon opposing premises, and decided to face the work ethic issue head-on. They stated flatly, in accepting an employment strategy as their first priority in reforming the social security system that, as the Minister of National Health and Welfare had said, "the first strategy in providing income security to Canadians must be to provide people with jobs — with income through employment.... [13] And the Conference of Welfare Ministers agreed to a "community employment policy ... designed specifically for the clients of the social security system."[14]

Reaching this conclusion gave rise to a good deal of argument, particularly among the public servants who were engaged in the social security review. There were social workers, particularly those familiar with the social assistance practices of earlier times, who raised the spectre of "work for welfare." People should not be coerced into working, they asserted. There were economists who saw in the community employment policy quite the opposite danger: the spectre of "guaranteed employment," and the government becoming the "employer of last resort." Others, who were concerned with welfare abuses, saw in the community employment policy the dawning recognition on the part of politicians that welfare recipients should simply be put to work. And not a few contemporary reformers saw in the program the opportunity of providing to everyone through community-service jobs "meaningful alternatives" to less attractive, lower-paying jobs in the private sector.

In the end the Conference set aside these arguments, and approved a community employment policy, as I have said, for "people who have particular and continuing difficulty in getting and keeping satisfactory employment." There were several forces which led to this decision. The most important, in my judgment, was the recognition by Ministers and officials alike that the vast majority of people on social assistance — the disabled, older people with limited skills, and single parents with pre-school children — would greatly prefer to be employed than to be "shelved" on social assistance. So providing employment was the humane, to say nothing of the productive, thing to do. And, it seemed obvious, it should be provided to those who needed it most — and those looking for a "meaningful alternative."

The second and equally important influence, again in my view, was the recognition by Ministers that the community generally held the same opinion as social assistance recipients — if for different reasons: they (the community) wanted a social security program which placed emphasis on making employment available, not one which emphasized making social assistance freely available. The evidence of a "welfare backlash" in Canada was enough to prove this.

The other force which led the Conference to accept an employment strategy as the first strategy, had to do with the "work for welfare" argument. My impression is that people involved in the Social Security Review in effect set this argument aside as being exaggerated. The *prima facie* evidence, so far as experienced politicians and public servants were concerned, was that precious few people preferred idleness to work. Moreover, the empirical evidence of the guaranteed income experiments in the United States tended to confirm this view. So the number of people who might be exposed to unwelcome pressure to take employment did not seem to warrant setting aside an employment strategy for fear that it might be distorted in application into a "work for welfare" measure.

The Search for a Simplistic Solution

The second policy issue confronted by the Conference, at least so it seems to me, was what I shall describe as "the search for a simplistic solution." The question was this: whether it wouldn't be possible to sweep away the great morass of federal and provincial income security programs in favor of a grand and simplified omnibus program. The siren song in this scenario — to use the jargon of the contemporary bureaucrat — was, of course, the guaranteed income. This after all was the classic solution of such economic luminaries as Friedman and Tobin — and what could be better than an economist's solution? It increasingly was being accepted by the business community as the efficient way of dismantling an allegedly incentive-less and much-abused welfare system. And it equally was the favorite of liberal-minded reformers who saw in it a simple, unstigmatized, and equitable way of getting money to the poor.

Interestingly enough the other simplistic solution — the payment of universal allowances large enough to meet the full costs of "child-caring" and child-raising, thus assuring, presumably, that wages plus allowances would always meet family income needs — was never really considered.[15] I say interestingly because universal allowances, or demogrants, as a mode of supporting family income are relatively well-developed in Canada, and, as we have seen, were employed by Ministers as the first steps toward reforming the social security system (in 1973). But obviously Ministers did not regard demogrants as the solution for the whole of the social security problem.

The other simplistic solution, the single guaranteed income system as a replacement for all existing programs, was also rejected by Ministers, without extensive debate or discussion. The reason was stated simply: "a single new program would not likely be found to be practical as an immediate goal." Moreover, "it would almost certainly result in unacceptable delays in the immediate reforms which are required in Canada's social security system."[16]

I suspect, however, that there were deeper reasons for this conclusion. It was recognized, at least so it seems to me, that most Canadians believe people should save for the contingencies of life, including retirement, not be guaranteed an income by others. This was reflected in the fact that social insurance is commonly accepted as the first line of defence for retirement, and against temporary income losses. The benefits are seen as a "right" — are relatively stigma-free, in other words; the apparently regressive payroll tax as a partial mode of financing is seen as savings; and the structuring of benefits on the basis of past income rather than on the basis of current need — with redistributive elements thrown in, of course — is accepted as normal. Social insurance, in short, is based upon a generally accepted community value — the "work and save" philosophy, if you will — and Ministers were not about to eliminate the plans involved in the name of efficiency or simplicity.

Finally, and on a much less intellectually elegant plane, there was the fact that politicians have a capacity for recognizing, as theoreticians sometimes do not, that you always start from where you are, not from where you might like to be. It is all very well to argue, as indeed a few people involved in the Review did, that the social security system would be simpler and more efficient and more equitable if those who are employed were to provide for those who are not, through a progressively-financed guaranteed income plan. But that did not reckon with the fact that social insurance plans exist in Canada, and the fact that people were not likely to accept the dissolution of these plans in favor of some unknown income support plan — however much the same constituency might argue that the country's social security system should be simplified.

So it was, in my opinion, that the second strategy, the social insurance strategy, survived, and that the Social Security Review came to address itself to the reform and harmonization of social insurance and social assistance, together, rather than to their replacement by a single grand scheme.

The Nature of the Guaranteed Income System

The third major issue the Social Security Review confronted was the form of the guaranteed income system which ought to be adopted. The arguments centered on two basic questions. The first of these was how to limit eligibility to a full guaranteed income in such a way as to avoid creating a system which apparently gave people a free choice between work and leisure, while at the same time avoiding the categorization of people as between those who are employable and those who are not. The second question was how to reconcile the objective of an adequate level of income support, or income guarantee, with the objective of a sufficient work incentive — without incurring enormous costs to the treasury.

The first of these questions was by far the most difficult one confronted in the Social Security Review. There was one school of thought which argued that eligibility for a full guaranteed income should be based upon income alone: if individual or family income were inadequate, that alone would be a sufficient measure of the need to pay a guaranteed income. The other school of thought argued that access to a full guaranteed income or full income support, should be limited to people who were "unable or not expected to work" — generally the mentally or physically handicapped, the retired, single parent families, and people unable to find employment by reason of a combination of factors such as age, lack of skills and length of time out of the labor market.[17]

Those supporting the first school of thought advanced a number of arguments in support of their cause. First, need was need, and if family income were insufficient, it was wrong in human terms to expect the family to live below established income standards. Secondly, it was argued that all of the evidence in the guaranteed income experiments in the United States suggested that very few people indeed would in fact choose not to work if a guaranteed income were available. Thirdly, the usual test for eligibility for a guaranteed income, other than income itself, was employability, and it was quite impossible to administer a guaranteed income system with impartiality and fairness and humanity if it were necessary to measure, medically, a person's capacity to work.

The second school of thought argued, essentially, that the credibility, even the acceptability, of a guaranteed income system depended upon some reasonable assurance against its abuse. If the system were to provide to the individual a free choice between leisure and work, the community would perceive in it a great potential for "free-loading," even if the numbers who were in fact to choose leisure were to turn out to be a very small fraction of total recipients. Consequently, said the advocates of this point of view, some measure of the ability of a person to support him/herself was a necessary condition to establishing eligibility for a full guaranteed income — perhaps even to establishing a guaranteed income system at all.

The problem of differentiating between the "unemployable" and the "employable," or between the "deserving" and "undeserving" poor, bedevilled even those who were most committed to the second school of thought — to the two-tier system. Everyone knew, for example, of the practical difficulties being encountered by the Canada and Quebec Pension Plans in determining eligibility for disability pensions. And everyone knew of the opposition of welfare workers generally to the "categorization" of welfare recipients.

The problem of "categorization" was ultimately set to rest by a suggestion made by the Minister of National Health and Welfare. It was that an *employment availability test* should be substituted for an *employability test* in determining eligibility for a full guaranteed income. Thus, as Mr. Lalonde put it, "a full guaranteed income should be provided to people for whom employment at provincial labor standards cannot or has not yet been found, whether by reason of disabilities of the individual, or by reason of the unavailability of jobs within a reasonable radius. Similarly a full guaranteed income should be provided to single parents whose family rearing responsibilities make it impossible for them to take employment outside the home."[18]

The Conference of Ministers agreed to this eligibility requirement for a full guaranteed income[19] — one Minister dissenting — and thus brought to an end, at least at the Ministerial level, the so-called "one tier *vs* two tier argument."[20]

The second question confronted by the Conference was the classic dilemma of the guaranteed income system. Indeed it was what lay at the heart of the failure of the Family Assistance Plan proposed in the United

States. It seemed obvious that people with little or no income — again, the handicapped, the old, the single parents with pre-school children — should be guaranteed an adequate income. It was equally obvious that there should be a financial incentive for people on a guaranteed income, particularly able-bodied people, to work. It was obvious, in other words, that these people should not have their income support reduced, as their earnings increased, at such a rate as to weaken their incentive to increase their income through work. Put these two propositions together, however — an acceptable income guarantee, say $5,000 or $6,000 for a family of four, and a low enough rate at which income support is reduced as earnings increase, say 50% — and you find yourself supporting incomes over a very wide range of income — up to $10,000 or $12,000 in this example. The result, in financial terms, would be a huge bill for the treasury, which is to say the taxpayers.

The solution to this dilemma was found to lie in the differentiation between people who are likely to have little or no income, and be on full income support, and those who are working and earning some income, but whose incomes are inadequate and require supplementation. The first of these groups is in fact, as I have said, made up largely of the handicapped, of older people who have difficulty in finding their way back into the labor force, and of single parents who find it difficult to take employment outside the home. These people are not kept from working by any financial disincentive; indeed they generally would welcome any employment they realistically could take as a means of relieving the isolation and often the desolateness of a life on social assistance or a guaranteed income. So for these people the answer lay more in finding them employment — and where required in fitting them for it — and less in providing them with a financial incentive.

So it was that the Community Employment Strategy came to be seen as the sensible solution for people with little or no income, *not* a lower reduction or tax-back rate in the guaranteed incomes provided to them. And so it was agreed, finally, that the reduction rate over the lower income ranges, where high levels of income support were being paid, would have to remain high — 75% has been suggested — higher than anyone would want to set it if there were no fiscal or economic constraints.

For the second group of people, on the other hand — those who are working but whose incomes are inadequate — it was generally accepted that the financial incentive was likely to be very much more important. Here one was more at the margin, so to speak, of choosing between additional hours of work, or fuller-time, higher-paid work on the one hand, and a reduction in free-time on the other. It was here, therefore, that the question of marginal financial gain could be expected to become relevant. So those engaged in the Social Security Review generally concluded that in the higher ranges of income where income supplements are being paid, the rate at which the supplements are reduced as earnings increased should be very much lower — even as low as 33⅓%.

These, then, were the two principal policy questions, as I see it, which were confronted in deciding upon the nature of the guaranteed income system. I have not referred here to the other two major issues which lie at the heart of establishing a guaranteed income system in Canada: the question as to which order of government will administer the guaranteed income, and in particular will "deliver" the income supplements; and the question as to the proportion of the guaranteed income which should be financed through national taxation — which has the greatest redistributive effect across the country, and the proportion which should be financed through provincial taxation — which carries with it greater sensitivity as to the degree of income redistribution desired within the province. These two questions — jurisdiction and finance — have, as I said in earlier pages, been carried over into the implementation phase of the Social Security Review, where, it seems obvious, they almost certainly will be the most difficult issues facing the Conference.

The Income Redistribution Issue

It will be evident to this audience that the major unarticulated issue in the Social Security Review has been — and necessarily is — the question of how much income redistribution there should be. It lies at the heart of the question as to how much reliance should be placed on wage-related social insurance as opposed to needs-related guaranteed incomes in meeting the income security requirements of Canadians. It lies at the heart, too, of the question as to the extent to which income transfers should be built into social insurance plans, or, alternatively, the extent to which such income transfers should be effected by the manner in which social insurance plans and the guaranteed income system are harmonized.

Even more, the extent of income redistribution desired will determine the design of the guaranteed income system. Which order of government should set the income support or guarantee levels? If it is the provinces, should a national minimum be established? Which order of government should determine the range of income over which income supplements should be paid to the so-called "working poor"? And should there be a national minimum here too? Should the income levels at which personal income taxes begin to be levied, be raised to the levels below which family incomes ought to be supplemented, or should the levels below which incomes are supplemented be kept down to the levels at which incomes now become taxable? And there are other characteristics of the system which can be designed so as to increase or decrease the degree of income redistribution inherent in it.

Beyond these questions as to the shape of the guaranteed income system, there is the issue as to how it will be financed — an issue to which I referred a moment ago — and the question as to what priority will be accorded to its implementation. The answer to these questions will depend, in substantial measure, upon the conclusion which is reached as to the appropriateness of present income distribution patterns in Canada, and the desirability of changing them. To be more precise, should the absolute income levels of the poor be raised in Canada, and should their share of the national income be increased?

Interestingly, there has not been a great deal of discussion of this underlying issue in the course of the federal-provincial meetings — at least not explicitly. Perhaps it is because welfare Ministers take it as axiomatic that the national income should be further redistributed in favor of the poor. Or perhaps it is due to the fact that ministries of welfare tend to think of individual families, and the design of income security programs so as to meet their needs, leaving income redistribution to be the result of the process rather than its explicit starting point. Or perhaps there is a less charitable explanation: that officials became too preoccupied during the course of the Review with the mechanics of the income security system, with Ministers being only too willing to be diverted from the abstract and underlying ethical questions involved — questions with which they don't always feel too comfortable.

My own judgment is that both federal and provincial Ministers simply didn't feel it necessary to discuss the income distribution issue in their Conferences. Rather they saw it as the public issue — as the issue to be taken to the public, to be settled in the political process.

The Minister of National Health and Welfare, for example, began putting the income distribution issue to the public in the fall of 1974. In a speech to the Empire Club in Toronto he spoke of the need "to define a national conscience in the field of social security" — of the need for Canadians to decide "the income levels which we...believe our less fortunate neighbors should be expected to live on, and the distribution of income which we believe to be fair as between higher and lower income people."[21] And in subsequent speeches he has posed the same issue.

I suspect, if I may be forgiven for looking into a crystal ball, that the question of income distribution will become more explicit rather than less as the Social Security Review proceeds into its operational phase. For it is in this phase that the difficult questions concerning the details of the guaranteed income system, its financing, its harmonization with social insurance and with the tax system, and the timing of its implementation will have to be decided upon.

The Place of Social Services in the Social Security System

The final policy issue which I should like to review has to do with place of social services in the social security system.

From the beginning of the Review there was a difference of approach as between the economists involved — who generally were engaged in the examination of social insurance plans and the guaranteed income system, and the social workers and manpower officials — who generally were engaged in the examination of social and employment services. The economists tended to talk in terms of incentives to work, and the provision of employment opportunities, while the social workers and manpower people tended to speak in terms of the services people required in order that they might be fitted into employment, and might achieve their "fullest functional potential." To further confuse matters, those concerned with employment and employment services were inclined to be suspicious of phrases like "fullest functional potential," and the social workers tended to regard the manpower people as being excessively preoccupied with employment rather than the "whole person."

It took some time before the economists, and rather less time before the manpower experts began to understand what the social workers were saying. Their argument, in its essence, was that the vast majority of people caught in the "welfare net" do not need financial incentives to work, nor even simply manpower training services: they need individual rehabilitation, occupational adaptation, transportation, home or day care services, and other social services, in order to make it possible for them to take employment, or indeed, in some cases, for them simply to care for themselves in their own homes.

The nexus between the employment strategy and the income supplementation strategy, in short, was as much — indeed more — the social services strategy, as it was the financial incentives built into a guaranteed income system, or, for that matter, general employment training and placement services.

The social workers learned from the economists, too. As time went on they recognized more that there were choices to be made in designing a complete social security plan: that it was unrealistic to develop and propose the complete and ideal social services system, despite the case which could be made for it in individual, human terms. They learned, too, I suspect, something of the vocabulary of politics: that it was better sometimes to speak in economic terms — for example, of the economies which would be effected by keeping people in their homes instead of in institutions — rather than always to speak in social terms, with such ringing phrases as the realization of the fullest functional potential of the individual.

In the event, the importance of social services was finally recognized — both as a means for getting people into employment and as a means for preventing the "withering of the individual," at home or in an institution. And the new plan for the financing of social services, under a new federal Social Services Act, was more readily accepted by the Conference than almost any other proposal.

Conclusion

These then were the central policy issues, as I saw them, during the policy and program development stages of the Social Security Review. It is tempting to go on into the federal-provincial and methodological issues which emerged during these two years, as well, but that would take me beyond my mandate. My purpose is limited to attempting to set the stage for this Symposium on Income Security in Canada, by describing how a politically directed review of the social security system proceeded, and what policy issues emerged in that process. It will be instructive to observe the differences between this approach to the analysis of Canada's social security system, and that which is followed by the rather more detached social scientists involved in this Symposium. I cannot refrain from saying again that it is the very engaging of these multiple perspectives on public policy issues which will enrich both public policy formulation and the development of knowledge and theory in the several social sciences.

NOTES

1. Symposium on Income Security held June 2, 1975 at Edmonton, a joint session of the Canadian Economics Association and the Canadian Political Science Association, sponsored by *Canadian Public Policy — Analyse de Politiques*.
2. Canada, Department of National Health and Welfare (1973), *Working Paper on Social Security in Canada*, Hon. Marc Lalonde, April 18.
3. "Statement by Conference Chairman at Concluding Session of Conference," Federal-Provincial Conference of Ministers of Welfare, April 25, 1973.
4. Communique of Meeting of Federal and Provincial Ministers of Welfare, April 30 and May 1, 1975: "The Ministers concluded that the major policy aspects of the Social Security Review having been agreed upon . . . it was appropriate to proceed now to the operational design stage . . . ."
5. Communique of Meeting of Federal and Provincial Ministers of Welfare, February 19 and 20, 1974.
6. Communique of Meeting of Federal and Provincial Ministers of Welfare, April 30 and May 1, 1975.
7. Communique of Interprovincial Conference of Ministers of Welfare, September 20, 1974.
8. Statement by the Honorable Marc Lalonde to the Conference of Federal and Provincial Ministers of Welfare, February 1975, p. 9.
9. Communique of Meeting of Federal and Provincial Ministers of Welfare, April 30 and May 1, 1975.
10. Statement by Conference Chairman at Concluding Session of Conference, Federal-Provincial Conference of Ministers of Welfare, April 25, 1973.
11. Communique of Meeting of Federal and Provincial Ministers of Welfare, April 30 and May 1, 1975.
12. This is the current basis for the sharing by the Government of Canada, under the Canada Assistance Plan, of the costs of provincial social services.
13. *Working Paper on Social Security in Canada*, p. 22.
14. Communique of Meeting of Federal and Provincial Ministers of Welfare, February 19 and 20, 1974.
15. Professor Brian Abel-Smith advanced such a proposal to the Canadian Conference on Social Welfare at Calgary in June 1974.
16. Communique of Meeting of Federal and Provincial Ministers of Welfare, February 19 and 20, 1974.
17. *Working Paper on Social Security in Canada*, p. 32.
18. Statement by the Honorable Marc Lalonde to the Conference of Federal and Provincial Ministers of Welfare, February 18, 1975.
19. See communique of Meeting of Federal and Provincial Ministers of Welfare, February 18 and 19, 1975.
20. The first tier of the guaranteed income system was to be the full guaranteed income, available to those who were unable to work or to find employment, and the second was to be the income supplementation available to people who *were* working, but at unacceptably low income.
21. Notes for an Address by the Honorable Marc Lalonde to the Empire Club of Canada, "Income Distribution: A Question of Community Ethics," October 31, 1974.

Income Maintenance Programs and Their Effect on Income Distribution in Canada

JOAN ST. LAURENT

Canada is one of a group of societies that can be described as an advanced capitalist society. The essential characteristics of such a society, as defined by Ralph Miliband (1974:8-9), are that the largest part of the means of economic production is privately owned and controlled and that it is highly industrialized. Based on the assumption that the social relationships in a society are primarily determined by the mode of production, these same societies can be said to have similar social structures and are regarded here as class societies in which a wide range of inequalities of material condition and power continue to exist. No particular political structure can necessarily be associated with advanced capitalism, but these societies have tended to be political democracies. In a political democracy, unlike in a fascist state, the state and the political system are not synonymous. Universal suffrage and certain liberal democratic freedoms, such as political competition on a more-than-one-part basis, representative assemblies, regular elections, freedom of speech and the press, and freedom to organize, etc., make it possible for class conflict to be openly expressed in a society dominated by one class (i.e., an economically dominant class).[1] This same set of societies has been characterized, particularly since the end of World War II, by a dramatic increase in state activity.

In Canada, total government expenditure as a percentage of Gross National Product (GNP)[2] rose about fivefold between 1869 and 1967, from 7% to 35% (Bird, 1970:13). A significant proportion of that expenditure has been on social programs which are purported to alleviate the negative consequences of industrialization under a system of private ownership, and thereby reduce the level of inequality in the society.[3] These negative consequences, in the very broadest terms, can be referred to as the social and economic insecurity experienced by large numbers of citizens at the lower levels of the class system. A Canadian Press release in the *Montreal Gazette* (March 9, 1978) observed that in 1977, 9% of the GNP was chanelled into social security, compared with 3% in the early 1950s and 5% in the mid-1960s. The social welfare programs discussed here refer to those social programs through which the state provides income to individuals and families. The first program of this type was the 1914 Ontario Workmen's Compensation Act. The Manitoba government introduced Mother's Allowances in

1916, and the first federal program came in the form of the 1927 Old Age Pensions Act. Since that time a large number of social welfare programs have been introduced in Canada.[4] The claim is still made in 1978, however, that large numbers of Canadians live in abject poverty in one of the most affluent countries in the world.

The National Council of Welfare (NCW) reported in March 1978 that the lowest-income 20% of Canadians received barely 4% of the total national income. In contrast, the highest-income 20% received more than 40% of the total national income — a share ten times as great. Based on the 1977 Statistics Canada figures on income distribution, three million Canadians still live in poverty. The extent to which the evidence supports this claim is the subject of this paper, which will attempt to reveal some of the structural mechanisms that tend to nullify the redistributive effects of income maintenance programs.

We shall begin with a brief discussion of the theoretical assumptions underlying the article and then outline the specific set of social welfare programs (i.e., income maintenance programs) to be discussed. We will also investigate the nature of government spending, the distribution of income, and the effects of income maintenance programs on that distribution. Finally, we will consider some aspects of the tax structure, on the assumption that the redistributive behavior of the state is reflected in government revenue as well as in government spending.

Theoretical Assumptions

It is assumed that Canada is an advanced capitalist society, exhibiting the characteristics mentioned in my opening remarks. It is not assumed (as it is by the pluralists) that the state is an impartial arbiter of the diversified interests in society, and that power is widely diffused among various interest groups. Rather, the persistence of sharp inequalities of material condition and security is, as Westergaard and Resler (1975:141) have argued, a product of the persistence of capitalist power. In demonstrating those inequalities, as we attempt to do here, one demonstrates the persistence of that power. While the state is not seen as an impartial arbiter, neither is it regarded as a repressive agency of the dominant economic class.

Piven and Cloward (1971:XV) are among those theorists who see the state as a repressive institution. They suggest, in their study of relief-giving in the United States, that reflief-giving is used to regulate the political and economic behavior of the poor, thereby counteracting what they refer to as "several strains toward instability inherent in capitalist economies" (1971:4). This approach assumes first, that the introduction of relief and similar programs, and their periodic expansion and contraction, always stabilizes, and secondly, that there is a homogeneous dominant class which knows its own best interest and is capable of directing the state in the maximization of those interests. Clearly, such programs do not always stabilize or mute the more disruptive aspects of social disorder. Unemployment relief measures introduced in Canada in response to social disorder in the 1930s, for example, led to an increase in social unrest due to the inadequacy of those programs.[5] With respect to Piven and Cloward's second assumption, on examination of the introduction of social programs in particular historical situations, it is impossible to identify a homogeneous class. One typically finds disagreement between the various fractions of the economically dominant class in relation to any particular program.[6] No single-factor explanation for social programs or any other type of government policy seems compatible with historical reality. Socioeconomic trends, class relationships, and the political strategy of the state all enter into the issue with varying degrees of importance depending on the program and the historical period. In the Canadian case, social programs introduced in other British Commonwealth countries, the constitutional divison of powers between the federal and provincial levels of government, as well as the efforts of social reformers such as J.S. Woodsworth are secondary factors[7] which must be considered in the analysis of the origins of social programs. The argument that social programs perform a social control function in society by integrating class conflict, does little to explain differences between social programs within or between societies, or how specific programs come into being and evolve over time. A theory of the state which sees state actions as determined by a variety of economic and class factors is, therefore, more fruitful for the study of government programs.

R. Miliband (1969) and N. Poulantzas (1973), frequently referred to as Neo-Marxist theorists, provide a basis on which to study state actions in advanced capitalism, taking into account these economic and class factors. While there are many differences between the theories of Miliband and Poulantzas, they both view the state as a relatively autonomous entity, which represents the political interests of the dominant classes and is situated within the field of class struggle. Conflict between fractions of the dominant class

> necessitates the existence of an "external" institution representing the common, longer term, political interests of the dominant class(es) as a whole. Without that they would degenerate into special-interest lobbying (Gough, 1975:65).

At the same time the state must set itself up as representing the general interest of the people as a whole and this role of the state is legitimized through universal suffrage, regular elections, and other liberal democratic freedoms. The relative autonomy of the state is necessary so that it may intervene in class conflict. The state offers compromises to the dominated classes, which are in the long-run interest of the dominant class as a whole, but which are not in their short-term interest, or even in the long-term interest of a particular fraction or fractions of the dominant class. This situation, in which the state is responsive to the ongoing class struggle between and within dominant and dominated classes has resulted in a long series of social as well as economic reforms. The social welfare programs, with which we are concerned, can be regarded as concessions made to the dominated classes. However, these reforms have not changed the distribution of resources because political power still resides in capital. We are not so much concerned here with the origins of social welfare programs, which are to be found in the historical circumstances under which specific programs are introduced, as with their ongoing function in Canadian society. These programs may well have been absorbed and adapted to the benefit of the dominant class. Nevertheless, social programs are part of the real wage level of the working class and as such continue to be fought for in a way similar to money wages. State expenditures for these programs do reflect the mediating role of the state.

Income Maintenance Programs

Canada can be regarded as a "welfare state" because a significant proportion of its increasing state expenditure has been on the socially related programs of education, health, and social welfare. Social programs can be distinguished from other state programs as the means through which goods and services, as well as income, are provided directly to individuals or families by the state. The social programs which provide income are the subject for discussion here.[8]

Income programs can be divided into three categories: social insurance, social assistance, and social benefits.[9] Social insurance programs are of a contributory nature, where contributions are made to a fund by workers and/or employers and payments are made to individuals for various reasons (e.g., unemployment, industrial accident). There are specific entitlement criteria related to these programs which exclude some workers who would otherwise receive benefits.[10] Social assistance makes available public relief and pension payments. These programs are not contributory and the main qualification is that the recipient is in need. They are, therefore, means-tested programs. Social benefit programs pay benefits to individuals who qualify for specific reasons (e.g., the aged, widows,

Table 1

Income Programs

Program	Type	Level of Government
Workmen's Compensation	Social insurance	Provincial
Mothers' Allowances	Social benefit	Provincial
Old Age Security	Social benefit	Federal
Veterans' Allowances	Social benefit	Federal
Unemployment Insurance	Social insurance	Federal
Family and Youth Allowances	Social benefit	Federal (except for Quebec which has a similar provincial plan)
Canada/Quebec Pension Plan	Social insurance	Federal/Provincial in the Quebec case
Canada Assistance Program	Social assistance	Federal/Provincial shared-cost plan
Old Age Security Guaranteed Income Supplement	Social benefit	Federal

veterans, etc.). Table 1 gives a classification of Canadian income programs and the levels of government which provide them.

As Table 1 shows, Mothers' Allowances and the Old Age Security Guaranteed Income Supplement (GIS), for example, are both means-tested programs in the same way as social assistance. These programs are social benefits and not social assistance, however, because need is not the primary criteria for eligibility. To be eligible for Mothers' Allowance one must first of all be a mother with children who are solely dependent on her for economic support, and to be eligible for GIS one must be at least 65 years old. Family Allowances, as well as Old Age Security, are universal programs, frequently referred to as "demogrants" — they apply to everyone who has children, or who is 65 years old or older, regardless of their wealth or income. The positive redistributive effects for the poor of such programs, because they provide equal benefits to rich and poor alike, can be expected to be minimal. These universal programs account for more than 80% of all the expenditures for income security administered by the federal Health and Welfare Department as reported by the NCW (March, 1978:2). The NCW found that universal programs only maintain the gap between rich and poor.

Government Spending in Canada

In his study of state expenditure in advanced capitalism, Ian Gough (1975) observed that there has been a growth of government expenditure at all levels of government on social services, infrastructure items, and aid to private industry. R.M. Bird (1970a:15), in his study of the growth of government expenditure in Canada, found that this was also true for Canada. Increasing federal government expenditure has been the norm since Confederation. The early federal expenditure in the late 1800s and early 1900s was related to the "national policy" and was mainly directed toward the economic development of the country. Provincial expenditure was insignificant until the early 1900s, when it took a dramatic climb upwards. Garth Stevenson (Panitch, 1977:71-100) observed that while health and welfare contributed substantially to this increased provincial expenditure, most of the growth was related to items such as transportation, hydro-electric power, and industrial subsidies, or to use Gough's terms, infrastructure items and aid to private industry. Bird's data also show a marked increase in municipal expenditure beginning in the early 1900s. This growing municipal expenditure may be more closely related to the growing demands for social services in an industrializing society as overburdened charitable institutions were forced to turn to the municipality for assistance. Bird's breakdown of government expenditure shows the dramatic appearance and rise in expenditure on education, health and social welfare, and veterans' pensions and benefits in the 1935 to 1965 period (1970b:29), supporting the view that such expenditure is largely a post-World War II phenomenon.

Taking into account the increases in prices and population, as well as the increase in real income per capita, Bird (1970:13) found that total government expenditure, as a percentage of GNP, still rose about fivefold between 1870 and 1967. Leo Johnson points out that the GNP and the total earned income both increased greatly between 1946 and 1971, as shown in Table 2.

Table 2

GNP and Earned Incomes of Canadians: Constant (1961) Dollars: 1946, 1961, and 1971

	1946	*1961*	*1971*
Consumer Price Index	60.0	100.0	133.4
GNP (in millions of dollars)	$20,493	$39,080	$69,786
Personal earned income (in millions of dollars)	8,860	21,480	41,991
Per capita GNP	1,667	2,143	3,236
Per capital earned income	721	1,178	1,947

Source: Leo Johnson, *Poverty in Wealth*, 1974, p.3.

Table 3

Relation between Expenditures for Selected Social Programs, Government Expenditures and Gross National Product, 1962-76 (in Billions of Current $, Unless Otherwise Stated)

Year	Expenditures for Social Programs	Government Expenditures	GNP	Social Programs as a % of Government Expenditures	Social Programs as a % of GNP	Government Expenditures as a % of GNP
1962	3.9	13.2	42.9	29.78	9.14	30.74
1963	4.1	13.9	46.0	29.73	9.00	30.30
1964	4.5	14.9	50.3	29.98	8.88	29.64
1965	4.9	16.6	55.4	29.77	8.89	29.90
1966	5.6	19.1	61.8	29.08	8.97	30.89
1967	6.8	21.8	66.4	31.07	10.21	32.87
1968	7.9	24.5	72.6	32.13	10.84	33.71
1969	9.1	27.2	79.8	33.41	11.40	34.11
1970	11.1	31.1	85.7	35.69	12.98	36.35
1971	13.0	35.2	94.4	36.90	13.75	37.27
1972	15.4	39.7	105.2	38.68	14.61	37.76
1973	17.0	45.0	123.6	38.86	13.90	36.46
1974	20.9	55.9	147.2	37.42	14.21	38.01
1975	25.4	68.4	165.4	37.10	15.35	41.37
1976	29.0	77.0	190.0	37.74	15.27	40.50

Source: Michel Bergeron, *Social Spending in Canada: Trends and Options*, Canadian Council on Social Development, Table 4, 1979, p. 17.

Table 4

Gross National Product for 10 Industrial Nations: 1975

Country	Gross National Product*	
	Total	Per Capita of Population
	In Billion $	In $
Belgium	63.1	6,438
Federal Republic of Germany	424.1	6,859
Finland	26.2	5,560
Great Britain	231.6	4,133
Canada	158.4	6,938
Netherlands	80.8	5,918
Austria	37.6	4,991
Sweden	69.5	8,484
Switzerland	56.0	8,743
U.S.A.	1,516.3	7,101

*Converted into dollars at average exchange rates for the year.

Source: Social Security in 10 Industrial Nations, Union Bank of Switzerland, 1977, p.3.

As increasingly large percentage of this growing GNP was channeled into social security. Figures released in 1979 by the Canadian Council on Social Development show the continuing trend in the relationship between expenditures on social programs, government expenditures, and GNP for the 1962-76 period (Table 3).

In 1962 government expenditure was 30.74% of the GNP and social programs accounted for 29.78% of that expenditure. By 1976 government expenditure was 40.50% with social programs accounting for 37.74%. In spite of this increased expenditure on social security, Canada fared poorly in a 1977 Union Bank of Switzerland study of social security in ten OECD (Organization for Economic Co-Operation and Development) countries. The study compared the level of benefits provided to individuals or members of their family through the various social insurance and social benefit schemes in the event of old age, death, invalidity, sickness, and unemployment. Social assistance programs, because of their extreme diversity within and between countries, were not compared. Although Canada ranked fourth highest in terms of national wealth (Table 4), Canadians ranked low in terms of benefits received, except for health insurance.

H.L. Wilensky (1975:124), in his book *The Welfare State and Equality,* showed similarly that compared to the other 22 countries he studied, Canada ranked very high in terms of GNP but very low in terms of the percentage of that GNP spent on social security.[11] These studies tend to support the view that Canada is a relatively affluent society, compared to other advanced capitalist countries, but that relative to most of the same countries, Canadians receive a smaller proportion of that wealth in social security.

Income Distribution in Canada

Leo Johnson, in his study *Poverty in Wealth* (1974:2), reported that between 1946 and 1971 the per capita GNP in Canada increased by 346%. For the same period the per capita earned income increased by 501%. This is a dramatic increase in both national wealth and the incomes of Canadians. Johnson suggested, however, that for many Canadians this increase in average income was meaningless because when the income of Canadians was broken down into deciles (i.e., 10% groupings) and the average income of each decile calculated, a very different picture emerged, as shown in Table 5.

Furthermore, the poorest paid workers were experiencing a rapidly declining level of purchasing power (Table 6). It has been argued by Richard Hamilton and Maurice Pinard (1977), that Johnson misrepresents the Canadian case and that, rather than a tendency to increasing disparity, the trend has been one of modest convergence between the incomes of rich and poor.

Hamilton and Pinard base their criticism of Johnson's study largely on the fact that he uses individual income data, which they argue includes principal and secondary earners of a given family. They state that individual income data ignores the substantial increase in part-time and short-term earners, many of whom are women and youths, which results in an increase in the average number of earners per family. Total family income is the only valid data for measuring the extent of poverty, according to Hamilton and Pinard. Johnson responded that in his work *Poverty in Wealth*, he was not describing the extent and character of poverty but rather, he was addressing the question of why increased welfare had not resulted in a decrease in income inequality. Johnson suggests that if one were attempting to measure the extent of poverty it would be necessary to know how many persons were dependent upon a particular income. Using the income concepts of

Table 5

Average Income of Income Earners by Decile: Constant
(1961) Dollars: 1946, 1961, and 1971

	1946	1961	1971
Bottom 10%	$ 411	$ 483	$ 286
10 - 20%	1,082	1,091	1,059
20 - 30%	1,472	1,755	1,705
30 - 40%	1,774	2,286	2,442
40 - 50%	2,157	2,805	3,204
50 - 60%	2,522	3,359	4,033
60 - 70%	2,884	3,938	4,973
70 - 80%	3,324	4,606	6,017
80 - 90%	4,012	5,541	7,432
Top 10%	8,325	10,148	12,900
Median	2,332	3,085	3,601
Average	2,802	3,601	4,405

Source: Leo Johnson, *Poverty in Wealth*, 1974, p. 4.

Statistics Canada one would want to know if a particular income is for an unattached individual, a family or a family unit.

A family is a group of people sharing a common dwelling unit and related by blood, marriage, or adoption (*Perspective Canada,* 1974:154). An unattached individual is a person living alone or in a household where he or she is not related to other household members. A family unit designates, collectively, unattached individuals and families with two or more members. It is this combination of data for unattached individuals and families which Johnson argues is most helpful in measuring the extent of

Table 6

Changes in Purchasing Power (1961 Constant Dollars) Received by Average Earners in Each Decile: 1946-71

Bottom 10%	$ −125
10 - 20%	− 23
20 - 30%	+233
30 - 40%	+668
40 - 50%	+1,047
50 - 60%	+1,511
60 - 70%	+2,089
70 - 80%	+2,693
80 - 90%	+3,420
Top 10%	+4,575
Average change	+1,603

Source: Leo Johnson, *Poverty in Wealth,* 1974, p. 6.

Table 7

Distribution of Income among Individuals[1]

	All Individuals					1971	
	1951	*1957*	*1961*	*1967*	*1971*	*Male*	*Female*
Mean income	$2,086	2,812	3,191	4,222	5,371	7,004	2,948
Median income	$1,768	2,351	2,651	3,553	4,170	6,331	2,000
Gini coefficient	0.4332	.4188	.4271	.4472	.4843	.4203	.4874
Shares of total income going to				*%*			
Lowest quintile	3.2	3.3	3.1	2.7	2.0	2.8	1.9
Second quintile	9.2	9.5	8.9	8.4	7.2	10.0	7.8
Middle quintile	17.4	17.5	17.2	16.8	15.5	18.0	14.1
Fourth quintile	25.2	25.4	26.0	25.8	26.0	25.1	26.3
Top quintile	45.0	44.3	44.8	46.3	49.2	44.1	50.0

[1]Farmers are not included before 1967. This however, has little effect on the comparability. All data shown are in current dollars.

[2]Each quintile contains one fifth of all income recipients; for example, the lowest quintile contains the fifth of recipients with the lowest incomes.

Source: Statistics Canada, *Perspective Canada,* 1974.

poverty. Perhaps the reasons for this are more clearly demonstrated by referring to Tables 7, 8, and 9. Table 7 shows the distribution of income for individuals in various years from 1951 to 1971.

One can observe a general decrease in the share of income going to the lowest quintile from 3.2% to 2.0% and an increase in the share going to the top quintile from 45% to 49.2%. The second and middle quintiles also show a general decrease while there is an increase for the fourth quintile. The Gini coefficient, which measures inequality of income distribution, has values ranging from 0 to 1. The higher the value of the Gini coefficient, the greater the degree of inequality. Table 7 shows, using the Gini coefficient as a measure of inequality, that the income inequality among individuals has increased from 0.4322 in 1951 to 0.4843 in 1971. This has not been a continuous process over the period. Income inequality among individuals declined in 1957 and in 1961 but rose again to even higher levels in 1967 and 1971. It is important to observe in Table 7 that, when broken down by sex, it is the females who show greater inequality of income. In Table 8 the distribution of income of family units still shows a decline in the shares of income going to the lowest three quintiles and an increase in the shares going to the upper two quintiles.

The most obvious conclusion to be drawn from the previous discussion is that, whichever way you choose to measure income, the multi-million dollar social security system has not significantly reduced income inequality. On the contrary, the distribution of income for family units, which seems to come closest to measuring the real level of income inequality, indicates that the gap between rich and poor is increasing. Using Statistics Canada data on non-farm families and individuals, the NCW (March, 1978b:1) observes that for the period between 1951 and 1976 the income gap separating the richest and poorest 20% of Canadians grew enormously. In 1951 the gap stood at $3,060, which, adjusting for inflation, is the equivalent in 1976 dollars of $6,900. By 1976 the gap between the richest

Table 8

Distribution of Income among Families and Unattached Individuals[1]

	1951	1957	All Units 1961	1967	1971	1971 Unattached	Families
Mean income	$ 3,185	4,269	4,815	6,519	8,845	4,346	10,368
Median income	2,703	3,624	4,262	5,859	7,832	3,214	9,347
Gini coefficient	0.3904	.3810	.3679	.3789	.4001	.4655	.3433
Shares of total income going to				%			
Lowest quintile	4.4	4.2	4.2	4.2	3.6	2.9	5.6
Second quintile	11.2	11.9	11.9	11.4	10.6	8.0	12.6
Middle quintile	18.3	18.0	18.3	17.8	17.6	14.8	18.0
Fourth quintile	23.3	24.5	24.5	24.6	24.9	25.8	23.7
Top quintile	42.8	41.4	41.1	42.0	43.3	48.6	40.0

Source: Statistics Canada, *Perspective Canada*, 1974.

and poorest fifths had increased to $18,000 or, expressed in dollars of equal value, the gap had multiplied by over two and a half times.

The distribution of money income is the most frequently used measure of inequality, largely because income inequality tends to underlie other types of inequality. Income distribution is, of course, only a partial measure of the extent to which governments redistribute resources. It includes only transfer payments and does not include government redistribution effected by the value of government goods and services received or by taxes paid. Many people argue that, while income distribution does not reveal a redistribution of income, if all government redistributive actions generated by taxes, transfers, and government services were measured and accounted for, this true measure of income distribution would reveal a reduction in income inequality. W.I. Gillespie (1976) tried to capture this broader picture of the effects of government redistributive behavior using fiscal incidence studies, which he refers to as measuring "command over resources."

Gillespie describes fiscal incidence as "a measure of the change in relative income positions of family units in response to the taxation and public expenditure policies of the entire public sector" (1976a:421). The estimates of fiscal incidence are derived by subtracting the distribution of effective tax rates from the distribution of effective expenditure rates. A positive value for the effective fiscal incidence rate for any income bracket indicates that the family units in the bracket are net gainers from the redistributive mechanism of the public sector, while a negative value indicates that they are net contributors (Gillespie, 1976b:428). Due to the inflation of money income, however, from one year to another, income brackets used to classify family units will not be directly comparable. This means that the effective rates measure of fiscal incidence will be more useful for describing the state of redistribution at one point in time than for describing changes in redistribution through time. Accordingly, Gillespie recast his results in a Lorenz measure of fiscal incidence, comparing, for a given percentage distribution of family units in each year, the percentage of income redistributed (Gillespie, 1976c:431). Using the Lorenz measure of fiscal incidence, Gillespie attempts to capture the change over time in the redistributive activity of the public sector, which regular income distributions tend to miss (Table 9).

Gillespie points out that during the 1960s there was a change which favored Groups 1, 2, and 5 (Table 9) at the expense of Groups 3 and 4. The total public sector was redistributive over time away from the middle and upper-middle-income classes toward the poorest and richest income classes. The decline in the fiscal incidence for Groups 3 and 4 was very small, at -0.008 and -0.077, respectively (Table 9b). The major gains were made by the rich Canadians in Group 5, prompting Gillespie to state, on the basis of these data,

> each rich Canadian family gained three times more than each poor Canadian family and six times more than each Canadian family in the lower-middle-income class (Gillespie, 1976d:432-33).

Table 10 shows the total command over resources after the redistributive activity of all three levels of government, and reveals considerable inequality in the command over those resources. Gillespie points out that a

Table 9

Fiscal Incidence in Canada, 1961-69, Using the Lorenz Measure of Fiscal Incidence

Lorenz Grouping	Family Units in Lorenz Group	Fiscal Incidence (% of Total Income Redistributed)		Change in Fiscal Incidence
		1961	*1969*	*1961-69*
a. *Share of total income redistributed within each Lorenz Grouping*				
1. Group 1 (poorest)	21.7	2.7	3.6	+0.9
2. Group 2 (lower-middle)	25.5	2.5	3.0	+0.5
3. Group 3 (middle)	25.5	0.1	−0.1	−0.2
4. Group 4 (upper-middle)	22.2	−2.0	−3.7	−1.7
5. Group 5 (richest)	5.0	−3.3	−2.7	+0.6
Total	100.0	0.0	0.0	0.0
b. *Share of total income redistributed for a percentile of family units within each Lorenz Grouping*				
6. Group 1	1.0	0.124	0.166	+0.042
7. Group 2	1.0	0.098	0.118	+0.020
8. Group 3	1.0	0.004	−0.004	−0.008
9. Group 4	1.0	−0.090	−0.167	−0.077
10. Group 5	1.0	−0.660	−0.540	+0.120
Total	1.0	1.0	1.0	1.0

Source: W.I. Gillespie, "On the Redistribution of Income in Canada," in this volume.

Table 10

Distribution of Total Command Over Resources[1], 1969

Income Class		% of Total Command over Resources	
(% of Family Units)[2]		*Within Each Income Class*	*For a Percentile of Family Units within Each Income Class*
1. Poorest	(21.7)	6.9	0.318
2. Lower-middle	(25.5)	17.9	0.702
3. Middle	(25.5)	25.7	1.008
4. Upper-middle	(22.2)	32.0	1.441
5. Richest	(5.0)	17.6	3.520
Total	(100.0)	100.0	1.000

[1]The adjusted broad income concept.

[2]The Lorenz Groupings in Table 9.

Source: W.I. Gillespie, "On the Redistribution of Income in Canada," in this volume.

representative rich family unit had almost 12 times the total income, after all public sector redistribution has taken place, as a representative poor family unit. Why is there this apparent lack of impact by government redistributive activity on income inequality? To answer this question, let us look first at some social programs on the government expenditure side and finally at taxation on the government revenue side.

Social Welfare Programs

Social welfare programs provide a variety of government goods, services, and income to individuals. Low income families, for a number of reasons, may be less likely to make use of goods and services (e.g., education and health care), thereby making them less redistributive than they might otherwise be. Social programs which provide income are not redistributive either.

The tendency for Statistics Canada data to underestimate the extent of poverty may mean that many individuals and families who actually require income assistance do not receive it. David Ross, of the Canadian Council on Social Development (CCSD), argues that the subsistence poverty lines used by Statistics Canada adjust for changes in the cost of living but not in the standard of living. Using the subsistence poverty line for the 1967 to 1973 period, the extent of poverty in Canada declined (Table 11). In 1967, 18.4% of families, 39.0% of unattached individuals, and 23.5% of total households (family units) were living below the poverty line; in 1973, only 12.0%, 31.6%, and 17.2%, respectively, were living below it. Using the relative measures of the CCSD and the Senate Committee poverty lines, the incidence of poverty was virtually unchanged for the same period. Ross interprets this tendency to measure poverty in subsistence terms (e.g., Statistics Canada I, Table 11) in the following way. Ross says that in terms of basic food, shelter, and clothing requirements, as determined using the subsistence approach, fewer low-income Canadians are going without the basics. In terms of possessing an adequate quality of goods and services, in relation to what the average Canadian possesses, the position of the low- income Canadian has not improved, despite the introduction of a variety of social welfare programs. The new Statistics Canada poverty line, introduced in 1973 (Statistics Canada II, Table 11), measures poverty in more relative terms than their previous subsistence measure but, compared to the other two more relative poverty lines in Table 11, it tends to show a considerably lower level of poverty. The problem of realistically defining poverty has not yet been solved. The problem of defining poverty and the inadequacy of social welfare programs is clearly demonstrated in relation to the working poor.

The NCW (June 1977) found that 60% of low-income family units headed by persons under 65 years of age rely on work rather than government assistance for their inadequate incomes. Using the 1973 revised Statistics Canada poverty line, this group consisted of 513,400 Canadians

Table 11

Extent of Poverty in Canada, 1967 and 1973

Poverty Line	Families		Unattached Individuals		Total Households	
	1967					
	No. ('000)	%	No. ('000)	%	No. ('000)	%
Statistics Canada I[1]	831	18.4	585	39.0	1,416	23.5
Statistics Canada II[2]	—	—	—	—	—	—
CCSD	819	18.1	548	36.5	1,367	22.7
Senate	1,052	23.3	606	40.4	1,658	27.5
	1973					
Statistics Canada I[1]	633	12.0	608	31.6	1,241	17.2
Statistics Canada II[2]	738	14.1	770	39.6	1,508	20.9
CCSD	960	18.2	691	35.9	1,651	22.9
Senate	1,171	22.2	802	41.7	1,973	27.4

[1]Statistics Canada I is the subsistence poverty line updated for changes in the cost of living.

[2]Statistics Canada II is the revised poverty line updated for changes in the standard of living, plus adjustments for size of area of residence.

Source: David Ross, *Canadian Fact Book on Poverty,* 1975, p. 12.

who were family heads. The total number of individuals in working poor families is close to one and a half million. The "marginal labor force," in which the working poor works, differs considerably from the "normal labor force."

The marginal labor force differs in terms of the level of wages, fringe benefits, and conditions of work. These workers enjoy none of the fringe benefits which unions and professional organizations gain for their members, such as private pension plans, paid sick leave, life, accident, and supplementary medical insurance, and full or partial payment by employers of provincial health insurance. A large number of factors, which the NCW discuss, leads them to believe that organization of such workers in the future is unlikely. Their jobs hold no promise of promotion or reward for performance, and they have little or no access to the normal work force, where conditions are better. Minimum wage legislation has not been effective in improving the condition of these workers. Employers have numerous and diversified ways of getting around the legislation. In any case, even if the minimum wage rate could be enforced, the council found that, in none of the five cities which they studied across Canada, could a family with one earner, a spouse, and one child earn enough at the provincial minimum wage to reach the poverty line.

The low minimum wage levels are closely related to a recurring theme which manifests itself in relation to almost every type of social program and which is closely related to liberal ideology. It is the notion that minimum wage levels, as well as level of benefits from social programs, must be kept low in order to give individuals an incentive to work. This idea is the most frequently expressed justification for the low level of benefits from social programs. The implicit assumption is that people would rather take a "free hand-out" than work. There is truth to this argument only to the extent that there are jobs in advanced capitalist society in which working conditions are so poor and/or the work is so repetitive and numbing to the intellect that no one could realistically be expected to take them on except under threat of severe economic and social hardship. Hence the argument is frequently parroted by significant numbers of all social classes, including some better-off members of the working class, that the level of Social Assistance and Unemployment Insurance, for example, must be kept low enough to induce beneficiaries of these programs to work and to take whatever jobs are available. The Guaranteed Annual Income (GAI) proposals are plagued with this same concern with the incentive to work. The concern is particularly ludicrous in relation to the working poor, who we found to be more than half of the Canadian poor. It is hard to imagine a group which could be expected to have less incentive to work, given conditions in the marginal labor force, and still they work rather than accepting government benefits. For the working poor, in particular, the present system of social security is clearly inadequate.

Workers who need assistance may not be eligible for benefits, which they might otherwise have received, due to specific entitlement criteria and gaps between programs. Benefits, if they are paid, may be so low as to spell further economic disaster. A worker injured on the way to work, for example, will not be eligible for Workmen's Compensation benefits, and if he/she hasn't been on the job for the minimum period required, will not be eligible for Unemployment Insurance benefits. Even if a worker is eligible under such a program, he/she is only guaranteed a portion of the previous income, which for the working poor was already inadequate. Workmen's Compensation will provide three-fourths of the pre-injury wage and Unemployment Insurance will provide two-thirds of the lost income. A minimum wage earner with an earned income of $6,000 in 1978 was entitled to a weekly Unemployment Insurance benefit of $76.92 and a weekly benefit of $102.56 if the earned income was $8,000. There is an insurable limit of $240 a week income, and therefore, workers with an earned income of $15,000 a year or more are entitled to the same maximum weekly benefit of $160.00 (NCW, 1978:10-11). In the case of pre-retirement disability a low-income worker can rely on the Canada/Quebec Pension Plan (C/QPP), which would provide 25% of the previous income. In 1977 the average monthly benefit payment under CPP for a disability pension was $137.12. The corresponding QPP for the same year was more generous at $209.59 monthly (Statistics Canada, 1978:458). Reliance on such programs means even greater economic disaster for families with a previously inadequate income and little, if any, savings. The future is not much brighter for the working poor after retirement.

The retirement situation of the working poor is seriously affected by their position in the labor market. They do not have the funds to take advantage of a Registered Retirement Savings Plan, which permits taxpayers to save at a tax saving for their retirement. In many cases they do not have access to employee or company pension plans because they are widely dispersed throughout the work world. In any case it is the better-off workers who receive the lion's share of the benefits from Registered Pension Plan Contributions. The NCW reports that the lowest-income 70% of tax filers get only 17% of the benefits from such pension plans (1976:25).

Because work-related retirement pensions are not available to workers in the marginal labor force, they must rely on C/QPP, Old Age Security Pensions, and the Guaranteed Income Supplement (GIS), the state programs which provide income for the aged and retired. Under C/QPP, 25% of an inadequate income will not be very helpful. The maximum pensionable earnings under CPP in 1977 was $9,300 (NCW, June 1977:16). The Old Age Security for the year 1976-77 paid a basic pension of $1,659.66 to anyone of age 65 who had been a beneficiary during all 12 months. For those pensioners with little or no income other than the basic pension, Old Age Security plus GIS paid a pension of $2,592.35. In October 1975 a Spouse's Allowance became payable to the spouses of Old Age Security pensioners, provided the spouse was between the ages of 60 and 64 and qualified on the basis of an income test. The average amount of the spouse's allowance (1976-77) was $1,569.32 annually (Statistics Canada, 1978: 546-47). These federal programs, plus varying but modest provincial supplements, do not in themselves provide a generous income for a comfortable retirement.

The Canada Assistance Plan (CAP) is a federal-provincial cost-shared program, established in 1966, primarily to fill the gap between previously existing programs. It is a social assistance program which means that, unlike the already existing social insurance and social benefit programs, the main criteria for eligibility is need and is therefore directed at only the poor. This program shares the shortcoming of all cost-sharing programs in Canada; that it provides an uneven standard of service from one part of the country to another.

In September 1977, the federal government proposed a new "block-funding" system for assisting the provinces to finance their social service programs. Instead of the present cost-sharing arrangement, by which the federal government reimburses half the cost of certain designated services (e.g., CAP), the provinces would be given unrestricted per capita grants based on the national average expenditure for services (NCW, March 1978a:1). There is some skepticism about whether or not this new system will result in a more even standard of services across Canada. As the NCW suggests, the uneven standard of services can only be partially explained by regional and demographic differences and the varying financial resources of the provinces. The quality and quantity of social services in large measure reflects the priority which provincial governments attach to such services. The NCW warns that the guarantee of federal funds not directly related to expenditures may make it easier for provinces not to expand social services or even cut them back because, unlike the existing cost sharing system, there will be no reduction in federal grants. Table 12 shows the disparity among provincial rates and, more generally, the low level of benefits throughout the country. In examining this table one must keep poverty levels in mind. The Senate Poverty Committee level of $6,200 and the

Table 12

Annual Benefits for a Couple with One, Two, and Three Children under Provincial Social Assistance Programs, by Province, April 1973

Province	Maximum Standards for a Couple with		
	One Child	Two Children	Three Children
	$	$	$
Newfoundland	2,640	2,940	3,240
Prince Edward Island	2,913	3,552	4,182
Nova Scotia	2,952	3,300	3,744
New Brunswick	3,120	3,408	3,672
Quebec	3,102	3,510	3,786
Ontario	3,456	4,032	4,608
Manitoba	3,504	3,864	4,174
Saskatchewan	3,456	3,972	4,488
Alberta	3,496	4,158	4,743
British Columbia	3,600	4,200	4,800

Source: Canadian Council on Social Development, *Social Security for Canada, 1973*, p. 25.

Statistics Canada level (revised) of $5,040 are both adjusted for a family of four to 1973 prices. It is the case, on comparing the level of welfare payments provided under CAP, that these payments alone do not permit families to escape poverty. CAP also contained a provision which allowed payment of assistance to the working poor but this was not taken up in any systematic way by any province. In most cases you either work, in which case you do not qualify for assistance, or you qualify for assistance and are not permitted to work and still receive assistance.

The Tax Structure

By the late 1950s there was a general realization that the existing social legislation was not having a significant impact on the distribution of resources or the elimination of poverty, despite the fact that the 1940s and 1950s had been periods of high economic growth. There was a growing suspicion that the basic reason for this resided in the tax structure. In 1962 the Royal Commission on Taxation (the Carter Commission) was set up but the subject of government payment programs to individuals was outside their terms of reference. The committee's report confirmed that government methods of taxation functioned to maintain a gap between rich and poor. The government White Paper on tax reform, which followed the Carter Commission report, contained a dilution of the Commission's recommendations (Adams, et al., 1971:140). The *Real Poverty Report* (Adams et al., 1971), described the whole tax system as regressive, pointing out that it taxes lower incomes more than higher ones up to about the average standard of living. It becomes slightly progressive, at least at the lower brackets of the affluent, but they found a lack of data about people in the top brackets. The Carter Commission suspected that those at the top paid a lower percentage of their income in taxes than people at the bottom of the over-average income bracket. Corporation taxes and indirect taxes make up the rest of the tax revenue.

Corporation income taxes are only partly regressive because they are only partly passed on to the consumer in higher prices. Indirect taxes, which include property and sales tax, and import duties and excise tax are totally regressive. The *Real Poverty Report* says of such taxes that they are directly tacked on to the cost of products and raise the prices, and everybody pays the same amount of tax regardless of their ability to pay. As can be seen in Table 13 indirect taxes made up more than half the tax collected in Canada in 1961. As compared to the other member countries of the OECD shown in the table, Canada ranks very high with respect to the proportion of taxes coming from indirect taxation. Gillespie's work on tax payments for 1969 shows a similar breakdown (1976e:437).

A Special Senate Committee on Poverty (the Croll Commission) reported in 1971 that the present welfare system was clearly inadequate and made a set of recommendations to correct the situation. They proposed a Guaranteed Income Program, using a negative income tax method on a uniform and national basis.[12] Social insurance programs such as C/QPP

Table 13

Canadian Tax Structure as Compared to That of Other OECD Countries

| Country | Percentage Composition of Taxes | | | |
	Direct Tax on Household	Direct Taxes on Corporations	Indirect Taxes	Total
Austria	48	7	45	100
Belgium	52	6	42	100
Canada	30	16	54	100
Denmark	37	4	49	100
France	48	5	47	100
Germany	51	8	41	100
Greece	36	2	62	100
Iceland	29	—	71	100
Ireland	23	9	68	100
Italy	57	—	43	100
Japan	38	21	41	100
Luxembourg	58	10	32	100
Netherlands	62	8	30	100
Norway	53	4	43	100
Sweden	60	6	34	100
Switzerland	56	10	34	100
United Kingdom	45	8	47	100
United States	50	16	34	100

Source: Ian Adams et al., *The Real Poverty Report,* 1971, p. 146.

and Unemployment Insurance, as well as certain contractual programs, such as Veterans' Allowances and programs related to native people, would be retained. Income programs such as Family Allowances, Youth Allowances, and Old Age Security would be repealed. Individuals would be guaranteed an income based on what the Croll Commission described as a new, more realistic poverty line. The individual requiring income assistance would no longer face the either-or situation where he/she must either work or accept social assistance, but not both. A GAI would permit its recipients to supplement their basic income through work. Earnings would be taxed back at a rate which provided that the recipient was always better off financially by working. The basic design of both the Canadian and American social experiments, purported to test the feasibility of such a program, is such that the incentive to work is the major determinant of both the level of basic income guarantee and the rate at which additional earnings will be taxed. In such an approach the economic and social conditions under which the recipients live are a secondary consideration. This pervasive concern with the incentive to work has been inhibitive of a satisfactory level of social and economic benefits for needy individuals in the past. There is no reason to believe that the effects should be different in relation to a GAI. Tax reform is not mentioned, except to say that no Canadians below the poverty line would be subject to income tax. Indirect taxation, which makes up such a large portion of the tax revenue and is most regressive, is not mentioned.

The NCW (1976) commented on yet another source of inequity in the tax system, which they refer to as "the hidden welfare system." They were referring here to the tax subsidies generated by the exemptions and deductions in the personal income tax system.[13] They argue that these subsidies most benefit the well-to-do. Such subsidies are of no benefit to those whose income is too low to pay taxes, they are of little benefit to the low-income taxpayer and only of modest benefit to the majority of middle-income taxpayers. Table 14 shows the estimated average benefit per taxpayer in 1974 from 17 subsidies, whose cost the NCW estimated.

The NCW argues that it is hard to imagine a government introducing a program which gave $244.00 to those with incomes less than $5,000, while giving ten times as much to those with incomes over $25,000. The hidden welfare system does exactly this and little protest is heard, partly because the public is unaware of the extent of its effects. The figures in Table 15, showing the percentage of benefits from the 17 tax subsidies going to persons in various groups, are also revealing. The lowest 70% of tax filers received only 40% of the benefits from tax subsidies, while the top 11% of tax filers received 33% of the subsidies. The NCW makes the important point that, unlike government expenditure, these tax subsidies are not continually open to scrutiny. Approval for direct government welfare payments must be won annually from the Treasury Board, Cabinet, and Parliament. Once established through the Income Tax Act, tax subsidies need no such approval. Their social and economic effects are rarely examined. Until these and other inequities built into the tax structure are rectified, no redistribution of income is likely to occur as the result of income or other social welfare programs, including a Guaranteed Annual Income.

Table 14

Estimated Average Benefit per Taxpayer from 17 Subsidies in 1974

Income Group	Average Benefit
Under $5,000	$ 243.75
$5,000-10,000	$ 484.65
$10,000-15,000	$ 788.06
$15,000-20,000	$1,177.46
$20,000-25,000	$1,786.93
$25,000-50,000	$2,426.73
Over $50,000	$3,989.78

Source: "The Hidden Welfare System," National Council of Welfare, 1976, p. 17.

Table 15

Percentage of Benefits from 17 Tax Subsidies Going to Various Income Groups

Income Group	Percentage of All Tax Filers	Percentage of Total Benefits from 17 Subsidies
Under $5,000	38.4%	12.5%
$5,000-10,000	31.5	27.9
$10,000-15,000	18.7	26.5
$15,000-20,000	6.8	14.3
Over $20,000	4.6	18.8
Total	100.0%	100.0%

Source: "The Hidden Welfare System," National Council of Welfare, 1976, p. 18.

Inequality, defined in terms of income distribution, does not suggest a decline in poverty. Examining inequality in terms of command over resources, which takes the redistributive function of the whole public sector, including the tax system, into account, Gillespie found no reduction in inequality. One can only conclude that social welfare programs have not been redistributive of money and resources from rich to poor.

Why has a tax structure which minimizes the other redistributive activity of government persisted? Why have social welfare programs, which have been relatively insignificant in their redistributive effects, not been terminated? Clearly, a marked decrease in indirect taxation, which most affects the poor, a decrease in tax subsidies, which most benefits the well-to-do, and a significant increase in corporate taxes would be a politically unpopular move by any government, particularly in view of the economically dominant class. Unless this type of change is made and new more realistic poverty lines are drawn, a Guaranteed Income will also be an ineffective mechanism by which to redistribute income. Similarly, if programs such as Family Allowances and Old Age Pensions were to be discontinued, one could expect extreme opposition from the middle and better-off working class, as well as from those who have a vested interest because they are employed by such programs. The working poor, who are largely pre-occupied with keeping the inadequate job they have and are generally poor-ly educated and unorganized, are unlikely to pose a serious political threat. It is the marginal population (i.e., women, youth, and the aged) who suffer most from income inequality, yet these same individuals are also lacking in political efficiency as compared to males between the age of 25 and 65. The latter group suffers much less frequently from poverty. Labor force statistics indicate that this is also true for unemployment, which often leads to poverty. The ineffectiveness of social welfare programs is unlikely to be explained by examining existing programs alone. It requires the study of state redistributive activity in the context of the economic and class en-vironment in which it operates. There are obviously economic and class fac-tors which have the effect over time of keeping the rich rich and the poor poor, in spite of the existence of a complex social security system.

NOTES

1. Member countries of the Organization for Economic Co-operation and De-velopment (OECD) are the most obvious set of advanced capitalist societies.

2. GNP is the total value of goods and services produced within the economy.

3. This is the view taken by a large range of theorists who can be loosely classified as pluralists. They view the state in liberal democracy as the impartial arbiter of diversified interests and given the democratic nature of these societies, they argue that no one class is able to insure its permanent political predominance. For them the growth of government has offset the unequal distribution of wealth and resources which results from the private ownership of property. See, for ex-ample, S.M. Lipset, *Political Man* (Anchor, 1963) and A.M. Rose, *The Power Structure: Political Process in American Society* (Oxford University Press, 1967).

4. Andrew Armitage, in his book *Social Welfare in Canada*, offers a compre-hensive chronology of these and other social programs between 1900 and 1970 (1975:213-20).

5. In 1935, workers were stopped in Regina by the RCMP on their way to Ottawa (the On-To-Ottawa-Trek) to protest inadequate relief programs and make-work projects, particularly the labor camps for young unattached men. Similarly, in-adequate programs for veterans were a contributing factor in the social unrest associated with the 1919 Winnipeg Strike.

6. Alvin Finkel (Panitch, 1977:357) observes, for example, that the financial and manufacturing fractions of the economically dominant class favored an Unemployment Insurance scheme when it was suggested by the Bennett Conser-vative government in 1935 and later in 1940 when it was finally introduced by King's Liberal government, while the resource industries were opposed to it.

7. They are secondary factors in that they are not determinant of government policy in the way in which economic and class factors are.

8. These definitions of the welfare state and social programs are, of course, operational definitions enabling us to distinguish between state expenditure on

social programs and other types of state expenditure (e.g., research and development, the building of public utilities, and communications systems). This is not to deny the benefits of social programs to business and industry or the benefits of public utilities, etc., to individuals and families. A comprehensive categorization of state expenditure is a topic which merits separate study, and mutually exclusive categories of state expenditure are yet to be developed. James O'Connor (1973:5-10) has made an interesting attempt to categorize state expenditure, working largely from basic Marxist economic categories. The fact that his categories are not mutually exclusive does not preclude their usefulness.

9. This classification of social welfare programs was suggested by C.I. Schottland in his 1967 book on the welfare state.

10. A worker must have worked a certain number of weeks to be eligible for Unemployment Insurance and, similarly, must have received an injury on the job to receive Workmen's Compensation.

11. A note of caution is necessary regarding Wilensky's study because not all the countries he compared were advanced capitalist societies in the way Miliband defined such societies. Comparability may be questionable with some of the countries compared such as the Soviet Union, Czechoslovakia, and East Germany, where state ownership prevails.

12. For a discussion of the negative income tax approach, refer to *Summary Report: New Jersey Graduated Work Incentive Experiment,* Office of Economic Opportunity, U.S. Department of Health, Education, and Welfare, 1973, and R.S. Hikel, M.E. Laub, and B.J. Powell, *The Manitoba Basic Annual Income Experiment,* Health and Welfare Canada, 1974.

13. They exclude from this group of subsidies the basic personal exemption and the deductions for expenses related to earning income. They include such items as child care deductions, registered retirement savings plans, registered pension plan contributions, interest income deductions, registered home ownership savings plans, etc.

REFERENCES

Adams, I. et al. *The Real Poverty Report.* Edmonton: Hurtig, 1971.

Armitage, Andrew. *Social Welfare in Canada.* Toronto: McClelland and Stewart, 1975.

Bergeron, Michel. *Social Spending in Canada: Trends and Options.* Ottawa: Canadian Council on Social Development, 1979.

Bird, R.M. *The Growth of Government Spending in Canada.* Toronto: The Canadian Tax Foundation, 1970.

Canadian Council on Social Development. *Social Security for Canada.* Ottawa, 1973.

Caskie, Donald M. *Canadian Fact Book on Poverty 1979.* Ottawa: Canadian Council on Social Development, 1979.

George, V. and P. Wilding. *Ideology and Social Welfare.* London and Boston: Routledge and Kegan Paul, 1976.

Gillespie, W.I. "On the Redistribution of Income in Canada," *Canadian Tax Journal,* Vol. 24, No. 4 (1976).

Gough, I. "State Expenditure in Advanced Capitalism," *New Left Review,* No. 92 (July/Aug. 1975).

Hamilton, Richard, and Maurice Pinard. "Poverty in Canada: Illusion and Reality," *Canadian Review of Sociology and Anthropology*, Vol. 14, No. 2 (1977), pp. 247-52.

Johnson, Leo. *Poverty in Wealth: The Capitalist Labour Market and Income Distribution in Canada*, 2nd. ed. Toronto: New Hogtown Press, 1974.

_____. "Illusions or Realities: Hamilton and Pinard's Approach to Poverty," *Canadian Review of Sociology and Anthropology*, Vol. 14, No. 3 (1977), pp. 341-46.

Miliband, Ralph. *The State in Capitalist Society*. London: Quartet Books, 1974.

National Council of Welfare. "The Hidden Welfare System," Ottawa, 1976; "Jobs and Poverty," Ottawa, 1977; "The Federal Government and Social Services," Ottawa, 1978a; "Baring the Burden, Sharing the Benefits," Ottawa, 1978b.

O'Connor, James. *The Fiscal Crisis of the State*. New York: St. Martin's Press, 1973.

Panitch, Leo, ed. *The Canadian State, Political Economy and Political Power*. Toronto and Buffalo: University of Toronto Press, 1977.

Piven, F. F. and Cloward, R. A. *Regulating the Poor*. New York: Pantheon Books, 1971.

Ross, David. *The Canadian Fact Book on Poverty*. Ottawa: The Canadian Council on Social Development, 1975.

Schottland, C. I. *The Welfare State*. New York: Harper and Row, 1967.

Special Senate Committee on Poverty. *Poverty in Canada*. Ottawa, 1971.

Statistics Canada. *Perspective Canada*. Ottawa: Information Canada, 1974.

_____. *Social Security, National Programs*, Catalogue 86-201 Annual, Ottawa, 1978.

Union Bank of Switzerland. *Social Security in Ten Industrial Nations*. Zurich, 1977.

Westergaard, J. and Resler, H. *Class in a Capitalist Society*. London: Heinemann Educational Books, 1975.

Wilensky, H. L. *The Welfare State and Equality*. California: University of California Press, 1975.

Poverty, Policy, and Politics: The Evolution of a Guaranteed Annual Income Experiment in Canada

SID GILBERT

> The Times They Are A-Changin'
> *Bob Dylan circa 1964*

Introduction

In the United States during the early 1960s there were civil rights marches, urban race riots, campus power struggles, free speech demonstrations, New Left initiatives, and of course, deep protests over the war in Vietnam. A War on Poverty was declared around the same time and it was highly unlikely this was mere coincidence. While Canada did not have an officially declared War on Poverty, in the early 1970s it did have a Special Senate Committee on Poverty (the Croll Commission), a *Real Poverty Report* (Adams et al.), and a guaranteed annual income experiment (the Manitoba Basic Annual Income Experiment). During those times in both countries many academics, researchers, and social commentators were proclaiming the reality of Dylan's song title. As W.E. Mann (1970:vii) notes, if speeches, reports, inquiries, and press coverage could beat an enemy then poverty in Canada would have been as extinct as the dodo by late 1969.

Almost a decade later little has changed. Poverty is still a major problem. This paper examines the relationships among poverty, social policies and politics, as demonstrated through the evolution of a guaranteed annual income experiment in Canada.

Background

Many factors contributed to the creation of the War on Poverty in the United States. On the popular front, Michael Harrington's *The Other America* (1962) and Dwight MacDonald's "Our Invisible Poor" in *The New Yorker* (1963) shocked and outraged a nation that had been led to believe poverty was a relatively minor residual or "afterthought" in American society (Galbraith, 1958).[1] Americans were startled to find that not only did a broader base for poverty exist but that the extent was massive — 40 to 50 million Americans, according to Harrington's figures. However, the new poor were largely invisible — off the social, political, and economic track.

U.S. president John F. Kennedy was reportedly among those shocked and horrified. Already more sensitive to domestic issues than his predecessor, Kennedy considered tyranny, poverty, disease, and war to be the major common enemies of man (1961 inaugural address). Kennedy was also undoubtedly aware that the irony of poverty amid plenty represented an excellent rallying principle for the 1964 election. He therefore initiated the attack which Lyndon Johnson was to later implement.

In addition to popular and political support, the War on Poverty was also influenced by the development of two key theories or perspectives.[2] The "culture of poverty" perspective (Oscar Lewis, 1959; 1961) came to be interpreted as a set of values, beliefs, psychological attitudes, and behavior that formed a way of life or culture among the poor that was detrimental to their success. Once in existence it represented a vicious circle, a self-perpetuating cycle of hopelessness and despair (Harrington, 1962:21-23). At the same time a somewhat broader "institutional critique" of the poverty program developed. The institutional critique stressed that poverty was not just the result of individual failures. Instead, something in the structure of the society itself, in the institutional arrangements, *systematically* generated the poor.

It will simply be noted at this point that only 20% of the poor were estimated to have this culture of poverty; that there was an obvious causal connection between the institutional structure and the culture of poverty; that this was later analytically, if not pragmatically, resolved; and that the institutional problem was dropped. I will return to these issues later.

U.S. President Lyndon B. Johnson launched the War on Poverty in his message to Congress on March 16, 1964. In introducing the Economic Opportunity Act, Johnson noted that previous wars had been waged against foreign enemies but that a domestic enemy was now threatening the strength of U.S. society and the welfare of its people. This program was intended to be much more than a mere skirmish against poverty:

> Rather it is a commitment. It is a total commitment by this President, and this Congress, and this Nation, to pursue victory over the most ancient of mankind's enemies . . . .
>
> I have called for a national war on poverty. Our objective: total victory. . . .
>
> Our history has proved that each time we broaden the base of abundance, giving more people the chance to produce and consume, we create new industry, higher production, increased earnings and better income for all.
>
> Giving new opportunity to those who have little will enrich the lives of all the rest.
>
> Because it is right, because it is wise, and because, for the first time in our history, it is possible to conquer poverty, I submit for the consideration of the Congress and the country, the Economic Opportunity Act of 1964 (Lyndon B. Johnson, 1964).

Unfortunately, the War on Poverty failed. It was the first of two wars the U.S. was to lose in a short period of time. Some of the reasons the War on Poverty failed can be seen in the passage above. First, it was oversold.

Second, the War on Poverty was waged by the Office of Economic Opportunity. It was expected that educational and occupational training programs in the human capital tradition could eliminate poverty. Emphasis was placed on eliminating the culture of poverty, not only by upgrading skills, qualifications, and experience but also by changing the values and attitudes of the poor, thereby enabling them to take full advantage of mobility opportunities — in other words, to make the poor fit in better with the achievement/attainment ethic. The problem was diagnosed as one of low labor market productivity. Skeptics have suggested that this approach represented a war on the poor, not a war on poverty. The major difficulties encountered were: (1) Not all the poor were candidates for the labor force. The aged, the disabled, single parents with young children would not benefit by educational and occupational upgrading. (2) An overwhelming majority of the poor were not thought of as having the culture of poverty, therefore, programs oriented in this direction would largely miss the mark. (3) Providing more opportunities and attempting to make the poor assimilate into the middle-class mobility paradigm was more difficult than expected. Human capital investment and an economy at full employment would not do it. It was not that easy to overcome years of primary socialization. And, even if overwhelmingly successful, which it was not, the enrichment of mobility and opportunity could only go so far toward the elimination of systematic inter-generational poverty. The generals of the War on Poverty had misidentified the specific nature of the structural problem. Perfect equality of opportunity or maximum mobility would simply create a new class of poor. Other reasons for the demise of war on poverty programs were underfunding and ambiguities in goals. In addition, the Community Action Program, which was hardly radical in content, turned out to be very radical in form, with the increased participation of the welfare poor not at all appreciated by program administrators and officials. Finally, the War on Poverty became a casualty of that other war, both in terms of attention and financing.

The ineffectiveness of its programs and mounting critical attacks dictated that a new approach was required. The first American guaranteed income experiment originated as a test of an alternative approach to the elimination of poverty. Canada was headed in a similar direction but with more discussion and less activity. The Economic Council of Canada (fifth and sixth annual reports) documented the severity of the situation and have remained unaccountably silent since then. Both the *Real Poverty Report* (Adams et al., 1971) and the report of the Special Senate Committee on Poverty in Canada (1971) recommended a guaranteed annual income. The former asserted that "the case for a guaranteed annual income is unassailable" (Adams et al., 1971:190) and the latter that "the Committee sees the Guaranteed Annual Income as the first firm step in the war against poverty" (1971:xvii). The Senate Committee saw a GAI as a pragmatic, reasonable, practical, flexible compromise between the radical solution of fundamentally altering the economic, social, and political structure towards complete equality and the traditional conservative solution of adding another program or layer to the social security system, thereby preserving the status quo. Data gathered a few years later showed that the public was also becoming supportive of the concept. Forty-three percent of Canadian adults predicted a GAI within ten years *and 58% approved of the idea* (The Canadian Institute of Public Opinion, February 2, 1974.[3] Although the Department of National Health and Welfare, in its white paper *Income Security for Canadians* (1970), rejected a GAI as a viable immediate solution, it was strongly supportive of further research on the potential impact of a guaranteed income program. Similarly, the comprehensive Castonguay-Nepveu report recommended consideration of a two-tiered guaranteed annual income.[4]

Clearly, a guaranteed annual income was an idea whose time had come. It had academic, administrative, and popular support. Political support came when the federal government announced the creation of a fund to cover 75% of the cost of any test projects, and Manitoba's NDP premier, Edward Schreyer, indicated a commitment to a pilot project testing whether or not the concept of a GAI could be translated into an effective program.

Accordingly, the Province of Manitoba submitted a research proposal (1973) to the Department of National Health and Welfare. It was approved in principle two months later, and a jointly-funded social experiment testing the effect of a GAI was announced February 22, 1974.

The Principles and Rationale of a Guaranteed Income

The essential features of a guaranteed income are attractively simple. Each individual or family is entitled to a certain basic income or support level, as it is called, if there are no other earnings or income. Families or persons having earnings or income receive a subsidy up to a cutoff or break-even point. Hence, the income units retain any and all independent income or earnings but have the amount of income supplementation reduced as independent income or earnings increase. Therefore, a positive monetary incentive to work always exists. The percentage by which independent earnings are taxed to reduce the payment is referred to as the offset tax rate or the reduction rate. Algebraically, this is expressed as follows:

$$P = S_t - jY \text{ where } P = \text{payment}$$
$$S_j = \text{the support level for a particular family size}$$
$$t = \text{the reduction rate}$$
$$Y = \text{family income}$$

An illustration will make this clear. Assume a family of four is guaranteed a support level of $6,000 a year. If there is no other income, the family would be entitled to receive the $6,000 or $500 a month for 12 months. However, if the family earns an additional $2,000 over the year, or let us say $200 in one particular month, then with a 50% reduction rate the family would receive in total:

	Month	Year
Basic guarantee	$500	$6,000
Less: reduction for earned income	100 (50% x $200)	1,000 (50% x $2,000)
Government payment	$400	$5,000
Family earnings	200	2,000
TOTAL INCOME	$600	$7,000

A GAI, therefore, is a universal, non-discretionary, income-conditioned transfer mechanism that attempts to minimize any work disincentive. Unlike traditional welfare programs where payments are reduced dollar for dollar if there are outside earnings, thus creating little incentive to get off welfare, the guaranteed income approach always maintains a positive monetary incentive to work through the less than 100% offset tax rate. A GAI is oriented primarily to the working poor, not to the disabled, the aged, etc. Incentives to join the labor force would not be *con* especially useful or appropriate in these cases. Poverty under this approach is defined mainly as a lack of income or money. In its pure form there is no social service philosophy or provision associated with it. As Lampman *pro* (1976:viii) has noted, the GAI approach "competed with the notion that the poor needed sympathetic counselling, job training, and public service employment or inkind transfers, such as food stamps, medical care, and housing." Other benefits anticipated from a guaranteed income program were a simplification of welfare administration and bureaucracy and a less stigmatizing payment process.

The Orange Paper on Social Security in Canada (April 1973), which initiated the federal-provincial Social Security Review, provides an excellent summary of the deficiencies of our social security system: it does not adequately respond to an economy operating at less than full employment; regional and sectoral differences in employment and sudden changes in the supply of labor are not handled well; it does not provide for the working poor; it does not provide an incentive to get off social assistance and back into the labor force; it does not adequately meet the needs of single parent families; it does not provide for horizontal equity, is not integrated with existing social insurance plans, and lacks overall coordination; it is stigmatizing and invites abuse.

A guaranteed income was expected to remedy these defects. The jor criteria by which such a program would be evaluated were work disincentive, cost and adminstrative feasibility. As Hum notes:

> The policy significance of obtaining reliable results concerning the work response is paramount. The extent of work disincentive, if any, for a guaranteed annual income will be a major factor in determining program costs, feasibility and public support (1977:5).

The Manitoba Basic Annual Income Experiment[5]

As in the U.S., a GAI *experiment* was created to ascertain just how significant the factors mentioned above might be. The Manitoba Basic Annual Income Experiment or "Mincome Manitoba" was established as a $17.3 million jointly funded federal-provincial project. The government of Canada provided 75% of the cost, the government of Manitoba 25% of the cost, with the design, planning, and research shared and the province made responsible for the administration and operation of the experiment.

This was not merely a pilot project or a test implementation of a GAI program to see if it would work. Instead it was a large-scale social experiment where one group, the participants or the experimental group, would be entitled to a GAI and another group, the control group, would not but would provide information for comparison purposes. Both groups would be interviewed extensively every four months for a three-year period. As indicated above, the major dependent variables were economic ones related to labor force response or work behavior such as hours of work and labor force participation, investment in human capital, job search processes, and job satisfaction. Secondly, administrative research on the overall program cost, administrative efficiency, responsiveness, and participants' comprehension of the administrative structure of the program was to be performed. Finally, some sociological research on self-esteem and achievement motivation, geographic mobility, family decision-making and family stability, stigma, community participation and youth behavior was to be developed, mainly for possible connections to work-related behavior.

The main features of a GAI are, of course, the support level and the offset tax rate. Mincome established three discrete guarantee levels to test for possible non-linear relationships. The generosity of the support levels was constrained by budgetary considerations, yet it could not be so low as to be non-competitive with existing welfare programs or no families or individuals would enroll in the voluntary GAI experiment. In January of 1975 when payments began, the support levels were $3,800, $4,800 and $5,800 for a family of four. After adjusting for inflation, these became $4,982, $6,114 and $7,246 by January 1977. Three offset tax rates of 25%, 50%, and 75% were employed, yielding the following nine-cell combination:

| | | January 1975 Support Levels | | |
		$3,800	$4,800	$5,800
Tax	35%	X_1	X_4	X_7
Rates	50%	X_2	X_5	X_8
	75%	X_3	X_6	X_9

Plan X_3, the lowest guarantee and the highest tax rate, was eliminated because it was not attractive enough, given existing welfare programs. Plan X_7, the highest guarantee and the lowest tax rate, was eliminated because it was considered "too far outside the bounds of policy relevance." This will be explained in the following section of the paper.

Some other features of the experiment were as follows: Stratified random samples were drawn from Winnipeg and selected rural Manitoba communities, and all families and individuals in the town and rural municipality of Dauphin were eligible to apply for enrolment in the program. (As of January 1, 1977, 1,057 families or individuals from Winnipeg, 178 from the rural dispersed areas, and 420 in the Dauphin saturated site, participated.) Support levels were indexed, taking into consideration family size. In order to control the participants' marginal tax rate and provide a basis of equality, all government cash transfers received by participants were taxed at 100% and income taxes were rebated. As a family's economic position depends on assets as well as income, a net worth tax was employed and payments were made for a three-year period (approximately January 1975 - December 1977) for most participants.

Assessment and Evaluation

Since no data are available yet from Mincome, the concept of a GAI will be assessed in theory and in practice, as operationalized by the experiment. What will a GAI do and not do? First, it will not break the culture of poverty where it exists nor will it propel lower-income adults and their children up the economic, social, and political hierarchies of the class structure. It will not produce a neat meritocracy in which everyone has an equal chance at success. In the first place no social services or training are provided, just money. The implicit hope is that it will be spent wisely — "invested" in human capital such as education.[6] Unfortunately, this financial policy solution or adherence to the "just pour more dollars in" philosophy is grounded in the convenient but completely unrealistic assumption of rational, economic man. It is unlikely that the provision of money alone would enhance motivation, drive, values, attitudes, interests, abilities, and performance.

If a GAI will not promote much upward mobility, it is argued by some that it will at least reduce the range of income inequality by establishing an adequate income floor and by giving a boost to earners near the floor. However, this appears to be an equally unwarranted expectation. The support levels, even the most generous ones, are far below existing poverty lines. Families and individuals actually would be "guaranteed" poverty level incomes.

Mincome Support Levels January 1975		Poverty Lines* January 1975	
	StatsCan	CCSD	Senate
$3,800			
$4,800	$7,608	$7,028	$7,871
$5,800			

*Source: David Ross, 1975:8-11.

Recall the point mentioned previously concerning the elimination of plan X_7, the combination with the highest support level and the lowest offset tax rate, because it was beyond the range of policy relevance. This catchy way of putting it really means "not politically expedient," "too generous," "might actually redistribute some income." When working in this area, one can not avoid the impression that a Catch-22 exists: adequate support levels ensuring a decent standard of living would mean somewhat less income inequality but would be politically terminal. On the other hand, a politically viable GAI program would maintain people at subsistence levels, would consequently not cost a great deal, and of course, would not accomplish anything. As Adams et al. (1971:192) noted, somewhat prophetically:

> In other words, a guaranteed annual income at a low level is a glorified welfare program. And a dangerous one — for its introduction would allow the Canadian government to make political hay out of a minor adjustment in bookkeeping.

Sadly, this appears to be borne out by the analysis above.[7]

This may be the place to speculate on the broader policy implication of this finding, which is not unique to the poverty/welfare area. With stunning regularity, social policies accepted in principle by politicians and by the public are rejected when the operational details become known or the actual consequences realized. It is easy to support bilingualism and biculturalism until you lose a promotion to a Francophone. It is easy to assert equality for women until women are selected for positions over equally qualified male applicants or until men find themselves up to their eyeballs in diarrhea, diapers, and crying babies. Similarly, it is easy to favor a GAI, as 58% of Canadians did in 1973, until it becomes painfully obvious that to be beneficial it would have to redistribute income — your income.

One further observation. It may appear that the GAI faltered in the "means" stage: it could not be designed exactly right, the precise operational details could not be established, it sounded good in theory but could not be made to work in practice. Some may think that agreement on the goals had been reached but that things went awry in working out the means. However, this was not the case. Agreement in principle was reached in this paticular instance, and this applies also to social policy in general because it was a vacuous, motherhood-type of generality. The debate over the acceptability of specific goals like the extent of income redistribution was simply deferred to the operational phase of policy implementation. But the initial phase, determination of the objective, was never really resolved.

The question of goals and the observation that it was not the state that accomplished the redistribution in the Robin Hood story, lead to the relationship between poverty policies and government. Naturally, policies are established by the political party in power. However, the important questions are: Does the government reflect the interests of the people in general or merely the interests of the dominant class? Another way to put it is: Does a voluntary social contract or a consensus on fundamental values exist or is there an imposition of the values of the dominant class? Or, what kind of consciousness supports the ideology that "if one group wins another has to lose"? Is this false consciousness or consciousness of another kind? Generally, there are two opposing positions on these questions. One group decries the tax burden on the professional and middle class; the diminishing of income rewards as inducements for achievement, productivity, effort, and success; the maintenance of idle, slack, welfare bums; and the inefficiency and coldness of yet another bureaucratic government program. The other group considers a GAI to be a cooling-out mechanism, one that produces false consciousness and mitigates against fundamental economic change, particularly in the system of property ownership. The co-optation of potential revolutionary fodder in the proletariat is seen by the second group as another mechanism of social control exercised by and for the bourgeoisie, or the ruling class.

Both of these positions are ideologies. There is no acceptable test between false and true on the question of values, nor is any possible. Therefore, the events concerning the evolution and impact of guaranteed income experiments in Canada and in the U.S. will be described, leaving interpretation to the reader.

The results of the U.S. GAI experiments in New Jersey, Gary, Indiana, and rural areas of Wisconsin and North Carolina all indicate that a GAI seems to have little effect on anything. There was no great increase in self-esteem and achievement motivation, no large investment in education, and certainly no significant work disincentive.[8] How smoothly were the experiments run, what was their contribution, and what was their impact? Accounts of the course of the New Jersey experiment (Kershaw and Fair, 1976; Rossi and Lyall, 1976) indicate major problems and a rocky history. Initial mass media coverage of the experiment gave rise to problems like the one concerning a man who was interviewed at home and at work on television and was later hassled at work, laid off, unemployed, separated from his wife, ordered by the court to make child support payments (which he was unable to do), and threatened with being jailed for non-support. It was not clear if the television program was the direct cause of his troubles but the impact convinced project officials not to release names of participants even with their written consent and, in fact, to provide no information to the media (Kershaw and Fair, 1976:181). Local welfare officials subpoenaed experiment records when it was suspected that some welfare families were accepting both GAI and welfare payments and not reporting the GAI payments to welfare. In addition, a four-month grand jury investigation was undertaken for possible welfare fraud involving criminal indictments on conspiracy charges. Both of these matters were eventually settled with no great harm to the experiment, but it was a trying period. The experiment was also under political pressure to release early findings that could be used in supporting President Nixon's Family Assistance Plan. Senior project officials provided the information and immediately lost their scientific credibility. They were seen as advocates of a GAI-type approach and not as objective researchers attempting to ascertain what impact a GAI would have, if any. Furthermore, the early release of data led to an investigation of the experiment by the General Accounting Office. These events reflect the difficulty of reform and its overwhelmingly political nature in this area.

The contribution of the experiments has largely been a technical one. As Rossi and Lyall note:

> It is one of the apparent ironies of the experiment that while its motivation sprang from a strong concern with poverty and a desire on the part of both the experimenters and OEO to affect national welfare reform, its most substantial

contributions may be of a more scholarly sort in the areas of experimental design and work behavioral response (1976:177).

However, it is more than ironic: it is sad.

The impact of the U.S. GAI experiments can be gauged by current policy research in the welfare/poverty area. The emphasis now is on employment and employment subsidies rather than on income maintenance (Lerman, 1976; Bishop, 1977; Danziger and Plotnick, 1978; Lerman and Skidmore, 1977; Haveman, 1977; Smeeding, 1977; Lampman, 1975; Lampman, 1976). A number of factors are related to this shift in orientation: first, welfare benefits actually became income-conditioned, thereby operating as a kind of GAI; second, unemployment is now considered of higher priority; third, the political system rejected both expensive and inexpensive GAI-type proposals; fourth, the public are more strongly supportive of job guarantees than income guarantees; and finally, the rapid expansion of cash and in-kind transfer programs creates the illusion that the problem has already been solved. As one economist put it, "advocates of a simple, straightforward negative income tax with a moderate tax rate built in are caught between a rock and a hard place" (Lampman, 1975:9), and another commented more generally that "although a relatively simple cash transfer program such as a negative income tax has great appeal to most economists, anti-poverty policies appear to be shaped by a wider variety of goals than economists often consider" (Smeeding, 1977:375). And lest the point be missed, it should be noted that these goals or values are non-technical and non-rational.

The course of events in the United States was dismal. However, things were worse in the Canadian situation. Initially, the Manitoba Basic Annual Income Experiment experienced a similar development as the New Jersey Income Maintenance Experiment. Press coverage was positive and favorable, but when the experiment refused, for excellent reasons, to release details on the participants and on the program, criticisms concerning "secrecy" and "bureaucracy" were mounted. More importantly, the political climate in the country had changed. The tax/welfare backlash era had arrived. All indications were that even the modest GAI being considered could be much more expensive than planned and hence completely unacceptable. This reflects the concept of eliminating poverty without any great cost ot the non-poor — increasing the incomes of the poor without decreasing anyone else's income. It would be ideal if income redistribution were a Doug Henning illusion, but it is not.[9]

It soon became obvious that Mincome Manitoba could not carry out its research mandate under the original $17.3 million budget. An Ontario tax study claimed that the net cost of implementing the income support and supplementation system proposed by the federal government would be three times the federal estimates. Furthermore, the cost of this guaranteed income proposal would escalate from $3.0 billion in 1975 to $4.4 billion in 1978, a growth of 46% in only three years (Cost of the Guaranteed Income Proposal, 1976). These factors, combined with the overall climate of fiscal restraint, did not augur well for the GAI experiment. There were internal problems as well. The sample, it was discovered, did not contain enough poor people and, therefore, the scientific and policy usefulness of the experiment was in question. Finally, discussions at the federal-provincial Social Security Review revealed a marked disinterest in the guaranteed income approach. Five issues emerged from the Social Security Review: the work ethic, the simplistic solution of a grand omnibus program, the nature of the GAI, the income redistribution issue, and the place of social services in social security (Johnson, 1975:464). The GAI option was rejected by the ministers without extensive debate or discussion because a GAI could not be implemented immediately and something practical and immediate was needed. Secondly, there was a stress on the insurance strategy, or the work-and-save philosophy as opposed to a minimum guaranteed "right"; thirdly, the idea that it is more appropriate to start from where you are, not from where you would like to be, was invoked;[10] and finally, there was a desire to avoid giving the participants a free choice between work and leisure (Johnson, 1975:466). There was little discussion of the income redistribution issue as well. Instead, the Social Security Review advocated a community employment strategy. The final result of these events was that on April 28, 1976, the Canadian GAI experiment was shelved. The Manitoba Basic Annual Income Experiment would provide no results or analyses, only a data base for future research. At that time there were no concrete plans for any further research. It appeared that a GAI was an idea whose time had come and had gone.

The Poverty of the Future

It is normal to speculate on future developments at the conclusion of a paper. Murphy's Law is that if anything can go wrong, it will. O'Tool's commentary on this was that Murphy was an optimist. The analysis above indicates that this is the case concerning poverty policy. Poverty will not be conquered in the next 20, 30 or even 40 years. This last statement is optimistic.

I will conclude by specifying errors that have been made in the past and some that will be made in the future regarding the elimination of poverty through social policy:

1. Poverty will not be eliminated by a general increase in the standard of living.
2. Full employment and employment policies by themselves will not eliminate poverty.
3. Increased opportunity, including perfect equality of opportunity, will not eliminate poverty.
4. Massive increases in government cash and in-kind transfers will not eliminate poverty.
5. Reform of the tax structure and increased government transfer payments will not eliminate poverty.
6. Attacks by rhetorical wizards will not eliminate poverty.
7. Moderate truncation of income distribution will not eliminate poverty.

8. Poverty will not be conquered without considerable cost to the non-poor.
9. Disagreement over the goal of equality versus inequality will continue to be a major problem.
10. Resolving this disagreement will be troublesome and lengthy and a political or power process.

What will the future look like? Much like the present and the past:

It was the best of times, it was the worst of times, it was the age of wisdom, it was the age of foolishness, it was the epoch of belief, it was the epoch of incredulity, it was the season of Light, it was the season of Darkness, it was the spring of hope, it was the winter of despair, we had everything before us, we had nothing before us, we were all going direct to Heaven, we were all going direct the other way — in short, the period was so far like the present period, that some of its noisiest authorities insisted on its being received, for good or for evil, in the superlative degree of comparison only (Dickens, 1962:1).

NOTES

1. According to this view, U.S. poverty in the 1950s was largely *case* or *insular.* Insular poverty existed as islands or pockets of poverty. This was not the result of individual inadequacy but was rather of the people's total frustration with their environment. Case poverty, it was thought, and this was later to become the dominant philosophy of the War on Poverty, "is commonly and properly related to some characteristic of the individuals so afflicted. Nearly everyone else has mastered his environment; this proves that it is not intractable. But some quality peculiar to the individual or family involved — mental deficiency, bad health, inability to adapt to the discipline of modern economic life, excessive procreation, alcohol, insufficient education, or perhaps a combination of several of these handicaps — have kept these individuals from participating in the general well-being" (Galbraith, 1958:252).

2. Perhaps these should be called metaphors because they are not theories in any rigorous sense of the term. The essential point, however, is that these ideas had a real impact on the course of events. As Popper would say, World 3, the world of abstract ideas or the world of objective contents of thought, exerts an immense influence on World I, the world of physical objects or states (Popper,1975:106,155).

3. Interestingly, education was inversely related to approval, but directly related to expectation within ten years.

4. A high support level and a high reduction rate for those with no strong attachment to the labor force and a low support level and reduction rate for those expected to work a considerable amount.

5. Details of the Experiment are from published public documents such as R.S. Hikel, M.E. Laub and B.J. Powell, "The development and design of the basic annual income experiment in Manitoba: a preliminary report," Working Paper X-7401 and Derek Hum, "Objectives, design and data contents of the basic income experiment in Manitoba." Paper presented to the Annual Meetings of the Canadian Economics Association, Fredericton, June 1977.

6. Human capital theory is in disrepute lately. It predicted economic growth would occur as a result of large expenditures in education. What occurred was little

economic growth, unemployment and large numbers of university graduates having difficulty finding a job.

7. Trevor Lloyd came to a similar conclusion: "In general terms, if the guaranteed income is applied at any level that ensures a decent standard of living it involves a large redistribution of income in an egalitarian direction, and it also involves freeing the able-bodied poor from the compulsion to accept any job available as a necessary condition of getting assistance from the government. ...Taken together, they are too much for governments to face. On the other hand, a guaranteed income at a level somewhat below a decent standard of living has neither of these effects, and so is much more acceptable to a state capitalist government. ... This is why, when Nixon's government in the United States and Heath's government in Britain suggest guaranteed income schemes, in both cases the suggested level of support is low enough to mean that nobody would live on it if they had any choice in the matter" (Lloyd, 1971:171-72). As the table shows, the same is true in the Canadian situation.

8. Except for secondary earners in families where a disincentive did exist. For a variety of reasons this was not considered undesirable.

9. An example of how to perform some sleight of hand with government taxation and expenditure policies to redistribute income is Wilensky's (1976:14-21) argument that socialist governments should rely on non-visible or less visible taxation to raise funds which can then be transferred via expenditure policies favoring those with low incomes. Invisible taxes are corporate income and profits taxes, property taxes paid by businesses, and sales taxes, while visible taxes are personal income taxes and household property taxes. The difficulty with this approach is that the invisible taxes are also the regressive ones. Money would simply be returned to the class from which it was collected in the first place.

10. This reasoning has also been used in the U.S. to justify piecemeal alterations to the welfare system: "Some will call the proposed measures only half a loaf. But in the welfare system as it now stands, this is certainly better than no bread at all. Given the uncertainties surrounding the outlook for and consequences of more dramatic proposals, a solid half loaf can be viewed as a real accomplishment" (Doolittle, Levy and Wiseman, 1977:87). The analysis in the present paper demonstrates this was the case with a guaranteed annual income. But the GAI was considerably less than half a loaf and the real accomplishment was a few crumbs.

REFERENCES

Adams, Ian et al. *The Real Poverty Report.* Edmonton: Hurtig, 1971.

Bishop, John. "The General Equilibrium Impact of Alternative Anti-Poverty Strategies: Income Maintenance, Training and Job Creation," *Institute for Research on Poverty.* Discussion Paper 386-77, University of Wisconsin-Madison, February 1977.

Canadian Institute of Public Opinion, as reported in *The Ottawa Citizen,* February 2, 1974.

Danziger, Sheldon and Robert Plotnick. "Can Welfare Reform Eliminate Poverty?" *Institute for Research on Poverty.* Discussion Paper 517-78, University of Wisconsin-Madison, August 1978.

Department of National Health and Welfare, *Income Security for Canadians,* Ottawa, 1970.

Dickens, Charles. *A Tale of Two Cities.* New York: Macmillan, 1962.

Doolittle, Frederick, Frank Levy and Michael Wiseman. "The Mirage of Welfare Reform," *The Public Interest,* No. 47 (Spring 1977).

Economic Council of Canada. *Fifth and Sixth Annual Reports.* Ottawa: Queen's Printer, 1968 and 1969.

Galbraith, John Kenneth. *The Affluent Society.* New York: Mentor Books, 1958.

Government of Canada, Department of National Health and Welfare. Working Paper on Social Security in Canada, April 18, 1973.

Harrington, Michael. *The Other America.* New York: Penguin Books, 1962.

Haveman, Robert H. "Poverty, Income Distribution, and Social Policy: The Last Decade and the Next," *Public Policy,* Vol. 25, No. 1 (Winter 1977).

Hikel, R.S., M.E. Laub and B.J. Powell. "The Development and Design of the Basic Annual Income Experiment in Manitoba: A Preliminary Report." Working Paper X-7401, Manitoba Basic Annual Income Experiment, 1974.

Hum, Derek. "Objectives, Design and Data Contents of the Basic Annual Income Experiment in Manitoba." Paper presented to the Annual Meetings of the Canadian Economics Association, Fredericton, June 1977.

Johnson, A.W. "Canada's Social Security Review 1973-75: The Central Issues," *Canadian Public Policy,* 1:4 (Autumn 1975).

Kershaw, David and Jerilyn Fair, eds. *The New Jersey Income Maintenance Experiment.* New York: Academic Press, 1976.

Johnson, Lyndon B. Message to the United States Congress March 16, 1964," in Herman P. Miller, ed., *Poverty American Style.* Belmont: Wadsworth, 1968.

Lampman, Robert J. "The Decision to Undertake the New Jersey Experiment" in David Kershaw and Jerilyn Fair, eds., *The New Jersey Income Maintenance Experiment.* New York: Academic Press, 1976.

_____. "Scaling Welfare Benefits to Income: An Idea That Is Being Overworked," *Policy Analysis,* Vol. 1, No. 1 (1975).

_____. "Employment versus Income Maintenance," in Eli Ginzberg, ed., *Jobs for Americans.* Englewood Cliffs: Prentice-Hall, 1976.

Lerman, Robert and Felicity Skidmore. "Welfare Reform: A Reappraisal of Alternatives," *Tax Notes,* Vol. V, No. 17 (April 25, 1977).

Lerman, Robert I. "A Reappraisal of Negative Income Tax and Employment Subsidy Approaches to Reforming Welfare," *Institute for Research on Poverty.* Discussion Paper 382-76, University of Wisconsin-Madison, December 1976.

Lewis, Oscar. *Five Families: Mexican Case Studies in the Culture of Poverty.* New York: Basic Books, 1959.

_____. *The Children of Sanchez.* New York: Random House, 1961.

Lloyd, Trevor. "State Capitalism and Socialism: The Problem of Government Handouts," in Laurier Lapierre et al., eds., *Essays on the Left.* Toronto: McClelland and Stewart, 1971.

MacDonald, Dwight. "Our Invisible Poor," *The New Yorker,* 38 (January 19, 1963).

Mann, W.E. *Poverty and Social Policy in Canada.* Toronto: Copp Clark, 1970.

Ontario Ministry of Treasury, Economics and Intergovernmental Affairs, Taxation and Fiscal Policy Branch. "Cost of the Federal Guaranteed Annual Income Proposal." Ontario Tax Study 10, April 1976.

Popper, Karl R. *Objective Knowledge: An Evolutionary Approach.* London: Oxford University Press, 1975.

Poverty in Canada. Report of the Special Senate Committee on Poverty. Ottawa: Queen's Printer for Canada, 1971.

Province of Manitoba. "A Proposal for a Guaranteed Annual Income Experiment." Manitoba Minimum Annual Income Project, March 2, 1973.

Ross, David. *The Canadian Fact Book on Poverty.* Ottawa: The Canadian Council for Social Development, 1975.

Rossi, Peter H. and Katharine C. Lyall. *Reforming Public Welfare: A Critique of the Negative Income Tax Experiment.* New York: Russell Sage Foundation, 1976.

Smeeding, Timothy M. "The Antipoverty Effectiveness of In-kind Transfers," *Journal of Human Resources,* Vol. XII, No. 3 (Summer 1977).

Wilensky, Harold. *The 'New Corporatism', Centralization, and the Welfare State.* Beverly Hills: Sage Publication 06-020, 1976.

Housing as Labor

CHARLES GORDON

> Woe unto them that join house to house, that lay field to field, till there be no place, that they may be placed alone in the midst of the earth (Isaiah, V, 8).

In defining the issue of housing, John F.C. Turner (1972) writes as follows:

> Some components of housing action are clearly measurable-dwelling units, for instance. It is also possible and practical to measure financial costs, time invested and even human effort. But the vital aspects of housing are not quantifiable at all. The most important "product" of any human activity is, of course, the satisfaction or frustration of human needs.

One could argue with Turner about whether or not it is possible to quantify the "needs" aspect of housing. But one must also go beyond the usual statistical descriptions of existing housing stocks and discuss the place of housing in the processes of human life. In the same article, Turner distinguishes between "housing" as a noun and as a verb — that is, between the house as object and artifact and housing as a social process, as something that people do. He proposes that the former should be ignored; I would suggest that both want discussion. And both need to be placed in a broader theoretical context in order to illuminate the related specific problems of housing, poverty, and social class.

Such an effort at illumination requires the suspension of certain taken-for-granted notions about housing as part of the social process. Because housing is assumed to be a necessity of human life, the nature of that necessity often has remained unexamined. The consequences of that necessity have also been left unexamined. Most studies look at the differential distribution of variable characteristics of housing, but those characteristics are the varying responses to more basic societal or environmental needs. It is these more basic needs that have been ignored and must form part of the theoretical context referred to above.

Primarily, housing is a form of shelter, that is, it is a form of protection. Particularly, it is the protection of physical existence: of the group, its organization and its artifacts, and ultimately, of the individual group member. It is a form of adaptation to and of the environment; thus, it is a form of culture (Lenski and Lenski, 1974:16). At minimum, the adaptive "need" involved is the protection of the biological entity of the person. There is a great deal more involved, of course, but that minimum is all too easily forgotten. *Homo Sapiens* (as we pretentiously call ourselves) is a relatively weak species, with only moderate endowments of eyesight, hearing, and smell. And it is a species that must create a barrier between the individual and the natural environment if it is to persevere. That fact is as true in Toronto as it is in Tierra del Fuego, for all the complex superstructure of the contemporary city. Beavers and bears have fur coats, and find (and to some extent, make), shelter; humans make clothes and build houses. In the obtaining of shelter, humans tend to systematically make what other species find instinctively (although this is a matter of degree). The purposeful nature of shelter-getting will be important in our consideration of housing.

The nature of the interchange between the biological entity of an individual and the natural environment has been described precisely by Fitch. He suggests that "building regulates the body's transactions."

> Because the external environment seldom affords the human body the precise "mix" that it requires at any given moment, man has perfected two ameliorating devices: clothing and building. Both act as interfaces between the internal micro-environment of the body and the macro-environment of external nature (1972:8-9).

Fitch continues to point out that both clothing and building function to create a "meso-environment" that is specific to human requirements. They are distinguishable from each other in that buildings shelter social as well as individual entities.

These aspects relate housing to the nature of the species and suggest that the ways in which specific social formations meet these species requirements are strongly characteristic of those formations. This is not the place for a social history of building, but it is the place to suggest that a capitalist industrial society provides a particular kind of housing and a particular kind of man-environment relationship. The way in which that relationship comes into being is not simply as a result of the class system; the form of housing and of cities is not simply a "determined" outgrowth of the relations of production. Rather, shelter relationships are relations of production and an integral part of the class system.

The notion that shelter relationships are relations of production comes from the more basic notion that the relations of production are the arrangements made to control labor, either by the laborer or, more likely, by somebody else.

> Labor is, first of all, a process between man and nature, a process by which man, through his own actions, mediates, regulates and controls the metabolism between himself and nature (Karl Marx, *Capital*, Vol. I:283).

Such a process is very close to the definition of the nature of housing cited from Fitch.

One should not put too fine a point on a semantic similarity (particularly when dealing with a translation), but there is an underlying sense to it. If labor is significant, if the relation between persons and the product of their labor is significant, it is because labor is the medium of subsistence and survival. The provision of shelter, of physical protection to biological or social entities would seem a kind of labor equivalent (if not identical) to the provision of other sorts of sustenance. This being the case, it would seem reasonable to extend the notion by which we discuss the labor process, such as class and alienation, to the shelter process. Housing is to the person the product of his or her labor. And an integral part of the defining of class position would be the kinds of control over shelter, as analagous to control of the means of production.

It is hardly new or profound to write that housing has become a commodity. But it must be remembered what is contained within such a statement. The relation of the individual to his or her shelter, as with labor, has been transformed from an integral relationship to an alienated form, where shelter has become an alienable, sellable, calculable quantity. The relation between the individual and the "provider" of his or her housing has, in varying degree, moved from one of tradition to a commercial fragmented relationship, an alienated relationship. The provision of housing is not done to meet that basic "need," individually or collectively, but to earn a profit higher than in other investments. Thus, the variation of housing relationships is a fundamental representation of social class. The broad sweep of housing policy in a society represents the imposed norms for the distribution of a commodity. But it is also the case, albeit a more speculative case, that the consequences of commodity housing are analogous to the effects of commodity labor in their impact on the lives of those whose relationships to the constructed environment are of an alienated kind. An even more speculative case can be made that the physical form of housing, the nature of its design, its aesthetic nature, are part of a similar process, as part of the dominant ideology and its hegemony.

One of the implications of this line of thought is that the person/house relationship must be framed in terms which encompass but go beyond those of assumed standards of physical safety, comfort, or other amenities. The control over shelter — the ability, in some sense, to create one's own shelter — is an equally important consideration. The ability to invest action with meaning and purpose is considered a defining human characteristic, in both Weberian and Marxian formulations. That ability, in relation to the physical environment, may be termed design. Papanek (1972) defines "design" as the purposeful manipulation of the environment. The limitation or denial of that ability through the loss of manipulability or of meaning, we will call "design alienation." And it would seem that the shelter process for the lower classes of the society is characterized by design alienation.

Historically, the processes of enclosure that helped to produce the working class (E.P. Thompson, 1970) had a strong parallel in the housing of the workers. Housing had become, under various forms of traditional mandate, a matter of social control and/or speculative profit. The provision of housing for the rural poor was a part of population control — not only had the poor man's animals to leave the land, he and his family had to leave the land as well. Among the farming landlords in 18th century Britain, there existed two sorts of population "policy": the "stock" theory and the "alien" theory. The former held that people on the land were to be regarded in the same way as cattle or sheep — as a valuable resource, to be housed in comfort sufficient to insure productivity. That view was seen as outmoded by the adherents of the "alien" theory, who saw the population on the land as alien, never to be allowed rights in the land, or the houses on it (Gouldie, 1974:30). Given a surplus of working population over housing, only the "best" were allowed to stay on the land. The shift in the view of housing was directly comparable to the changes in work organization occurring at the same time.

The role of housing in the control of and reproduction of labor was evident in the industrial setting as well. There was considerable argument as to whether the employer should provide housing for the workers in 19th-century Britain. On the one hand, if rents were increased so as to go beyond the 4% return on investment that employers got from renting to their own employees, the employers might have to raise wages. And there were competing demands for the employers' capital, while unemployment lessened the need for housing as an inducement for workers. But "the power over employees given by the provision of tied housing, however, could still be a great advantage" (Gouldie, 191). As late as 1906, strikes were broken by the threat of eviction from tied housing and in general, housing was part of the process of the control of labor. Gouldie suggests that as this was insufficiently profitable for private enterprise, the help of the state was sought. This is a continuing theme in the development of housing: in the narrow sense, it is seen as part of the process of managing a labor force; in a broader sense, it becomes an element of social control.

Crowding and Density

Basically, the problem of protection is a problem of control over the immediate physical environment. In abstract terms, this is a matter of control over what has been termed "personal space" (Hall, 1966; Sommer, 1969). In less abstract terms it is a matter of density, crowding, and the consequences which ensue from them.

High density has for some time been considered as a major cause of the pathologies of urban life. In its most basic sense, crowding is the inability to protect a given space from intrusion; and it is related to isolation as an inability to obtain a desired level of interaction in a given space. Density is an aggregate measure of the number of people in a given space; the question of "desirability" is not inherent in it nor is the choice of the kind of area which serves as a part of the unit of measurement for density. The selection of that unit will bias the relationship to the putatively "pathological" consequences. And it would seem that the selection of the indicators of pathology are just as biasing. Indeed, the viewing of certain activities as "pathological" is itself a bias. What, for example, is to be made of vandalism? It is costly and disruptive, but perhaps the only form of design available to certain classes of people.

The distinction between crowding and density has been made by numerous authors. Rapoport suggests that "density and crowding (the negative perception of density) are related to the experience of other people (and their environmental products) while privacy can be understood as the ability to exclude such experiences at will in the various sensory modalities" (1977:201). Isolation is the inability to include these experiences. Rapoport continues:

The critical factor in all this is *choice* — it is unwanted interaction which is the

problem, and there is actually more socializing when choice is available.
. . . Thus the ability to withdraw at will may enhance collective life, since the
more the individual can protect his own life and reduce information flows at
will the more he will enter into social relations with others and the more intense the interaction at such times (1977:203).

Hirsch has suggested that private space, areas where one can choose the
level of interaction, will become one of the scarcest commodities in industrial society. Lofland (1973) has suggested a vast range of activities,
from waste disposal to political activity, which once were public but are
now seen as private. While the general norm is that such activities are
private, the ability to maintain the privacy will increasingly be a matter of
stratification, that is, an unevenly distributed resource.

This is not as abstract, or as individualized a matter as it may seem.
Making it less abstract is a matter of selecting the appropriate level of
analysis:

> It is now fairly clear that while density at the macro level has some minor
> 'pathological' effects, it is not a variable of major substantive importance. In
> contrast, the evidence on overcrowding in the home is much less consistent.
> . . . [R]elationships in the home are more enduring and play an important role
> in determining the well being and behaviour of the individual. Disruption of
> these relationships due to overcrowding is thus apt to have serious conse-
> quences (Gove et al., 1979:59).

The rather mixed, if not contradictory, evidence in regard to crowding
and density is partly due to the misconceptualization of the issue. If the
issue is one of choice, as Rapoport suggests, then the concern is not with
density or crowding *per se*, but with *privacy*. As Margulies defines it,
privacy "as a whole, or in part, represents the control of transactions between person(s) and other(s), the ultimate aim of which is to enhance
autonomy and/or to minimize vulnerability" (Margulies, 1977:10). That
control (or lack of it) may be seen in spatial terms; it may be enforced by
means of the built environment. In the former instance, we are speaking of
the concerns of the literature on crowding; in the latter, we are speaking of
housing in the critical sense of its providing protection from other people as
well as from "the elements."

The parentheses in Margulies' definition above must be noted as well.
Privacy may be a group phenomenon as well as an individual one; that is, it
may be access to or by a group that one wishes to control. Certainly, the in-
vasions of the home to which poor families are subject are often a matter of
institutional demands rather than of individual actions. The "man-in-the-
house" regulations characteristic of welfare systems in Canada and the U.S.
have demanded that welfare recipients have their homes examined to insure
that no employable males are present. New proposals in Ontario would
allow the fire marshall powerful rights of search, and there are minimal
restrictions on entry for landlords. (Arguably, the poor are less able to enforce what rights do exist.) In all of these cases, physical invasion cannot be
countered by the particular dweller in a residence, because of the "rights" of
the state or of property.

At the other end of the scale, there are issues on the inability to obtain interaction when it is desired, that is, the problem of isolation. One thinks of this in its extreme form, as in the "segregation" cells of a prison. And certainly there are questions on the effects of sensory deprivation. Rapoport (1977:195-201) sees the problem in information terms — the urban setting presents problems of both sensory overload and deprivation, which have negative consequences for the individual.

The traditional image of life in the city is that of isolated individuals. This was an image both in novels (see, for example, the work of Theodore Dreiser) and in sociological literature. The inner zones of Burgess's concentric circles were the zones of isolated men — the men examined in the studies of the Chicago school, such as Anderson's work on the hobo. The notion of urban anomie was essentially one of the isolation of the urban dweller, in contrast to the assumed tightly-knit and supportive community in the rural setting.

As with crowding, the discussion of isolation is critically dependent on the selection of an appropriate unit of analysis and on the mode of interaction. Who is more isolated, a resident in a bachelorette apartment who rarely goes out but who is constantly on the phone or a member of an orthodox religious community who rarely interacts with anyone outside the community? The answer depends on what one wishes to see happen as a result of the interaction and to whom one allows the choice and range of interaction.

It is possible to speak in a more technical fashion about the kind of interaction which is sought or avoided. For the most part, we speak of face-to-face interaction, or of verbal interaction (as with the phone). But there are other sorts as well. Living in a dense situation may present problems of noise, smell, and ventilation, as well as of visual privacy. Even with these factors, it would seem a matter of control — for instance, it is the unpredictability of noise, rather than its level *per se*, which produces stress in the hearer (Glass et al., 1977).

Such intrusions at a technical or an organizational level represent a breakdown in the function of a boundary, which is to protect those within it, to mediate the relationship with the environment. Such alienation can be seen as a result of the development of the capitalist economic process — not only in financing and ownership patterns, but also in the development of house form, site, and even materials. If noise is a problem, then the choice of acoustic barriers in the design is a problem as well. Some barriers are mandated in codes and regulations, but they are often as much a part of the problem as they are a solution.

Defensible Space

The choice of the boundary for control is an obvious point of interest. As cities grew past the point where they were homogeneous systems, internal boundaries had to exist. (Indeed, the growth of such boundaries could be seen as a spatial reflection of the division of labor and organic solidarity.) Lofland (1973) argues that special areas and locations became necessary to identify people as the city became, in his terms, "a world of strangers."

It is also important to recognize that such differentiation was a process of struggle, negotiation, and flux. The origins of the "ghetto" are illustrative. Initially, they were much sought-after recognition of a legal standing for Jews, who had existed on the margins of medieval society. The grant of a "quarter" in the city was a reward for loyal services. Only later did the term come to have the sense of repressive isolation it now bears. Again, the selection and maintenance of a boundary becomes a matter of choice, control, and power.

Traditionally, the maintenance of community boundaries has been sought in the maintenance of neighborhood units or of the institutions within those boundaries. The locus of interaction was not within the houses, but in the streets between the houses (Gans, 1962; Jacobs, 1961; Whyte, 1955). But more recent work has examined the ways in which communities are maintained within large buildings. The economics of land, if for no other reason, have militated for the development of large buildings, and the development of high-rise public housing presents particular problems.

In the lower class particularly, the maintenance of boundaries is a matter of physical safety in its simplest sense. There are symbolic and expressive rewards to be found in the nature of housing, of course— for example, a display of social status — but as sociologists we may emphasize those over some important aspects of physical protection. In an article entitled "Fear and the House-as-Haven in the Lower Class," Lee Rainwater argues that security and safety are the primary factors that the lower class seeks in their homes (1966). They seek protection from both human threats to themselves and to their possessions and from non-human threats that stem from the poor quality of the construction and maintenance of their homes. The kinds of things that Rainwater lists are threats in themselves; and they also "destabilize" the life of the individuals involved. It is not only that the plumbing may not be working; it is also that it is not predictable when it will be working. That, in turn, creates problems of coping with the uncertainty. Rainwater tells the story of a pediatric out-patient clinic whose patients come only after the working day. The mothers won't come in with their children until another family member is home because the appliances in the home cannot be left unattended for fear of theft.

Would changes in the quality of such housing make any difference? One side of the argument is that a slum is a slum is a slum because of social conditions irrelevant to the physical quality of the housing. In another sense, it can be said that lower-class life is a chancy business in general — employment is less stable, housing tenure is less stable. The threats perceived are very real ones. The housing unit is perceived as the appropriate boundary or at least the most practical boundary to be maintained.

It has also been argued that housing quality itself is not determined within the structure of the local neighborhood. In the case of public housing, there are questions of design and the bureaucratic management of the housing. In the case of private-sector housing for the lower class, it may not be in the interest of the owner to maintain the housing. Barton (1977) argues that the deterioration of housing is a "natural and even profitable" consequence of a rental housing market under conditions of income inequality and segregation based on the same.

Oscar Newman (1971), in seeking to understand the nature of crime in public housing, provides some suggestions about the alternatives. The buildings that were the worst in terms of crime (within Newman's study) were high-rise buildings. Developments with a similar area density (but with a low-rise configuration) had less crime. For reasons of scale (fewer people in each of the low-rise units) and configuration (the entrances, lobbies, and approaches were more observable), it was easier for a sort of community to be maintained in each low-rise building. Presumably, a smaller population means that any one resident is apt to know who lives in the building and face-to-face interaction becomes more possible. Newman also suggests design changes that would increase the extent to which a resident identifies with his or her residence and therefore want to preserve and protect it.

Underlying Newman's considerations is the issue of the extent to which changes in the physical environment can determine the growth of community. Without resolving that dubious issue, it is possible to draw support from it that a critical protective boundary exists at some level of community. This would seem to be true in the most squalid of settings:

> That ties of reciprocal help should bind neighbours in the shanty towns is to be expected. Here certainly there is a contrast with the domestic independence found in more affluent suburbs. But the bonds are often much stronger than this. The residential community in the shanty town may seem very like a village — not, as is often argued, because its people still betray their rural origins, but because it is a small and largely self-contained unit with a stable membership, having its own mode of social stratification, competing with neighbouring units in its relationships with the outside world. (Lloyd, 1979:163-64).

The descriptions of the ethnic urban areas of North America present a similar picture (Gans, Jacobs, 1961). And as Gans details, things done in the name of improving the quality of urban life in fact damage the ability of the community to provide a useful boundary.

It seems to be the case that the nature of the housing market within such a community tends to keep the housing in better shape. Krohn and his associates studied the nature of local housing markets in Montreal, and found that:

> First, the areas of increasing property values are in the hands of professional owners, with results ranging from maintenance through neglect to demolition, but not renovation. . . . Secondly, amateur-owned areas, although confined to neighborhoods with stable or declining property values, normally have well maintained or even improved buildings (1977:118).

Amateur housing is part of a local, community set of institutions, with what Krohn calls "efficiencies of small scale." The local owner, in developing only a few units (one of which may well be his own) is able to assemble new "non-market" resources, in terms of unemployed labor and leisure time, and to substitute labor for borrowed capital.

> These non-market resources are further expanded by multi-faceted relations between owners and their relatives and friends and between owners and their tenants, which allow the conversion of, for example, the obligations of kin-

ship into improved housing via free labor time or extra care for a relative's house (Krohn et al., 1977:121).

No More Barn Raisings: The Deskilling of Urban Life

The relationships that Krohn and his associates describe in the paragraphs cited above presuppose the distribution of certain basic construction skills in the population. That supposition in itself can be questioned, but there is an underlying question — what opportunities are there for employing such skills?

If our analogy between housing and labor is valid, then the construction of one's own housing, and its continuing maintenance, is much a part of that labor. It is a form of mediating the relationship, on a continuing basis, with the natural environment. In urban settings, and as part of the process of capitalism in those settings, it becomes more and more difficult to exercise what I will call "domestic" skills. The maintenance of that labor-like relationship must be left to specialists; it must be purchased. In that sense, a part of urban life is "deskilled."

At the point of the first move into the non-rural setting, the rural poor come with considerable construction skills. In a sense they are vernacular architects. The barrios or shantytowns of the Third World are executed with incredible ingenuity. And similar skills are applicable here in Canada. S.D. Clark writes of the rural-urban move in New Brunswick:

> The steps in a building of a typical house, usually spread out over several years were described as follows:
> 1. The building of a one-room tar-paper shack; the single room often very large.
> 2. The laying of a foundation, either directly under the house or next to the house so that the house could be jacked up and moved.
> 3. The building of additional rooms.
> 4. The addition of paint and shingles.
> 5. The addition of running water and an indoor toilet (1978:79).

Clark is concerned about the limited quality of such housing. But he misses the point that this is housing built by the occupant, using his own labor instead of capital.

In rental housing, many of the tasks of maintaining or improving the house are required by regulation to be left to the owner of the building. The minimum standards for housing, and the other aspects of building codes, have the effect of requiring a certain level and kind of financing to build a house (Turner, 1972). But they also mean that a great deal of work on a house must be done by professionals.

There has been a growth in recent years in "do-it-yourself" home improvements. But one can speculate that such improvements are made by those who own their homes — in general, the middle class — and that the ability to use domestic skills is distributed much as the use of skill in work is distributed.

Indeed, what might be considered as home improvement in one sense could well be considered vandalism in another. Stanley Cohen (1973) refers to "tactical vandalism," the destruction of property as a conscious means to a non-monetary end. He also points out that vandalism is a label applied to discredit certain actions. In a sense, vandalism is illegal architecture, and what has been labeled as vandalism is the unregulated use of domestic skills to modify the environment.

The discussion to this point has centered on ways in which individuals are limited in the extent to which they control their immediate physical environment. Further, the ability to exercise that control is differentially distributed, and a lesser degree of control is, by definition, a form of alienation. To complete the discussion, we must look at the other side of the formulation. That is, we must examine the ways in which those who exercise control over the housing of others do so. If housing is labor, then we must look at that control as we look at the ownership of the means of production. This, in turn, concerns us not only with the decisions to build houses, but also with the decisions on where to build them and what form they should take.

In another sense, we are dealing with the house as commodity. We must also deal with the ways that such a commodity is formed and transferred. According to Heimsath, there are three major roles in the building process:

1. the architect, who designs the building for the owner;
2. the owner who commissions the building and manages it after it is built;
3. the regulatory government, acting through zoning laws, building codes, etc. (1977:25).

Heimsath, however, may be a bit behind the times because the division of labor has divided up these roles and created new ones. In the design process, there are a number of stages of conceptual refinement, ranging from broad concepts to working and detailed drawings; and special occupations have grown up in relation to most of these stages. A new specialty called "architectural programming" has emerged, whose function is to work out the purposes and relationships of the intended building, short of giving them physical form. At the detailed end, a number of sub-specialties (such as that of quantity surveyor) and a number of building systems (such as ventilation) are designed by specialist engineers.

Similarly, the role of owner has been divided. The legal owner of a building is unlikely to be the eventual resident; he is also unlikely to be the financier of the building; and indeed, maintenance may be left to the tenant, or subcontracted to specialists in building maintenance and security. The regulator role of the state is similarly divided among different agencies and levels of government.

Underlying all of this is the development of housing policy in the various levels of government. That policy is significant in its substance; but it is also important as an indication of the manner in which those with power and capital view housing. Heimsath also suggests that every building is the product of three things:

1. the need of the owner, defined by the owner;
2. the regulatory guidelines of the governmental agencies protecting health and safety;

3. the experience and insight of the architect as expressed in the design (1977:25).

Although the owner is not the resident, the owner's needs and his interpretation of the residents' needs will affect the form of the buildings. It is also the case that the "experience and insight" of the architect sums up a view of the potential tenant as well. In both cases, we are dealing with the ideological bases for the location and form of housing.

The ideology of the architect has a number of aspects, some of them contradictory. On one hand, there is a frequent belief in "architectural determinism," a belief that design changes will produce the desired behavior in the tenants. This conflicts with another notion that whatever is designed will be misused by an ignorant tenant: "Poor people mess up nice buildings; if they wanted nice buildings they would keep them nice." The latter is very likely a rationalization for the failures of the former. Heimsath summarizes the problem as follows:

> Theory in architecture has concentrated on aesthetics, or glorified the expression of the ordinary, or looked to utopian tomorrows. A more meaningful theory focusing on people's needs, seen dynamically, is hampered by half truths about the relation between people and buildings (1977:46).

In addition, Lipmann has written of a rather romantic view of community that is held by architects, and which influences their design. The problem is that it is a view of community which has little to do with the views held by the actual residents of the communities involved.

There is also a dilemma in the notion of design itself. In taking a commission, and indeed, in being a professional, the architect accepts a position of power and control. In a sense, the fact that the position of architect exists at all (and thus, that people do not design their own houses) indicates that the relation between person and housing is an alienated one.

> When the house becomes a commodity supplied through paternalistic agencies, there is no room for the enjoyment of the process itself. To the professional trapped by institutional frameworks, or isolated by his own secretiveness, all measures of value are invested in the material end product. To the extent that I and my colleagues were associated with institutionalized housing, we contributed to the human and material costs imposed on those least able to afford them (Turner, 1972:133).

The division of labor in housing, it would seem, creates not only an alienated resident, but an alienated architect as well.

There have been various attempts at an "advocacy" role for the designer that would help the resident deal with the structure of housing. But, as Harms points out, that term still has a "caretaker" connotation to it: "another professional who knows what is good for the poor (Harms, 1972:189).

More intriguing are attempts to design in ways that allow for the maximum participation of the residents in the creation of their housing. This has taken various forms. One architect set up his design office in a storefront next to the site of the project he was designing, and the local population continually dropped in to check out and help with the design. Nicholas

Habraken, in his book *Supports,* suggests a kind of design that provides a basic shell of services within which the tenant completes the design and construction of his own unit from standard elements. The challenge, in fact, is to design in ways that allow for the use of skills, rather than in ways which further the deskilling process.

Ownership as Ideology

It has been written by many (C.B. Macpherson, most prominently) that the development of private property and related institutions is a key aspect in the development of capitalism. In the planning and development of housing, to own is good and to rent is bad; indeed, not owning one's home would seem to be the same sort of "sin" as not having a job. Not as serious a sin perhaps, but similar in kind. And this is not just a matter of the stigma placed on public housing; there is something of a stigma placed on renting in general. On the other hand, one of the major reasons for a move from apartments to single homes is the desire for ownership (Michelson, 1977). More significant, however, is the distinction between owners and renters that is to be found among those who plan and develop housing. That is, the stigma of non-ownership is part of the class ideology of the developers.

Constance Perrin has written a remarkable book in which she examines the relationship between social order and land use. Much of the book looks at the way in which the decisions on land use are reflections of ideology. Generally, she writes, it is expected that one moves in the course of the life cycle from renter to owner. Renting is a stage to be passed through.

> The owners once renters have ... negotiated life's hazards and passed through its less blessed stages toward salvation in a sacred home.... [Renters] are in transit, but in fact they might never cease being renters. They may never become safe and sacred owners of single-family-detached houses. They may never attain complete social personhood in terms of the American Dream. Not 'full-fledged citizens', they are socially marginal (Perrin, 1978:56).

That marginality is compounded by the nature of real property law.

There is little question that property law, and more importantly zoning regulations, reflect the workings of local political interest. Particularly, they work, as Perrin points out, to stabilize property values so as to limit the risks to the investors in property. These regulations are part of the stratification of location in housing and to some extent create that stratification. They are based on the ideology of those who influence their nature. To quote Constance Perrin yet again:

> The cultural conceptions providing social meanings to newcomers and old-timers, renters and owners, those arriving and those arrived, high and low density settlements, stability and change, and suburbs and cities powerfully guide actual practice in land-use matters. These conceptions also reveal more than we may have known before about some fundamental sources of stratification and differential social evaluation, more fundamental than those

conditions summed up in objective measures of wealth and power, for example (1977:210).

In the broadest sense, housing policy is a similar reflection and creator of social stratification. The choices that are made to define a housing market, to determine what kinds of financing are available for which sorts of housing, and the numerous other "policy" questions, are in essence part of an ideology. It is an ideology that controls the housing relationship in the same way that scientific management was an ideology as well as a managerial practice in the control of work.

That ideology shows up in a variety of policy settings. As Belanger (1978:391) points out, the taxation system was geared toward home ownership, a tendency increased by the institution of the home ownership savings program. The new Conservative government has proposed mortgage interest deductibility that increases this trend. Not only do such policies create benefits for those who are already well-off, but the value of home ownership and the importance of its protection is made clear.

Indeed, the thrust behind much of Canadian housing has been "home ownership assistance for young Canadian families of modest means" (Patterson, 1978:293). It has done this by attempting to supplement or aid people in entering the housing market. Yet as Patterson points out, less than 3% of the Canadian housing stock is located outside the private market.

Those who do live in "non-market" homes are seen to be stigmatized. But that stigma, often used as an excuse for discontinuing public housing programs, is most often generated by the officials who make the decisions, in response to the fears of middle-class property owners and "propertied" interests (Canadian Council on Social Development, 1977:14).

The parallels to ideologies in regard to labor are clear. The emphasis on ownership is very similar to the emphasis on individualism and the emphasis on labor as an alienable commodity. The emphasis on the housing market is very much like the myth of the labor market: with modest assistance, everyone should be able to participate. And everyone is "equal," much as the lone laborer was "equal" in bargaining with the large employer.

Both the shelter process and the labor process involve the mediating of the man/nature relationship; both have become commodities with the development of capitalism. Both have become the basis for speculative profit of the capitalist while remaining essential in the livelihood of the worker. The control of labor and shelter have posed problems, both for the individual and for larger collectivities. Both processes are, in essence, alienated.

The maintenance of that alienated labor/shelter process has been achieved by means of the "deskilling" of both, by the increasing division of labor in both, and by parallel legitimating myths of individualism and market access, with parallel stigmatization of those who do not succeed in terms of those myths. Housing is not an outgrowth of a particular stratification system; it *is* the stratification system. The characteristic inequality of housing is part of the character of a particular economic formulation and is integral to the understanding of it.

REFERENCES

Anderson, Nels. *The Hobo*. Chicago: University of Chicago Press, 1923.

Barton, Stephen E. "The Urban Housing Problem: Marxist Theory and Community Organizing," *Review of Radical Political Economics*, 9, 4 (Winter 1971), pp. 16-30.

Belanger, Gerard. "Housing Policy and the Poor," in D. Glenday, H. Guindon and A. Turowitz, eds., *Modernization and the Canadian State*. Toronto: Macmillan of Canada, 1978.

Canadian Council on Social Development. *A Review of Canadian Social Housing Policy*. Ottawa: Canadian Council on Social Development, 1977.

Clark, S.D. *The New Urban Poor*. Toronto: McGraw-Hill Ryerson, 1978.

Cohen, Stanley. "Property Destruction: Motives and Meanings," in Colin Ward, ed., *Vandalism*. New York: Van Nostrand Reinhold, 1973, pp. 23-53.

Fitch, James Marston. *American Buildings: Volume 2 - The Environmental Forces That Shape Them*. New York: Houghton Mifflin, 1972.

Gans, Herbert. *The Urban Villagers*. New York: The Free Press, 1962.

Gauldie, Enid. *Cruel Habitations*. London: Allen and Unwin, 1974.

Glass, David, Jerome Singer and James Pennebaker. "Behavioral and Physiological Effects of Uncontrollable Events," in David Stokols, ed., *Perspectives on Environment and Behavior*. New York: Plenum, 1977.

Gove, Walter, Michael Hughes and Omar Galle. "Overcrowding in the Home: An Empirical Investigation of Possible Consequences," *American Sociological Review*, 44, 1 (1979), pp. 59-80.

Habraken, N.J. *Supports: An Alternative to Mass Housing*. London: Architectural Press.

Hall, Edwin. *The Hidden Dimension*. Garden City, New York: Doubleday, 1966.

Harms, Hans. "User and Community Involvement in Housing and Its Effects on Professionalism," in J. Turner and R. Fichter, eds., *Freedom to Build*. New York: Macmillan, 1972.

Hay, Douglas et al. *Albion's Fatal Tree*. New York: Pantheon, 1975.

Heimsath, Clovis. *Behavioral Architecture*. New York: McGraw-Hill, 1977.

Jacobs, Jane. *The Death and Life of Great American Cities*. New York: Random House, 1961.

Krohn, Roger, Berkeley Fleming and Marilyn Manzer. *The Other Economy: The Internal Logic of Local Rental Housing*. Toronto: Peter Martin Associates, 1977.

Lenski, Gerhard and Jean Lenski. *Human Societies: An Introduction to Macrosociology*, 2nd. ed. New York: McGraw-Hill, 1974.

Lipman, Alan. "The Architectural Belief System and Social Behavior," *British Journal of Sociology*, 20 (1969), pp. 190-204.

_____. "Professional Ideology: 'Community' and 'Total' Architecture," *Journal of Architectural Research and Teaching*, 1, 3 (1971), pp. 39-49.

Lloyd, Peter. *Slum of Hope? Shanty Towns of the Third World*. Harmondsworth, England: Penguin, 1979.

Lofland, Lyn. *A World of Strangers*. New York: Basic Books, 1973.

Macpherson, C.B. *The Political Theory of Possessive Individualism*. Oxford: Oxford University Press, 1962.

Margulis, Stephen T. "Conceptions of Privacy: Current Status and Next Steps," *Journal of Social Issues, 33*, 3 (1977), pp. 5-21.

Marx, Karl. *Capital, Volume 1,* Ben Fowkes, trans. London: Penguin Books, in association with the New Left Review, 1976.

Newman, Oscar. *Defensible Space.* New York: Macmillan, 1971.

Papanek, Victor. *Design for the Real World.* New York: Pantheon, 1972.

Patterson, Jeffrey. "Distributional and Social Impacts of Canadian National Housing Policy: Leasing It to the Market," in L.S. Bourne and J.R. Hitchcock, eds., *Urban Housing Markets: Recent Directions in Research and Policy.* Toronto: University of Toronto Press, 1978.

Perrin, Constance. *Everything in Its Place: Social Order and Land Use in America.* Princeton, N.J.: Princeton University Press, 1977.

Rainwater, Lee. "Fear and the House-as-Haven in the Lower Class," *Journal of the American Institute of Planners, 32*, 1 (1966).

Rapoport, Amos. *Human Aspects of Urban Form.* New York: Pergamon, 1977.

Smith, Michael P. *The City and Social Theory.* Oxford: Oxford University Press, 1978.

Sommer, Robert. *Personal Space: The Behavioral Basis of Design.* Englewood Cliffs, N.J.: Prentice-Hall, 1969.

Thompson, E.P. *The Making of the English Working Class.* Harmondsworth: Penguin, 1970.

Turner, John F.C. "Housing as a Verb," in John F.C. Turner and Robert Fichter, eds., *Freedom to Build.* New York: Macmillan, 1972.

Whyte, William Foote. *Street Corner Society,* rev. ed. Chicago: University of Chicago Press, 1955.

BIBLIOGRAPHY

I. The Basis of Concern

Adams, Ian et al. *The Real Poverty Report*. Edmonton: Hurtig, 1971.

Asimakopulos, A. "A Kaleckian Theory of Income Distribution," *Canadian Journal of Economics*, Vol. VIII (Aug. 1975), pp. 313-33.

Baetz, Reuben C. and David Critchley. "Two Poverty Reports," *Canadian Welfare*, Vol. 48 (Jan.-Feb. 1972).

Bailey, Don. "Both Sides of the Poverty Wall," *Canadian Forum*, Vol. 50 (Sept. 1970), pp. 206-7.

Black, Errol. "One Too Many Reports on Poverty in Canada," *Canadian Journal of Political Science*, Vol. 5 (Sept. 1972), pp. 439-43.

Buchbinder, Howard I. "The Politics of Anti-Poverty," *Canadian Forum*, Vol. 49 (Sept. 1969), pp. 127-29.

Canada. *The Measurement of Poverty*. Ottawa: Queen's Printer, 1970.

Canadian Chamber of Commerce. *Submission on Poverty, June 1970*. Montreal, 1970.

Copp, Terry. *The Anatomy of Poverty: The Condition of the Working Class in Montreal, 1897-1929*. Toronto: McClelland and Steward, 1974.

Courchene, T.J. "Some Reflections on the Senate Hearings on Poverty." Research Report 7118, Department of Economics, University of Western Ontario, n.d.

Eastman, Sheila. "Uncertainty and the Time Profile of Wages," *Canadian Journal of Economics*, Vol. X (1977), pp. 472-73.

Firth, Sophia. *The Urbanization of Sophia Firth*. Toronto: Peter Martin Associates, 1975.

Ford, George and Steven Langdon. "Just Society Movement: Toronto's Poor Organize," *Canadian Dimension*, Vol. 7 (June-July 1970), pp. 19-23.

Gonick, C.W. "Poverty and Capitalism," *Canadian Dimension*, Vol. 6, No. 5 (Oct.-Nov. 1969), p. 26.

Hardin, Hershel. *A Nation Unaware: The Canadian Economic Culture*. Vancouver: J.J. Douglas, 1974.

Harp, John and John Hofley, eds. *Poverty in Canada*. Scarborough, Ont.: Prentice-Hall of Canada, 1971.

Health and Welfare Canada. *The Distribution of Income in Canada: Concepts, Measures and Issues*. Ottawa, 1977.

Information Canada. *Families: Incomes of Families, Family Heads and Non-Family Persons Showing Selected Characteristics*. Ottawa, 1975.

_____. *Incomes and Opportunities*. Ottawa, 1973.

Jencks, Christopher et al. *Inequality: A Reassessment of the Effect of Family and Schooling in America*. New York: Basic Books, 1972.

Johnson, Leo. A. *Incomes, Disparity and Impoverishment in Canada since World War II.* Toronto: New Hogtown Press, 1973.

_____. *Poverty in Wealth: The Capitalist Labour Market and Income Distribution in Canada.* Toronto: New Hogtown Press, 1974.

Knight, Bryan M. "Poverty in Canada: An Overview," *Our Generation,* 4 (1967), pp. 8-21.

Larner, Jeremy and Irving Howe, eds. *Poverty: Vision from the Left.* New York: William Morrow and Co., 1971.

Lederer, K.M. *The Nature of Poverty: An Interpretative Review of Poverty Studies, with Special Reference to Canada.* Edmonton: Human Resources Research Council, 1972.

Lithwick, N.H. "Poverty in Canada: Some Recent Empirical Findings," *Journal of Canadian Studies,* 6 (May 1971), pp. 27-41.

Mann, W.E., ed. *Poverty and Social Policy in Canada.* Toronto: Copp Clark, 1970.

McCormack, Thelma. "Poverty in Canada: The Croll Report and Its Critics," *Canadian Review of Sociology and Anthropology,* Vol. 9 (Nov. 1972), pp. 366-72.

Parliament of Canada. *Senate Special Committee on Poverty, 1969/70.* Ottawa: Information Canada, 1972.

Podoluk, Jenny R. "Low Income and Poverty," in James E. Curtis and William G. Scott, eds., *Social Stratification: Canada.* Scarborough, Ont.: Prentice-Hall of Canada, 1973.

Puxley, Evelyn. *Poverty in Montreal.* Montreal: Dawson College Press, 1971.

Robertson, Heather. *Grass Roots.* Toronto: James, Lewis and Samuel, 1973.

Roby, Pamela, ed. *The Poverty Establishment.* Englewood Cliffs, N.J.: Prentice-Hall, 1974.

Ross, David. *Canadian Fact Book on Poverty.* Ottawa: The Canadian Council on Social Development, 1975.

Ryan, Thomas I. *Poverty and the Child: A Canadian Study.* Toronto: McGraw-Hill Ryerson, 1972.

Schlesinger, Benjamin. "Profile of Poverty," *Canadian Health and Welfare,* Vol. 25, No. 3 (Nov.-Dec. 1970), pp. 16-19; Ottawa: Information Canada, 1971.

_____. *What About Poverty in Canada?* Toronto: Guidance Centre, Faculty of Education, University of Toronto, 1975.

Senate Special Committee on Poverty. *Poverty in Canada.* Ottawa: Queen's Printer, 1971.

Sheffe, Norman, ed. *Issues for the Seventies: Poverty.* Toronto: McGraw-Hill Ryerson, 1970.

Terkel, Louis. *Working: People Talk about What They Do All Day and How They Feel about What They Do.* New York: Pantheon Books, 1974.

Thurow, L. *Poverty and Discrimination.* Washington: Brookings Institution Press, 1969.

Velk, Tom. "Good News — Changes in Income Distribution," *Canadian Forum,* Vol. LVI (May 1976), pp. 21-23.

Weisbrod, Burton Allen, ed. *Economics of Poverty: An American Paradox.* Englewood Cliffs, N.J.: Prentice-Hall, 1965.

II. Perspectives on Inequality

Bachrach, Peter and Morton S. Baratz. *Power and Poverty: Theory and Practice.* New York: Oxford University Press, 1970.

Baldus, Bernd. "Social Control in Capitalist Societies: An Examination of the 'Problem of Order' in Liberal Democracies," *Canadian Journal of Sociology,* Vol. 2, No. 3 (Summer 1977), pp. 247-63.

Bell, David V.J. *Power, Influence and Authority: An Essay in Political Linguistics.* Don Mills, Ont.: Oxford University Press, 1975.

Blackburn, Robin, ed. *Ideology in Social Science.* Glasgow: Fontana/Collins, 1972.

Charles, K.J. "The Economics of Modern Capitalism," *Canadian Dimension,* Vol. 11, No. 7 (Oct. 1976), pp. 39-42.

Coser, Lewis. "The Sociology of Poverty," *Social Problems,* 13:2 (Fall 1965), pp. 140-48.

Crook, Rodney K. "Men, Situations and Structure: An Essay," *Canadian Review of Sociology and Anthropology,* Vol. 10 (Aug. 1973), pp. 252-65.

Faber, Seymour. "Working Class Organization," *Our Generation,* Vol. 11, No. 3 (Summer 1976), pp. 13-26.

Glaberman, Martin. "Work and Working Class Consciousness," *Our Generation,* Vol. 11 (1976), pp. 24-32.

Grabb, Edward G. "Canada's Lower Middle Class," *Canadian Journal of Sociology,* Vol. 1, No. 3 (Fall 1975), pp. 295-311.

Lebowitz, Michael A. "Marx's Falling Rate of Profit: A Dialectical View," *Canadian Journal of Economics,* Vol. 9 (1976), pp. 232-54.

Manzer, Ronald. *Canada: A Socio-Political Report.* Toronto: McGraw-Hill Ryerson, 1974.

Marchak, M. Patricia. *Ideological Perspectives on Canada.* Toronto: McGraw-Hill Ryerson, 1975.

Marx, Karl. *Capital,* Volume 1. Chicago: Charles H. Kerr, 1912.

Rawls, J. *A Theory of Justice.* Cambridge: Harvard University Press, 1971.

Valentine, Charles. "Culture and Poverty: Critique and Counter-Proposals," *Current Anthropology* (April-June 1969), pp. 181-201.

Wachtel, Howard M. "Looking at Poverty from Radical, Conservative and Liberal Perspectives," in Pamela Roby, ed., *The Poverty Establish-* ment. Englewood Cliffs, N.J.: Prentice-Hall, 1974.

Waxman, Chaim I. *The Stigma of Poverty.* New York: Pergamon Press, 1977.

Westell, Anthony. *The New Society.* Toronto: McCelelland and Stewart, 1977.

ˡWestergaard, John and Henrietta Resler. *Class in a Capitalist Society.* New York: Basic Books, 1975.

III. Sources of Variation: The Political Economy of Inequalities

Aba-Laban, S.B. and B. Aba-Laban. "Women and the Aged as Minority Groups: A Critique," *Canadian Review of Sociology and Anthropology,* Vol. 14 (1977), pp. 103-16.

Acton, Janice, Penny Goldsmith and Bonne Shepard, eds. *Women at Work: Ontario, 1850-1930.* Toronto: The Women's Press, 1974.

Adams, Ian et al. "Education and Poverty," in W.E. Mann and Les Wheatcraft, eds., *Canada: A Sociological Profile,* 3rd ed. Toronto: Copp Clark, 1976.

Adler-Karlsson, Gunnar. *Reclaiming the Canadian Economy, A Swedish Approach through Functional Socialism.* Toronto: Anansi, 1970.

Altman, Dennis. *Homosexual: Oppression and Liberation.* New York: Outerbridge and Dienstfrey, 1971.

Anderson, Grace M. *Networks of Contact: The Portuguese in Toronto - Waterloo.* Ottawa: Wilfred Laurier University Press, 1974.

Archibald, Kathleen. *Sex and the Public Service,* Report to the Public Service Commission of Core. Ottawa: Information Canada, 1970.

Armstrong, Donald E. *Education and Achievement, Studies of the Royal Commission on Bilingualism and Biculturalism, No. 7.* Ottawa: Queen's Printer, 1970.

Balakrishnan, T.R. "Ethnic Residential Segregation in the Metropolitan Areas of Canada," *Canadian Journal of Sociology,* Vol. 1, No. 4 (Winter 1976), pp. 481-98.

Balakrishnan, T.R. and J.D. Allingham. *Fertility and Family Planning in a Canadian Metropolis.* Montreal: McGill-Queen's University Press, 1975.

Balakrishnan, T.R. and George K. Jarvis. "Socio-economic Differentiation in Urban Canada," *Canadian Review of Sociology and Anthropology,* Vol. 13 (May 1976), pp. 204-16.

Baldus, Bernd. "The Study of Power: Suggestions for an Alternative," *Canadian Journal of Sociology and Anthropology,* Vol. 1, No. 2 (Summer 1975), pp. 179-99.

Baldwin, Elizabeth G. "On Methodological and Theoretical 'Muddles' in Clement's Media Study," *Canadian Journal of Sociology,* Vol. 2, No. 2 (Spring 1977), pp. 215-20.

Ballentine, J. Gregory and Wayne R. Thirsk, "Labour Unions and Income

Distribution Reconsidered," *Canadian Journal of Economics,* Vol. 10 (1977), pp. 141-48.

Barber, Bernard. "Social Stratification and Trends of Social Mobility in Western Society," in James E. Curtis and William G. Scott, eds., *Social Stratification: Canada.* Scarborough, Ont.: Prentice-Hall of Canada, 1973.

Beatty, Christopher. *Minority Men in a Majority Setting.* Toronto: McClelland and Stewart, 1975.

Bladen, V.W. "Command over Labour: A Study in Misinterpretation," *Canadian Journal of Economics,* Vol. 8 (Nov. 1975), pp. 504-19.

Blishen, Bernard and Hugh A. McRoberts. "A Revised Socioeconomic Index for Occupations in Canada," *Canadian Review of Sociology and Anthropology,* Vol. 13, No. 7 (Feb. 1976), pp. 71-79.

Blishen, Bernard. "Social Class and Opportunity in Canada," *Canadian Review of Sociology and Anthropology,* Vol. 7, No. 2 (1970), pp. 110-27.

Booker, Fred. "The Part That Does Not Die. My Visit to a Black Canadian Ghost Town," *Canadian Forum,* Vol. XLIII, No. 669 (Mar. 1977), pp. 9-11.

Boulet, Jac-Andre and J.C.R. Rowley. "Measurement of Discrimination in the Labour Market: A Comment," *Canadian Journal of Economics,* Vol. 10 (1977), pp. 149-54.

Braverman, Harry. *Labour and Monopoly Capital: The Degradation of Work in the Twentieth Century.* New York: Monthly Review Press, 1974.

Breton Raymond. "Academic Stratification in Secondary Schools and the Educational Plans of Students," in James E. Curtis and William G. Scott, eds., *Social Stratification: Canada.* Scarborough, Ont.: Prentice-Hall of Canada, 1973.

Breton, Raymond and Howard Roseborough. "Ethnic Differences in Status," in Bernard Blishen, Frank Jones et al., eds., *Canadian Society.* Toronto: Macmillan of Canada, 1971.

Brinkerhoff, Merlin B. "Women Who Want to Work in a Man's World: A Study of the Influence of Structural Factors on Role Innovativeness," *Canadian Journal of Sociology,* Vol. 2, No. 3 (Summer 1977), pp. 283-304.

Brody, Hugh. *Indians on Skid Row.* Ottawa: Northern Science Research Group, Department of Northern Development, 1971.

_____. *The Peoples Land: Eskimos and Whites in the Eastern Arctic.* Markham, Ontario: Penguin Books of Canada, 1975.

Caloren, Fred. "The Revolutionary Struggle of Native People of the Northwest," *Our Generation,* Vol. 12, No. 3 (Spring 1978). A Review of the film "Mishikata."

Campbell, Maria. *Half-breed.* Toronto: McClelland and Stewart, 1973.

Canadian Council on Social Development. *The One-Parent Family:*

Report of an Inquiry on One-Parent Families in Canada. Ottawa: Canadian Council on Social Development, 1971.

Canning, Stratford. "The Illusion of Progress: Rural Development Policy since 1949," *The Canadian Forum* (Mar. 1974), p. 22.

Carter, George E. "Financing of Post-Secondary Education under the Federal-Provincial Fiscal Arragenments Act: An Appraisal," *Canadian Tax Journal,* Vol. 24 (Sept.-Oct. 1976), pp. 505-22.

Clairmont, David H. and Dennis W. Magill. "Nova Scotia Blacks: Marginality in a Depressed Region," in W.E. Mann and Les Wheatcroft, eds., *Canada: A Sociological Profile,* 3rd. ed. Toronto: Copp Clark, 1976.

Clark, S.D. *The New Urban Poor.* Toronto: McGraw-Hill Ryerson, 1978.

Clement, Wallace. *The Canadian Corporate Elite: An Analysis of Economic Power.* Toronto: McClelland and Stewart, 1975.

———. *Continental Corporate Power.* Toronto: McClelland and Stewart, 1977.

———. "Inequality of Access: Characteristics of the Canadian Corporate Elite," *Canadian Review of Sociology and Anthropology,* Vol. 12, No. 1 (Feb. 1975), pp. 33-52.

———. "Overlap of the Media and Economic Elites," *Canadian Journal of Sociology,* Vol. 2, No. 2 (Spring 1977), pp. 205-14.

Coburn, David and Virginia L. Edwards. "Objective and Subjective Socio-economic Status: Intercorrelation and Consequnces," *Canadian Review of Sociology and Anthropology,* Vol. 13, No. 2 (May 1976).

Coleman, J. et al. *Equality of Opportunity.* Washington: U.S. Government Printing Office, 1966.

Collison, Robert. "War of the Elites: Two Factions Due for Power in the New Quebec," *Saturday Night,* Vol. 93, No. 4 (May 1978), pp. 19-25.

Comay, Yochanan, A. Melnick and M.A. Pollatschek. "Dropout Risks, Option Values, and Returns to Investment in Schooling," *Canadian Journal of Economics,* Vol. 9 (1976), pp. 45-56.

Connelly, Patricia M. and Linda Christiansen-Ruffman. "Women's Problems: Private Troubles or Public Issues?" *Canadian Journal of Sociology,* Vol. 2, No. 2 (Spring 1977), pp. 167-78.

Couchman, Robert. "Project Interval: A Community Development Response to C.E.L. D.I.C.," *The Social Worker,* Vol. 44, No.4 (Winter 1976), pp. 113-19.

Cummings, P.A. and N.H. Mickenberg, eds. *Native Rights in Canada.* Toronto: Indian Eskimo Association of Canada, General Publishing, 1972.

Cuneo, Carl J. and James E. Curtis. "Quebec Separatism: An Analysis of Determinants within Social Class Levels," *Canadian Review of Sociology and Anthropology,* Vol. 11 (Feb. 1974), pp. 1-29.

———. "Social Ascription in the Educational and Occupational Status Attainment of Urban Canadians," *Canadian Review of Sociology and An-*

thropology, Vol. 12 (Feb. 1975), pp. 6-24.

Dales, J.H. "Beyond the Marketplace," Presidential Address, *Canadian Journal of Economics,* Vol. 8 (1975), pp. 483-503.

Davis, Arthur K. "Canadian Society and History as Hinterland versus Metropolis" in Richard J. Ossenberg, *Canadian Society: Pluralism, Change, and Conflict.* Scarborough, Ont.: Prentice-Hall of Canada, 1971.

Denton, Frank T. and Sylvia Ostry. *Working-Life Tables for Canadian Males.* Ottawa: Dominion Bureau of Statistics, 1969.

Dofny, Jacques. "The P.Q. Government: Year One," *Our Generation,* Vol. 12, No. 2 (Fall 1977), pp. 25-34.

Dominion Bureau of Statistics. *Post-Secondary Student Population Survey, 1968-69.* Ottawa: Education Division, Information Canada, 1970.

Dosman, Edgar J. *Indians: The Urban Dilemma.* Toronto: McClelland and Stewart, 1972.

Editorial. "Unemployment: A New Analysis," *Our Generation,* Vol. 8, No. 2 (Winter 1972).

Eichler, Margrit. "Women as Personal Dependents," in M. Stephenson, ed., *Women in Canada.* Toronto: New Press, 1973.

Ekeland, Robert B. Jr. and Robert D. Tollison. "The New Political Economy of J.S. Mill: The Means to Social Justice," *Canadian Journal of Economics,* Vol. 9 (1976), pp. 213-31.

Elliott, Jean Leonard, ed. *Minority Canadians, Volume 1. Native Peoples.* Scarborough, Ont: Prentice-Hall of Canada, 1971.

Faber, Seymour. "Rank and File Insurgency: The State and the Unions," *Our Generation,* Vol. 2 (1976), pp. 38-43.

Farid, Z. and J. Kuyek. "Who Speaks for Working-Class Women?" *Canadian Dimension,* Vol. 10, No. 8 (June 1975), p.80.

Fisher, Robin. *Contact and Conflict: Indian-European Relations in B.C., 1774-1890.* Vancouver: University of British Columbia Press, 1977.

Forcese, Dennis. *The Canadian Class Structure.* Toronto: McGraw-Hill Ryerson, 1975.

Fournier, Pierre. "The Parti Quebecois and the Power of Business," *Our Generation,* Vol. 12, No. 3 (Spring 1978), pp. 3-15.

_____. *The Quebec Establishment: The Ruling Class and the State.* Montreal: Black Rose Books, 1976.

Frechette, P. R. Jouandet-Bernadat and J.P. Vezina, Introduction de Jacques Parizeau. *L'économie Québécoise.* Anjoy, Québec: Les éditions HRW, 1975.

Frideres, James S. *Canada's Indians: Contemporary Conflicts.* Scarborough Ont.: Prentice-Hall of Canada, 1974.

Friere, Paulo. *Education for Critical Consciousness.* New York: The Seabury Press, 1973.

_____. *Pedagogy of the Oppressed.* New York: The Seabury Press, 1970.

Fulford, Robert. "Have the Amish a Place in our Liberal Society?" *Saturday Night,* Vol. 92, No. 10 (Dec. 1977), pp. 19-21.

Fumoleau, Rene. "The Treaties: A History of Exploitation," *Canadian Forum,* Vol. 56 (Nov. 1976), pp. 17-34.

Gagnon, Lysiane. "Growing Poor in Quebec," *Canadian Dimension,* Vol. 17, Nos. 5 & 6 (Dec. 1970), p. 55.

Gelber, Sylvia. "Women and Work — The Legislative Base," *Canadian Labour/Le Travailleur Canadien,* XX, 2 (June 1975), pp. 7-10, 8-11, 38.

Geoffroy, Renée and Paule Sainte-Marie. *Attitude of Union Workers to Women in Industry,* Study No. 9. Royal Commission on the Status of Women in Canada. Ottawa: Queen's Printer, 1971.

Gilbert, S. and H. McRoberts. "Academic Stratification and Educational Plans," *Canadian Review of Sociology and Anthropology,* Vol. 14 (Feb. 1977), pp. 34-47.

Gingrich, Paul. "Unemployment: A Radical Analysis of Myth and Fact," *Our Generation,* Vol. 12 (Spring 1978), pp. 16-28.

Gonick, Cy. "The Scourge of Unemployment. 10 Lessons in Capitalist Economics," *Canadian Dimension,* Vol. 8 (June 1971), pp. 15-21.

Gordon, Myron J. "Employment and Productivity Productivity," *Canadian Forum,* Vol. 51 (Jan.-Feb. 1972), p. 49.

Goyder, J.C. and J.E. Curtis. "Occupational Mobility in Canada over Four Generations," *Canadian Review of Sociology and Anthropology,* Vol. 14 (1977), pp. 303-19.

Green, Alan G. *Immigration and the Postwar Canadian Economy.* Toronto: Macmillan of Canada, 1976.

————. *Regional Aspects of Canada's Economic Growth.* Toronto: University of Toronto Press, 1971.

Greenglass, Esther. "The Psychology of Women: Or, the High Cost of Achievement," in M. Stephenson, ed., *Women in Canada.* Toronto: New Press, 1973.

Grubel, Herbert G., Dennis Maki and Shelly Sax. "Real and Insurance Induced Unemployment in Canada," *Canadian Journal of Economics,* Vol. 8 (May 1975), pp. 174-91.

Gunderson, Morley. "Logit Estimates of Labour Force Participation Based on Census Cross-Tabulations," *Canadian Journal of Economics,* Vol. 10 (1977), pp. 453-62.

Guidon, Hubert. "Social Unrest, Social Class and Quebec's Bureaucratic Revolution," in James E. Curtis and William G. Scott, eds., *Social Stratification: Canada.* Scarborough, Ont.: Prentice-Hall of Canada, 1973.

Guppy, L.N. and J.L. Siltanen. "A Comparison of Male and Female Occupational Prestige," *Canadian Review of Sociology and Anthropology,* Vol. 14 (1977), pp. 320-30.

Gwyn, Sandra. "She Thinks Like a Man," *Saturday Night* (Jul.-Aug. 1977), pp. 21-26.

Haimey, John. "Special Status in Immigration," *Canadian Forum*, Vol. LVIII (May 1978), p. 4.

Hall, Oswald. "The Canadian Division of Labour Revisited," in James E. Curtis and William G. Scott, eds., *Social Stratification: Canada*. Scarborough, Ont.: Prentice-Hall of Canada, 1973.

Hamilton, R. and M. Pinard. "Poverty in Canada: Illusion and Reality," *Canadian Review of Sociology and Anthropology*, Vol. 14 (May 1977), pp. 247-52.

Harvey, Edward and Lorna R. Harvey. "Adolescence, Social Class, and Occupational Expectations," *Canadian Review of Sociology and Anthropology*, Vol. 7 (May 1970), pp. 138-147.

Harvey, Edward B. *Education and Employment of Arts and Science Graduates: The Last Decade in Ontario, Commission on Post-Secondary Education in Ontario.* Toronto: Queen's Printer, 1972.

Harvey, E. *Educational Systems and the Labour Market.* Don Mills, Ont.: Longman, 1974.

Heap, James L., ed. *Everybody's Canada: The Vertical Mosaic Reviewed and Re-examined.* Toronto: Burns and MacEachern, 1974.

Henderson, Vernon, Peter Mieszkowski and Yvon Sauvageau. *Peer Group Effects and Educational Production Functions.* Ottawa: Economic Council of Canada, 1976.

Henry, Francis. *Forgotten Canadians: The Blacks of Nova Scotia.* Don Mills, Ont.: Longman, 1973.

Hiller, Harry. *Canadian Society: A Sociological Analysis.* Scarborough, Ont.: Prentice-Hall of Canada, 1976.

Holmes, Jeffrey. "Demography Affects Employment Promotion," *University Affairs* (Mar. 1974).

Howard, Leslie and Jack Wayne. "Ethnicity in Canada: A Social Structural View," *Journal of Comparative Sociology*, 2 (1974-75), pp. 35-52.

Hughes, D.R. and E. Kallen. *The Anatomy of Racism: Canadian Dimensions.* Montreal: Harvest House, 1974.

Hughes, David R. and Evelyn Kallen. "The Persistence of Systems of Ethnic Stratification" in W.E. Mann and Les Wheatcroft, eds., *Canada: A Sociological Profile.* Toronto: Copp Clark, 1976.

Hunter, A.A. "A Comparative Analysis of Anglophone-Francophone Occupational Prestige Structures in Canada," *Canadian Journal of Sociology*, Vol. 2, No. 2 (Spring 1977), pp. 179-94.

Hutcheon, Pat Duffy. *A Sociology of Canadian Education.* Toronto: Van Nostrand Reinhold, 1975.

Iannucci, Amilcare A. "The Italian Immigrant— Voyage of No Return," *Canadian Forum*, Vol. LVII (Mar. 1977), pp. 12-15.

Information Canada. *The Law Relating to Women.* Ottawa, 1973.

_____. *The Rights of Man, and the Status of Women.* Ottawa, 1973.

_____. *Royal Commission on the Status of Women, Report.* Ottawa, 1971.

———. *Women in the Labour Force.* Ottawa, 1973.

———. *Working Mothers and Their Child-Care Arrangements.* Ottawa, 1970.

Ishwaran, K., ed. *The Canadian Family*, rev. ed. Toronto: Holt, Rinehart and Winston, 1976.

Ishwaran, K. *Family, Kinship and Community: A Study of Dutch Canadians.* Scarborough, Ont.: McGraw-Hill Ryerson, 1977.

Jackson, Brian and Dennis Marsden. *Education and the Working Class.* Penguin Books, 1966.

James, Alice. *Poverty: Canada's Legacy to Women.* Vancouver: Vancouver Women's Caucus, n.d.

Jewell, Gary. "The History of the I.W.W. in Canada," *Our Generation.* Vol. 2 (1976), pp. 35-45.

Johnson, Leo A. "The Development of Class in Canada in the Twentieth Century," in this volume.

Johnson, L.A. "Illusions or Realities: Hamilton and Pinard's Approach to Poverty," *Canadian Review of Sociology and Anthropology,* Vol. 14 (1977), pp. 341-46.

Johnson, Walter. "Ste. Thérèse En Grève," *Our Generation,* Vol. 2 (1976), pp. 44-49.

———. *Working in Canada.* Montreal: Black Rose Books, 1976.

Jones, Frank and John Selby. "School Performance and Social Class," in Thomas J. Ryan, ed., *Poverty and the Child: A Canadian Study.* Toronto: McGraw-Hill Ryerson, 1972.

Jones, Frank. "Some Social Consequences of Immigration for Canada," in Bernard Blishen, Frank Jones et al., eds., *Canadian Society.* Toronto: Macmillan of Canada, 1971.

Kalback, Warren E. and Wayne McVey. *The Demographic Bases of Canadian Society.* Toronto: McGraw-Hill Ryerson, 1971.

Kaliski, S.F. "Real and Insured Induced Unemployment in Canada: A Comment," *Canadian Journal of Economics,* Vol. 8 (1975), pp. 600-3.

———. "Unemployment and Unemployment Insurance: Testing Some Corollaries," *Canadian Journal of Economics,* Vol. 9 (1976), pp. 705-12.

Kealey, G.S. *Hogtown: Working Class Toronto at the Turn of the Century.* Toronto: New Hogtown Press, 1973.

Kelner, M. "Ethnic Penetration into Toronto's Elite Structure," *Canadian Review of Sociology and Anthropology,* Vol. 7 (May 1970), pp. 128-37.

Kerton, R. *Active Manpower Programs in Canada.* Canada: Prices and Incomes Commission, 1972.

Kew, Mike. "100 Years of Making Indians in B.C.," *Canadian Dimension,* Vol. 8, No. 3 (Nov. 1971), p. 35.

Kirsch, Chantel. "Relations entre les differenciations biologiques et sociales des sexes," *Canadian Review of Sociology and Anthropology,* Vol. 13 (1976), pp. 435-47.

Kurelek, William and Abraham Arnold. *Jewish Life in Canada.* Edmonton: Hurtig Publishers, 1976.

Lanphier, C.M. and R.V. Morris. "Structural Aspects of Differences in Income between Anglophones and Francophones," *Canadian Review of Sociology and Anthropology,* Vol. II (Feb. 1974), pp. 53-56.

Laschuk, Maureen Wilson and George Kurian. "Employment Status, Feminism, and Symptoms of Stress: The Case of a Canadian Prairie City," *Canadian Journal of Sociology,* Vol. 2, No. 2 (Spring 1977), pp. 195-204.

Lawlor, S.D. "Social Class and Achievement Orientation," *Canadian Review of Sociology and Anthropology,* Vol. 7 (May 1970), pp. 148-53.

Laxter, Robert. *Canadian Unions.* Toronto: James Lorimer and Company, 1976.

Lazar, Fred. "Regional Unemployment Rate Disparities in Canada: Some Possible Explanations," *Canadian Journal of Economics,* Vol. 9 (1976), pp. 112-29.

Lewis, David. *The Corporate Welfare Bums.* Toronto: James, Lewis and Samuel, 1972.

Limonchik, Abe. "The Colonization of the Urban Economy: Montreal," *Our Generation,* Vol. 12, No. 2 (Fall 1977), pp. 5-24.

Lipset, Seymour M. "Social Class," in James E. Curtis and William G. Scott, eds., *Social Stratification: Canada.* Scarborough, Ont.: Prentice-Hall of Canada, 1973.

Lorimer, James and Myfanwy Phillips. *Working People: Life in a Downtown City Neighbourhood.* Toronto: James, Lewis and Samuel, 1971.

Lubka, Nancy. "The Ins and Outs of Women's Liberation," *Canadian Dimension,* Vol. 7 (June-July 1970), pp. 24-29.

Mackie, M. "On Congenial Truths: A Perspective of Women's Studies," *Canadian Review of Sociology and Anthropology,* Vol. 14 (1977), pp. 117-28.

Macmillan, James A., Chang Mei Lu and Charles F. Framingham. *Manitoba Interlake Area: A Regional Development Evaluation.* Ames, Iowa: Iowa State University Press, 1975.

Maki, Dennis. "The Direct Effect of the Occupational Training of Adults Program on Canadian Unemployment Rates," *Canadian Journal of Economics,* Vol. 5 (Feb. 1972), pp. 125-31.

Manuel, George. "An Appeal from the Fourth World," *Canadian Forum* (Nov. 1976), pp. 8-12.

Manuel, George and Michael Posluns. *The Fourth World: An Indian Reality.* New York: The Free Press, 1974.

Marchak, Patricia. "A Critical Review of the Status of Women Report," *Canadian Review of Sociology and Anthropology,* Vol. 9 (Feb. 1972), pp. 72-85.

————. "Women Workers and White-Collar Unions," *Canadian Review of Sociology and Anthropology*, Vol. 10 (May 1973), pp. 134-47.

Marsden, Lorna R. "Why Now? The Mirage of Equality," *Canadian Forum*, Vol. LV (Sept. 1975), pp. 12-17.

Martel, George. *The Politics of the Canadian Public School*. Toronto: James, Lewis and Samuel, 1975.

Matheson, Gwen, ed. *Women in the Canadian Mosaic*. Toronto: Peter Martin, 1976.

Matthiasson, John S. and W.S. Chow. "Relocated Eskimo Miners," in *Occasional Papers*, No. 1. Winnipeg: Centre for Settlement Studies, University of Manitoba, 1970.

McDonald, Lynne. "Wages of Work: A Widening Gap between Women and Men," *The Canadian Forum*, Vol. LV (April-May 1975), pp. 4-7.

Meissner, Martin. "At Work — At Home: Women and Inequality," *Our Generation*, Vol. 2(1976), pp. 59-71.

Milner, Henry. "The Marxist-Leninist Left in Quebec," *Our Generation*, Vol. 12, No. 2 (Fall 1977), pp. 35-42.

————. "Quebec Sovereignty and the Canadian Interest,"*Canadian Forum*, Vol. LVII (May 1978), pp. 11-15.

Morris, Dave and Joseph F. Krauter. *The Other Canadians: Profiles of Sex Minorities*. Toronto: Methuen, 1971.

Morris, Raymond N. and Michael C. Lanphier. *Three Scales of Inequality*. Don Mills, Ont.: Longman, 1977.

Morton, Desmond. "Labour's New Political Direction: Is the C.L.C. Serious?" *Canadian Forum*, Vol. LVII (Oct. 1977), pp. 11-13.

Morton, Peggy. "Women's Work Is Never Done — or the Production Maintenance and Reproduction of Labor Power," in *Women Unite! An Anthology of the Canadian Women's Movement*. Toronto: The Women's Press, 1972.

Mowat, Farley. *Canada North Now*. Toronto: McClelland and Stewart, 1976.

Murphy, R. "Societal Values and the Reaction of Teachers to Students' Backgrounds," *Canadian Review of Sociology and Anthropology*, Vol. 14 (1977), pp. 48-56.

Myers, Gustavus. *A History of Canadian Wealth*. Toronto: James, Lewis and Samuel, 1972.

Nagler, Mark. *Natives without a Home*. Don Mills, Ont.: Longman Canada, 1975.

————. *Perspectives on the North American Indians*. Toronto: McClelland and Stewart, 1973.

Newman, Peter C. *The Canadian Establishment*. Toronto: McClelland and Stewart, 1975.

Noble, Gaile P. "The Canadian North: Economic and Social Development," *The Social Worker,* Vol. 44, No. 1 (Spring 1976), pp. 12-14.

Ogmudson, R. "Mass-Elite Linkages and Class Issues in Canada," *Canadian Review of Sociology and Anthropology,* Vol. 13, No. 7 (Feb. 1976), pp. 1-12.

Ontario, Department of Labor. Research Branch, Employment Information Series, No. 7. *Characteristics of Low-Wage Workers in Ontario.* Ontario: Queen's Printer, 1974.

Overton, D.J.B. "Regional Development — Realities of Exploitation — The National Park System in Newfoundland," *Our Generation,* Vol. 12, No. 3 (Spring 1978), pp. 57-66.

Page, Robert. "Northern Pipelines: On to the Yukon," *Canadian Forum,* Vol. LVII (Sept. 1977), p. 37.

Park, Frank and Libby Park. *Anatomy of Big Business.* Toronto: James, Lewis and Samuel, 1973.

Patterson, E. Palmer. *The Canadian Indian.* Don Mills, Ont.: Collier Macmillan Canada, 1972.

Peitchinis, Stephen G. *The Canadian Labour Market.* Toronto: Oxford University Press, 1975.

Pineo, Peter C. and John Porter. "Occupational Prestige in Canada," in James E. Curtis and William G. Scott, eds., *Social Stratification: Canada.* Scarborough, Ont.: Prentice-Hall of Canada, 1973.

Porter, John. "The Economic Elite and the Social Structures in Canada," in James E. Curtis and William G. Scott, eds., *Social Stratification: Canada.* Scarborough, Ont.: Prentice-Hall of Canada, 1973.

————. "Social Class and Educational Opportunity," in James E. Curtis and William G. Scott, eds., *Social Stratification: Canada.* Scarborough, Ont.: Prentice-Hall of Canada, 1973.

Porter, Marion R., John Porter and Bernard R. Blishen. *Does Money Matter? Prospects for Higher Education.* Toronto: York University Institute for Behavioural Research, 1973.

Prentice, Alison. *The School Promoters: Education and Class in Mid-Nineteenth Century Upper Canada.* Toronto: McClelland and Stewart, 1977.

Prentice, Alison and Susan Mann Trofimenkoff. *The Neglected Majority: Essays in Canadian Women's History.* Toronto: McClelland and Stewart, 1976.

Quebec Teacher's Corporation Manifesto. *Our Schools Serve the Ruling Class.* Toronto: New Hogtown Press, 1973.

Raynauld, Andre, Marion Gerald and Richard Beland. "Structural Aspects of Differences in Income between Anglophones and Francophones: A Reply," *Canadian Review of Sociology and Anthropology,* Vol. 12, No. 2 (May 1975), pp. 221-28.

Rea, Samuel A. Jr. "Unemployment Insurance and Labour Supply: A Simulation of the 1971 Unemployment Insurance Act," *Canadian Journal of Economics,* Vol. 10 (1977), pp. 263-78.

Reety, Jeffrey. "Analysis of Changing Group Inequalities in a Changing Occupational Structure." Paper presented at the Annual Meeting of the Canadian Sociology and Anthropology Association, Toronto, Aug. 21-24, 1974.

Resnick, P. *The Land of Cain: Class and Nationalism in English Canada, 1945-1975.* Vancouver: New Star Books, 1976.

Rex, John. "Nations, Nationalism, and the Social Scientist," *Canadian Journal of Sociology,* Vol. 1, No. 4 (Winter 1976), pp. 501-14.

Richardson, C. James. "Education and Social Mobility: Changing Conceptions of the Role of the Educational System," *Canadian Journal of Sociology,* Vol. 2 (Fall 1977), pp. 417-34.

Richmond, Anthony H. "Social Mobility of Immigrants in Canada," in Bernard Blishen, Frank Jones et al., eds., *Canadian Society.* Toronto: Macmillan of Canada, 1971.

Rinehart, James W. and Ishmael O. Okraku. "A Study of Class Consciousness," *Canadian Review of Sociology and Anthropology,* Vol. 2, No. 3 (Aug. 1974), p. 197.

Rinehart, James W. *The Tyranny of Work.* Don Mills, Ont.: Longman Canada, 1975.

Roberts, Albert R., ed. *Childhood Deprivation.* Springfield, Ill.: Charles C. Thomas Co., 1974.

Robertson, Heather. "Grey Liberation," *Saturday Night* (Jan.-Feb. 1978), pp. 18-25.

Robinson, H.L. "Hidden Unemployment," *Canadian Forum,* Vol. 57 (April 1977), p. 5.

_____. "The Secondary Majority: The Hidden Unemployed," *Canadian Forum,* Vol. LVII (Oct. 1977), pp. 15-18.

_____. "Unemployment in 1976," *Canadian Forum,* Vol. LVII (Mar. 1977).

_____. "Who Pays for Foreign Investment?" *Canadian Forum,* Vol. 53 (May 1973), p. 8.

Robson, R.A.H. and Mireille Lapointe. *A Comparison of Men's and Women's Salaries and Employment Fringe Benefits in the Academic Profession, Studies of the Royal Commission on the Status of Women in Canada,* No. 1. Ottawa: Queen's Printer, 1971.

Romaniuk, A. and V. Piche. "Nationality Estimates for the Canadian Indians by Stable Population Models, 1900-1969," *Canadian Review of Sociology and Anthropology,* Vol. 9 (Feb. 1972), pp. 1-20.

Roseborough, Howard and Raymond Breton. "Perception of the Relative Economic and Political Advantages of Ethnic Groups in Canada," in Bernard Blishen, Frank Jones et al., eds., *Canadian*

Society. Toronto: Macmillan of Canada, 1971.

Ross, Donald. "Waiting Down East," *The Last Post*, Vol. 1, No. 6 (Feb. 1971), p. 34.

Rowley, J.C.R. and N. Leckie. "A Further Look at Determinants of Educational Achievement," *Canadian Journal of Sociology*, Vol. 2 (Fall 1977), pp. 339-54.

Royal Commission on Bilingualism and Biculturalism. "Ethnicity, Religion and Educational Advancement," in James E. Curtis and William G. Scott, eds., *Social Stratification: Canada*. Scarborough, Ont.: Prentice-Hall of Canada, 1973.

Royal Commission on the Status of Women. "Women in the Work Force: Paid Work," in W.E. Mann and Les Wheatcroft, eds., *Canada: A Sociological Profile*. Toronto: Copp Clark, 1976.

Runciman, W.G. *Relative Deprivation and Social Justice*. Berkeley: University of California Press, 1966.

Russell, Peter H. "The Dene Nation and Confederation," *Canadian Forum*, 56 (Nov. 1976), pp. 35-40.

Schecter, Stephen. "Urban Politics in Capitalist Society: A Revolutionary Strategy," *Our Generation*, Vol. 11, No. 1 (Fall 1975), pp. 28-41.

Schlesinger, Benjamin. "The Unmarried Mother Who Keeps Her Child," *The Social Worker*, Vol. 44, No. 4 (Winter 1976), pp. 108-13.

Schrank, William E. "Sex Discrimination in Faculty Studies," *Canadian Journal of Economics*, Vol. 10 (1977), pp. 411-33.

Shapiro, H. "Poverty — A Bourgeois Economist's View," in Officer and Smith, eds., *Canadian Economic Problems and Policies*. Toronto: McGraw-Hill, 1970.

Sharples, Brian. "Provincial Disparities in Educational Expenditures," *Canadian Tax Journal*, Vol. XXIII, No. 4 (July-Aug. 1975), pp. 383-93.

Smith, Allan. "Quet Revolution in the West," *Canadian Forum*, Vol. LVIII (June-July 1978), pp. 12-15.

Smith, David and Lorne Tepperman. "Changes in the Canadian Business and Legal Elites, 1870-1970," *Canadian Review of Sociology and Anthropology*, Vol. 11, No. 2 (May 1974), pp. 97-109.

Smith, Dorothy E. "Women, the Family and Corporate Capitalism," in M. Stephenson, eds., *Women in Canada*. Toronto: New Press, 1973.

Smith, Janet. "Equal Opportunity in the Public Service," *Canadian Labor/Le travailleur canadien*, XX, 2 (June 1975), pp. 13-15, 14-16, 37.

Smollet, Eleanor. "Schools and the Illusion of Choice: The Middle Class and the Open Classroom," in W.E. Mann and Les Wheatcroft, eds., *Canada: A Sociological Profile*. Toronto: Copp Clark, 1976.

Stanbury, W.T., assisted by Jay H. Siegel. *Success and Failure: Indians in Urban Society.* Vancouver: University of British Columbia Press, 1975.

Statistics Canada. *Incomes of Unemployed Individuals and Their Families, 1971.* Ottawa: Information Canada, 1973.

Stephenson, Marylee, ed. *Women in Canada.* Toronto: New Press, 1973.

Stoakes, J.W., John Richards, J.W. Steadtler et al. "A Special Survey on Labour's Response to Wage Controls," *Canadian Dimension,* Vol. 11, No. 3 (Feb. 1976), pp. 11-15.

Tepperman, Lorne. "'A Simulation of Social Mobility in Industrial Societies," *Canadian Review of Sociology and Anthropology,* Vol. 13, No. 7 (Feb. 1976), pp. 26-42.

———. "Demographic Aspects of Career Mobility," *Canadian Review of Sociology and Anthropology,* Vol. 12, No. 2 (1975), pp. 163-77.

———.*Social Mobility in Canada.* Toronto: McGraw-Hill Ryerson, 1975.

Traprock, Walter J. "Native Peoples Use and Need All of Their Ancestral Lands," *The Last Post,* No. 5 (Dec. 1975), pp. 4-7.

T'Seleie, Frank. "My People Are Waking Up," *Canadian Forum* (Nov. 1976), pp. 13-16.

Turrittin, H.H. "Social Mobility in Canada: A Comparison of Three Provincial Studies and Some Methodological Questions." Paper presented at the Eighth World Congress of Sociology, Toronto, 1974.

Van Stolk, Mary. "The Battered and Abused Child," *The Social Worker,* Vol. 43, No. 3 (Fall 1975), pp. 138-42.

Verrall, Marg. "Women and the Labor Market," *The Last Post,* Vol. 1, No. 6 (Feb. 1971), p. 28.

Warnock, John W. "The Political Economy of the Food Industry in Canada: Oligopoly and American Domination," *Our Generation,* Vol. 11, No. 4 (1976), pp. 52-72.

Warnock, John. "Unemployment and Foreign Ownership: A Cause or a Solution?" *Canadian Dimension,* Vol. 7, No. 8 (April 1971), p. 4.

Wheeler, Susan. "Liberation, Feminism and Marxism," *Our Generation,* Vol. 11, No. 3 (Summer 1976), pp. 6-12.

———. "Women and the Political Economy — Wages for Housework," *Our Generation,* Vol. 11, No. 1 (Fall 1975), pp. 44-61.

Winks, Robin. *The Blacks in Canada.* Montreal: McGill-Queen's University Press, 1971.

Women Unite! An Anthology of the Canadian Women's Movement. Toronto: Canadian Women's Educational Press, 1972.

Wood, Myrna. *Equality for Working Class Women.* Toronto: New Hogtown Press, n.d.

Wuttunee, William I.C. *Ruffled Feathers.* Calgary: Bell Books, 1971.

Young, Bert. "Canadian Society: Social Justice or Social Control," *Our Generation,* Vol. 11, No. 4 (Winter 1976), pp. 13-25.

Zuker, Marvin A. and June Callwood. *Canadian Women and the Law.* Toronto: Copp Clark, 1971.

IV. Strategies and Programs

Abouchar, Alan. "Indexing Inflation, Lessons from Brazil," *Canadian Forum,* Vol. LV (Aug. 1975), pp. 12-14.

"The AIB's Obituary," *Canadian Dimension,* Vol. 13 (1976), p. 10.

Allan, J.R., S.N. Poddar and N.D. LePan. "The Effects of Tax Reform and Post-Reform Changes in the Federal Personal Income Tax, 1972-1975," *Canadian Tax Journal,* Vol. XXVI, No. 1 (Jan.-Feb. 1978), pp. 1-30.

Anti-Inflation Board. "Three Questions for Canadians," *Saturday Night* (July-Aug. 1977), pp. 47-54.

Archibald, G.C. and D. Donaldson. "Non-Paternalism and the Basic Theorems of Welfare Economics," *Canadian Journal of Economics,* Vol. 9 (Aug. 1976), pp. 492-507.

Armitage, Andrew. *Social Welfare in Canada: Ideals and Realities.* Toronto: McClelland and Stewart, 1975.

_____. "The Work-Social-Security Link Up and Its Effect on Social Services," *Canadian Welfare,* Vol. 50 (Mar.-Apr. 1974), pp. 14-15, 31.

Baetz, Reuben C. "New Developments in Social Security and Income Maintenance, *Canadian Welfare,* Vol. 48 (Sept.-Oct. 1972), pp. 4-8.

Barker, Penny and Wally Seccombe. "The Developers," *Canadian Dimension,* Vol. 9, Nos. 2 & 3 (Jan. 1973), pp. 19-50.

_____. *Highrise and Superprofits.* Toronto: Dumon Press Graphix, 1973.

Berger, Sara. "The House that CMHC Built," *Canadian Dimension,* Vol. 8, No. 8 (Aug. 1972), p. 11.

Black, Don, Harry Newton and Tom Sweeting. "Personal Income Tax Reform: An Ontario Assessment," *Canadian Tax Journal,* Vol. XXVI, No. 1 (Jan.-Feb. 1978), pp. 54-67.

Bryant, R.W.G. "Housing," *Canadian Dimension,* Vol. 6, No. 5 (Oct.-Nov. 1969), p. 19.

Bourne, Lang et al., eds. *Urban Futures for Central Canada: Perspectives on Forecasting Urban Growth and Form.* Toronto: University of Toronto Press, 1974.

Bryden, Kenneth. *Old Age Pensions and Policy Making in Canada.* Montreal and London: McGill-Queen's University Press, 1974.

Buchbinder, Harold. "Guaranteed Annual Income: The Answer to Poverty for all but the Poor," *Canadian Dimension,* Vol. 7, No. 4 (Oct.-Nov. 1970), p. 27.

Burgess, David F. "The Income Distributional Effects of Processing Incentives," *The Canadian Journal of Economics,* Vol. 9 (1976), pp. 595-612.

Caloren, Fred. "The Economics of Misery," *Our Generation,* Vol. 10, No. 4 (Winter 1975).

Central Mortgage and Housing Association. *Housing the Elderly.* Ottawa: Central Mortgage and Housing Corporation, 1972.

Cohen, Steven D. "John Turner's Budget: The Depression: Guess Who'll Pay?" *The Last Post,* Vol. 4, No. 8 (Aug. 1975).

Crowley, R. and D. Dodge. "Cost of the Guaranteed Annual Income," *Canadian Tax Journal* (Nov.-Dec. 1969), pp. 395-408.

Culpepper, Roy and Cy Gonick. "AIB — One Year Later," *Canadian Dimension*, Vol. 11, No. 8 (Nov. 1976), pp. 8-9.

Davies, Gordon W. "A Model of the Urban Residential Land and Housing Markets," *Canadian Journal of Economics*, Vol. X, No. 3, pp. 393-410.

Deaton, Rick. "The State's Fiscal Crisis," *Our Generation*, Vol. 8, No. 4 (Oct. 1972).

Dennis, Michael and Susan Fish. *Programs in Search of a Policy: Low Income Housing in Canada*. Toronto: Hakkert, 1972.

Denton, Frank and Byron G. Spencer. "Health Care Costs When the Population Changes," *Canadian Journal of Economics*, Vol. VIII, No. 1, pp. 34-48.

Deutsch, Antal. "Inflation and Guaranteed Formula Pension Plans," *Canadian Journal of Economics*, Vol. 8 (1975), pp. 447-48.

Drummond, Ian M. *Economics: Prinicples and Policies in an Open Economy*. Georgetown, Ontario: Irwin Dorsey, 1976.

Gingrich, Paul. "Defining Unemployment Out of Existence," *Canadian Dimension*, Vol. 12, Nos. 4 & 5 (1977).

Gonick, Cy and Fred Gudmundson. "Food Glorious Food," *Canadian Dimension*, Vol. 9, Nos. 7 & 8, pp. 26-46.

Gonick, Cy. *Inflation or Depression*. Toronto: James Lorimer, 1975.

———. "Planned Unemployment," *Canadian Dimension*, Vol. 12, No. 3 (July 1977), pp. 2-4.

———. "Taxes and Welfare," *Canadian Dimension*, Vol. 8, No. 2 (Aug. 1971), p. 6.

Gonick, Cy and Leo Panitch. "Wage Control," *Canadian Dimension*, Vol. 11, No. 3 (Feb. 1976), pp. 34-44.

Government of Canada. *Working Paper on Social Security in Canada*. Ottawa: Queen's Printer, 1973.

Gray, Anthony. "Nôtes sur les programmes et Approches en matière de Secétrité du Revenu," *The Social Worker*, Vol. 43, No. 4 (Winter 1975), pp. 182-85.

Green, Christopher. *The Negative Income Tax*. Washington: The Brookings Institution, n.d.

Green, Christopher and Jean-Michel Cousineau. *Unemployment in Canada: The Impact of Unemployment Insurance*. Ottawa: Supply and Services Canada for the Economic Council of Canada, 1976.

Hamovitch, Eric. "The Low-Cost Myth: Housing for Those Who Can Afford It," *The Last Post*, Vol. 2, No. 7 (Oct. 1972), p. 10.

Information Canada. *Income Security for Canadians*. Ottawa, 1970.

Jackson, Anthony. "A Rose By Any Other Name," *Canadian Forum*, Vol. 53 (Aug. 1973), p. 10.

Jump, G.V., and T.A. Wilson. "Macro-Economic Effects of Federal Fiscal

Policies, 1974-1975," *Canadian Tax Journal*, Vol. XXIII, No. 1 (Jan.-Feb. 1975), pp. 55-62.

_____. "Fiscal Policy in Recession and Recovery," *Canadian Tax Journal*, Vol. XXIV, No. 2 (Mar.-Apr. 1976), pp. 132-43.

Kaliski, S.F. and D.C. Smith. "Inflation, Unemployment and Incomes Policy," *Canadian Journal of Economics*, Vol. 6 (1973), pp. 574-91.

Kardouche, George K. *Wage and Price Controls for Canada?* Montreal: C.D. Howe Research Institute, 1975.

Kelly, Michael G. *The Short-Run Impact of Foreign Inflation on Canadian Prices.* Prepared for the Prices and Incomes Commission. Ottawa: Information Canada, 1972.

Khetan, C.P. and S.N. Poddar. "Measurement of Income Tax Progression in a Growing Economy: The Canadian Experience," *The Canadian Journal of Economics*, Vol. 9 (1976), pp. 613-29.

Kuyek, Joan. "Housing: A Corporate Conglomerate," *Our Generation*, Vol. 7, No. 4 and Vol. 8, No. 1 (Feb. and June 1971).

Liskeard, Richard. "Sudbury's Trailer Camp," *The Last Post*, Vol. 1, No. 6 (Feb. 1971), p. 39.

Lithwick, N.H. *Urban Poverty: Research Monograph No. 1.* Ottawa: Canadian Mortgage and Housing Corporation, 1971.

Loyns, R. *An Examination of the Consumer Price Index and Implicit Price Index as Measures of Recent Price Change in the Canadian Economy.* Canada: Prices and Incomes Commission, 1972.

MacDonald, Lorne P. "Social Priorities for Social Security: A Comment," *The Social Worker*, Vol. 44, No. 2-3 (Summer-Fall 1976), pp. 71-73.

Manitoba. Department of Health and Social Development. *Report on a Guaranteed Annual Income Experimental Project in Manitoba Prepared by M.D.T. Associates.* Manitoba: Queen's Printer, 1972.

Marine, G. and Judith V. Allen. *Food Pollution: The Violation of the Inner Ecology.* Toronto: Holt, Rinehart and Winston, n.d.

Marsh, Leonard. "G.A.I.: A New Look at Welfare Policy," *Canadian Welfare*, Vol. 49, No. 6 (Nov.-Dec. 1973).

Maslove, Allan M. and J.C.R. Rowley. "Inflation and Redistribution," *Canadian Journal of Economics*, Vol. 8 (1975), pp. 399-409.

Maslove, Allan M. *The Pattern of Taxation in Canada.* Economic Council of Canada. Ottawa: Information Canada, 1973.

McCollum, J. *Inflation and Interest Rates in Canada: A Study Prepared for the Prices and Incomes Commission.* Canada: Prices and Incomes Commission, 1972.

Mcfayden, Stuart and Robert Hobart. "An Alternative Measurement of Housing Costs and the Consumer Price Index," *Canadian Journal of Economics*, Vol. 11 (1978), pp. 105-12.

Mitchell, Don. *The Politics of Food.* Toronto: James Lorimer, 1975.

Morton, Desmond. "The Great Anti-Guidelines Crusade: A Second Opinion," *Canadian Forum*, Vol. LVI, No. 659 (Mar. 1976), pp. 18-20.

Murphy, Rae. "Home is Where the Mortgage Is," *The Last Post,* Vol. 4, No. 2 (Aug. 1974), p. 29.

National Council of Welfare. *Beyond Services and Beyond Jobs: People's Need to Grow.* Ottawa: Queen's Printer, 1974.

———. *Directory of Low Income Citizen Groups in Canada.* Ottawa: Information Canada, 1973.

———. *Guaranteed Incomes and Guaranteed Jobs.* Ottawa: Information Canada, 1972.

———. *Poor People's Groups.* Ottawa: Information Canada, 1973.

———. *The Press and the Poor: A Report on How Canada's Newspapers Cover Poverty.* Ottawa: Information Canada, 1973.

———. *Prices and the Poor.* Ottawa: Information Canada, 1974.

———. *Seminar on Self-Help Problem Solving by Low-Income Communities,* Smith Falls, Ontario, 1972.

Naylor, Tom. "Commentary," *Our Generation,* Vol. 11, No. 1 (Fall 1975), pp. 17-24.

Neave, Davis. "Housing of Welfare Recipients in Calgary," *Canadian Welfare,* Vol. 49, No. 4 (July-Aug. 1973).

New Brunswick. Economic Advisor. *Income Distribution in Canada, the Atlantic Provinces and New Brunswick, 1951-1971.* New Brunswick: Queen's Printer, 1973.

Ontario Welfare Council. *A Study of Housing Policies in Ontario: General Report.* Ontario Welfare Council, 1973.

Palys, T.S. *Social Indicators of Quality of Life in Canada: A Practical Theoretical Report.* Manitoba: Department of Urban Affairs, Queen's Printer, 1973.

Panitch, Leo. *Workers, Wages and Controls: The Anti-Inflation Programme and its Implications for Canadian Workers.* Toronto: New Hogtown Press, 1976.

Phillips, Paul. "The Rationale for Wage Controls," *Canadian Dimension,* Vol. 11, No. 2 (Feb. 1976).

Pitchford, J.D. "Expectations and Income Claims in a Two Sector Model of Inflation," *Canadian Journal of Economics,* Vol. X, No. 4, pp. 637-52.

Pollution Probe. *Rule of the Tame: A Handbook for Tenants and Homeowners.* Toronto: Pollution Probe, 1972.

Prices and Incomes Commission. *Inflation, Unemployment and Income Policy: Final Report.* Ottawa: Information Canada, 1972.

Rea, Jr., Samuel A. "Investment in Human Capital Under a Negative Income Tax," *Canadian Journal of Economics,* Vol. 10 (1977), pp. 607-720.

Rinehart, James W. "In Canada: Wage Controls, Unions and Class Conflict," *Our Generation,* Vol. 11 (1976), pp. 27-34.

Robinson, H.L. "Notes on Inflation," *Canadian Forum,* Vol. LV (Aug. 1975).

_____. "Notes on Inflation II,"*Canadian Forum* (Oct. 1975), p. 18.

_____. "Notes on Inflation III," *Canadian Forum,* Vol. LV (Dec. 1975, Jan. 1976), pp. 11-15.

_____. "Unravelling the Guidelines," *Canadian Forum,* Vol. LVI (May 1976), pp. 18-20.

Rosenblum, Simon. "Economic Nationalism and the English Canadian Socialist Movement," *Our Generation,* Vol. 11, No. 1 (Fall 1975), pp. 5-16.

_____. "A Reply to Tom Naylor,"*Our Generation,* Vol. 11, No. 2 (Winter 1976).

Rutman, Leonard. "Evolution of Community Health Centers," *The Social Worker,* Vol. 43, No. 4 (Winter 1975), pp. 188-92.

Ryant, Joseph C. "Personal Social Services in a Period of Economic Constraint," *The Social Worker,* Vol. 44, No. 4 (Winter 1976), pp. 95-100.

Scarfe, B. *Price Determination and Process of Inflation in Canada.* Ottawa: Prices and Incomes Commission, 1972.

Siemiatycki, Jack. "The Distribution of Disease-Like Income, Disease Is Not Distributed Equally under Capitalism," *Canadian Dimension,* Vol. 10, No. 2 (June 1974), p. 15.

Silver, J.R. *Housing and the Poor.* Canada. Ministry of State for Urban Affairs. Ottawa: Information Canada, 1971.

Smiley, Donald V. "The Non-Economics of Anti-Inflation," *Canadian Forum,* Vol. LV, No. 659 (Mar. 1976), pp. 11-14.

Smith, Lawrence B. "Canada's Incomes Policy: An Economic Assessment," *Canadian Tax Journal,* Vol. XXIV, No. 1 (Jan.-Feb. 1976), pp. 67-73.

Smith, Wallace F. *Housing: The Social and Economic Elements.* Berkeley: University of California Press, 1971.

Spencer, Byron G. *A Preliminary Paper on Family Food Expenditures in Canada; An Analysis of the 1974 Survey.* Ottawa: Food Prices Review Board, 1976.

Surette, Ralph. "Who's to Blame for the Food Prices?" *The Last Post,* Vol. 3, No. 4 (July 1973).

Tussing, Dale. "The Dual Welfare System," *Transaction,* Vol. 11, No. 2 (Jan.-Feb. 1974).

_____.*Poverty in a Dual Economy.* New York: St. Martin's Press, 1975.

Van Stolk, Mary. *The Battered Child in Canada.* Toronto: McClelland and Stewart, 1972.

Ward, Colin. *Housing: An Anarchist Approach.* Montreal: Black Rose Books, 1976.

Warrion, Peter. *Occupational Health Anthology.* Toronto: New Hogtown Press, 1976.

Watt, Bryan. "Patterns of Association in Low Income Housing." Unpublished paper, University of Calgary, 1973.

Westergaard, John and Henrietta Resler. *Class in a Capitalist Society.* New York: Basic Books, 1975.

Wilson, T.A. and G.V. Jump. "Economic Effects of Provincial Fiscal Policies, 1975-1976," *Canadian Tax Journal,* Vol. XXIII, No. 3 (May-June 1975).

Winnipeg Urban Renewal Commission. *Presentation by the Housing Committee of Mount Carmel Clinic re: Housing Conditions in North Point Douglas.* Manitoba: Queen's Printer, 1970.